Mountain Tourism

Experiences, Communities, Environments and Sustainable Futures

_____

Mountain Tourism

Experiences, Communities, Environments and Sustainable Futures

Harold Richins

Thompson Rivers University

John S. Hull

Thompson Rivers University

www.cabi.org

CABI is a trading name of CAB International

CABI
Nosworthy Way
Wallingford
Oxfordshire OX10 8DE
UK

CABI
745 Atlantic Avenue
8th Floor
Boston, MA 02111
USA

Tel: +44 (0)1491 832111
Fax: +44 (0)1491 833508
E-mail: info@cabi.org
Website: www.cabi.org

Tel: +1 (617) 682 9015
E-mail: cabi-nao@cabi.org

A catalogue record for this book is available from the British Library, London, UK.

Library of Congress Cataloging-in-Publication Data

Names: Richins, Harold, editor of compilation. | Hull, John, 1963- editor of
    compilation.
Title: Mountain tourism : experiences, communities, environments and
    sustainable futures / edited by Harold Richins, and John Hull.
Description: Wallingford, Oxfordshire ; Boston, MA : CABI, [2016] | Includes
    bibliographical references and index.
Identifiers: LCCN 2015042009 | ISBN 9781780644608 (hbk : alk. paper)
Subjects: LCSH: Mountain tourism. | Mountain tourism--Case studies. |
    Sustainable tourism. | Sustainable tourism--Case studies. |
    Tourism--Environmental aspects. | Tourism--Environmental aspects--Case
    studies.
Classification: LCC G156.5.M68 M68 2016 | DDC 338.4/791--dc23 LC record
    available at http://lccn.loc.gov/2015042009

ISBN-13: 978 1 78064 460 8

Commissioning editor: Claire Parfitt
Editorial assistant: Emma McCann
Production editor: Tracy Head

Typeset by SPi, Pondicherry, India.
Printed and bound in the UK by CPI Group (UK) Ltd, Croydon, CR0 4YY.

Contents

_____

PART VII   MOUNTAIN TOURISM IMPLICATIONS

Contributors

Jovel Francis Ananayo is Assistant Professor and Chairperson of the Department of Tourism and Home Science of the Ifugao State University in Ifugao Province, Philippines. He earned a BA from the University of the Philippines in Baguio City, an MSc from the School of Travel Industry Management of the University of Hawaii at Manoa in the USA, and a PhD from the Department of Tourism of the University of Otago in New Zealand. Prior to his academic career, Dr Ananayo held positions both in the government and private sectors. He has served as Tourism Operations Officer at the Tourism Office of the Ifugao Provincial Government and has worked with non-governmental organizations that embarked on community-based tourism in the Ifugao rice terraces of the Philippine Cordilleras, a UNESCO World Heritage Site. He has been engaged in tourism development planning and heritage conservation initiatives, which were implemented in the mountainous province of Ifugao, the home of the Ifugao indigenous peoples group, to which he belongs.

Thorvarður Árnason is an environmental humanist who lives and works in Hornafjörður, south-east Iceland. His primary research areas are landscape studies and protected area management. Thorvarður has also engaged in many tourism projects, both academic and applied, concerning, e.g. sustainable tourism, educational tourism, geotourism and seasonality in tourism. He has over the years forged strong links with VisitVatnajokull, the local tourism cluster, and Vatnajökull National Park. Thorvarður is currently working with a group of local adventure tourism entrepreneurs in the SAINT project and with local photographers and tour guides in the group Vatnajokull Photo. A landscape photographer and filmmaker, Thorvarður has also been exploring ways of developing visual research methods, e.g. using repeat photography to document the changes taking place in Hornafjörður and Vatnajökull National Park due to glacier recession. Thorvarður is the Director of the University of Iceland's Hornafjörður Regional Research Centre.

Dani Blasco is professor and project manager at the University of Girona. His research topics are Tourism Destination Management, Tourism Governance and Human Capital in Tourism. He has published in academic journals such as *Annals of Tourism Research*, *Tourism Geographies*, *Journal of Heritage Tourism* and *Tourism Planning and Development*. Since 2005, he has participated in several research projects related to tourism at local, regional and international levels. At the moment, he is involved in the promotion of a tourism cluster within the University of Girona and Catalunya region, called 'Campus UdG Tourism'.

Philipp E. Boksberger received his BA in Business Administration from the University of St Gallen in 1999. He continued studying at the University of St Gallen and finished his MA in Tourism Management with cum laude honours. Parallel to his studies, he worked as a research assistant at the Institute for Public Services and Tourism (IDT-HSG) for Prof. Dr Thomas Bieger. In order to gain more international experience and deepen his industry experience, he undertook an internship at the World Tourism Organization in Madrid in 2002 and an internship at THR (Consultant Company in Tourism and Hospitality) in Barcelona in 2003. At the same time he started his post-graduate studies at the University of St Gallen. In 2004 he received a grant from the federal government to continue his studies at the University of Queensland in Australia, where he finished his PhD in Consumer Behaviour (awarded by the University of St Gallen in 2006) and started his teaching and research career. At the end of 2005 he took over the task of establishing a tourism consulting and research unit at the University of Applied Sciences (HTW Chur) in Switzerland and supporting their undergraduate program in tourism. In 2007 he was promoted to become the Head of the School of Tourism at HTW Chur. Under his management the school not only increased student numbers and turnover to become the biggest unit within the university, but also internationalized its research, consulting and executive education activities. At the same time he continued to lecture, research and publish in top academic journals. At the end of 2011 he was asked by Prof. Dr Peter Lorange to take over the role of COO at the Lorange Institute of Business Zurich with the objective of executing the turnaround of the Business School and further developing the business. In 2014 he was appointed CEO of the Lorange Institute of Business Zurich.

Federica Buffa is Assistant Professor in Economics and Business Management at the Department of Economics and Management at the University of Trento (Italy). In 2007, she earned a PhD in Business Economics at the Ca' Foscari University of Venice (Italy). Since 2001 she has been a member of the eTourism – currently EMASUS (Economics, Management and Sustainable Consumption) – research group, headed by Prof. Franch, at the University of Trento. Her research topics are related to Economics and Business Management. The main research areas concern: strategies and management of small and medium tourism enterprises; governance and management of multi-stakeholder territorial systems; consumer behaviour, with particular attention to decision making processes; and sustainability attitude of tourist demand. The research is mainly focused on community destinations in Alpine areas. She is author of more than 60 academic publications.

Alison S. Burke is an Associate Professor of Criminology and Criminal Justice at Southern Oregon University. She holds a PhD in Criminology from Indiana University of Pennsylvania and a Master of Criminal Justice from University of Colorado Denver. While her areas of expertise and interest reside within the field of criminology, topics such as gender and juvenile justice and delinquency prevention, Dr Burke has also taught special topic seminars on environmental crime and green criminology. The topic of environmental crime has sparked her interest in pursuing further research related to crime and tourism. Dr Burke is a member of the Ashland Woodlands and Trails Association (AWTA), which is a non-profit group that helps to preserve and maintain the Ashland woodlands. She actively supports mountain tourism through participation in the trail-running community, which host races and events that fundraise for AWTA and other community organizations. Alison is an avid trail runner and can often be found running on the Pacific Crest Trail or the vast and beautiful trails around Ashland.

Kellee Caton is Associate Professor of Tourism Studies at Thompson Rivers University in Canada. She holds a PhD from the University of Illinois. Her research focuses on how we come to know tourism as a sociocultural phenomenon, and also on how we come to know and reshape the world through tourism; in particular, she is interested in the moral dimensions of these two epistemic processes. Kellee is currently co-chairing the Critical Tourism Studies international network, as well as its new North American chapter. She sits on the editorial boards of *Annals of Tourism Research* and *Tourism Analysis* and serves on the executive of the Tourism Education Futures Initiative.

Lisa Cooke is Assistant Professor of Cultural Anthropology in the Department of Sociology and Anthropology at Thompson Rivers University in Kamloops, British Columbia, Canada. Her research interests revolve around examining indigenous–settler relations in Canada as they play out in, through and between places. She has found ethnographic examinations of tourism and the production of touristic spaces a great entry point to exploring contemporary settler colonial cultural forms and the ways that indigenous–settler relations shape and are shaped by them. Earlier work conducted in Whitehorse and Dawson City in Canada's Yukon Territory informs her current examination of relations as they play out in the southern interior of British Columbia. It is her strong belief that by better understanding the ways that settler colonialism works as an ongoing structural and cultural project, often articulated through the production of particular kinds of places that serve to structure indigenous–settler relations in oppositional terms, that we might collectively find a way past these literal and figurative 'roadblocks' to nurture spaces of actualized solidarity where settler Canadians stand alongside our indigenous neighbors in their struggles for recognition of land-rights, Aboriginal title, self-determination and lived reconciliation.

Carolyn Deuchar is a Senior Research Fellow at the New Zealand Tourism Research Institute at the Auckland University of Technology. She holds a PhD from Auckland University of Technology where her work focuses on understanding the processes that underlie small tourism enterprise and community network formation in rural areas drawing on a case from Western Southland – the southernmost mountainous area at the very bottom of New Zealand's South Island. Carolyn's other research interests include community informatics and tourism, incorporating regulation theory and the concept of flexible specialization as tools to understand STE networks and the ways in which they can contribute to regional social and economic development. Carolyn has been a member of a number of commercial research and evaluation projects in New Zealand, Canada and the South and Central Pacific including those sponsored by the European Union and the United Nations Environment Program. She is also a member of the New Zealand Tourism Data Industry Reference Group.

Tracey J. Dickson is an Associate Professor of Event and Tourism Management in the Faculty of Business, Government and Law at the University of Canberra, Australia. Tracey's diverse academic qualifications reflect a spirit of curiosity and lifelong learning (BCom (Accounting), GradDipEd (Adult Ed), MEd (Adult Ed), MHRM, Master of Public Health and a PhD in Experiential Learning). Her professional life started in accounting and finance before switching to outdoor education and then on to an academic life thinking, teaching, researching and writing on snowsports, risk management and event volunteer management. Throughout this she has maintained a connection with the Australian alpine areas through her membership of one of the oldest ski clubs in Australia, Cooma Ski Club, where she has served on the board for over 10 years, and an ongoing enjoyment of the mountains through skiing, hiking and biking. Recently Tracey has been appointed to the state minister's advisory council for national parks due to her knowledge and experience in ecotourism and outdoor recreation.

Axel Dreyer is Professor for Tourism Management/Marketing at the Hochschule Harz, University of Applied Sciences, Wernigerode, Germany (since 1993) and Honored Professor for Sport Management at the University of Goettingen (since 1996), where he earned his PhD. Prof. Dr Dreyer is co-founder of the German Society of Tourism Research (DGT - Deutsche Gesellschaft für Tourismuswissenschaft e.V.). He is founding director of the Institute of Tourism Research and works in different positions as researcher at the Hochschule Harz. Prof. Dr Dreyer has published a lot in the fields of tourism markets and tourism marketing. Special issues among others are service quality and customer satisfaction, the impact of demographic change on tourism, sports tourism and cultural tourism. At present he is working on hiking tourism, cycling tourism and wine tourism.

Marit Gundersen Engeset is an Associate Professor of Marketing at the School of Business, South East Norway University College. She has a PhD in Marketing from Norwegian School of Economics, and an MSc in International Hotel and Tourism Management from the Norwegian School of Hotel Management, University of Stavanger. Engeset has more than 20 years' teaching experience, including Bachelor, Master and PhD level courses in marketing, tourism and scientific methods, and she has been involved in development of study programmes at Bachelor, Master and PhD levels. She has experience in collaborating with the tourism industry in different research projects focusing on development of competitive advantages for tourism destinations. Her area of expertise is within measurement of customer and employee value, as well as customer co-creation and creative consumption. She has published in several leading international journals, including *Journal of Marketing Research*, *Journal of Travel Research* and *Cornell H.R.A. Quarterly*.

Hugues Francois is a research engineer at Irstea. His research focuses on ski resorts in the scope of local development and spatial planning. During his PhD, he investigated the case of mid-mountain resorts and the impact of the valuation of specific territorial resources on their economic model and local anchorage. Nowadays he is the administrator of the BD Stations, a socioeconomic and technical database about ski resorts in France. His present works focus on the modelling of ski areas and their snow cover to study their resilience in the perspective of climate change.

Linda-Louise Geldenhuys was born and resides in Cape Town, South Africa. She is a researcher, lecturer and Head of Department at Prestige Academy in Tourism Management. Currently busy with her PhD, she obtained her BCom degree in 2011, Honours degree in 2012 and Master's degree in 2013 at the North-West University, Potchefstroom Campus. She operates within the fields of ecotourism and marine tourism. She has published three articles in peer-reviewed journals and five research reports. She attended two international conferences and two national conferences. In 2014 she became a member of the Golden Key Honour Society and in 2015 she was awarded with the African SunMedia award for Best Published Post-Graduate Article.

Emmanuelle George-Marcelpoil is the head of the research unit 'Development of Mountain Territories' at the Irstea Grenoble center. After a PhD in Economy at the Pierre Mendès France University in Grenoble, her early research focused on ski resorts' governance. Empirical studies conducted in the Alps have highlighted the diversity of governance arrangements between private and public actors in the stations. These early works continued with the analysis of land dynamics and leisure real estate and most recently with the impacts of climate change on the economy of winter sports. This research, conducted across the Alps as in other massifs, allowed scientific publications but also contributed to a decision aid to public actors (diagnostic tools, policy evaluation and operational recommendations).

Alison M. Gill is a Professor at Simon Fraser University with a joint appointment in the Department of Geography and the School of Resource and Environmental Management. She holds a PhD in Geography from the University of Manitoba, an MA from the University of Alberta and a BA from the University of Hull (UK). Dr Gill's research has for many years focused on issues of growth and change associated with tourism in mountain resort communities. Institutional arrangements and the politics of place are important theoretical constructs underpinning her work on tourism and the transformation of place. Much of her empirically based research has been conducted in the mountain resort of Whistler. Dr Gill serves on the editorial boards of several major tourism journals including *Annals of Tourism Research*, *Journal of Travel Research* and *Tourism Geographies*. She is a Fellow of the International Academy for the Study of Tourism and also the Royal Canadian Geographical Society.

Bryan Grimwood is Assistant Professor in the Department of Recreation and Leisure Studies at the University of Waterloo, Canada. His research explores human–nature relationships and advocates social justice and sustainability in the contexts of tourism, cultural livelihoods, and environmental learning and management. He is an engaged scholar and emerging specialist in participatory and Aboriginal research, northern landscapes, responsible tourism development and experiential education. Recent and ongoing projects involve collaborations with indigenous and tourist communities to document and dialogue culturally diverse relationships and responsibilities associated with a special and changing Canadian Arctic riverscape. As a parent and outdoor educator, Bryan is also interested in the 'nature stories' we tell ourselves and live, what these stories tell about our being human and the extent to which they foster resilient children, communities and ecologies.

Sven Gross is Professor of Transport Carrier Management at the Harz University of Applied Sciences in Wernigerode, Germany. He studied Tourism Geography and Economics at the University of Trier and Spatial Planning at the Technical University of Dortmund in Germany. Sven got his Master's degree in 1998 and was a management and community consultant for several years, personal assistant to a mayor and research associate at the Chair of Tourism Economics and Management at the Dresden University of Technology. From 2008 to 2013 he was co-head of the tourism department in the Competence Center of Information and Communication Technologies, Tourism and Services at the Harz University, from 2013 to 2015 he was vice-director of the Institute for Tourism Research (ITF) at the Harz University and since 2007 he has been a member of the New Zealand Tourism Research Institute (NZTRI) based in Auckland/New Zealand. In 2010 and 2014/15 Sven was as a Visiting Professor at the Auckland University of Technology. His main research areas include tourism and transport (e.g. airline management, cruise ship management, car rental management), business travel management and tourist market research. He has authored more than 80 publications on these subjects, including 12 books.

Jaume Guia is Associate Professor in the Faculty of Tourism of the University of Girona. His background is in management and organization theory and his research interests in tourism governance, organizational networks, collaboration and relationship management. He has published research articles on these and other related topics and participated in research projects in collaboration with the industry. Currently he is programme director of the European Master's in Tourism Management (EMTM).

C. Michael Hall is a Professor in the Department of Management, Marketing and Entrepreneurship, University of Canterbury, New Zealand; Docent in the Department of Geography, University of Oulu, Finland; and a Visiting Professor, Linneaus University, Sweden. He has wide-ranging interests in tourism, regional development, global environmental change and environmental history.

Elizabeth Halpenny is an Associate Professor at the Faculty of Physical Education and Recreation at the University of Alberta. She received a PhD in Recreation and Leisure Studies from the University of Waterloo in 2006. Previous to this she worked with an international NGO around the world helping entrepreneurs and government agencies develop ecotourism infrastructure and programmes. She also has an MES in Environmental Studies from York University and a BA in Geography from Wilfrid Laurier University. She currently teaches and conducts research in the areas of tourism, marketing, environmental psychology and protected areas management. Elizabeth's research focuses on individuals' interactions with nature environments, tourism experience and environmental stewardship. Current research projects include: the affect of mobile digital technologies on visitors' experiences; the impact of World Heritage designation and other park-related brands on travel decision making; individuals' attitudes towards and stewardship of natural areas; and children's access to nature as a place to play and the outcomes that arise from these activities.

Louise Hudson, who introduced Simon Hudson to skiing, is a freelance journalist living in South Carolina. She co-wrote *Winter Sport Tourism*, *Golf Tourism* and *Customer Service for Hospitality & Tourism*. Originally trained in journalism in England, she writes about skiing for many publications including *Ski Canada Magazine*, *LA Times*, *The Dallas Morning News Travel*, *Houston Chronicle*, *Boston Globe*, *Canada's Globe and Mail*, *Dreamscapes* magazine, *Calgary Sun*, *Calgary Herald*, *Edmonton Sun*, *Vancouver Sun*, *Ottawa Citizen*, Canada's *MORE* magazine, *Eat Drink Travel*, *Opulence*, *Alberta Parent*, *Calgary's Child*, *Travel Alberta*, *Fresh Tracks*, *Alberta Hospitality* magazine and several UK publications. A committed ski bum, Louise has skied every season for the past 42 years all over Europe and North America. She is also a prolific ski blogger on http://www.onetwoski.blogspot.com and a ski tweeter @skiblogger.

Simon Hudson, as well as being a keen skier, is an Endowed Chair in Tourism at the University of South Carolina. He has held previous academic positions at universities in Canada and England, and has worked as a visiting professor in Austria, Switzerland, Spain, Fiji, New Zealand and Australia. Prior to working in academia, Dr Hudson spent several years working in the ski industry in Europe. Dr Hudson has written over 60 journal articles and published seven books: *Snow Business*; *Sports and Adventure Tourism*; *Marketing for Tourism and Hospitality: A Canadian Perspective*; *Tourism and Hospitality Marketing: A Global Perspective*; *Golf Tourism*; *Customer Service for Hospitality & Tourism*; and *Winter Sport Tourism: Working in Winter Wonderlands*. The marketing of tourism is the focus of his research, and he is frequently invited to international conferences as a keynote speaker.

John S. Hull is an Associate Professor of Tourism Management at Thompson Rivers University in British Columbia, Canada. He is Co-director of the Alliance for Mountain Environments (AME) and has served on the organizing committee for the triennial Thinking Mountains Conference at the University of Alberta. He is also a visiting professor at South East Norway University College, Norway and at Harz University of Applied Sciences, Germany. His research addresses the sustainability of tourism in peripheral regions focusing on creative tourism, cruise tourism, geotourism, Arctic tourism, mountain tourism and wellness tourism. At present he is a member of the New Zealand Tourism Research Institute (NZTRI), the International Competence Network for Tourism Research and Education (ICNT) and the International Tourism Studies Association (ITSA). He enjoys spending time in the mountains and lives along Guerin Creek in an intentional community that promotes cooperative, sustainable living.

Sydney Johnsen is a former instructor at Thompson Rivers University and is now the principal of Peak Planning Associates, a consulting firm providing policy and planning services in the tourism, cultural and recreation fields. Sydney is a professional member of the Canadian Institute of Planners and a Director on the Fraser Basin Council (FBC) and sits on the policy committees of the Tourism Industry Association of BC and Kamloops Chamber of Commerce. Sydney lives in Kamloops where she enjoys playing on her yoga mat, mountain bike and hiking trails in the summer, and on skis during the winter.

Aurelia Kogler is founder and CEO of MONTCON Tourismus, a consultancy specializing in the strategic support of Ski Resorts and Alpine Destinations mainly in Austria and Switzerland (www.montcon.at). Furthermore she is Professor for Tourism and Leisure Research at the University of Applied Sciences in Chur (HTW Chur) in Switzerland. Being business-school educated, her special academic and practical research interests are strategic marketing and management topics related to health tourism, luxury tourism, mountain tourism and leisure management. Aurelia was a member of the Board of Directors of the World Leisure Organization (www.worldleisure.org) and is currently a member of the Board of Directors at Pizolbahnen AG (www.pizol.com), a Swiss ski resort. She has published research articles in both scientific journals and popular magazines and has been invited as a speaker at academic and professional events around the world.

Michael Lück is Head of Department in the School of Hospitality and Tourism, Associate Director for the Coastal and Marine Tourism research programme at the New Zealand Tourism Research Institute at Auckland University of Technology, and founding co-chair of the International Coastal & Marine Tourism Society (ICMTS). He has more than 10 years' work experience in the tourism industry and his research interests include wildlife tourism, the cruise industry, ecotourism, mountain tourism, the impacts of tourism, and aviation. He has published in a number of international journals, is founding editor-in-chief of the academic journal *Tourism in Marine Environments*, and editor of the *Journal of Ecotourism and Marine Policy*. He has edited or co-edited volumes on ecotourism, marine and polar tourism, events and low cost airlines, as well as the *Encyclopedia of Tourism and Recreation in Marine Environments* (CABI), and co-authored the introductory text *Tourism* (CABI).

Lena-Marie Lun is researcher at the Institute for Regional Development and Location Management at the European Academy Bozen/Bolzano (EURAC research), Italy. She graduated in geography at the Albert-Ludwigs-Universität Freiburg (Germany) and obtained a Master's degree in Sustainable Resource Management from the Technische Universität München (Germany). At the European Academy Bozen/Bolzano her main areas of expertise include rural tourism, sustainable tourism, destination governance, climate change and tourism and regional products.

Byron Marlowe, MBA is the Instructor of Hospitality and Wine Business Management at Washington State University Tri-Cities. Previously, Byron was the Senior Instructor and Hospitality and Tourism Program Coordinator at Southern Oregon University. In addition to teaching in the USA, Byron has a Visiting Lecturer post at University of Applied Sciences, Hochschule Harz. Byron spent several years in food and beverage and tourism publishing in Arizona before his academic career. Byron received his Master of Business Administration with a concentration in Hospitality Management from Colorado Technical University – Denver. Byron is developing his academic literature on wine hospitality and tourism as a researcher. Byron is currently enrolled as a PhD student in Lodging and Food-service Management at Iowa State University.

Umberto Martini, PhD in Business Economics, is Full Professor of Business Management within the Department of Economics and Management at the University of Trento (Italy), where he is responsible for the courses Tourism Marketing (in the Master's of Management of Sustainability and Tourism) and Marketing Advanced (in the Master's of Management). From 2003 to 2009 he was also the director of the Master's of Tourism Management at the same university. His main research interests concern destination management and marketing, focusing on community-based approaches and sustainability. In this field, from 2009 to 2011 he was the scientific coordinator of the Central European Research Project 'LISTEN to the Voice of Villages', and from 2010 to 2012 of an Italian research group on sustainability and management in tourism involving ten universities and research centres. He is author of 145 scientific publications.

Anne Menzel completed her Diploma in Tourism Management at the Hochschule Harz, University of Applied Sciences, Wernigerode, Germany in 2006. She takes part in several research projects at the Hochschule Harz and is publishing in the field of hiking tourism.

Michael Meyer started his career as a consultant on management of tourism facilities, working for 15 years on quality assessment and training of staff. In 1999 he became a member of the board of Ecological Tourism in Europe (ETE) to work on the topic of sustainable tourism development in and around protected areas, foremost within Central and Eastern Europe. From 2006 he has also been working for the World Tourism Organization (UNWTO), giving advice to member states on sustainable tourism planning and biodiversity-based tourism product development. He is a member of the roster of experts of the Convention on Biological Diversity (CBD) and co-author of the International Guidelines on Biodiversity and Tourism Development of the CBD. His specialties are coaching of tourism planning processes, capacity-building of local communities and entrepreneurs, and sustainable tourism product development.

Simon Milne's research focuses on creating a better understanding of the economic significance of tourism, and developing strategies and tools to sustain the natural, social and cultural resources upon which the industry depends. For the past 30 years Simon has focused in particular on the ability of information technology to improve the economic performance and sustainability of destinations and regions around the world. Recent years have seen Simon's research take on an increasingly applied focus, often in international settings and often in mountain environments. A number of his research programmes have been funded through major international donor organizations (UNDP, UNEP, EU, World Bank). The New Zealand Tourism Research Institute (www.nztri.org), which Simon directs at the Auckland University of Technology in New Zealand, is a major generator of externally funded research projects that support graduate student training and development.

Farhad Moghimehfar is a doctoral candidate at the Faculty of Physical Education and Recreation at the University of Alberta. He has an MSc in Tourism Management and a BSc in Industrial Engineering. Farhad integrates social science into the planning and management of tourism and outdoor recreation. He examines social psychological aspects of visitors' behavior, with an emphasis on tourism and outdoor recreation in an effort to understand factors that influence people's pro-environmental behaviour. Farhad's recent project examines campers' pro-environmental behavior in Alberta's provincial parks. He also explores hunters' and bird watchers' behaviours in North America. Focused on human dimensions of natural resources management, he uses a mixed methods approach to investigate people's motivations and constraints to engage in waterfowl hunting and bird watching.

Sanjay K. Nepal is Professor in the Department of Geography and Environmental Management at the University of Waterloo, Canada. He received his Master's degree in Rural and Regional Development Planning from Asian Institute of Technology in Thailand in 1991, and a PhD in Geography from the University of Berne in Switzerland in 1999. He is broadly trained, which is reflected in his research papers and diversity of topics. Most of his tourism research is focused on remote regions, parks and protected areas, and mountainous regions. The bulk of his academic work is based on field research conducted in Nepal, Thailand and Canada (British Columbia). Initially trained as a quantitative geographer, his most recent research is qualitative due to his shifting interests on issues relevant to globalization, landscape studies and political ecology. His research has been funded by the Social Sciences and Humanities Research Council (SSHRC), Natural Sciences Research Council (NSERC), United States Department of Agriculture, and various other sources in Canada, the USA and Switzerland. In 2012, he was awarded the Association of American Geographers (AAG) Roy Wolfe Award. He is one of the co-editors of a forthcoming book on tourism and political ecology.

Terry Palechuk is an Instructor and Program Coordinator in the Adventure Studies Department at Thompson Rivers University (TRU). With over 25 years of professional guiding together with academic teaching experience in leadership, expedition planning and nature-based community development, Terry has finally decided he has a legitimate base from which to study people's interactions with recreation and nature-based recreation. This has been facilitated with an MBA in Community Economic Development with a research focus on the socio-economics of recreational infrastructure. Terry presently sits on the Board of Directors for Avalanche Canada and Backcountry Lodges of British Columbia and serves as Chair of the Instructor Training Committee for Avalanche Canada and is a member of the Association of Canadian Mountain Guides (Ski Guide and Hiking Guide) as well as a Professional Member of the Canadian Avalanche Association.

Joe Pavelka is an Associate Professor of Ecotourism and Outdoor Leadership in the department of Health and Physical Education at Mount Royal University in Calgary, Alberta, Canada. He holds a PhD from University of Calgary, an MA from the University of Alberta and two undergraduate degrees from Lakehead University in Thunder Bay, Ontario, Canada. Joe has served as the Coordinator of the Ecotourism and Outdoor Leadership Program and the World Leisure Organization Visiting Scholar in Sustainable Leisure Management at Vancouver Island University. Previously Joe held senior positions in public recreation and he is the founder and President of Planvision Consulting, which provides consultancy to tourism destination management and marketing initiatives. Joe is also the founder of Canoes for Peru, a not-for-profit that supports the reintroduction of canoes and canoeing to parts of the Peruvian Amazon. Joe has been operating ecotourism-based field schools to Latin America since 2003 and is currently operating in Peru. Joe's research involves lifestyle migration, experiential education and the analysis of communities in early transition into tourism.

Harald Pechlaner holds a Chair in Tourism and is Director of the Center for Entrepreneurship at the Catholic University of Eichstätt-Ingolstadt (Germany), and is Director of the Institute for Regional Development and Location Management at the European Academy Bozen/Bolzano (EURAC research), Italy. Since 2014, he has been Adjunct Research Professor at the School of Marketing (Tourism Research Cluster) of Curtin University, Perth (Australia). Harald has graduated with a PhD in Social and Economics Sciences from the University of Innsbruck (Austria). He is the president of AIEST (Association Internationale d'Experts Scientifiques du Tourisme). His main areas of expertise include destination governance, resort and location management and entrepreneurship.

Lluís Prats is Assistant Professor at the Faculty of Tourism of the University of Girona in the Business Management and Product Design Department. He is co-director of the Organizational Networks, Innovation and Tourism (ONIT) research group. He obtained a PhD in Tourism Economics and a PhD in Marketing and Business Administration, linking this with his main topics of interest, planning and managing tourism destinations and product development. He is chairman of the Academic Committee of NECSTOUR, an international network for tourism sustainability and competitiveness. He has participated actively in national and international research projects under several initiatives.

László Puczkó is the Group Managing Partner at APP and he has been working as a travel and tourism expert for over 20 years. He graduated as an economist specialized in tourism at Budapest University of Economics and following his interests in culture, arts and experiences, he also graduated from Art & Design Management from the Hungarian University of Applied Arts. He completed his PhD in 2000. He became a Certified Management Consultant (CMC) in 2003. He was manager at KPMG TLT (EMEA) between 2001 and 2004. He founded The Tourism Observatory for Health, Wellness and Spa (2012). He participated in more than a hundred projects in research, planning, product development, experience mapping and design, impact assessment and marketing. László has been lecturing at various international professional and academic conferences. He is the co-author of numerous specialized books (e.g. *Health, Tourism and Hospitality*, *Impacts of Tourism*) and articles in professional journals.

Frieda Raich graduated from Innsbruck University with a PhD in Social Sciences, is currently teaching and researching at MCI Tourism at the Management Center Innsbruck (MCI) and is responsible for the modules 'Management of tourism organizations' and 'Trends in tourism and in the hotel industry' at the SRH Fernhochschule Riedlingen. She is a lecturer, a member of the scientific board and examination committee (Tourism Marketing and Destination Management) at the Hotel Management School Kaiserhof Meran (I). Her research fields are destination governance and leadership, networks in tourism and regional development.

Robin Reid is an Assistant Professor in the Tourism Management Department at Thompson Rivers University (TRU), Kamloops, British Columbia, where she is also a member of the Pedagogy of Place Group at TRU, an interdisciplinary research group. Robin's research interest in cultural narrative, community engagement and sense of place in urban and wilderness landscapes has resulted in publications within a wide range of interdisciplinary and pedagogical contexts. She is the recipient of the 2014 Thompson Rivers University Teaching Excellence Award and continues to merge her research interests with scholarship of teaching.

Harold Richins is Professor of Tourism and former Dean of the Faculty of Adventure, Culinary Arts and Tourism and Co-Director of the Alliance for Mountain Environments at Thompson Rivers University in British Columbia, Canada. He holds a PhD from James Cook University in Australia and BSc and MSc degrees from University of Oregon. Harold has served as Chair of the Graduate Program in the School of Travel Industry Management at University of Hawaii, Professor and Chair of the Mountain Resort Management Program at Sierra Nevada College, and Program Developer and Coordinator of the Entrepreneurship and Small Business Management Program at Mt Hood College, Oregon. He has held academic leadership positions for over 15 years in Australia and New Zealand including Waikato University, University of Newcastle and University of the Sunshine Coast. Richins' management background is with larger sport and technology corporations (Nike, Tektronix) as well as within retail and tourism operations. This included developing and owning an adventure and island cruising tourism enterprise, co-founding a consulting company (Sierra Research Associates), working with the mountain resort industry, and consulting for tourism enterprise startups. Richins has served on numerous community, environmental and tourism boards and has published widely.

Melville Saayman is the director of TREES (Tourism Research in Economic Environs and Society) at the North-West University (Potchefstroom Campus) in South Africa. He is married to Andrea, a tourism economist at the same university, and they have two daughters, Dominique and Anaïs. His field of research is tourism economics and management and he has published more than 130 scientific articles, 20 tourism books and more than 300 technical reports.

Joel Schmidt is Dean of the Faculty of Key Competencies and Professor of English/Business English at the University of Applied Management (Erding, Germany). Originally from Vancouver, Canada, he pursued undergraduate studies at the University of Alberta (BA) and the University of British Columbia (BEd) and worked for 3 years as a secondary school teacher in Vancouver before moving to Germany with his family for further studies at the University of Munich-LMU (MA and DPhil) in the area of Educational Science. At UAM Joel has held leadership roles in teaching and research as well as international development, including the management of joint degree programmes (Educational Management), summer school programmes (delivered in China and Russia), and an innovative cooperative doctoral programme in Education (with Latvian university partner, Riga Teacher Training & Educational Management Academy). Additional international projects with Thompson Rivers University in the area of tourism together with the UAM Institute of Winter Sport (located in Garmisch-Partenkirchen, Germany) have led to a continuing research interest in the areas of adventure and mountain tourism combined with experiential learning and outdoor education.

Donna Senese was born and raised in the Niagara Region of Ontario and has lived in Canada's other prominent wine region, the Okanagan Valley, since completing a PhD in Geography at the University of Waterloo in 1991. Donna is an Associate Professor of Geography at the University of British Columbia Okanagan; her research and teaching interests are in the geographies of tourism, parks and protected areas, food systems and wine. Donna is also the North American Director of Academics at the Sonnino Centre for International Studies in Montespertoli, Tuscany, where she continues her research and instructs experiential courses in rural sustainability, tourism, food and wine.

Hubert J. Siller is Professor and long-time Head of MCI Tourism at the Management Center Innsbruck (MCI). He serves on various advisory and executive boards and accompanies personalities, companies and institutions in strategic questions in the national and international field of tourism and leisure. His research and consulting focus is in the field of strategic management, leadership and destination development. Hubert posseses a distinct experience and knowledge in alpine tourism.

Ivett Sziva, Xellum Ltd, Budapest, Hugary.

Franz Tschiderer has been President of the Tirol Tourism Board since 2013. He graduated with a Master's in 1977 and a PhD in 1980 at the University of St Gallen, where he served as research assistant at the Institute of Tourism from 1977 to 1979. From 1979 to 2011 Franz Tschiderer was a hotel owner–manager. Since 1989 he has been President of the Tourism Board Serfaus (which since 2005 has been named Serfaus-Fiss-Ladis SFL) and CEO of SFL Marketing.

Peet van der Merwe was born in Kuruman, South Africa and is currently living in Potchefstroom, South Africa. He is a senior lecturer and researcher in tourism management at North-West University, Potchefstroom Campus, School for Business Management. As researcher he also forms part of the NRF research unit TREES (Tourism Research in Economic, Environs and Society). Peet obtained his Bachelor's degree in 1994, Honours degree in 1995 and Master's degree in 1999. He completed his PhD (2004) in Tourism Management; in 2010 he was promoted to Associate Professor and in 2014 to Full Professor. His field of expertise lies in wildlife tourism, hunting tourism and ecotourism (sustainable tourism). Research outputs are: peer-reviewed articles (30), popular articles (27), projects (27), research reports (34), books (2), chapters (2), completed Master's and PhD students (17), international conferences (34), national conferences (14) and international quest lectures (3). Peet is married to Madelein and they have two sons, Armand and Richter.

Jan Velvin is an Associate Professor of Business Management at School of Business, South East Norway University College. He has previously been Director at the Center of Tourism Management at Buskerud and Vestfold University College and Visiting Associate Professor at the Scandinavian College in Brazil. Jan has worked on issues in tourism since 1994. His research interests encompass protected areas and rural development, second home tourism, tourism statistics and service management. Velvin also works as a consultant with strategic planning, training and coaching both at management and employee level in the tourism industry, and he has served on several boards and as director of the board of several companies over the years.

Michael Volgger has been a research fellow at the Institute for Regional Development and Location Management at the European Academy Bozen/Bolzano (EURAC research) in Italy since 2010. Michael is currently studying for his doctorate at the Catholic University of Eichstätt-Ingolstadt in Germany. His main areas of expertise include destination governance and location management, product development and innovation in tourism, inter-organizational cooperation and qualitative research. He has conducted several applied research projects in European tourism destinations, with particular regard to mountain contexts.

Martina Voskarova, Ecological Tourism in Europe (ETE), Bonn, Germany.

Johannes T. Welling is a doctoral candidate in Tourism Studies within the Faculty of Geography and Tourism at the University of Iceland, Reykjavik. He holds an MA in Political and Socio-Cultural Science from the University of Amsterdam and an MSc in Environment and Resource Management from the Free University of Amsterdam. His PhD project concerns the impacts of climate change and variability on glacier tourism actors in Iceland. For this project he received a grant from the Icelandic Tourism Board and the Nature Conservation Fund of Pálmi Jónsson.

Christian Werner is active in a broad range of fields pursuing his passion for teaching, research and university leadership in various roles at multiple universities in Europe, including Professor of Organisational, Market and Advertising Psychology at the University of Applied Management (Erding, Germany), and Professor of Sport and Leisure Management at the University of Health & Sport, Technology & Arts (Berlin, Germany). Following his international education and training in the areas of Business/Economics (BA/MA, doctorate), Political Science (BA/MA), and Educational Science (doctorate) from universities in Germany (Landshut and Munich) and Hungary (Budapest), his professional career spans many years in business consultancy and training, with a current focus on business development in the field of higher education. As founder and CEO of the University of Applied Management (Erding, Germany) and President of the International University Network (IUN), Christian is dedicated to innovations in higher education. Ongoing development of the UAM Adventure Campus (Treuchtlingen, Germany) allow him to combine the area of experiential learning in outdoor and adventure contexts with regional development in sport, leisure and tourism. Other research interests include educational management, innovations in teaching and learning, applied creativity, and strategic management.

Peter Williams is a strategic planner and educator whose professional interests focus on tourism destination management. As a strategic planner, he works extensively with government agencies, business associations and communities on issues related to the development, marketing and ongoing management of tourism regions. Many of these projects involve emerging mountain destination development issues across North America and Europe. As an educator, Peter conducts tourism policy, planning and development courses for academic and professional audiences around the globe. An important part of his teaching identifies aspects of destinations governance systems that move tourism organizations towards more sustainable outcomes. He is a past Chair of the Board for the International Travel and Tourism Research Association, which is dedicated to nurturing excellence in tourism research practice. He has also served as a Governor of the Royal Canadian Geographic Society. He currently is on the Board of the International Association of Scientific Experts in Tourism – an international organization of tourism researchers and practitioners – and a member of the prestigious International Academy for the Study of Tourism. Peter is a Professor Emeritus in the School of Resource and Environmental Management at Simon Fraser University, British Columbia.

Anita Zehrer graduated from Innsbruck University with a PhD in Social Sciences. Currently she is Professor at MCI Tourism at the Management Center Innsbruck (MCI), Deputy Head of the

MCI Academic Council and Adjunct Professor at the University of Canberra, Australia. From 2007 to 2015 she was Deputy Head of MCI Tourism. She serves as Vice-President of the Deutsche Gesellschaft für Tourismuswissenschaft DGT e.V. (German Association for Tourism Research) and since 2014 has been a member of the Tourism Advisory Board of the Federal Ministry of Foreign Affairs and Energy, Germany. Her research interests are diverse and include consumer behaviour in tourism, service experiences and service design, destination entrepreneurship and leadership, family business management, epistemology in tourism and tourism education. Zehrer currently serves on several editorial boards such as *The Journal of Travel Research*, *Journal of Vacation Marketing*, *Tourism Analysis*, *The Tourism Review* and *The Journal of Hospitality and Tourism Management* and is reviewer for a range of tourism and hospitality journals.

Jeff Zukiwsky is a professional planner and consultant based in the Canadian Rocky Mountain town of Fernie, British Columbia. He holds a Bachelor of Tourism Management from Thompson Rivers University and a Master's in Resource and Environmental Management from Simon Fraser University with specialization in tourism and recreation policy. For the past decade Jeff has consulted on numerous projects for municipalities, provincial and federal government, and the private sector focused on strategic planning related to tourism and recreation, climate resiliency, risk management and economic development. His work in the tourism and recreation field has focused primarily on helping government agencies better manage tourism and recreation use in the Rocky Mountains. Jeff has served on numerous community and regional boards and committees, and currently chairs the Kootenay-Rockies Chapter of the Planning Institute of BC.

1 Overview of Mountain Tourism: Substantive Nature, Historical Context, Areas of Focus

Harold Richins,[1]* Sydney Johnsen[2] and Dr John S. Hull[1]
[1]*Thompson Rivers University, Kamloops, British Columbia, Canada;*
[2]*Peak Planning Associates, Kamloops, British Columbia, Canada*

The Aim of This Book on Mountain Tourism

The aim of this book is to advance the literature in the field of mountain tourism. In particular, this book aims to broaden the discussion on the diversity of perspectives, interactions and roles of mountain tourism, through an interdisciplinary and management context that addresses communities, impacts, development approaches, planning and governance, natural environment, and creation of mountain tourism experiences.

Mountain Tourism: Experiences, Communities, Environments and Sustainable Futures contains five thematic areas, each with an overview and relevant case studies. These themes include: (i) the creation of mountain tourism experiences; (ii) people and communities in mountain tourism; (iii) natural environments in mountain tourism; (iv) impacts and solutions in mountain tourism; and (v) development, planning and governance approaches in mountain tourism. Mountain areas from around the world are covered in this edited book including areas within Europe, Asia-Pacific, North America, Africa and South America.

Authors included in this publication on mountain tourism address the five thematic areas listed above through scholarly or professional synthesis and review, systematic evaluation of specific issues, or through theoretically-informed empirical research. Most have developed an innovative theoretical approach or framework, and then have applied and assessed their topic empirically and qualitatively. The editors orientate readers to each thematic area through a short introductory chapter. An introductory chapter and concluding chapter serve to introduce and summarize the major themes of the book.

Significance of Mountains and Mountain Tourism

Mountains cover about 24% of the world's land surfaces, are found in every continent, exist in 139 countries and in all major types of ecosystems, from deserts and tropical forests to polar icepacks (Denniston, 1995; Charters and Saxon, 2007; People and Planet, 2008; Keller, 2014). Mountain areas are second only to coasts and islands as popular tourism destinations, generating 15–20% of annual global tourism.

Globally, development of mountain tourism is unique in time and place. For many

---

* Corresponding author: hrichins@tru.ca

regions the development process has been characterized by a period of exploration or discovery, followed by community/regional development that results in the creation of destinations for travel and tourism. In Canada, explorers in the late 19th and 20th centuries blazed the trails that opened up the mountains for others to follow. They travelled through unfamiliar mountain passes, up steep rocky routes, seeking adventure and fortune. Mountain communities became important centres for travel and tourism, known for their beauty, natural assets and as places to experience the outdoors. In a Canadian context, survey crews following the paths of early explorers charted a route through the Rocky Mountains. The survey camps eventually became well-known mountain communities (e.g. Golden, Revelstoke). The Canadian Pacific Railway company followed these routes, built the glamorous Banff Springs Hotel on the shores of a mountain lake and brought in Swiss guides to take rail passengers on mountaineering expeditions (Nepal and Jamal, 2011). The routes opened new industrial opportunities and provided the impetus for fortune seekers to follow. More mountain communities sprung up, many based on mining (e.g. Fernie, Kimberley, Rossland), energy (e.g. Revelstoke) and/or forestry along British Columbia's mountainous west coast.

The United Nations Environmental Programme (UNEP) declared 2002 as the 'International Year of Mountains', noting that mountain tourism accounted for a significant piece of the worldwide tourism pie, and the World Tourism Organization (WTO) predicted that mountain tourism would continue to grow and develop (UNEP, 2002; see Fig. 1.1). International tourism arrivals reached a record 1087 billion arrivals in 2013 with receipts totalling US$1159 billion (UNWTO, 2014). With an estimated 15–20% of tourism occurring in mountain regions, global estimates identify that there were as many as 163–217 million arrivals to mountain regions in 2013 with estimated receipts amounting to US$174–232 billion.

Many mountain regions of the world have seen a strong rise in visitation with the development of tourism (Nepal, 2002; Nepal and Chipeniuk, 2005; Nepal and Jamal, 2011). In the 18th century, the Alps were transformed from a region of poor alpine agricultural settlements to prosperous mountain resorts and villages that now host 30 million international arrivals annually (CIPRA, 2015). The Snowy Mountains of Australia welcomed 1.3 million visitors in 2012 with visitor spending estimated at AUS$468 million (Tourism Snowy Mountains, 2013). In South Africa, Table Mountain's designation as one of the 'New 7 Wonders of Nature' has resulted in a rapid growth in visitation, with over 2.4 million visitors in 2012 (Westgro, 2013). In North America, the Rocky Mountain National

Fig. 1.1. Dolomites UNESCO World Heritage Site (photography courtesy of Harold Richins).

Park in the USA and Banff National Park in Canada both welcome approximately 3–4 million visitors annually (Banff National Park, 2015; Rocky Mountain National Park, 2015). For more remote regions such as the Andes and the Himalayas, mountain tourism has become a phenomenon of explosive growth over the past two decades, with over 1 million tourists flocking annually to Macchu Picchu in South America and over 600,000 trekking in Nepal each year (Government of Nepal, 2011; Dunnell, 2015).

Mountain tourism does not just refer to high-level Alpine environments, but embraces lower-level rural environments and geographically diverse areas with varying weather patterns, temperatures and climatic conditions. Mountain tourism includes, for example, areas with the highest mountain on earth, Mount Everest, in the Himalayas at 8850 m (29,035 feet) to the low-lying Blue Mountains near Sydney, Australia, which contrasts with its rare beauty at only 1189 m high (3901 feet). About 12% of the world's human population lives in the mountains, with another 15% living next to or very near mountain areas. Billions of people throughout the world are dependent on fresh drinking water that originates from mountain areas (United Nations Agenda 21, 1992; Denniston, 1995; People & Planet, 2008).

People Seeking Experiences and the Attraction of Mountains

Marković and Petrović (2013) believe people are seeking experiences that restore their sense of health and wellness in the 'clean, cool air [and] varied topography'. Urry (1990) noted, tourists come to the mountains to 'gaze' upon them and Godde et al. (2000) add that 'people look to mountain environments for their serenity' seeking 'a sense of renewal and spiritual well-being'. Pfister (2000) mentions that the attraction to mountain environments is, 'the mystery and spiritual value of travel to inaccessible, less known, and remote locations in mountainous regions'.

As populations have migrated from rural to intensely urban areas, mountainous regions have become increasingly attractive as destinations because people want to escape the 'artificiality of modern civilization' and 'our too-muchness' (Cronon, 1996, 15). The attraction of mountains, as Pfister (2000) suggests, is the result of our 'desire to experience nature on its own terms and get back to the basics of observing what it is to live close to the land' (116). In mountain areas where indigenous people have settled, visitors are often attracted by the opportunity to become more deeply connected through authentic intercultural experiences (Deng et al., 2002). Many visitors come to the mountains drawn to the underlying symbolic imagery of untouched nature, clean, cool air, restoration and cultures living in harmony with their surroundings (Silva et al., 2011; see Fig. 1.2).

Mountain tourism experiences have significance in the notion of special interest or special niche tourism, which engages in mindful and authentic experiences that have been characterized based on levels of customer participation (passive to active) and the relationship (absorption to immersion) to the environment in which the experience is occurring (Fitzsimmons and Fitzsimmons, 2006; Steiner and Reisinger, 2006; Pine and Gilmore, 2007; Moscardo, 2008; Sundbo and Sørensen, 2013). This may include going to an extraordinary destination, having experiences in authentic settings, staying at unique places (lodging), interacting with extraordinary people, utilizing a distinctive transportation method, taking care of special needs and/or being involved in an exceptional activity (Smith and Eadington, 1992; Weiler and Hall, 1992; Pearce et al., 1998; Scarinci and Richins, 2003; Novelli, 2005).

Visitors may seek opportunities to appreciate and learn about the natural environment and/or are attracted to take part in mountain-based activities. Figure 1.3 shows activities that may be offered in natural mountain settings. Tourists are periodically involved in activities that relate to travel for nature or adventure tourism, travel for sport, health, personal wellbeing, interest in learning or serious leisure, seeking cultural tourism in natural settings, or having other interests related to the journey or the place (Weiler and Hall, 1992; Douglas et al., 2001; Scarinci and Richins, 2003; Novelli, 2005; Tourism British Columbia, 2005; Trauer, 2006; Newsome et al., 2013; Elkington and Stebbins, 2014).

Fig. 1.2. Hiking tour of White Cloud Wilderness, Idaho, USA (photograph courtesy of Harold Richins).

The attraction of mountains can be seen to be 'steeped in actual and symbolic representations of adventure' (Beedie and Hudson, 2003, 626) and in the sense of 'inherent dangers that attract some daring tourists' for sports and leisure activities (Marković and Petrović, 2013). For these adventure-seeking tourists, the natural landscape is simply just the 'backdrop or place in which the activity takes place' rather than being the focus of attention (Newsome *et al.*, 2013, 30). Within this context, adventure tourism activities range from 'hard' to 'soft', with soft adventure (lower-skilled activities) in mountain environments including activities such as camping, hiking, biking, animal watching, horseback riding, canoeing and photography. These activities are most often sought after by those interested in adventure at a relatively lower level of risk (Godde *et al.*, 2000; Beedie and Hudson, 2003; Newsome *et al.*, 2013). Alternatively, hard adventure (normally involving higher-skill-based activities) may include activities

such as mountaineering, rock climbing, remote area backpacking, white-water rafting and mountain biking. These attract adventurers more comfortable with a higher level of risk and exertion and possessing specialized skills (Newsome *et al.*, 2013).

Sport and Adventure Activities in Mountain Areas

In 2003, the Canadian Tourism Commission (CTC) studied the Canadian domestic market of outdoor adventure enthusiasts. The Travel Activities and Motivation Survey (TAMS) identified the soft adventure market as comprising 4.4 million adults, with 30–60% going hiking/backpacking, wildlife viewing, fishing, cycling (see Fig. 1.4), kayaking/canoeing, motor boating, golfing and wildflower viewing. In contrast, the CTC estimated the Canadian hard adventure market size as being significantly smaller at only 1.6 million

Fig. 1.3. Matrix of nature-based speciality travel that may take place in mountain settings (photographs courtesy of Harold Richins).

Fig. 1.4. Road biking Lake Garda, Italian Alps (photograph courtesy of Harold Richins).

adults. Mountain biking was the most popular outdoor activity, followed by rock climbing, scuba diving and white-water rafting. Over half of the hard adventure tourists also enjoyed soft adventure activities and most often the outdoor adventurer's interests and capabilities lie somewhere along a hard/soft continuum (CTC, 2003a,b). Internationally, outdoor adventure continues to have significant economic benefits, and a 2013 study estimated the value of the global outbound adventure travel sector to be US$263 billion, excluding airfare. This represents a very high average growth rate of 63% per year from 2009 to 2012 (Adventure Tourism Report, 2013). Many activities in this fast-growing sector of tourism occur within mountain settings, utilizing the compelling natural mountain resources.

Those seeking leisure and tourism experiences in the mountains now have a myriad of opportunities to engage in recreational sport (Weed and Bull, 2004; Musa *et al.*, 2015). Outdoor winter recreation activities were the impetus behind the development of many mountain destinations 'allowing the mountains to become playgrounds' (Marković and Petrović, 2013, 82). In the early days of mountain-based tourism, winter activities included snowshoeing and skiing (backcountry, alpine and cross country) and summer activities included hiking/mountaineering activities (Godde *et al.*, 2000). As technology changed and improved and the desire for adventure grew, snowmobiling and cat/heli-skiing followed in the winter, and all-terrain vehicles (ATVs) (e.g. motorcycles, quads) with mountain bikes

and other adventure sports, including white-water paddling and rafting, becoming more common in the drier summer months.

Also growing is the trend towards commercially sponsored competitive events in natural areas (Newsome *et al.*, 2013). This includes activities such as multi-sport adventure racing (i.e. a race including a variety of activities such as running, biking and paddling) or single sport racing (e.g. downhill mountain bike races). These competitive events are still adventure tourism, but distinguished from those activities where participants are actively engaged on their own or in small groups. These larger group mountain tourism activities attract an audience of spectators, which plays a significant role in the economic benefit of tourism in mountain destinations.

The Transition of Mountains Toward Visitation and Stewardship

Snowdon *et al.* (2000) have observed how mountains have become places where the economy has transitioned from resource extraction to places where tourism 'acquired a central position in thinking about the future of rural, upland and mountain economies' (138). Unlike valley bottoms, where the flat land and warmer temperatures support agriculture and manufacturing activities (and thriving service centres), mountains are generally devoid of broad-scale, intensive economic activity. Between 1870 and 1940, many countries set aside these 'worthless' lands for protected areas and parks (Hall and Higham, 2000). Policy makers believed, however, that these areas had future tourism potential as they would be aesthetically pleasing to visitors. To meet this potential, luxurious lodges were established to attract visitors and the development of railways allowed them to reach these often remote destinations (e.g. Banff, Canada; Hall and Higham, 2000).

By the 1970s–1980s, a paradigm shift occurred from more of an interest in development and visitation in mountain areas to that of preservation and stewardship (example, see Fig. 1.5). Previously considered visitor-friendly places, new policies limited visitor infrastructure

Fig. 1.5. Northstar California Resort Village, Lake Tahoe, California (photograph courtesy of Harold Richins).

in order to maintain a 'state of nature' as referred to in the 1952 New Zealand National Parks Act (Hall and Higham, 2000). The tension between the visitor-centric and preservation viewpoints is often exacerbated, however, when the mandates of differing government agencies come into stark contrast with each other. For example, the New Zealand (NZ) Department of Conservation (DOC) was originally responsible both for conservation and for fostering tourism and recreational use in all national parks – a task that was somewhat manageable under one department. However, the role of a separate agency, the Tourism Marketing Board, was to significantly increase tourist numbers by promoting NZ as a clean, green destination using the marketing slogan, '100% Pure New Zealand'. The subsequent growth in visitor numbers (many of whom visit these parks) meant that the DOC's dual mandate was particularly difficult to deliver, and became more so when their budget was significantly reduced at the same time that funding for the marketing

board was substantially increased (Hall and Higham, 2000). This is an example in New Zealand, but examination in other countries, such as Canada and the USA, produces similar observations.

Emphasis on Mountain Destination Resort Communities

Today, the focus on tourism in many mountain destinations centres is around resorts. For example, the government of the province of British Columbia in Canada has actively pursued the development of mountain resorts to 'revitalize the dwindling economies of interior BC communities' (Nepal and Jamal, 2011, 89) with the development of the 'All Season Resort Policy' in 2005. This signals a significant shift from the previous focus on winter-only destinations (see Fig. 1.5). While this has led to mountain resorts now offering golf, horse riding and mountain biking activities in the summer, resorts have expanded mountain activity offerings throughout all seasons of the year (Buckley *et al.*, 1999). Moving from being destinations where activities primarily took place slopeside (ski/snowboard), many resorts now offer a multitude of activities, including, for example, cat-skiing, tubing, skating, or snowmobiling as ways to recuperate intensive capital and operating costs. They have also increasingly turned to events, competitions (attracting both participants and viewers), meetings and conventions and cultural events (i.e. concerts, art shows). These are now becoming a large draw for additional resort visitors. Not only has this attracted short-stay visitors, but amenity migrants too – 'the combination of tourism, second homes, and amenity migration has fueled the economy of many mountain regions', according to Nepal and Jamal (2011).

Brief Summary of This Book on Mountain Tourism

Mountain Tourism: Experiences, Communities, Environments and Sustainable Futures has wide-reaching geographic coverage of mountain regions, and includes areas of focus within Europe, Asia-Pacific, South America, Africa and North America. Figure 1.6 shows the dispersion of continental regions covered by authors. European geographic mountain regions represent 33% of the coverage, North America 22%, and Asia and Pacific regions are represented in approximately 14% of the book chapters. Twenty-five per cent of the chapters could be considered in an international context.

Of the 36 chapters, 19 countries are included as a geographic focus, and eight chapters have a broader international or multi-state reach. Table 1.1 lists the geographic distribution for chapters based on subject coverage, and Figs 1.7 and 1.8 below show these regions on world and European maps.

There are 58 different contributors from 34 academic and associated organizations residing in 15 countries. In some instances more than one country is covered within a particular chapter, as comparisons are drawn or a region is covered (such as the Alps of Europe) that includes a number of countries.

The following provides a broader summary of each section of *Mountain Tourism: Experiences, Communities, Environments and Sustainable Futures*, including the introductory and concluding chapters.

Part I: Mountain Tourism Introduction

This section provides a brief introduction to mountain tourism in its theoretical and historical context as well as describing the management themes of the book relevant to mountain tourism.

Part II: Experience Provision in Mountain Tourism

Part II introduces and focuses on experience development and delivery within mountain tourism settings. This includes contextual and historical development of experience studies and application in mountain environments, within the sphere of customer experiences and motivations, the relevance to shorter-term and longer-term residents, and also in aspects of organizational and destination success within these unique environments.

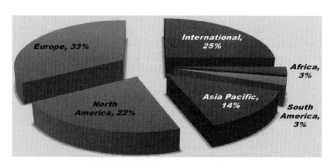

Fig. 1.6. Geographic distribution of chapters in *Mountain Tourism* by continent/region.

A number of examples of organizational commitment within a mountain tourism context are presented through a basic content exploration of tourism enterprise communication and promotion that emphasizes customer experience service provision.

Table 1.1. Geographic distribution of chapters by country in *Mountain Tourism*.

Country	Number of chapters
Australia	2
Austria	1
Canada	7
France	2
Germany	3
Iceland	1
Iran	1
Italy	1
Nepal	1
New Zealand	1
Norway	1
Peru	1
Philippines	1
Romania	1
Slovakia	1
South Africa	1
Spain	1
Switzerland	1
USA	2
International	8

Part III: People and Communities in Mountain Tourism

Part III explores aspects of people and communities in mountain tourism. This includes a focus on mountain communities and the people that visit and/or reside within these mountain regions. Many mountain communities are vibrant tourism destinations offering attractions beyond those experiences available in the natural mountain outdoors. Attractions may include historical areas, art galleries, wineries, craft breweries, hot springs and mineral pools, and festivals centred on music, food and drink. Understanding the players involved in mountain tourism and development as well as the role of local participants is critical for realizing change.

Part IV: Natural Environments and Their Connection to Mountain Tourism

Part IV explores mountain tourism and its connection and integration to natural environments through an overview of relevant literature. Mountains attract visitors for a variety of reasons, including: adventure; summer and winter sporting activities; festivals and events within natural

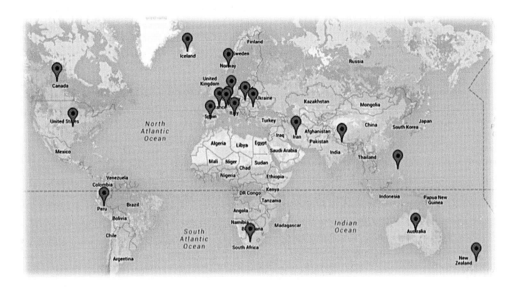

Fig. 1.7. World map of chapter geographic distribution in *Mountain Tourism* (from Google Maps).

Fig. 1.8. European map of chapter geographic distribution in *Mountain Tourism* (from Google Maps).

settings; experiencing flora and fauna; exploration; getting away, enjoying solitude, serenity and beauty; and engaging or visiting unique human settlements or mountain communities.

Part V: Impacts and Solutions in Mountain Tourism

The fifth section explores the diversity of impacts, approaches and solutions in mountain tourism through utilization of a number of case studies and pertinent writings. Each of the chapters in this section helps the reader develop a greater understanding of the complex effects and approaches used to achieve viable outcomes and successful results, while minimizing adverse consequences in mountain tourism.

Part VI: Development, Planning and Governance in Mountain Tourism

This section focuses on development, planning and governance in mountain tourism. This

includes an exploration of associated literature and presents a number of case studies and further writings in this area. This includes addressing approaches through networks, partnerships and community engagement; facilitating success through community-based tourism and small tourism enterprises and regional collaboration and governance in the context of mountain tourism.

Part VII: Mountain Tourism Implications

This final section provides a brief conclusion to Mountain Tourism in its theoretical and applied context. A model for management is presented (referred to as the Sustainable Mountain Tourism Experience Model) which endeavours to address many of the complex issues and circumstances of visitation to, and within mountains, the interactions and associations with relevant communities, as well as addressing the inherent need for effective management and emphasis on sustainable futures in the mountain tourism experience.

References

Adventure Tourism Report (2013) Available at: www.adventuretravelnews.com/new-adventure-tourism-report-reveals-263b-market-up-65-per-annum-since-2009 (accessed 15 February 2015).

Banff National Park (2015) Quick Facts. Available at: http://www.banfflakelouise.com/About-the-Area/Quick-Facts (accessed 1 May 2015).

Beedie, P. and Hudson, S. (2003) Emergence of mountain-based adventure tourism. *Annals of Tourism Research* 30(3), 625–643.

Buckley, R.C., Pickering, C.M. and Warnken, J. (1999) Environmental management for alpine tourism and resorts in Australia. In: Godde, P., Price, M.F. and Zimmermann, F.M. (eds) *Tourism and Development in Mountain Regions*. CAB International, Wallingford, UK, pp. 27–45.

Canadian Tourism Commission (2003a) Canadian Soft Outdoor Adventure Enthusiasts. Available at: http://en-corporate.canada.travel/sites/default/files/pdf/Research/Product-knowledge/TAMS/Canadian%20Travellers%20Outdoor%20Activity/tams_Canadian_soft_adventure.pdf (accessed November 2014).

Canadian Tourism Commission (2003b) Canadian Hard Outdoor Adventure Enthusiasts. Available at: http://en-corporate.canada.travel/sites/default/files/pdf/Research/Product-knowledge/TAMS/Canadian%20Travellers%20Outdoor%20Activity/tams_report_Canadian_hard_adventure.pdf (accessed November 2014).

Charters, T. and Saxon, E. (2007) Tourism and Mountains: A Practical Guide to Managing the Environmental and Social Impacts of Mmountain Tours. United Nations Environment Programme. Available at: http://www.unep.fr/shared/publications/pdf/DTIx0957xPA-MountainsEN.pdf (accessed 27 August 2015).

CIPRA (2015) What Role Do the Alps Play Within World Tourism? Available at: http://alpsknowhow.cipra.org/background_topics/alps_and_tourism/alps_and_tourism_chapter_introduction.html (accessed May 2015).

Cronon, W. (1996) The trouble with wilderness: or, getting back to the wrong nature. *Environmental History* 1(1), 7–28.

Deng, J., King, B. and Bauer, T. (2002) Evaluating natural attractions for tourism. *Annals of Tourism Research* 29(2), 422–438.

Denniston, D. (1995) *High Priorities: Conserving Mountain Ecosystems and Cultures*. Worldwatch Paper 123. Worldwatch Institute, Washington, DC.

Douglas, N., Douglas, N. and Derrett, R. (eds) (2001) *Special Interest Tourism: Context and Cases*. John Wiley and Sons, Australia.

Dunnell, T. (2015) Macchu Picchu Facts. Available at: http://goperu.about.com/od/sightsandattractions/tp/Machu-Picchu-Facts.htm (accessed 1 May 2015).

Elkington, S. and Stebbins, R.A. (2014) *The Serious Leisure Perspective: An Introduction*. Routledge, Abingdon, UK.

Fitzsimmons, J.A. and Fitzsimmons, M.J. (2006) *Service Management: Operations, Strategy, and Information Technology*. Irwin/McGraw-Hill, New York.

Godde, P., Price, M.F. and Zimmermann, F.M. (2000) Tourism and development in mountain regions: moving forward into the New Millennium. In: Godde, P., Price, M.F. and Zimmermann, F.M. (eds) *Tourism and Development in Mountain Regions*. CAB International, Wallingford, UK, pp. 1–25.

Government of Nepal (2011) Nepal Tourism Misses 1 Million Arrivals Target. Available at: http://www.eturbonews.com/27171/nepal-tourism-misses-1-million-arrivals-target (accessed 2 May 2014).

Hall, M.C. and Higham, J. (2000) Wilderness management in the forests of New Zealand: historical development and contemporary issues in environmental management. In: Font, X. and Tribe, J. (eds) *Forest Tourism and Recreation: Case Studies in Environmental Management*. CAB International, Wallingford, UK, pp. 143–160.

Keller, P. (2014) Mountainlikers: New trends of mountain tourism for the summer season. *8th World Congress on Snow and Mountain Tourism*. Andorra-la-Vella, Principality of Andorra, 9–10 April 2014.

Marković, J.J. and Petrović, M.D. (2013) Sport and recreation influence upon mountain area and sustainable tourism development. *Journal of Environmental and Tourism Analyses* 1(1), 80–89.

Moscardo, G. (2008) Understanding tourist experience though Mindfulness Theory. In: Kozak, M. and Decrop, A. (eds) *Handbook of Tourist Behavior: Theory and Practice*. Routledge, New York, pp. 99–115.

Musa, G., Higham, J. and Thompson-Carr, A. (eds) (2015) *Mountaineering Tourism*. Routledge, London.

Nepal, S.K. (2002) Mountain ecotourism and sustainable development: ecology, economics and ethics. *Mountain Research and Development* 22(2), 104–109. Available at: www.bioone.org (accessed 15 November 2014).

Nepal, S.K. and Chipeniuk, R. (2005) Mountain tourism: toward a conceptual framework. *Tourism Geographies* 7(3), 313–333.

Nepal, S.K. and Jamal, T.B. (2011) Resort-induced changes in small mountain communities in British Columbia, Canada. *Mountain Research and Development* 31(2), 89–101. Available at: www.bioone.org (accessed 30 November 2014).

Newsome, D., Moore, S.A. and Dowling, R.K. (2013) *Natural Area Tourism: Ecology, Impacts and Management* (2nd edn). Channel View, Bristol, UK.

Novelli, M. (ed.) (2005) *Niche Tourism: Contemporary Issues, Trends and Cases*. Elsevier Butterworth-Heinemann, Burlington, Massachusetts.

Pearce, P.L., Morrison, A. and Rutledge, J. (1998) *Tourism: Bridges Across Continents*. McGraw-Hill, Sydney.

People and Planet (2008) Mountains: Vital for Human Survival. Available at: www.peopleandtheplanet. com/index.html@lid=26651&section=41&topic=44.html (accessed 13 March 2015).

Pfister, R.E. (2000) Mountain culture as a tourism resource: aboriginal views on the privileges of storytelling. In: Godde, P., Price, M.F and Zimmermann, F.M. (eds) *Tourism and Development in Mountain Regions*. CAB International, Wallingford, UK, pp. 115–136.

Pine, B. and Gilmore, J. (2007) *Authenticity: What Consumers Really Want*. Harvard Business School Press, Boston, Massachusetts.

Rocky Mountain National Park (2015) Park Statistics. Available at: http://www.nps.gov/romo/learn/management/statistics.htm (accessed 2 May 2015).

Scarinci, J. and Richins, H. (2003) Motivations for visiting bed and breakfast accommodation: Implications for niche marketing. *Refereed Proceedings of the Asia Pacific Tourism Association Ninth Annual Conference*. Asia Pacific Tourism Association, Sydney.

Silva, C., Kastenholz, E. and Abrantes, J.L. (2011) An overview of social and cultural meanings of mountains and implications on mountain destination marketing. *Journal of Tourism* 12(2), 73–90.

Smith, V.L. and Eadington, W.R. (eds) (1992) *Tourism Alternatives: Potentials and Problems in the Development of Tourism*. University of Pennsylvania Press, Philadelphia, Pennsylvania.

Snowdon, P., Slee, B. and Farr, H. (2000) The economic impacts of different types of tourism in upland and mountain areas of Europe. In: Godde, P., Price, M.F. and Zimmermann, F.M. (eds) *Tourism and Development in Mountain Regions*. CAB International, Wallingford, UK, pp. 137–155.

Steiner, C., and Reisinger, Y. (2006) Understanding existential authenticity. *Annals of Tourism Research* 33, 299–318.

Sundbo, J. and Sørensen, F. (eds) (2013) *Handbook on the Experience Economy*. Edward Elgar Publishing, Cheltenham, UK.

Tourism British Columbia (TBC) (2005) Characteristics of the Commercial Nature-Based Tourism Industry in British Columbia. Available at: http://www.wilderness-tourism.bc.ca/docs/Commercial_Nature-Based%20 Tourism.pdf (accessed 7 January 2016).

Tourism Snowy Mountains (2013) Snowy Mountains Annual Report 2011–12. Available at: http://www.arcc. vic.gov.au/uploads/publications-and-research/ARCC-AnnualReport-2011to2012-Web.pdf (accessed 7 January 2016).

Trauer, B. (2006) Conceptualizing special interest tourism – frameworks for analysis. *Tourism Management* 27(2), 183–200.

United Nations Agenda 21 (1992) United Nations Conference on Environment & Development: Rio de Janerio, Brazil. Agenda 21. Available at: http://sustainabledevelopment.un.org/content/documents/Agenda21.pdf (accessed 22 November 2014).

United Nations Environmental Programme (2002) Mountains. United Nations Environment Programme. Available at: http://www.unep.org/resourceefficiency/Home/Business/SectoralActivities/Tourism/WorkThematicAreas/EcosystemManagement/Mountains/tabid/78801/Default.aspx (accessed 22 November 2014).

UNWTO (2014) *UNWTO Tourism Highlights*, 2014 Edition. World Tourism Organization, Madrid.

Urry, J. (1990) *The Tourist Gaze: Leisure and Travel in Contemporary Societies*. Collection Theory, Culture & Society. Sage Publications, London.

Weed, M. and Bull, C. (2004) *Sports Tourism: Participants, Policy and Providers*. Elsevier Butterworth, Oxford, UK.

Weiler, B. and Hall, C.M. (1992) *Special Interest Tourism*. Belhaven Press, London.

Westgro (2013) Table Mountain Aerial Cableway Annual Report 2013. Available at: http://www.tablemountain. net/uploads/files/18284_TM_Annual_Report_2013_Flipping_Brochureindd_1_1.pdf (accessed 3 May 2015).

2 Experience Provision in Mountain Tourism: Overview, Contextual Development and Emphasis

Harold Richins*

Thompson Rivers University, Kamloops, British Columbia, Canada

Introduction

This chapter introduces Part II by providing an overview of experience provision within mountain tourism settings. Included is a contextual emphasis on experiences in mountain environments, both within the sphere of visitor experiences and services and also concerning the significance of organizational commitment and destination emphasis on experience provision within these unique environments. Numerous examples of organizational commitment within a mountain tourism context are presented through a basic content exploration of tourism enterprise communication and promotion, which emphasizes customer experience service provision. This introduction summarizes the chapters included in Part II.

The notion of experience studies incorporates the understanding, creation, development, and provision of human experiences and services, and has progressed toward more complexity, inclusion, application, and focus over the 45 years since Toffler (1970) first wrote about the upcoming experience industries. The literature has advanced concepts in specific areas including: extraordinary experience; products and services as experiences; and the concept of the experience society

(Abrahams, 1981; Holbrook and Hirschman, 1982; Schulze, 1992, 2005; Arnould and Price, 1993). Additionally, there has been a growing body of knowledge on the importance of the development and provision of experiences to raise the bar on value within the service industries, particularly through tourism experiences (Cohen, 1979; Mannell and Iso-Ahola, 1987; Aho, 2001; Uriely, 2005). Over the last two decades, there has been added scholarship and conceptual development utilizing relevant aspects of experience creation, customer service experience, experience behavior, experience economy, as well as the creative economy (Jensen, 1996; Pine and Gilmore, 1998 ,1999; Jensen, 1999; Schmitt, 2003; Andersson and Andersson, 2006; Fleming, 2007; Moscardo, 2008).

Tourism, Leisure and Visitor Experiences

The provision of quality experiences is of particular interest in the study of tourism, leisure, and visitor experiences (Cohen, 1979; Mannell and Iso-Ahola, 1987; Buhalis and Paraskevas, 2002; Michelli, 2006; Andersson, 2007; Fleming, 2007; Hayes and MacLeod, 2007; Oh *et al.*, 2007; Moscardo, 2008; Michael *et al.*, 2009; Kaplanidou and

* Corresponding author: hrichins@tru.ca

Vogt, 2010; Tung and Brent Ritchie, 2011; Richins, 2013). Key components in the provision of tourism and leisure experiences have been acknowledged including gaining an understanding of the participant, the place in which the experience occurs, the focus of the experience, the state of mind of the participant(s), the structure, provision and communications which enhance or create success in the experience, the themes or narrative of the experience, and the outcomes which occur as a result of the experience (Quan and Wang, 2004; Mossberg, 2007; Moscardo, 2008). Tourism Australia, for example has been emphasizing a commitment to identifying and promoting authentic tourism experiences for a significant period of time. Developed in 2006, the Australian Experiences Framework: 'focuses on seven Key Australian Experiences which are based on Australia's core strengths' (Tourism Australia, 2014).

Canada has also taken a leadership role in emphasizing the value of providing tourists with more meaningful, memorable, and authentic visitor experiences with destination marketing organizations building experiential travel into their strategic directions as an integral part of positioning their brand in regional, provincial, and national markets. Examples include the Thompson Okanagan Tourism Organization's principle of 'developing and promoting distinctive quality experiences' (TOTA, 2014), Destination British Columbia's tourism goal to provide 'world class visitor experiences' (JTST, 2014) and the Canadian Tourism Commission's priority to 'enhance visitor experiences through quality service and hospitality' (CTC, 2014). The Canadian Tourism Commission has also prioritized the development and marketing of quality customer experiences leading to the successful creation of 'Signature Experiences', which identifies leading Canadian tourist/visitor experience products (CTC, 2014).

Emphasis on leisure and tourism experiences in mountain communities

Mountain resort communities have often integrated daily life and leisure experiences with visitor and customer experiences (Sun Peaks, 2014; Whistler, 2014a; Zermatt, 2014). As an example, the Resort Municipality of Whistler (Whistler 2014b) indicates that it acts 'as a steward for resort interests and serving the needs of both residents and visitors. The organization is committed to progressive and deliberate community planning and management to create a vibrant and healthy resort community.' The first two priorities of Whistler's 2020 community vision includes enriching community life and enhancing the resort experience (Whistler, 2014c). These normally dynamic and active communities frequently involve the development of unique specialist or niche activities, balancing leisure and tourism experiences, and often include high levels of experience engagement and customer focus (Smith and Eadington, 1992; Weiler and Hall, 1992; Pearce et al., 1998; Douglas et al., 2001; Novelli, 2005; Trauer, 2006; see Fig. 2.1).

Basic Content Exploration of Tourism Enterprises Emphasizing Customer Experience Service Provision

There has been a clear and applied focus by industry players, particularly in mountain regions, regarding the development and provision of quality and engaging experiences (Mountain Experience NP, 2014; New Zealand Travel Experiences, 2014; Vermont, 2014; Wiegele, 2014). Mountain environments offer a myriad of opportunities for engaging recreation and tourism experiences. People who visit mountain regions often do so for challenging and physically active experiences connected with the natural assets of the mountain regions.

A number of companies focus on prioritizing the concept of experiences in the mountain environments or settings. Sun Peaks, a resort municipality in British Columbia (BC), was purpose-built in the 1990s with a long-term plan to develop a community and attractive tourism and recreational environment that focuses on outdoor winter and summer activities. Their Mission Statement is 'To provide the finest mountain resort experience'. This mission is incorporated into both the company's operational culture as well as the important focus on customer experience management (Sun Peaks, 2014; see Fig. 2.2). This experience focus has propelled Sun Peaks Resort, Canada's second-largest ski

Fig. 2.1. Visitor experience provision with the *Siora Veronica*, the oldest sailing vessel on Lake Garda, Italian Alps (photograph courtesy of Harold Richins).

Fig. 2.2. Sun Peaks Mountain Resort Municipality: a focus on the experience, British Columbia, Canada (photograph courtesy of Harold Richins).

area, towards becoming one of the Top Ten Family-friendly Ski Resorts in North America (Condé Nast Traveler, 2014).

There are numerous examples in the niche mountain adventure tourism segment of helicopter skiing. All of the following heli companies emphasize the creation, development, and provision (and promotion) of enhanced customer experiences. There are several British Columbia examples, beginning with Canadian Mountain Holidays (CMH). CMH opened in 1959 and started providing heli-skiing services into the wilderness areas of British Columbia starting in 1965. CMH promises guests 'an experience like never before' and expresses significant details in the many ways they provide visitors with unparalleled experiences and 'one of life's ultimate experiences' (CMH, 2014):

> Canadian Mountain Holidays has always set out to bring people to the peak of an experience like never before ... there's only one company that delivers heart-thumping terrain along with exceptional lodge experiences to forever ignite a person's spirit of adventure. That's CMH.

Mike Wiegele Helicopter Skiing, which started in 1970, uses a catchy tag line, 'Elevate Your Experience'. They are pioneers in the provision of high level and fully integrated mountain experiences (Wiegele, 2014). Ruby Mountains Heli-experience, which started in 1977, incorporates experience into their name and offers a remote Nevada wilderness ski experience (Ruby, 2014) and they demonstrate through communication and customer feedback their strong commitment to personal engaged experiences. Last Frontier Heliskiing, began operating in 1991 within a 2.2 million acre tenure in northern BC offering 'the ultimate helicopter skiing experience' (Last Frontier, 2014). Lastly, Majestic Heli Ski, located within Alaska's Chugach and Talkeetna Mountains proudly discusses 'the majestic heli ski experience' and shows a major commitment towards added value in the provision of its participant mountain experiences (Majestic, 2014). Other global examples of tourism enterprises include Mountain Experience Trekking and Expedition, operating out of Nepal, which is built on their commitment to the visitor experience:

> Mountain Experience Pvt. Ltd. Trekking and Expedition was founded with a vision to provide our clients with a unique travel experience that brings enjoyment and creates an understanding of local cultures. We offer cultural journeys on foot. Walking is the best way to explore a country, and combined with a high standard of comfort and with experienced, well-informed guides, will ensure that each one of you enjoys an outstanding experience that will be fondly remembered for many years. At Mountain Experience we plan our trips with you in mind so that you can experience the scenic sights and local cultures at a leisurely pace. Our itineraries are well-structured and offer flexibility, fun and education.
>
> (Mountain Experience, 2014)

Intrawest, 'a premier North American mountain resort and adventure company' states that 'what sets Intrawest apart and propels the company forward is the very fact that we create places where amazing experiences happen. Unique, memorable, ultimate body-and-soul satisfying experiences.' They also speak of how these exceptional experiences lead to their success: 'Our ability to consistently deliver exceptional experiences forms the foundation of our financial success.' Intrawest's vision also expresses this focus: 'Intrawest is committed to being the best in the world at guiding our guests through an evolving range of great experiences which connect them to fun, a sense of discovery and rejuvenation' (Intrawest, 2014a).

Other companies that emphasize personal experiences include: Ontario's Blue Mountain resort can 'customize your mountain experience' (Blue Mountain, 2014); Western Australia's Montafon Mountain resort community emphasizes 'real mountains; real experiences' (Montafon Mountain, 2014); and Europe's The True Collection emphasizes 'the colours of the Alps, true experiences deliver once in a lifetime memories and lasting relationships' (True Collection, 2014). Canada's Rocky Mountaineer rail tours, has offered mountain train travel for over two decades in Canada. They emphasize '25 years of life changing experiences' in their tag line (Rocky Mountaineer, 2014).

Zermatt, a mountain community with extensive history in the southern Swiss Alps, has long been known for mountain tourism. In the late 1800s, mountaineering had reached a prominent age of accomplishment, and even though there were tragic deaths in the success of summiting the peak, there was significant growth of mountain tourism to the region. Now, close to 150 years later, Zermatt has continued to be a prominent mountain tourism and recreation community (Matterhorn, 2014). The resort community continues to indicate this emphasis in communicating the following: 'mountain experiences once in Zermatt, always in Zermatt' and 'unforgettable experiences lure everyone' (Zermatt, 2014).

A number of mountain tourism enterprises have incorporated 'experience' into their name. Examples include the following: 'Experience MTB' focuses on mountain bike experiences in the Karkonosze Mountains in southwestern Poland, along the border with the Czech Republic (Experience MTB, 2014); 'Japan Experience' offers special tours in the Alpine region of Nagano, Japan (Japan Experience, 2014); 'Mountain Experience', also from Japan, describes their service as, 'Mountain Experience ... founded with a vision to provide our clients with a unique travel experience that brings enjoyment and creates an understanding of local cultures' (Mountain Experience NP, 2014); the UK's 'River Mountain Experience' concentrates on backcountry guiding as well as guide and mountain training in North Yorkshire in the UK (River Mountain Experience, 2014); 'Mountain Experience', also based in the UK, focuses on training for mountain experiences and leading mountain expeditions for all ability levels (Mountain Experiences UK, 2014); the USA's 'White Mountain Experience', which focuses on offering adventures off the beaten track in the mountain region of northern New Hampshire (White Mountain Experience, 2014); and 'Mountain Experience Org' out of Bridgend County in the UK, which emphasizes 'Adventures off the Beaten Track' (Mountain Experience Org, 2014). A final example from Canada is 'Selkirk Mountain Experience', which offers a backcountry lodge experience near Revelstoke, British Columbia where 'Guests come from all over the world to experience our mountains and our hospitality' (Selkirk Mountain, 2014).

'New Zealand Travel Experiences' emphasizes the visitor experience in this quote: 'The team at Experience New Zealand has been carefully matchmaking travelers with wonderful New Zealand experiences for more than 12 years. We are passionate about our clients' entire journey, from dream, to experience, to memory' and 'Whatever your chosen mode of travel, our goal is always the same – to provide you with a truly memorable New Zealand travel experience' (New Zealand Travel Experiences, 2014). Also from New Zealand is 'Kiwi Experience', a unique coach transportation system for international travellers to New Zealand, that has spent over two decades emphasizing experiences both on and off the bus as well as the flexibility in access to transport. The following demonstrates this emphasis:

> You're here to see the country – not the inside of a bus. You're here to meet people – not have the backseat to yourself. You're here to experience a legendary place and be guided by those who know New Zealand best ... Kiwi Experience is the leading hop-on, hop-off backpacker New Zealand bus experience designed by travelers for travelers. We know when to stop the bus and soak it in, and when to keep on driving and leave the tourist traps behind. We'll show you New Zealand's big highlights, and incredible places so hidden even Peter Jackson couldn't find them. Whether you're an adrenalin junkie, a culture seeker, a beach bum, or have come to see the most awe-inspiring landscapes in the world, Kiwi Experience is the trip of a lifetime! You couldn't have a bad time if you tried ... Over 25 years our reputation, passenger numbers, awards, and word of mouth from thrilled travelers and New Zealand backpackers has spoken for itself. As the country's largest, leading, and legendary bus experience we'd love you to continue the story and experience New Zealand with us – the way it should be seen.
>
> (Kiwi Experience, 2014)

Organizational Focus and Priority on the Provision of Experiences

Over the last two decades there has been a growing understanding of the interest and need to have an organizational focus and priority on the design, development, provision, and management of experiences in order for enterprises to achieve success within their respective industry sectors (Shaw and Iven, 2004; Pine and Gilmore, 2007; Darmer and Sundbo, 2008; Prahalad and Krishnan, 2008; Sundbo and Darmer, 2008; Hyken, 2009; Pine and Gilmore, 2011; Tung and Brent Ritchie, 2011). This involves building inclusive capacity within the organization to create and put into action extraordinary visitor experiences. As an illustration of improving the organizational culture of experience-based management within tourism organizations, Intrawest shows its priority for customer experience excellence:

> We set the stage for amazing vacations. Our difference is our dedication to the experience our guests have in every single one of our unique locations. It's about embracing every visitor in a way that's genuine and down-to-earth in a fun mountain atmosphere. It starts with our people and the level of commitment they bring to what they do every day. It results in every visitor feeling welcomed into each and every place they visit, which takes their vacation experience to a whole new level. And it all happens against the backdrop of our unique collection of mountain properties and resorts, which makes it even easier to recognize the appeal of our authenticity and hospitality.
>
> (Intrawest, 2014b)

This brief content analysis of customer experience provision points to how numerous organizations within the mountain tourism sector are prioritizing the provision of high-quality and engaging experiences. Though further work may be done in understanding the depth of accomplishment and success in experience provision in mountain tourism, a number of enterprises are demonstrating through promotional tag lines and descriptions of their offerings, as well as through company names, mission and vision statements, the emphasis they are placing on experiences, and in particular the visitor and participant experiences.

Summary of Chapters in Part II: Experience Provision in Mountain Tourism

The chapters in this section explore this important area of experience provision in mountain tourism. The literature and brief case studies provide a context for mountain tourism-based experience studies discussing informal interactions and activities and also more formal or purposeful experience creation and provision within the context of mountain tourism destinations. The following briefly summarizes the authors' efforts to describe the significance of experience development in mountain tourism settings. Topics explore: (i) rural and peripheral alpine tourist experiences; (ii) wellness and mountain resort tourism experience provision; (iii) unique experience-based trail networks as tourism products (iv) innovation in high-end heli-ski mountain experiences; (v) the setting of mountain destinations in building small organized event experiences; and (vi) the commitment to excellence in customer experience provision within a winter sports destination. These chapters are summarized further below.

Chapter 3. Wellness Tourism Experiences in Mountain Regions: The Case of Sparkling Hill Resort, Canada

Author: John S. Hull

Wellness tourism is perhaps one of the oldest types of activities that has attracted visitors to mountain areas. From Roman resort communities to hot springs hotels in Canada to Japanese baths ('onsen') in mountain areas, people have gravitated toward these natural hot spring and spa areas and travelled long distances with the expectation of improving their health and fitness with the mineral waters resulting from volcanic and geologic processes in mountain regions. Other mountain assets such as the natural beauty, the clean mountain air and water, and a sense of serenity have also been attractors for visitors seeking health and wellness.

Author John S. Hull discusses wellness tourism through a case study of a wellness tourism resort in the Okanagan region of British Columbia (BC). His chapter looks at the emerging sophistication of wellness experiences in mountain areas. Through in-depth discussions with Sparking Hill supervisory staff, the author ascertained important themes connecting the wellness and spa customer experience with the mountain and lake landscape. The research discussed in this chapter involved both an audit of health and wellness facilities within the province of BC, and a case study of Sparkling Hill Resort. The findings suggest key indicators of success in attracting and satisfying guests interested in wellness tourism in mountain areas.

Chapter 4. Creating Tourist Experiences in European Alpine Areas: Beyond Mass Tourism

Authors: Umberto Martini and Federica Buffa

Experience-based tourism focuses on building and providing engaging and memorable experiences for tourists. Another emerging area related to the customer experience has been referred to as creative tourism. This has aspects of experienced-based tourism with the added components of authentic learning experiences related to creative activities as well as outcomes related to the unique qualities of a destination.

Chapter 4 provides a case study of the development of experience-based tourism with a key motivation to build unique tourist experiences for visitors and enhance the competitiveness of rural mountain regions in northern Italy. The authors discuss the challenges of rural valley communities surrounded by mountain terrain as traditional lifestyles change over the decades. Remote communities are even further challenged due to difficult access and limited economic diversity.

The case study in this chapter focuses on the relatively remote region of Trentino in Italy referred to as Valle del Chiese, which includes a number of small municipalities, many with fewer than 500 residents. Through the support of a Central European programme, which focuses on village redevelopment and viability, the rural area has begun to develop and provide unique tourism offerings of high relevance to their regional assets, and cultural and social attributes. This case provides examples of the potential for positive outcomes when the community works in a collective fashion in the development and provision of remote rural-based tourism experiences.

Chapter 5. Motivations for a Destination Wedding in Canada's Mountain Parks

Author: Elizabeth A. Halpenny

While there is a large body of research work on travel tourist behaviour and motivations, only nominal research has been conducted in examining mountain tourist behaviour. Elizabeth A. Halpenny reviews tourist behaviour literature and provides insight on mountain tourist behaviour motivations, focusing on the speciality tourism sectors of couples, friends, and family travelling to mountain tourism destinations to participate in weddings at these destinations. She found that many wedding groups who travel to destinations specifically for a wedding also participate in tourist activities at either the same or a similar location.

Mountain tourism destination settings provide a significant backdrop for small, organized event experiences. Halpenny provides a context for the findings related directly to the destination wedding tourism experience, particularly within national parks in mountain regions of Canada. The interest in tourist destination wedding experiences is increasing, with 15–25% of weddings involving travelling to tourist destinations for both their wedding ceremonies and celebrations, in addition to the honeymoon. This exploratory study allows the reader to understand more thoroughly the destination wedding practices, activities, experiences, and the motivational factors (some push, some pull) with regard to this newer niche marketing area of destination weddings in some of the significant mountain tourism destinations of Canada.

Chapter 6. Stamp Books in the Harz Mountains, Germany – Fun Not Just for Children

Authors: Michael Lück and Sven Gross

Tourism and leisure activities and experiences in mountain environments normally involve active participation and engagement. Experiencing the outdoors has mental and physical aspects, and has long been touted as one of the major reasons for travel to mountain areas.

The most common mountain activities often involve hiking, walking or trekking. Michael Lück and Sven Gross explore this significant tourism activity and make the case that the use of stamp books may, perhaps, be an extension of the historic way in which families experienced natural areas in the past, particularly mountain regions.

This chapter provides a case study of the most mountainous region of former East Germany, the Harz Mountains. The authors discuss the importance of hiking tourism, both economically, in terms of destination-based mountain tourism, and in the provision of peripheral economic outputs. Perhaps, along with wildlife viewing and fishing, hiking is one of the most commonly practised activities in natural environments (particularly within mountain environments).

The case study describes motivational and beneficial aspects of hiking as an outdoor activity and also provides for a discussion of a more structured approach to hiking within Germany and particularly within the Harz Mountain region. The trail network system and a method of utilizing a stamp-book approach for demonstrating hiking accomplishments is discussed, and the benefit of motivating hikers to be active in the completion of distinctive trails in the region is examined. The case attempts to demonstrate unique experience-based tourism products, which bring economic value, community cooperation, and build awareness of the range of regional assets for visitors. The authors note how this adds significant value to the tourist experience for families holidaying in the region.

Mike Wiegele was involved as an early pioneer in the development of motorized access to winter backcountry experiences. This chapter emphasizes, through the lens of innovation, the historical development of accessing and skiing in remote winter mountain terrain. The chapter provides insight into the development of a best-practice iconic tourism experience that started with strong emphasis on providing exceptional and personal customer service, and building high-quality visitor amenities.

Though access to backcountry skiing did not start in the Canadian Rockies, the innovative development of multi-run heli-skiing on world-class terrain began and grew over a 50-year period in British Columbia, Canada. The chapter explores this development through product and experience innovation within a small-to-medium-sized and community-based luxury tourism enterprise.

The author discusses the development of backcountry terrain tenure, the use of motorized equipment for access, innovation regarding personal equipment for heli-skiing, and the provision and development of innovative and personal iconic experience development within the industry. Other innovative aspects are exemplified in the safety programme development and certification methods, the provision and access to non-expert backcountry experiences, and innovative measures to create excellence in the accommodation and hospitality experience offered to guests. Finally, the chapter discusses the shift towards developing an integrated winter sports village with access to backcountry experiences.

Chapter 7. Significant Innovation in the Development and Provision of Heli-ski Mountain Experiences: The Case of Mike Wiegele Helicopter Skiing

Author: Harold Richins

Mountain terrain has had a history of access-related issues. Over the last century, various attempts have been made to improve access for those wishing to enjoy mountain experiences and activities. In this chapter by Harold Richins, the progression of innovative and enterprising approaches to providing winter snow sports experiences is discussed.

Chapter 8. From Winter Destination to All-year-round Tourism: How Focus on Service Can Reduce Fluctuation in Demand Due to Seasonality

Authors: Marit Gundersen Engeset and Jan Velvin

In winter-dominated mountain tourism destinations, seasonality has traditionally been a major challenge in achieving long-term destination success. Some mountain resorts only operate during a relatively short winter season (2 to 4 months) while others have found ways to operate beyond that period. The off-season, or what is called in tourism circles the 'between seasons', is a challenge even in mountain destinations that have opportunities to expand their summer business given easy access to lakes, rivers, and other mountain features.

Customer experience provision relates to the customer service provided by tourism organizations. Authors Marit Gundersen Engeset and Jan Velvin provide an alternative position on building customer interest and longer-term commitment to mountain destinations. This involves commitment to excellence in developing and providing quality customer experiences. The chapter argues that the commitment to customer service and experience provision provides for a foundation that grows the overall business year-round.

The authors use the case of Hemsedal, Norway and a 3-year research project focused on a customer-service training programme. It describes various phases of the programme, including employee and leadership training that is related to building the customer service experience, collection of data related to measuring satisfaction and tensions, and providing feedback to enterprises regarding their progress. Results from the efforts have shown positive preliminary outcomes, and the intent is to build upon these through future commitment to the process. With today's emphasis on customer feedback through personal recommendation using web-based methods such as TripAdvisor and Booking.com, it is becoming increasingly important to focus attention in the area of customer experience development and provision.

Concluding Remarks Regarding this Chapter on Experience Provision in Mountain Tourism

This chapter has provided an introduction to Part II and has given an overview of experience provision in mountain tourism. A number of illustrations of organizational commitment within a mountain tourism context were presented through a basic content exploration of tourism enterprise communication and promotion, which emphasizes customer experience service provision.

The literature and the summaries of chapters in this section has introduced the reader to the dynamic topics pertinent to experience creation in mountain tourism and gives an overview and contextual understanding to the topic of Part II: the development and provision of mountain tourism experiences. The chapters represent the diversity in this field, and provide specific examples of issues and influences that have both a direct and indirect impact on achieving effective customer and organizational experience development within mountain tourism settings.

References

Abrahams, R.D. (1981) Ordinary and extraordinary experiences. In: Turner, V. (ed.) *The Anthropology of Experience.* University of Illinois Press, Chicago, Illinois, pp. 45–72.

Aho, S.K. (2001) Towards a general theory of touristic experiences: modelling experience process in tourism. *Tourism Review* 56(3), 33.

Andersson, A.E. and Andersson, D.E. (2006) *The Economics of Experiences, the Arts and Entertainment.* Edward Elgar, Cheltenham, UK.

Andersson, T.D. (2007) The tourist in the experience economy. *Scandinavian Journal of Hospitality and Tourism* 7(1), 46–58.

Arnould, E.J. and Price, L.L. (1993) River magic: extraordinary experience and the extended Service Encounter. *Journal of Consumer Research* 20(1), 24–45.

Blue Mountain (2014) Blue Mountain website. Available at: http://www.bluemountain.ca (accessed 16 November 2014).

Buhalis, D. and Paraskevas, A. (2002) Entrepreneurship in tourism and the contexts of experience economy, University of Lapland, Rovaniemi, Finland, 4–7 April 2001. *Tourism Management* 23(4), 427–428.

CMH (2014) Canadian Mountain Holidays website. Available at: http://www.canadianmountainholidays.com (accessed 16 November 2014).

Cohen, E. (1979) A phenomenology of tourist experiences. *Sociology* 13(2), 179–201.

Condé Nast Traveler (2014) Top 10 Family-friendly Ski Resorts in North America. Available at: http://www.cntraveler.com/galleries/2014-12-03/tahoe-sun-valley-mont-tremblant-top-10-family-friendly-ski-resorts-in-north-america/8 (accessed 17 November 2014).

CTC (2014) Canada's Federal Tourism Strategy: Welcoming the World. Available at: http://www.tourism.gc.ca/eic/site/034.nsf/eng/00218.html (accessed 10 November 2014).

Darmer, P. and Sundbo, J. (2008) *Creating Experiences in the Experience Economy (Services, Economy and Innovation)*. Edward Elgar, Cheltenham, UK.

Douglas, N., Douglas, N. and Derrett, R. (eds) (2001) *Special Interest Tourism: Context and Cases*. John Wiley, Milton, Queensland, Australia.

Experience MTB (2014) MTB Treks. Available at: http://www.mtbtreks.com (accessed 16 November 2014).

Fleming, T. (2007) *A Creative Economy Green Paper for the Nordic Region*. Nordic Innovation Centre, Oslo, Norway.

Hayes, D. and MacLeod, N. (2007) Packaging places: designing heritage trails using an experience economy perspective to maximize visitor engagement. *Journal of Vacation Marketing* 13(1), 45–58.

Holbrook, M.B. and Hirschman, E.C. (1982) The experiential aspects of consumption: Consumer fantasies, feelings, and fun. *Journal of Consumer Research* 9(2), 132–140.

Hyken, S. (2009) *The Cult of the Customer: Create an Amazing Customer Experience That Turns Satisfied Customers Into Customer Evangelists*. Wiley, Hoboken, New Jersey.

Intrawest (2014a) Intrawest website. Available at: http://www.intrawest.com (accessed 16 November 2014).

Intrawest (2014b) Intrawest: What We Do. Available at: http://www.intrawest.com/about-us/what-we-do.aspx (accessed 20 November 2014).

Japan Experience (2014) Japan Experience website. Available at: http://www.japan-experience.com (accessed 16 November 2014).

Jensen, R. (1996) The Dream Society. *The Futurist* 30(3)), 9–13.

Jensen, R. (1999) The story of the future. *Across the Board* 36(1), 33–36.

JTST (2014) Ministry of Jobs, Tourism and Skills Training: Tourism Policy Branch. Available at: http://www.jtst.gov.bc.ca/tourismstrategy (accessed 14 November 2014).

Kaplanidou, K. and Vogt, C. (2010) The meaning and measurement of a sport event experience among active sport tourists. *Journal of Sport Management* 24(5), 544–566.

Kiwi Experience (2014) Kiwi Experience website. Available at: http://www.kiwiexperience.com (accessed 10 November 2014).

Last Frontier (2014) Last Frontier Heliskiing website. Available at: http://www.lastfrontierheli.com (accessed 14 December 2014).

Majestic (2014) The Majestic Heli Ski Experience. Available at: http://majesticheliski.com/the-experience (accessed 30 October 2014).

Mannell, R.C. and Iso-Ahola, S.E. (1987) Psychological nature of leisure and tourism experience. *Annals of Tourism Research* 14(3), 314–331.

Matterhorn (2014) Matterhorn – Symbol for Switzerland. Available at: http://www.myswitzerland.com/en-ca/the-matterhorn-in-your-sights.html (accessed 14 October 2014).

Michael, M., Elbe, J. and Curiel, J. (2009) Has the experience economy arrived? The views of destination managers in three visitor-dependent areas. *International Journal of Tourism Research* 11(2), 201–216.

Michelli, J. (2006) *The Starbucks Experience: 5 Principles for Turning Ordinary into Extraordinary*. McGraw-Hill, New York.

Mike Wiegele (2014) Mike Wiegele Helicopter Skiing. Available at: http://www.wiegele.com/heliski-experience.htm (accessed 22 November 2014).

Montafon Mountain (2014) Montafon website. Available at: http://www.montafon.at (accessed 24 October 2014).

Moscardo, G. (2008) Understanding tourist experience though Mindfulness Theory. In: Kozak, M. and Decrop, A. (eds) *Handbook of Tourist Behavior: Theory and Practice*. Routledge, New York, pp. 99–115.

Mossberg, L. (2007) A marketing approach to the tourist experience. *Scandinavian Journal of Hospitality and Tourism* 7(1), 59–74.

Mountain Experience NP (2014) Mountain Experience Trekking & Expeditions website. Available at: http://www.mountainexperience.com.np (accessed 16 November 2014).

Mountain Experience Org (2014) Mountain Experience: Adventures Off the Beaten Track. Available at: http://www.mountain-experience.org (accessed 10 November 2014).

Mountain Experiences UK (2014) Available at: http://www.mountainexperiences.co.uk (accessed 27 August 2015).

New Zealand Travel Experiences (2014) Experience New Zealand Travel. Available at: http://www.experiencenz.com (accessed 10 November 2014).

Novelli, M. (ed.) (2005) *Niche Tourism: Contemporary Issues, Trends and Cases*. Elsevier Butterworth-Heinemann, Burlington, Massachusetts.

Oh, H., Fiore, A.M. and Jeoung, M. (2007) Measuring experience economy concepts: tourism applications. *Journal of Travel Research* 46(2), 119–132.

Pearce, P.L., Morrison, A. and Rutledge, J. (1998) *Tourism: Bridges across Continents*. McGraw-Hill, Sydney.

Pine, B. and Gilmore, J. (1998) Welcome to the experience economy. *Harvard Business Review* (July–August), 97–105.

Pine, B. and Gilmore, J. (1999) *The Experience Economy, Work is Theatre and Every Business a Stage*. Harvard Business School Press, Boston, Massachusetts.

Pine, B. and Gilmore, J. (2007) *Authenticity: What Consumers Really Want.* Harvard Business School Press, Boston, Massachusetts.

Pine, B. and Gilmore, J. (2011) *The Experience Economy* (updated edn). Harvard Business School Press, Boston, Massachusetts.

Prahalad, C. and Krishnan, M. (2008) *The New Age of Innovation: Driving Co-created Value through Global Networks*. McGraw-Hill, New York.

Quan, S. and Wang, N. (2004) Towards a structural model of the tourist experience: an illustration from food experiences in tourism. *Tourism Management* 25(3), 297.

Richins, H. (2013) Experience studies in tourism: a movement, or just another way of offering specialized service or authentic tourism? Extended abstract for *International Critical Tourism Studies Conference V. Tourism Critical Practice: Activating Dreams into Action*. Sarajevo, Bosnia and Herzegovina.

River Mountain Experience (2014) River Mountain Experience website. Available at: http://www.rivermountain-experience.com (accessed 10 November 2014).

Rocky Mountaineer (2014) Rocky Mountaineer: Our History. Available at: http://www.rockymountaineer.com/en_CA_BC/about_us/our_history (accessed 16 November 2014).

Ruby (2014) Available at: http://www.helicopterskiing.com/the-experience (accessed 30 October 2014).

Schmitt, B. (2003) *Customer Experience Management*. The Free Press, New York.

Schulze, G. (1992) *Erlebnisgesellschaft: Kultursoziologie der Gegenwart.* Campus Verlag, Frankfurt.

Schulze, G. (2005) *The Experience Society*. Sage, London.

Selkirk Mountain (2014) Selkirk Mountain Experience website. Available at: http://www.selkirkexperience.com (accessed 10 October 2014).

Shaw, C. and Iven, J. (2004) *Building Great Customer Experience*. Palgrave Macmillan, Basingstoke, UK.

Smith, V.L. and Eadington, W.R. (eds) (1992) *Tourism Alternatives: Potentials and Problems in the Development of Tourism*. University of Pennsylvania Press, Philadelphia, Pennsylvania.

Sun Peaks (2014) Sun Peaks Resort: About Us. Available at: http://www.sunpeaksresort.com/corporate/about-us (accessed 16 November 2014).

Sundbo, J. and Darmer, P. (2008) *Creating Experiences in the Experience Economy*. Edward Elgar, Cheltenham, UK.

Toffler, A. (1970) *Future Shock*. Random House, New York.

TOTA (2014) Thompson Okanagan Tourism Association: Embracing Our Potential. Available at: http://www.totabc.org/corporateSite/regional-strategy (accessed 14 November 2014).

Tourism Australia (2014) The Australian Experiences Framework. Available at: http://www.tourism.australia.com/industry-advice/the-australian-experiences-framework.aspx (accessed 12 November 2014).

Trauer, B. (2006). Conceptualizing special interest tourism – frameworks for analysis. *Tourism Management* 27(2), 183–200.

True Collection (2014) True Collection website. Available at: http://www.thetruecollection.com/experiences (accessed 24 October 2014).

Tung, V.W.S. and Brent Ritchie, J.R. (2011) Exploring the essence of memorable tourism experiences. *Annals of Tourism Research* 38(4), 1367–1386.

Uriely, N. (2005) The tourist experience: conceptual developments. *Annals of Tourism Research* 32(1), 199–216.

Vermont (2014) The Mountain Experience. Available at: http://www.vermont.org/mountains (accessed 10 October 2014).

Weiler, B. and Hall, C.M. (1992) *Special Interest Tourism*. Belhaven Press, London.

Whistler (2014a) Resort Municipality of Whistler website. Available at: http://www.whistler.ca (accessed 16 January 2015).

Whistler (2014b) Resort Municipality of Whistler: About the RMOW. Available at: http://www.whistler.ca/about/about-rmow (accessed 16 January 2015).

Whistler (2014c) Resort Municipality of Whistler: Whistler2020. Available at: http://www.whistler.ca/municipal-gov/strategies-and-plans/Whistler2020 (accessed 20 January 2015).

White Mountain Experience (2014) White Mountain Experience website. Available at: http://www.whitemountainexperience.com (accessed 16 November 2014).

Zermatt (2014) Zermatt Tourismus website. Available at: http://www.zermatt.ch (accessed 14 November 2014).

3 Wellness Tourism Experiences in Mountain Regions: The Case of Sparkling Hill Resort, Canada

John S. Hull*

Thompson Rivers University, Kamloops, British Columbia, Canada

Introduction

Resorts have been a feature of travel for centuries. Their origins in Europe are traced to Roman times when their typical structure was defined by an atrium surrounded by recreational or sporting amenities, restaurants, rooms and shops (Mill, 2001). The purpose of Roman resorts focused on promoting health and social benefits as well as relaxation for legionnaires and consuls throughout the Empire (Mill, 2001; Murphy, 2008). Murphy (2008, 9) defines a modern-day resort as a 'planned vacation business ... that can operate at a variety of scales and with a selection of target markets through the creation of a valued experience'. The purpose of a resort is to provide a place of escape or restoration from the world of work and daily care by providing holiday-makers with high-quality experiences and services that include accommodations, food and beverage, entertainment, recreation, health amenities and social opportunities (Krippendorf, 1987; Gee, 1996; Ernst and Young, 2003). Once a retreat for the wealthy, over time these developments have become accessible to the masses through improved accessibility and globalization (Murphy, 2008).

Resort concepts have been developed over the last two centuries by corporations and communities in mountainous regions of western Canada for two main reasons: to encourage westward expansion (e.g. the Banff Springs Hotel, which opened on 1 June 1888, and is one of Canada's 19th-century grand railway hotels); and to develop the hinterland of industrial-rural regions. The government of Canada's most westerly province, British Columbia (BC), launched the Heartlands Economic Strategy in 2003. The goal was to promote resort development in rural mountain areas by investing CAN$2–3 billion over a 10-year period (Murphy, 2008; Nepal and Jamal, 2011).

The purpose of this chapter is to explore the evolving role of the visitor experience at health resorts in mountainous regions of western Canada through an exploratory case study of Sparkling Hill Resort in British Columbia. The chapter will first provide a review of current literature examining trends in mountain tourism, health and wellness tourism, and the case study of the Okanagan Valley. The second section will outline the mixed-methods approach used to define the nature of the visitor experience at BC mountain resorts followed by the results/analysis based on a web audit of health and wellness facilities in BC and a series of in-depth interviews with the management of Sparkling Hill Resort in the Okanagan

---

* Corresponding author: jhull@tru.ca

Valley. Results will identify key themes and elements of the supply side of resort development to understand the importance of the mountain landscape and wellness experiences in attracting, holding, and satisfying guests (Murphy, 2008).

Literature Review

Mountains are attractive as tourism destinations offering numerous health and wellness experiences for visitors (Beedie and Hudson, 2003; Nepal and Jamal, 2011). Travellers are often attracted to mountain regions for renewal and spiritual well-being, and to escape urban pollution, noise, crime, and related stress (Godde *et al.*, 2000). Mountain regions are also places to play, retire and invest in tourism services and facilities. Recently many mountain communities in British Columbia are experiencing growth from second homes and resort accommodations (Nepal and Jamal, 2011). The following section provides a context for understanding the important issues defining the visitor experience linked to wellness tourism in mountain destinations.

Mountain Tourism

Mountain tourism is defined as any tourism activity occurring in mountain areas. It is a multifaceted phenomenon that raises the economic status of mountain residents by: providing alternative employment opportunities and income in the service sector; strengthening indigenous traditions and cultures; and providing an opportunity for year-round outdoor recreation activities for which mountains have a comparative advantage, such as snow sports, hiking, mountaineering, white-water rafting, mountain biking, cultural tourism, and pilgrimages (Godde *et al.*, 2000; Nelson, 2004; Kruk *et al.*, 2007). These recreational opportunities are influenced by six resource characteristics of mountain areas: (i) natural and cultural diversity; (ii) marginality; (iii) lack of accessibility; (iv) fragile environments; (v) niche products/services; and (vi) aesthetics (Nepal and Chipeniuk, 2005).

The rapid growth of mountain tourism has raised a number of specific challenges in a development context in the form of changing cultural values, environmental degradation, economic inflation, labour shortages, user conflicts, and a lack of community cohesion (Gill and Williams, 1994; Nepal and Chipeniuk, 2005; Nepal and Jamal, 2011).

In summarizing the global market demand for mountain tourism, mountain regions are identified as second in global popularity after coastal regions, representing 15–20% of the global demand for tourism, and generating US$70–90 billion annually (Mieczkowski, 1995; Kruk *et al.*, 2007). Three principal users of mountain attractions and services are: local recreationists, visitors/tourists and amenity migrants (Chipeniuk, 2005; Nepal and Chipeniuk, 2005). As a trip motivator, mountain areas carry a desirable image for many travellers offering a return to simplicity and wholesome living. They offer pristine and untouched scenic beauty that supports a notion of romantic idealism for people jaded by urbanization, industrialization, and information technology. They also provide an opportunity to seek adventure through participation in outdoor activities and recreational sports (Godde *et al.*, 2000). A large segment of migrants and visitors to mountain areas are baby boomers, who are demanding a range of health- and service-based products such as gym and spa facilities, yoga classes, meditation centres, spiritual retreats, organic goods, complementary and alternative medicines that are part of the health and wellness industry that is expanding globally (Nepal and Jamal, 2011).

Wellness Tourism

The health and wellness industry is recognized as one of the fastest-growing tourism niche markets (Pilzer, 2007; Yeoman, 2008; Voigt and Pforr, 2014). Wellness tourism is differentiated from medical and health tourism and is defined by Smith and Puczkó (2014, 25) as 'trips aiming at a state of health where the main domains of wellness (body, mind, spirit) are harmonized or balanced. There is emphasis on prevention rather than cure, but some medical treatments may be used in addition to lifestyle-based therapies.' The Global Spa Summit (2011) also adds that wellness tourism involves people who are maintaining or enhancing their personal health and well-being and who are seeking unique, authentic, location-based experiences. Wellness is described as including the following dimensions: multidimensional; holistic; changing over time; personal; influenced by the environment; and encouraging self-responsibility (GSS, 2010).

In defining where tourists travel to participate in wellness tourism, one of the main destinations is resort spas. A resort spa is described as a resort in a remote location or beautiful natural setting normally detached from civilization, offering a wide array of wellness services and programmes in an all-inclusive arrangement to guests. The wellness services are professionally administered spa services that integrate fitness and wellness components (ISPA, 2007; Smith and Puczkó, 2014). Over 90% of resorts offer spa services (Mill, 2001). The Province of British Columbia has been recognized as a destination for

wellness tourism and is increasingly recognized for its resort spas; one of the popular destinations for wellness tourism is the Okanagan Valley in BC's interior.

The Okanagan Valley

The Okanagan Valley (see Fig. 3.1), located in south-central BC, is a region best described as a land of mountains, forests, and vines (Aspler, 2013). The Valley was formed during the Pleistocene glacial period 9000 years ago and is characterized by low mountains with numerous lakes that drain into the Columbia River. The Valley is approximately 200 km long and 20 km wide and is located between the Columbia and Cascade Mountain Ranges creating a hot, sunny, dry climate with 2000 hours of sunlight per year and about 250–400 mm of precipitation (Marsh, 2006). The warm arid climate, agricultural landscapes and recreational amenities linked to the lakes and scenic

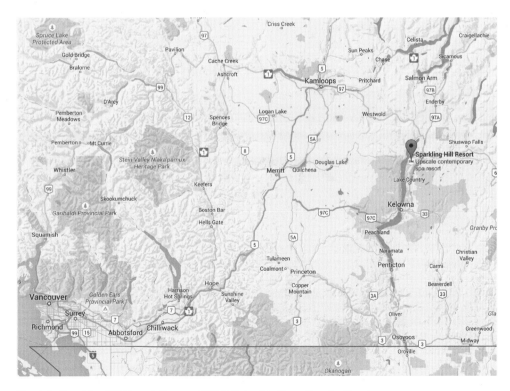

Fig. 3.1. Sparkling Hill Resort, Vernon, British Columbia (from Google Maps).

mountains have produced a valuable tourism economy that is centred on the wine industry and local rural aesthetic associated with a contemporary cultural landscape, recreation facilities, and associated amenities (Senese et al., 2012). As a result, the region is known for its wine and culinary tourism, outdoor adventure and wellness experiences (TOTA, 2012).

The Okanagan Valley is part of the Thompson Okanagan Tourism Region, one of six tourism regions in the province. The region welcomes 3.5 million visitors annually, generating over CAN$1.7 billion to the regional economy, and employing approximately 15,000 residents. Over 64% of visitors to the region are from British Columbia, with 19% from the rest of Canada, 9% from overseas, and 8% from the USA (TOTA, 2012). These markets are attracted to the region for wine and culinary experiences, soft and extreme nature-based adventure, golf and winter snow sports, aboriginal cultural tourism, festivals and events and an emerging wellness experience (TOTA, 2012). Senese et al. (2012, 87) points out that 'wine tourism regions have emerged as the logical receptors of increasing adoration by aging baby boomers and urbanites in search of class attachment and health benefits associated with epicurean consumption'. Another Canadian wine enthusiast claims 'British Columbia has the most beautiful winescape in Canada. The hills and mountains that enclose the Okanagan and Similkameen valleys offer vistas of incredible beauty' (Aspler, 2013, 13). The physical environment and natural capital are acknowledged as the main motivators for visiting the region (Senese and Wilson, 1998; Carmichael and Senese, 2012).

Methodology

In order to gain a greater understanding of the development of wellness tourism and visitor experience in British Columbia, a case study approach was adopted using mixed methods. Case studies provide flexibility when using multiple data collection methods and they also provide a strategy for understanding people, events, experiences, and organisations in their social and historical context (Veal, 2006; Singh

et al., 2012). Case studies also provide both exploratory and evaluative research results through the application of both quantitative and qualitative methods (Beeton, 2005; Stark and Torrance, 2005).

This research adopted two specific research aims: (i) to examine the intensity of the emerging wellness tourism sector through a product audit (identification, categorization) of health and wellness tourism facilities promoted in British Columbia to determine the size and scope of the wellness tourism industry; and (ii) to examine the visitor experience at Sparkling Hill Resort through a series of qualitative in-depth interviews with knowledgeable informants on staff and in management positions at the resort. The researcher used a purposeful sampling strategy to select employees at the resort with considerable knowledge of the visitor experience at Sparkling Hill (Merriam, 1998; Wray et al., 2010). Interviews lasted approximately one hour. A semi-structured interview guide was used with open-ended questions to understand perceptions and opinions and to avoid bias. Results are summarized and analysed in the following section.

Results/Analysis

BC Wellness Tourism Product Audit

In order to gain a greater understanding of the size and scope of the BC wellness industry linked to resort spas, a product audit based on a review of Destination BC's tourism website and regional tourism websites in the Province was completed. Results of the inventory reveal that the province supports a well-developed sector of 81 resorts in the Province (Destination BC, 2015). Of these resorts, 73 offer wellness facilities and services (see Table 3.1). Not surprisingly, the majority of BC's resort spas are located in tourism regions where 91.5% of the province's tourism businesses operate: Vancouver Island, Vancouver Coast Mountains, and the Thompson Okanagan (Destination BC, 2015). Resort spas are included in BC's food and beverage and accommodation sectors, which make up approximately two-thirds (66.7%) of the province's tourism-related businesses;

Table 3.1. British Columbia wellness tourism product audit (source: Destination BC, 2015).

Region / Category	Vancouver Coast and Mountains	Vancouver Island	Thompson Okanagan	Cariboo Chilcotin Coast	Northern BC	Kootenay Rockies
Resort spas	21	19	14	3	3	13

accommodation alone generated CAN$1.5 billion in 2012 (Destination BC, 2015).

The 2015 Health and Wellness Development forecast for North America (TREC, 2015) reports that the top driver for vacationers is brand/reputation. BC's highly successful revitalized branding campaign, 'Super Natural BC, The Wild Within', showcasing 'the unique beauty and power of the British Columbia wilderness' was awarded First Prize at the 2015 ITB Berlin 14th Annual International Tourism Film, Print and Multimedia competition. The brand is a testament to the province's success in attracting the leisure market, 'aspiring to enrich life by fulfilling dreams, connecting peoples of the world and refreshing the human spirit' to provide a unique experience for travellers (Destination BC, 2015, 15). Smith and Puczkó (2014) argue that branding health and wellness tourism must integrate some kind of health element. BC's new branding focuses on what travellers will see, do, and how they will feel when experiencing BC's landscape. Visitors' accounts of their experiences to BC, collected as part of the new corporate strategy, describe personal, heartfelt experiences in nature – finding truth, rediscovering their better selves, energizing their body, inspiring creativity, and providing time for intense introspection (Destination BC, 2015). These statements reinforce how the province's natural attractions are providing functional and emotional wellness benefits for targeted visitors.

In addition, many of BC's resort spas provide added value to travellers with an outdoor wellness experience. Spa facilities and services are the second-highest driver for vacationers on a wellness holiday (TREC International/Tourism Observatory, 2015). Table 3.2 provides a summary of the signature spa facilities and services that are available at provincial resorts in BC.

Results of the inventory point out that BC has a resort spa industry focused mainly on

Table 3.2. British Columbia resort signature spa facilities and services (adapted from Voigt, 2014).

Signature facilities/services	Number
Water-based treatments	19
Exercise/fitness	17
Educational activities	13
Manipulative body-based therapies/ massage	11
Body/facial beauty treatments	4
Expressive/energy therapies	4
Meditation/relaxation	3
Natural remedies/nutrition	2
Total	73

water-based treatments, exercise/fitness, educational activities, and manipulative body-based therapies. According to Erfut-Cooper and Cooper (2009, 3) the wellness concept historically has its origins in a natural and holistic approach to health that includes the use of water, and the minerals within the water, to cure various human ailments. In the 19th to 21st centuries, wellness is aimed more broadly at greater health awareness, prevention of illness, and lifestyle choices not just from the use of thermal waters, but also as a result of informed health promotion, education and encouragement of a holistic approach to nutrition, and achieving mental and spiritual balance through attendance at spa facilities (Erfut-Cooper and Cooper, 2009, 3).

BC has approximately 80 hot springs with a long tradition of use (Erfut-Cooper and Cooper, 2009; Woodsworth and Woodsworth, 2014) although not all of them are associated with resorts. The broad range of wellness facilities and services available in BC reinforces the notion that the province has a well-developed wellness tourism sector. The following section analyses the visitor experience at one of these resort spas to understand their strategy in attracting, holding, and satisfying guests. Sparkling Hill Resort (see Fig. 3.2), built in 2010 on a site overlooking Okanagan Lake,

Fig. 3.2. Sparkling Hill Resort conference facility including Swarovski crystal lighting (photograph courtesy of Harold Richins).

is a premier European-style wellness resort with 149 luxury rooms, and 40,000 ft^2 of spa and therapy facilities (TOTA, 2015).

Visitor Experience at Sparkling Hill Resort

A number of researchers and policy makers have argued that visitor experiences are the result of a four-stage tourism production process that includes: (i) Primary Inputs (Resources/Commodities); (ii) Intermediate Inputs (Facilities/Goods); (iii) Intermediate Outputs (Services); and (iv) Final Outputs (Experiences) (Smith, 1994, 592; Pine and Gilmore, 1999). The Canadian Tourism Commission (2011) points out that in order to create lasting memories for tourists, visitor experiences must incorporate elements from all stages of the production

process. In analysing experience creation at a destination or business, it is therefore necessary to consider three important aspects of the tourism production process: the consumer purchasing the experience, the organization delivering the product, and the experience (Leiper, 1993; Smith, 1994; Sundbo and Darmer, 2008; CTC, 2011). The following section analyses the wellness experience at Sparkling Hill Resort in a context of the consumer, the organization, and the experience to evaluate their success in attracting, holding, and satisfying customers (Murphy, 2008).

The Consumer Purchasing the Experience

Resort spas often differentiate themselves by targeting a selection of visitor markets that are focused on a specific sport/recreation activity or on a specific phase of life such as the seniors' market (Porter, 1980; Murphy, 2008). In the case of Sparkling Hill, interviews with management indicated that the resort's main target group is the 55+ age demographic, concerned with maintaining optimal health.

> Thirty per cent of our guests are in the 55+ age demographic. They are mainly from North America and they are enrolling in our one-week wellness packages, focused on staying young and healthy, whole-body wellness, healthy weight loss, and cleanse and detox. These packages offer proactive steps to prevent age-related disease and functional decline to optimize overall health. In ten years we hope that 80% of our guests will be participating in these programmes.
> (Respondent 1)

> In addition to the week-long wellness market, the resort also focuses on regional and corporate markets. In winter the resort relies on local and regional markets from BC and Alberta, as well as the heli-ski market through a partnership with a local business. Local and regional visitors are interested in two-to-three-night stays and the steam and sauna experiences. They often like to come when it is less busy. In addition to the winter markets, we also are a popular destination for corporate retreats with CEOs and executive programmes. These tend to be more high-end meetings that incorporate workshops and gatherings as well as wellness breaks.
> (Respondent 2)

The summer months also attract longer-haul national and international markets.

> The summer is crazy busy with out-of-towners flying in from Vancouver, Toronto and Los Angeles to tour the scenic Okanagan Valley. The direct flights have made a huge difference. The American market increased 7% in 2013.
> (Respondent 3)

In summarizing the Sparkling Hill consumer, it is evident that the resort has differentiated itself by targeting visitor markets that focus mainly on an older age demographic. Successful resorts must align their products and experiences to profitable market segments such as the baby boomers who are increasingly demanding alternative and efficient forms of health services (Murphy, 2008). The resort also attracts regional markets in the winter and summer seasons with a local market in winter and an increasing number of Americans in summer. In order for resorts to meet the challenges of changing seasonal conditions and human activities within them, visitor experiences need to be blended to assist the resorts to maximize their opportunities. Sparkling Hill has done this by catering to specific seasonal recreational activities such as the heli-ski winter market or the American summer touring market.

The Organization Delivering the Product

Resort management operates at a variety of scales. At the micro- and meso-scales the resort is meant to hold guests and satisfy their needs for the whole day through their accommodation, restaurant opportunities, and onsite entertainment and recreation activities. The resort requires not only a critical mass of activities but also must provide a high level of hospitality, quality service from professionals, freedom of choice, and involvement of visitors in the experience (Murphy, 2008; Xu, 2010). At Sparkling Hill there are a number of ways in which guests are served.

> Sparkling Hill is different from any other hotel because guests are treated like family and friends. They come on a personal journey to improve their health that can change their life in one or two weeks. You develop a personal relationship with guests and call them by their name. You help them accomplish their goals. When they leave, they thank you rather than you thanking them.
> (Respondent 2)

This response speaks of the importance of hospitality and service quality – intangible elements required to satisfy visitor needs and deliver a memorable visitor experience through building personal relationships (Smith, 1994; Xu, 2010). Freedom of choice is also recognized as an important tangible element (Smith, 1994; Xu, 2010) where guests are offered a range of options to satisfy their needs as is conveyed in the following comment.

> On the first day of the wellness package, there is a meet-and-greet session, where there is an

orientation of the week's activities. Senior management greets guests, in addition to the two doctors and also the support staff. The main goal is to design a personalized health programme focused on individual needs in the form of a schedule of treatments, nutrition and service for guests. There is no standard package for health at Sparkling Hill. There are customized programmes to help guests improve their personal health. Every guest is important to us.

(Respondent 1)

Finally, the involvement of guests in the delivery of services (Smith, 1994) is also identified as a critical measure of success. Guests at Sparkling Hill are able to take personal responsibility for their wellness programme, so they can continue once they return home.

There is a unique service culture at Sparkling Hill, with people on staff now for a few years supporting a whole-body wellness concept. At most resorts, the experience is about the room. Here it is about the rest of your experience with staff. There are physical assessments that highlight what guests need to work on to solve movement problems or problems linked to nutrition or psychological issues. There are personal training sessions during the week that help staff develop a personal relationship with guests. You work with them every day and, as you know them, you determine what they need. It is about educating and informing guests through their wellness programme, so that they can walk out of here and work on and continue to improve their health when they go home.

(Respondent 3)

At the macro-scale, the resort's efforts to work collaboratively with the destination stakeholders is important in uniting and building consensus on regional strategic planning and management objectives (Murphy, 2008). The Thompson Okanagan Tourism Association's (TOTA's) 10-year tourism strategy, 'Embracing Our Potential', argues that creating exceptional visitor experiences in the region requires building a partnership approach that focuses on the iconic; reveals the story; and expands personal horizons through self-discovery and wellness in the region (TOTA, 2012).

In 2014, Sparkling Hill Resort hosted a Health and Wellness workshop, sponsored by TOTA and delivered by two local educational institutions, Thompson Rivers University and Okanagan College (TOTA, 2015). Approximately 50 representatives from local businesses attended the 1-day event that featured three speakers focusing on health and wellness tourism impacts at the international, regional, and local level. Two of the featured speakers reported on public and private efforts in the region to promote the region as a wellness destination (TOTA, 2015). The workshop keynote presenter, Dr László Puczkó (TOTA, 2015), argued that the current trend towards health and wellness travel has many aspects which draws visitors, and destinations can focus on different themes that include: eco-adventure; natural healing features; local concepts of well-being; spirituality; and destination spas.

Moscardo (2010) points out that the different themes such as those mentioned by Puczkó, assists visitors in developing meaning from their experiences. One of these themes – the natural healing features – will be explored in more detail in the following section.

The Role of 'Place' in the Visitor Experience at Sparkling Hill

The scenic mountain landscape of the Okanagan Valley and the Sparkling Hill resort is acknowledged as one of the main motivators, or pull factors, for visitors to the region. Researchers argue that this attachment to place is a result of the characteristics of the area and the activities that are available for visitors (Kianicka et al., 2006; Cutler and Carmichael, 2010). Sparkling Hill staff acknowledge that the unique location and the resort's 'sense of place' are main factors in providing a wellness experience for visitors.

We are located here in Vernon because we were looking for serene nature. The resort is sitting on top of a mountain with only good views. It is a gift. It doesn't matter what room a visitor has – everyone has a breathtaking view. For our generation, stress is a huge factor. Looking out the window calms you down. Here you can breathe – there is open space to see the Monashee Mountains to the east and Okanagan Lake to the west. The difference in the resort's location compared to European spas is that in Europe the majority of spas are in the valleys, not up on the top of the mountains.

(Respondent 1)

When you look out into the landscape, you can experience the change of seasons all year round. Springtime brings a lush green forest. There are deer along the trail. In the fall you have the colourful autumn leaves and in winter there are the snow-covered mountains. The location gives you a sense of the wild – of reconnecting with nature, a sense of seclusion, where you can have space and time to yourself to live in the moment. The experience is not only about the physical environment. There is also a service culture developing here. We build personal relationships with visitors. You work with them every day and help them personally to reach their goals. It is an ongoing journey for them and the programme affects them more than they expect.

(Respondent 3)

Another manager also speaks of the importance of the resort's physical design in allowing visitors to experience the landscape as a place to rejuvenate.

The view alone is amazing. The resort with the large floor-to-ceiling windows invites nature in. You don't need pictures on the walls. Taking in the scenery allows visitors to relax and rejuvenate.

(Respondent 2)

The mountain experience at Sparkling Hill provides place attachment for visitors – an emotional and affective bond between humans and the environment. In addition, the resort also provides opportunities for visitors to explore their self-identity through a wellness experience that allows them to commune with nature, connect with other people, and renew the self (Arnould and Price, 1993; Cutler and Carmichael, 2010).

Conclusions

In the mid-19th and early 20th centuries, the natural thermal springs in the mountains of western Canada drew visitors for bathing and relaxation (Erfut-Cooper and Cooper, 2009). In the 21st century, these hot springs continue to serve as a basis for the development of a diversified spa and wellness industry in the region focused on water-based treatments, exercise/fitness, educational activities, and manipulative body-based therapies.

Smith and Puczkó (2014) argue that in North America, wellness and lifestyle services based on leisure, recreational spas, and wellness resorts will become the norm as travellers continue to seek meditative tranquility, spiritual experiences, and opportunities for rest and relaxation (Schweder, 2008). Spa and wellness travellers are looking for local, traditional and unique experiences that acknowledge location, geography and people (Global Spa Summit, 2011; McDonald, 2012).

British Columbia has a well-developed wellness market focused on resort spas and the outdoor activities associated with the natural beauty of the mountain landscape. The case study of Sparkling Hill resort in the Okanagan Valley supports the current trends in the wellness industry in North America by attracting, holding, and satisfying its guests through: (i) its unique geographic location on a mountain top; (ii) its service culture focused on building personal relationships with the guest; and (iii) its wellness experiences that offer customized opportunities for personal discovery of self, restoration of personal wellness, an escape from a busy lifestyle, and a search for aesthetic meaning (Cohen, 1979; Ooi, 2005; Cutler and Carmichael, 2010).

References

Arnould, E.J. and Price, L.L. (1993) River magic: extraordinary experience and the extended service encounter. *Journal of Consumer Research* 20(1), 24–45.

Aspler, T. (2013) *Canadian Wineries*. Firefly Books, Richmond Hill, Ontario, Canada.

Beedie, P. and Hudson, S. (2003) Emergence of mountain-based adventure tourism. *Annals of Tourism Research* 30(3), 625–643.

Beeton, S. (2005) The case study in tourism research: a multi-method case study approach. In: Ritchie, B., Burns P. and Palmer C. (eds) *Tourism Research Methods: Integrating Theory with Practice*. CAB International, Wallingford, UK, pp. 37–48.

Canadian Tourism Commission (CTC) (2011) *Experiences: A Toolkit for Partners of the CTC* (2nd edn). CTC, Vancouver, British Columbia, Canada.

Carmichael, B. and Senese, D. (2012) Competitiveness and sustainability in wine tourism regions: the application of a stage model of destination development in two Canadian wine regions. In: Dougherty, P. (ed.) *The Geography of Wine: Regions, Terroir and Techniques*. Springer Science+Business Media B.V., Dordrecht, Netherlands, pp. 159–178.

Chipeniuk, R. (2005) Planning for the advent of large resorts: current capacities of interior British Columbian mountain communities. *Environments* 33(2), 57.

Cohen, E. (1979) Rethinking the sociology of tourism. *Annals of Tourism Research* 6(1), 18–35.

CTC (2011) *Experiences: A Toolkit for Partners of the CTC*, 2nd edn. Canadian Tourism Commission (CTC), Vancouver, British Columbia, Canada.

Cutler, S.Q. and Carmichael, B.A. (2010) The dimensions of the tourist experience. In: Morgan, M., Lugosi, P. and Brent Ritchie, J.R. (eds) *The Tourist and Leisure Experience: Consumer and Managerial Perspectives*. Channel View Publications, Bristol, UK, pp. 3–26.

Destination BC (2015) Corporate website. Victoria, British Columbia, Canada. Available at: http://www.destinationbc.ca (accessed 15 April 2015).

Erfut-Cooper, P. and Cooper, M. (2009) Introduction: development of the health and wellness spa industry. In: Erfut-Cooper P. and Cooper M. (eds) *Health and Wellness Tourism: Spas and Hot Springs*. Channel View Publications, Bristol, UK, pp. 1–24.

Ernst and Young (2003) *Restoring to Profitability*. Tourism Task Force Australia (TTF), Sydney, New South Wales, Australia.

Gee, C. (1996) *Resort Development and Management*, 2nd edn. Educational Institute of the American Hotel and Motel Association, East Lansing, Michigan.

Gill, A. and Williams, P. (1994) Managing growth in mountain communities. *Tourism Management* 15(3), 212–220.

Global Spa Summit (2011) *Wellness Tourism and Medical Tourism: Where Do Spas Fit?* Global Spa Summit, Bali, Indonesia.

Godde, P.M., Price, M.F. and Zimmermann, F.M. (2000) Tourism and development in mountain regions: moving forward into the New Millennium. In: Godde, P.M., Price M.F. and Zimmermann, F.M. (eds) *Tourism and Development in Mountain Regions*. CAB International, Wallingford, UK, pp. 1–25.

GSS (2010) *Spas and the Global Wellness Market: Synergies and Opportunities*. Global Spa Summit, New York.

ISPA (2007) 2007 ISPA Global Consumer Report. Available at: www.experienceispa.com (accessed 10 April 2015).

Kianicka, S., Buchecker, M., Hunziker, M. and Muller-Boker, U. (2006) Locals' and tourists' sense of place. *Mountain Research and Development* 26(1), 55–63.

Krippendorf, J. (1987) *The Holiday Makers*. Heinemann, London.

Kruk, E., Hummel, J. and Banskota, K. (2007) *Facilitating Sustainable Mountain Tourism. Volume 1: Resource Book*. International Centre for Integrated Mountain Development (ICIMOD), Kathmandu, Nepal.

Leiper, N. (1993) Industrial entropy in tourism systems. *Annals of Tourism Research* 20(1), 221–226.

Marsh, J. (2006) Okanagan Valley. Available from Historica Canada at: www.thecanadianencyclopedia.ca/en/article/okanagan-valley/#h3_jump_0 (accessed 3 April 2015).

McDonald, A. (2012) *Global spa and wellness industry briefing papers 2012*. Global spa and wellness summit, New York.

Merriam, S.B. (1998) *Qualitative Research and Case Study Applications in Education*. Jossey-Bass Publishers, San Francisco, California.

Mieczkowski, Z. (1995) *Environmental Issues of Tourism and Recreation*. University Press of America, Lanham, Maryland.

Mill, R.C. (2001) *Resorts: Management and Operation*. Wiley-VCH, New York.

Moscardo, G. (2010) The shaping of the tourist experience: the importance of stories and themes. In: Morgan, M., Lugosi, P. and Brent Ritchie, J.R. (eds) *The Tourist and Leisure Experience: Consumer and Managerial Perspectives*. Channel View Publications, Bristol, UK, pp. 43–58.

Murphy, P. (2008) *The Business of Resort Management*. Elsevier, London.

Nelson, F. (2004) *The Evolution and Impacts of Community-based Ecotourism in Northern Tanzania*. Issue paper 131. International Institute for Environment and Development, London.

Nepal, S. and Chipeniuk, R. (2005) Mountain tourism: toward a conceptual framework. *Tourism Geographies: An International Journal of Tourism Space, Place and Environment* 7(3), 313–333.

Nepal, S. and Jamal, T.B. (2011) Resort-induced changes in small mountain communities in British Columbia, Canada. *Mountain Research and Development* 31(2), 89–101.

Ooi, C.-S. (2005) A theory of tourism experiences. In: O'Dell, T. and Billing, P. (eds) *Experiencescapes: Tourism, Culture and Economy*. Copenhagen Business School Press, Kogen, Denmark, pp. 51–68.

Pilzer, P.Z. (2007) *The New Wellness Revolution* (2nd edn.) Wiley-VCH, Hoboken, New Jersey.

Pine, B.J. and Gilmore, J.H. (1999) *The Experience Economy*. Harvard Business School Press, Boston, Massachusetts.

Porter, M. (1980) *Competitive Strategy*. Free Press, New York.

Schweder, I. (2008) The emergence of a new global luxury business model: a case study of the spa at the Mandarin Oriental. In: Cohen, M. and Bodeker, G. (eds) *Understanding the Global Spa Industry: Spa Management*. Butterworth Heinemann, Oxford, UK, pp. 171–188.

Senese, D. and Wilson, W. (1998) *Wine Tourism in the Okanagan*. British Columbia Wine Institute, Kelowna, British Columbia, Canada.

Senese, D., Wilson, W. and Momer, B. (2012) The Okanagan wine region of British Columbia, Canada. In: Dougherty, P. (ed.) *The Geography of Wine: Regions, Terroir and Techniques*. Springer Science+-Business Media B.V., Dordrecht, Netherlands, pp. 81–94.

Singh, E., Milne, S. and Hull, J.S. (2012) Use of mixed methods case study to research sustainable tourism development in South Pacific SIDs. In: Hyde, K., Ryan, C. and Woodside, A. (eds) *Field Guide to Case Study Research in Tourism, Hospitality and Leisure*. Emerald, Bingley, UK, pp. 457–478.

Smith, M. and Puczkó, L. (2014) *Health, Tourism and Hospitality*, 2nd edn. Routledge, Abingdon, UK.

Smith, S.L.J. (1994) The tourism product. *Annals of Tourism Research* 21(3), 582–595.

Stark, S. and Torrance, H. (2005) Case study. In: Somekh, B. and Lewis, C. (eds) *Research Methods in the Social Sciences*. Sage Publications, London, pp. 33–40.

Sundbo, J. and Darmer, P. (2008) *Creating Experiences in the Experience Economy*. Edward Elgar, Cheltenham, UK.

TOTA (2012) *Embracing Our Potential: A Ten-Year Strategy for the Thompson-Okanagan Region 2012–2022*. TOTA, Kelowna, British Columbia, Canada.

TOTA (2015) TOTA corporate site: News. Available at: www.news.totabc.org (accessed 10 April 2015).

TREC International/Tourism Observatory (2015) *2015 Health and Wellness Development Forecast for North America*. Xellum Ltd, Budapest.

Veal, A.J. (2006) *Research Methods for Leisure and Tourism: A Practical Guide,* 3rd edn. Pearson Education, London.

Voigt, C. (2014) Towards a conceptualization of wellness tourism. In: Voigt, C. and Pforr, C. (eds) *Wellness Tourism: A Destination Perspective*. Routledge, Abingdon, UK, pp. 19–44.

Voigt, C. and Pforr, C. (eds) (2014) *Wellness Tourism: A Destination Perspective*. Routledge, Abingdon, UK.

Woodsworth, G. and Woodsworth, D. (2014) *Hot Springs of Western Canada: A Complete Guide*, 3rd edn. Gordon Soules Book Publishers, West Vancouver, Canada.

Wray, M., Laing, J. and Voigt, C. (2010) Byron Bay: an alternate health and wellness destination. *Journal of Hospitality and Tourism Management* 17(1), 158–166.

Xu, J.B. (2010) Perceptions of tourism products. *Tourism Management* 31(5), 607–610.

Yeoman, I. (2008) *Tomorrow's Tourists: Scenarios and Trends*. Elsevier, Oxford, UK.

4 Creating Tourist Experiences in European Alpine Areas: Beyond Mass Tourism

Umberto Martini* and Federica Buffa
University of Trento, Trento, Italy

Introduction

The Alps have experienced profound economic and social change in recent decades, with the landscape having been considerably modified due to the development of the tourist industry. The key pillars of the tourist industry in the Alps are skiing in winter and hiking and climbing in summer. The success of the Alps' main tourism products has led to the development of a mass tourism model, where large sums have been invested in areas such as accommodation capacity, cable car systems, and transport and mobility, and where tourist flows are concentrated in short, seasonal peaks of no more than a few weeks. The sustainability of mass mountain tourism is being called into question due to both internal and external factors. The latter includes the impact of global warming on snow reliability during the ski season (Elsasser and Bürki, 2002; Agrawala, 2007) and ongoing changes in international tourist demand (Dwyer *et al.*, 2009).

Increasingly, European alpine areas previously not involved in mass tourism (either because of their location, altitude, or lack of local interest), have begun to diversify their economies into tourism, combining it with their traditional activities (i.e. agriculture, handicrafts, and industry)

in order to combat economic decline and consequent depopulation of the Alpine valleys. The development of tourism is, in fact, an opportunity to exploit European alpine resources (both material and immaterial) increasing the participation of local stakeholders and institutions.

It is, therefore, becoming increasingly important for European alpine destinations to develop differentiation strategies, which give their tourism products an ongoing competitive advantage, based on their roots in authentic territorial elements that target particular niche market segments. In this sense, the 'creative' tourism products being offered need to target specific alternative niche market segments, rather than target a mass tourism market.

This chapter describes the planning and creation of experience-based tourist products in Trentino, Northern Italy. Tourism in these territories is being integrated with farming, pastoralism, forestry, and the historical-cultural context of community in very practical, concrete ways. An initial literature review of factors required to develop and promote creative tourism in European alpine areas is summarized. In the second section, the description and evaluation of the emerging mountain destination (Valle del Chiese) describes the territory's creative tourism strategy and results and

* Corresponding author: umberto.martini@unitn.it

identifies the factors that have fostered the creation of experiential tourism products. Finally, a summary of conclusions and recommendations provides a number of policy considerations for other mountain tourism destinations promoting creative tourism development.

Literature Review Regarding Creative Tourist Experiences

Alternative tourism products can find inspiration in the emerging model of creative tourism 'which offers tourists the opportunity to develop their creative potential through active participation in courses and learning experiences which are characteristic of the destination where they are undertaken' (Richards and Raymond, 2000, 18). According to Richards (2011), UNESCO (2006, 3) has defined creative tourism as 'travel directed toward an engaged and authentic experience, with participative learning in the arts, heritage, or special character of a place, and it provides a connection with those who reside in this place and create this living culture'. Raymond (2007, 145) defined creative tourism as being 'a more sustainable form of tourism that provides an authentic feel for a local culture through informal, hands-on workshops and creative experiences. Workshops take place in small groups at tutors' homes and places of work; they allow visitors to explore their creativity while getting closer to local people.' The most important feature of creative tourism is that it allows tourists to learn more about the local skills, expertise, traditions, and unique qualities of the places they visit (Richards and Wilson, 2006; Richards and Wilson, 2007; Tan et al., 2013).

Creativity-based tourist products may involve learning (workshops, courses), tasting (experiences, open ateliers), seeing (itineraries) and buying (shops, handicrafts) (Richards, 2011, 1239), and making creative tourists the active co-creators or co-producers of their own experience (Binkhorst and den Dekker, 2009; Scott et al., 2009; Prebensen and Foss, 2011; Tan et al., 2014). Creative tourism can clearly lead to innovative new offers in the European Alpine territories, where the products being consumed are not goods and services, as they are in mass destinations, but experiences – a development consistent with current economic trends (Pine and Gilmore, 1999). It is generally recognized that tourism can be considered an experience (Quan and Wang, 2004; Uriely, 2005; Andersson, 2007), and that the core product of tourism is the beneficial experience that tourists gain (Prentice et al., 1998). Above all, tourism becomes an experience when the tourists' offer focuses not only on services and productivity, but also on the emotional reactions and environmental perceptions of the consumers (Otto and Ritchie, 1996).

The real challenge for tourist destinations is, therefore, to provide tourists with memorable experiences (Sun Tung and Ritchie, 2011). Whether or not this challenge can be met depends increasingly on a destination's ability to create a recognizably unique tourist product. When planning creative tourism product offers, territories must identify those activities closely linked to their region (its history, culture, and traditions), and then base the tourist experience they offer on these elements, thus differentiating themselves through resource-specific activities and actions. To quote Richards:

> Creative tourism implies that not just the tourists need to be creatively involved, but the destination itself needs to become more creative in designing 'characteristic' experiences. This means that the destination needs to think carefully about the aspects of creativity that are linked to place, and which give creative tourists a specific motivation to visit. This also makes it important that creativity is also embedded or anchored in the destination. Every location has the potential to provide a unique combination of knowledge, skills, physical assets, social capital and 'atmosphere' which make certain places particularly suited to specific creative activities.
> (Richards, 2011, 1238)

Creative experiences for destinations require innovative strategies that must integrate a number of specific management considerations that are linked to the geography of place. Alpine valleys, in fact, are community destinations (Murphy, 1985; Taylor, 1995; Joppe, 1996; Murphy and Murphy, 2004), as the tourism experiences they offer are based on a deep connection with their territory. The 'tourism territory' can be understood as a geographically distinct area, with natural and administrative borders, culturally characterized by the anthropological notion of 'place' as a historical, relational, and identity-related entity. These territories have many stakeholders, among whom diverse relationships and partnerships are developed. The available resources are also territory-specific (Sheehan and Ritchie, 2005).

In order to understand cooperative-based management in these destinations (Jamal and Getz, 1995; Beritelli, 2011; Laws et al., 2011), it is useful to consider a local development approach that emphasizes the deep connection between a territory and its identity, recognizing this as fundamental to its competitiveness. According to this approach, the region gains importance, becoming a place whereby its resources, competences, and specific knowledge can territorially diversify production and therefore represent a potential competitive advantage. Local systems can therefore be based on a specific local milieu, which is a permanent set of socio-cultural elements gathered within a geographical area during the evolution of inter-subjective relationships. Such elements are vital for the process of experience creation, providing labour, entrepreneurship, material, and immaterial infrastructure, as well as social, cultural, and organizational skills. The territory may thus be seen as a cognitive multiplier, which generates knowledge that is transferred to local productions and increases the economic competitiveness of its stakeholders (Rullani, 2003; Bathelt et al., 2004; Cooke and Lazzeretti, 2008).

Endogenous development is directly connected with local innovation capability. This means that the survival of a territorial system depends on its ability to manage natural and artificial resources, which may also involve the attraction of external resources and skills (Garofoli, 2002). These processes are neither automatic nor spontaneous (Sharpley and Telfer, 2015), but they need to be driven and supported by meta-management organizations, involving public and private stakeholders and the local community. By so doing, these processes lead to the emergence of a new consciousness of the concept of 'local', linked to a recognition of the contribution the local community makes to territorial heritage in the creation of long-lasting wealth. Territorial identity

becomes a 'constructive energy' that can configure development models based on the recognition of socio-cultural peculiarities and the development of local resources and non-hierarchical exchange networks within a society (Murphy, 1985; Bramwell and Lane, 2000; Beeton, 2006). These 'geographic' considerations for creative tourism development will now be explored in more detail through the case study of Valle del Chiese in northern Italy.

Experience-based Products and Creative Tourism in an Emerging Rural Destination

Valle del Chiese (altitude range 200–3400 m) is a typical rural mountain area in Trentino, Italy, marginalized both geographically and socio-economically. From an administrative viewpoint, the valley is divided into 14 municipalities, seven of which have a population of fewer than 500 people. The area is about 400 km^2, which is approximately 6% of the whole of Trentino. The towns that are more populated lie at the bottom of the valley, which is surrounded by mountains covered almost entirely by woodland. The total number of inhabitants is about 13,000, making up 2% of the population of the whole province of Trento. Twenty per cent of the population is 19 years old and under and 45% is represented by people aged 46 and over (year 2008). Valle del Chiese is peripheral to the core of the province and far from the main production, administrative, and service centres. The valley is located far from the main business and industrial areas; however, there is a main trunk road, which connects the valley to these areas both in Trentino and in the nearby Lombardia region. The large number of cars and trucks that travel along the valley to reach industrial areas located at its far ends cause pollution and congestion.

The main drivers of local economic development are manufacturing (particularly mechanical engineering and timber) and construction. Although the valley has been the focus of numerous publicly funded (with both local and EU money) development projects designed to involve and support the local business community and residents generally, the potential of the tourist industry has still not been realized. While there is activity in the sector, and accommodation is available (mainly small scale and non-hotel accommodation), until a few years ago the contribution of tourism to the local economy was restricted to certain areas.

Since 2009, however, Valle del Chiese has been experiencing a process of balanced and sustainable development. Thanks to the European Project, 'Listen to the Voices of Villages', promoted by the Central European Programme,[1] the valley has begun to redevelop and highlight the local products of the territory. This process has been raising the profile of the tourism sector and encouraging its integration into the different economic sectors, while also further engaging several local stakeholders (public and private). This result has been achieved thanks to the creation of tourist products, which celebrate the authentic, distinctive resources of the destination and seek to fully – even emotionally – engage tourists. The first creativity workshop was held in the summer of 2011, and in 2013, arrivals and presences had increased by 10% and 11%, respectively.

The case of the Valle del Chiese can thus be seen as emblematic: here, endogenous territorial development has showcased many of the area's particular features, introducing, and then widening, the offer of experiential tourist products. The destination has thus responded innovatively to the requests of the emerging demand segments interested in creative tourism. Its tourist offerings have thus been aligned with the sustainable tourist development of the territory. The 'creation' of these tourism products corresponds with particular themes illustrated in the literature of this chapter, which are analysed below.

The underlying premises for the tourist development of the destination

The marginal nature of the Valle del Chiese and the characteristics of the tourist sector, both on the supply (small enterprises) and demand (tourist flows restricted to particular areas) sides indicate development choices that focus on alternatives to mass tourism models. The integration of authentic features, the knowledge base, the traditions and the identity

of the territory then stimulates local participation – both by business (hotel keepers, craft and small industry, farmers, retailers), and on the part of the local population – in the creation of the offer. The valley's unspoiled rural nature has been identified as key in the presentation of its tourist products and the territory has numerous, still largely intact, natural attractions with great development potential. It also produces some distinctive food products (e.g. the yellow flour of Storo, Spressa cheese from Roncone[2], speck and brook trout), and has an interesting complementary cultural offer (e.g. First World War itinerary). The creation of products that highlight these resources and integrate them into the rural context helps to differentiate the offering from the 'traditional' Alpine experience.

Specificities of the process involved in creating the tourist product

Since 2009, the concept of the Valle del Chiese has referred to 'a rural experience', 'a slow holiday', 'getting to know the area' and is divided into three product clusters targeted at attracting three distinct niche markets: DINK (double income no kids); families; and outdoor sports lovers. All three clusters value the rural dimension, though in different ways and to different degrees, depending on their interests. The creation of the products, particularly those for the first two clusters, has fostered the integration of the accommodation and agriculture sectors, in line with the tenets of creative tourism. Local food and wine and the opportunity to taste them are of particular interest to the first cluster. The second cluster is particularly attracted by creativity workshops in which tourists come into direct contact with local people and learn to get to know the area's resources, customs, and traditions and costumes. Any creativity workshop that takes place is publicized as part of the territory's wider tourist offer during that week. The rural context and its natural resources, the third cluster, are the background against which they will engage in their various sporting activities, and the offers targeted at them cut across those offered for the other two clusters.

Specificities of experiential tourist products

The most innovative aspect of the tourist product offerings has been the setting up of creative workshops, intended particularly to appeal to families. The workshops, with their claim: 'If I do, I'll learn!' provide the space for creative encounters between tourists and the territory, awakening and encouraging curiosity and interest in authentic features of the destination. Tourists are active co-creators of the product, and their subsequent engagement thus becomes a unique, creative experience.

The area's most striking features were linked initially to the forest (along with timber products). The valley's tourist product offerings have now been widened, and with the rediscovery and creative production of local resources, like water (there are more than 140 waterfalls in the Valle del Chiese, and a number of big hydroelectric plants, which are open to the public), other farm products evoke the destination's rural nature such as a local maize flour (Storo Yellow Flour), honey, wool, herbs and milk.[3]

The creativity workshops carried out in the Valle del Chiese are a part of the experiential product offering which emphasizes the learning dimension of creative tourism (Richards, 2011). Set within unspoiled, natural surroundings, many of them guide tourists in the tasting of products and allow them to come into direct contact with the host community. The creativity workshops offer tourists the opportunity to get in touch with their own creative energies. A visit to the territory also gives tourists the chance to combine the typical creative tourism experiences of learning and seeing. Local hosts become much more involved and tourists more aware and appreciative of the 'unique qualities of the visited place' (Richards and Wilson, 2006; Richards and Wilson, 2007; Tan et al., 2013).

At the end of each creativity workshop the participants can take home whatever they've made (e.g. bread, biscuits, wooden objects, skin creams). See Table 4.1 for a listing of these experience-based products. These keepsakes add an extra dimension to tourists' memories of their holiday, helping them recall a pleasant time in a way in which the simple *buying* (the most passive of the creative activities described by Richards (2011)) of souvenirs or local products cannot. The more engaged activities of *seeing*, *tasting* and *learning* involved in creative tourism consolidate visitors' lived experiences. From a managerial perspective, the creation of experiential products contributes to the achievement of two objectives: (i) on the demand side, the active participation of the tourist in the creation of a product authenticates his or her experience; and (ii) on the supply side, the product's value increases and it benefits from the competitive advantage gained through differentiation.

Conclusions

The Valle del Chiese is a success story of a European alpine territory promoting creative forms of tourism that contributes to the sustainable development of the area. The success of the project can be traced back to the direct involvement of local actors right from the planning stage. These were people whose grasp of the territory's potential and of the opportunities offered by the integration of tourism with other economic sectors has facilitated their acceptance of both planning proposals and suggested marketing strategies. Experiential tourism products cannot, in fact, be created unless operators and tourists interact. The engagement of tourists, local enterprises, and the local community in the definition and use of the product offerings, moreover, enhances the co-creative nature of the product – a central feature of creative tourism. This focus on the creative dimension of the product has benefitted both from operators' knowledge and understanding of the various emerging forms of tourism and from the feedback left by tourists after they have participated in creativity workshops. This feedback has been used to improve and widen the product offerings, and has led to very positive results, both in terms of visitor satisfaction and increased tourist flow since the first creativity workshop was held. The Valle del Chiese's recent development path connects this case study to the key elements of creative tourism, as defined in the literature. As shown earlier, it 'implies that not just the tourists need to be creatively involved, but

Table 4.1. Experience-based products and creative tourism in Valle del Chiese (source: our analysis of Richards 2011, 1239; information on creativity workshops retrieved from www.visitchiese.it/it/esperienze/laboratori-didattici).

		Modes of creative tourism		
Resource	Description of the experience-based products	Learning	Tasting	Seeing
Wood	The creativity workshop describes the forest habitat and the characteristics of different trees. Participants also learn how to make something from wood.	X		X
Water	The creativity workshop introduces children to recreational fishing and allows them to try fishing in the valley's streams. They visit a river trout nursery farm and learn about the reproductive cycle of fish. They also learn how to make little craft objects using leaves, cones and twigs collected in the woods.	X	X	X
Flour	The creativity workshop takes place in an old mill, and introduces participants to this highly prized local resource through its processing and the making of bread and biscuits.	X	X	X
Honey	The creativity workshop is a learning experience, which includes a visit to a beekeeper, the making of products with beeswax, and honey tasting.	X	X	X
Milk	Participants visit an Alpine farm with its cow barns and a cheese maker. They see the milking parlour and where the milk is processed and are invited to taste the farm's products and to experiment with butter making.	X	X	X
Wool	This creativity workshop focuses on the techniques of wool production and making clothes and crafts with felt.	X		X
Herbs	Participants learn about the properties and uses of certain herbs, go on a guided tour of an educational garden and make a simple herbarium and a natural cosmetic.	X		X

the destination itself needs to become more creative in designing "characteristic experiences"' (Richards, 2011, 1238).

In conclusion, this European project, with its clear emphasis on the fundamental role of local stakeholders, has contributed to the spread of a new way of creating tourism products and of stimulating local enterprises and communities to engage with the development of tourism in their area. This process fosters and supports the project going into the future (unlike previous experiences) and encourages product innovation inspired by the interaction between demand and supply and by the integration of tourism with traditional local economic activities.

Notes

[1] The 3-year project (2009–2011) has involved nine European partners, including the eTourism research group of the Department of Economics and Management (University of Trento), which is the scientific leading partner (for further information, see http://www.central2013.eu).The authors thank Prof. Franch, coordinator of the eTourism research group, for her help; Serena Barbera, Fabio Sacco and Stefano Andreotti for

their collaboration in the field research; Paolo Grigolli of TSM – Trentino School of Management and Division for European Affairs and Local Development (Autonomous Province of Trento) for the support and collaboration in the research process.

[2] Storo and Roncone are municipalities in the Valle del Chiese.

[3] For more information about the natural heritage of the Valle del Chiese, visit http://www.visitchiese.it/en/territory/nature.

References

Agrawala, S. (2007) *Climate Change in the European Alps: Adapting Winter Tourism and Natural Hazards Management*. OECD-CABI, Paris, France.

Andersson, T.D. (2007) The tourist in the experience economy. *Scandinavian Journal of Hospitality and Tourism* 7(1), 46–58.

Bathelt, H., Malmbert, A. and Maskell, P. (2004) Cluster and knowledge. *Progress in Human Geography* 28(1), 31–56.

Beeton, S. (2006) *Community Development through Tourism*. Landlinks Press, Collingwood, UK.

Beritelli, P. (2011) Cooperation among prominent actors in a tourist destination. *Annals of Tourism Research* 38(2), 607–629.

Binkhorst, E. and den Dekker, T. (2009) Agenda for co-creation tourism experience research. *Journal of Hospitality Marketing and Management* 18(2–3), 311–327.

Bramwell, B. and Lane, B. (eds) (2000) *Tourism Collaboration and Partnerships*. Channel View Publications, Clevedon, UK.

Cooke, P. and Lazzeretti, L. (eds) (2008) *Creative Cities, Cultural Clusters and Local Economic Development*. Edward Elgar, Cheltenham, UK.

Dwyer, L., Edwards, D., Mistilis, N., Roman, C. and Scott, N. (2009) Destination and enterprise management for a tourism future. *Tourism Management* 30(1), 63–74.

Elsasser, H. and Bürki, R. (2002) Climate change as a threat to tourism in the Alps. *Climate Research* 20(2), 253–257.

Garofoli, G. (2002) Local development in Europe. *European Urban and Regional Studies* 9(3), 225–239.

Jamal, T.B. and Getz, D. (1995) Collaboration theory and community tourism planning. *Annals of Tourism Research* 22(1), 186–204.

Joppe, M. (1996) Sustainable community tourism development revisited. *Tourism Management* 17(7), 475–479.

Laws, E., Agrusa, J. and Richins, H. (eds) (2011) *Tourist Destination Governance: Practice, Theory and Issues*. CAB International, Wallingford, UK.

Murphy, P.E. (1985) *Tourism. A Community Approach*. Methuen, New York.

Murphy, P.E. and Murphy, A.E. (2004) *Strategic Management for Tourism Communities: Bridging the Gaps*. Channel View Publications, Clevedon, UK.

Otto, J.E. and Ritchie, J.R.B. (1996) The service experience in tourism. *Tourism Management* 17(3), 165–174.

Pine, J. and Gilmore, J. (1999) *The Experience Economy*. Harvard Business School Press, Boston, Massachusetts.

Prebensen, N.K. and Foss, L. (2011) Coping and co-creating in tourist experiences. *International Journal of Tourism Research* 13(1), 54–67.

Prentice, R.C., Witt, S.F. and Hamer C. (1998) Tourism as experience. *Annals of Tourism Research* 25(1), 1–24.

Quan, S. and Wang, N. (2004) Towards a structural model of the tourist experience: an illustration from food experiences in tourism. *Tourism Management* 25(3), 297–305.

Raymond, C. (2007) Creative tourism New Zealand: the practical challenges of developing creative tourism. In: Richards, G. and Wilson, J. (eds) *Tourism, Creativity and Development*. Routledge, London, pp. 145–157.

Richards, G. (2011) Creativity and tourism: the state of the art. *Annals of Tourism Research* 38(4), 1225–1253.

Richards, G. and Raymond, C. (2000) Creative tourism. *ATLAS News* 23, 16–20.

Richards, G. and Wilson, J. (2006) Developing creativity in tourist experiences: a solution to the serial reproduction of culture? *Tourism Management* 27(6), 1209–1223.

Richards, G. and Wilson, J. (eds) (2007) *Tourism, Creativity and Development*. Routledge, London, UK.

Rullani, E. (2003) The Industrial District (ID) as a cognitive system. In: Belussi, F., Gottardi, G. and Rullani, E. (eds) *The Technological Evolution of Industrial Districts*. Springer Science+Business Media, New York, pp. 63–87.

Scott, N., Laws, E. and Boksberger, P. (2009) The marketing of hospitality and leisure experiences. *Journal of Hospitality Marketing & Management* 18(2–3), 99–110.

Sharpley, R. and Telfer, D. (eds) (2015) *Tourism and Development: Concepts and Issues*. Channel View Publications, Bristol, UK.

Sheehan, L.R. and Ritchie, J.R.B. (2005) Destination stakeholders. Exploring identity and salience. *Annals of Tourism Research* 32(3), 711–734.

Sun Tung, V.W. and Ritchie, J.R.B. (2011) Exploring the essence of memorable tourism experiences. *Annals of Tourism Research* 38(4), 1367–1386.

Tan, S.K., Kung, S.F. and Luh, D.B. (2013) A model of 'creative experience' in creative tourism. *Annals of Tourism Research* 41(April), 153–174.

Tan, S.K., Luh, D.B. and Kung, S.F. (2014) A taxonomy of creative tourists in creative tourism. *Tourism Management* 42(June), 248–259.

Taylor, G. (1995) The community approach: does it really work? *Tourism Management* 16(7), 487–489.

UNESCO (2006) Towards Sustainable Strategies for Creative Tourism: Discussion Report of the Planning Meeting for 2008 International Conference on Creative Tourism, Santa Fe, New Mexico. Available at: http://portal.unesco.org/culture/fr/files/34633/11848588553oct2006_meeting_report.pdf/oct2006_meeting_report.pdf (accessed 15 March 2015).

Uriely, N. (2005) The tourist experience. Conceptual developments. *Annals of Tourism Research* 32(1), 199–216.

5 Motivations for a Destination Wedding in Canada's Mountain Parks

Elizabeth A. Halpenny*

University of Alberta, Edmonton, Alberta, Canada

Introduction

This chapter recounts couples' decisions to engage in a destination wedding in Canada's Rocky Mountain parks. The motivations for choosing to travel to a particular destination have been studied extensively by tourism researchers; however, few of these studies have examined mountain tourists' motivations and even fewer studies have examined motivations for engaging in destination wedding travel. Understanding couples' motivations will enhance practitioners' understanding of what mountain tourists and destination wedding tourists seek. This will not only assist tourism sector operators, but also the managers of mountain landscapes who are assigned the achievement of management goals that include conservation, recreational enjoyment, and opportunities to make a living in mountain regions. This chapter briefly reviews published destination wedding and mountain tourism literature, followed by a more in-depth review of visitor motivations related to these two forms of tourism, an explanation of the study's methodology, and discussion of findings.

Background

Destination weddings

A destination wedding can be defined as a wedding that occurs in a location other than where one or both parts of a couple are from, and in which they are not currently living (Daniels and Loveless, 2011). Destination weddings are a fast-growing segment of the travel market and wedding industry. In Canada the total number of destination weddings more than doubled between 2009 and 2014 and now account for 15% of all weddings (Weddingbells, 2014). In the USA this rate is higher, with 24% of couples opting for a destination wedding (XO Group Inc., 2012). While a large percentage of these weddings occur in tropical destinations such as Mexico and Hawaii (www.travelweekly.com, 2013), other locations such as mountain resorts are also experiencing growth in wedding tourism. For mountain communities, destination weddings have important implications as couples not only purchase wedding specific services such as flowers and food, but *The Knot's 2012 Destination Wedding Survey* observed that one in three couples plans a group activity

---

* Corresponding author: halpenny@ualberta.ca

for their guests such as sightseeing tours, as well as rehearsal dinners, next-day breakfasts and so on. Moreover, seven in ten couples have their honeymoon at the wedding location (XO Group, 2012). The expenditures of the wedding couples along with the expenditures of companions who join their nuptials bring significant revenues to local businesses (Daniels and Loveless, 2011; Durinec, 2013).

While these industry-related sources provide some understanding of the significance of destination weddings from a financial and tourist flow standpoint, few scholarly studies of destination weddings have been undertaken. Exceptions include Johnston's (2006) examination of New Zealand wedding tourism and the use of nature-based contexts as heteronormative landscapes, Boyd's (2008) critique of the gay wedding tourism market, and McDonald et al.'s (2005) cross-cultural study of Japanese and North American tourists' use of Hawaii as a wedding destination. Additionally, wedding culture and practices have received some attention from anthropology and sociology scholars (Leeds-Hurwitz, 2002; Boden, 2003; Daas, 2005).

Mountain tourism

Mountains as destinations have been studied in many different ways including examinations of: impacts of mountain tourism (Sun and Walsh, 1998; Nyaupane et al., 2006; Pickering and Hill, 2007; Fredman, 2008; Geneletti and Dawa, 2009); the role of mountain communities as high amenity landscapes and second home enclaves (Shumway and Otterstrom, 2001; Müller, 2005; Kaltenborn et al., 2008); effects of climate change on mountain tourism (Scott, 2006; Bourdeau, 2009; Pickering, 2011; Steiger, 2011); development and positioning of mountain destinations (Price, 1992; Heberlein et al., 2002; Williams et al., 2004; Hudson and Miller, 2005); management and structure of mountain tourism destinations (Gill and Williams, 1994; Draper, 2000; Bodega et al., 2004); and studies of who mountain tourists are (Fredman and Emmelin, 2001; Lin, 1997; Tesitel et al. 2003). However, no studies have been published that explicitly explore the growing

phenomenon of visiting friends and relatives (VFR) tourism in mountain contexts and, in particular, destination weddings.

Motivations defined and reviewed

Motivations are factors that influence an individual to take action. Push and pull factors offer a framework for understanding tourists' decision making (Dann, 1977; Crompton, 1979; Klenosky et al., 2000) regarding the location of a wedding. Push motivations are internal cognitions that impel the tourists to travel to a particular destination. Pull motivations are external to the tourist and are often related to the features of a destination (Dann, 1981). While tourism researchers have produced many studies over the last 30 years that document the role of motivations, few have examined the role of motivations in selecting wedding venues. Guan's (2014) Master's thesis is an exception to this. In a study of Chinese consumers' selection of a wedding banquet venue, she identified four push factors: (i) 'seeking relaxation and knowledge'; (ii) 'fulfilling prestige'; (iii) 'escaping from daily routine'; and (iv) 'social networking'; and six pull factors: (i) 'budget'; (ii) 'atmosphere'; (iii) 'facilities'; (iv) 'wedding services'; (v) 'transportation'; (vi) 'service and quality'. Other studies have examined the importance of destination and venue attributes to perspective brides and grooms. These attributes inform pull motivations. For example, Lau and Hui's (2010) study of wedding banquet venue attributes deemed most important by Hong Kong wedding couples revealed the importance of employee attitude, cleanliness and food quality.

Industry sources suggest several factors appear to be driving the rapid increase in popularity of destination weddings. Richard Markell of the Association for Wedding Professionals International suggests 'the new elopement' allows couples to combine the wedding with the honeymoon, and avoids the 'one-night wedding' phenomenon, which 'just turns into a blur the next day'; instead the couple can experience a longer wedding process and have more time to share it with friends and family (Bernstein, 2005, 1). Wally Martin of the Traveller's Hotel B&B in Langley, British Columbia, suggests that, while their guests' primary purpose is attending the wedding, they often stay on for a number of extra days to go golfing, participate in adventure tourism, and so on (Anon., 2007).

Motivations for travel to mountain environments have been more extensively studied. Examples of mountain visitation motivations include: (i) spiritual (Pandey, 1994; Rátz et al., 2009); (ii) dark tourism and memorializing (Tang, 2014); (iii) risk taking and adventure (Beedie and Hudson, 2003; Pomfret, 2006); (iv) recreation-specific amenities and landscapes, particularly related to ski tourism and hiking (Mills et al., 1986; Williams et al., 1994; Richards, 1996; Hudson and Shephard, 1998; Klenosky et al., 2000; Fredman and Heberlein, 2005; Alexandris et al., 2007; Needham et al., 2011); (v) the desire to experience mountain cultures (Pandey, 1994); and (vi) mountain scenery (Pandey, 1994; Holden and Sparrowhawk, 2002; Needham et al., 2011). Mountain tourists' motivations have been used to segment visitors to mountain destinations, to inform management and planning efforts in these regions (Kim et al., 2003; Needham et al., 2011; Pan and Ryan, 2007).

Methodology

Context

Two of Canada's Rocky Mountain parks, Banff National Park and Jasper National Park served as the context for this study. Both parks host a variety of tourism activities each year; Banff National Park receives the greater number of tourists (>3 million/year). Iconic sites within the parks such as Jasper's Pyramid Island (see Fig. 5.1) serve as popular nuptial backdrops; however, larger weddings (>50 people) are also held on hotel properties. Data collected for this project were part of a larger effort to understand the characteristics and impacts of special events in Canada's national mountain parks. The project was funded by Parks Canada, the management agency for Banff and Jasper National Parks.

Methods

This naturalistic inquiry utilized a multi-methods case-study approach (Stake, 2000; Patton, 2002).

Fig. 5.1. Pyramid Island, Jasper National Park (photograph courtesy of Parks Canada).

A non-random sample of study participants were recruited using two approaches. Wedding commissioners (justices of the peace) who perform wedding ceremonies in the two parks were asked to send recruitment letters drafted to potential and past clients. The clients could choose to contact the researchers if they wanted to participate. Snowball sampling was the second method used to recruit participants. Acquaintances and friends of the researchers were asked to inform friends and relatives who had married in the mountain parks during the last year about the project and supply them with a letter that explained the project and contact information for the researchers. Incentives to participate in the project were given to each couple as they completed their interviews; these included an annual family park pass to Canada's national parks, a gift certificate for a local restaurant, or a donation to a local charity. Equal representation of couples who married in the two parks was sought. Data collection continued until the descriptions of couples' wedding experiences became repetitive; at this stage it was felt a saturation of data had been achieved.

Seventeen individuals were interviewed, all but one as a couple. A semi-structured format (Newman, 2004) was used to guide this process. An interview guide featured ten questions which explored the wedding experience, why the couples chose the mountain park as the setting over another setting, previous experience with the park and other parks, and childhood interaction with parks and natural settings. Answers to these questions were posed to both members of each couple simultaneously; each individual was encouraged to provide their full response to the question prior to commencing the next question. The researcher was careful to ensure neither spouse dominated the conversation; however, because their responses were given in the presence of the other spouse, a group effect (Newman, 2004) likely characterizes the information derived from this process.

Aware of this aspect, the researcher administered four additional tasks to the participants; they were instructed to complete each task on their own without comparing notes with their spouse. The questions were tailored to the particular park in which they were married. The results were then shared with the researcher and the spouse simultaneously. These tasks included: (i) draw a picture of the most significant moment at your wedding; (ii) draw a picture of Jasper/Banff National Park; (iii) write three words or phrases that describe Jasper/Banff National Park; and (iv) complete the following statement: 'I am Jasper/Banff National Park at your wedding. I am … '. The latter question was modified from a previous environmental attitudes study. The drawings were utilized primarily as a catalyst to inspire conversation about the wedding, and served as a memory cue during data analysis. Constant comparison method (Glaser and Strauss, 2009) was employed to identify shared and distinct motivation themes expressed by the couples. Interviews ranged in length from 45 minutes to 1.5 hours.

Findings

The experiences and motivations of nine couples were documented. Interviewees ranged in age from their late 20s to mid-50s. Prior to their weddings, they all lived with their partners, some for many years before marrying. Three of the couples had children from previous marriages; five couples had no children and were not married previously. All couples married outdoors, seven in the summer/autumn and two in the winter. Three couples married at scenic publicly accessible locations within the Jasper and Banff (i.e. Pyramid Island and Bald Mountain) and the remaining couples married on or adjacent to hotel properties. One couple asked their wedding commissionaire to arrange for witnesses, as they had no friends or family travelling with them. Three couples travelled with just one other couple or their children. Five of the couples had larger weddings with guest numbers ranging from 20 to 120 people. While all the couples spent at least one night in the destination, four couples travelled elsewhere for their honeymoons. Motivations that appeared to 'push' and 'pull' couples to marry in Canada's Rocky Mountain parks are described in Table 5.1.

Table 5.1. Motivations for weddings in the mountain parks.

Pull factors	Push factors

■ Scenic landscape
■ Well-developed wedding services and infrastructure
■ Hospitality and recreation offerings
■ Distance for guests and ease of access; distance from relatives and obligatory invitations
■ Appeal to wedding guests
■ Family tradition of visiting destination
	■ Avoidance
	  • Minimize wedding-related stress
	  • Avoid hustle and bustle (of city setting or Banff)
	■ Seeking
	  • Spiritual connections and experiences
	  • Closeness to and immersion in nature
	  • Relaxation
	  • Novelty
	  • Distinction, uniqueness
	  • Familiarity seeking
	  • Reconnection with (attachment to) place
	■ Expression of identity
	  • Maturity/life stage of couple-hood and individuals
	  • Identity reflected in mountain/park setting
	  • Status of getting married in iconic location
	■ Social
	  • To connect with each other, and connect families
	  • To party

Pull motivations for destination weddings in the mountains and parks

Interviewees noted the importance of wedding-specific services, such as the availability of wedding commissioners to perform the ceremony and registry offices where marriage licences could be obtained. Hotel and restaurant services were highlighted as essential by each couple; for some, the services of hotel event planners and the settings that hotels provided for outdoor and indoor (weather contingent) ceremonies were the deciding factors in marrying in Jasper and Banff. Several couples indicated they did not want their ceremony to be on display for other tourists: 'At the Rim Rock Hotel ... you were going to be a tourist attraction by virtue of where you were located ... you'd have lots of Japanese tourists snapping photos' (Heidi). Heidi and her spouse assessed many locations in Banff, as well as tropical destinations; venue characteristics and especially views of the mountains were very important to them and others:

> We didn't want the big pretentious Banff Springs Hotel wedding, much as I love the Banff Springs. We wanted to be outside and

we looked at a number of facilities in Banff, but the Juniper Hotel offered that terrace on the front that had a little bit of noise from the highway, which was ... a compromise we made, but the ultimate scenario was we were able to get married on the deck in the snow with amazing pictures just of the ceremony, because Mount Rundel is behind there and Sulphur Mountain, and you can see Banff Springs nestled in the valley there.

Marrying in a nature destination was important to all study participants. The reasons for this ranged from the utilization of a scenic backdrop, to having nature as a guest and/or host of the ceremony. Several participants were thrilled to have nature insert itself into the ceremony:

> I didn't think I was going to get choked up but I guess it was a really important thing, eh? Just as I'm saying my lines, this loon [an iconic Canadian water bird] lets out a wail [*laughs*] and it was like ... oh, the timing!
>
> (Jane)

> It really felt like we were part of the natural environment, like it really was part of the wedding.
>
> (Daryl)

The first thing Daryl and his wife did when planning their wedding was to think about 'how do we want to feel at our wedding and words like party and natural, easygoing and calm' were identified; he stressed that this was how important it would be to him, his partner and friends. Some participants wanted to marry in a national park, stressing the protection that park status brings. Mary, an older bride, stated:

It's a national park so you know that the animals you see probably won't get shot at and that you won't have someone roaring up behind you on an ATV and in the Okanogan that happens. I mean you can't go anywhere without ATV tracks and beer cans and it's really sad, and we just don't want to be part of that culture.

Later Mary also stated that the park designation brought permanence, which was important for her in the selection of the place they would marry:

I'm very transient when it comes to houses … for our wedding I wanted it to be somewhere that you could always come to and that is a national park, right? Like the park is always going to be there.

A destination wedding in the mountains was chosen by approximately half the study participants to avoid the necessity of inviting others to the ceremony; they wanted an intimate, uncomplicated experience. For others, the destination was often selected because it was located between two groups of relatives, and thus a midway point to travel. In addition to logistical and financial considerations of guest travel, the overall appeal of the destination to friends and relatives was also considered salient. Iconic nature scenery and world-class wildlife viewing opportunities were important:

You don't have big horn sheep in Ontario, you don't see elk. [In Jasper] you can mountain bike, downhill ski, hang out in the hot springs, where in the hell are you going to go in a hot spring in Ontario?

(Jane)

Other couples reported they selected Banff or Jasper because of sentimental reasons, as it was the site of their first trip together, or a place frequently visited in childhood. An example of family traditions of travel to the site is provided by Peter:

Every year we went to Banff and you got your park permit. You used to have a park permit in the window of your car, so we had a 1978 Ford Fairmont station wagon and around the back of the car were all the park permits … that goes way back, you know, so anytime you see an old car, you can always tell how long somebody's been around if they've got the old Banff park stickers in the window of their car.

He illustrated this relationship with Banff during the drawing exercise that requested the study participants to draw a picture of the park (see Fig. 5.2). This illustration also elucidates the deep attachment that characterized many of the study participants' relationships with Jasper and Banff and is discussed in the following section about push motivations.

Push motivations for destination weddings in the mountains and parks

Iso-Ahola (1982, 1999) has categorized motivations as seeking or avoiding. All couples interviewed expressed a desire to marry in a destination that inspired calm and restoration.

Fig. 5.2. Use history and abiding attachment to Banff National Park (illustration by Peter).

They wanted to 'avoid the hustle and bustle of the city' (Trish). Participants who married in Jasper rather than Banff felt even more strongly about this, claiming they actively chose Jasper over Banff as it was more relaxing: 'it's just more laid back and more real, you don't have to blink for clothing stores' (Troy). A second avoidance motivation, alluded to in the pull motivations section, was related to the complexities of organizing and paying for large weddings that are characterized by obligatory invitations of friends and family.

Seeking motivations were more prevalent. The benefits derived from visiting a nature destination encouraged couples to select the mountains for their weddings. For example, Meg describes these positive effects: 'I think of the clean air and just getting away from the city and I mean the quiet and it just feels clean like you're shedding everything.'

A smaller number of participants indicated the importance of spirituality to their wedding experience and their visitation to Jasper and Banff's nature. Only a few participants dwelled on this motivation, but because it was an especially powerful factor for them, it is highlighted here. A search for spiritual significance is reflected in Mary's statement when speaking of Jasper's national park status:

> In the way some people would choose to be married in a church of their choice because that is a haven that represents the values that they share and that they will continue to support throughout their life together and wherever it takes them right – so to us Jasper National Park is like the cathedral . . . in fact, we do sometimes talk about this with other people, that being outdoors in nature is like a churchlike experience.

Novelty seeking is often a motivation that inspires travel. For most couples in this study, Banff and Jasper were not new destinations, but they were utilized in a novel way. As a location for a wedding ceremony, they were repurposing a much loved space, which resulted in a distinct and unique event for themselves and their guests:

> I mean Banff was the perfect venue because it took us out of the city and eliminated the familiarity of the city and added . . . I wouldn't say an exotic element so much as the refreshingly different.
>
> (Heidi)

The motive to seek out familiar settings, practices and objects also inspired the couples to select the Banff and Jasper, as most had camped as children in these parks or similar parks, spent time on ski hills and/or found employment as ski instructors or lift operators as young adults. Familiarity with these settings and the related sentimentally that can arise from this use history likely influenced their destination selection.

Extended use history of a site leads to place attachment. This served to influence all study participants, with the exception of an American couple. However, even the American couple, who had not visited the Canadian Rocky Mountain Parks previously, still expressed a profound attachment to natural areas, including Michigan's 'North Country' and the West's mountain landscapes. After extensive research they chose Jasper.

> Our ultimate goal wasn't to come to the Canadian Rockies to get married. We were originally going to just go on vacation, and the more I researched, it was a no-brainer. This was the most beautiful place on earth. This is exactly what we've been waiting for. This is what we both really wanted, and from then on it was full speed ahead with the [wedding] planning.
>
> (Carrie)

Additional push motivations that emerged from the data included motivations relating to the expression of individuals' and couples shared identities (see Halpenny, 2008). Several participants appeared to engage in wedding destination as a means of expressing their identity as mature, accomplished individuals. Heidi described this:

> We're older, we're paying for it ourselves, it's our first wedding although we haven't been previously married, we were very driven by our professions so by the time we got around to getting married in our mid-30s we had a pretty good idea of what we wanted.

Place identity, how individuals form and express their identity through interactions with a particular location (Proshansky et al., 1983; Korpela, 1989), emerged as an important motivator. Identities as environmental stewards were conveyed through the selection of a national park location for a wedding. Identities as 'outdoors people,' 'snow bunnies' and 'nature lovers' were communicated through study participants' selection of outdoor wedding venues and engagement in nature-based recreational activities. See Fig. 5.3, which Troy drew to explain his thoughts of Jasper as a protected landscape where interactions with nature are valued.

A final cluster of push motivations were related to social considerations. Participants expressed the importance of having a setting for their ceremony where: (i) they could bond as a couple; (ii) their immediate families could bond (especially in the case of blended families); and (iii) their distinct families could have the opportunity to meet and connect. Jane, who married at Pyramid Island, explained that she and her partner wanted an intimate setting, with just their immediate family: 'The most important people are the ones that are in our family and that's the four of us' (see Fig. 5.4).

Fig. 5.3. Troy's illustration of Jasper as a protected landscape, which offers recreational amenities. It's 'clean, green, and serene' (illustration by Troy).

Fig. 5.4. Jane's desire for an intimate setting 'just the family' (illustration by Jane).

In contrast, Trish described the importance of multiple recreation options before and after the ceremony – not only would this appeal to and entertain their guests, but it would provide opportunities to build connections between their distinct families.

Discussion

Motives for destination weddings

Motivations for travel are diverse and dynamic. As Pearce and Lee (2005) suggest, they change with age, life-cycle and the influence of other people. Couples interviewed for this study can be characterized as mature in many different ways. For example they were older, had long-running relationships and well-established careers, and, for some, they were engaging in a second marriage with children. These characteristics of destination wedding couples have been documented by other researchers (McDonald et al., 2005; Daniels and Loveless, 2011). These characteristics are likely to have shaped some of their motives to engage in a destination wedding. Mature individuals who have been living separately from their parents and have set their own path for many years may feel more comfortable in forgoing wedding traditions, such as the white dress and the church wedding (McDonald et al., 2005). Instead they chose to express their identity through the uniqueness of a mountain setting for their wedding (Brooks et al., 2004; Brooks et al., 2006).

Additionally, due to the complexity of second marriages and the stresses of blending large extended families, some of the study's couples chose a destination wedding to avoid these challenges. Others sought to reduce costs by having an intimate wedding far from their family and friends who would expect an invitation. McDonald et al. (2005) observed this with Japanese couples who chose to marry in Hawaii to avoid the high expenses associated with weddings in Japan. She also observed that Japanese and North American couples were motivated to have a destination wedding to avoid the obligations and conflicts that can arise with marrying in a home setting.

The maturity and life stage of these couples may also help explain two other motives. The motive to marry in an exotic or iconic destination may have been a form of seeking status through consumption – a demonstration of financial success that affords their ability to travel to a desirable location to marry. In short, a 'we've made it' statement that was enabled by their career stage and financial security. Engaging in a destination wedding may also be a statement of uniqueness and desire to differentiate themselves from their peers (Bourdieu, 1984; McDonald et al., 2005).

Some couples in this study were experienced travellers who travel to seek novel experiences. The desire to consume destinations and continually seek new destinations is well documented in the tourism literature (Snepenger, 1987; Urry, 1995; Assaker et al., 2011; Urry and Larsen, 2011). However, for most couples in this study, Banff and Jasper were not destinations that would be visited once and then ignored. Most couples expressed high levels of attachment to the Canadian Rocky Mountains and parks. Instead they conceptualized Jasper and Banff as novel because they were 'not the city' and represented an important change of pace and atmosphere.

A set of wedding destination motives that were not influenced by the couples' characteristics were pull factors such as the amenities offered by Jasper and Banff National Parks. The importance of wedding-specific services have been cited in reports on destination weddings (McDonald et al., 2005; Daniels and Loveless, 2011). Major et al. (2010) claim that developing relationships with couples before their arrival at the destination can reassure couples who marry abroad, and increase the tangibility of wedding service offerings; this type of communication between commissioners, hospitality providers, and couples prior to the wedding trip was observed in this case study. Well-developed Internet-based sources of information and images enticed and facilitated each couple's efforts to organize their weddings from a distance, but also further motivated their selection of Jasper and Banff through fuelling their fantasies about the wedding.

The availability of recreational activities at a destination in addition to wedding specific activities has been highlighted by destination wedding professionals as an important consideration for prospective brides and grooms (Daniels and Loveless, 2011; XO Group, Inc., 2012). Certainly this was the case for couples in this study as well.

Motivations for marrying in the mountains

Choosing to get married in a nature-based tourism destination was important to participants, as nature brought intimacy, relaxation, peace and a sense of connection. Holden and Sparrowhawk (2002) found similar results when surveying hikers in Nepal. The hikers agreed strongly with the item 'To feel close to nature' when asked about their motivations for visitation the destination. Pan and Ryan (2007) found that relaxation was a major category of motives of visitors to New Zealand's mountains. Johnston (2006), in her critique of wedding tourism in New Zealand, noted that wedding ceremonies in nature are seen to enhance social well-being, reduce the stress of a traditional wedding, and allow the couple to fully commit to each other: 'To be married in what has become one of the world's premier nature spaces – New Zealand – implies a total commitment to the relationship which is contrasted to the unnatural stress and fuss of weddings at home with family' (p. 203). McDonald et al. (2005) suggest that weddings in parks allow friends and family to congregate and relax, sharing the original spirit of romanticism that rejects social conventions, values nature, and pursues self-expression.

The search for connections with others and nature, and the benefits arising from nature contexts paralleled participants' search for spiritual experiences during their wedding, which nature appeared to facilitate. Brooks et al.'s (2004, 2006) studies documented a woman's relationship with Rocky Mountain National Park, located in Colorado, USA. The woman reported getting married in the park, and then engaging in a hike with friends and family the same day. The woman suggested that a spiritual aspect of the ceremony for her and her partner was for them to commit themselves to the state of marriage and the rootedness of being married in that particular park. The authors suggest she was expressing the deeper realities of commitment involved with marriage to the difficult realities of a backcountry hike. A few Jasper and Banff study participants echoed the importance of their wedding locations in enabling spiritual experiences.

Related to this discussion was the role of attachment to place as a motivator for locating the wedding in Jasper and Banff. Often cited as a reason – and explained in this study by personal recreation use, sentimental ties, and a history of family visits – was place attachment, which was a powerful influence on many couples' selection of Jasper and Banff as wedding locations. This corroborates Fredman and Heberlein's (2005) findings arising from a study of mountain tourists in Sweden, and Pan and Ryan's (2007) observations of New Zealand hikers. Attachment has been identified as a motivator for return visitation in other contexts as well (Halpenny, 2006; Halpenny, 2007; Yuksel et al., 2010). Fredman and Heberlein's study also examined the impact of recreation activity commitment on visitation to mountain areas. Activity commitment was more important to downhill skiers than hikers, but attachment was an even more powerful predictor. In the Banff and Jasper wedding tourism study, participants were also motivated by recreation activities opportunities offered by the parks, for their own enjoyment and their guests. This is similar to findings in other studies that highlight the importance of recreation activities unique to a mountain context as an important motivator for mountain visitation (Klenosky et al., 2000; Alexandris et al., 2007; Needham et al., 2011). Additionally, a long history of pursuing hiking, skiing and related activities helped to build the participants' attachment to these places, thus securing the park's appeal as wedding locations (Williams et al., 1992).

Additional parallels between this study and other investigations of mountain tourists' motivations are summarized here. First the importance of scenery is always a highly motivating pull factor in tourists' decision making. Aesthetic appeal was observed as an important deciding factor for this study's participants and others (Needham et al., 2011). Connectedness to nature and enjoyment of nature, two additional motivations, have also been observed in studies of mountain tourists (Holden and Sparrowhawk, 2002).

Conclusion

When comparing this study's findings with other contexts and populations, a note of caution when interpreting study findings should be sounded. This is due to the sample of couples interviewed. Only two couples lived more than 4 hours' drive from Banff and Jasper National Parks, resulting in a sample of short-haul tourists. Additionally, all couples were heterosexual, white and of European heritage. Banff and, to a lesser degree, Jasper are international destinations, with large numbers of visitors from Asia and Europe. Couples from these regions are likely to differ from the sample interviewed for this present study, particularly in terms of culturally related norms, practices, and expectations related to what a wedding should be and what to expect from a mountain tourism environment. One can speculate that the family traditions of visiting Banff and Jasper and strong levels of place attachment do not exist for the international couples who travel to Banff and Jasper to marry; however, they are likely to share some characteristics such as a desire for a scenic setting, as well as the appeal of hospitality, transport, and wedding-related services. Cultural significance may also be negligible for certain push motivations such as a desire to marry in a novel, status-elevating destination, or the desire to avoid wedding-related stress factors, such as addressing extended family obligations and expectations (McDonald et al., 2005).

In this study several similarities were observed between the motives of this study's participants and established knowledge of mountain tourist motivations. This study corroborates the observations of previous scholars' work in other mountain contexts. The advancement of understanding of destination wedding tourists' motivations – in particular, short-haul tourists – is a novel contribution. Neither push nor pull motivations appeared to dominate the decision making of the participants in this study; however, the mountain setting, with its protected alpine landscapes, scenic visits, and hospitality infrastructure appeared to be universally important.

The ongoing protection of Banff and Jasper's mountain landscapes and wildlife, along with a continued commitment to hospitality and recreation provision excellence would appear to be the best way forward in ensuring that these destinations are sustainable and competitive (Franch *et al.*, 2008). Promotion of awareness of these offerings via the internet and other channels will be essential if mountain destination wedding tourists, especially long-haul tourists, are to be attracted to the Canadian Rocky Mountains region.

References

Alexandris, K., Kouthouris, C. and Girgolas, G. (2007) Investigating the relationships among motivation, negotiation, and alpine skiing participation. *Journal of Leisure Research* 39(4), 648–667.

Anon. (2007) Weddings: an MC&IT Product? Available at: http://www.corporate.canada.travel/corp/media/app/en/ca/magazine (accessed 29 October 2007).

Assaker, G., Vinzi, V.E. and O'Connor, P. (2011) Examining the effect of novelty seeking, satisfaction, and destination image on tourists' return pattern: a two factor, non-linear latent growth model. *Tourism Management* 32(4), 890–901.

Beedie, P. and Hudson, S. (2003) Emergence of mountain-based adventure tourism. *Annals of Tourism Research* 30(3), 625–643.

Bernstein, B. (2005) Destined to be different: in their search for paradise, more and more contemporary couples are choosing destination weddings. *Lustre*, 1 March. Available at: http://www.highbeam.com/doc/1G1-131785588.html (accessed on 13/07/15).

Bodega, D., Cioccarelli, G. and Denicolai, S. (2004) New inter-organizational forms: evolution of relationship structures in mountain tourism. *Tourism Review* 59(3), 13–19.

Boden, S. (2003) *Consumerism, Romance and the Wedding Experience*. Palgrave Macmillan, New York.

Bourdeau, P. (2009) Mountain tourism in a climate of change. In: Jandl, R. *et al.*, *Global Change and Sustainable Development in Mountain Regions (Alpine space – man & environment)*, (volume 7). Innsbruck University Press, Innsbruck, Austria.

Bourdieu, P. (1984) *Distinction: A Social Critique of the Judgement of Taste* (trans. R. Nice). Harvard University Press, Cambridge, Massachusetts.

Boyd, N.A. (2008) Sex and tourism: The economic implications of the gay marriage movement. *Radical History Review* 100, 223–235.

Brooks, J.J., Titre, J.P. and Wallace, G.N. (2004) What does it mean to visit a place like Rocky Mountain National Park? Visitors tell their stories in Colorado. *Global Challenges of Parks and Protected Area Management: Proceedings of the 9th ISSRM: October 10–13, 2002*. La Maddalena, Sardinia, Italy, p. 87.

Brooks, J.J., Wallace, G.N. and Williams, D.R. (2006) Place as relationship partners: an alternative metaphor for understanding the quality of visitor experience in a backcountry setting. *Leisure Sciences* 28, 331–349.

Crompton, J.L. (1979) Motivations for pleasure vacation. *Annals of Tourism Research* 6(4), 408–424.

Daas, K. (2005) Women, weddings, and popular culture: An intertextual analysis of college women's negotiation of the wedding-industrial complex. Unpublished dissertation. University of Nebraska, Lincoln, Nebraska.

Daniels, M. and Loveless, C. (2011) Wedding Planning and Management: Consultancy for Diverse Clients. Available at: https://archive.org/details/Wedding_Planning_and_Management (accessed 7 January 2016).

Dann, G. (1977) Anomie, ego-enhancement and tourism. *Annals of Tourism Research* 4(4), 184–194.

Dann, G. (1981) Tourist motivation: an appraisal. *Annals of Tourism Research* 8(2), 187–219.

Draper, D. (2000) Toward sustainable mountain communities: balancing tourism development and environmental protection in Banff and Banff National Park, Canada. *AMBIO: A Journal of the Human Environment* 29(7), 408–415.

Durinec, N. (2013) Destination weddings in the Mediterranean. In: Rathnayake, D. *et al.* (eds) *Proceedings of the 1st International Conference on Hospitality and Tourism Management – 2013: The Way Forward to Tourism (ICOHT– 2013) 28th and 29th October, 2013*. Leap Business Management, Colombo, Sri Lanka, pp. 1–17.

Franch, M., Martini, U., Buffa, F. and Parisi, G. (2008) 4L tourism (landscape, leisure, learning and limit): responding to new motivations and expectations of tourists to improve the competitiveness of Alpine destinations in a sustainable way. *Tourism Review* 63(1), 4–14.

Fredman, P. (2008) Determinants of visitor expenditures in mountain tourism. *Tourism Economics* 14(2), 297–311.

Fredman, P. and Emmelin, L. (2001) Wilderness purism, willingness to pay and management preferences: a study of Swedish mountain tourists. *Tourism Economics* 7(1), 5–20.

Fredman, P. and Heberlein, T.A. (2005) Visits to the Swedish mountains: constraints and motivations. *Scandinavian Journal of Hospitality and Tourism* 5(3), 177–192.

Geneletti, D. and Dawa, D. (2009) Environmental impact assessment of mountain tourism in developing regions: a study in Ladakh, Indian Himalaya. *Environmental Impact Assessment Review* 29(4), 229–242.

Gill, A. and Williams, P. (1994) Managing growth in mountain tourism communities. *Tourism Management* 15(3), 212–220.

Glaser, B.G. and Strauss, A.L. (2009) *The Discovery of Grounded Theory: Strategies for Qualitative Research*. Transaction Publishers, New Jersey.

Guan, L. (2014) Push and pull factors in determining the consumers' motivations for choosing wedding banquet venues: a case study in Chongqing, China. Iowa State University, Graduate Theses and Dissertations. Paper 13851. Available at: http://lib.dr.iastate.edu/cgi/viewcontent.cgi?article=4858&context=etd (accessed 20 October 2014).

Halpenny, E.A. (2006) Environmental behaviour, place attachment and park visitation: a case study of visitors to Point Pelee National Park. PhD dissertation. University of Waterloo, Waterloo, Ontario, Canada.

Halpenny, E.A. (2007) Fostering return visitation to nature-based destinations: the role of place attachment, length of affiliation, frequency of visitation and distance between residence and destination. Oral presentation at the *Tourism and Travel Research Association Annual Meeting*, 18–22 September 2007, Charlottetown, Prince Edward Island. Available at: http://www.ttracanada.ca/sites/default/files/uploads/10._halpenny_elizabeth._fostering_repeat_visitation_to_nature-based_destinations.pdf (accessed October 2014).

Halpenny, E.A. (2008) Wedding tourism in the Mountain Parks: an exploration of place identity. Poster and abstract of paper presented at the *12th Canadian Congress on Leisure Research*, 13–16 May 2008, Montreal Quebec, pp. 166–170. Available at: http://lin.ca/sites/default/files/attachments/CCLR12MAY-13to162008.pdf (accessed 20 October 2014).

Heberlein, T.A., Fredman, P. and Vuorio, T. (2002) Current tourism patterns in the Swedish mountain region. *Mountain Research and Development* 22(2), 142–149.

Holden, A. and Sparrowhawk, J. (2002) Understanding the motivations of ecotourists: the case of trekkers in Annapurna, Nepal. *International Journal of Tourism Research* 4(6), 435.

Hudson, S. and Miller, G.A. (2005) The responsible marketing of tourism: the case of Canadian Mountain Holidays. *Tourism Management* 26(2), 133–142.

Hudson, S. and Shephard, G.W. (1998) Measuring service quality at tourist destinations: an application of importance-performance analysis to an Alpine ski resort. *Journal of Travel & Tourism Marketing* 7(3), 61–77.

Iso-Ahola, S.E. (1982) Toward a social psychological theory of tourism motivation: a rejoinder. *Annals of Tourism Research* 9(2), 256–262.

Iso-Ahola, S.E. (1999) Motivational foundations of leisure. *Leisure studies: Prospects for the Twenty-First Century*, 35–51.

Johnston, L. (2006) 'I do down under': naturalizing landscapes and love through wedding tourism in New Zealand. *ACME* 5, 191–209.

Kaltenborn, B.R.P., Andersen, O., Nellemann, C., Bjerke, T. and Thrane, C. (2008) Resident attitudes towards mountain second-home tourism development in Norway: the effects of environmental attitudes. *Journal of Sustainable Tourism* 16(6), 664–680.

Kim, S.S., Lee, C.K. and Klenosky, D.B. (2003) The influence of push and pull factors at Korean national parks. *Tourism Management* 24(2), 169–180.

Klenosky, D.B., Gengler, C.E. and Mulvey, M.S. (2000) Understanding the factors influencing ski destination choice: a means-end analytic approach. *Consumer Behaviour in Travel and Tourism* 59–79.

Korpela, K.M. (1989) Place-identity as a product of environmental self-regulation. *Journal of Environmental Psychology* 9(3), 241–256.

Lau, C.K. and Hui, S.H. (2010) Selection attributes of wedding banquet venues: an exploratory study of Hong Kong prospective wedding couples. *International Journal of Hospitality Management* 29(2), 268–276.

Leeds-Hurwitz, W. (2002) *Wedding as Text: Communicating Cultural Identities through Ritual*. Lawrence Erlbaum Associates, Mahwah, New Jersey.

Lin, L. (1997) A study of motivations of tourists in mountain resorts – a case study of tourists in Huangshan Mountain. *Human Geography* 1.

Major, B., McLeay, F. and Waine, D. (2010) Perfect weddings abroad. *Journal of Vacation Marketing* 16(3), 249–262.

McDonald, M.G., Cartier, C. and Lew, A.A. (2005) Tourist weddings in Hawai'i – consuming the destination. In: Cartier, C. and Lew, A.A. (eds) *Seductions of Place: Geographical Perspectives on Globalization and Touristed Landscapes*. Routledge, Abingdon, UK, pp. 171–192.

Mills, A.S., Couturier, H. and Snepenger, D.J. (1986) Segmenting Texas snow skiers. *Journal of Travel Research* 25(2), 19–23.

Müller, D.K. (2005) Second home tourism in the Swedish mountain range. In: Hall, C.M. and Boyd, S. (eds) *Nature-Based Tourism in Peripheral Areas: Development or Disaster?* Channel View Publications, Bristol, UK, pp. 133–148.

Needham, M.D., Rollins, R.B., Ceurvorst, R.L., Wood, C.J., Grimm, K.E. and Dearden, P. (2011) Motivations and normative evaluations of summer visitors at an alpine ski area. *Journal of Travel Research* 50(6), 669–684.

Newman W.L. (2004) *Basics of Social Research: Qualitative and Quantitative Approaches*. Pearson Education, Boston, Massachusetts.

Nyaupane, G.P., Morais, D.B. and Dowler, L. (2006) The role of community involvement and number/type of visitors on tourism impacts: a controlled comparison of Annapurna, Nepal and Northwest Yunnan, China. *Tourism Management* 27(6), 1373–1385.

Pan, S. and Ryan, C. (2007) Mountain areas and visitor usage – motivations and determinants of satisfaction: the case of Pirongia Forest Park, New Zealand. *Journal of Sustainable Tourism* 15(3), 288–308.

Pandey, M.B. (1994) International visitor attitudes to Sagarmatha (Mt. Everest) National Park, Nepal. Master's thesis. University of Nebraska-Lincoln, Nebraska.

Patton, M.Q. (2002) *Qualitative Research and Evaluation Methods*, 3rd edn. Sage Publications, Thousand Oaks, California.

Pearce, P.L. and Lee, U.I. (2005) Developing the travel career approach to tourist motivation. *Journal of Travel Research* 43, 226–237.

Pickering, C. (2011) Changes in demand for tourism with climate change: a case study of visitation patterns to six ski resorts in Australia. *Journal of Sustainable Tourism* 19(6), 767–781.

Pickering, C.M. and Hill, W. (2007) Impacts of recreation and tourism on plant biodiversity and vegetation in protected areas in Australia. *Journal of Environmental Management* 85(4), 791–800.

Pomfret, G. (2006) Mountaineering adventure tourists: a conceptual framework for research. *Tourism Management* 27(1), 113–123.

Price, M.F. (1992) Patterns of the development of tourism in mountain environments. *GeoJournal* 27(1), 87–96.

Proshansky, H.M., Fabian, A.K. and Kaminoff, R. (1983) Place-identity: physical world socialization of the self. *Journal of Environmental Psychology* 3(1), 57–83.

Rátz, T., Pohner, T. and Berki, T. (2009) Religious and pilgrimage tourism as a special segment of mountain tourism. *Journal of Tourism Challenges and Trends* (2.1), 27–42.

Richards, G. (1996) Skilled consumption and UK ski holidays. *Tourism Management* 17(1), 25–34.

Scott, D. (2006) Global environmental change and mountain tourism. *Tourism and Global Environmental Change* 54–75.

Shumway, J.M. and Otterstrom, S.M. (2001) Spatial patterns of migration and income change in the Mountain West: the dominance of service-based, amenity-rich counties. *The Professional Geographer* 53(4), 492–502.

Snepenger, D.J. (1987) Segmenting the vacation market by novelty-seeking role. *Journal of Travel Research* 26(2), 8–14.

Stake R.E. (2000) Case studies. In: Denzin, N.K. and Lincoln, Y.S. (eds) *Handbook of Qualitative Research*. Sage Publications, Thousand Oaks, California, pp. 435–454.

Steiger, R. (2011) The impact of snow scarcity on ski tourism: an analysis of the record warm season 2006/2007 in Tyrol (Austria). *Tourism Review* 66(3), 4–13.

Sun, D. and Walsh, D. (1998) Review of studies on environmental impacts of recreation and tourism in Australia. *Journal of Environmental Management* 53(4), 323–338.

Tang, Y. (2014) Dark touristic perception: motivation, experience and benefits interpreted from the visit to seismic memorial sites in Sichuan province. *Journal of Mountain Science* 11(5), 1326–1341.

Tesitel, J., Kusova, D. and Bartos, M. (2003) Tourists' reasons for visiting mountain areas: a case study of the Sumava Mountains. *Landscape Research* 28(3), 317–322.

Travel Weekly (2014) Weddings to go. Travel Weekly: The Travel Industry's Trusted Voice (web newsletter). Available at: http://www.travelweekly.com/Travel-News/Travel-Agent-Issues/Weddings-to-go (accessed 12 February 2014).

Urry, J. (1995) *Consuming Places*. Routledge, New York.

Urry, J. and Larsen, J. (2011) *The Tourist Gaze 3.0.* Sage Publications, Thousand Oaks, California.

Weddingbells (2014) Annual Reader Survey. Available at: http://www.weddingbells.ca/planning/wedding-trends-in-canada-2014 (accessed 7 January 2016).

Williams, D.R., Patterson, M.E., Roggenbuck, J.W. and Watson, A.E. (1992) Beyond the commodity metaphor: examining emotional and symbolic attachment to place. *Leisure Sciences* 14(1), 29–46.

Williams, P.W., Dossa, K.B. and Fulton, A. (1994) Tension on the slopes: managing conflict between skiers and snowboarders. *Journal of Applied Recreation Research* 19(3), 191–213.

Williams, P.W., Gill, A.M. and Chura, N. (2004) Branding mountain destinations: the battle for 'placefulness'. *Tourism Review* 59(1), 6–15.

www.weddingbells.ca (2014) Wedding Trends in Canada 2014. Available at: http://www.weddingbells.ca/planning/wedding-trends-in-canada-2014 (accessed 21 October 2014).

XO Group, Inc. (2012) The Knot Market Intelligence Destination Weddings Study, 2012 (online press release). Available at:http://www.xogroupinc.com/press-releases-home/2012-press-releases/2012-06-18-destination-weddings-study-results.aspx (accessed 21 October 2014).

Yuksel, A., Yuksel, F. and Bilim, Y. (2010) Destination attachment: effects on customer satisfaction and cognitive, affective and conative loyalty. *Tourism Management* 31(2), 274–284.

6 Stamp Books in the Harz Mountains, Germany – Fun not Just for Children

Michael Lück[1]* and Sven Gross[2]
[1]*Auckland University of Technology, Auckland, New Zealand;*
[2]*Harz University of Applied Sciences, Wernigerode, Germany*

Introduction

Hiking has long been a popular leisure and holiday activity. This is, in part, because it is seen as an inexpensive activity (there is no need to purchase and maintain expensive equipment), can be undertaken almost anywhere, and can be enjoyed by all age groups, from children to seniors. Dreyer *et al.* (2010) talked about a renaissance of hiking in the last 15 years in Germany, and noted that tourism destinations have increasingly promoted hiking and provided the necessary infrastructure in a fiercely competitive market. These hiking destinations are mostly located in the German mid-mountain and alpine ranges, with the most popular hiking regions in Germany being the Black Forest (12%), followed by the Elbsandsteingebirge in Saxonia (8%), the Bayerische Wald in Bavaria (7%), and the Harz region (6%) (Menzel *et al.*, 2008). Despite not being seen as a luxurious activity, hiking, Brämer (2003) estimated, contributed approximately €12 billion to Germany's economy: €2.5 billion for specialized clothing; €1.5 billion for other gear/equipment; €3 billion for transport; and €2.5 billion each for accommodation, and food and beverages (Menzel *et al.*, 2008).

This chapter reviews hiking in Germany, followed by the introduction of a specific hiking programme in the Harz Mountains region: The 'Harzer Wandernadel' (HWN, the 'Hiking Pin Harz'). The findings of a survey undertaken in the Harz region with a specific focus on the HWN is then presented and discussed. The aim is to better understand the users of the HWN, including a demographic profile, purchase behaviour, loyalty, and an evaluation of the programme. The chapter concludes with the benefits of the project and recommendations to introduce similar ventures in other mountain regions.

Hiking in Germany

Hiking is popular mostly because it does not require specific landscapes or any expensive equipment (though today clothing and gear are available in all price ranges). Although delineating hiking from walking/strolling is difficult, the German Ministry for Economic Affairs and Technology (BMWI) defines hiking as 'a leisure activity with varying strong physical demand, promoting both mental and physical wellbeing. Typical for a hike are: a period of

---

* Corresponding author: michael.lueck@aut.ac.nz

more than 1 hour, appropriate planning, the use of specific infrastructure, and customized equipment' (BMWI, 2010, 23). In a study published in 2010, BMWI attempted to identify the activities that respondents associate with the term 'hiking'. Despite the difference between hiking and walking/strolling, 51% of respondents associate the term 'hiking' with 'strolling'. In addition, 14.5% think of geocaching, 43% think of Nordic walking, 43.5% think of trekking, 41.5% think of pilgrimage, and 17% think of climbing/mountaineering (BMWI, 2010).

Germany's hiking propensity is relatively high, and thus offers excellent potential for the development of hiking offers at destination levels. For example, Project M (2014) identified that 11% of the respondents stated that they regularly hike, 23% occasionally, 35% say that they rarely hike, and 29% never hike. Thus, 34% can be considered moderately active hikers. When it comes to the intensity, 15.8% of respondents claimed that they hiked more than once a month, 14.2% at least five or six times per half-year, 21.3% at least once or twice a year, and 4.4% less than once or twice a year (BMWI, 2010).

Trendscope (2009) differentiates between day hikers (i.e. hikers who do not require accommodation, and hike in and around their

home environment), and 'holiday hikers', (i.e. hikers who engage in the activities during holiday trips). In their study of holiday hikers, they found that 40% of the respondents took 1–5 hikes, 22% took 6–10 hikes, 16% took 11–20 hikes, 12% took 21–50 hikes, and 3% more than 50 hikes. The figures for day hikers were very similar: 44% of the holiday hikers took 1–5 hikes, 20% took 6–10 hikes, 14% took 11–20 hikes, 11% took 21–50 hikes, and 3% more than 50 hikes (Trendscope, 2009).

When BMWI asked respondents to identify their reasons for hiking, the majority of respondents indicated that the natural environment is important, and cited benefits such as experiencing nature, fresh air, the beauty of nature and landscape, fauna, and flora. Another main motivator is the physical aspect, including being active, regeneration, doing something for your health, and mountain climbing. Lastly, social aspects such as social contacts and a change from the daily routine are important motivators (BMWI, 2010). Figure 6.1 represents these motives for hiking.

In Kreilkamp et al.'s (2012) study of hikers, the main motive was to experience nature and landscapes (84.8%), followed by 'doing something for your health' (50.3%), 'hiking as personal tradition' (45.5%), 'change from daily routine'

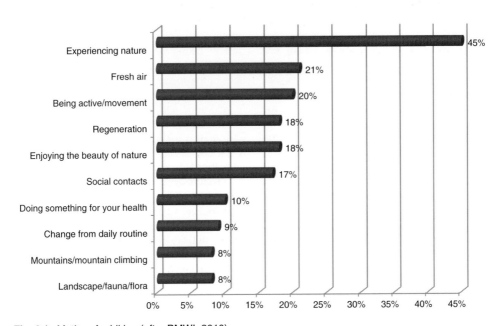

Fig. 6.1. Motives for hiking (after BMWI, 2010).

(44.1%) and 'spending time with family and friends' (30.3%).

The Harz Region and the Harzer Wandernadel (HWN)

The Harz region ('The Harz') is a German tourist destination extending beyond the three states of Lower Saxony, Saxony-Anhalt and Thuringia. The area has a long tradition and high brand recognition (86% of German residents today are aware of the Harz as a destination (IMT, 2012). Of the approximately 6.2 million overnight stays in the Harz in 2013, about 54% are apportioned to the Lower Saxony part of the Harz and approximately 46% to the Harz areas in Saxony-Anhalt and Thuringia. While the western part of the region has noted decreasing overnight stays over the past 5 years, an opposite trend can be observed in the eastern part. As a result, the eastern Harz continuously gains influence to the outcome of the entire central mountain region (Landesbetrieb für Statistik Niedersachsen, 2014; Statistisches Landesamt Sachsen-Anhalt, 2014). Hiking, nature experiences, recreation, and visiting cultural attractions are the focus of stay for most tourists in the Harz Mountains (inspektour GmbH/ift GmbH, 2012).

Since 2006, the Harzer Wandernadel ('Hiking Pin Harz') has offered an intriguing opportunity to combine hiking, health and fun. Within more than 8000 km of sign-posted hiking trails in the Harz region, a total of 222 stamp stations are positioned at attractions and on hiking trails (Fig. 6.2). In addition there are a number of 'special stamps', related to events and attractions, which may vary from year to year (Harzer Wandernadel, 2014a).

This network of hiking trails stretches across three states and six regions, and includes the Harz National Park (Gesund älter werden im Harz e.V., n.d.). Located in former East Germany, the regional council agency for employment (Kommunale Beschäftigungsagentur Landkreis Harz) in cooperation with the not-for-profit organization 'Ageing Healthily in the Harz Region' (Gesund älter werden im Harz e.V.) created the HWN, with the main goals of employment creation and health benefits/prevention in mind. Endreß (2009) emphasized that hiking

Fig. 6.2. A total of 222 stamp stations are spread around the Harz region (photograph courtesy of M. Lück).

and Nordic walking promotes significant cardiovascular benefits.

The HWN system consists of a stamp book and a set of three maps, which can be purchased at various outlets in the region. The detailed hiking maps also indicate the locations of the 222 stamp stations, as well as the locations of the special stamps. Upon reaching a station, the hiker stamps their stamp book (Fig. 6.3). In addition, a third party developed a new Android App, offering maps and satellite images with stamp locations, GPS navigation, and a tracking system (www.androidpit.de/app/de. dherz.hwn).

To further motivate hikers, the HWN offers various levels of achievement as shown in Table 6.1.

Once a level is achieved, the hiker can visit one of the distribution outlets in the region, to get their stamp book validated, and to purchase the respective pin (between €3.50 and €5).

As part of the trail network, the HWN also developed four specially themed trails, reflecting the rich history of the area: The 'Goethe im Harz' trail, which revisits the famous poet's

Fig. 6.3. HWN stamp book.

Table 6.1. Levels of the HWN (source: Gesund älter werden im Harz e.V., 2009).

Minimum requirement	Award
8 different stamps	Harz Hiking pin – bronze
16 different stamps	Harz Hiking pin – silver
24 different stamps	Harz Hiking pin – gold
50 different stamps	Harz Hiking King
All 222 stamps	Harz Hiking Emperor
Themed Trails	
11 stamps of the themed 'witches trail'	HWN Harzer-Hexen-Stieg (Harz Witches Trail)
111 different stamps, including 22 stamps from themed mining stations	Harzer Steiger (Harz Miner)

travels in the region; the 'Harzer-Hexen-Stieg', which is based on the myths and legends about witches on and around the largest mountain in the area, the Brocken (1141 m); the 'Harzer Grenzweg', along the former border between East and West Germany; and the 'Harzer Steiger', which showcases the important mining history in the region.

After only a few years, the HWN has developed into a successful project in many ways. The organization has sold tens of thousands of stamp books, and by mid-2009 a total of 507 hikers had already registered as 'Harzer Wanderkaiser' (Harz Hiking Emperor) signifying that they have visited all 222 stamp stations. By 2014, only 8 years since inception, this number increased to 2555 'Harzer Wanderkaiser' (Harzer Wandernadel, 2014b).

The Gesund älter werden im Harz e.V. is illustrating the success of the project, highlighting that it has holistic benefits for the region, and beyond. Economically, it supports the hospitality and tourism industry in the area, as well as suppliers of hiking gear and gadgets. Socially, the project supports jobs and brings a number of volunteers together, who are helping to maintain the trails and stamp stations. In terms of health, hiking is heralded as an inexpensive form of exercise, which has significant health benefits, both as a measure of prevention and a form of rehabilitation. Furthermore, hiking is an activity that can be enjoyed by all age groups, from children to senior citizens (Gesund älter werden im Harz e.V., n.d.). It is an activity that is particularly suited for families, since children can enjoy hiking without having to learn new skills. Despite the initial goal of employment creation and the promotion of health benefits, the HWN has also developed a loyalty programme that attracts repeat visitors to the region.

Methodology

The methods used in this study included paper-and-pen surveys, distributed at a number of locations in the Harz region in May and June of 2012. Locations included the castle, the Westerntor railway station, car parks at various hiking trailheads, and the city centre of Wernigerode. The questionnaire included questions about hiking in general, the HWN, and about the respondents' demographics. The majority of questions were closed-ended items in a six-point Likert scale format and simple multiple-choice questions. A total of 187 surveys were successfully distributed. Univariate and bivariate analyses, as well as Analyses of Variance (ANOVA) were used in order to gain information about respondents' opinions concerning the HWN, their usage of the HWN, and demographics. Data were processed with the IBM Statistical Package for Social Sciences (SPSS), version 22.

This study represents a relatively small sample (n=187), and thus the findings cannot be generalized to the larger population. However, they represent a good indication of the trends, and build the basis for a larger study in the same area.

Results and Discussion

A demographic profile of Harz visitors

This section provides a basic demographic profile of the respondents (Table 6.2). When considering the gender profile of respondents, it is interesting to note that this closely matches Kreilkamp *et al.*'s (2012) research in the Harz area, which identified more male (60.7%) than female (39.3) respondents, with a majority of hikers in the 46–55 age group. This correlates

Table 6.2. Demographic details of respondents.

Category	Percentage
Gender (n = 187)	
Male	53.5
Female	46.5
Age (n = 186)	
18–25	5.9
26–35	7.0
36–45	17.2
46–55	30.1
56–65	19.4
66–75	17.2
>75	3.2
Employment status (n = 186)	
Employed	50.6
Self-employed	14.5
Student/military or civil service	5.9
Homemaker	2.2
Retired	25.8
Currently unemployed	1.1
Education (n = 187)	
Still at school	0.6
Secondary school qualification	44.8
University qualification	35.4
Vocational/trade qualification	18.8
No qualification	0.6
Income (€/month) (n = 147)	
< €900	18.2
€901–1499	17.1
€1500–1999	15.0
€2000–2499	15.5
€2500–3000	5.9
>€3000	7.0
Not indicated	21.4

to other studies, such as the 2008 research conducted by Menzel *et al.*, which suggested the average hiker in Germany is between 40 and 60 years of age (although they note that almost all age groups can be found among hikers); and the 2012 research conducted by Kreilkamp *et al.* in the Harz, which found 32.8% of respondents were between 50 and 59 years old and 28.5% were 60 years or older.

Menzel *et al.*'s (2008) research also found that the typical hiker in Germany had an above-average education. The vast majority of respondents originated from the wider regions around the Harz National Park, with a maximum of approximately 250–300 km away. For example, 47.73% of the respondents indicated a postal code beginning with the numbers 38 and 39, which represent the area around the Harz, and another to the east. The next highest category of respondents originated from Berlin, and two regions to the West of the Harz (across the former border to West Germany), and finally, respondents originated from other regions came mostly from northern Germany, with one respondent being from Austria.

The Harzer Wandernadel (HWN) system

The stamp books, maps and hiking pins can be purchased through a number of outlets. These include the HWN service office in Blankenburg, various hotels, tourist information offices, souvenir shops, the map publisher, and online. Table 6.3 identifies how respondents found out about the HWN and where they obtained their stamp book.

When rating the number of stamp stations on a six-point Likert-type scale, and their distance to each other, the vast majority of respondents felt that the number of stations and the distance between the stations was right (75.4%) or slightly too far apart (21.1%), with a mean of 2.82. A total of 70.2% found that the stamp stations were easy to find (mean = 2.16). Occasionally, stamps are damaged or stolen (vandalism), which causes some level of frustration to hikers. In order to ensure hikers still received credit for their completed hikes, the Gesund älter werden im Harz e.V. attached

Table 6.3. How did you learn about the HWN, and where did you purchase the stamp book?

	How did you learn about HWN (%) (n=186)	Where did you purchase the stamp book? (%) (n=186)
Tourist Information	40.8	91.4
Friends/family	15.8	–
Newspaper	14.5	–
Other	10.5	–
Internet	7.9	3.4
HWN service office	5.3	3.4
Launch of the HWN	–	1.7
Hotel	2.6	–
Magazine	–	–
Brochure/leaflet	2.6	–

a unique code on a small plate at each station, and if hikers copy that code into their stamp book, it is counted as a stamp (Fig. 6.3). A total of 44.8% of the hikers reported one or more missing stamps during their hikes, and 34.3% noted that this negatively impacted their hiking experience.

Overall, respondents rated the HWN offerings as good value for money (Table 6.4). The nominal charges for the maps, stamp books, and pins appear to be acceptable. The stamp book, the maps, and the hiking pins were all rated as good or very good value for money.

Repeat hikers and loyalty

One of the main goals of the HWN is the creation of repeat usage, through the introduction of various levels. During the survey, only one respondent had achieved all levels (Fig. 6.4). About one-quarter of the respondents had not achieved any level yet and just over one-quarter stated that they were not targeting any particular level. When respondents were asked to rate the steps between the various achievement levels, 26% rated this as very good, and 50% as good (mean 2.43).

There was no significant difference between gender and the highest achieved level, .05 significance level (F = .686; Sig. = .622), but a significant difference could be found between age and highest achieved level (F = 6.250; Sig = .000). For the differences between gender, age, and the targeted level, no significance was found (F = .403; Sig = .873 and F = 1.154; Sig = .349, respectively).

When asked directly, the vast majority of respondents felt that the HWN had enriched their holiday experience and more importantly, almost half of the respondents stated that the HWN was a reason to visit the Harz region (Table 6.5).

It is important to note that the HWN can be a powerful pull factor for the Harz region. A total of 98.6% in Kreilkamp *et al.*'s (2012) study stated that hiking and walking were the preferred activities during their leisure time. When it comes to repeat visits, Trendscope (2009) found that 44% of the 'holiday hikers'

Table 6.4. Value for money.

	Stamp book (%) n = 186 (Mean = 1.72)	Hiking maps (%) n = 182 (Mean = 2.19)	Hiking pins (%) n = 175 (Mean = 2.40)	Additional booklets (%) n = 175
1 Very good	44.8	31.6	29.8	7.0
2	44.8	47.4	49.1	17.5
3	8.6	12.3	8.8	0.0
4	0.0	1.8	0.0	0.0
5	0.0	0.0	0.0	0.0
6 Very poor	0.0	0.0	0.0	0.0
Not applicable	1.7	7.0	12.3	75.4

Table 6.5. HWN and loyalty.

	To what extent did the HWN add to your holiday experience? (%) (n = 184) (Mean = 2.10)	The HWN was a reason to visit the Harz region (%) (n = 184) (Mean = 3.35)	The HWN is a reason to return to the Harz region (%) (n = 184) (Mean = 2.47)
1 Very much	31.3	18.4	31.9
2	39.6	24.5	31.9
3	20.8	16.3	17.0
4	6.3	10.2	4.3
5	0.0	6.1	6.4
6 Not at all	2.1	24.5	8.5

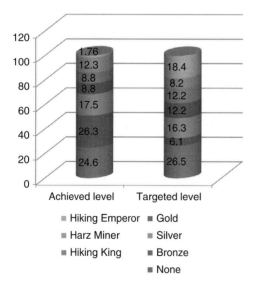

Fig. 6.4. Targeted and achieved HWN levels (in per cent).

and 38% of the 'day hikers' are likely to return to their hiking destination. In the current study, almost 70% agreed that the HWN is a reason to return to the Harz region, indicating a likeli-hood of doing so. These results suggest that the HWN can be an important tool to create loyalty among hikers, and thus generate repeat visits to the region.

Conclusions

Hiking has experienced a new renaissance as an important leisure and holiday activity in Germany. In a highly competitive market, tourism destinations have recognized the economic value of this activity, and the value of increased purchases of equipment, accommodation, food and beverage, and transport. In addition, governments support hiking as an important health initiative, aiding prevention and rehabilitation, and as a means of job generation. The Gesund älter werden im Harz e.V., in cooperation with many local partners, initiated the Harzer Wandernadel (HWN), a project that was primarily meant to support new jobs. In less than a decade, the HWN has grown significantly, with tens of thousands of participants, many of them returning on a regular basis. In a survey among visitors to the Harz region, it became clear that the demographic profile of the respondents largely matched that of other studies, both in the Harz region and in Germany in general. The typical hiker is between 40 and 60 years old, relatively highly educated, and is either employed full time or retired.

When it comes to the HWN in particular, the majority of hikers enjoyed the offerings, and agreed that the HWN added to their holiday experience. Most importantly, a substantial number of respondents agreed that the HWN was a reason to visit the area, and an even larger number stated that it is a reason to return to the Harz region. This is supported by the fact that many hikers have reached various levels of the HWN, and are targeting a higher level. Only a quarter of the respondents indicated that they would not attempt to achieve a higher level. These findings are important for the destination Harz, since they support the strength of the HWN as a pull factor to the Harz region. While hikers have the choice of a number of excellent hiking opportunities in various low mountain ranges across Germany, the HWN represents a unique selling proposition for the Harz region. Not only does it draw people to the region, it also creates loyal repeat visitors, benefiting the region economically, providing hikers with an enhanced experience and important health benefits. It is thus suggested that similar stamp book systems may be a viable option for other regions around Germany and abroad.

Acknowledgement

The authors would like to thank the students of the 2012 Postgraduate Project Course (Praxisprojekt II) at Harz University of Applied Sciences for their help with data collection and analysis.

References

BMWI (2010) Grundlagenuntersuchung Freizeit- und Urlaubsmarkt Wandern, Forschungsbericht Nr. 591, Forschungsbericht, Langfassung. Available at: https://www.bmwi.de/BMWi/Redaktion/PDF/Publikationen/Studien/grundlagenuntersuchung-freizeit-und-urlaubsmarkt-wandern,property=pdf, bereich=bmwi,sprache=de,rwb=true.pdf (accessed 13 November 2014).

Brämer, R. (2003) Megatrend Wandern – Problem oder Chance. In: Neuerburg, H.-J. and Wilken, T. (eds) *Sport und Tourismus*, Dokumentation des 10. Symposiums zur nachhaltigen Entwicklung des Sports, Heft 21 der Schriftenreihe, Sport und Umwelt. Deutscher Sportbund, Frankfurt am Main, Germany, pp. 62–77.

Dreyer, A., Menzel, A. and Endreß, M. (2010) *Wandertourismus: Kundengruppen, Destinationsmarketing, Gesundheitsaspekte*. Oldenbourg Verlag, Munich, Germany.

Endreß, M. (2009) *Prävention & Sport im Urlaub: Präventions- und Sportreisen auf dem deutschen Touristikmarkt*. ITD-Verlag, Hamburg, Germany.

Gesund älter werden im Harz e.V. (2009) *Mit Stempelstellen zum Harzer Wanderkaiser!* Gesund älter werden im Harz e.V., Blankenburg, Germany.

Gesund älter werden im Harz e.V. (n.d.) *Harzer Wandernadel: Das Wanderstempeln im Harz*. Gesund älter werden im Harz e.V., Blankenburg, Germany.

Harzer Wandernadel (2014a) Die Stempelstellen der Harzer Wandernadel. Available at: http://www.harzer-wandernadel.de/home/stempelstellen.php (accessed 21 November 2014).

Harzer Wandernadel (2014b) Kaiserjahrgang 2014. Available at: http://www.harzer-wandernadel.de/home/2014_kaiserliste.php (accessed 21 November 2014).

IMT (2012) *Destination Brand 12*. Institut für Management und Tourismus, Heide, Germany.

inspektour GmbH/ift GmbH (2012) *Permanente Gästebefragung Sachsen-Anhalt 2011/12 – Berichtsband mit Endergebnissen*. inspektur, Cologne/Hamburg/Potsdam, Germany.

Kreilkamp, E., Kirmair, L. and Kotzur, A. (2012) *KLIFF Gästebefragung Harz – Sonderauswertung Wanderurlauber*. Leuphana Universität Lüneburg, Lüneburg, Germany.

Landesbetrieb für Statistik Niedersachsen (2014) *Beherbergung im Reiseverkehr – Jahr 2013*. Landesbetrieb für Statistik Niedersachsen, Hannover, Germany.

Menzel, A., Endreß, M. and Dreyer, A. (2008) *Wandertourismus in den Deutschen Mittelgebirgen*. ITD-Verlag, Hamburg, Germany.

Project M (2014) *Wanderstudie: Der Deutsche Wandermarkt 2014*. Project M GmbH, Münster, Germany.

Statistisches Landesamt Sachsen-Anhalt (2014) Beherbergungen im Reiseverkehr (einschließlich Camping) nach Reisegebieten nach Jahren. Available at: https://www.statistik.sachsen-anhalt.de/Internet/Home/Daten_und_Fakten/index.html (accessed 7 January 2016).

Trendscope (2009) *Wandern in Deutschland 2009*. Trendscope GbR, Cologne, Germany.

7 Significant Innovation in the Development and Provision of Heli-ski Mountain Experiences: The Case of Mike Wiegele Helicopter Skiing

Harold Richins*

Thompson Rivers University, Kamloops, British Columbia, Canada

Innovation in Special Niche Tourism Experience Development

Tourism, and particularly special niche tourism, has advanced through a multitude of innovative practices over the last 50 years (Poon, 1993; Rachman and Richins, 1997; Benckendorff *et al.*, 2014; Neuhofer *et al.*, 2014). These innovative practices are found in both major and minor tourism product/service experience provision developments; through innovation in channel/promotion methods; and in the methods for accessing these experiences (Novelli, 2005; Swarbrooke and Horner, 2005; Scarinci and Richins, 2008).

Innovation has been defined and conceptualized in diverse ways (Peters and Pikkematt, 2005). The Organisation for Economic Co-operation and Development defined enterprise innovation as: 'The implementation of a new or significantly improved product (good or service), or process, a new marketing method, or a new organizational method in business practices, workplace organization or external relations' (OECD, 2005). The Conference Board of Canada (2013) expanded on this concept of innovation to create a more comprehensive definition: 'the process through which economic and social value is extracted from knowledge through the generation, development, and implementation of ideas to produce new or improved strategies, capabilities, products, services, or processes'.

Four types of innovation identified by the Conference Board of Canada (2013) are: (i) radical change to products and services; (ii) radical change to processes; (iii) incremental improvement to products and services; and (iv) incremental improvement to processes. Hertog *et al.* (2010) expresses services innovation as a multidimensional phenomenon and identifies dimensions of service innovation, which are significantly applicable to tourism and, in particular, the development of the heli-ski speciality tourism sector. These are referred to as 'new service experiences and solutions', and involve the six dimensions of: (i) new service concepts; (ii) new customer interactions; (iii) new business partners; (iv) new multi-shared revenue models; (v) new delivery system through organizational/personal means; and (vi) new delivery system through technological means. This chapter explores innovation in the development of a distinctive niche segment or sector of the tourism industry; that is, utilizing air-based transportation, particularly helicopters, in accessing

* Corresponding author: hrichins@tru.ca

© CAB International 2016. *Mountain Tourism: Experiences, Communities, Environments and Sustainable Futures* (eds H. Richins and J.S. Hull)

environments for active participation in remote alpine winter sports (primarily alpine skiing).

History and Development of Air-based Winter Sports Access

Mountain tourism, and in particular alpine skiing, has perhaps been related to access since people first decided to utilize mountain environments for recreational activity. The equipment utilized to access winter activities has progressed in the last 60 or 70 years at a consistent pace with numerous technological advances, as well as service and product advancements in winter sports (Fry, 2006a; Kresbach, 2014; Yarvin, 2014).

There was strong motivation to develop new ways to move skiers uphill. Prior to the mid-1930s, skiers had to walk uphill on skis or other devices to have a run downhill and then return for the difficult trek back uphill to do maybe one more run in a full day. Then various surface and aerial lifts were devised to assist with more frequent downhill opportunities over snow. Ways to move skiers and mountain tourism parties uphill developed from large vehicles, such as snow cats or snow trucks, to large railways and funiculars, and finally aerial means (tramways, chairlifts, detachable chairlifts, funitels, gondola lifts, hybrid lifts); and surface means or lifts including j-bars, t-bars, magic carpets, platter/button/poma lifts, rope tows and handle tows (Skilifts, 2014). Though many of these uphill mountain transport methods opened up vast areas to explore, most commonly near mountain villages, true wilderness/backcountry access was still very difficult.

The first use of aircraft to access downhill terrain probably occurred as early as 1952 in the Banff region of the Canadian Rockies. Also between 1952 and the early 1960s, a number of flights were made on the glaciers in the Alps of Switzerland (Fry, 2006b). By 1955, only a few years later, New Zealand's Southern Alps also had airplane flights onto the Franz Joseph and Tasman Glaciers that included skiing experiences (Mt Cook, 2014). By 1962, the French Alps became a major destination for

accessing untracked skiing terrain through the use of adapted glacial ski planes (Fry, 2006a). Looking at older photographs, there is some evidence of helicopters being utilized for skiing in the early-to-mid-1950s (Atwater, 1968; Tordrillo, 2014), but the Canadian Rockies is generally attributed with the advent of heli-skiing in the early 1960s.

In 1959, Canadian Mountain Holidays (CMH) was incorporated in Banff, Alberta by Austrian immigrant, Hans Gmoser, a mountain guide who led trips into the alpine areas near Mount Assiniboine. In 1962, a plane was used for skiing in the Cariboo Mountains in British Columbia, and by 1963, the Association of Canadian Mountain Guides was formed to build and lead the growing field of mountain-based winter and summer backcountry experiences in western Canada (Skiing History, 2014).

In this same year, Hans gave a speech to the Canadian Ski Instructors' Alliance promoting the benefits of utilizing helicopters as a means of building versatility and mobility to access backcountry winter areas. The first helicopter to access skiing was used in Canada in 1965 when CMH operated the first helicopter ski tour into the Bugaboos Mountain Range (Donahue, 2008, 2013; Backcountry, 2014). The Bugaboo Lodge was opened in 1968, becoming the first lodge to be used for heli-skiing. In 1969, skiing by helicopter began in Valemount, British Columbia. Some other early heli-ski operators soon developed their own pioneering operations (rk heliski, 2014; Wiegele, 2014). CMH opened a second lodging facility, Cariboo Lodge, in 1974, and in 1978, the first heli-hiking tour was developed for summer activities (Fry, 2006a).

Today heli-ski experiences exist in almost 20 countries: USA, Canada, Iceland, Switzerland, Italy, Greenland, India, Chile, Turkey, Georgia, Sweden, New Zealand, Nepal, Norway, Finland, Argentina, Russia, Japan, Austria, as well as Antarctica (Wanrooy and Anthony, 2006; Last Frontier, 2014; Robbins, 2014). With the vibrant, expansive and pre-eminent mountain terrain available, Western Canada has dominated the provision of heli-ski experiences since its inception (Helicopter Skiing, 2014). In British Columbia, there are more than 30 (23 heli-ski and 16 cat-ski) operations listed on the BC tourism website, including some with dual operations (Hello BC, 2014).

One of the pioneers of heli-skiing still engaged in the development of the industry, and the particular operation he established in the early 1970s, is located in the small community of Blue River, British Columbia (Fig. 7.1). This chapter discusses, in some depth, the Mike Wiegele winter sports enterprise as a meaningful example of innovation in mountain experience provision. Aspects of innovation are covered in the chapter, encompassing customer service and experience development, community development and lifestyle integration, equipment and facility innovation, adventure tourism safety, and expansion of exclusive and high-end winter sports offerings.

Development of Winter Sports Access in Backcountry British Columbia – The Mike Wiegele Helicopter Skiing (MWHS) Operation

During the decade of the 1960s, at the time Hans Gmoser was developing his Canadian Mountain Holidays, another Austrian, Mike Wiegele, was also considering ideas for changing the face of access to backcountry skiing. After having been involved with a diversity of outdoor employment exploits in Western Canada, Wiegele's love of skiing eventually led to his involvement in the Banff winter sports scene. Wiegele became the Director of the Lake Louise Ski School, where he assisted numerous young skiers to become internationally successful as

Fig. 7.1. Location of Blue River, British Columbia, Canada (source: Google Maps).

competitors. Following this, he became interested in accessing the mountainous backcountry in winter, and in the early 1970s started a small heli-ski operation within the Cariboo and Monashee Mountain Ranges of British Columbia (Skinet, 2014). This relatively remote backcountry wilderness heli-skiing experience grew to serve a vast terrain system larger than all of the lift-served runs in North America. The geographic location was crucial – it was both accessible and contained unique and expansive mountain ranges, which also had the outstanding advantage of having abundant and reliable snow.

In a region that had been known for logging and transportation (Blue River, 2014), a new type of transportation sprung up to enable adventure skiers to access untouched runs in a 1.2 million acre mountain area. Today, explored alpine terrain of MWHS now includes an area shaped rather like a rectangle of 64 km by 128 km, with more than 1000 peaks, 4500 km², and more than 550 named runs (Wiegele Press Room, 2014). From its early days this area developed into a small community, supporting numerous individuals and families with a focus on winter sports activities. There are currently close to 500 people served by the unincorporated region of Blue River (Blue River, 2014). Summer activities are also important to the region, with access to numerous mountains and to Murtle Lake in Wells Gray Provincial Park, the largest paddle-only lake in North America (Wells Gray, 2014). The major catalyst, however, in the regional community's more recent vitality, particularly over the last 30 years, is the world-class winter niche tourism operation of Mike Wiegele Helicopter Skiing (Blue River, 2014).

of Canada, 2013), the pioneer spirit of Mike Wiegele Helicopter Skiing was paramount in building a specialist tourism activity within remote locations in interior British Columbia. These innovative breakthroughs included: integrated resort innovation; innovative community tourism development; building unlimited access to mountain environments; innovation in weather, safety, and prediction systems; innovation in winter sports equipment and facility management; innovation in building and incorporating higher-end culinary and lodging experiences in remote locations; innovative personalized approaches to speciality tourism products; and finally, innovation in the customer experience development and provision arena.

Over the past 45 years, the enterprise has built an extremely successful reputation and now has a strong customer following as one of the premier heli-ski operations in North America, or the 'largest single base helicopter skiing operation in the world' (Harley, 2014). This consists of providing a full service experience with holistic, encompassing daytime and night-time activities including luxury sport, culinary, and health and wellness amenities within a rustic mountain lodge setting. MWHS promotional materials combine the idea of the mountains and the importance of the experience using the tag line 'Elevate Your Experience'. They also show their commitment, primary focus, and an organizational culture dedicated to providing the highest-quality customer experience: 'At Mike Wiegele Helicopter Skiing our experience makes your experience extraordinary' (Wiegele, 2014).

Innovation in Mountain Experience Provision

From the beginnings of heli-skiing in remote mountain regions of British Columbia, Mike Wiegele became one of the world's early pioneers and innovators in this high-end adventure sport. Innovation is the process by which conditions exist to convert opportunities into marketable and practical ideas (Okpara, 2007). Known for both incremental as well as breakthrough innovation (OECD, 2005; Conference Board

Customer Experience Development and Provision

Service innovation has been shown to occur through the development and commitment to personalized approaches regarding speciality tourism products, and an organizational commitment to customer experience development and provision (Hertog et al., 2010). Throughout the development of adventure snow sports luxury tourism experiences, MWHS has been a leader in innovation in many areas, including: high levels of personalized customer service;

quality amenity provision including complimentary use of most available on-site and off-site facilities and activities; seamless transportation and transfer services; attention to detail in every aspect of the experience; opportunity for positive and constructive social and individual interaction (including various languages); the integration of employees within the customer experience as appropriate; learning and active participation as a key quality in the experience; opportunity for custom-designed group packages; a significant focus on health and wellness, as well as fitness and skill in the context of snow sports; and the provision of high-quality food and beverage experiences utilizing up-to-date culinary ingredients, presentation, and nutrition, plus an extensive wine cellar (Powder, 2014). These aspects of innovation are relevant to Hertog et al.'s (2010) new service experiences and solutions and, in particular, new service and customer interactions as well as new delivery of service through an integrated organizational culture.

As mentioned on the website, guides and hosts from Michael Wiegele's are:

> chosen for their ability to provide our guests with an exciting and memorable vacation, while caring for their safety and comfort at all times. In addition to their technical qualifications, they also possess strong interpersonal and communication skills.
>
> (Wiegele, 2014)

The unique, personalized service component is emphasized in these same marketing materials:

> Our guides are also your resort hosts – they meet you on arrival, take you to your accommodations, and show you our facilities. Every evening after their detailed guides meeting, they will meet you in the Powder Max Dining Room and the Silver Buckle Lounge for your gourmet dining experience and conversation.
>
> (Wiegele, 2014)

Winter Sports Equipment and Transport Access Innovation

When helicopter skiing started in the late 1960s and 1970s, equipment was not set up well to access the challenging terrain. There were no snowboards then, nor was there such specialized equipment as powder skis. Also, helicopters were small and could only accommodate a few people at a time and there was great difficulty getting to challenging alpine spots to let off skiers. Another challenge was weather reliability and accessibility. Three innovations have provided potential solutions to these earlier issues.

Two of the key innovations in the further development of heli-skiing gear and transport equipment occurred throughout the 1990s. One is the more radical innovation in the development of purpose-built fat powder skis. Mike Wiegele had been partnering with Atomic Ski Company for many years in the provision of the most appropriate skis for backcountry experiences. Traditional ski resorts were focusing on improvements for the majority of the skiing participants, which meant attention being given to grooming technique changes and slopes accessed by uphill lifts. The focus on equipment improvement revolved around the same priority group, i.e. the groomed run skiers. Minimal effort, therefore, was being placed on improving equipment for alternative snow sports experiences, including powder and backcountry gear.

Two aspects of ski innovation occurred at this time: (i) the experimentation of much wider, longer and more flexible skis; and (ii) the decision to provide equipment to guests as part of the full package skiing experience. At the same time, major changes were under way to provide snowboards as a means of accessing deep snow experiences (Snowboarding History, 2014).

These innovations resulted in major shifts in the ability of heli-ski guests to access helicopter-served backcountry skiing. No longer reserved for just the higher-end experts, the sport expanded to include a wealthier clientele who might have lower skill levels, and included even intermediate skier abilities. Both skiers and the growing snowboarder market became a focus of Wiegele in meeting their needs and interests, and this effectively expanded their market reach. Today, MWHS ski and snowboard equipment, developed in partnership with major international ski manufacturers, is provided as part of the heli-ski package, and can be allocated based on skier ability, conditions and terrain. This has greatly enhanced and broadened the experience for many guests.

A second, more incremental innovation has been the improvement of helicopters in accessing backcountry deep snow conditions (see Fig. 7.2). This included the development and provision of larger helicopters to accommodate up to ten guests, whereas earlier helicopters were only

Fig. 7.2. Mike Wiegele helicopter skiing drop in the Cariboo Mountains (photograph courtesy of Harold Richins).

able to accommodate around four guests. This allowed ten guests to come down the runs while ten other guests were being taken to the drop-off point, thus accommodating up to 20 guests at any one time. Improvements also included more comfort in transport equipment, and becoming more customer-focused with improved safety systems in place, while allowing for an increased number of rides per day (Wiegele, 2014).

A third innovation relating to access, which has occurred over the last 15 years, has been the partnership arrangement with the forest industry in combining approved logging operations with careful alpine trail development for snow cat operations. The Eight Peaks Ski Resort Master Plan (SRMP) dealt with the designated Eight Peaks area with close proximity to and surrounding the Blue River area. As mentioned in the brief description of the plan:

> The objective of this was to improve the reliability of the skiing product on the skiable terrain in close proximity to the Heli-Village and base facilities in Blue River. This offers the operational benefit of quick access and egress

> to the skiing, reducing concerns about being unable to fly due to bad weather.
>
> (Harley, 2014)

Building Unlimited Access to Mountain Environments

Helicopters are very expensive to operate. Added to this is the expense and challenge of heli-ski operation within extreme winter conditions. High-level maintenance, well-trained guides, knowledge of weather conditions and snowpack, and other risk factors all add to the costs of operation. Due to this, the cost of a visitor experience with a heli-ski company can be quite high. Different operators have dealt with this challenge in different ways. Most operators have a maximum amount of vertical terrain covered in the price, with sharp added fees once this maximum is reached. Mike Wiegele's enterprise established the approach for unlimited access to backcountry skiable terrain and unlimited number of runs over the course of a week in the heli-ski experience. This is often referred to as 'unlimited vertical'. The unlimited vertical MWHS price structure incorporates an average of most participants' daily and weekly mountain terrain experience. Therefore this allows those interested in an extensive number of runs to achieve their highest levels, while most are more than satisfied with a smaller number of uphill heli-ski rides. In adding to the unlimited access and vertical, an all-inclusive activity approach (with the exception of alcohol and some personal spa experiences) helps customers feel more relaxed and able to enjoy a simpler approach to their high-end mountain tourism experience.

Developing and Incorporating Higher-end Culinary and Lodging Experiences in Remote Locations

For many years in the early stages of the development of remote heli-ski operations, overnight facilities were quite basic, and they offered rather rudimentary culinary fare. Other amenities such as health and wellness offerings, sports equipment and even organized transport to the sites simply did not exist (Helicopter Skiing, 2014).

This has significantly changed over the last 20 years. A number of operators have developed fully fledged, upscale mini-resorts with transport access to accommodate the needs and interests of their guests. Over this period, Michael Wiegele has built a number of facilities, including smaller stand-alone lodges such as the 17-room Albreda Lodge for groups of up to 20 people, the Bavarian House estate to accommodate smaller groups, and individual, rustic houses with full kitchens within walking distance of the 22,000 ft^2 main lodge. There is also a substantial administrative, reservations, and conference facility. The state-of-the-art dining room and bar facilities in the main lodge serve as a major gathering place for guests. There is a significant international market (primarily from the USA and Europe) that has the desire and an expectation for rustic luxury within a remote mountain environment, yet they want to be able to access the area with relative ease. Wiegele responded to this by setting up weekly 2-hour airport transfers to allow access to the relatively remote location, and this organization stresses the importance of meeting the clients' needs, and in fact, sees this as paramount in the overall success of their programme.

The following quote from the MWHS website gives a flavour of the rustic luxury and exclusivity offered by the company:

> Mike Wiegele's Heli Village Resort provides exclusive luxury in a self-contained resort setting. Unique in the heli skiing industry, the Resort allows guests to enjoy the best of the day's powder skiing/boarding and then return to their exclusive log chalet accommodation and village amenities.
>
> With our team of highly talented professionals, MWHS delivers the most exhilarating ski experience, yet uniquely applies a boutique touch for exclusive service that creates memorable vacations.
>
> (Mike Wiegele Helicopter Skiing, 2014)

Community Tourism Development: Integration of Community, Organization, Employees, Families, Lifestyle and Visitor Experience

Successful tourism enterprise development in mountain communities can have significant impacts on such areas as employment and community development; social well-being; recreational resources; sense of place and community culture; community governance; and may act as a catalyst for further economic activity which results in significant change of a community over a period of time, especially in smaller population centres (Nepal and Jamal, 2011). The Blue River area, where the Wiegele heli-ski operations are located, has experienced the opportunities and benefits as well as the challenges of small community tourism development. These are briefly discussed below.

Employees and residents within small communities such as Blue River face difficulties associated with living in remote mountain areas. However, an integrated approach has been taken in Blue River to both successfully grow the winter snow sport enterprise and to support employees and their families living and working in the community. This is consistent with other small tourism community capacity building (Richins, 2008), and has slowly built a sense of community spirit and commitment to resource, health, education, and other socio-economic attributes.

Perhaps the following quote from Mike Wiegele best represents the commitment to responsibility a company such as MWHS has on influencing a small town and its community members:

> I don't believe in the industrial approach. We are in the people business. That's why we've worked so hard to establish a mountain community. We want our people to be able to build a full life – to start families, and put down real roots in the region. As I've often said: We may be in the tourism business, but our hearts and minds are not for sale.
>
> (Wiegele, 2014)

This commitment and passion, is further demonstrated by the following quote regarding potential employment at MWHS:

> Are you looking for a great job and a great lifestyle? Do you love snow? Would you like to work for the finest heli-ski resort in the world? If you share a passion for excellence, then learn more about the employment opportunities at Mike Wiegele Helicopter Skiing where we work hard … and play harder.
>
> (Wiegele, 2014)

Innovation in Guiding, Weather Systems, Safety and Prediction

An incremental innovation of the Mike Wiegele Helicopter Skiing enterprise is the extensive focus on safety, which, in a harsh mountain environment, has been one of the major challenges. Virtually all trips by heli-ski operations are guided trips with highly trained and qualified individuals possessing a number of mountain and safety certifications. In the case of MWHS operations, this normally includes the equivalent of the following: (i) the Canadian Ski Instructors Alliance (CSIA) (all are certified ski instructors); (ii) the Canadian Avalanche Association (CAA) membership and involvement, with extensive knowledge of avalanche prevention, risk aversion, and on-slope incident management; and (iii) the Canadian Ski Guide Association (CSGA), which offers extensive training in ski guiding. Another organization, the Association of Canadian Mountain Guides (ACMG), is a somewhat parallel, but broader organization offering certified mountain guide training through Thompson

Rivers University in British Columbia. All of these organizations were founded, built, and in a number of ways, influenced by interest in high mountain access within Western Canada during the same period as the development of heli-skiing. The ACMG and the CSGA were both formed by the founders of Canadian heli-ski companies (Hans Gmoser and Mike Wiegele, respectively).

In addition to the important guide qualification and certification advances, some of the important innovations with MWHS include: (i) the use of second guides; (ii) intensive safety team management; (iii) avalanche research; (iv) medical clinics; and (v) weather and snow condition forecasting. One of the key aspects here is the commitment to what is referred to as a tail guide, the guide who is involved at the rear of the group during the skiing experience. This was developed and pioneered by Mike Wiegele, and essentially has meant losing a seat in a ten-passenger helicopter (see Fig 7.3), while gaining the desired targeted focus on customer service, safety and high-level guest skiing and boarding experiences.

On team-oriented safety management, the Guide Haus was developed as a means of providing integrated and intensive communication sharing among guides, operations, and pilots. Creating this communication centre, allowed the sharing of more comprehensive, important information such as: (i) the historical snow and weather reporting system information (built in consultation with experienced personal and pilot guides); (ii) incident and near-miss incident reporting; and (iii) reports of successes.

Information at this site has also been augmented with periodic statistics or reports from the University of Calgary's Avalanche Research Centre and reports from the Canadian Ski Guide Association. A five-step checklist was developed over a number of years, and prioritized as an important step in the MWHS team's daily procedure. This checklist included: (i) daily weather data; (ii) graphs to show patterns; (iii) snow pack profiles; (iv) field observations; and (v) snow stability ratings. Additional information from weather patterns, the Canadian Avalanche Association, and other sources, is brought in to assist in making predictions to help in daily decision making as well as over the longer periods of time (Avalanche, 2014).

Fig. 7.3. Morning heliport pickup at Wiegele's Blue River Resort Site (photograph courtesy of Harold Richins).

Mike Wiegele Helicopter Skiing has also pioneered training in the use of mountain medical assistance and practice, and often includes medical personnel in larger groups of guests. For a number of years, there has been a medical clinic on-site, and often an on-site physician is incorporated as part of the Guide Haus. Guests are expected to participate in snow safety and helicopter safety orientation, and are trained in the use of a state of the art avalanche transceiver and shovel pack, which includes a snow probe in case of an incident. As mentioned on the website, 'We approach safety in a multi-faceted way that includes guest and guide training, helicopter maintenance, on-site doctors, sophisticated weather analysis, and avalanche forecasting' (Wiegele, 2014).

Future Innovation in the Development of Saddle Mountain Integrated Winter Sports Village

A number of mountain resorts have added helicopters or snow cats as a means of accessing terrain near their resorts. These are usually located in very accessible mountain regions, with day experiences to the slopes nearby. The MWHS enterprise, however, has been developing a new concept in integrated snow sports access and amenity. This essentially augments the extensive backcountry experience currently available by adding a substantial front country experience. The master development plan, referred to as the Saddle Mountain Master Development Agreement, expects to open and operate a sustainable, integrated, and holistic visitor and village experience to a higher-end clientele. The expected focus will be on: (i) the lifestyle of people who purchase property within the large resort; (ii) the complete visitor snow sports experience located in a remote mountain environment; and (iii) accommodating individuals and groups in an integrated way (i.e. the lifestyle of people who live and work in the community within a comprehensive recreational and community experience).

With the new Saddle Mountain Resort (see Fig. 7.4), there is expected to be a merging

Fig. 7.4. Site of proposed Saddle Mountain Resort at Blue River (photograph courtesy of Harold Richins).

of backcountry and front-country experiences served by a combination of uphill ski lifts, snow cats, and helicopters with ample access to terrain to suit a variety of abilities and interests creating more space and limited crowding. The purpose-built village design allows for unified ski-in/ski-out lodging facilities, as well as private residences. It is expected to have a village core, base lodge, and 'over 4,300 feet of lift-serviced, vertical skiing, making it one of the biggest lift-serviced mountains in North America' (Harley, 2014). The combination of mountain access lifts and machines also allows for a variety of weather conditions such as severe storms, fog, or temperature variation. Utilizing the lower facilities will allow downhill experiences to take place in the unlikely event that unusual weather conditions prevent heli-skiing. The following quote from the planners of the Saddle Mountain project, explains the focus of this project:

> The vision is to develop a mountain retreat that caters to the pursuit of powder skiing. It will include a powder skiing academy, enable down-day skiing for heli-skiers and facilitate a range of lift serviced/heli-skiing packages for a wider spectrum of the high end skier marketplace.
>
> (Harley, 2014)

The village is expected to have educational and training facilities, community services, and amenities, and will follow the historical approach from the 45-year-old heli-ski enterprise, which values providing strong support to employees and their families. In discussing the expanding and innovative new development, 'I want Saddle Mountain to become an international skiing mecca. Not for its size, necessarily, but for the quality of the experience it will provide' (Mike Wiegele Helicopter Skiing, 2014).

Concluding Remarks on Innovation in the Development of Heli-ski Mountain Experiences

This chapter has attempted to briefly explore a case study highlighting innovation in mountain tourism access, relating specifically to the heli-ski industry. This has included a very brief history of the challenges and development of air-based winter sport access, and provide a case study example to examine a 45-year-old enterprise, Mike Wiegele Helicopter Skiing. In addition, a number of innovation aspects were explored through the examples in both incremental and more profound (or radical) innovation developments (Conference Board of Canada, 2013). This has included areas of innovation regarding the higher end – the fully active and engaged niche tourism experience of heli-skiing. The parallel innovative developments regarding winter sports equipment and transport access and service were also discussed as an integral and key part of the ongoing success of this special interest tourism product.

This chapter also included the following innovation developments: (i) the provision of higher-end culinary and lodging experiences in remote and wilderness mountain regions; (ii) looking at regional tourism and community development facets as innovation aspects; (iii) innovations in guiding and safety (i.e. moving from lower-end basic survival practices in the backcountry when heli-skiing was in its infancy, to much greater sophistication and prediction, and, therefore lowered risk and increased safety) in winter mountain wilderness backcountry experiences. These considerable developments are primarily relevant to Hertog *et al.*'s (2010) dimensions of new service concepts, new customer interactions, new delivery system through organizational/personal means and new delivery system through technological means. Finally, the chapter included a discussion with regard to an innovative new mountain resort development, Saddle Mountain, outlining the expected long-term benefits for this higher-end integrated, village experience project.

The commitment to providing quality tourism experiences, product and organizational innovation, and organizational and client-focused commitment and emphasis on the dynamic and engaged tourist experience in this case study, is best captured in the following two quotes:

> Since 1970, we have led the helicopter skiing industry with our excellence in operations, unparalleled safety record and distinctive customer service – all within a unique Heli Village Resort setting.
>
> (Mike Wiegele, 2014)

> Over 40 years of experience guarantees guests a once in a lifetime experience with the best powder, dining, and guiding in the business.
>
> (Heli-cat-guide, 2014)

References

Atwater, M. (1968) *The Avalanche Hunters*. Macrae Smith, Philadelphia, Pennsylvania.

Avalanche (2014) Available at: http://www.avalanche.ca/training#overview (accessed 26 November 2014).

Backcountry (2014) Backcountry Skiing History. Available at: http://www.wildsnow.com/backcountry-skiing-history/backcountry-skiing-ski-mountaineering-chronology (accessed 20 November 2014).

Benckendorff, P., Sheldon, P. and Fesenmaier, D. (2014) *Tourism Information Technology*. CAB International, Wallingford, UK.

Blue River (2014) Available at: http://www.blueriverbc.ca/planning-your-trip/about-blue-river (accessed 12 November 2014)

Conference Board of Canada (2013) Innovation Defined. Available at: www.conferenceboard.ca/cbi/innovation (accessed 22 November 2014).

Donahue, T. (2008) *Bugaboo Dreams: A Story of Skiers, Helicopters and Mountains*. Rocky Mountain Books, Victoria, British Columbia.

Donahue, T. (2013) The First Heli-Ski Helicopter. Available at: http://www.canadianmountainholidays.com/about-us/50th-timeline.aspx (accessed 7 January 2016).

Fry, J. (2006a) Up by air: the adventure filled golden years of Heli-skiing. *Skiing Heritage* 18(3), 8–14.

Fry, J. (2006b) *The Story of Modern Skiing*. University Press of New England, Hanover, New Hampshire.

Harley (2014) Available at: http://www.brentharley.com/portfolio-item/mwhs/ (accessed 7 January 2016).

Heli-cat-guide (2014) Available at: http://www.powder.com/heli-cat-guide/mike-wiegele-helicopter-skiing (accessed 12 November 2014).

Helicopter Skiing (2014) Helicopter Skiing in BC Canada – A Brief History and Outlook. Available at: usconsum-ersplace.com/helicopter-skiing-in-bc-canada-a-brief-history-and-outlook (accessed 20 November 2014).

Hello BC (2014) Available at: http://www.hellobc.com/british-columbia/things-to-do/winter-activities/heli-skiing-cat-skiing.aspx (accessed 10 November 2014).

Hertog, P. den, van der Aa, W. and de Jong, M.W. (2010) Capabilities for managing service innovation: towards a conceptual framework. *Journal of Service Management* 21(4), 490–514.

Kresbach (2014) History of Heli Skiing. Available at: http://www.tordrillomountainlodge.com/history-heli-skiing (accessed 20 November 2014).

Last Frontier (2014) The History of Heli Skiing. Available at: http://www.lastfrontierheli.com/news/215/then-and-now-the-heli-skiing-scene (accessed 12 November 2014).

Mike Wiegele Helicopter Skiing (2014) Available at: www.wiegele.com/about-mike-wiegele-helicopter-skiing (accessed 15 November 2014).

Mt Cook (2014) Mt. Cook Ski Planes History. Available at: http://www.mtcookskiplanes.com/About-Us/Mt-Cook-Ski-Planes-history.asp (accessed 22 November 2014).

Nepal, S. and Jamal, T. (2011) Resort-induced Changes in Small Mountain Communities in British Columbia. *Mountain Research and Development* 31(2), 89–101.

Neuhofer, B., Buhalis, D. and Ladkin, A. (2014) A typology of technology enhanced tourism experiences. *International Journal of Tourism Research* 16(4), 340–350.

Novelli, M. (2005) *Niche Tourism: Contemporary Issues, Trends and Cases.* Elsevier, Butterworth-Heinemann, Oxford.

OECD (2005) *Science, Technology and Industry Scorecard 2005: Towards a Knowledge-Based Economy.* OECD Publications Service, Paris, France.

Okpara (2007) The value of creativity and innovation in entrepreneurship. *Journal of Asia Entrepreneurship and Sustainability* 2(2).

Peters, M. and Pikkematt, B. (eds) (2005) *Innovation in Hospitality and Tourism.* Harworth Hospitality, Binghampton, New York.

Poon, A. (1993) *Tourism, Technology and Competitive Strategies.* CAB International, Wallingford, UK.

Powder (2014) Mike Wiegele Helicopter Skiing. Available at: http://www.powder.com/heli-cat-guide/mike-wiegele-helicopter-skiing (accessed 15 November 2014).

Rachman, Z.M. and Richins, H. (1997) The Status Of New Zealand Tour Operator Web Sites. *Journal of Tourism Studies* 8(2).

Richins, H. (2008) Building sustainable tourism as an integral part of the resort community. *International Journal of Tourism Policy* 1(4), 315–334.

rk heliski (2014) How it All started – rk heliski History. Available at: http://www.rkheliski.com/the-rk-story (accessed 20 November 2014).

Robbins, T. (2014) Fifty Years of Heli-skiing. Available at: http://www.ft.com/cms/s/2/70fd5378-5968-11e4-9546-00144feab7de.html#axzz3KfZ4xWuC (accessed 20 November 2014).

Scarinci, J. and Richins, H. (2008) Specialist lodging in the USA: motivations of bed and breakfast accommodation guests. *Tourism and International Interdisciplinary Journal* 56(3), 271–282.

Skiing History (2014) Hans Gmoser, Heliski Pioneer. Available at: http://www.skiinghistory.org/lives/hans-gmoser (accessed 5 November 2014).

Skilifts (2014) Cable Tramway Terms. Available at: http://www.skilifts.org/old/glossary.htm (accessed 27 August 2015).

Skinet (2014) Heli-skiing: Where We've Been and Where We're Going. Available at: http://www.skinet.com/warrenmiller/history-of-Heli-skiing (accessed 12 November 2014).

Snowboarding History (2014) Available at: http://www.abc-of-snowboarding.com/snowboardinghistory.asp (accessed 27 August 2015).

Swarbrooke, J. and Horner, S. (2005) *Consumer Behaviour in Tourism,* 2nd edn. Butterworth-Heinemann, Oxford, UK.

Tordrillo (2014) History of Heli-skiing. Available at: http://www.tordrillomountainlodge.com/the-history-of-heli-skiing (accessed 15 November 2014).

Wanrooy, B. and Anthony, C. (2006) *Dream Season: Worldwide Guide to Heli and Cat Skiing/Boarding.* Lulu.com, Raleigh, North Carolina.

Wells Gray (2014) Explore Wells Gray. Available at: http://www.explorewellsgray.com/index.php/activities/paddling (accessed 15 November 2014).

Wiegele (2014) Mike Wiegele Helicopter Skiing – Experience. Available at: http://www.wiegele.com/heliski-experience.htm (accessed 20 November 2014).

Wiegele Press Room (2014) Mike Wiegele Helicopter Skiing – Media Press Room. Available at: http://www.wiegele.com/press-room.htm (accessed 20 November 2014).

Yarvin, B. (2014) A Brief History of Ski Lifts and Cable Cars. The Bulletin. Bend, Oregon. Available at: www.bendbulletin.com/news/1351807-151/a-brief-history-of-ski-lifts-and-cable (accessed 24 July 2015).

8 From Winter Destination to All-year-round Tourism: How Focus on Service can Reduce Fluctuation in Demand due to Seasonality

Marit Gundersen Engeset* and Jan Velvin
Buskerud Vestfold University College, Kongsberg, Norway

Introduction

Fluctuation in demand causes challenges with tourism, related to capacity management, workforce retention, and profitability (Allcock, 1989; Butler, 2001; Higham and Hinch, 2002; Koenig-Lewis and Bischoff, 2005; Pegg *et al.*, 2012). A major reason for fluctuation is the seasonality of the tourism product, where demand is concentrated during a few months of the year. Many tourism destinations and companies meet this challenge by targeting business markets when the leisure market is off-season. For mountain resorts relying on snow tourism, this strategy is difficult, since high season in the leisure market coincides with peak demand in the business market. Competition from other vacation forms and changes in climate will affect the future earnings of the destinations that focus only on winter tourism (Moen and Fredman, 2007). Mountain resorts therefore need to develop their attractiveness in the leisure market in all seasons. Tourism destinations dedicated to breaking out of seasonal fluctuations typically focus on developing off-season products or marketing activities such as price discounts and promotions to increase demand during low-season (Higham and Hinch, 2002). In order to be

competitive, companies and destinations must also ensure high-quality offerings throughout the year. This is particularly challenging when demand fluctuates and the pressure on services and infrastructure is unstable.

An important part of the tourism product consists of personal services that rely on courteous and skilled staff. Research suggests that the service encounter – that is, the meeting between the guest and the service worker, is central to consumers' overall service experience and contributes extensively to perceptions of service quality (Troye *et al.*, 1995). Perceptions of service, unlike perceptions of, for example, the skiing area, are not linked to or limited to a specific season. Therefore, promoting a destination that has a reputation for providing excellent personal service can build positive brand associations that are not limited to high season. To investigate this assumption and to understand the importance of service excellence, not only the satisfaction and perceptions of quality, but also for increasing off-season demand, the authors systematically studied a case in Hemsedal, Norway.

Hemsedal is a skiing destination that over the last 4 years has worked to improve service by providing employee and management training. The purpose of this case study is to understand

* Corresponding author: marit.engeset@hbv.no

how training and motivation of staff and management can be a successful strategy for resorts dedicated to reducing their vulnerability to seasonal changes. The focus is on systematic measurement of employee and customer value, as well as monitoring revisit intentions among guests both during low and high seasons.

The chapter is organized as follows. First, how seasonality creates a negative demand fluctuation spiral is discussed. Next, the importance of service quality for guest satisfaction and revisiting behaviour is discussed. Then, the details of service training and results from the Hemsedal case are discussed, before concluding with recommendations for winter tourism destinations.

Seasonality

Seasonality is defined by Koenig-Lewis and Bischoff (2005) as the 'recurring movements in a time series during a particular time of the year'. Frechtling (1996, 2012) identified climate/ weather as an important cause of seasonality in tourism demand. Since mountain destinations typically offer outdoor activities, they are highly climate-dependent (Smith, 1990), and fluctuation in demand due to seasonality is difficult to avoid. Pegg *et al.* (2012) identified a number of costs of seasonality for both companies and the local communities. Companies are challenged off-season because of over-capacity, non-utilization of infrastructure, reduction in the workforce, and non-attraction of investments. This results in problems with recruitment and retention of full-time employees. During peak season, companies and the local communities suffer from overuse of infrastructure and high demand on services. Demand on both physical infrastructure and service employees often exceeds capacity – leading to higher waiting time, overcrowding, less time for staff to serve the individual guests' needs, and less attention to detail. The intensity in demand combined with the unstable workforce due to part-time and seasonal employees makes it difficult to maintain satisfactory levels of service quality when seasonal fluctuation is high.

To meet the challenges caused by high concentration of people in time and space, highly skilled, stable, and motivated service staff are needed. This requires a level of investment in recruiting, training, motivating, and retaining staff that most seasonal companies cannot afford. In addition, recruiting highly skilled staff is a challenge, as seasonal work is often regarded as inferior due to lack of career opportunities (Ainsworth and Purss, 2009). High workforce turnover combined with low skills and lack of focus on systematic training make it difficult to maintain high levels of service quality – something that in turn leads to lower guest satisfaction. Lower satisfaction will hurt demand during low season more than during high season, since the attractiveness of the physical product is lower than during peak season when activities and physical surroundings have higher pull-factor on the market. These factors create a negative spiral that it is difficult to break out of. Figure 8.1 illustrates these effects: high seasonal demand fluctuation leads to layoff of staff during low season, which in turn results in high employee turnover. The unattractiveness of seasonal workplaces coupled with general low levels of competencies among workers in the tourism sector and limited resources to training lead to less skilled staff. This in turn contributes to lower service quality and lower guest satisfaction. It becomes more difficult to attract customers during low season, and higher seasonal demand fluctuation can be expected.

To break out of this negative spiral, destinations typically focus on developing attractive off-season products, working towards becoming four-season destinations. While this is necessary, it is not sufficient to attract tourists outside high season. Being able to deliver high-quality physical facilities and attractive activity opportunities is important, but not sufficient to be competitive. People are inseparable from the service product, and the overall experience for the guest depends on the employee's ability and motivation to provide service in all aspects of the experience. To motivate tourists to come back during other seasons, they must believe that the overall experience, including attractions and activities as well as service, will meet their expectations. Hence, we argue that focus on service quality will not only increase satisfaction and repeat visitation during peak season, it will also result in higher demand during other seasons.

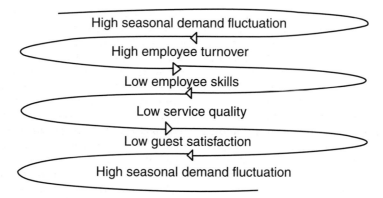

Fig. 8.1. The demand fluctuation spiral.

Service Quality and Guest Satisfaction

Service quality is conceptualized as consumers' evaluations of different aspects of the service (Brady and Cronin, 2001). Early definitions of service quality were based on the disconfirmation paradigm, which posits that service quality is a result of consumers' comparison between experienced and expected service (Grönroos, 1982; Parasuraman et al., 1985; Parasuraman et al., 1988). Later research has concluded that expectations can be dropped from the model altogether and that service quality can be assessed directly by focusing on performance only (Cronin and Taylor, 1992). Service quality is a key factor in building competitive advantage and creating high-value customer experience; it has been shown to have significant impact on guest satisfaction, behavioural intentions and loyalty, both in tourism research (Žabkar et al., 2010) and in the general marketing literature (Sivadas and Baker-Prewitt, 2000). Service quality research has focused on the structure of the quality construct – i.e. what it is about the service that can be subject to quality evaluations. Different models have been suggested – The Nordic Model (Grönroos, 1984) distinguishes between technical quality – what is being delivered, and functional quality – how it is delivered.

The SERVQUAL model (Parasuraman et al., 1988) identifies five dimensions: (i) reliability; (ii) responsiveness; (iii) empathy; (iv) assurances; and (v) tangibles. Other models have also been suggested and tested (Rust and

Oliver, 1993; Troye, 1996; Brady and Cronin, 2001). Common for all these models is that they include both quality of the tangibles, or physical attributes of the product, and the more immaterial attributes relating to quality of the encounter between the customer and the employee. While the physical product is easier to standardize at a defined level of quality, the quality of the service encounter is more difficult to manage and ensure, since the service is produced and consumed at the same time, and the quality depends to a large extent on the abilities and willingness of that particular employee in that particular encounter. Žabkar et al. (2010) argue that quality in the tourism product is created partly by the process of service delivery (e.g. friendliness, courtesy, efficiency, reliability, staff competence). Bearing in mind that service satisfaction influences both overall satisfaction with the experience and satisfaction with other facets of the offering (Troye et al., 1995), and that the customer experience of the service encounter is an important driver of loyalty (Bove and Johnson, 2001; Castro et al., 2004), enabling the employee to provide the best possible service in their encounters with guests is a worthwhile investment for companies and destinations dedicated to high service quality of their offerings.

Training for Service Excellence

Training staff to increase their ability to provide the personal service is important for consumer quality evaluations and satisfaction. Testa and

Sipe (2012) identified 'people savvy' as an important category of service-leadership competencies. These competencies focus on managers' interactions with employees and customers, interactions that form the 'foundation of employee and customer satisfaction' (Testa and Sipe, 2012), competencies that can be enhanced through leadership training. Positive relationships among training, job satisfaction, and intention to stay have been established in the general management literature (Heskett et al., 1994). Chiang et.al. (2005) investigated these relationships in a tourism setting, and found that high-quality training of front-line employees led to higher training satisfaction, which in turn influenced both job satisfaction and intention to stay with the employer. Wirtz et al. (2008) document the importance of extensive training and retraining for the high-quality services provided by staff in Singapore

Airlines. Training for better-qualified and motivated service workers results in better quality services and more satisfied guests. Research shows a high correlation between employee satisfaction and customer satisfaction (Schneider and Bowen, 1993). Thus, a training programme that is successful in increasing employees' skills and competencies as well as motivating them to provide higher-quality services is likely to result in higher levels of customer satisfaction. A training programme focusing on improving service quality at the company and destination level must be based on customer-based feedback to assess the actual level of service quality and identification of areas for improvement in all aspects of the service. The Service Quality Excellence Model in Fig. 8.2 shows the proposed relationships between customer feedback, training, motivation, quality, satisfaction and retention.

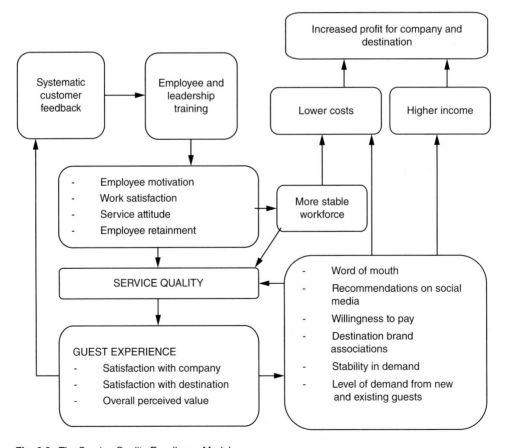

Fig. 8.2. The Service Quality Excellence Model.

Training for increased interaction competencies is important to ensure high-quality services. Employee and leader training, service quality, customer satisfaction, and outcome factors at both the company and the destination levels are interrelated and mutually dependent. When customer-based feedback on company and destination performance are used in employee and leadership training, companies become better able to ensure high quality in all aspects of the service. This will, in turn, lead to more satisfied guests and higher perceived value and consequently more positive word-of-mouth referrals, social media posting, higher willingness to pay, more repeat visits and a more stable demand over time. Employee and leadership training combined with more stable demand will have positive effects on the stability of the workforce as there will be more full-time positions available and the competence built into the workforce is retained at the destination. Over time, this will reduce costs connected to recruitment and training of new employees. Focusing on service excellence is therefore proposed to have a dual effect on company profitability: higher income from increased demand and willingness to pay coupled with lower costs connected to reduced need to advertise to new visitors and less recruitment/training of new employees.

The Case of Hemsedal

The service excellence model has been the basis for a 3-year research-based training programme in Hemsedal, Norway. Hemsedal is a skiing resort with high seasonal fluctuation in demand. Since tourism is the main source of income in this area, businesses and the local community have been dedicated to developing Hemsedal's summer-product in order to reduce fluctuation in demand. During the years 2004–2008, Hemsedal was part of an ARENA project called Innovative Mountain Tourism. The focus in that project was on developing attractive summer products in winter destinations, resulting in a number of successful new products, which helped Hemsedal in their effort to increase the attractiveness of their summer products. To take the success further, Hemsedal decided to participate in a service

excellence project with Buskerud County and Buskerud University College as partners in a project funded by the Regional Research, Development and Innovation programme at the Norwegian Research Council. Participants from Hemsedal included Skistar, the biggest commercial enterprise in the area, with ownership of the ski-area, various types of accommodation, restaurants, and shops, as well as a booking and distribution system. Other participants in the project were: HTTL, the local destination management operation in charge of marketing communication and branding as well as tourist information; and 18 individually owned and operated tourism businesses. Overall, the project involved ten restaurants/bars, seven shops, three hotels, the welcoming centres, one transport company, the tourist information centre, and three operations relating to the ski-area.

To increase competitiveness of the destination as a whole by focusing on service quality, it was essential in the beginning to create a common understanding of the importance of employee training and motivation as a necessary basis for customer service, service quality, and guest satisfaction as outlined in the Service Quality Excellence Model (Fig. 8.2). The first step in the project was therefore to develop reliable indicators of guest satisfaction and employee motivation and service attitude. Then, guest satisfaction and employee motivation and service attitudes were measured to identify areas for potential improvement, and to create a benchmark for comparisons and evaluations. The results were used to provide direct feedback to the business owners and to HTTL, and they were used as input to a training programme focusing on employee motivation and leadership training. Figure 8.3 illustrates the phases of the project.

Phase 1. Development and validation of measures. Guest satisfaction measures were derived from a number of previous studies on customer satisfaction (Yoon and Uysal, 2005; Ekinci and Hosany, 2006; Meng *et al.*, 2008). The items were chosen and developed to measure different aspects of the experience: (i) overall satisfaction and behavioral intentions at the destination level; (ii) attribute satisfaction at the company level – satisfaction with service, physical aspects, and availability (service satisfaction items were the same across

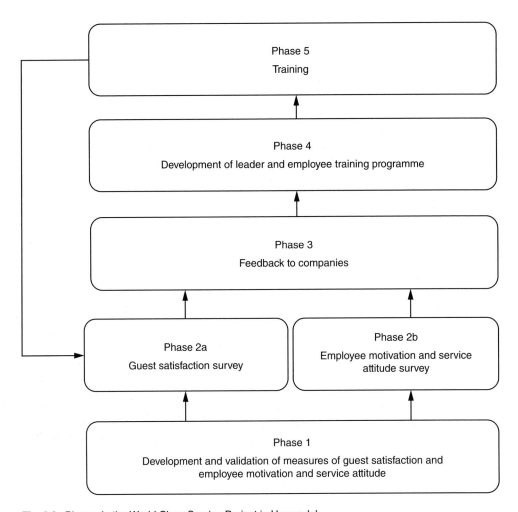

Fig. 8.3. Phases in the World Class Service Project in Hemsedal.

companies, but physical attributes and availability were adjusted to the type of company – all the stores got one set of items, the restaurants another, etc.); (iii) overall satisfaction and behavioural intentions at the company level; and (iv) travel motives. Employee motivation and service attitude measures were derived from the National Institute of Occupational Health in Norway (www.stami.no) and from the literature on employee value, satisfaction, and motivation (Davidson, 2003; Lundberg *et al.*, 2009). To measure employee service attitude, a set of questions relating to affective, cognitive, and conative aspects of providing personal service to guests was developed and validated.

Phase 2. Data collection. The project collects data from guests throughout the winter season every year. Participating companies collect guests' email addresses and the guests are followed up after seven days with an electronic survey measuring: (i) satisfaction with the company that recruited them to the survey; and (ii) overall satisfaction with their stay in Hemsedal, as well as their motives for visiting Hemsedal, their word-of-mouth intentions, and intentions to visit Hemsedal again during winter, autumn, summer or spring for the next 3 years. Employees in partner companies are surveyed once in the middle of the season.

Phase 3. Feedback to companies. Each company is given a presentation of their performance on guests' satisfaction with important attributes benchmarked against their own performance the year before, and against the average performance of other companies that year. These results are then used to provide concrete feedback to decide on which area management should focus in order to improve their guests' satisfaction. Similarly, an evaluation of their employees' level of motivation and service attitude compared to previous years and to the average is also presented to each company's manager.

Phases 4 and 5. Leadership and employee training programme. The results from the surveys are used systematically to develop the content of the training programme that takes place every autumn/winter at the destination. Over the 3 years the programme has been operating, the main focus has been on aligning employee service skills and attitudes with guests' expectations. Results from the employee surveys as well as research literature (Suh et al., 2012; Testa and Sipe, 2012; Chen, 2013) suggest that managers' human relation skills along with reflections over their own performance would give Hemsedal's companies important tools for improvement and development of their employees' skills as service providers. A development programme focusing on leadership skills for management and motivational seminars for staff was developed and implemented in cooperation with the Administrative Research Institute in Norway. The programme addresses the challenges discovered by investigating the customers' and employees' feedback. The management training focuses on how to motivate employees, goal targeting, the difficult conversation, service attitude, and organizational/employee change. Focus in employee training is to heighten the consciousness of the customers' needs, to motivate the employees to provide excellent service in all aspects of their jobs, and to provide them with the skills necessary to do so.

Results from 3 Years of Training

The 'World Class Service' programme in Hemsedal started in 2011 with development and validation of instruments (Phase 1), and has developed since with three waves of customer and employee surveys, feedback, and training. Investing for service quality excellence requires cooperation between companies, destination management and marketing organizations, local authorities, as well as professional trainers and researchers. This is costly in terms of time, effort and money. It is therefore crucial to monitor the effects of the investments.

Results from these years support the relationships proposed in the Service Quality Excellence Model. At the company level, customers' satisfaction with service attributes contributes far more to overall satisfaction and repurchase intentions/word-of-mouth referrals than satisfaction with other aspects of the experience (physical attributes and availability). These results are consistent across types of companies and over time. At the destination level, we see that revisit intentions in low season (spring, summer, and fall) are significantly predicted by guests' service satisfaction.

We also see positive effects of the training. Over time, participating companies have developed a more motivated and service-oriented staff, their employee turnover is lower, and the most dedicated companies see significant effects on customer satisfaction with service. Employees' levels of service attitudes show significant effect on customer satisfaction with service and overall satisfaction with the companies. Managers report that they experience an upswing in demand both during high and low season (10% increase in demand in 2012–2013), and they claim that this is partly attributed to their new focus on service.

Analysis of customer value over the 3 years of training for service excellence in Hemsedal show that focusing on enhancing guests' satisfaction with the service provided by employees has positive impact on demand during low season. Linear regression analysis shows that service satisfaction has a stronger impact than satisfaction with the physical aspects on intention to come back to the destination in low season. To assess the nature of the relationships between service satisfaction, loyalty to the destination, and intention to come back during low season, structural equation analyses were performed using LISREL. Three competing models were compared, and results show that loyalty to the destination fully mediates the effect of service satisfaction on intention to

**: p<.01

Goodness of fit measures: Chi square = 592.73 (df=33), RMSEA=.048, CFI=.99, SRMR=.022

Fig. 8.4. Relationships between service quality, destination loyalty and low-season visit intentions.

come back during low season. Results from SEM analyses of the model that achieved best fit is presented in Fig. 8.4.

Conclusion

For mountain destinations relying on snow tourism, efforts to reduce seasonal fluctuation in demand should include both development of attractive off-season products and focus on employee and leadership training to enhance service quality. Associations relating to high-class service are not directly tied to seasonality, reducing the barriers for entering the guests' consideration sets during low season. More stable demand throughout the year will benefit the companies by enabling them to reduce recruitment cost, to utilize the infrastructure they invest in, and to increase revenues from more return visits and higher number of visitors during low season. This benefits the workers and the society at large, since more all-year-round

jobs will be available, securing a more stable job market and a higher income tax to the community. Less fluctuation in demand will also make it possible to invest in infrastructure to meet the demand on services, something that will be of benefit to both tourists and local society. Results from the Service Excellence Project in Hemsedal show that investing in training and employee value has a positive effect that goes far beyond the direct effects on employee motivation and retention. When training is based on knowledge about guests' experiences, training can be tailored to focus on areas of importance to guest satisfaction. Such focused training has had a positive effect on service employees' attitudes towards providing service, their motivation, and job satisfaction. For customers, more positive service attitudes among employees lead to higher-quality services, which in turn influence satisfaction with service, loyalty to the destination, and intentions to revisit the destination during low season.

References

Ainsworth, S. and Purss, A. (2009) Same time, next year? Human resource management and seasonal workers. *Personnel Review* 38, 217–235.

Allcock, J.B. (1989) Seasonality. In: Witt, S.F. and Moutinho, L. (eds) *Tourism Marketing and Management Handbook*. Prentice-Hall, Englewood Cliffs, New Jersey, pp. 387–392.

Bove, L.L. and Johnson, L.W. (2001) Customer relationships with service personnel: do we measure closeness, quality or strength? *Journal of Business Research* 54, 189–197.

Brady, M.K. and Cronin Jr, J.J. (2001) Some new thoughts on conceptualizing perceived service quality: a hierarchical approach. *Journal of Marketing* 65, 34–49.

Butler, R. (2001) Seasonality in tourism: issues and implications. In: Baum, T. and Lundtorp, S. (eds) *Seasonality in Tourism*. Pergamon, London, UK, pp. 5–22.

Castro, C.B., Armario, E.M. and Ruiz, D.M. (2004) The influence of employee organizational citizenship behavior on customer loyalty. *International Journal of Service Industry Management* 15, 27–53.

Chen, W.J. (2013) Factors influencing internal service quality at international tourist hotels. *International Journal of Hospitality Management* 35, 152–160.

Chiang, C.F., Back, K.J. and Canter, D.D. (2005) The impact of employee training on job satisfaction and intention to stay in the hotel industry. *Journal of Human Resources in Hospitality and Tourism* 4(2), 99–118.

Cronin Jr, J.J. and Taylor, S.A. (1992) Measuring service quality: a reexamination and extension. *Journal of Marketing* 56, 55–68.

Davidson, M.C. (2003) Does organizational climate add to service quality in hotels? *International Journal of Contemporary Hospitality Management* 15, 206–213.

Ekinci, Y. and Hosany, S. (2006) Destination personality: an application of brand personality to tourism destinations. *Journal of Travel Research* 45, 127–139.

Frechtling, D.C. (1996) *Practical Tourism Forecasting*, Butterworth-Heinemann, Oxford, UK.

Frechtling, D.C. (2012) *Forecasting Tourism Demand*. Routledge, London.

Grönroos, C. (1982) An applied service marketing theory. *European Journal of Marketing* 16, 30–41.

Grönroos, C. (1984) A service quality model and its marketing implications. *European Journal of Marketing* 18, 36–44.

Heskett, J.L., Jones, T.O., Loveman, G.W., Sasser, W.E.J. and Schlesinger, L.A. (1994) Putting the service profit chain to work. *Harvard Business Review* 72, 164–174.

Higham, J. and Hinch, T. (2002) Tourism, sport and seasons: the challenges and potential of overcoming seasonality in the sport and tourism sectors. *Tourism Management* 23, 175–185.

Koenig-Lewis, N. and Bischoff, E.E. (2005) Seasonality research: the state of the art. *International Journal of Tourism Research* 7, 201–219.

Lundberg, C., Gudmundson, A. and Andersson, T.D. (2009) Herzberg's Two-Factor Theory of work motivation tested empirically on seasonal workers in hospitality and tourism. *Tourism Management* 30, 890–899.

Meng, F., Tepanon, Y. and Uysal, M. (2008) Measuring tourist satisfaction by attribute and motivation: the case of a nature-based resort. *Journal of Vacation Marketing* 14, 41–56.

Moen, J. and Fredman, P. (2007) Effects of climate change on Alpine skiing in Sweden. *Journal of Sustainable Tourism* 15, 418–437.

Parasuraman, A., Zeithaml, V.A. and Berry, L.L. (1985) A conceptual model of service quality and its implications for future research. *Journal of Marketing* 49, 41–50.

Parasuraman, A., Zeithaml, V.A. and Berry, L.L. (1988) SERVQUAL. *Journal of Retailing* 64, 12–40.

Pegg, S., Patterson, I. and Gariddo, P.V. (2012) The impact of seasonality on tourism and hospitality operations in the alpine region of New South Wales, Australia. *International Journal of Hospitality Management* 31, 659–666.

Rust, R.T. and Oliver, R.L. (1993) Service quality: insights and managerial implications from the frontier. In: Rust, R.T. and Oliver, R.L. (eds) *Service Quality: New Directions in Theory and Practice.* Sage Publications, Thousand Oaks, California.

Schneider, B. and Bowen, D.E. (1993) The service organization: human resources management is crucial. *Organizational Dynamics* 21, 39–52.

Sivadas, E. and Baker-Prewitt J.L. (2000) An examination of the relationship between service quality, customer satisfaction, and store loyalty. *International Journal of Retail & Distribution Management* 28, 73–82.

Smith, K. (1990) Tourism and climate change. *Land Use Policy* 7, 176–180.

Suh, E., West, J.J. and Shin, J. (2012) Important competency requirements for managers in the hospitality industry. *Journal of Hospitality, Leisure, Sport & Tourism Education* 11, 101–112.

Testa, M.R. and Sipe, L. (2012) Service-leadership competencies for hospitality and tourism management. *International Journal of Hospitality Management* 31, 648–658.

Troye, S.V. (1996) *Markedsorientering av servicebedrifter: med fokus på reiselivet*. Tano, Oslo, Norway.

Troye, S.V., Ogaard, T. and Henjesand, I.J.(1995) *The Triple Importance of Service: An Alternative Model of Service and Product Quality.* SNF Report no 35/95, NHH, Bergen, Norway.

Wirtz, J., Heracleous, L. and Pangarkar, N. (2008) Managing human resources for service excellence and cost effectiveness at Singapore Airlines. *Managing Service Quality* 18, 4–19.

Yoon, Y. and Uysal, M. (2005) An examination of the effects of motivation and satisfaction on destination loyalty: a structural model. *Tourism Management* 26, 45–56.

Žabkar, V., Brencic, M.M. and Dmitrovic, T. (2010) Modelling perceived quality, visitor satisfaction and behavioural intentions at the destination level. *Tourism Management* 31, 537–546.

9 People and Communities in Mountain Tourism: Overview, Contextual Development and Areas of Focus

John S. Hull* and Harold Richins

Thompson Rivers University, Kamloops, British Columbia, Canada

Introduction

This chapter provides an introduction to Part III, which explores aspects of people and communities in mountain tourism, including a broad range of topics, diverse geographical areas, and discussion regarding communities that have evolved in mountain areas. The people that visit and/or reside in mountain regions are normally significant participants in recreation and tourism activities. Meeting and integrating their interests with the diverse residential needs specific to mountain communities introduces opportunities, challenges, impacts, and outcomes. Planning processes and efforts to build infrastructure and services in what is often a harsh mountain environment that is dynamically changing, can be extremely challenging, but it is this very circumstance that requires careful consideration and the need for issues to be addressed.

Introduction to Literature on People and Communities in Mountain Tourism

People and communities

In mountain destinations, the welfare of people and community – all those who live within a destination area – has been a central tenet of tourism development (Mathieson and Wall, 1982; Ives *et al.*, 1997; Swarbrooke, 1999; Godde *et al.*, 2000; Nepal and Chipeniuk, 2005). Many mountain communities have been identified as some of the poorest and most marginalized in the world (Ives *et al.*, 1997; Godde *et al.*, 2000; Kruk *et al.*, 2007). Tourism is recognized as a significant tool for the development of community particularly in marginal and peripheral regions (Beeton, 2006). Understanding the actors involved in mountain development as well as the role of local participation is critical for realizing positive change.

Actors in mountain destinations

Murphy (1985) points out that tourism as an industry uses the host community as a resource and sells it as a product, affecting the lives of everyone. Understanding the role of tourism in a community requires looking at the complex interaction of visitors or 'guests' demanding a wide range of services, facilities, and inputs, as well as locals or 'hosts' who provide these services (Smith, 1989; Price *et al.*, 1997; see Fig. 9.1). The main actors who participate in the mountain tourism system have been categorized into three

---

* Corresponding author: jhull@tru.ca

Fig. 9.1. A mountain community within Canada's first national park – a World Heritage Site: Banff, Alberta, Canada (photograph courtesy of Harold Richins).

main groups of recreationists: tourists, amenity migrants and local residents (Table 9.1).

The presence and association of tourists, local residents, and amenity migrants gives rise to conflict and co-existence between recreationists in mountain destinations as a result of not only differences in perspectives, values, traditions and beliefs, but also as a result of differences in levels of use and resource consumption, and frequency and intensity of contact (Jurowski *et al.*, 1997; Lankford *et al.*, 1997; Nepal and Chipeniuk, 2005; Kruk *et al.*, 2007; Pavelka and Draper, 2015; see Fig. 9.2). Nepal and Chipeniuk (2005) have identified five potential kinds of conflict between various groups: (i) local residents and tourists; (ii) amenity migrants and local residents; (iii) amenity migrants and tourists; (iv) conflicts within each category; and (v) conflicts involving all three categories, resulting in numerous challenges for tourism

planners in mountain regions. The success of tourism depends on the mutual benefits created and exchanged between these groups (Smith, 1989).

Community capacity building and local participation

Researchers argue that tourism destinations are complex networks of co-producing actors that deliver a range of products and services (Beritelli *et al.*, 2007; Haugland *et al.*, 2011). Securing benefits from tourism are dependent upon the links, connections, and working relationships between community members participating in the development process (Beritelli *et al.*, 2007; Pearce, 2008; Haugland *et al.*, 2011). One of the challenges of planning is the political nature

Table 9.1. Characteristics of recreationists in mountain tourism (adapted from Nepal and Chipeniuk, 2005).

Characteristic	Tourists/guests	Local residents/hosts	Amenity migrants
Sense of place	Images of place important	Place attachment	Strong sense of place as self-expression
Degree of familiarity with destination	Low degree of familiarity with local culture and environment	High degree of familiarity with local culture and environment	Moderate degree of familiarity with local culture and environment
Accessibility	Restricted/regulated access to recreational space	Less restricted use of space	Regulated access to recreational space
Territoriality	Less territorial	May exhibit NIMBY syndrome – territorial	Moderate territoriality, resistance to change
Use of attractions, facilities	Intensive use of facilities at specific time periods (high season)	Well defined pattern of recreation frequency and intensity year round	Moderate frequency and intensity at specific time periods
Local participation in civic life	No participation in civic life	High degree of participation in civic life	High degree of participation in civic life
Type of environment required	High quality environments desired	High quality environments important	Demand for high-quality environments
Motivation	Escapism	Easy access	New forms of recreation
Frequency of visit	Some will be repeat visitors; some will be first time visitors only	High degree of repeat visitation to attractions/facilities	Moderate degree of repeat visitation to attractions/facilities

Fig. 9.2. Mountain tourism community of Mittenwald, German Alps (photograph courtesy of Harold Richins).

of the planning process that often highlights the power imbalances and lack of social capacity in a community (Sofield, 2003; Beeton, 2006). Moscardo (2008, 9) argues that there is a need to increase the collective knowledge and ability within a community and to use this knowledge for effective planning, coordination, and involvement of local stakeholders as part of a participatory planning process that builds community capacity. Local participation is a key factor in realizing sustainable development.

Historically, mountain communities have been neglected in development priorities resulting in increased dependency, unequal terms of exchange, loss of autonomy in decision making, and resource use that has resulted in poverty and uncertainty. Policy makers argue that there is a need for participatory approaches to planning in mountain regions that integrate local consultations with key stakeholders, local inputs in monitoring of ecological and social indicators, and preferential treatment in income and employment to ensure the well-being of local residents (Nepal and Chipeniuk, 2005; Kruk et al., 2007). Mountain destinations have used a variety of tools for involving local stakeholders that include social mobilization, appreciative participatory planning and action, the development wheel, participatory resource mapping, the seasonal calendar, and the natural step. Without involving local people in tourism strategies, implementation will be difficult, as tourism will fail to have the support of local residents and will not realize its potential as a tool for local development (Waldon and Williams, 2002; Kruk et al., 2007; see Fig. 9.3).

Sustainable Principles for Mountain Communities

Principles of sustainable mountain tourism development that have been proposed by UNEP

Fig. 9.3. Sun Peaks Community – British Columbia's first designated mountain resort municipality, Canada (photograph courtesy of Harold Richins).

and UNWTO (2005) outline the importance of people and community to the development in mountain destinations. These 12 principles are important considerations for policy makers in mountain regions as part of the strategic planning process. They advocate not only visitor fulfilment for guests, but also the importance of economic opportunities, social equity, local control, community well-being, cultural richness, physical integrity, biological diversity, resource efficiency and environmental purity for hosts in mountain destinations (Table 9.2).

Summary of Chapters in Part III: People and Communities in Mountain Tourism

This chapter introduces Part III, which explores various aspects of people and communities that reside in or visit mountain tourism environments. A contextual background of the relevant literature related to people and communities provides an introduction and understanding of the importance of the diverse challenges facing planners, developers, operators, community participants, and other relevant mountain tourism stakeholders. Engagement and collaboration strategies that focus on the variety of needs and interests found in mountain tourism are included.

The following are brief summaries of the six chapters within Part III, covering these topics: (i) networks and partnerships for sustainable tourism; (ii) amenity migration in a small mountain town; (iii) understanding visitors to Australia's alpine areas; (iv) community-based tourism in Peru; (v) sustainable tourism in the Carpathian mountains in Eastern Europe; and (vi) a focus on second-home leisure activity within the Alps.

Chapter 10. Tourism-led Amenity Migration in a Mountain Community: Quality of Life Implications for Fernie, British Columbia

Authors: Peter W. Williams, Alison M. Gill and Jeff M. Zukiwsky

A topic associated with tourism is the broader concept of short-term human mobility, which includes all forms of impermanent movement of people to a new location. This may include voluntary, involuntary, and undocumented mobility. Related to this chapter, voluntary mobility includes movements of people for purposes of family reunion, education, tourism, and/or for labour reasons.

An unprecedented increase in human mobility globally is the result of a number of innovations, openness of socio-political environments, influences due to improved technological and transportation systems, and increased opportunities with economic improvement. Due to these influences, mountain resort communities attract people seeking quality-of-life amenities in these locales. These 'tourism-led migrants' often become interested in purchasing second homes, which may eventually lead to an increased number of visits, longer stays and, potentially even lead to full-time relocation to the mountain community.

Utilizing a 'tourism-led amenity migration framework', Williams, Gill, and Zukiwsky employ a case study of second-home migrants in the small mountain town of Fernie, British Columbia. The chapter provides insight into the

Table 9.2. Principles of sustainable mountain tourism development (source: Kruk *et al.*, 2007).

Economic viability	To ensure the viability of tourism destinations and enterprises
Local prosperity	To maximize tourism's contribution to the host destination
Employment quality	To strengthen the number and quality of local jobs
Social equity	To seek a fair distribution of economic and social benefits
Visitor fulfilment	To provide a safe, satisfying, and fulfilling experience for visitors
Local control	To engage and empower local communities in planning
Community well-being	To maintain and strengthen the quality of life in local communities
Cultural richness	To respect and enhance the historic heritage and authentic culture of host communities
Physical integrity	To maintain and enhance the quality of the landscapes
Biological diversity	To support the conservation of natural areas
Resource efficiency	To minimize the use of non-renewable resources
Environmental purity	To minimize pollution and generation of waste

quality-of-life aspects and implications for planning and development within amenity-rich mountain communities. In addition to the more traditional short-stay tourists, destination mountain resort communities are increasingly interested in building more permanent residential communities by encouraging amenity migrants. These new residents can affect the development and vibrancy of the mountain community; these effects, or what the authors term, 'transformational effects', include: environmental, economic, socio-cultural and quality of life. Williams *et al.* explore these transformational effects in Fernie and utilize this case study to discuss important implications for planning in destination mountain communities in the area of tourism-led amenity migration.

Chapter 11. In the Shadow of Machu Picchu: A Case Study of the Salkantay Trail

Author: Joe Pavelka

Cultural and natural World Heritage sites have been a strong draw for tourists since the time of the Grand Tour of the 17th and 18th centuries, and this strong interest continues with today's international travellers. Accessing these sites can be done either directly (transport systems like bus tours with direct access to the site) or indirectly through more traditional routes (e.g. pilgrimage trails) historically established and related to local cultures and traditional transportation methods. Tourists are often interested in these indirect, traditional routes to access sites of world prominence such as the 15th-century Inca site, Machu Picchu, in Peru. Over time, it has been observed that this more popular route, which is significantly controlled and managed by authorities, receives an increasing number of tourists, leading to some people seeking out more authentic experiences using alternative routes such as the Salkantay Trail.

Machu Picchu, in the Cusco Region of Peru, is arguably one of the world's most prominent World Heritage sites, often described as the largest tourist attraction in South America. The site was abandoned and unknown for many centuries, but after it was rediscovered in 1911, it received international attention. Author Joe Pavelka presents a case study of tourism in this region, highlighting capacity building and

impacts on mountain communities along the more remote Salkantay Trail, and describes a recent programme intended to provide small business tourism capacity building for families living along the trail.

Chapter 11 explores the Salkantay Trail from a historic, political, cultural and community development point of view, and compares this to the more widely visited Inca Trail. The research results shed light on both the challenges and constraints of developing community-based tourism along the trail, as well as suggesting opportunities for responsibly developing tourism capacity with local Salkantay families and community tourism operators.

Chapter 12. Transformational Wine Tourism in Mountain Communities

Author: Donna M. Senese

Tourism in mountain regions is often associated with gastronomy and consumption of beverages representative of, or endemic to, the region. Wine has unique properties related to a regional landscape: it is influenced by the relevant fertile areas suitable for growing certain varieties as a result of climate and soil, and also by cultural paradigm of the viticulturist and the vintner.

This chapter by Donna Senese explores the development and transformative nature of wine tourism in a region through a case study of the Okanagan region of British Columbia within an international context. The article describes the value and development of wine tourism internationally, and reflects on this in the discussion of the regional case study that includes practitioners in the Okanagan wine tourism industry. Observation and comments resulting from the study articulate the nature of wine tourism to the development of the Okanagan tourism and community experience and its mountain and rural community tourism development.

Key points of the chapter demonstrate that tourism and wine industries are compatible, as the lifestyle and aesthetics of wine culture are transferred into a unique rural ideal. However, rural areas with a traditional agricultural focus in mountainous regions may be dramatically affected by the advent of tourism, as visitors expect the provision and quality of certain amenities (e.g. food, beverage and shopping outlets). Also, the development of wine tourism has been a key aspect of this ideal, due to the unique landscapes, the varieties of grapes, and rich cultural heritage of the region.

Chapter 13. Sustainable Tourism in the Carpathians

Authors: László Puczkó, Michael Meyer, Martina Voskarova and Ivett Sziva

This chapter describes the development of a strategy across seven countries in the Carpathian Mountains of Eastern Europe regarding sustainable tourism. The strategy is to create a catalyst for an integrated effort among the seven countries so that they work together to coordinate the responsible use, conservation, and development of the region as an emerging mountain tourism destination.

Part of Chapter 13 gives a background of the Carpathian mountain region, and a description of tourism visitation to that area. The uniqueness of this area in a European and global context is discussed – it is one of Europe's largest, but less-developed mountain ranges, meaning that it has some of Europe's cleanest streams and greatest expanses of pristine forest, with high biological diversity, and a relatively small human population density. The chapter deepens readers' understanding of the Carpathian mountain region with discussion of its strengths related to natural, cultural, and heritage assets, its relatively undeveloped nature, and the emerging interests of visitors in discovering the region. Affordability and improvement of access to the region is also considered.

Some challenging aspects in the region, such as language diversity, the difficulties of cross-border access, and coordination with multi-country destinations, are discussed. Visitors do not currently see the region as an integrated destination. This may be because of the lack of cohesiveness in areas such as destination management, infrastructure, service quality, planning and communication. Finally, the chapter discusses the vision and objectives of the strategy and the challenges ahead in achieving

success in both the development and implementation of the strategy.

Chapter 14. Leisure Living in the Alps

Authors: Aurelia Kogler and Philipp Boksberger

Mountain communities grow up around the development of industries related to the particular assets of a region. When industrial activities stop or reduce in size as access to natural assets diminishes (e.g. forestry, mining and agriculture), some residents leave or pursue other economic opportunities. However, other residents sometimes arrive in their place, as people seeking leisure and tourism activities in alpine regions become interested in living the mountain lifestyle. In a number of communities around the world, this has prompted the development of second homes where these new temporary residents stay on a periodic basis. This chapter discusses the challenges of the lodging industry in alpine regions where the increasing demand for second homes, often only used for a few weeks each year, may produce negative impacts for the resort in the form of temporary (or cold) beds.

Kogler and Boksberger explore new ideas and models in ownership, financing, management, and taxation of hospitality projects in order to move from 'cold' to 'hot beds'. Financing the development of hotel projects by selling resort/hotel units to private investors is explored, and analysis on investment and performance key factors present the advantages and disadvantages of new business models from developer, management and investor viewpoints. The authors suggest that future research be conducted in the areas of overseeing these new business models, with particular investigation of shared ownership models.

Chapter 15. Australia's Alpine Areas: Motivations, Experiences and Satisfaction of Visitors to Mt Kosciuszko

Author: Tracey Dickson

The interest and fascination with high mountain regions is explored in this chapter on mountain tourism in Australia. Tracey Dickson deepens our understanding of wilderness and what it is that draws tourists to alpine areas, looking at visitor motivation, perceptions and satisfaction in the Snowy Mountains. This in-depth look at an important semi-wilderness area within the expansive New South Wales mountainous region provides further understanding regarding visitation and motivation.

The Snowy Mountain National Park, one of the most prominent national parks in Australia, has not been formally designated a wilderness area – even though it is looked upon by visitors as wilderness. Dickson surveyed tourists along major summer walking tracks to better understand tourist motivations, expectations and experiences concerning wilderness.

This important study was conducted in an area with a 150-year history of tourism that generates close to 60% of the Australian snow sports winter business. Though the region is primarily a winter sports area, almost 45% of visitation is in the summer. The research gives a comparative profile of wilderness visitors and their key interest priorities categorized by escape, personal goals, socialization and engaging with nature.

Concluding Remarks

This chapter has provided an introduction to Part III and has presented an overview of literature and knowledge relating to people and communities in mountain tourism. Communities, and the diversity of people within them, have long been integral to the development and sustainability of mountain tourism regions. The chapters in Part III demonstrate in more detail the variety and the dynamic nature of mountain tourism communities, and their diversity with regard to geographic regions, providing the reader with a deeper understanding of the people and the communities engaged in mountain tourism.

References

Beeton, S. (2006) *Community Development through Tourism*. Landlinks Press, Collingwood, Australia.

Beritelli, P., Bieger, T. and Laesser, C. (2007) Destination governance: using corporate governance theories as a foundation for effective destination management. *Journal of Travel Research* 46(1), 96–107.

Godde, P., Price, M.F. and Zimmermann, F.M. (2000) Tourism and development in mountain regions: moving forward into the new millennium. In: Godde, P., Price, M. and Zimmermann, F. (eds) *Tourism and Development in Mountain Regions*. CAB International, Wallingford, UK, pp. 1–25.

Haugland, S.V., Ness, H., Gronseth, B.-O. and Aarstad, J. (2011) Development of tourism destinations. *Annals of Tourism Research* 38(1), 268–290.

Ives, J.D., Messerli, B. and Spiess, E. (1997) Mountains of the world: a global priority. In: Messerli, B. and Ives, J.D. (eds) *Mountains of the World: A Global Priority*. Parthenon Publishing Group, New York and Carnforth, UK.

Jurowski, C., Uysal, M. and Williams, R.D. (1997) A theoretical analysis of host community resident reactions to tourism. *Journal of Travel Research* 36(2), 3–11.

Kruk, E., Hummel, J. and Banskota, K. (2007) *Facilitating Sustainable Mountain Tourism: Volume 1: Resource Book*. International Centre for Integrated Mountain Development (ICIMOD), Kathmandu, Nepal.

Lankford, S.V., Williams, A.L. and Knowles-Lankford, J. (1997) Perceptions of outdoor recreation opportunities and support for tourism development. *Journal of Travel Research* 35(3), 65–69.

Mathieson, A. and Wall, G. (1982) *Tourism: Economic, Physical and Social Impacts*. Longman, London.

Moscardo, G. (2008) Understanding tourist experience though mindfulness theory. In: Kozak, M. and Decrop, A. (eds) *Handbook of Tourist Behavior Theory and Practice*. Routledge, London.

Murphy, P. (1985) *Tourism: A Community Approach*. Routledge, London.

Nepal, S. and Chipeniuk, R. (2005) Mountain tourism: towards a conceptual framework. *Tourism Geographies* 7(3), 313–333.

Pavelka, J. and Draper, D. (2015) Leisure negotiation within amenity migration. *Annals of Tourism Research* 50, 126–142.

Pearce, D. (2008) A needs-function model of tourism distribution. *Annals of Tourism Research* 35(1), 148–168.

Price, M.F., Moss, L.A.G. and Williams, P.W. (1997) Tourism and amenity migration. In: Messerli, B. and Ives, J.D. (eds) *Mountains of the World: A Global Priority*. Parthenon Publishing Group, New York and Carnforth, UK.

Smith, V. (1989) *Hosts and Guests: The Anthropology of Tourism*. University of Pennsylvania Press, Philadelphia, Pennsylvania.

Sofield, T. (2003) *Empowerment for Sustainable Tourism Development*. Pergamon, Oxford, UK.

Swarbrooke, J. (1999) *Sustainable Tourism Management*. CAB International, Wallingford, UK.

UNEP/UNWTO (2005) *Making Tourism More Sustainable. A Guide for Policymakers*. UNEP/UNWTO, Paris and Madrid.

Waldon, D. and Williams, P. (2002) Steps towards sustainability monitoring: the case of the Resort Municipality of Whistler. In: Harris, R., Griffin, T. and Williams, P. (eds) *Sustainable Tourism: A Global Perspective*. Elsevier, Oxford, UK, pp. 180–194.

10 Tourism-led Amenity Migration in a Mountain Community: Quality of Life Implications for Fernie, British Columbia

Peter W. Williams,[1]* Alison M. Gill[1] and Jeff M. Zukiwsky[2]

[1]*Simon Fraser University, Burnaby, Canada;*
[2]*Zumundo Consultants, Fernie, Canada*

Introduction

Globalization forces linked to changes in sociopolitical systems, as well as innovations in communications, transportation, and workplace technologies, have fuelled unprecedented opportunities for people to visit, live, work, and/or retire in areas possessing high quality of life (QoL) amenities (Sheller and Urry, 2006). These amenities include attractive recreation and cultural facilities, scenic and healthy natural environments, efficient transportation and communication systems, and vital community support services (Moss, 2006). The flows of people drawn to places possessing such attributes are often referred to as amenity-led migrations, and the participants are amenity migrants.

Because of their unique combination of tourism and community QoL assets, mountain resort communities are increasingly the destination of choice for amenity migrants (Chipeniuk and Rapport, 2008). Those motivated primarily to move to such places because of the presence of tourism-related assets and opportunities are referred to as tourism-led amenity migrants (Williams and Hall, 2000). A particularly important subset of this group comprises those who eventually purchase second homes in the community for intermittent and/or eventually permanent use (Stewart, 2000). While much research attention exists concerning tourism-led amenity migrations, less is known specifically about the QoL effects of second-home migrants who frequent their properties on an intermittent basis. Understanding such entanglements in resort communities is critical for planners and policy makers seeking to guide tourism-led amenity migrations in ways that contribute in positive ways to overall QoL. This chapter employs Williams and Gill's (2011) 'Tourism-led Amenity Migration Framework' to investigate how second-home migrants are transforming QoL in the amenity-rich mountain community of Fernie, British Columbia (BC), Canada. Unlike several purpose-built resort communities in BC, Fernie has evolved its economic base and supportive services in a more incremental than strategically planned fashion in order to accommodate its growing flow of second-home migrants. As such, it provides useful insights into the types of QoL issues and strategies that less tourism-oriented communities must consider when hosting such migrants.

* Corresponding author: peterw@sfu.ca

Guiding Framework

The chapter's guiding frame is embedded within a broader paradigm of mobility that explores the movements in people, capital, and knowledge into amenity-rich destinations (Sheller and Urry, 2006). Tourism-led amenity migration is increasingly understood within this paradigm (Coles and Hall, 2006). The framework directs the focus towards how this type of migration influences the politics of place (Williams, 2002) and subsequent transformations in host destinations. Marsden (2006) sees these new forms of mobility as forces creating both vulnerabilities and opportunities for communities. The framework is further refined by tourism destination management perspectives, which centre on understanding the effects of amenity migration on policy and management decisions (Ritchie and Crouch, 2003). In Fig. 10.1, tourism-induced migrations (e.g. consumption- and/or production-based) lead to influxes of people, capital, and knowledge to amenity-rich destinations. The effects of these flows have potentially transformational landscape, environmental, social, economic, political, and quality-of-life implications. These ensuing changes may be perceived as either positive or negative, depending on the meaning and values that affected stakeholders attribute to them. Depending on power structures and issues, contestation between varying stakeholder groups (e.g. second-home migrants and permanent residents) will vary in character and outcome. Tourism-led amenity migrants tend to introduce a range of new stakeholders, perspectives, and contestation into the politics of place (Low, 2005; Mair *et al.*, 2005). This in turn potentially leads to the reshaping and refinement of host community policy and management strategies.

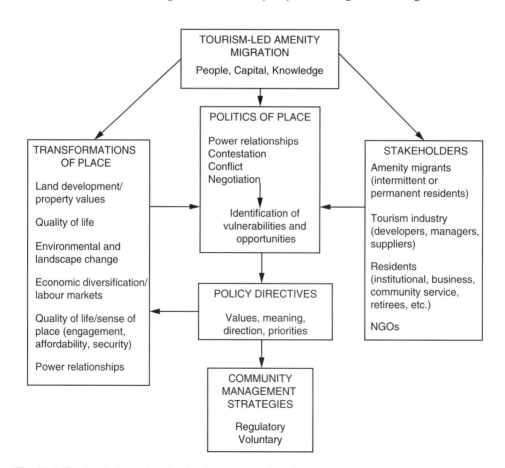

Fig. 10.1. Tourism-led amenity migration framework (adapted from Williams and Gill, 2011).

On a more applied level, the framework provides touch points for case studies of QoL challenges and management strategies in mountain resort communities dealing with influxes of second-home migrants. It helps focus attention on management strategies designed to help such places proactively respond to second-home inflows in ways that contribute to broader community QoL objectives.

Tourism-led Amenity Migration Dynamics

Transitioning tourists into longer-term second-home owners is alluring for resort communities because of the longer-term financial, intellectual, and social capital they might contribute as second-home migrants. Many destinations initially focused primarily on hosting short stay tourists are now aggresively seeking such migrants. This strategy is reflected in the increasing array of timeshare, multi-unit strata, fractional and single family accommodation options marketed to visitors in tourism resort communities (Rodriguez, 2001). While the complexity and range of second-home ownership options tends to blur the lines between short-term tourist and potentially more commited second-home migrants, it is clear that market interest 'purchasing a piece of paradise' in amenity-rich resort communities continues to expand. This adds a subtle but important layer of complexity to planning tourism destinations, particularly with respect to the effect these second-home migrants may have on overall community QoL.

Estimates to the extent and distribution of second-home ownership on a global scale are at best guestimates. However, Halseth (2004) suggests that second-home ownership is widespread across all regions of Canada. For instance, an estimated 145,000 second homes existed in BC in 2006 (BC Stats, 2006). A deeper review of this data suggests that while such ownership is widespread in the province, it is particulary concentrated in or near to rich amenity tourism areas such as Whistler (55%), Radium (55%), Fernie (29%), and Tofino (28%) (BC Stats, 2006). In the context of this chapter's case study, second-home ownershsip is also strong in the Eastern

Kootenay Regional District near Fairmont and Invermere (59%) (Zukiwsky, 2010).

Transformational Effects

The transformational effects of second-home migrations span a variety of changes ranging from those linked to land use, economic, social and environmental issues to changes in overall community quality of life and sense of place (Fig. 10.1).

Previous reviews of second-home development impacts in Europe have focused primarily on effects in rural areas (Gallent et al., 2005) as opposed to communities with tourism-based economies. However, there is a growing stream of investigations especially in mountain and coastal regions in North America and elsewhere (Moss, 2006; Williams and Gill, 2006; Glorioso and Moss, 2007). Existing reviews suggest that second-home developments may have positive and/or negative implications, depending on how they are planned and managed.

Environmental effects

High-quality natural environments are important attractions for most second-home migrants, and are significant contributors to the the quality of life of residents. Several studies suggest that second-home owners bring with them strong conservation and environmental ethics that constrain further development (Smith and Krannich, 2000; Hall and Müller, 2004; Gill and Welk, 2007). In this respect, environmental concerns stem almost exclusively from second-home siting and development footprint issues that lead to the loss of wildlife habitat, forested areas, water quality, and overall ecosystem health (Venturoni et al., 2005; Williams and Gill, 2006). In some instances, these and many other localized impacts can be mitigated through development and planning policies that respect important community values and priorities.

Economic effects

For communities once dependent on natural resource extraction, attracting second-home owners may serve as a new economic diversification opportunity (Chipeniuk, 2004; Glorioso and

Moss, 2007). Much of the economic stimulus comes from the construction and renovation of second homes. In the USA, the construction, marketing, financing, and maintenance of second homes is a US$19 billion industry (Francese, 2003). In north-west Colorado, where approximately 55% of residential properties are owned by non-residents (NWCCOG, 2006), about 45% of the jobs and 38% of the total economic spending are believed to be linked to the second-home industry. In addition, Venturoni (2003) suggests that second-home owners spend significantly more than local residents on community services related to home maintenance (e.g. lawn care, home security, etc.), and charities (e.g. churches, environmental NGOs, etc.). Other studies highlight how the infusion of second-home owner wealth and entrepreneurial spirit into host economies adds another layer of prosperity to these communities (Desrosiers-Lauzon, 2015).

Despite the preceding benefits, such contributions do not always flow readily (Buxton, 2008). Economic contributions are frequently associated with the level of second-home use, and frequently such occupancy is both intermittent and limited (NWCCOG, 2006). Resort community economies depend in large part on commercial and private accommodation being used year round and users spending money locally. Under-utilization of homes (aka 'cold beds') can have a devastating effect on local businesses and the overall vibrancy of resort communities (Bieger *et al.*, 2007).

It is also generally assumed that second-home developments increase local taxes while placing less stress on local community services (e.g. waste management, sewer and water services, etc.) due to intermittent owner use. While property taxes and development cost charges (DCCs) are meant to help host communities finance or recoup associated infrastructure development and service costs (Venturoni *et al.*, 2005), often taxes and charges secured from second-home owners and developers are inadequate to cover long-term servicing and infrastructure support costs (Fodor, 2009). Much of this mismatch in charges and service costs is linked to the more costly siting of such developments (e.g. large lots removed from core service centres) (NWCCOG, 2006). In addition, Clifford (2002) suggests second-home owner migrations lead retail businesses to refocus and gentrify their products and services to the chagrin of more permanent residents. He and others (e.g. Paradis, 2000) believe this reorientation threatens the vitality of such business districts and reduces community cohesiveness and overall sense of place.

Socio-cultural effects

The most recurrent socio-cultural effects of second-home development in resort communities are associated with housing and cost of living issues. Second-home migrants tend to drive up real estate prices and associated living expenses, which can lead to displacement of permanent residents and/or affordability challenges for other resort workers (Hettinger, 2005; Glorioso and Moss, 2007). In addition, tourism service employees and other community employees seeking seasonal rental accommodation may find it harder to find appropriately priced accommodation and be subsequently obliged to reside beyond the host community (Hettinger, 2005; Moore *et al.*, 2006).

The replacement of permanent residents with second-home owners can lead to a permanent population decline and/or a 'cold bed' situation in which accommodation remains uninhabited for signficant portions of the year. Empty homes can lead to negative neighbourhood appeal, reduced sense of place, and poorer QoL (Bush, 2006; Thompson, 2006). The key lesson is that growing demand for second-home properties plays a critical role in shaping affordable housing options in many resort communities (Hettinger, 2005). However, the extent and form of its contribution to displacement is contextual. For instance, in communities with vacant or derelict properties available, displacement is limited; while in situations where demand for limited accommodation is high, displacement occurs (Gallent *et al.*, 2005).

Tensions between permanent and second-home owners often exist over their respective roles in shaping growth and development, as well as community sense of place and associated QoL (Clifford, 2002; Buckley, 2005). Overall, there is a sense among many researchers that second-home owners are less apt to be engaged in resort community affairs, community elections, community service reporting, and other local activities than their permanent resident counterparts (Gill, 2000; Venturoni et al., 2005). Often they are perceived to have less community attachment, although their primary motives for moving to such places are typically linked to strong QoL and sense of place priorities. They also show lower levels of support for the development of community services (schools, community centres, day cares, etc.) than do permanent residents (Gill, 2000). This situation exists despite a commonly held belief that they possess signficant potential human and social capital that can be tapped to enhance the overall QoL in resort communities.

Quality-of-life effects

QoL generally refers to pereceptions of those natural, socio-cultural and economic attributes that contribute to personal and collective well-being (Dissart and Deller, 2000). A combination of subjective (e.g. values, experiences, perceptions) and objective (e.g. behaviours, costs, benefits, etc.) indicators provide the basis for measuring its status in communities (CMHC, 1993). While many QoL attributes are valued similarly by second-home migrants and permanent residents in resort communities, variations in priorities tend to emerge based on the extent to which second-home migrants reside in the destination. For instance, while second-home migrants normally place a high value on the presence and protection of scenic and natural landscapes central to their vacation experiences, they tend to be less committed than their permanent resident counterparts in activities enhancing broader community social development initiatives (Putney, 2003; Vesley, 2007). Paradoxically, while second-home migrants view small-town atmosphere as an important QoL asset, excessive levels of second-home development can lead to a loss of such 'local atmosphere' appeal among second-home migrants and permanent residents alike (Korber and Rasker, 2001; Clifford, 2002). The following case study explores relationships between second-home migrants and QoL in Fernie, BC.

Fernie Case Study

Fernie is a small mountain community situated in a north–south-running valley just east of the Canadian Rocky Mountain Trench, and west of the Continental Divide. The larger urban centres near to Fernie (Fig. 10.2) are Cranbrook, Nelson, Revelstoke and Calgary. The largest centre, Calgary, Alberta, provides Fernie with transportation access to large domestic and international tourism markets. For more than a century, Fernie's economy has revolved around mining and resource extraction employment. Currently, there are five operating coal mines in the surrounding Elk Valley region. However, spurred on by the initial development of its first ski hill, Fernie Snow Valley, in 1963, and the subsequent acquisition of this development by a major investor – Resorts of the Canadian Rockies in 1997 – Fernie's economy has gradually transitioned to one that is increasingly focused on tourism-related development. During this period, it has also gradually matured into an internationally recognized snow sports destination, as well as a provincially designated 'resort municipality' in 2009. This status gives it access to the BC Government's Resort Municipality Initiative (RMI), an ongoing programme that provides such communities with incentive-based funding designed to support tourism-related infrastructure and amenity development (Government of BC, 2015). For example, in 2013 Fernie received approximately US$440,000 from the RMI for such purposes (Free Press, 2013).

In recent years, second-home development has become an increasingly prominent component of Fernie's tourism-led economy (City of Fernie, 2009). For instance, despite its permanent population decreasing 23% to 4217 people between 1981 and 2006 (BC Stats, 2009), Fernie accommodated 552 new housing starts between 1991 and 2005. Many of these homes were designed to accommodate second-home purchasers (Pringle and Owen, 2006; City Spaces Consulting, 2007). Based on forecasts of ongoing increases in demand for second homes, as well as anticipated increases in home purchases by other amenity-led migrants, Fernie has plans in place to almost double its households from 2800 in 2003 to 5000 by 2023 (City of Fernie, 2003). While the prospects of

Fig. 10.2. Fernie location map (source: City of Fernie, 2015).

achieving this level of development have been dampened by the advent of the 2008 global recession, the trend towards increased (albeit slower) rates of second-home development in amenity-rich tourism destinations continues across British Columbia (Moore *et al.*, 2006; Ness, 2009; Johnson, 2010; Zukiwsky, 2010).

While Fernie's growth in second-home development has ensued, so has concern for maintaining the community's QoL. In response to this issue, Fernie's Official Community Plan (City of Fernie, 2003) identified the maintenance and/or protection of valued QoL amenities as a critical governance priority. Aligning with this objective, local government leaders have

pursued a suite of strategies designed to meet its QoL goals. It has also implemented its own resident-based QoL monitoring programme (Fernie QoL).

In a complementary initiative, Zukiwsky (2010) conducted an investigation examining the effects of second-home development on QoL in Fernie. His findings are based on information derived from Fernie's second-home owners, as well as permanent resident stakeholder populations.

An online survey with a sample of 23% or 237 of Fernie's estimated 998 second-home owners was conducted to identify their Fernie-related behaviours and QoL priorities.

The priorities explored were based on those identified and used in other QoL studies mentioned elsewhere in this chapter (e.g. CMHC, 1993). In addition, 23 key informants from the town's permanent resident population were interviewed, to gain their perceptions of how the second-home migrants were affecting Fernie's QoL and to identify what strategies might work to capitalize on the human, social and economic capital these second-home owners possessed. The informants included members of the community's municipal government, non-government organizations, economic development, and social service organizations who were familiar with Fernie's evolution as a mountain community and the role that second-home migrants were playing in this transition. The following sections highlight findings emanating from the second-home migrant surveys and community-based key informant interviews.

Fernie's second-home migrants

Fernie's second-home migrants tended to be comparatively older and wealthier, more formally educated and less fully employed than their permanent resident counterparts. Their second homes were also more likely to be townhouses, condominiums and apartments than were the accommodations of permanent residents. Their behaviours are briefly described in the following paragraphs.

Migration motivations

About 87% of Fernie's second-home migrants lived permanently elsewhere. The majority (62%) purchased their Fernie property for vacation purposes or with the intent (24%) to eventually retire there. Another 14% considered these houses to be primarily investment assets. About 38% also owned vacation properties in addition to their Fernie second home and permanent residence.

Overall, natural attractions such as the scenery, built attractions (e.g. ski areas) and a healthy environment were the most important attributes driving second-home purchase decisions. However, socio-cultural attributes such as high

quality of life, mountain culture and small-town atmosphere were also important. Potential job opportunities were markedly the least important factor.

From a community planning and management perspective, those factors rated most important to their QoL were primarily environmental amenities such as high-quality drinking water, natural scenery and recreation trails. Middle-range priority factors tended to be associated with socio-cultural features (e.g. small-town atmosphere, and sense of place features such as community festivals, arts and culture). Of less importance, but still some significance, were economic development traits related to type and rate of business growth and diversification.

Property use and community engagement

Fernie second-home use patterns varied considerable among the second-home owners. Overall, almost two-thirds of them (64%) used their Fernie homes between 30 and 129 days annually. On average their properties were occupied by them as vacation residences for 65 days, about 18% of the year. Visitation was highest during the winter months (an average of 26 days). Overall, during their visits, household occupancy was higher (avg. 3.9) than was the case for BC households in general (avg. 2.5 people) or Fernie's permanent resident homes (avg. 2.2 people) (BC Stats, 2009).

Most of the respondents (75%) did not rent their second home to others, preferring the flexibility to use it when they wished. Among those who did rent, rentals occurred an average of 42% of the year, and especially (47%) during the summer season.

Most (80%) of the second-home migrants planned to either maintain or increase their current use levels in the future. About a quarter of them (27%) expressed intentions of moving permanently to Fernie, either to work or to retire in the future. Few (12%) indicated they planned to sell their Fernie property and buy elsewhere.

For the most part (80%), second-home migrants stated that they were not particularly engaged in local Fernie affairs. Beyond attending promoted community (64%) and sporting events (46%), their involvement in local clubs, teams, cultural, volunteer or political events was limited (<5%). Most prominent reasons for their relatively minor engagement were: limited periods of time in Fernie (66%); commitments in their home community (21%); and perceptions of Fernie being solely a vacationing place (19%).

Fernie's Transformations

Perceptions of the transformational effects of second-home migration were derived from key informants in Fernie's permanent community. Their overall sentiment was that second-home development was making positive contributions to Fernie's QoL. However, the strength of that sentiment varied depending on the quality-of-life dimension discussed. Overall, they felt that second-home migrants brought new people with experiences, perspectives and capital that contributed to a more vital, energized and diverse social and economic fabric. They indicated that manifestations of second-home migrant tastes, interests and purchasing power were increasingly reflected in improvements to Fernie's commercial retail and food sectors, recreational amenities, as well as social and recreation services. A key informant articulated this position particularly well:

> They have new and diverse views and preferences, Fernie ... benefits with respect to the amenities, social services, retail and entertainment options available. All of which enhances the social fabric and diversity of the community.
>
> (Key Informant 17)

Notwithstanding this generally positive sentiment, some tension and ambivalence concerning specific impacts were identified. Much of the tension was attributed to underlying concerns about the rate and extent of second-home development in general and the potential (but largely unknown) implications of it on permanent residents and the QoL. Some key informants suggested that overall community tension seemed to be tapering as awareness, understanding and approaches to managing the implications of second-home development emerged. However, some issues still persisted and represented potentially challenging transformation effects for Fernie QoL.

Community engagement

While most of the informants felt that second-home migrants had much to contribute to local QoL, they were less sure of the extent to which such expertise was being captured and used. Some informants felt that many second-home owners were very engaged and contributing members to Fernie's social and cultural fabric:

> They get involved ... [T]hose that have become community drivers, many fall into that category [they were previously second-home migrants]; they have made the leap and now make a significant contribution to the community. They volunteer ... a large portion of second-home migrants get very involved.
>
> (Key Informant 6)

Others suggested that more had to be done to extend migrant contributions beyond purely monetary infusions, if these second-home owners were to be truly contributors to the community's QoL:

> They aren't involved. The tax dollars and money they spend when they are here ... don't really contribute to the fabric of the community. The fabric of the community is made up of more than just tax dollars and grocery money ... [it] is made up of people who volunteer and get involved in community issues. The higher the number of them, the lower the overall quality of life is for people that call Fernie their home and want to contribute to a strong sustainable community.
>
> (Key Informant 21)

Other informants suggested that engagement varied along a continuum. At one end were second-home migrants who purchased a home in a residential neighbourhood with intentions to live permanently in Fernie. They tended to be very involved in the community. On the other side were those migrants who purchased their property as a place solely for vacationing without becoming involved locally. One informant explained this non-engaged faction's behaviour as follows:

> I know many people that come to Fernie and don't speak to their neighbours. They come here to have an escape and a getaway from their urban existence ... they treat their residence as a cabin ... I'm not sure you will

reach these people with outreach, because I don't think they want to be engaged.

(Key Informant 21)

Regardless of whether respondents perceived second-home migrant community involvement as high or low, there was general agreement that the community should strive to further engage and get them involved in community affairs. Moreover, some key informants felt that Fernie had underachieved when it comes to nurturing such involvement. As one interviewee explained:

They bring a wealth of experience and education ... It's valuable to have people with time, who are educated and experienced. It's a valuable resource. I think we could tap into that more than we do.

(Key Informant 19)

Housing effects

Housing issues were perceived by most key informants to be a particularly challenging transformational effect of second-home development. They felt that such developments were pushing up housing and living costs. In particular, they believed that Fernie's low-income earners, seniors, seasonal workers and entry-level home buyers were particularly vulnerable to these escalations. Informants identified three transformational effects meriting attention. The most prominent concerned the displacement of local workers in the community:

They [second-home migrants] purchase smaller houses and take them out of the market, so there is less of that available for people that can only afford in that range.

(Key Informant 8)

Some interviewees noted that such displacements also affected the ability of local businesses to retain employees. As one local business informant stated:

Potential employees who find Fernie an attractive community can't afford to buy and settle in Fernie. We've had people in the past who, because they couldn't find a residence ... that was attainable in Fernie, they've declined employment ... These are the people who were looking for the mountain culture atmosphere.

(Key Informant 21)

Other informants mentioned that many permanent residents were moving from Fernie, not because they were being pushed out by affordability issues, but rather due to perceived opportunities to 'cash out' on their earlier Fernie home investments. In all these instances, the general sentiment was that second-home purchasers had hastened the movement of many past and potential residents away from Fernie.

From a 'sense of place' perspective, the presence of under-occupied second homes in some parts of the community (especially during tourism's shoulder seasons) was detrimental to Fernie's QoL. The impact of this 'cold bed' phenomenon was eloquently expressed by one of the informants:

My daughter lives in ... [a] building [that] is virtually empty. This is a detriment to some neighbourhoods. It's a darkened community; there is no life in the neighbourhood, no kids in the street.

(Key Informant 15)

Overall, there was a sense among key informants that increasing the frequency and duration of second-home occupancy would lead to an enhanced sense of community, and a more enhanced QoL in Fernie.

Economic effects

Overall, key informants felt that second-home migrants favourably contributed to the diversification of Fernie's economic base. Speaking in the context of second-home migration, one informant indicated:

[We] have tourism, mining, forestry, the public sector. There are so many legs that if one falls off, or is hurting, the other legs can pick up the slack.

(Key Informant 14)

The informants also agreed that numerous skilled trade jobs were created as a result of second-home construction, renovation, and maintenance, and that expenditures by second-home owners extended well beyond the typical development services to include other retail, service and hospitality industries. In many cases, the interviewees felt that second-home migrants were invaluable in helping sustain much of Fernie's retail and service sector. An informant confirmed that:

They support many of the local businesses and without them there would be quite a negative impact on local business.

(Key Informant 15)

Beyond the positive effects generated, some informants noted that such benefits were not without costs. For instance, they felt that as the diversity of retail offerings increased, so too had the prices paid for those services. An informant suggested that this was:

[An] economic challenge for people who work here … trying to keep up with rising costs of living, food, services.

(Key Informant 2)

Environmental effects

Informant perceptions were mixed concerning the extent and ways in which second-home migrants affected Fernie's environment values and priorities. Some of the interviewees felt that second-home migrants did not always live up to their self-professed high environmental ethics. However, others believed that these owners demonstrated a real willingness to pay for the protection of such natural assets. They felt that this demonstration of commitment could possibly be leveraged to pressure other resource based industries in the area to become more environmentally proactive. As one informant suggested:

They … could place significant political pressure against coal mining … We haven't had full scale opposition to [coal] operations, but the potential is there.

(Key Informant 22)

Conversely, other key informants felt that without greater engagement in local matters, the values of second-home migrants might not be realized in decisions impacting Fernie's environmental assets.

Discussion and Conclusions

Second-home developments and their migrants play a role in shaping Fernie's QoL. Many important planning lessons can be taken from this case. This section discusses

the findings in the context of Williams and Gill's (2006) 'Tourism-led Migration and the Transformation of Place' framework, and then identifies planning strategies designed to capture and reinforce QoL values expressed by Fernie residents and leaders.

Framework implications

Williams and Gill (2011) suggested that tourism-led amenity migration and the subsequent transformation of resort communities was shaped by the flow of people, capital and knowledge into these places. Such flows were capable of reshaping the local economy, landscape, social fabric, and political structure of host communities. They also asserted that host communities could use voluntary and regulatory planning intitiatives to mitigate vulnerabilities and exploit opportunities. To a large extent, the outcomes of this case study research confirm these assertions. Most second-home respondents were specifically drawn by Fernie's tourism-related recreational amenities prior to purchasing their property, and were transforming aspects of the community through their social and financial capital. However, the key informants felt that Fernie itself could become more proactive in escalating the extent of second-home migrant contributions to the social and economic fabric of the community. In addition, they recognized that not all second-home migrants were drawn to the area because of tourism-induced factors, and that efforts were needed to draw the capacities of other types of amenity migrants into Fernie's community networks. As suggested by Kuentzel and Ramaswamy (2005), other socio-economic and demographic forces were opening up new opportunities to capture the talents and capital of amenity migrants.

From a more applied perspective, Williams and Gill (2006) suggest that tourism-led migration can create challenges for host destinations. Some of the more prevalent challenges identified by the respondents were tied to QoL issues such as: affordability displacement effects; under-utilized accommodation 'cold bed' impacts; and second-home development environmental concerns.

Displacement

Housing affordability and cost of living costs are recurring issues in resort communities. Past research suggests that second-home demand, through the inflationary pressure put on real-estate prices, exerts a displacement effect on local populations (Gallent *et al.*, 2005), which in turn results in a loss of important local populations. This perspective was held by many Fernie key informants. In Fernie's case, displacement was not only affecting neighbourhood sense of place, but was also threatening the extent of provincial government funding for social services such as schools and hospitals. It must be recognized, however, that other variables beyond housing prices influence population decline. These include external forces such as broader demographic trends (rural exodus to urban centres), declines in resource extraction employment, as well as growing competition and product diversity in the tourism marketplace. There was clear recognition among community informants that diversifying Fernie's economy would be critical to reducing permanent resident displacement trends. Central to such strategies were commitments to retaining and enhancing Fernie's QoL attributes.

Key informants supported Sheller and Urry's (2006) perspective that investments in contemporary telecommunication and transportation infrastructure would encourage skilled professional workers to live and work in different locales such as high-amenity rural tourism communities. They felt that such investments would enhance the 'hard wiring' required to attract a range of 'footloose' industries and employees. From a more social and environmental infrastructure perspective, more contemporary versions of the types of 'comfort amenities' suggested by Moss (2006) represent useful QoL assets for not only holding existing residents, but also drawing new migrants. Examples of these amenities include: environmentally friendly multi-mode transport corridors; energy and waste management systems; as well as proximate medical, wellness, recreation and learning facilities.

Cold beds

Under-utilized and/or vacant second homes (aka 'cold beds') were considered detrimental to Fernie's vitality and sense of place. They represented lost opportunities to capitalize on the economic, social, and human capital that second-home migrants embodied. While many key informants recognized that not all second-home migrants intended to eventually move to the community full-time, they did feel that even those visiting on an intermittent basis could be encouraged to stay longer and become more engaged. Their suggestions for encouraging such transformations largely involved creating and promoting more vibrant tourism, and recreational and cultural amenities suited to the interests during non-traditional use periods. Recommended methods of promoting greater second-home uses and community engagement included: scheduling community events at times that aligned with their availability; promoting such events through social media that matched with their preferences; and orchestrating community orientation programmes that welcomed them to share their expertise and talents with local residents.

Environmental planning

Concerns about the environmental implications of second-home developments in Fernie mirror those noted in the literature. Clifford (2002) and Chipeniuk (2004) suggested that second-home development in amenity-rich tourism areas tends to increase the ecological footprint on resort communities. This case study identified that such impacts are primarily caused by inappropriate development siting and zoning controls implemented by local and, in some cases, provincial government authorities. The take-home lesson was that care must be taken to ensure that stakeholder interests in capturing second-home development opportunities are not fast-tracked at the cost of longer-term environmental quality.

Summary

Collectively, the preceding findings highlight the role that second-home migrants play in transforming the character of amenity-rich resort communities. In recent years, Fernie has taken a proactive approach to protecting those amenities that make it a desirable destination for second-home migrants. However, its ability to capitalize on the contributions that such migrants can potentially bring to the community's QoL is tempered by an overriding challenge. Despite being property owners, many of Fernie's second-home migrants are primarily intermittent visitors with relatively limited interest (or time) for greater community engagement. For the most part, they are there for leisure-oriented purposes. This makes capturing their 'community attention' more than a passing exercise. It requires keeping a close pulse on second-home migrant values and aspirations, and then implementing strategies that may help align them and their activities with Fernie's QoL goals. The insights provided in this chapter are intended as planning and management guides designed to steer tourism-led amenity migrations to outcomes that improve the QoL for all resort community stakeholders.

References

BC Stats (2006) Socio-economic Profiles. Government of British Columbia, Victoria, British Columbia, Canada.

BC Stats (2009) 2006 Census Profile: Fernie. Government of British Columbia, Victoria, British Columbia, Canada.

Bieger, T., Beritelli, P. and Weinert, R. (2007) Understanding second home owners who do not rent: insights on the proprietors of self-catered accommodation. *International Journal of Hospitality Management* 26(2), 263–276.

Buckley, R. (2005) Social trends and ecotourism: adventure recreation and amenity migration. *Journal of Ecotourism* 4(1), 56–60.

Bush, D.E. (2006) From collaboration to implementation: local policies to preserve agriculture, wildlife habitat, and open space in the mountain resort towns of the rocky mountain west. In: Thomas, C., Gill, A. and Hartman, R. (eds) *Mountain Resort Planning and Development in an Era of Globalization.* Cognizant Communications Corporation, New York, pp. 202–220.

Buxton, G. (2008) Planning for amenity migration: can amenity migration pay for itself? In: Moss, L.A., Glorioso, R.S. and Krause, A. (eds) *Understanding and Managing Amenity-led Migration in Mountain Regions.* Banff Centre, Banff, Alberta, Canada, pp. 103–106.

Chipeniuk, R. (2004) Planning for amenity migration in Canada: current capacities of British Columbian interior mountain communities. *Mountain Research and Development* 24(4), 327–335.

Chipeniuk, R. and Rapport, E. (2008) What is amenity migration and how can small mountain communities measure it? In: Moss, L.A., Glorioso, R.S. and Krause, A. (eds) *Understanding and Managing Amenity-led Migration in Mountain Regions.* Banff Centre, Banff, Canada, pp. 212–218.

City of Fernie (2003) Official Community Plan. Available at: https://fernie.civicweb.net/filepro/documents/603 (accessed 7 January 2016).

City of Fernie (2009) Fernie and Area Resort Municipality Tax Transfer Program: Five Year Resort Development Strategy. City Hall, Fernie, British Columbia, Canada.

City of Fernie (2015) Map of Southern BC. Available at: http://www.fernie.ca/assets/Residents/docs/Map-Southern-BC.pdf (accessed 21 August 2015).

City Spaces Consulting (2007) Fernie Affordable and Attainable Housing Strategy. City Hall, Fernie, British Columbia, Canada.

Clifford, H. (2002) *Downhill Slide: Why the Corporate Ski Industry is Bad for Skiing, Ski Towns, and the Environment.* Sierra Club Books, San Francisco, California.

CMHC (1993) Developing quality of life indicators for municipalities. Research and development highlights. Canada Mortgage and Housing, Ottawa, Ontario, Canada.

Coles, T. and Hall, C.M. (2006) Editorial: the geography of tourism is dead. Long live geographies of tourism and mobility. *Current Issues in Tourism* 9(4 and 5), 289–292.

Desrosiers-Lauzon, G. (2015) *Florida's Snowbirds: Spectacle, Mobility and Community Since 1945.* McGill-Queen's University Press, Montreal and Kingston.

Dissart, J.C. and Deller, S.C. (2000) Quality of life in the planning literature. *Journal of Planning Literature* 15(1), 135–161.

Fodor, E. (2009) *Fiscal and Economic Impacts of Destination Resort in Oregon.* Central Oregon Land Watch, Eugene, Oregon.

Francese, P. (2003) The second home boom. *American Demographics* 25(5), 40–42.

Free Press (2013) Fernie to Receive over $400,000 in RMI Funding. *The Fress Press*, 18 January 2013.

Gallent, N., Mace, A. and Twedyr-Jones, M. (2005) *Second Homes: European Perspectives and UK Policies*. Ashgate, Aldershot, UK.

Gill, A. (2000) From growth machine to growth management: the dynamics of resort development in Whistler, BC. *Environment and Planning* 32, 1083–1103.

Gill, A. and Welk, E. (2007) Natural heritage as place identity: Tofino, Canada, a coast resort on the periphery. In: Agarwal, S. and Shaw, G. (eds) *Managing Coastal Tourism Resorts: A Global Perspective*. Channel View Publications, Clevedon, UK, pp. 169–184.

Glorioso, R.S. and Moss, L.A. (2007) Amenity migration to mountain regions: current knowledge and strategic construct for sustainable management. *Social Change* 37(1), 137–161.

Government of BC (2015) Resort Municipality Funding. Available at: http://www2.gov.bc.ca/gov/topic.page?id=30A40BDA6D8346798E15C6050063F719 (accessed 31 March 2015).

Hall, M.C. and Müller, D.K. (2004) *Tourism, Mobility and Second Homes: Between Elite Landscape and Common Ground*. Channel View Publications, Cleveland, UK.

Halseth, G. (2004) The 'cottage' privilege: increasingly elite landscapes of second homes in Canada. In: Hall, M.C. and Müller, D.K. (eds) *Tourism, Mobilty and Second Homes: Between Elite Landscape and Common Ground*. Channel View Publications, Cleveland, UK, pp. 35–54.

Hettinger, W. (2005) *Living and Working in Paradise: Why Housing is too Expensive and What Communities Can Do About It*. Thames River Publishing, Windham, Connecticut.

Johnson, S. (2010) Managing residential tourism in British Columbia's South Okanagan. Masters Report. Resource and Environmental Management, Simon Fraser University, Burnaby, British Columbia, Canada.

Korber, D. and Rasker, R. (2001) *Measuring Change in Rural Communities: An Economics Workbook for Western Canada*. Chinook Institute for Civic Leadership, Kelzen, Oregon.

Kuentzel, W.F. and Ramaswamy, V.M. (2005) Tourism and amenity migration. *Annals of Tourism Research* 32(2), 419–438.

Low, M. (2005) 'Power' and politics in human geography. *Geografiska Annaler* 87B(1), 81–88.

Mair, H., Reid, D. and George, W. (2005) Globalization, rural tourism and community power. In: Hall, D., Kirkpatrick, I. and Mitchell, M. (eds) *Rural Tourism and Sustainable Business*. Channel View Publications, Clevedon, UK, pp. 165–179.

Marsden, T. (2006) Denial or diversity: creating new spaces for sustainable development. *Journal of Environmental Policy & Planning* 8(2), 183–198.

Moore, S.R., Williams, P.W. and Gill, A. (2006) Finding a pad in paradise: amenity migration effects on Whistler, British Columbia. In: Moss, L.A. (ed.) *The Amenity Migrants: Seeking and Sustaining Mountains and Their Cultures*. CAB International, Wallingford, UK, pp. 135–147.

Moss, L.A. (ed.) (2006) *The Amenity Migrants: Seeking and Sustaining Mountains and Their Cultures*. CAB International, Wallingford, UK.

Ness, J. (2009) Managing stakeholder contestation and negotiation in amenity-driven land-use planning. Masters Report. Resource and Environmental Management, Simon Fraser University, Burnaby, British Columbia.

Northwest Colorado Council of Governments (NWCCOG) (2006) *Transitions in Mountain Communities: Resort economies and Their Secondary Effects*. Northwest Colorado Council of Governments, Silverthorne, Colorado.

Paradis, T.W. (2000) Main street transformed: community sense of place for nonmetropolitan tourism business districts. *Urban Geography* 21(7), 609–639.

Pringle, T. and Owen, S.M. (2006) *How Growth in the Recreation and Resort Property Market is Driving Change in the East Kootenay Region*. Communities in Transition. Real Estate Foundation of BC, East Kootenay, Canada.

Putney, A. (2003) Perspectives on the value of protected areas. In: Harmon, D. and Putney, A.D. (eds) *The Full Value of Parks: From Economic to Intangible*. Rowman & Littlefield, Lanham, Maryland, pp. 3–12.

Ritchie, J.R.B. and Crouch, G.I. (2003) *The Competitive Destination: A Sustainable Tourism Perspective*. CAB International, Wallingford, UK.

Rodriguez, V. (2001) Tourism as a recruiting post for retirement migration. *Tourism Geographies* 3(1), 52–63.

Sheller, M. and Urry, J. (2006) The new mobilities paradigm. *Environment and Planning A* 38, 207–226.

Smith, M.D. and Krannich, R.S. (2000) Culture clash revisited: newcomer and longer term residents' attitudes toward land use, development, and environmental issues in rural communities in the Rocky Mountain West. *Rural Sociology* 65, 396–421.

Stewart, S.I. (2000) Amenity migration. In: Luft, K. and MacDonald, S. (eds) *Trends 2000: Shaping the Future: 5th Outdoor Recreation and Trends Symposium.* Department of Park, Recreation and Tourism Resources, Lansing, Michigan, pp. 369–378.

Thompson, S. (2006) Gateway to Glacier: will amenity migrants in north-western Montana lead the way for amenity conservation? In: Moss, L.A.G. (ed.) *The Amenity Migrants: Seeking and Sustaining Mountains and Their Cultures.* CAB International, Wallingford, UK, pp. 108–119.

Venturoni, L. (2003) The Social and Economic Effects of Second Homes. Available at: http://www.eagle county.us/uploadedFiles/ECG_Website/Housing_and_Development/Developers/SocEcon%20Ef fect%281%29.pdf (accessed 27 August 2015).

Venturoni, L., Long, P. and Perdue, R. (2005) The economic and social impacts of second homes in four mountain resort counties in Colorado. Paper presented at the *Annual Meeting of the Association of American Geographers, Tourism and the Tourist in the American West, 7 April,* Denver, Colorado.

Vesley, E. (2007) Green for green: the perceived value of a quantitative change in the urban tree estate of New Zealand. *Ecological Economics* 63, 605–615.

Williams, A.M. and Hall, C.M. (2000) Tourism and migration: new relationships between production and consumption. *Tourism Geographies* 2(1), 5–27.

Williams, D. (2002) Leisure identities, globalization, and the politics of place. *Journal of Leisure Research* 34(4), 351–367.

Williams, P.W. and Gill, A.M. (2006) A research agenda for tourism amenity migration destinations. *Tourism Recreation Research* 31(1), 92–98.

Williams, P.W. and Gill, A.M. (2011) Blending amenity migrants with locals in host destinations: residential tourism in British Columbia. In: Gross, M.J. (ed.) *CAUTHE 2011 National Conference Proceedings: Tourism: Creating a Brilliant Blend.* University of South Australia, Adelaide, Australia, pp. 1369–1373.

Zukiwsky, J. (2010) Understanding and managing the effects of residential tourism on quality of life in Fernie. Resource and Environmental Management, Simon Fraser University, Masters Report, Burnaby, British Columbia, Canada.

11 In the Shadow of Machu Picchu: A Case Study of the Salkantay Trail

Joe Pavelka*

Mount Royal University, Calgary, Canada

Introduction

Travel to Peru has risen sharply in the past two decades from 479,000 in 1995 to over 3.1 million in 2013 (Index Mundi, 2014) and so has travel to the cultural site of Machu Picchu, Peru's primary attraction. Just over 70% of all international travellers to Peru visit Machu Picchu (Pavelka, 2010). There are few attractions in the world with such a prominent role in a nation's tourism and identity (Shullenberger, 2008) as Machu Picchu, which stands as a visual focal point of indigenous cultural reawakening. It acts as the economic engine of tourism, and it fuels constant debate of its environmental carrying capacity, with arguments that daily visitor limits threaten its ecological integrity (Lincoln and Neelam, 2012). Machu Picchu differs from many other attractions because the experience of Machu Picchu involves two distinct components: getting to the site and the site itself. Machu Picchu receives about 2500 visitors each day (Zan and Lusiani, 2011), but the way these visitors get to the site is often as important as the visit itself. There are four ways visitors get to Machu Picchu: the most common way is by train, and there are three hiking routes, the Inca Trail, the Salkantay Trail and the Lares Trek. There is a car route as well, but this is downplayed (Pavelka, 2010).

Increased visitation to Machu Picchu has placed capacity stress on the routes to the site. The most popular of the routes is the Inca Trail, which allows a maximum of 500 people each day, including trekkers, guides and porters (Zan and Lusiani, 2011). Guidebooks stress the need to book the Inca Trail up to a year in advance. The Salkantay is presently marketed online under 'Alternatives to the Inca Trail', along with the Lares Trek, variations of the Inca Trail, and the Vilacabamba or Choquequirao, as it is locally known (although the latter is an indirect route to Machu Picchu). It is tourism businesses, not the government, who promote alternate trails. A trail promoted by the government, such as the Inca Trail, must be controlled, meaning that trekkers must use an approved guiding company. There is considerable local speculation about whether the Salkantay will become a controlled trail in the future. Despite the lack of official communication, government-sponsored trail development has occurred along the Salkantay since 2010 in the form of providing washrooms and a gate, which has only fuelled more speculation about the government's future intentions. The Salkantay Trail is transitioning from an informal trail, used by random groups of independent trekkers, to one that is presently promoted by numerous guiding companies. Changes in

---

* Corresponding author: jpavelka@mtroyal.ca

the type and scale of tourism and the status of the Salkantay trail have important implications for the small communities residing along the trail. The purpose of this chapter is to present a case study of how tourism impacts the Salkantay Trail. It reports on research carried out during the summer of 2012 as part of a programme to support tourism capacity building of the communities along the trail, and represents the first known published research on the Salkantay Trail.

Background to the Research

The Salkantay Trail is the only route of the three treks that can be hiked as an independent trekker; that is, it can be hiked without the services of a guiding company. In 2008, the author first trekked the Salkantay as an independent trekker and began learning about the relationship local families have with tourism. Since then he has included the Salkantay Trail as part of an ecotourism field school with post-secondary students. Some of the insight presented herein is based on observations and conversations from numerous visits.

Most of the families living along the trail have traditionally survived on subsistence farming and only recently have they decided to venture into tourism, providing either *arriero* (horse-packing) services to independent trekkers, camp cooking services, or the provision of rustic camping areas. The families have expressed a desire to expand their involvement in tourism, but with no English language skills or guide certification, their involvement is limited. Families along the trail fear that as the Salkantay grows in popularity, there will be fewer independent trekkers and more guided groups who often by-pass locals and create their own trekking infrastructure. A more critical consideration is that the trail may become a 'controlled' trail, as is the Inca Trail, in which case independent trekkers will not be permitted, all trekkers will have to travel with an approved guiding company, and horse-packing support may be eliminated in lieu of the porter system in place at the Inca Trail.

By invitation of the local families we carried out a programme in 2012 to support tourism capacity building. Our initial investigation revealed no published material on the Salkantay Trail beyond trip accounts and promotional material on the internet, so we endeavoured to undertake our own research. Three senior ecotourism students were engaged over a 3-month period to carry out two research projects. The first was a study of tourists in the city of Cusco, where all Machu Picchu travel and treks are launched, and the second examined trekkers along the Salkantay Trail. The two studies were purposefully planned to support small business development for the families along the trail. The study of tourists in Cusco attempted to determine what is important to tourists in the selection of a route/trek to Machu Picchu, and their perceptions of Machu Picchu. Tourists in Cusco were targeted because it was observed that a good proportion booked their trip to Machu Picchu upon arrival at Cusco, implying an opportunity to capture these 'undecideds' if preferences were well understood. The second study involved a survey of trekkers already on the trail to better understand ways to expand and improve the Salkantay experience with involvement of the families. Results of the two studies were drafted into a summary format, translated into Spanish and provided to the families along the trail with informal workshops during May of 2013 and continues today.

Background to the Salkantay Trail

The Salkantay Trail is currently known as the main alternative trek to the classic Inca Trail. It offers a wider variety of ecological niches than the Inca Trail, but lacks the archaeological ruin sites that the Inca Trail offers. Ecosystems including glaciers, tropical vegetation/birds, coffee plantations, and bananas can be found along the route. The trail allows for better interaction with local people who live and work in the area. The Salkantay is promoted as a four-night trek into Machu Picchu, while the Inca Trail is a three-night trek, and the Lares Trek is two or three nights, although all trip itineraries tend to vary.

The Salkantay Trail begins in the town of Mollepata, located 90 km (3.5 hours) from Cuzco (see Fig. 11.1). From Mollepata, Soraypampa is the first camp, approximately 20 km

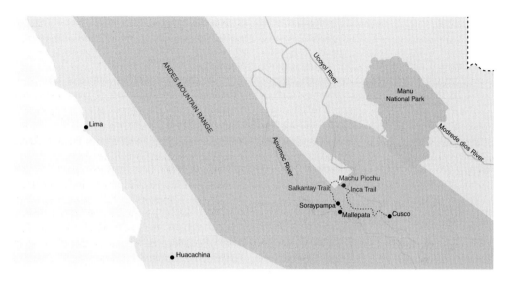

Fig. 11.1. Salkantay Trail, including Mallepata and Machu Picchu.

along a dirt road or animal trails. Soraypampa lies in a valley that includes a node of 16 families that work as *arrieros* and numerous temporary tent camps operated by trekking companies. The valley sits in the shadow of the Salkantay (mountain) at an elevation of 6271 m. The trail continues over the Salkantay Pass, which represents the highest point on the trail at 4600m or 15,000 feet. The highest point on the Inca Trail is Dead Woman's Pass at 4215 m. SAS Travel, a popular Andes tour company, describes the Salkantay as 'a great alternative to the Inca Trail trek, better suited to the more adventuresome trekkers who are able to handle more altitude and distance . . .' (SAS Travel Peru, 2015).

Trekkers pass from an arid alpine environment to a semi-tropical forest during the descent from the high pass, and encounter the small villages of Huarac Punku, Chaullhay and Collpapampathat, which offer camping on a *'lo que sea su voluntad'* (whatever is your will) basis. A small portion of the trip is carried out by van from La Playa to Santa Teresa, and then to a Hydro Electric plant and an 8 km hike to the Pueblo of Aguas Caliente (renamed Machu Picchu Village) at the base of Machu Picchu. The distance from Mollepata to Santa Teresa is about 56 km in total. Languages spoken along the Salkantay Trail are mainly Quechua (the Indigenous language of the area)

and Spanish. The people who live along the trail speak almost no English.

The families formed an *arriero* association in 2002 to garner more respect from outside agencies and the government, and to establish rules among themselves. Members of the association have different motivations for making money and for doing well at their jobs. Respect is important to the Quechua people and is acquired by hard work with a positive attitude. The men claim to enjoy their work with tourists; they earn decent wages and take pride in a job well done. *Arrieros* are often able to send their children to school in larger communities, where it is hoped they will have more opportunities.

The Emergence of Tourism and Adventure Trekking to Machu Picchu

The purpose of this section is to shed light on the struggle of the families living along the Salkantay Trail to better access the tourism economy and, therefore, background on tourism in Peru relevant to Machu Picchu and the Inca Trail is provided. The Salkantay Trail exists in the shadow of Machu Picchu; both in geography and touristic prominence, and the families living along the trail are affected by the broader historic macro socio-political factors even today.

Tourism in the Cusco region emerged during the 1960s, largely driven by exposure from decades of scientific expeditions by Peruvians and others (Carey, 2012). But it was a modernization effort following a devastating earthquake in 1950, coupled with sharp interest in Machu Picchu by UNESCO, which resulted in a surge in travel to Machu Picchu during the 1960s and 1970s. Numbers dropped considerably during the 1980s as a result of economic depression, and the de-stabilization of the Maoist group the *Sendero Luminoso* (Shining Path), whose terrorist activities kept tourists away (Hill, 2007). At the same time, tourism around the world was growing, and rumour of a trek through sacred mountains, ending at a mystical cultural site, was all too attractive. But as with most sectors of the Peruvian economy, tourism relied on the government for investment, regulation, and direction. The government established a variety of national agencies to promote and develop tourism during that time, but real growth did not occur until the 1990s.

It was not until the arrival of the controversial President Alberto Fujimoro in 1990 that the country and its tourism took a sharp turn. Fujimoro instituted wide-ranging neo-liberal policies that resulted in a new relationship between government and business, with much control handed over to business interests (Desforges, 2000). In 1992, Fujimoro's government quashed the Shining Path and captured its leader Abimael Guzman, which resulted in a return of both international and domestic tourists. All the while Peru was re-embracing its Inca heritage in relation to a national identity, also known as *incanismo*, and created a perfect storm for the increase of tourism to Machu Picchu and the Inca Trail (Hill, 2007).

Numbers travelling along the Inca Trail had risen sharply from 6263 in 1984 to 130,454 by 2006 (Maxwell, 2012). In 2000, new regulations were instituted to limit the number of people on the trail to 500 each day and to make the Inca Trail 'controlled', meaning that to hike the trail, one had to hire an approved guiding company. But as the Inca Trail's 500 person per day limit was put in place, visitation to Machu Picchu continued to increase from just over 400,000 in 2000 to over 1.1 million in 2013 (Peruvian Times, 2014). Most of the increased visitation to Machu Picchu has been accommodated by train travel, but there are few options for those insisting on a trek, except to explore the Salkantay and Lares Treks – alternatives to the Inca Trail.

The controversial neo-liberal policies instituted by Fujimoro have largely persisted under a succession of Presidents attempting to balance economic investment and maintain domestic control over national resources and cultural treasures. Tourism, with its connection to cultural identity, has been under particular scrutiny during this time as residents of Cusco protest the way tourism is progressing. However, Hill (2007) points out that the real issue is not that their *incanismo* heritage is used to attract tourists, but it is the residents' lack of access to meaningful participation in the tourism economy that is at issue. The problem of social and economic exclusion from tourism has been previously attached to the Inca Trail porter situation and their lack of access to meaningful engagement (Arellano, 2011). Structural constraints to meaningful participation usually appear as a lack of education and language skills, and a real, but less tangible 'club' mentality to accessing business opportunities. Tourism, and guiding in particular, is a lucrative area of employment in this part of Peru and many people, especially from smaller villages, aspire to work in tourism. McGrath (2004) maintains that the guide is an important figure in Peruvian tourism, but access to the guiding profession is highly regulated. Full guides are university-educated (usually in history or cultural studies), while a second tier of guides is college-tourism-educated, and the third tier is local guides. Local guides tend to live near the tourism attraction and have exceptional local knowledge, but lack English language skills and certifications, making them the lowest tier of guides, therefore easy to by-pass.

The families along the Salkantay are local guides, which explains in part their exclusion from the tourism industry that surrounds them. This means the families have limited ability to earn higher wages, all the while the number of guiding companies on the trail from outside increase, and the families' ability to have input on government driven trail changes are limited at best. Salkantay residents experience a similar type of social and economic exclusion as Arellano (2011) reports with the Inca Trail porters, although families along the trail own their land, which affords some power. But the central issue is a shared one of constraints to meaningful social and economic participation, due to a variety of socio-economic and political structural inequalities.

Method

Research reported for this chapter was part of a larger tourism capacity building programme to support families living along the Salkantay Trail. The ultimate aim of the project was to support increased tourism capacity building of families along the trail in light of the socio-political and economic challenges previously highlighted. Therefore, the aim of the two studies was to better understand the consumer decision making of the tourist/trekker in Cusco and along the Salkantay Trail, and to bring this information back to the residents along the trail.

Data collection occurred during the summer of 2012 in the form of a semi-structured survey of English-speaking tourists in Cusco and on the Salkantay Trail. The interviews were carried out in person using a systematic sample of every fifth person in Cusco, and every second person on the trail. A total of 290 interviews were carried out in Cusco and 186 along the trail. In Cusco, data collection was carried out in 2-hour periods in the busy Plaza de Armas, rotating the time of day for data collection. Along the trail, data collection occurred when a group was encountered in either Soraypampa or Chaullahay.

Two questionnaires were developed, with approximately 20 items each. The brevity of the instrument was viewed as essential in getting people to agree to participate. The two instruments shared two separate measures for comparison. The first is a measure on perceptions of Machu Picchu, because it is reasonable to assume that a critical motivation for any trekker or train occupant is to visit Machu Picchu. Therefore, we wanted to check for differences in the way Machu Picchu is perceived by those who took other routes from those who trekked the Salkantay. The second shared measure is concerned with the importance of various route features to better understand how visitors choose their respective route to Machu Picchu.

The Salkantay Trail questionnaire included sections directly related to soliciting feedback about the trail and what else could be offered.

Results

Data from fieldwork was input into SPSS15 and checked for inconsistencies. Descriptive statistics were first carried out by item for both samples. Later, bivariate and factor analysis were conducted on the two primary measures related to perceptions of Machu Picchu and the importance of factors in the selection of a route to Machu Picchu. Presented in this section is a description of the samples, basic comparison of perception of Machu Picchu, and factors important in the selection of a route by each sample. Additionally, other descriptive data relevant to the discussion is presented.

Table 11.1 presents a description of the two samples by three descriptors: how they are travelling, age, and self-reported 'adventuresomeness' – that is, a self-reporting of how adventurous people perceive themselves to be. Overall, the two samples (which included Cusco and along the trail) are more similar than different. In general, two of three travellers to the area are fully independent travellers, versus those travelling in a guided group. This result suggests that over 60% of visitors may decide for themselves what route they take into Machu Picchu, without the influence of a tour company. Tourists in Cusco were asked what route to Machu Picchu they intended to take. A total of 46% indicated it was to be 'By Train', followed by 'Inca Trail' at 19%, then the 'Salkantay' with almost 13%. 'Lares Trek' and 'By Car' made up a total of 12%. Trekkers specifically along the Salkantay Trail were asked whether they were hiking in a guided group or as independent trekkers, with the result that 91% of trekkers along the trail travel in a guided group. The two samples are similar and reflect a younger traveller, with 82% of both samples between the ages of 18 and 34. Both samples report themselves to be adventurous, with just over 70% of both samples reporting themselves to be adventurous, or very adventurous. The latter item is important to developing marketing materials that reflect the audience and how they like to see themselves.

Table 11.2 presents results of perceptions of Machu Picchu based on a five-point agree/ disagree scale, whereby 1 is strongly agree, and 5 is strongly disagree. The Pearson Chi Square test revealed a significant difference in four of the 11 items. The four significant items (*) may be interpreted in two statements about the two samples, with respect to their different perceptions of Machu Picchu. The first is that the Cusco group agrees more strongly than the Salkantay group that Machu Picchu is important to the economy of the people; and that it is simply something to do while in the Cusco area. The second statement is that the Salkantay group agrees more strongly that Machu Picchu is a well-managed attraction for locals and tourists and that it is a place that may change how one sees the world.

Table 11.3 provides a ranking of perceptions of Machu Picchu by means. What is revealed is a contradiction of the high-ranking perceptions for both groups. Machu Picchu appears to

Table 11.1. Description of sample (all responses in per cent).

How they travel	Cusco sample (N=273)	Salkantay sample (N=190)
Group travel	37	33
FIT (fully independent traveller)	63	67

Age categories	Cusco sample (N=290)	Salkantay sample (N=186)
18–24	41	32
25–34	41	50
35–44	8	9
45–54	5	6
55–64	2	1
65+	2	0

Self-report adventuresome	Cusco sample (N=272)	Salkantay sample (N=186)
Very adventurous	20	15
Adventurous	53	55
Not sure	24	26
Not adventurous	2	1
Not at all adventurous	0	0

Table 11.2. Perception of Machu Picchu by Cusco and Salkantay samples.

Item	Cusco mean (N=288)	Salkantay mean (N=184)	Pearson Chi Square
Machu Picchu is a beautiful place	2.05	2.17	.442
It is important to the cultural identity of the local people	2.22	2.28	.516
It is overrun by tourists	1.99	1.96	.071
Machu Picchu is a spiritual place	3.01	2.81	.363
It is important to the economy of the local people	1.33	1.57	.017*
It is a well-managed attraction for tourists and locals	3.78	3.63	.040*
It is the primary reason I came to Peru	3.78	3.82	.997
It is a place that may help me change how I see the world	2.18	2.15	.017*
It is simply something to do while I am in the Cusco area	3.25	3.47	.024*
It is an old and worn-out tourist attraction	1.97	1.97	.116
It is a place that will help me change who I am	3.56	3.63	.521

Table 11.3. Ranking of perceptions of Machu Picchu by mean.

Rank	Cusco sample	Salkantay sample
1	It is important to the economy of the local people	It is important to the economy of the local people
2	It is an old and worn-out tourist attraction	It is overrun by tourists
3	It is overrun by tourists	It is an old and worn-out tourist attraction
4	Machu Picchu is a beautiful place	It is a place that may help me change how I see the world
5	It is a place that may help me change how I see the world	Machu Picchu is a beautiful place
6	It is important to the cultural identity of the local people	It is important to the cultural identity of the local people
7	Machu Picchu is a spiritual place	Machu Picchu is a spiritual place
8	It is simply something to do while I am in the Cusco area	It is simply something to do while I am in the Cusco area
9	It is a place that will help me change who I am	It is a place that will help me change who I am
10	It is a well-managed attraction for tourists and locals	It is a well-managed attraction for tourists and locals
11	It is the primary reason I came to Peru	It is the primary reason I came to Peru

present a conflicted image to tourists. These results should be of concern to managers of Machu Picchu, but they are not particularly surprising. In recent years, criticism has become more common, both in scholarship and in guidebooks (Pavelka, 2010). More recently, the tension between Machu Picchu and UNESCO over perceived mismanagement of visitor numbers and overcrowding has garnered attention (Zan and Lusiani, 2011). Yet Machu Picchu manages to maintain global iconic status as a sacred and spiritual place (Shullenberger, 2008).

Table 11.4 provides the results of the importance of factors in the selection of a route based on a five-point Likert importance scale, whereby 1 is very important and 5 is not at all important. The Pearson Chi Square yielded four significant results (*) out of the seven items. The significant items may be interpreted in two statements about the samples. The first is that the Salkantay group is more likely than the Cusco group to select a trip that is less expensive, more authentic, and presents the opportunity to see fewer people. The second statement is that the Cusco group is more likely than the Salkantay group to select a route that affords more personal status in relation to what Kerr *et al.* (2012) refer to as 'bragging rights', and one's choice of destination.

The mean ranking of factors important to the selection of a route are presented in Table 11.5.

The ranking reveals an important difference in the two groups, especially in light of the factors pertaining to 'fewer tourists', ranked most important by the Salkantay group, and least important by the Cusco group. A similar outcome is observed for the 'status' item. With respect to project aims, data in Table 11.4 and 11.5 offer direction to product development and marketing for the Salkantay Trail, and suggests that Salkantay trekkers may differ from the majority of tourists to Machu Picchu.

Trekkers along the trail were asked what features would make the Salkantay experience even stronger. The results appear in Table 11.6. They are based on a five-point Likert scale of desirability, whereby 1 is very desirable, and 5 is not at all desirable. Table 11.6 data suggest that there is a strong interest in learning more about local culture and daily life and they are keen to participate in more local cooking and ceremonies. There is support for the addition of trekking options not involving Machu Picchu as the final destination, and slightly less for adding up to 2 more days to explore the local area, and to see more local guides offering experiences. The results suggest there is potential to develop products specific to the Salkantay that is appealing to the market.

Finally, trekkers along the trail were asked when they booked their Salkantay trip.

Table 11.4. Importance of factors in the selection of a route.

Item	Cusco sample (N=273)	Salkantay sample (N=178–187)	Pearson Chi Square
The price – it is less expensive	2.74	2.70	.001*
Amount of time – it is more convenient	2.70	2.96	.106
Cultural value – it has more cultural value than other options	2.46	2.66	.069
Fewer tourists – I will see fewer tourists than other options	2.99	2.40	.000*
Physical – it fits my physical needs better than other options	2.94	2.84	.436
Authentic – it is more authentic than other options	2.67	2.48	.005*
Status – it provides more status than other options	2.54	2.92	.017*

Table 11.5. Ranking of factors important to the selection of a route.

Rank	Cusco sample	Salkantay sample
1	Cultural value – it has more cultural value than other options	Fewer tourists – I will see fewer tourists than other options
2	Status – it provides more status than other options	Authentic – it is more authentic than other options
3	Authentic – it is more authentic than other options	Cultural value – it has more cultural value than other options
4	Amount of time – it is more convenient	The price – it is less expensive
5	The price – it is less expensive	Physical – it fits my physical needs better than other options
6	Physical – it fits my physical needs better than other options	Status – it provides more status than other options
7	Fewer tourists – I will see fewer tourists than other options	Amount of time – it is more convenient

Table 11.6. What trekkers along the Salkantay would like to see along the trail.

Item	Mean
Learn more about local culture and daily life (N=182)	1.89
Eat more local food prepared by local people (N=187)	2.22
Learn more about and participate in local ceremonies (N=182)	2.24
See more trekking options not involving Machu Picchu (N=183)	2.36
Add more time (up to two days) to explore the trail (N=183)	2.67
See local operators offer more guided experiences (N=184)	2.68

The result is that 43% reported booking their trip while in Cusco, 31% booked the trip up to 4 months in advance, and the remaining 26% booked their trip between 5 and 18 months in advance.

Recommendations and Conclusions

The purpose of this chapter is twofold. First, to bring to light the situation of the communities residing along the Salkantay Trail, and the structural constraints they face in fully engaging in tourism. Second is to present market development research, designed to support the tourism capacity building of those families. It is hoped the two aims together have presented a case study of tourism along the Salkantay Trail. The struggle of the families to fully engage in tourism involves many issues, including those attached to decades of neo-liberal policies, which this chapter cannot fully address. However, the research presented in this chapter points to a cautiously positive future for community-scale tourism in the region. Three recommendations capture the basic implications of the data for the families, as outlined below.

1. Opportunity: Data suggests that there is a realistic opportunity to increase the number of trekkers along the Salkantay Trail, given that 43% of tourists do not select and book their route to Machu Picchu until they arrive in Cusco. The families along the trail – perhaps working with 'friendly' local guiding companies out of Cusco – can work to capture the 'undecideds' in Cusco by better appealing to those seeking traits known to be important to potential hikers.

2. Distinct Market: In addition to opportunity, data suggests that those trekking along the Salkantay Trail represent a distinct group, at least from a marketing perspective. This is evidenced by the level of importance placed on key variables, such as seeing fewer other trekkers, and the desire to have an authentic experience.

3. Product Development: The data further suggests there is opportunity to develop and enhance the Salkantay experience by focusing more on the inclusion of local foods, and education regarding daily life, customs and ceremonies. There is some opportunity to develop trekking itineraries that do not involve Machu Picchu, or even to extend the trek by 1 or 2 days with additional day hikes.

The Salkantay Trail represents an important area of growth for tourism in the Cusco region. It presently accommodates 13% of all visitors to Machu Picchu and it will likely have to accommodate more in the future. But unlike the Inca Trail, it includes more human settlement, which adds to the cultural appeal of the trek, but complicates its operation from a traditional 'parks' perspective. There is a long history of park–people conflict in protected areas the world over, whereby it is easier to operate a park for tourists without locals living and working in the park. Maxwell's (2009) comprehensive assessment of the Inca Trail begins by explaining that some of the problems faced by Machu Picchu and Inca Trail can be attributed to a 'Yellowstone Model' of management that focuses on creating pristine wilderness environments and marginalizing local residents. Further development of the Salkantay needs to respect the fact that it is different from the Inca Trail in a variety of ways, as mentioned above. The implication is that it represents more of a 'working landscape' and it is the embodiment of the dynamic human–environment relationship. Ironically, it represents an authentic view of Andean mountain life – something of particular value to many travellers to the area. The Salkantay Trail functions as well as it currently does because of the local residents and their genuine spirit of cooperation and respect. It would be wise to develop the trail further in a manner that permits long-term, meaningful contributions from the local guides already there.

Acknowledgements

The author would like to acknowledge funding support from the Association of Universities and Colleges of Canada and the invaluable work of the student researchers: Kelly Cytco, Roberto Donoghue and Mike Overend. A short film of the families along the Salkantay Trail, entitled *In the Shadow of Machu Picchu*, can be viewed on https://vimeo.com/45927236

References

Arellano, A. (2011) Tourism in poor regions and social inclusion: the porters of the Inca Trail to Machu Picchu. *World Leisure Journal* 53(2), 104–118.

Carey, M. (2012) Mountaineers and engineers: the politics of international science, recreation, and environmental change in twentieth century Peru. *Hispanic American Historical Review* 92(1), 107–141.

Desforges, L. (2000) State tourism institutions and neo-liberal development: a case study of Peru. *Tourism Geographies: An International Journal of Tourism Space, Place and Environment* 2(2), 177–192.

Hill, M.D. (2007) Contesting patrimony: Cusco's mystical tourist industry and the politics of incanismo. *Ethnos: Journal of Anthropology* 72(4), 433–460.

Index Mundi (2014) Peru – international Tourism: International Tourism, Number of Arrivals. Available at: http://www.indexmundi.com/facts/peru/international-tourism (accessed 28 July 2015).

Kerr, G., Lewis, C. and Burgess, L. (2012) Bragging rights and tourism marketing: a tourism bragging rights model. *Journal of Hospitality and Tourism Management* 9, 15–24.

Lincoln, R.L. and Neelam, C.P. (2012) Developing sustainable tourism through adaptive resource management: a case study of Machu Picchu, Peru. *Journal of Sustainable Tourism* 20(7), 917–938.

Maxwell, K. (2009) Making Machu Picchu: history and embodying nature in the Peruvian Andes. Presented at the *Yale Program in Agrarian Studies Colloquium Series*, 10 April 2009.

Maxwell, K. (2012) Tourism, environment and development on the Inca Trail. *Hispanic American Historic Review* 92(1), 143–171.

McGrath, G. (2004) Including the outsiders: the contribution of guides to integrated heritage tourism management in Cusco, Southern Peru. *Current Issues in Tourism* 7(4–5), 426–432.

Pavelka, J. (2010) Survey Finds that Visitors to Machu Picchu are Satisfied. Available at: https://ecoclub.com/education/articles/389-100614 (accessed 7 August 2015).

Peruvian Times (2014) Drastic New Rules Coming Very Soon for Visitors to Machu Picchu [quoting data from Ministerio de Cultura – Direccion Regional de Cultura – Cusco (MINCETUR)]. Available at: http://www.peruviantimes.com/12/drastic-new-rules-coming-very-soon-for-visitors-to-machu-picchu/21727 (accessed 7 August 2015).

SAS Travel Peru (2015) Salkantay, Machupicchu & Huaynapicchu 5 Day/4 Night – Group Service. Available at: http://www.sastravelperu.com/english/program/342/salkantay-machupicchu-huaynapicchu-5-day-4-night-group-service (accessed 28 July 2015).

Shullenberger, G. (2008) That obscure object of desire: Machu Picchu as myth and commodity. *Journal of Latin American Cultural Studies: Travesia* 17(3), 317–333.

Zan, L. and Lusiani, M. (2011) Managing change and master plans: Machu Picchu between conservation and exploitation. *Archaeologies: Journal of the World Archaeological Congress* 7, 329–371.

12 Transformative Wine Tourism in Mountain Communities

Donna M. Senese*

University of British Columbia–Okanagan, Kelowna, British Columbia, Canada

Introduction

Wine regions are classified according to their landscape, climate, and geological origin. These are factors that also help define 'terroir', a complex term that delimits geographical space constructed in the interaction of the natural environment and human factors over time (Unwin, 2012). Terroir is widely discussed and hotly contested wherever wine is produced, and this is especially true in unique environments with difficult growing conditions such as mountain regions. Mountain regions and cultures also possess conflicted economic landscapes, where the amenities of primordial nature compete, often unsuccessfully, with the needs of industry. Tourism and wine industries share a potential to co-exist sustainably in amenity-rich mountain environments where the lifestyle and aesthetic of wine culture transforms mountain landscapes into a unique rural idyll. The author examines the transformative potential of mountain wine tourism to address some of the issues facing rural mountain communities beginning with presentation of the potential of wine tourism to join the cast of niche tourism sectors as it transforms the landscape and worldview of hosts and guests. The value of mountain wine-producing areas in a global perspective is introduced and

a position on the potential of wine tourism to act as a transformative agent in the Okanagan wine region of British Colombia is presented.

Wine Tourism and Transformation

Wine tourism appeared in the academic literature in the 1980s with market-based research (Spawton, 1986) and through the 1990s research continued to grow, especially in new world wine regions (Gilbert, 1992; Dodd, 1995; Macionis and Cambourne, 1998). By the end of the decade attention turned to links between wine tourism and sustainability (Carmichael, 2004; Getz and Brown, 2006; Poitras and Getz, 2006). By 2006, three books amalgamating research on wine tourism were published: Getz (2000), Hall *et al.* (2000) and Carlsen and Charters (2006). The 2008 Congresso Internzionale sul Turismo Enogastronomico Mondo Globale highlighted an unprecedented wine tourism growth in new world wine regions (Senese, 2008). Links between wine tourism and sustained competitiveness (Hall *et al.*, 2003; Hashimoto and Telfer, 2003; Carmichael and Senese, 2012) appeared in transitioning rural environments. The most recent work in wine tourism explores the idea of image in the process of regional

---

* Corresponding author: donna.senese@ubc.ca

wine tourism growth. Duarte Alonso and Northcote (2009) examine heritage landscape characteristics for wine tourism origin branding and the attention to a rural idyll. Overton and Murray interrogate the idyll of wine and explore a class culture or rural bourgeoisie in the consumption of landscape in wine and wine tourism branding (Overton, 2010; Murray and Overton, 2011; Overton et al., 2012; Overton and Murray, 2013).

Wine tourism promotes or produces transitioning landscapes wherever it is developed. But is the transition transformative? Weaver (2014) notes interest in tourism models that perpetuate the ethics ideal but dismisses them 'beyond their small, mostly academic circles of enthusiastic and idealistic proponents' (p. 525). Pritchard et al. (2011) define hopeful tourism as a reciprocal partnership for co-learning among hosts and guests derived from the concept of transformational learning theory developed by Mezirow in 1978 (Mezirow, 1978). Tourism is not inherently transformational but it can offer transformative possibilities (Pritchard and Morgan, 2013, 12). There appear to be many avenues for all kinds of significant change in tourism, 'the transformation of meanings or consciousness can take place in almost any context-place if the individual concerned is ready for change' (Reisinger, 2013, 29) but not all types of tourism offer transformational potential.

At first glance wine tourism may not appear to hold promise as transformational, but the author argues that it has left a mark of transformational change, especially in mountain wine regions. There is a quality of life associated with visiting a winery and running a winery (Senese et al., 2012) that is related to a widespread notion of 'countryside' in the middle-class system of values (Harvey, 1989; Urry, 1990) and disillusionment with modernity and the regimentation of urban life. Rural mountainous areas are now more accessible to the middle-class notion of countryside evolving into a post-productive space, where rurality is exploited as a playground of consumption (Travis, 2007). The production of wine is paramount within the economies of some rural areas transitioning as post-productive landscapes, but it is the discovery, consumption and experience of wine and the lifestyle associated with it that holds transformative potential.

Mountain Wine Tourism

The mountain landscapes that produce wine vary considerably from the deeply eroded ancient basements of South Africa and Douro Region of Portugal to the faulted plains of France (Fanet, 2004, 12). Among those landscapes, only relief is generally accepted as a common denominator. Relief provides the drainage of air and water that provide perfect growing conditions in a variety of climatic conditions. The grape vine, a woody perennial, requires diurnal and seasonal change in temperature and moisture conditions provided by landscape relief to encourage bud break, vine growth, and the delicate balancing act between flesh and skin, sugar and acid in the fruit of the vine. In mountainous regions where relief is a dominant characteristic, wine is produced both because of the landscape and despite the landscape.

The Centre for Research, Environmental Sustainability and Advancement of Mountain Viticulture (CERVIM) in the European Union promotes, protects and valorizes mountain viticulture. CERVIM refers to mountain viticultural areas as 'heroic' and characterizes these as small, non-contiguous, often terraced vineyards with orographic conditions that create impediments to mechanization and produce niche grape varieties with tightly defined geographical range (Piscolla, 2007). Therefore these areas are highly valued landscapes for the provision of both grape and wine production and consumption. So valued, in fact, that eight of the heroic mountain wine regions are UNESCO World Heritage Sites representing tangible monuments of the cultural landscape or 'heritage-scape' (Di Giovane, 2008).

The mountain wine regions of the new world, though devoid of world heritage status are also valorized as productive landscapes. The decisive factor in the development of Chile's vineyards is the coastal cordillera that provides for the varied terroir of Mendoza (Fanet, 2004). The West Coast wine regions of North America lie in some of the most complex mountainous formations on the continent including the premier vineyards of California (Fanet, 2004, 208). In the Pacific Northwest, the Coast Range lines up as a sheltering sea wall, bringing rain and modifying temperatures to wine regions in Washington, Oregon, and Idaho (Johnson and

Robinson, 2009). Further to the north, the Okanagan wine region of British Columbia (BC) is protected by the Monashee Mountain Range to the east and the Coast Mountain Range to the west which provides a rain shadow with a mild, dry, continental climate (Belliveau et al., 2006). The desert conditions provide for exceptional diurnal summer temperature variation in the Okanagan where early ripening grapes are favoured (Johnson and Robinson, 2009). Physiographically, the Okanagan is a rolling upland, with extensive kame and outwash terraces and an assortment of glacial and alluvial features that hold well-drained soils, an ideal setting for grape production (Senese et al., 2012).

The Okanagan wine industry has experienced rapid and sizeable growth; however, grapes have been a part of the rural landscape since the 1860s. The valley remained relatively quiet as a wine producer until the Free Trade Agreement of 1988 and the new BC regulations in 1990 that created VQA (Vintner's Quality Assurance) standards. VQA standards also provided regional, localised brand recognition and ultimately the synergy of wine amenities and tourism that has made the industry more economically viable (Senese, 2008). The images of the Okanagan used to attract settlers a century ago emphasized the lush, oasis-like qualities of orchards and lakes set among a dramatic, arid and mountainous backdrop. Today, the orchardists are displaced by a new generation of settlers who come to retire, attracted to the region and its wine culture, or who come to make their living in the wine tourism industry (Wagner, 2008).

Transformative Wine Tourism in the Okanagan

The nascent Okanagan wine region is part of the transitioning rural economy and culture of the post-industrial era (Senese, 2010). Wine tourism has been widely acknowledged as an economic cushion throughout that transition. A 2008 BC Tourism survey of visitor flows show the impact of increasing wine tourism as visitors surveyed were more interested in wine travel, more experienced in wine travel and more likely to choose the Okanagan wine region as a primary destination (Tourism BC Research and Planning, 2009). The British

Columbia Wine Institute's economic impact report of the wine industry shows a CAN\$476 million yearly revenue in tourism and business revenues generated from approximately 800,000 wine visitors yearly (BCWI, 2013).

Beyond economics, an understanding of how transformational the wine tourism experience is, and the potential it might have in sustaining rural communities is not well understood. Twelve semi-structured interviews were conducted with expert wine industry proprietors and wine makers in the Okanagan to articulate the transformative change in the landscape and aesthetic of the Okanagan and the role of the wine industry in constructing that change. Photographs were made to illustrate the reflections caught in those interviews. Interviews took place at the winery or vineyard of the subjects and were between 1 and 3 hours in length. The interviews took on a fluid conversational form and varied according to the interests, experiences, and views of the interviewees. The surface contents of the interview transcripts were assessed for manifest content using NVivo. Using emergent themes, a latent content analysis of the transformative nature of the respondent's words was then performed.

The interviews progressed in ways and towards thematic areas that were not always anticipated. Four transformative themes were teased out of the interview transcripts: transformative mobility of the subjects; personal perspective change expressed as a moment or turning point; viticultural order out of natural chaos in the mountain idyll; and living the dream and sharing the work with others. The author was struck by the passion of those interviewed, their struggle to articulate a particular value of the wine landscape and intrigued by the personal change that had driven all of them into the industry and their eagerness to share that change.

Transformative Mobility (Fig. 12.1) in Mountain Regions

The transformative nature of life-course change is a common element that drives amenity migrants to mountain environments (Chipeniuk, 2004) and this kind of mobility is often driven by the initial appeal of mountain tourism.

Fig. 12.1. Transformational Mobilities (photograph courtesy of Andrew T. Barton).

The mountain wine regions of North America have experienced significant influx of amenity migrants and a rural gentrification (Travis, 2007) based on that mobility. Among those interviewed in the Okanagan, ten had moved to the region from elsewhere to work in the wine industry and not one of the twelve interviewed began their working lives in wine. The stories of that mobility and transition varied, but the role of tourism was significant and most shared a sense of how the move into wine and the Okanagan had changed their lives.

> My husband and I worked in the investment business. I was not a farmer. I had no farm experience. I am a city girl and we started the farming and wine making from scratch. There is a tourism piece to the story. I grew up in Calgary and we vacationed here for the mountains and the beaches, long before there was wine.
> (Interview 2)

The experiences of transitioning mobility among the hosts of wine tourism were demonstrated as life changing, transformational and occasionally dreamlike:

> Well, I did work for a quarter-century in investment banking. Life was not too bad, but I was miserable. I grew up in a wine family and this is always what I wanted to do. One of those classic things is how do I describe it?

> I turned left out of UBC and woke up 26 years later in a career in wine.
> (Interview 3)

The transformation from city life to running a winery was almost always propelled by tourism:

> We came to the Okanagan four years ago; we were vacationing here. Step by step we bought vineyards. It's everyone's dream. I am an engineer; there are lots of engineers in this wine industry.
> (Interview 4)

The Transformative Turning Point (Fig. 12.2)

The struggle to articulate the value or a single variable that makes the transitioning wine landscape uniquely attractive to visitors was common. Many mentioned the role of the mountain landscape in transforming the experience of place or consciousness and the single experience or turning point that changed their perspective.

> We've got a deck that looks out there [the lake]. For reasons I don't know, one day we sat down here and faced the other way, east, and we're looking at the mountain backdrop, kind of like what the tourists see and ... my god, it was a moment where we realized,

Fig. 12.2. The Turning Point (photograph courtesy of Andrew T. Barton).

it's not just the lake or the mountains or the vineyard, it is the whole package.

(Interview 3)

While lifestyle changes are often incremental, they were often described as abrupt turning points in the transitioning mountain environments:

I'm a Vancouver boy, this was life-changing. I'm sitting up top on the bluff and a moment that only living in the mountain valley will give you happens. It was absolutely silent for a moment ... when the water is flat, absolutely silent. There I am, cup of coffee in my hands, I go out, moon is there, sun coming up and my dog starts howling like a wolf, I figure there is a bear behind me and I'm about to get eaten and my heart jumped and I think, hell, I might as well face death head-on, and I turn around and there is nothing there, just the dog wagging his tail, and all of a sudden I could hear cars and crickets and trucks and I look at the dog and I'm alive. So that's it; that was the moment that changed everything.

(Interview 6)

Transforming Mountain Chaos into Order (Fig. 12.3)

The cultivation of valleys between the rugged rock profiles of the mountains presents a significant contrast of landscapes that has transformed the way visitors experience mountain settings in wine regions.

It is the contrasts between wild and cultivated. Especially the rocks against the vines.

(Interview 1)

It was anticipated that the interview subjects would capture the importance of bucolic agricultural life in the transitioning landscape. However, the importance of that rural idyll appeared central to the touristic experience, especially in contrast to the narrative of chaos, nature, and wildness of the mountain landscape. The soothing balm of the mountain setting was not anticipated.

Here is paradise. We have the vineyards, the mountains, the trees, and we have a lot of nightlife. In winter we have [cougars] in the mountains, we have bears that like to dine on grapes. We have everything, wild and not wild.

(Interview 4)

Some positioned the mathematical precision of the vines as a soothing balm against the chaos of nature.

It is my new perspective, you are sitting among the rows of vines that are very mathematically precise, ordered – people love that kind of order. The chaos is in between the

Fig. 12.3. Order and Chaos: Where the Mountain Meets the Vineyard (photograph courtesy of Andrew T. Barton).

rows – weeds and things like that. We train these trellises like soldiers in a Chinese tomb, these magical, geometric patterns. Looking at those things and the backdrop is the lake, and behind that is the silhouette of the mountains and people just stand there and go, 'Oh!', and they are changed.

(Interview 5)

While others confirm the inspirational value of wildness connected to cultivated order.

Those really old sage brushes that grow from the mountain … I'm curious about whether it is part of terroir, does the sage show up in the wine? I would argue that it does. The property I'm working on today, it's high, but about mid-bank is an amphitheatre of sage; it's incredible and, you know, the smells that come from that are just inspiring.

(Interview 2)

Living the Dream (Fig. 12.4) and Sharing the Work

Finally, the transformational, practical, and sometimes magic or spiritual idea of how the work of wine is the dream to be passed on to the tourist was often articulated in the interviews.

Beauty is in the eye of the beholder. I look at that vineyard, that order, and I see how well my trimmer is working. Am I going for the aesthetics? No, I'm going for the crop. I love the agricultural scene, I think it is beautiful. I had a group come, they knew they were coming to a winery and one of the first comments they made was: 'Where are we? What is this? This is a farm, we thought we were going to a winery.' I said, 'You are at a winery, wineries have vineyards, and vineyards are farms'. His vision of it was that a winery wasn't agriculture, he had no idea you grew grapes to make wine. See, it takes all kinds, it was quite an education I gave him!

(Interview 5)

The idea of transforming lives through tourism is key to notions of hopeful tourism, those interviewed expressed this principle through the contrasting experience of mountain and city life.

When the visitors come, they are surrounded by happy people and what's not to like? Those vineyard rows are part of our psyche, they lead you somewhere, like an escape route from something, I don't know what it is, but I sense that's what happens to them here. They love the wine, sure. It's easy, it is not a struggle like city life, it is a breath of fresh air they take home with them.

(Interview 12)

Fig. 12.4. The Dream on the Deck (photograph courtesy of Andrew T. Barton).

Others described this transformation of the touristic experience as ritual or even spiritual.

> The whole experience, people consume it when they visit and drink wine. Wine is not part of Canada food rules, we need social time and we need relaxation and we need rituals to rally around, but people drink wine to treat themselves and depending how good they have been, they treat themselves even more. So when they come to an actual winery, they are looking for the source of that treat, that ritual. Like they are at the source of life, chickens come home to roost or like they are at church. So there is some sort of fun in the whole thing and some reverence and some enjoyment.
>
> (Interview 1)

In mountain settings, the experience of landscape is often a dreamlike sequence. One winery proprietor gazed at his vineyard framed by the mountain vista for several moments, and then summed up the touristic experience in this setting.

> Everyone is in love with the vineyard and my deck is popular. On good days it is full of people enjoying my dream.
>
> (Interview 7)

Conclusion

Rural mountain communities have faced a barrage of difficulties in transitioning economic times. The downward spiral of resource economies and globalized competition for agricultural products in particular have made production-based economic activities unsustainable in many areas. Where agricultural landscapes meet the mountains, little to no succession planning among ageing farmers has serious repercussions for the fate of the family farm. Tourism has been used, with varying levels of success, as a tool of consumption to transition mountain communities through changing times. In particular, wine tourism in mountain communities holds some promise as a tool for transformative change as it links the amenities of mountain life and lifestyle with the productive capacity and culture of agricultural production. While amenity migrants, eager to leave city life for the dream of a winery in the country has been a driving force in winery growth, wine tourism has also meant a future for the family farm through succession plans that include winery production.

The transformational, often life-changing ideals articulated in these interviews and visualized in photographs indicate that the experience of winery visitation and working the winery can influence worldview of visitors and proprietors alike. Key themes articulated in this research include the nature of lifestyle mobility in mountain regions and the turning point that marks transformation, a contrast between the order of cultivation and the chaos of the mountains and sharing the transformative dream. The nostalgia for and a connection to rural winescapes as a salve to the effects of modernity sets a course for the life world change of hopeful tourism (Ateljevic *et al.*, 2013). The Okanagan experience reveals more than a simple understanding of the value of wine landscapes and wine touring that has been widely discussed in the academic literature, it shows the potential for hopeful tourism in this setting where mountain meets vineyard.

References

Ateljevic, I., Morgan, N. and Pritchard, A. (eds) (2013) *The Critical Turn in Tourism Studies: Creating an Academy of Hope*. Routledge, New York.

Belliveau, S., Smit, B. and Bradshaw, B. (2006) Multiple exposures and dynamic vulnerability: evidence from the grape industry in the Okanagan Valley, Canada. *Global Environmental Change* 16(4), 364–378.

British Columbia Wine Institute (BCWI) (2013) *The Economic Impact of the Grape and Wine Industry in Canada*. A report prepared by. F. Rimmerman and Company, St Helena, California.

Carlsen, J. and Charters, S. (eds) (2006) *Global Wine Tourism*. CAB International, Wallingford, UK.

Carmichael, B.A. (2004) Understanding the wine tourism experience for winery visitors in the Niagara Region, Ontario Canada. *Tourism Geographies* 7(2), 185–204.

Carmichael, B.A. and Senese, D.M. (2012) Competitiveness and sustainability in wine tourism regions: the application of a stage model of destination development to two Canadian wine regions. In: Dougherty, P.H. (ed.) *The Geography of Wine*. Springer, Netherlands, pp. 159–178.

Chipeniuk, R. (2004) Planning for amenity migration in Canada. *Mountain Research and Development* 24(4), 327–335.

Di Giovane, M. (2008) *Heritage-Scape: UNESCO, World Heritage and Tourism*. Rowman and Littlefield Publishers, Lanham, Maryland.

Dodd, T.H. (1995) Opportunities and pitfalls of tourism in a developing wine industry. *International Journal of Wine Marketing* 7(1), 5–16.

Duarte Alonso, A. and Northcote, J. (2009) Wine, history, landscape: origin branding in Western Australia. *British Food Journal* 111(11), 1248–1259.

Fanet, J. (2004) *Great Wine Terroirs*. University of California Press, Los Angeles, California.

Getz, D. (2000) *Explore Wine Tourism: Management, Development and Destination*. Cognizant Communication Corporation, New York.

Getz, D. and Brown, G. (2006) Benchmarking wine tourism development: the case of the Okanagan Valley, British Columbia, Canada. *International Journal of Wine Marketing* 18, 78–97.

Gilbert, D.C. (1992) Touristic development of a viticultural region of Spain. *International Journal of Wine Marketing* 4(2), 25–32.

Hall, C.M., Sharples, E., Cambourne, B. and Macionis, N. (eds) (2000) *Wine Tourism Around the World: Development, Management and Markets*. Butterworth-Heinemann, Oxford, UK.

Hall, C.M., Sharples, L., Mitchell, R., Macionis, N. and Cambourne, B. (2003) *Food Tourism Around the World: Development, Management and Markets*. Butterworth-Heinemann, Oxford, UK.

Harvey, D. (1989) *The Condition of Postmodernity*. Blackwell, Oxford, UK.

Hashimoto, A. and Telfer, D.J. (2003) Positioning an emerging wine route in the Niagara Region: understanding the wine tourism market and its implications for marketing. *Journal of Travel & Tourism Marketing* 14(3–4), 61–76.

Johnson, H. and Robinson, J. (2009) *The Concise World Atlas of Wine*. Mitchell Beazley, London.

Macionis, N. and Cambourne, B. (1998) Wine tourism: just what is it all about? *Australian & New Zealand Wine Industry Journal* 13(1), 41–47.

Mezirow, J. (1978) *Education for Perspective Transformation. Women's Re-entry Programs in Community Colleges*. Teachers College, Columbia University, New York.

Murray, W.E. and Overton, J. (2011) Defining regions: the making of places in the New Zealand wine industry. *Australian Geographer* 42(4), 419–433.

Overton, J. (2010) The consumption of space: land, capital and place in the New Zealand wine industry. *Geoforum* 41(5), 752–762.

Overton, J. and Murray, W.E. (2013) Class in a glass: capital, neoliberalism and social space in the global wine industry. *Antipode* 45(3), 702–718.

Overton, J., Murray, W.E. and Silva, F.P. (2012) The remaking of Casablanca: the sources and impacts of rapid local transformation in Chile's wine industry. *Journal of Wine Research* 23(1), 47–59.

Piscolla, I. (2007) *Guida alle Strade del Vino e dei Sapori*. Centro Studi e Servizi Strade del Vino e dei Sapori, Associazione Nazionale del Vino, Castelnuovo del Beredenga, Tuscany, Italy.

Poitras, L. and Getz, D. (2006) Sustainable wine tourism: the host community perspective. *Journal of Sustainable Tourism* 14(5), 425–448.

Pritchard, A. and Morgan, N. (2013) Hopeful tourism: a transformational perspective. In: Reisinger, Y. (ed.) *Transformational Tourism, Tourist Perspectives*. CAB International, Wallingford, UK. pp. 3–14.

Pritchard, A., Morgan, N. and Ateljevic, I. (2011) Hopeful tourism: a new transformative perspective. *Annals of Tourism Research* 38(3), 941–963.

Reisinger, Y. (2013) Connection between travel, tourism and transformation. In: Reisinger, Y. (ed.) *Transformational Tourism, Tourist Perspectives*. CAB International, Wallingford, UK, pp. 27–32.

Senese, D. (2008) Turismo enogastronomico Canadese, la nuova frontiera del turismo combinata all'ecoturismo e al turismo culturale. *Biteg: Congresso Internatzionale Sul Turismo Enogastronomico*, Saint Vincent, Italy.

Senese, D. (2010) Amenity resources and rural change in the Okanagan Valley of British Columbia. In: Beesley, K.B. (ed.) *The Rural–Urban Fringe in Canada: Conflict and Controversy*. Brandon University, Rural Development Institute, Brandon, Manitoba, Canada, pp. 158–175.

Senese, D.M., Wilson, W. and Momer, B. (2012) The Okanagan wine region of British Columbia, Canada. In: Dougherty, P.H. (ed.) *The Geography of Wine*. Springer, Netherlands, pp. 81–91.

Spawton, T. (1986) Understanding wine purchasing. *Wine Industry Journal* 1(2), 54–57.

Tourism BC Research and Planning (2009) *Okanagan Valley Wine Consumer Research Study 2008 Results*. Tourism British Columbia, Victoria, British Columbia, Canada.

Travis, W.R. (2007) *New Geographies of the American West. Land Use and Changing Patterns of Place*. Island Press, Washington, DC.

Unwin, T. (2012) Terroir: at the heart of geography. In: Dougherty, P.H. (ed.) *The Geography of Wine. Regions, Terroir and Techniques*. Springer, Netherlands, pp. 37–48.

Urry, J. (1990) *The Tourist Gaze: Leisure and Travel in Contemporary Societies*. Sage, London.

Wagner, J.R. (2008) Landscape aesthetics, water, and settler colonialism in the Okanagan Valley of British Columbia. *Journal of Ecological Anthropology* 12(1), 22–38.

Weaver, D. (2014) The sustainable development of tourism. A state of the art perspective. In: Lew, A.A., Hall, C.M. and Williams, A.M. (eds) *The Wiley Blackwell Companion to Tourism*. Wiley, Chichester, UK, pp. 524–533.

13 Sustainable Tourism in the Carpathians

László Puczkó,[1]* Michael Meyer,[2] Martina Voskarova[2] and Ivett Sziva[1]
[1]Xellum Ltd, Budapest, Hungary; [2]Ecological Tourism in Europe (ETE), Bonn, Germany

Introduction

This chapter describes the development of a sustainable tourism strategy for the Carpathian mountain system. Seven countries share the Carpathians, the second-longest mountain range in Europe. The Carpathians have great potential for tourism, though they are relatively unknown and less developed when compared to the Alps. The seven countries follow unique strategies and use different methods of tourism development, which may limit the expected positive contributions from tourism and/ or allow tourism to have a negative impact on local communities and the mountainous landscape.

The efforts of developing sustainable tourism in the Carpathians crystallized in preparation of a joint tourism development strategy. The purpose of the strategy was to determine common actions and measures in order to value and sustainably use the outstanding natural and cultural assets for sustainable tourism development of the Carpathians. The strategy, which provides the basis for this chapter, aims at harmonizing and coordinating country-specific approaches by providing a common understanding and umbrella platform for planning and management. The preparation of the strategy is not a stand-alone activity; it is part of a comprehensive effort of the group referred to as Parties to the Carpathian Convention (http://www.carpathianconvention.org) with a key purpose to coordinate the responsible use, protection and promotion of the Carpathians as a tourism destination.

The Carpathians

The Carpathian mountain system is unique on both a European and global scale. The Carpathians are one of Europe's largest mountain ranges, which cover about 210,000 km². Spreading widely towards the North and South, they extend in an arc for 1450 kilometres from the Eastern part of Czech Republic to the Iron Gate in Serbia. These mountains form one of the very last regions in the centre of Europe particularly rich in great beauty of natural resources, due to its wide diversity of landscapes and vegetation types, traditional cultural landscape and forms of land use, as well as a rich and diverse folklore.

The Carpathian region provides some of Europe's cleanest streams and drinking water

---

* Corresponding author: lpuczko@xellum.hu

supplies, and contains Europe's greatest reserve of pristine forest. The area represents a unique composition of ecosystems with an exceptionally high biological diversity. Relatively small population densities, difficult access to many mountain ranges and a considerable number of large forests have allowed a rich and diverse flora and fauna to exist in the Carpathians. As a result of far-reaching transformations of the natural environment in Central Europe, the Carpathians have remained either the only or the most important refuge for many plant and animal species, playing a significant role in the preservation of biological diversity in Europe (Fig. 13.1).

The Carpathians share geography with seven Central and Eastern European countries: Czech Republic, Hungary, Poland, Romania, Serbia, Slovak Republic and Ukraine, five of which (Slovakia, Hungary, Romania, Czech Republic and Poland) are members of the European Union (EU). The Carpathians are currently home to an estimated 18 million people. Ties linking the Carpathian countries are notice-able in languages, music, similar folklore, etc. Looking at historical information, many of the areas in question have a deeply rooted common heritage. For example, south-eastern Poland and Czech Republic, Slovakia, western Ukraine and Hungary have cultural and political traditions associated with Austro-Hungarian spheres of interest and trading partnerships.

Tourism in the Carpathians

Europe is the most-visited region of the world, accounting for 54.8% of all international travellers. UNWTO figures (2014) showed that before 2005, Central and Eastern Europe (CEE), in which the Carpathians are located, did not really play a significant role in international tourism. The Central and Eastern European region attracted 10.9% (87.9 million) of all international travellers (806 million). Since 2010, tourism in Central and Eastern Europe has improved with the number of international arrivals reaching 113.7 million in 2012. It must

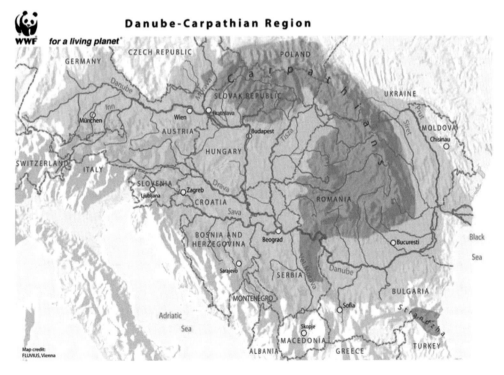

Fig. 13.1. Map of the Danube-Carpathian Region (source: http://www.internationalrivers.org/resources/defending-the-danube-1809).

be highlighted that the CEE has low performance among the European regions, with a
share of 21.1% from all European international
arrivals. Trend data suggest that CEE enjoys
the highest rate of growth in terms of tourism
development of all the regions in Europe. It is
estimated the actual Carpathian region (i.e.
considering only those regions and counties
that are geographically located in the mountain
range) receives close to 45 million overnight
stays (including both domestic and international
travellers) in a year.

The recent global financial crisis impacted
tourism within the Carpathian countries when
incoming tourist numbers as well as guest nights
fell. Only a couple of years after the crisis, however, tourism rebounded in all of the Carpathian
countries (after Bieger and Keller, 2011).

In terms of tourist arrivals and guest
nights, Poland, Hungary and the Czech Republic showed the strongest revival. It is estimated that domestic tourism is most important
in Poland (with 47.5 million guest nights). The
average length of stay is rather high in Ukraine
(4.97 days in 2011), while 3 days seems to be
the average in the other countries (where Pol-
and represents above-average stays, while Romania and Serbia both average 2.1 nights;
Popovic *et al.*, 2012).

Based on the data regarding the volume of
international excursionists (i.e. tourists who
visit a country and do not spend a night; EC,
2012; IPK, 2012), Poland (47 million) and
Hungary (31 million) seem to have the greatest
potential to switch same-day trips to longer-
stay visits. For example, Table 13.1 shows the
current number of overseas guests that spend
at least one night. By converting a relatively
small percentage of day visitors to overnight
visitors, this could have a significant increase in
international overseas visitation.

Several CEE countries built the international communication on the 'natural' theme,
i.e. mainly the Carpathian regions of the respective countries (Fig. 13.2). Poland used 'The
Natural Choice' slogan; in the logo of Romania
the Carpathians are resembled. In Hungary
2007 was the 'Year of Green Tourism'.

Interestingly, and not unrelated to the
Carpathian tourism theme, many countries in
the region from Poland to Austria refer to
themselves as 'The country in the Centre/
Heart of Europe'.

Background to the Strategy

The Carpathian Convention is a sub-regional
treaty to foster the sustainable development and
the protection of the Carpathian region. The
seven Carpathian countries signed it in May
2003. The basis for comprehensive international
cooperation in the Carpathians was laid down by
'The Framework Convention on the Protection
and Sustainable Development of the Carpathians'
(Carpathian Convention), which was adopted
and signed by the seven Parties (Czech Republic, Hungary, Poland, Romania, Serbia, Slovak

Table 13.1. Key Tourism Data in CEE Countries
(source: EC, 2012; IPK, 2012; UNWTO, 2013, 2014).

Country	Overnight stays of non-resident tourists in all types of accommodation establishments (millions)
Poland	10.6
Hungary	9.0
Czech Republic	6.3
Ukraine	6.0 (based on estimations)
Slovakia	4.0
Romania	3.0
Serbia	1.6

Note: Data based on country figures. It would have
been highly important to analyse the Intra-Carpathian
tourism flow, but due to the lack of the entity of
Carpathians, there are no relevant data available.

explore the Carpathian garden

Fig. 13.2. Logos used to promote tourism in the
Carpathians (logos courtesy of www.poland.travel
and romaniatourism.com).

Republic, Ukraine) in May 2003 in Kiev, Ukraine, and entered into force in January 2006 (http:// www.carpathianconvention.org/the-convention-17.html).

Tourism has been one of the priority areas of the Convention. In line with the objectives of the Carpathian Convention, the 3rd Conference of the Parties adopted the 'Protocol on Sustainable Tourism for the Framework Convention on the Protection and Sustainable Development of the Carpathians' in May 2011. In 2013, as a first implementation step, the Parties decided to develop and adopt the 'Strategy on Sustainable Tourism Development in the Carpathians' (Carpathian Convention, 2013). The most relevant chapters in the Protocol set out the fundamentals of the Strategy and are translated into a common action plan (e.g. Article 6: Participation of stakeholders; Article 7: International cooperation; Article 8: Promotion of the Carpathian region; Article 9: Development of regional sustainable tourism products; Article 10: Ensuring common high quality standards; Article 11: Enhancing the contribution of tourism to local economies, etc.).

The Convention signed a cooperation agreement (Advisory Assistance Programme for Environmental Protection in the Countries of Central and Eastern Europe, the Caucasus and Central Asia) with the German Federal Ministry for the Environment, Nature Conservation, Building and Nuclear Safety. As an element of this agreement, the German partner provided financial support for the preparation of the Sustainable Tourism Strategy for the Carpathians in 2013–2014. The planning process was supervised by the German Federal Agency for Nature Conservation (Bundesamt für Naturschutz (BfN).

In the years 2013 and 2014 more than 800 individuals and organizations provided feedback on the strategy during a number of country consultation meetings. During the project, seven country experts were identified, and they implemented a consultation process in each country of the Carpathians in order to collect comments from the stakeholders to improve the strategy draft and discuss the geographical scope for the Carpathian Tourism Strategy. The comments and recommendations of these consultations were considered and incorporated in the final version of the strategy. The Ecological Tourism in Europe (ETE) with the help of its partners Central Eastern Europe (CEE) web for Biodiversity (http://www.ceeweb.org/work-areas/working-groups/sustainable-tourism), WWF-Danube-Carpathian Programme Office (WWF-DCPO) and the Secretariat of the Carpathian Convention (UNEP-SCC) carried out coordination of the consultation process in the years 2013–2014.

Critical Assessment of the Carpathians

During the strategy development process, detailed analysis of the existing strengths and weaknesses was compiled and analysed (Table 13.2). It was understood that the Carpathians could be seen as a geographical region but not yet as a destination. This is probably the most important weakness identified by the strategy.

In spite of the numerous weaknesses, the mountain range can consider several opportunities that can help or facilitate tourism development in the region. Various EU funds are available in European Union member countries and non-EU countries in the form of cross-border cooperations. These funds, according to the priorities of the national development plans, tend to support tourism, infrastructure and social developments, although in various cases and countries the use of these funds was not fully explored. All of the Carpathian countries, to different degrees, are considered as economies in transition, which directly affects domestic and international tourism (e.g. in terms of frequency of trips and spending power). Since trips in general are getting shorter, it can be expected that people visit other places rather than the distant coastal areas, such as new destinations in mountains or inland lakes. For those using budget airlines, air travel definitely can and does play a significant role.

There are certain threats that may adversely influence the implementation and management of the strategy. Existing tourism product supply (skiing, snowboarding, mountain climbing, trekking, bird watching, hunting, fishing, rafting, parachuting, spas, city visits, festivals, events, gastronomy, folk traditions) is

Table 13.2. Strengths and weaknesses of the Carpathians as a tourism destination.

Strengths	Weaknesses
Strong natural and cultural assets, which are seen as 'exotic'	Strong natural and cultural assets, which are not yet well known
Widespread pristine environment, which can be attractive to guests from (over-)populated and polluted urban areas	High seasonality of tourism demand
Relatively underdeveloped, which makes the Carpathians seem and feel natural and not artificial	Tourism marketing and targeting is not always focused
Traditional and rich culture and heritage (e.g. languages, folk and culinary art, events)	There are seven countries involved, which also means seven languages, legislation, organizational structures, etc.
'New destination' status makes prospective visitors curious and interested	Non-governmental sector is not of the same strength in every Carpathian country. NGOs (like Greenways or CEEweb) have limited funds and resources
Natural beauty of the landscape	Lack of maintenance of already existing services and facilities
Multi-seasonal natural and cultural assets	Weakly developed social capital, mistrust and unwillingness to cooperate (political, historical and economic reasons)
Development and operational local and regional tourism organizations in most areas	Difficult to coordinate cross-border entry and various other administrative issues – two of the seven countries (Serbia and Ukraine) are not yet members of the EU
Good location in terms of international tourism	The link and communication between 'nature' and 'culture'
Attractive price/quality ratios of services	Ad-hoc planning and management is typical to many areas. Every EU member country prepares its National and Regional Development Plans, in which sustainable tourism had to be taken into account, but the ways in which these plans are to be implemented are not always transparent
Availability of nature and adventure tourism services (e.g. skiing, nature trails)	Monitoring and assessment of developments are rarely implemented
Improving access (growing number of regional airports)	Destination management practices are just in the beginning phase at Carpathian level (with good practices at local levels in numerous destinations)
	Everyday social problems dominate politics and budget negotiations (i.e. fighting poverty and unemployment). Sustainability may not be a priority. Quick (financial) returns and benefits are always favoured, while long-term impacts are not considered.
	Other economic activities (e.g. forestry, extracting industry) do influence natural and cultural environments
	Infrastructure system is underdeveloped, which makes tourism access very difficult
	Lack of necessary skills, knowledge and experience in sustainable practices among entrepreneurs, local communities and governmental sector
	Quality of services varies and is not reliable
	Lack of trustworthy and comparable data on tourism and related fields at Carpathian level
	The role of politics and that of some pressure groups (e.g. land owners, agriculture or hunters) put a pressure on conservation and integrated development and management

a great baseline for sustainable tourism, though the impacts should be monitored, the quality should be controlled and sound development is needed. Without integrated planning, developers will want more locations to be involved and to have more visitors, which leads to more intensive use of resources. The travel and tourism industry shows more interest in sustainable practices, especially if these can be translated to higher financial returns and/or decreased costs. In Europe the demand for responsible tourism is growing, which is a key market-generating factor for the Carpathians. There are efforts and initiatives by NGOs within the region significantly focusing on conservation, preservation and development of natural areas and local heritage.

The once favourable price/quality ratio made the region attractive, but price-led image and competition is always very dangerous and not sustainable. Inexpensive prices may seem to be tempting for Western visitors, but this may lead to price competition, where sustainability is much less of a priority. Development funds (e.g. provided by the EU) are used for quick-win economic developments, not taking nature and culture into consideration. There is pressure from developers/municipalities for quick (visible) results, which may lead to unsustainable but maintainable developments or 'greenwashing'. Nature conservation and management are in continuous competition with other user activities such as forestry or hunting. Also the success of the implementation of the strategy very much depends on local communities, but apathy by rural communities is an important challenge and is in numerous cases widespread.

Vision and Objectives

The vision of the proposed strategy encompasses three dimensions – competitiveness, conservation and cooperation – all of which are fundamental to adding value to tourism.

1. The Carpathians are a top competitive sustainable tourism destination in Europe, based on their unique natural and cultural heritage preserved and maintained over large integral areas.

2. The people in the Carpathians are successful in, and proud of, maintaining their local authentic traditions, cultures and landscapes, which contribute to unique tourist experiences.
3. Good cooperation, local management and partnerships contribute to the high quality of responsible tourism and ecosystem services, which ensures continuous benefits for local communities and economies.

The three objectives address the necessary conditions and management of sustainable tourism as well as referring to educational and awareness-raising aspects. In order to become a top sustainable tourism destination, it was agreed that three objectives form the targets to accomplish the vision by 2024.

The first objective is defined as 'Establish supportive conditions for sustainable tourism products and services, including development of a marketing scheme for the promotion of the Carpathians as a unique sustainable destination'. Under consideration is the possible creation of a certification and/or labelling system for sustainable tourism for the Carpathian Brand, supported by a Carpathian-wide marketing strategy. The creation of a Carpathian identity and making use of a logo/slogan is expected to be compulsory for all those service suppliers who joined and were labelled under the Carpathians product-line. It is also considered to be necessary to develop a Carpathian-wide quality standard system, local products and local services (e.g. 'Local food', 'Local accommodation', 'Local experience – how to guide tourists', 'Code of Conduct for Tourists in the Carpathians'). Common principles and guidelines on tourism infrastructure and activities are being developed to make them sustainable.

Another aspect is the establishment of a tour operator's cooperation platform, and designing and introducing, where applicable, a common system of marking trails throughout the Carpathians, which would support the feel of belonging to a single destination. This would need to be supported through the development and the use of a common online Carpathian platform for sustainable tourism, including a products and services database, trans-boundary products and mapping, as well as good practices, with continuously updated information, and the preparation of a Carpathian tourist map.

Finally, to complement tourism services it is necessary to develop and to manage an online platform promoting labelled products, linking with the websites of National Tourist Offices (NTOs).

A second objective of the strategy declares that it has to 'Develop innovative tourism management, fully integrating the needs of local people and economies and other supporting sectors, and respecting the preservation of natural and cultural heritage'. In terms of innovative tourism management, the strategy initiates resource mobilization for the implementation of the strategy at national and international levels involving all relevant stakeholders. This mobilization would include the development of a common communication paper on the Carpathian Brand and define the Carpathian Brand and its management structure with relation to other sectoral or geographical brands. Member countries would need to analyse their tourism resources, based on research to identify the key areas and products, and undertake further detailed research. The development of guidelines for the contribution of the tourism sector to the conservation of natural and cultural resources would also be necessary.

The development of a methodology for monitoring the impact of existing and planned tourism development on biodiversity and landscapes, including the social, economic and cultural impact, would facilitate implementation. Such a methodology would necessitate the definition and implementation of a common set of indicators on the effects of implemented policies and strategies for developing sustainable tourism in the Carpathians. The strategy initiates the establishment of an organizational unit (Carpathian Observatory on Sustainable Tourism), and also contributes to the implementation of the Sustainable Tourism Protocol and this strategy by monitoring and evaluation of tourism activities in the Carpathians. The Parties are invited to develop methods for the protection of 'brand-making' elements of the Carpathians' cultural heritage by implementing common projects for the preservation of cultural heritage. The seven countries are expected to support the setting up of a common mechanism for the implementation of the strategy. The definition and implementation of common guidelines for the support of sustainable local

supply chains, as well as for a scheme to monitor traffic to destinations and within destinations, will also be necessary.

The third objective states that it should establish a continuous process of awareness raising, capacity building, education and training on sustainable tourism development and management at all levels. To achieve this objective, the creation of an online platform for education, training and sharing of best practices available to all stakeholders will be necessary. Also, the development of a programme of workshops, conferences and study visits in order to exchange innovative experience on sustainable tourism development will be an important component. This is expected to include exchanging know-how and cooperation with other destinations on the contribution of tourism to biodiversity and cultural heritage conservation.

Challenges Ahead

During the consultations, stakeholders emphasized that this mountain area is facing a number of challenges, to be tackled with this strategy in joint efforts. Based on the critical assessment of the current situation, we judge that the most challenging tasks are coordination and communication-related activities. The future of the Carpathians as an attractive sustainable tourism destination, which is able to compete on the international tourism market, is largely dependent on the cooperation of all the sectors (governmental, business, non-governmental) to plan, develop and manage activities in the region in such a way that the existing natural and cultural resources are maintained in order for domestic and international visitors to enjoy a great experience.

Sustainable tourism that benefits local communities and national economies requires sound communication between all the involved stakeholders. The growing popularity of mountain areas, however, poses a potential threat to the health of their natural and cultural resources. The tourism sector's competitiveness is closely linked to the sustainability of its base, i.e. the natural and cultural assets. There is a challenge in coordinating tourism infrastructure developments, managing tours and tourist activities to avoid impacts on fragile ecosystems, as well as on the communities that inhabit mountain regions. The sustainability of nature and culture covers a number of considerations, including: (i) a large number of stakeholders; (ii) the responsible use of natural resources, taking account of the environmental impact of activities (pollution, production of waste, pressure on biodiversity, water and land resources, etc.); (iii) the use of 'clean' energy; (iv) protection of the heritage and preservation of the natural and cultural integrity of destinations; (v) the quality and sustainability of jobs created; (vi) local economic fallout; and (vii) customer care.

Product development in relation to sustainable tourism leaves the seven countries with many challenges. Several tourism products and leisure activities are very similar all across the Carpathians (e.g. nature walks, skiing, bird watching). This leaves the private and non-profit sector parties across the region with the challenge of working together for mutual benefit and advantage. Also, development plans and incentives may foster the development of services and products that are based on and/or are using local ingredients and materials (e.g. signature products to the region).

Climate change may leave the region with irreversible alterations of both natural and cultural systems and the tourism products that are built on them. The challenges are how to predict irreversible changes, and how to prepare alternative plans and management solutions to avoid a destination becoming dependent on a single form of tourism. Governments, either national or local, need sufficient and applicable planning and monitoring structures regarding infrastructure and superstructure developments all across the region.

Tourism as a cross-industry activity requires not only the harmonization of services but that of quality, too. Common standards can be used as a means of creating cohesion between market players and management organizations. The acceptance of similar standards that are applicable across the region and the tourism industry may improve industry knowledge and attitude towards quality. Development of the Carpathian-wide standards such as for rural accommodation, nature trails and guides, skiing or mountaineering,

however, requires close cooperation and coordination of all the sectors involved. Sustainable development-oriented approaches necessitate the presence and use of harmonized criteria and indicators. Without the involvement of governments, monitoring and assessment cannot be performed across the regions and against similar standards and thresholds.

Common branding and marketing of the Carpathians as a sustainable tourism destination leaves marketers with significant challenges, since such branding requires permanent market surveying, flexible and progressive market responses. Without joining forces, this common branding can only be performed partially and in a fragmented manner. A common Carpathian brand would need jointly accepted brand architecture (personality, identity, etc.), so that target markets (including two key groups for the future of European tourism selected by the European Commission within the framework of social tourism, family or children, and the 60+ age group) and have a better understanding of the great assets and resources of the Carpathians. Successful common branding cannot take place without coordination and communication between stakeholders or harmonized product development and industry standards. Table 13.3 translates the objectives and challenges of the sustainable tourism strategy for the Carpathian mountain system to tourism product-related focus areas.

Monitoring of the Implementation

The adoption of the strategy was only the first step in a long process. The strategy defined a series of monitoring activities and milestones against which implementation can be checked and actions or changes to the original tasks can be agreed upon.

Governments are expected to adjust their voluntary and legal frameworks for the support of sustainable tourism based on common assessments. It is understood that the strategy needs a coordination and operational platform for product development, promotion, marketing and monitoring. A number of laboratories and incubators are to be established as learning institutions on sustainable tourism practices for

Table 13.3. Key tourism products: objectives and activities envisioned.

Focus areas	Products/services investors find interesting	Sustainable practices needed	Countries
Rural tourism	Repositioning the existing accommodation, green practices	Using local materials, products, building authentic, green facilities, identifying the unique experience promises of 'Carpathians Rural Lifestyle'	Carpathian-wide
Slow movement	Developing new agrotourism networks	Sustainable agriculture, broaden the Carpathian Culinary Heritage Network	Carpathian-wide
Heritage tourism	Hotel developments in (historic and business) cities	Complex and balanced supply of accommodation at destinations, development of thematic roads	Carpathian-wide
Geotourism	Specialized tour operator services	Sustainable management, maintenance of the paths, code of behaviour for tourists	Carpathian-wide
Adventure tourism	Specialized tour operator services	Sustainable management, maintenance of the paths, parks, code of behaviour for tourists (walking, horse riding, cycling/ biking)	Poland, Slovakia, Ukraine, Romania
Ecotourism	Building eco-friendly, green lodges	Visitor management issues in national parks, green certification, code of behaviour for tourists	Carpathian-wide
Baths, mountain healing	Repositioning existing spas and developing new ones, using climate therapy as USP of Carpathians	Assuring access for locals, offering local products, therapies, treatments	Romania, Hungary, Ukraine, Serbia, Slovakia
Dark Sky Parks	Developing special themed parks, e.g. Dark Sky Parks (see Appendix)	Visitor management, code of behaviour for tourists	Poland, Slovakia, Ukraine, Romania, Serbia
Tourism products that can be considered but requiring special attention and considerations			
Skiing and cross-country skiing	Building green lodges, developing ski resorts	Reconsideration of the 'Sustainable Slopes' concept	Poland, Slovakia, Romania, Ukraine
Service elements			
Accommodation	Developing eco-lodges, eco-certification and identifying 'Carpathian accommodation style'	Consideration of how architecture, gastronomy and additional services can be incorporated to 'Carpathian accommodation style'	Carpathian-wide
Transportation	Developing and coordinating transportation infrastructure and services (esp. airports, trains)	Complex transportation infrastructure developments, zoning, identifying non-motorized areas, villages, developing local public transport (e.g. bus transfers)	Carpathian-wide

providers and communities. An information system is expected to be established throughout the Carpathians, which will provide online solutions and data for monitoring and serving visitors. A properly managed network of hiking, biking, skiing and horse riding trails is also expected to be created. Qualified products and services following common quality standards are to be integrated into a labelling system (i.e. the so-called 'The Carpathian Experience' label). The implementation is expected to include the establishment of a network of ecotourism destinations, which involves Carpathian service providers communicating to tourists the value of this mountain region based on a code of practice.

Since there is no formal destination management organization (DMO) at the regional level (and often at local levels), the collection of specific data may be rather unrealistic at this stage. However, if all the involved governments and stakeholders applied the step-by-step approach, the collection of data and reporting would become feasible (see suggested monitoring steps and activities in Appendix).

Summary

The first regional tourism strategy for the Carpathians aims at the sustainable development of the region. There are numerous destinations that have already become popular with domestic as well foreign tourists (especially skiing). Still, members of the Carpathian Convention look at the examples of already established destinations, especially the Alps. The lessons learned from such examples, whether favourable or unfavourable, can support the development efforts in the Carpathians.

The strategy has a very complex set of tasks and a plan to accomplish. The application of the strategy to the seven countries and to the relevant regions and communities requires not only substantial training, but also the adoption of a meta-management concept of destination management and, focusing on local initiations, monitoring.

The Parties to the Carpathian Convention have not yet decided on the geographical application of the objectives and the protocols in force of the Convention (see more at http://www.unep.org/ecosystemmanagement; UNEP, 2011). According to the results of the consultations with stakeholders in the seven countries during summer 2013, the interest was expressed to enlarge the scope of application for the Carpathian Tourism Strategy to an area that covers more than just the mountain territories of the Carpathians.

The implementation of the objectives of this strategy may well increase the competitiveness of the Carpathians as a mega-destination. To the seven countries, the mega-destination status refers to the international or global appeal. The Carpathians have the natural and cultural assets that, with careful planning and management of a competitive as well as a sustainable destination, may emerge and become successful.

Appendix
Steps and Elements of the Monitoring System

Phase 1 (2015)

1. Choose one destination in each of the seven countries, which is representative for tourism development in mountains in the Carpathians.
2. Collect data according to the set of indicators.
3. Apply TQoL methodology (Puczkó and Smith, 2011).
4. Deliver the data to the national statistical office for further processing.
5. Launch hotel/accommodation performance benchmarking (online system to indicate impacts of events, festivals, etc.). Present quarterly data.
6. Deliver the data to the Carpathian Coordination Centre for reporting.

Phase 2 (2016–2020)

7. Review set of indicators according to lessons learned in the destinations.
8. Establish a number of destinations, which cover the entire region of the Carpathians (if necessary, establish trans-boundary destinations).
9. Collect data in each destination according to the revised set of indicators.
10. Apply TQoL methodology to indicate changes.
11. Deliver the data to the national statistical office for further processing.
12. Deliver the data to the Carpathian Coordination Centre for reporting.
13. First comprehensive report on 'Tourism Impacts in the Carpathians' is accomplished in 2020.

Phase 3 (2021–)

14. Review set of indicators according to lessons learned in all the destinations.

15. Implement data collection and reporting in all destinations according to steps 7–9 in Phase 2.
16. Publish a report on 'Tourism Impacts in the Carpathians' at intervals of 4 years.

References

Bieger, T. and Keller, P. (2011) *Tourism Development after the Crises: Global Imbalances – Poverty Alleviation.* Erich Schmidt, Berlin, Germany.

Carpathian Convention (2013) Protocol on Sustainable Tourism for the Framework Convention on the Protection and Sustainable Development of the Carpathians. Available at: http://www.carpathian convention.org/tl_files/carpathiancon/Downloads/01%20The%20Convention/1.1.1.1_Carpathian Convention.pdf (accessed 9 September 2014).

EC (2012) Brussels Declaration on Via Carpathia.

IPK (2012) ITB World Travel Trends Report December 2012. Available at: http://www.itb-berlin.de/media/itbk/ itbk_dl_all/itbk_dl_all_itbkongress/itbk_dl_all_itbkongress_itbkongress365/itbk_dl_all_itbkongress_ itbkongress365_itblibrary/itbk_dl_all_itbkongress_itbkongress365_itblibrary_studien/ITB_World_ Travel_Trends_Report_2012_2013.pdf (accessed 7 January 2016).

Popovic, V., *et al.* (2012) Sustainable tourism development in the Carpathian region in Serbia. *SPATIUM International Review* 28(December), 45–52.

Puczkó, L. and Smith, M. (2011) Tourism-specific quality-of-life index: the Budapest model. In: Budruk, M. and Phillips, R. (eds) *Quality-of-Life Community Indicators for Parks, Recreation and Tourism Management.* Social Indicators Research Series, Volume 43, Springer, Dordrecht, Netherlands, pp. 163–183.

UNEP (2011) Strategic Action Plan for the Carpathian Area. Available at: http://www.unep.at/carpathian convention/tl_files/carpathiancon/Downloads/02%20Activities/2.1.2%20Strategic%20Action %20Plan%20for%20the%20Carpathian%20Area.pdf (accessed 30 August 2014).

UNWTO (2013) Factbook. Available at: http://www.e-unwto.org (accessed 16 August 2014).

UNWTO (2014) *Yearbook of Tourism Statistics, Data 2008–2012,* 2014 edn. UNWTO, Madrid, Spain.

14 Leisure Living in the Alps

Aurelia Kogler[1]* and Philipp Boksberger[2]
[1]*MONTCON Tourism, Austria and HTW Chur, Switzerland;*
[2]*Lorange Institute, Switzerland*

Introduction

Alpine tourism has evolved slowly but steadily from an isolated phenomenon in the 19th century to a mature tourism market in the 21st century. Not surprisingly, tourism in the Alps has been the focus of various scientific contributions. It is therefore well recognized that the following four factors significantly influence the spatial development in the Alpine region in general (Schuckert and Boksberger, 2008).

First, the usable space is very limited in the Alps. Between 5% and 20% of the alpine surface only can be used for private or commercial activities. Compared to other regions, the space for tourism development is very limited. Second, the real-estate situation in the Alps can be described as highly fragmented in consequence of small lots of land as a result of the historic agricultural structure of land ownership. This leads to the characteristic situation that various stakeholders (land owners) need to be democratically involved in the development of alpine destinations. Third, tourism is generally in competition and, sometimes, conflict with other non-compatible industries that may create even higher value added for the region. Additionally, for many of the typical small and medium-sized tourism enterprises (SME) in the

Alps, property (real estate) is the only source of equity capital. Fourth, the market for tourism real estate is in conflict with private real-estate markets for domestic living or second homes as well as retirement homes for non-domestic parties.

In addition, the evolution of tourism in the Alps from growth to maturity has resulted in some significant consequences for the lodging industry. In the context of steady or declining numbers of destination arrivals and the tendency towards fewer overnight stays over the last couple of years, the number of commercial guest beds shrank in many Alpine destinations, while at the same time, the demand and supply for vacation homes increased (Bieger *et al.*, 2005; Stettler and Giovanni, 2008). In Switzerland the development of second homes in most destinations is restricted following a referendum in March 2012. In contrast, the development of vacation ownerships, classic timeshare resorts (e.g. Hapimag) and second homes with an obligation to let, which usually generate higher frequencies and bring more benefits for the destination, will still be possible.

This chapter reports on business models in the Alpine lodging industry, using examples from French, Swiss and Austrian Alpine destinations. The explorative research is focusing

---

* Corresponding author: aurelia.kogler@htwchur.ch

explicitly on the relationship between developer, hotel management organization and buyer/owner in order to answer the following research questions:

- What are the most common usage rights for owners?
- What are the return rates for individual owners of shared ownership developments?
- What central facilities are offered at the hotel/resort?
- What are the risks for investors?

Particularities of the Alpine Lodging Industry

The lodging industry in the Alps is characterized by volatile demand (seasonality) and SMEs typically with family-owned and -operated properties. A few SMEs are affiliated with a hotel chain or participate in any kind of co-operative marketing activities. The most common feature among the SMEs, however, is the need to invest in high-cost lodging infrastructure. Hybrid business models that are characterized by the split of real estate ownership and resort hotel management are well established in the lodging industry (Bieger and Laesser,

2007). However, due to strict risk rating rules in the finance sector, it is difficult to secure loans for tourism infrastructure development; this in turn has aroused interest in alternative approaches to financing lodging projects (Deuber and Laesser, 2008).

For decades, ownership and use of vacation homes was sold to customers in order to defray property costs, even though these are often used infrequently (Hobson, 2002; Weinert et al., 2007). But it has only been in recent years that this ownership model has gained credence in the commercial lodging industry (Nash, 1997; Manikis, 1998). The impacts of real-estate private equity investments on the business development strategy of international hotel companies in European tourism destinations have been studied by Weiermair and Frehse (2008). Table 14.1 highlights the review of the most commonly used shared-ownership models in the Alpine region (Hobson, 2002; PWC, 2005).

The changing face of classical timeshare models and its derivatives has been analysed by PricewaterhouseCoopers (2005) and supported the findings of Lefebvre (2004) who identified that this type of shared ownership is typical in the French Alps' winter sport destinations, where international companies started to develop timeshare models in the 1960s.

Table 14.1. Shared ownership models.

Models	Characteristics	Examples
Vacation ownership	Right-to-use Purchasers buy either weeks or points that entitle them to use units over a set of years Time usage depending on points or weeks bought by the customer	Hapimag (e.g. Austria, France, Switzerland) Vacation Clubs in various countries worldwide
Fractional ownership	Fractional ownership of unrelated parties (1/4 or 1/7 or 1/12) Distinctive differentiation from timeshare through not more than 12 owners Nowadays upscale luxury home, which often incorporates five-star service and the exclusivity of a private club	Especially popular in North America, hardly established in Europe
Buy to use & let (BTUL)	Hotel or Resort with units that are individually owned (individual investors purchase whole ownership units) Whole ownership units including participation in rental programme (BTUL model with obligation to let) Mix of personal use and return rates Marketed and operated collectively and professionally	Landal Green Parks (e.g. Austria) Pierre et Vacances (e.g. France) IntraWest (e.g. France) Individual Hotels (e.g. Switzerland)

Leisure real estate with lease-back components can optimize the use of properties based on increased occupancy of owners and guests, and thus increase the revenue potential in comparison to classic second homes. All presented shared-ownership models have been utilized by developers and hotel management companies in the Alpine region. Depending on the model, the emphasis is more on lifestyle and the right of use (RoU) with classical timeshare and fractional ownership models, but more on investment and revenue with the BTUL models.

Particularities of Selected Business Models

Based on literature review, a market analysis and expert interviews, this chapter examines selected business models in the Alpine lodging industry by means of five explorative case studies that are described in terms of the shared-ownership model along with the following key features (see Table 14.2).

- Characteristic of shared ownership model.
- Spatial and structural considerations.
- Finance and performance indicators.
- Owners' rate of return and rights to use.
- Risks.

In evaluating the various models within the Alps, the following are characteristics. The sizes of units range from $19\,m^2$ (studios) to $140\,m^2$ (Chateau & Residence, Megève, 4*, Oceanis) and prices reach up to €9.50 per m^2 (Les Terrasses d'Eos, Flaine Montsoleil). Most units are sold furnished to grant a certain uniformity and better market the property, especially when the units are to be distributed via a rental pool. Standards and design of onsite amenities are strongly dependent on the category in which the hotel and resort is positioned (generally speaking, the higher the category, the more comprehensive the amenities). Restaurants and bars are normally available; upscale hotels and resorts offer a spa; while conference facilities that extend the season and increase occupancy rates are available in two of the analysed locations, namely Hotel Latitudes du Golf and Les Terrasses d'Eos.

The available units are often sold via real-estate agencies or subsidiary companies or specialized departments of the development company (e.g. Pierre & Vacances, Oceanis, Intrawest). Developers often provide financial blueprints for private investors (e.g. Landal, Intrawest). Some countries offer the possibility of pre-tax deduction for objects with the obligation to let (e.g. France, Austria). Most shared-ownership developments are sold 'off the plan', meaning that investors are buying before construction work starts (i.e. after 60% of the units are sold). Vast resorts are usually constructed in several stages (e.g. Les Terrasses D'Eos, Flaine Montsoleil, where 260 units had been constructed by the end of 2008 and more followed, according to the master plan).

The underlying business ownership and management models of selected examples are compared in Table 14.3 and subsequently discussed.

Resident Management has often been delegated to specialized companies, where unit owners may be shareholders of those (local) companies (Landal Ferienpark Hochmontafon), or General Management is shifted to international brands (Pierre & Vacances Group (P&V)). Gastronomy may be internally managed as a service/profit centre (P&V) or sourced out to local operators (Landal Ferienpark Hochmontafon). With most models, units are looked after professionally, thus it is hassle-free for absent owners.

Depending on the project and the developer, return rates can be guaranteed or not. Likewise, business models with or without RoU are on the market. Return rates ranging from 2.6% (with 6 weeks RoU per year, Résidence Maeva Le Montana) to up to 4.5% guaranteed Return Rates (without RoU, Les Terrasses d'Eos) have been found.

Discussion and Conclusion

The findings of this explorative study reveal a number of critical issues with shared-ownership models and more explicitly, the discrepancies that can appear within the stakeholder relationships (Warnken and Guilding, 2009). The structuring of the contractual relationships between developer, private investor/owner and management company is crucial; hence, many

Table 14.2. Description of selected properties.

	Résidence Maeva Le Montana 2*	Hôtel Latitudes du Golf 3*	Chateau & Residence, Megève 4*	Les Terrasses d'Eos 4*	Ferienpark Hochmontafon 4*
Resort					
Destination Developer, Owner, Manager/Operator	La Mongie, France Development: Pierre & Vacances Group (P&V) Ownership: private owners Management: Maeva (P&V)	Arc 1800, France Development: Pierre & Vacances Group Ownership: mostly private owners Management: Latitudes Hotel (P&V)	Megève, France Development: Oceanis Ownership: mostly private owners Management: Suites Residence Groupe (Oceanis)	Flaine, France Development: Intrawest Ownership: mostly private owners Management: Intrawest Hotels & Residences	Gargellen, Austria Development: Jägerbau Ownership: mostly private owners Management: Landal
Number of units	69	246	69	260	93
Size of units (examples)	Studio 26.6 m² 1 Bedroom 35–54 m² 1.5 Bedroom 45 m²	1 Bedroom 41–43 m²	Studio 19 m² 2 Bedrooms 40 m² Suites 140 m²	1 Bedroom 38 m² 2 Bedroom 50–65 m² 3 Bedroom 68–80 m²	2 Bedrooms, 64 m²
Central facilities, on-site amenities	Ski access, ski lockers, restaurant, parking (central facilities are property of P&V)	Ski access, ski lockers, restaurant, bar, parking, spa (gym, outdoor pool, sauna, steam bath), safe (reception), luggage deposit, conference facilities (central facilities are property of P&V)	Restaurant, bar, gym, in/outdoor pool, spa, parking	Ski in–ski out restaurant, café, bar, shopping, in/outdoor wellness facilities, luggage deposit, laundry room, parking, conference facilities	Ski in–ski out restaurant, bar, reception, shop, spa (indoor pool, sauna, steam bath, jacuzzi), playground, parking (central facilities are property of unit owners)
Owners' return rate (RR)	3.6% RR and 3 weeks RoU or 2.6% RR and 6 weeks RoU	4.5% RR and no RoU	3.0% RR and 3 weeks RoU	4.5% RR guaranteed and no RoU or up to 3.75% RR guaranteed and 4 weeks of use	Different models, e.g. 3.0% to 3.5% RR and 4 weeks of use

Table 14.3. Selected business ownership and management models in the Alpine lodging industry.

	Pierre et Vacances (example: Résidence Maeva Le Montana)	Landal (example: Ferienpark Hochmontafon)	Intrawest Europe (example: Flaine Montsoleil)
Business Model	Lease-back to P&V (minimum duration 9 years) Operations, Marketing incl. Distribution, Controlling via P&V	Lease-back to local management company, Marketing incl. Distribution, Controlling via Landal	Lease-back (minimum duration 12 years) to Intrawest
Resident Management	P&V	Local management company	Intrawest Hotels & Residences
Return Rate (RR)	Guaranteed RR (if booked or not) mostly between 2.6% and 3.6 %	No RR guarantee Offers found between 3.0% and 3.5% plus 4 weeks of use	Different models: Investors Formula: Guaranteed RR up to 4.5% (for 12 years)
Right of Use (RoU)	RoU optional (in the case of Résidence Maeva Le Montana additional RoU)	RoU: 3–4 weeks per year	Lifestyle Formula: Guaranteed RR up to 3.75% plus 4 weeks RoU

questions about future hotel and resort operations, facility management and re-investment needs have to be anticipated. Rights and obligations of all stakeholders must be regulated in these contracts. For example, the postponement of mission-critical investments by the owners or other fields of conflict have to be excluded from the very beginning by an adequate contractual framework. The statute of the operating body regulates the use of different parts of the property, such as the units or on-site amenities. In particular, the obligation to let has to be pre-arranged, if applicable, at least for a minimum duration. As the management organization is in charge of marketing and distribution of the units collectively, service fees and conditions, as well as service times and opening hours of onsite amenities, have to be defined in advance. Similarly, the calculation for dividend payout has to be pre-arranged in a transparent way.

The most common issues with shared ownerships, however, relate to maintenance and upkeep problems, and responsibilities and problems caused by time limitations of usage. As a reaction to these issues, developers have started to offer shared ownership products that allow them to manage and maintain the property in a more professional and efficient way,

by employing professional management companies to formalize and standardize the rights and obligations of both the owner and management company. One of the most striking features of these models is that single accommodation units are sold in the real-estate market, often under the compulsion of letting. Investor benefits vary according to the underlying business model, but consist in general of two major components. First, the monetary return on investment results from the possible valorisation of the real estate; and second, the intangible value of a private holiday apartment with its ease of use. While the benefit to the investor can be manifold, it is in the particular interest of the management to make a profit in the operations of the hotel. These shared-ownership models minimize the operational risk and generate a constant cash flow by the functional split of real-estate ownership and management.

The interests of developer and owners of shared-ownership projects are not always congruent. The most important risks for individual investors of these new business models are summarized as follows.

• Dependency of the return rate on the quality of hotel-management company (especially projects without guaranteed return rate).

- Temporal and spatial constraints of own use, including psychological barriers and perceived value of ownership.
- Depending on the drafting of the related contract, investors might become co-owner of onsite amenities, such as restaurants or spas, without having expertise of these operations – the investor ends up bearing part of the economic risk of these amenities.
- Although rights and seasons of use are specified in detail in most contracts, which

costs for maintenance have to be defrayed by the owners is not always transparent.

The authors suggest that future research should therefore concentrate on the governance of these business models in the Alpine lodging industry, and the identification of added value for hotel developers and potential investors. In addition, the implication of the real-estate market as well as the destination attractiveness in general should be investigated in the context of shared-ownership models.

References

Bieger, T. and Laesser, C. (2007) *Neue, hybride Formen der Beherbergung – Implikationen für Raumplanung und Destinationsentwicklung*. Institut für Oeffentliche Dienstleistungen und Tourismus, St Gallen, Switzerland.

Bieger, T., Beritelli, P. and Weinert, R. (2005) *HotBeds. Überwindung sozio-oekonomischer Barrieren bei der Vermietung von privatem Wohneigentum in Schweizer Tourismusregionen*. Wissenschaftlicher Schlussbericht, St Gallen, Switzerland.

Deuber, A. and Laesser, C. (2008) *Mit innovativen Betriebsmodellen die Schweizer Hotellerie befluegeln. Veralteter Hotelbegriff in der Lex Koller verhindert Wachstumsmoeglichkeiten*. Neue Zürcher Zeitung, Zurich, Switzerland.

Hobson, W. (2002) A research report on private residence clubs: a new concept for second home ownership. *International Journal of Hospitality Management* 21(3), 285–300.

Lefebvre, V. (2004) Malerisch oder Erhaben: Flaine and Avoriaz. In: Fakultät für Architektur der Technischen Universität Graz (Hrsg) *GAM. Graz Architecture Magazine 01*. Tourism and Landscape, Springer, Vienna, Austria.

Manikis, D. (1998) Timesharing. A disregarded tourist institution with substantial perspectives. *Tourist Market* 109, 144–145.

Nash, C. (1997) Vacation-ownership industry needs global thinking to thrive in the new millennium. *Lodging Limited Quarterly* April, 12–14.

PricewaterhouseCoopers (PWC) (2005) The changing face of timesharing in Europe. *Hospitality Directions Europe Edition*, Issue 12.

Schuckert, M.R. and Boksberger, P.E. (2008) Development of destinations and real estate in a tourism region – an application of life cycle theory. In: Keller, P. and Bieger, T. (eds), *International Association of Scientific Experts in Tourism (AIEST), Real Estate and Destination Development in Tourism, Successful Strategies and Instruments*. Erich Schmidt Verlag, Berlin, Germany, pp. 233–247.

Stettler, J. and Giovanni, D. (2008) Image, truth and illusion in tourism promotion: the problem of the rapid spread of second homes in Switzerland and planning strategies. In: Keller, P. and Bieger, T. (eds), *International Association of Scientific Experts in Tourism (AIEST), Real Estate and Destination Development in Tourism, Successful Strategies and Instruments*. Erich Schmidt Verlag, Berlin, Germany, pp. 249–265.

Warnken, J. and Guilding, C. (2009) Multi-ownership of tourism accommodation complexes: a critique of types, relative merits, and challenges arising. *Tourism Management* 30(5), 704–714.

Weiermair, K. and Frehse, J. (2008) Real estate private equity investment and its impacts on the business development strategy of international hotel companies in European tourism destinations. In: Keller, P. and Bieger, T. (eds), *International Association of Scientific Experts in Tourism (AIEST), Real Estate and Destination Development in Tourism, Successful Strategies and Instruments*. Erich Schmidt Verlag, Berlin, Germany, pp. 217–231.

Weinert, R., Laesser, C. and Beritelli, P. (2007) Customer value for second home ownership. Insights from a mature market (Switzerland). *Australian and New Zealand Marketing Academy Conference, 2007*. Dunedin, New Zealand, S. 34–42.

15 Australia's Alpine Areas: Motivations, Experiences and Satisfaction of Visitors to Mt Kosciuszko

Tracey Dickson*

University of Canberra, Canberra, Australian Capital Territory, Australia

'From the forest and wilderness come the tonics and barks which brace mankind.'

Henry David Thoreau, *Walking* (1862)

Introduction

The natural areas in alpine and mountain regions, especially summits, have been key attractions for tourists in winter and summer for decades. Mt Kosciuszko is one of those alpine summit destinations. Mt Kosciuszko is Australia's highest point, and is located in the Snowy Mountains, New South Wales (Fig. 15.1). It is of environmental and cultural significance to local Aboriginals as well as to current generations. Mt Kosciuszko in Kosciuszko National Park (KNP) is a popular winter destination, but the summit also has special appeal for summer visitors when the snow has gone. This chapter explores the issues related to understanding why people are drawn to alpine natural areas; how people experience their natural world; how to support their ongoing and sustainable participation in often fragile environments; and to support the visitation to, and management of, those areas for future generations.

The alpine areas of Australia are considered barometers of climate change in Australia (Turton *et al.*, 2010). If climate change predictions are accurate (Hennessy *et al.*, 2008; Bhend *et al.*, 2012), the existing dependence upon winter tourism may be terminal by 2070, as there would be insufficient natural snow to support a snowsport industry. As climate change threatens the viability of offering snowsport visitor products, summer mountain tourism may provide alternatives. The economic impact of nine months of non-winter tourism to the Snowy Mountains area is estimated to be just 30% of the winter tourism economic impact, but growing (National Institute of Economic and Industry Research, 2012). Should the visitation mix continue to shift towards summer visitation, it is essential to effectively manage one of the key attractors, Mt Kosciuszko.

Understanding the motivations and experiences of tourists year-round will be essential for tourism operators and land managers alike wanting to offer quality and sustainable summer tourism experiences. The 'increasing emphasis on quality tourism experiences and … experience as the essence of tourism' (Tussyadiah, 2014, 543) is even more important for tourism-dependent economies such as the Snowy Mountains of Australia that are susceptible to the vagaries of economic, social and climate impacts (Tourism Research Australia, 2011). Improved

---

* Corresponding author: tracey.dickson@canberra.edu.au

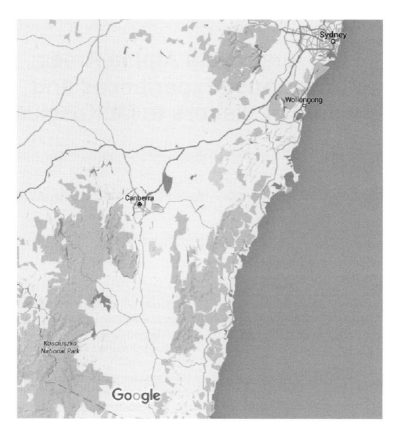

Fig. 15.1. Location of Mt Kosciuszko National Park in New South Wales, Australia (map data © 2015 Google).

understanding will also assist those offering tourism products and services in the area to better develop, focus and market their wares to meet the needs of their current and future clients seeking summer mountain tourism experiences.

Motivations

Tourism research has many longstanding models to draw upon when seeking to understand tourists' behaviours and motivations, but it is beyond the scope of this chapter to review the extensive literature available. To be motivated implies that one is moved to do something, be that via intrinsic or extrinsic motivations. In tourism research, the 'something' is travel. Iso-Ahola (1982) significantly proposed a two-dimensional model of human motivation with the dimensions: escaping from life's routines and seeking psychological (intrinsic) rewards.

Wilderness, Backcountry, Front Country and Wilderness Experiences

This research is further located within literature on wilderness, backcountry, front country and wilderness experiences.

Wilderness

There are at least four approaches to defining wilderness: pristine, phenomenal, perceptual, and legislated and pseudo-wilderness. These definitions reflect the relative importance given to the scientific and aesthetic qualities of environments as determined and constructed by people in positions of power and influence (O'Neill, 2002).

'Pristine wilderness' is 'areas of pristine ecology that are completely free of any human disturbance' (Higham, 1998, 29). 'Phenomenal wilderness' is a broader definition, where 'the imprint of humanity is largely unnoticeable' (Higham, 1998, 29). How noticeable the impact is may depend upon who is looking (e.g. a person from an urban area with no prior experience of the area may see very little impact, while an alpine ecologist or previous indigenous inhabitant may see very different levels of impact). This leads us to the next definition, 'perceptual wilderness', which reflects the 'eye of the beholder'. Each person's experience and perception of what wilderness is will be filtered though their individual array of life experiences; thus perceptions of wilderness may differ from what is legislated or designated as wilderness by others.

Next, legislation provides a fourth approach to defining wilderness and varies depending upon political structures. The National Parks and Wildlife Service of New South Wales (NPWS), works within the *National Parks and Wildlife Act 1974* and *Wilderness Act 1987*, and defines wilderness as 'large natural area of land that, together with its native plant and animal communities, is essentially unchanged by human nature' (National Parks and Wildlife Service, 1995, 1). Mt Kosciuszko is a unique and fragile natural area bordering a declared wilderness area. 'Pseudo-wilderness' is used to distinguish between areas legislated as wilderness and/or deemed to be phenomenal wilderness, versus those experienced as wilderness by those visiting, an important distinction when marketing wilderness areas and wilderness experiences.

Backcountry and front country

Intertwined with the definitions of wilderness are the concepts: backcountry and front country. Backcountry in KNP is defined as:

> Those parts of the park that are without public vehicle road access and not included in declared wilderness areas. Generally, these places are remote from vehicular access and display high degrees of naturalness ... The Back Country Zone covers approximately 49% of the total area of the park.
> (Department of Environment and Conservation, 2006, 25)

Front country is not a term used frequently in Australia, but in New Zealand it is understood to be 'any area directly accessible from formed tracks, within 1–2 hours' walk of major roads' (Cessford and Dingwall, 2001, 40).

Wilderness perceptions and experiences

There is a paucity of Australian wilderness research, in contrast to the long tradition of wilderness research in New Zealand (NZ) and the USA, including experiences in backcountry or designated wilderness areas (e.g. Turner, 1914; Higham, 1997; Higham *et al.*, 2000; Kearsley, 2000; Watson, 2000; Borrie and Roggenbuck, 2001; Cessford and Dingwall, 2001; Heintzman, 2003). The NZ and US research highlights the significance of individual experiences of wilderness rather than the importance of wilderness labels applied by marketers, land managers, legislators, academics or tourism operators. Kearsley, from NZ, points to the diversity of wilderness experiences:

> An essential part of the value of wilderness to the individual lies in the emotions and state of mind that are stirred in that person by the wilderness experience. People themselves experience wilderness in many different settings, not simply formally designated Wilderness Area.
> (Kearsley, 2000, 79)

Borrie and Roggenbuck (2001) concur, suggesting that 'wilderness experience is dynamic, complex and evolving' (p. 225). Further, multiphasic in that the experience and attitudes change during the time one is in the wilderness environment (Borrie and Roggenbuck, 2001), and with changes in culture, technology and the economy (Watson, 2000). Watson challenges wilderness managers to move 'beyond stewardship of our transactions with wilderness, like counting the number of campsites we find in an area or the number of people we encounter during a hike there – to stewardship of the relationship people have with this area' (pp. 6–7).

This study adds to our understanding of the motivations of visitors to Mt Kosciuszko, as well as their wilderness perceptions of a place not designated by legislation as wilderness, but potentially perceived and experienced as wilderness by visitors. This was the first research exploring motivations, experiences, or wilderness perceptions of visitors to Mt Kosciuszko.

Research Context

The history of KNP has been, and still is, a mix of conflicting, contested and evolving uses and agendas, of aboriginal and European uses, impacted by conservation, recreation and commercial agendas (Dickson *et al.*, 2006). Prior to European occupation, aboriginal use of the area was for ceremonial purposes and for catching Bogong Moths over summer (Young, 2000). European use has included summer grazing of cattle in the 1800s and early 1900s and then tourism, beginning in the early 1900s with construction of The Hotel Kosciusko (1906) and The Chalet at Charlotte Pass (1931). In the 1950s and 1960s, alongside a growing snowsport industry, the Snowy Mountains Hydroelectric Scheme saw construction of numerous tunnels through the mountains and the damming of a number of rivers (Independent Scientific Committee, 2002; Department of Environment and Conservation, 2006).

The recreation and conservation values were first recognized in 1906, when a 160-km² area around Mt Kosciuszko was set aside for recreation and preservation of game. In 1944 this was expanded to a 518,229-ha state park. In 1967 Kosciuszko National Park was established, but not without opposition from earlier users of the area (Department of Environment and Conservation, 2006).

The conservation, recreation and commercial developments with Kosciuszko National Park occurred in the context of an emerging international recognition of the uniqueness of KNP: listed in 1977 as a biosphere reserve under UNESCO's Man and the Biosphere Programme; then the Blue Lake area was acknowledged as a wetland of international significance under the Ramsar Convention (Department of Environment and Conservation, 2006).

Today, KNP is best known as a winter destination where thousands flock to the four snowsports resorts: Perisher, Thredbo, Charlottes Pass and Mt Selwyn, accounting for 57% of Australia's 2 million skier visits (Australian Ski Areas Association, 2012) and bringing in excess of AUS$1 billion into the state economy (National Institute of Economic and Industry Research, 2012).

The chapter reports on research that draws upon tourism motivation literature and addresses a gap in wilderness experience research in Australia and, in particular, visitor experiences in wilderness and pseudo-wilderness environments. Wilderness perceptions and experiences are an individual construct, influenced by a range of factors (e.g. temporal, spatial and experiential). To better plan, manage and utilize those areas, it is essential to understand the motivations and experiences of people in those places defined and/or experienced as wilderness. Drawing on the literature on wilderness experiences, the research sought to answer the following research questions asked of summer visitors to Mt Kosciuszko summit:

1. What are their motivations?
2. What are their expectations and experiences of wilderness?
3. How satisfied were they with their experience?

The focus of this research is upon the 45% of visitors who arrive outside the winter months to participate in other activities, e.g. bushwalking, mountain biking and scenic drives (Tourism Research Australia, 2008). Mt Kosciuszko is primarily accessed in summer along two tracks: (i) a 6-km, primarily metal track from the top of a chairlift in Thredbo; and (ii) a 9-km walk along a maintained service track from Charlotte Pass.

Research Design and Analysis

The questionnaire used for this study was adapted from Kearsley *et al.* (1998), who surveyed backcountry users in New Zealand. Changes were made to reflect the language, facilities and potential users in the Mt Kosciuszko area (e.g. hiking instead of tramping, deleting references to jet boats and hunters that are not relevant to KNP). The anonymous self-completion questionnaire explored: prior experience; motivations; wilderness expectations and experiences; and overall satisfaction (Dickson, 2007, 2008).

Data were collected over 4 days during Easter in the first year and a further 19 days over the summer (through to Easter) in Year 2. These peak periods were chosen as 2500–3000 people may daily visit the summit (Johnston and Growcock, 2005). Here, for the first time, the data sets from the two data collection periods have been combined to gain further insight into visitor motivations and experiences.

Participants were a convenience sample of adults who summited Mt Kosciuszko during the data collection periods. Having arrived at the summit and settled for a rest, potential respondents were invited to participate (Fig. 15.2). Once the questionnaire was completed, respondents were given a small chocolate in appreciation of their time.

Data from the two periods were combined in SPSS 21 for analysis, including a principal components analysis (PCA) of the motivation items. Between-group differences were analysed using Pearson's Chisquared, independent samples t-tests and odds ratios as applicable. The suitability of the motivation items for the PCA was confirmed via a Kaiser Meyer Olkin value of .820 exceeding the recommended level of 0.6 (Kaiser, 1970 cited in Pallant, 2011) and Bartlett's Test of Sphericity reaching statistical significance (p<.001) supporting the factorability of the correlation matrix (Bartlett, 1954 cited in Pallant, 2011).

The total number of responses was 3030: 542 in Year 1 and 2488 in Year 2. This is the largest survey of summer visitors to Mt Kosciuszko ever conducted. The results and discussion are presented in order of the three research questions, preceded by a summary of who responded to the survey.

Fig. 15.2. Data collection on the summit of Mt Kosciuszko (photograph courtesy of Tracey Dickson).

Visitors to the summit

Table 15.1 provides a summary of respondents, showing a similar number of males (51.1%) and females (48.9%). Most hiked to the summit (96.8%), with the majority using the track from Thredbo (74.4%). The Chi-squared analysis revealed that males indicated a significantly higher experience level in their mode of travel that day than females (p<.001).

Motivations to visit

Motivational items were scored on a five-point Likert scale from *1=Not at all important* to *5= Extremely important*. Most important were: scenic beauty, enjoying the outdoors and climbing Mt Kosciuszko; solitude, learning about nature and meeting new people were the least important (Table 15.2).

To determine patterns and structures, further interrogation on the motivational items was undertaken using PCA with oblimin rotation, retaining components with: eigenvalues >1; item loadings >0.40; and including at least three items (Costello and Osborne, 2005). This yielded a four-component solution accounting for 58.7% of the variance

(Table 15.3). Internal consistency for each of the scales was examined using Cronbach's alpha with none reaching the benchmark of 0.7, though component 1 is close, suggesting further refinement of the items would be necessary in future research. No improvement in reliability was achieved by reducing the items.

The first component, *Escape* ($\underline{M}$=3.86), reflects a motivation to get away, relax, enjoy the outdoors and engage in physical activity that resonates with Iso-Ahola's (1982) 'escape from routine life'. While *Goals* ($\underline{M}$=3.66) highlights personal goals, including climbing Mt Kosciuszko, the highest point in Australia, that reflects Iso-Ahola's (1982) second dimension of seeking rewards. *Socialise* ($\underline{M}$=2.49) includes meeting new people, solitude and challenges, which accounted for 9.14% of the variance, but was not such an important component with the lowest mean. *Engage with nature* ($\underline{M}$=3.46) reflects the draw of the scenery and untouched nature.

The highest-ranked motivation items reflect the pull of nature, the outdoors and the unique experience of climbing Australia's highest point, while the dominant motivation component *Escape* may be influenced by the timing of the research over peak summer holiday periods, rather than the specific destination itself.

Table 15.1. Profile of summer visitors to the summit of Mt Kosciuszko.

	Females % (n)	Males % (n)	Total % (n)	p
Mode of transport				
Hiking	97.3 (1348)	96.3 (1388)	96.8 (2736)	.11
Biking	2.7 (37)	3.7 (54)	3.2 (91)	
Experience level in mode of transport				
First time	15.7 (218)	14.2 (205)	15.0 (423)	<.001
Occasional (e.g. 1–2 times per year)	44.2 (612)	37.8 (545)	40.9 (1157)	
Regular (3 or more times per year)	40.1 (555)	48.0 (693)	44.1 (1248)	
Track used				
Summit Walk from Charlotte Pass (18 km)	19.9 (267)	19.0 (267)	19.4 (534)	.36
Main Range (22 km)	5.4 (73)	6.8 (96)	6.0 (169)	
Kosciuszko from Thredbo (14 km)	74.4 (1000)	74.0 (1037)	74.4 (2037)	
Other	0.3 (4)	0.1 (2)	0.3 (6)	
Total	48.9 (1391)	51.1 (1451)		

Table 15.2. Means and modes for motivational items.

Motivation items	n	Mean	Mode
Scenic beauty/naturalness	2911	4.35	5
To enjoy the outdoors	2909	4.29	5
To climb Mt Kosciuszko	2925	4.26	5
Relax with family, friends or partner	2894	3.77	4
To undertake physical exercise	2895	3.74	4
To get away from life's pressures	2881	3.54	4
To achieve personal goals	2887	3.46	5
To encounter wilderness/untouched nature	2867	3.43	4
For a totally new and different experience	2869	3.25	4
To face the challenges of nature	2883	2.95	3
To experience the solitude of being with no one but my own group	2859	2.69	1
To learn about Australian plants and wildlife	2869	2.60	2
To meet new people and make friends	2864	1.83	1

Table 15.3. Pattern matrix for principal components analysis of motivation items.

Component: Variance explained (Cronbach's alpha)	Mean	Component			
		Escape	Goals	Socialize	Engage with nature
1: 29.96% (.692)	3.86				
Relax with family, friends or partner	3.77	.841			
To get away from life's pressures	3.54	.821			
To enjoy the outdoors	4.29	.583			
To undertake physical exercise	3.74	.442			
2: 11.85% (.612)	3.66				
To climb Mt Kosciuszko	4.26		.877		
To achieve personal goals	3.46		.772		
For a totally new and different experience	3.25		.496		
3: 9.14% (.600)	2.49				
To meet new people and make friends	1.83			−.786	
To experience the solitude of being with no one but my own group	2.69			−.559	
To face the challenges of nature	2.95			−.557	
4: 7.80% (.607)	3.46				
Scenic beauty/naturalness	4.35				−.846
To encounter wilderness/ untouched nature	3.43				−.662
To learn about Australian plants and wildlife	2.60				−.618

Extraction Method: Principal Component Analysis.
Rotation Method: Oblimin with Kaiser Normalization

Expectations and experiences of wilderness

Responses to *How much does this track/area represent wilderness to you?* were scored on a five-point Likert scale from *1=Not wilderness at all* to *5=Pure wilderness* (M=2.85, SD=1.28). Respondents also indicated whether they had expected wilderness at this location and whether they believed they had experienced

Table 15.4. Expectations and experiences of wilderness.

		Experienced wilderness			
		Yes	No	Total	Odds
Expected wilderness	Yes	88.8% (1377)	11.2% (174)	69.1% (1551)	7.91
	No	27.3% (190)	72.7% (505)	30.9% (695)	0.38
	Total	69.8% (1567)	30.2% (679)	2246	21.03

wilderness (Table 15.4). Most expected wilderness (69.1%), with similar levels experiencing wilderness (69.8%). An odds ratio revealed that people who expected wilderness were 21 times more likely to experience wilderness (95% CI=16.7–26.5).

The results on wilderness experiences are consistent with previous research that suggested that people may experience wilderness in places not classified as such by the 'experts' (Kearsley, 2000). What clearly emerges from the research that is of importance to land managers and tourism operators alike, are two key findings: (i) those who expected wilderness were most likely to experience the area as wilderness; and (ii) those who expected wilderness were less satisfied with their overall experience. With scenic beauty being the main motivation, how Mt Kosciuszko is visually marketed to potential visitors may influence their expectations about usage and wilderness, and thus their overall satisfaction.

The fact the most people experienced wilderness in a very busy, highly modified and managed area may mean that more sensitive areas and declared wilderness areas can be better protected and managed by strategies such as limiting access and de-marketing. This may support conservation objectives across the whole of the KNP, often with limited resources, while maintaining visitor satisfaction in areas of high demand, such as Mt Kosciuszko.

Satisfaction

Responses to *How satisfied were you with your experience of this track today?* were scored on a nine-point Likert scale from *1=Extremely dissatisfied* to *9=Extremely satisfied*. The mean ($\underline{M}$=6.87, $\underline{SD}$=2.23) (n=2916)

is just below 7 on the scale indicating satisfaction. An independent-samples t-test was conducted to compare the overall satisfaction levels for those who did and did not expect wilderness. There was a significant difference in overall satisfaction between those expecting wilderness ($\underline{M}$= 6.78, $\underline{SD}$=2.36) and those not expecting wilderness ($\underline{M}$=7.09, $\underline{SD}$=1.85; t(2004.2)=3.76, p<.001). Similarly, there was a significant difference in overall satisfaction between those who said they did experience wilderness ($\underline{M}$= 7.91, $\underline{SD}$=1.14) and those who did not experience wilderness ($\underline{M}$=7.49, $\underline{SD}$=1.18; t (1201.9)=7.72, p<.001).

Conclusion

This exploratory research of summer visitors to the summit of Mt Kosciuszko highlights the motivational components of escape and achieving personal goals that reflect Iso-Ahola's (1982) two dimensions. Regardless of experience levels, summit visitors both expected and indicated that they experienced the area as wilderness, even though it is classified as a backcountry zone, not wilderness. Further, even though data was collected during peak periods when hundreds of people were in the area, visitors were still satisfied with their experience.

Future research could explore what, if any, changes in motivations, experiences and satisfaction may have arisen with the growth in mountain biking in the intervening period (Office of Environment and Heritage NSW, 2011; NPWS Planner National Parks and Wildlife Service, 2014). In addition, surveying those who avoid these peak periods may also give rise to further insights for tourism operators and land managers alike.

References

Australian Ski Areas Association (2012) Australian Skier Visits Statistics. Available at: http://asaa.org.au/ stats (accessed 7 October 2012).

Bhend, J., Bathols, J. and Hennessy, K. (2012) *Climate Change Impacts on Snow in Victoria*. CSIRO Marine and Atmospheric Research, Aspendale, Australia.

Borrie, W.T. and Roggenbuck, J.W. (2001) The dynamic, emergent, and multi-phasic nature of on-site wilderness experiences. *Journal of Leisure Research* 33(2), 202–228.

Cessford, G. and Dingwall, P. (2001) Wilderness and recreation in New Zealand. In: Cessford, G. (ed.) *The State of Wilderness in New Zealand*. Department of Conservation, Wellington, New Zealand, pp. 35–42.

Costello, A.B. and Osborne, J.W. (2005) Best practices in exploratory factor analysis: four recommendations for getting the most from your analysis. *Practical Assessment, Research & Evaluation* 10(7), n.p. Available at: http://pareonline.net/getvn.asp?v=10&n=7 (accessed 6 August 2015).

Department of Environment and Conservation (2006) *2006 Plan of Management: Kosciuszko National Park*. Parks and Wildlife Division, Queanbeyan, New South Wales, Australia.

Dickson, T.J. (2007) Mt Kosciuszko: wilderness expectations and experiences in a non-wilderness area. *Australasian Parks and Leisure* 10(3), 25–29.

Dickson, T.J. (2008) Importance-satisfaction analysis: the case of Mt Kosciuszko. Paper Presented at the *Council for Australian University Tourism and Hospitality Education Conference 2008: Where the Bloody Hell are We?* Griffith University, Gold Coast, Queensland, Australia.

Dickson, T.J., Laneyrie, F. and Pritchard, A. (2006) Australian snowsports: gendered and contested spaces? *Tourism: An International Interdisciplinary Journal* 54(1), 17–32.

Heintzman, P. (2003) The wilderness experience and spirituality: what recent research tells us. *JOPERD: The Journal of Physical Education, Recreation & Dance* 74(6), 27–31.

Hennessy, K.J., Whetton, P.H., Walsh, K., Smith, I.N., Bathols, J.M., *et al.* (2008) Climate change effects on snow conditions in mainland Australia and adaptation at ski resorts through snowmaking. *Climate Research* 35(3), 255–270.

Higham, J.E.S. (1997) Sustainable wilderness tourism: motivations and wilderness perceptions held by international visitors to New Zealand's backcountry conservation estate. In: Hall, C.M., Jenkins, J. and Kearsley, G.W.A. (eds) *Tourism Planning and Policy in Australia and New Zealand: Cases, Issues and Practice*. Irwin Publishers, Sydney, New South Wales, Australia, pp. 75–85.

Higham, J.E.S. (1998) Sustaining the physical and social dimensions of wilderness tourism: the perceptual approach to wilderness management in New Zealand. *Journal of Sustainable Tourism* 6(1), 26–51.

Higham, J.E.S., Kearsley, G.W.A. and Kliskey, A.D. (2000) Wilderness perceptions scaling in New Zealand: An analysis of wilderness perceptions held by users, nonusers and international visitors. Paper presented at the *Wilderness Science in a Time of Change Conference – Volume 2. Wilderness within the Context of Larger Systems*, Missoula, Montana.

Independent Scientific Committee (2002) *An Assessment of the Values of Kosciuszko National Park: Interim Report*. National Parks and Wildlife Service, Sydney, New South Wales, Australia.

Iso-Ahola, S.E. (1982) Toward a social psychological theory of tourism motivation: a rejoinder. *Annals of Tourism Research* 9(2), 256–262.

Johnston, S.W. and Growcock, A.J. (2005) Visiting the Kosciuszko Alpine area: visitor numbers, characteristics and activities. In: Cooper, C. (ed.) *Technical Report*. Available at: http://www.crctourism.com.au (accessed 6 August 2015).

Kearsley, G.W.A. (2000) Balancing tourism and wilderness qualities in New Zealand's native forests. In: Font, X. and Tribe, J. (eds) *Forest Tourism and Recreation*. CAB International, Wallingford, UK, pp. 75–90.

Kearsley, G.W.A., Coughlan, D.P., Higham, J.E.S., Higham, E.C. and Thyne, M.A. (1998) *Impacts of Tourist Use on the New Zealand Backcountry*. Centre for Tourism, University of Otago, Dunedin, New Zealand.

National Institute of Economic and Industry Research (2012) The Economic Significance of the Australian Alpine Resorts: Winter Season 2011. Available at: http://www.siaaustralia.com.au/_uploads/res/9_238. pdf (accessed 6 August 2015).

National Parks and Wildlife Service (1995) *Pamphlet: Wilderness – Experiences for Everyone*. National Parks and Wildlife Service, Hurstville, New South Wales, Australia.

NPWS Planner National Parks and Wildlife Service (2014) Kosciuszko Cycling Track Amendments. Available at: http://www.haveyoursay.nsw.gov.au/consultations/kosciuszko-cycling-track-amendments/ ?date=2014-02-14 (accessed 11 April 2014).

O'Neill, J. (2002) Wilderness, cultivation and appropriation. *Philosophy and Geography* 5(1), 35–50.

Office of Environment and Heritage NSW (2011) Sustainable Mountain Biking Strategy. Available at: http://www.environment.nsw.gov.au/resources/parks/cycling/110649SustMountainBikingStrategy.pdf(accessed 6 August 2015).

Pallant, J. (2011) *SPSS Survival Manual*, 4th edn. Allen and Unwin, Crows Nest, New South Wales, Australia.

Tourism Research Australia (2008) Tourism Profiles for Local Government Areas in Regional Australia: New South Wales, Snowy River Shire, Three or Four Year Average to June 2007. Available at: http://www.tra.australia.com (accessed 6 August 2015).

Tourism Research Australia (2011) The Economic Importance of Tourism in Australia's Regions. Available at: http://www.savannahway.com.au/resources/tra-regionalimpact2.pdf (accessed 27 August 2015).

Turner, F.J. (1914) The west and American ideals. *The Washington Historical Quarterly* 5(4), 243–257.

Turton, S., Dickson, T.J., Hadwen, W., Jorgensen, B., Pham, T., *et al.* (2010) Developing an approach for tourism climate change assessment: evidence from four contrasting Australian case studies. *Journal of Sustainable Tourism* 18(3), 429–447.

Tussyadiah, I.P. (2014) Toward a theoretical foundation for experience design in tourism. *Journal of Travel Research* 53(5), 543–564. DOI: 10.1177/0047287513513172.

Watson, A.E. (2000) Wilderness use in the year 2000: societal changes that influence human relationships with wilderness. In: Cole, D.N., McCool, S.F., Borrie, W.T. and O'Loughlin, J. (eds), *Wilderness Science in a Time of Change*. US Department of Agriculture, Forest Service, Rocky Mountain Research Station, Ogden, Utah, pp. 53–60.

Young, M. (2000) *The Aboriginal People of the Monaro*. NSW National Parks and Wildlife Service, Hurstville, New South Wales, Australia.

16 Natural Environments and Their Connection to Mountain Tourism: Overview, Contextual Development and Areas of Focus

Sydney Johnsen[1]* and Harold Richins[2]

[1]*Peak Planning Associates, Kamloops, British Columbia, Canada;*
[2]*Thompson Rivers University, Kamloops, British Columbia, Canada*

Introduction

This chapter, as an introduction to Part IV, examines mountain tourism and its connection and integration to natural environments. Relevant literature is explored here, and a summary of each chapter within this section is included at the end.

Visitors are drawn to visit and explore the natural setting in mountain environments. For some it is the physical aspect – being active, getting healthy – that motivates them to undertake leisure activities in the peaks and valleys of the mountain environment. For others it has more of an indescribable or spiritual meaning, or a sense of place where one finds wonder, enchantment or calming peacefulness. Authors Reid and Palechuck explore these benefits in Chapter 21, referencing research conducted by Kyle *et al.* (2004) that points out the relationship between place motivation and place attachment. Also, authors Dreyer and Mensel in Chapter 19 discuss spirituality and this deeper connection, referring to research by Antz (2009), and relate this to mountain environment experiences.

Whether it is this physical aspect or the 'pleasure' to be found 'in the pathless woods',

mountains first drew scientists, mountain explorers and, eventually, guide outfitters, who facilitated clients' access to wilderness. Reid and Palychuk discuss this in detail in Chapter 21, referring to earlier research by Beedie and Hudson (2003). In Chapter 17, Michael Hall makes the point that mountains weren't always places of pleasure, but rather that 'the dominant attitude' in Western civilization towards mountains is that they were 'wild places to be avoided'. Before discussing how these 'wild places' became places of 'pleasure', let's first talk about mountains: what they are, how they are formed, how mountains are both subject to and influencers of climate and what host of living things resides on their peaks and in the valleys.

Understanding Diverse Mountain Concepts and Geological Places of Interest to Visitors

First, what is a mountain? The answer to this question, like many other questions, depends on various aspects and perspectives (Beniston, 2002; Eagles *et al.*, 2002; UNEP, 2007).

---

* Corresponding author: sydney.johnsen@gmail.com

The *Oxford English Dictionary* defines a mountain as 'a large natural elevation of the earth's surface, esp. one high and steep in form (larger and higher than a hill) and with a summit of relatively small area.' (Oxford English Dictionary, 2015). The United Nations Environmental Programme mentions that 'All mountains have one major common characteristic: rapid changes in altitude, climate, vegetation and soil over very short distances that lead to dramatic differences in habitat and high levels of biodiversity' (UNEP, 2007, 6).

A geographer will tell you about mountain ranges and belts. A mountain range is 'a succession of many closely spaced mountains covering a particular region of the earth' (Pidwirny, 2006); a mountain belt is simply a group of mountain ranges running roughly parallel to each other. The Andes, located in South America,

are the world's longest mountain chain and the Himalayas are the world's highest mountain range. The Rockies, Sierra Madre (Mexico), Sierra Nevada, Cascade and Coast ranges (US) and Coast, Gold and Selkirk ranges (Canada) are North American examples of mountain belts. Over the last 50–60 years many of these ranges have become major visitor attractions. For example, Yosemite National Park, in California and Nevada's Sierra range, attract over 4 million day visitors yearly; over 55,000 of those are backcountry explorers (Yosemite Park, 2014). Lake Tahoe, with its expansive dark blue high mountain lake and numerous mountain villages, has over 3 million visitors experiencing a diversity of summer and winter activities including 17 nordic and alpine snowsports centres and resorts (Antonucci, 2014; Lake Tahoe, 2014).

Fig. 16.1. Tram access to Alpspitze, Garmisch-Partenkirchen, Germany (photograph courtesy of Harold Richins).

Some would simply say that mountains are places higher than the surrounding land, but that opens a discussion of how mountain heights are measured. Geologists and geographers measure mountain heights in terms of: (i) height above sea level; (ii) distance from Earth's centre or the moon and stars; and/or (iii) topographic prominence. When measured at height above sea level, Mount Everest, standing at 8850 m above sea level, is the Earth's highest mountain, followed on other continents by South Amercia's Aconcagua at 6962 m, North America's Mount McKinley (Denali) at 6194 m and Africa's Kilimanjaro (Kibo Summit) at 5895 m. The 100 peaks in central and southern Asia's mountain belt are all above 7200 m. When the distance from the earth's centre (or moon and stars) is used to measure height, Mount Chimborazo in Ecuador is higher than Everest. The difference is explained by the bulge in Earth's surface at the equator, making those mountains near or on the equator just a little bit closer to the moon and stars. A mountain that is topographically prominent is one that is circled by the lowest elevation contour line compared to other peaks. Islands are the exposed peaks of undersea mountains; Hawaii's Mauna Kea rises 10,203 m from the ocean floor, making it the earth's tallest mountain when measured from base to peak, although it only stands at 4205 m above sea level (Elert, n.d.). Size also matters in determining greatness of mountains; Mount Logan, the highest mountain in Canada and second-highest in North America, is the most massive mountain on Earth, as measured by the circumference of its base (Mt Logan Climb, 2014). However their height or size is measured, for over 200 years explorers, what we now generally call 'adventure tourists' (Swarbrooke et al., 2003; UNEP, 2007), have sought out ways to surmount the greatest and highest of Earth's massifs.

Mountain Tourism Illustrations

The eventual location and height of mountains is dependent on the forces of 'Mother Nature'. Tectonic forces build mountains through volcanic, fold or block pressures. The prominence of these mountains has long attracted the fascination of adventurous visitors; examples include Mt Hood in Oregon (USA), Mt Fuji in Japan, Mt Kosciuszko in Australia, and Mt Cook and Mt Ruapehu on New Zealand's South Island and North Island, respectively. Ojos del Salado in Argentina/Chile is the world's highest active mountain, meaning that it has shown signs of volcanic activity within the past 10,000 years. The world's highest dormant volcanic mountain is Mount Kilimanjaro (5895 m) in Africa. It was first climbed in 1889 and now an estimated 50,000 people a year attempt to climb this monolith (Johnston, 2014), contributing close to US$50 million in revenue to Tanzania's economy. Mountain tourism has generated employment for hundreds of guides and cooks and thousands of porters. The improved livelihoods of local people living near Kilimanjaro National Park has led to local children achieving the highest levels of literacy and high school enrolment rates in the country (World Bank, 2013; Christie et al., 2014). The Swiss Alps and the North American Appalachians are examples of 'folds' where the earth's crust is pushed together in a folding and rippling pattern and areas in the Sierra Nevada provide examples of a 'block' mountain – those distinguished by sheer rock faces, caused by enormous pressure forcing a rock mass to break away and rise on one side and fall on the other (Pidwirny, 2014).

The Attraction of Diversity and Variation in Mountain Shapes, Latitudes, Biodiversity and the Effects of Climate and the Weather

What goes up must come down, and so it is true with mountains as the environmental forces of glaciers, water and wind gradually erode them. The level of erosion helps dictate the shape or relief of a mountain; less erosion leaves sharper peaks and valleys where more erosion leads to rounder shaped mountains. Mountain altitude and relief give rise to a great variety of biogeoclimatic zones on mountains. Temperatures are cooler at higher than lower elevations because the thin air is less able to absorb water and therefore less heat (Smith,

Fig. 16.2. A mountain walk on the Pali, Oahu, Hawaii (photograph courtesy of Harold Richins).

2014). Mountain peaks influence wind flow and subsequently precipitation in both local and distant environments. Evidence of this is seen in South America – the world's driest desert, the Atacama to the west of the Andes and the Amazon Rainforest on the east side.

Latitude also affects mountain climates. Variations in climate and in latitude mean that mountains are places of high biodiversity, typically host to approximately 200 diverse plant species (Smith, 2014). Mountains near the equator experience spring-like conditions year-round, whereas mountains at more temperate latitudes experience great seasonality during the course of the year (Mountain, 2015). The weather patterns can shift from dry to wet, sunny to cloudy quite quickly – a phrase often heard on mountains is 'Wait ten minutes, the weather will change'. These variations and this diversity can be of significant interest and fascination to those wishing to experience novelty, escape, learning or nature and the environment (Sung *et al.*, 1996; Swarbrooke *et al.*,

2003; Pearce, 2005). Climate certainly plays a role in which mountain destinations attract the interest of potential tourists and what time of year they are likely to visit.

Unlike valley bottoms, where the flat land and warmer temperatures support agriculture and manufacturing activities (and thriving service centres), mountains are generally absent of broad-scale, intensive economic activity, although mining has been the economic driver of many mountain communities around the world. Mining drives La Rinconada in southern Peru, the world's highest mountain community at 5100 m; the community has boomed with close to 30,000 people drawn by the lure of gold (West, 2002; Larmer, 2009).

Tourism is the newcomer to the mountain economy in many countries. Many mountain economies have transitioned from resource extraction to places where tourism has 'acquired a central position in thinking about the future of rural, upland and mountain economies' (Snowdon *et al.*, 2000, 138). Now mountain

Fig. 16.3. Dolomite Mountains World Heritage Site, Italian Alps (photograph courtesy of Harold Richins).

areas are second to coastal areas as tourism destinations in terms of visitation as well as the generation of revenue for the communities that reside within these diverse regions (Beedie and Hudson, 2003; UNEP, 2007; Holden, 2008).

Summary of Chapters in Part IV: Natural Environments and Their Connection to Mountain Tourism

The chapters in this section explore this important area of natural environments in mountain tourism. The editors, Richins and Hull, have sought to provide the reader with a wide range of case studies and writings from around the world. Clearly mountains have become attractions – tourism assets. Visitors undertake a wide variety of activities in the mountains. Hiking, either for a few hours or over several days, is one of the most popular mountain-based activities undertaken in distant, 'exotic' destinations (e.g. Iceland, Borneo) or nearer to home (e.g. hiking in Germany, Chapter 19). Depending on the perceived or actual level of risk or challenge, people will either travel independently or on guided expeditions. Guide

outfitting companies have sprung up to assist mountaineers wanting to climb the 'Seven Summits', the highest peak on each of the world's seven continents (7 summits, 2009). Readers will learn about guides introducing visitors to the landscape in Iceland (in Chapter 18) and Iran (in Chapter 20), and how they become connected to place such as in British Columbia (Chapter 21).

The chapters following provide diverse examples of natural assets and the environments where mountain tourism is nurtured and developed. Summaries of chapters contained in this section are presented below and address the diversity of scholarship in this focus area, and provide illustrations showing areas with both direct and indirect influences on natural environments and mountain tourism. Chapters in this section include: (i) influence and changing attitudes towards mountains; (ii) development challenges of glacier tourism in Iceland; (iii) a study of hiking tourism within the Harz mountains of Germany; (iv) sustainable hiking tourism within mountain environments; and (v) the development of mountain tourism in the Rockies. These chapters are summarized further below.

Chapter 17. Tourism, Environmental Pragmatism and Changing Attitudes Towards Mountains

Author: Michael Hall

This chapter provides an overview of people's changing attitudes regarding mountains, using examples from North America and Australia. The author begins by looking at attitudes towards mountains through a spiritual and historical lens, discussing the changing attitudes toward mountains. Early religious groups saw mountains as places where people were tested or where survival is emphasized; Hall makes readers aware of how religious beliefs have influenced these attitudes both as an attractor and detractor. He discusses early Australian and North American settlers, who first saw the wilderness as ominous and a formidable barrier to settlement. Hall shows how attitudes concerning mountains shifted towards a desire to conquer the New World, eventually giving rise to the romantic notion of taming the wild. Over the past few decades, a new interest in the natural environment has driven increased attention toward conservation and a growing desire to experience mountain areas.

The author discusses the debate about right of access and ways in which mountain areas are valued and managed; he particularly emphasizes the ways that varied and sustainable opportunities for the public to access natural areas through tourism and leisure activities were created.

Chapter 18. External and Internal Challenges of Glacier Tourism Development in Iceland

Authors: Johannes Welling and Thorvarður Árnason

People are often fascinated and intrigued by glaciers. Even as glaciers are decreasing in length and size over the last few decades, tourists are increasingly interested in exploring and experiencing these natural wonders in rather remote locations. In this chapter, Johannes Welling and Thorvarður Árnason explore the historic and modern expansion of glacial visitation to the Scandinavian country of Iceland.

In order to understand this growing aspect of tourism, the authors present evidence of the entrepreneurial activity of more than 40 small, hard and soft adventure tourism operators in this niche sector. The authors discuss a number of issues and challenges and address the pressure on these sensitive iconic sites as a result of a sevenfold increase in tourist visits to a limited number of accessible glacial sites.

Additional challenges are described further as they relate to glacier tourism, including: (i) building the customer experience between larger group operators and small specialized operators; (ii) lack of operator guidelines for visitation management to sites; (iii) challenges of natural volcanic uncertainties including eruptions, ash dispersion and poisonous gas emissions; (iv) retreating glacial areas; and (v) ensuing issues of access, interest in particular sites and the viability of experiences at these sites.

Chapter 19. Hiking Tourism in Germany's Low and High Mountain Regions

Authors: Axel Dreyer and Anne Menzel

Walking has historically been one of the most significant ways in which humans have accessed natural mountain environments. Trail systems have allowed people to interact with mountain environments; some trails were naturally created by animal movements, others by humans intentionally moving from one area to another to find food and water, and to move grazing herds to summertime mountain meadows or to visit, and perhaps live, in small mountain communities.

Many of the trail systems through the mountains of Europe evolved from being used primarily as a means of making a livelihood, into trails which provide access for recreation and sport activities. Chapter 19 discusses walking as a recreational activity in both the low mountain and the higher alpine regions of Germany. The authors discuss demand, motivation and tourism trends as they relate to hiking tourism in Germany.

This case study reveals that there is a diversity of demand for hiking which shifts with age and/or changes in the desired level of hiking frequency. The chapter also discusses key motivations for hiking tourism based on relaxation, health, novelty, physical activity and sophistication of the niche offerings. Trends of hiking tourism in Germany are discussed in detail and include: health benefits of hiking, the tendency to explore spirituality through hiking in mountain environments, growing quality standards for hiking trails, accessing small communities to learn about historical and cultural aspects, experience and interpretation, and building information and technology (e.g. GPS) to understand and access trail systems and their augmented services and activities.

Chapter 20. Sustainable Mountain Hiking Practices in Isfahan, Iran

Authors: Farhad Moghimehfar and Elizabeth A. Halpenny

Mountain tourism occurs in wide-ranging and diverse geographic locations throughout the world. Mountain tourism experiences take place in a variety of pristine natural environments, where visitors' behaviour and attitudes are sometimes influenced by the intrinsic values and challenges of the environments themselves. The experiences people have in mountain locations can have long-lasting impressions due to overcoming challenges (as thoroughly described in Cheryl Strayed's recent popular book, *Wild*; Strayed, 2013), their interactions with the natural environments, and their social interactions during these activities. Chapter 20 focuses on mountain areas in the Middle East, and more specifically, Iran.

Authors Farhad Moghimehfar and Elizabeth Halpenny provide a case study involving hiking and camping within Iranian mountain areas, and look at the constraints experienced during these outdoor activities. The literature on tourism and pro-environmental behaviour

and the constraints on environmental behaviours forms the basis for this study. A comparison between positive environmental actions and its influence and constraints on mountain tourist behaviour is made, and a classification of constraints on behaviour is developed within the chapter. Broad groupings of these categories included intrapersonal, interpersonal and structural constraints.

These exploratory studies are among the first to focus on the Middle East and Central Asia in terms of socio-psychological aspects of mountain tourism (particularly with environmental impacts and influences on tourists in mountain areas). The authors suggest that there can be effective tools in mitigating potential negative environmental impacts in sensitive mountain tourism regions.

Chapter 21. Two Canadian Mountaineering Camps: Participant Motivations and Sense of Place in a Wilderness Setting

Authors: Robin Reid and Terry Palechuk

Groups or clubs that brought people interested in mountains together may, very possibly, be the initiators of mountain tourism. Mountain clubs have been formed and have operated primarily as volunteer organizations since the mid-1800s, starting with the Alpine Club of Great Britain, and later with alpine regions of Europe and North America. A long tradition, and an important activity included in most alpine clubs, is the organization and provision of mountain camps. Chapter 21 describes the historical foundation, motivations and value of camps within alpine regions of Canada.

The authors involved participants at two different annual camp experiences – one with a long history of over 100 years providing mountaineering camps to approximately 30 guests in remote regions within the Canadian Rockies, and a second camp that started less than 5 years ago offering similar experiences to smaller groups of around 12 guests. Alpine Club of Canada's General Mountaineering Camp has been operating since 1906 and is, perhaps, the flagship and catalyst for mountain tourism in Canada. The more recently developed and operated camp, the Boutique Mountaineering Camp, was established in 2012, and works toward offering more personalized experiences to wilderness mountain areas in British Columbia and Alberta.

In both instances, participants are flown into remote locations by helicopter, and experience week-long adventures in high mountain glacial regions. A key focus of the chapter is to explore the motivations and experiences related to sense of place in the mountain wilderness and the attachments and impressions participants have with and of the camps and the high alpine areas.

Concluding Remarks

This chapter introduces the reader to Part IV, 'Natural Environments and Their Connection to Mountain Tourism', and provides an overview of the literature and relevant knowledge in this area. The chapters in this section include a wide range of geographic areas, from hiking in Germany and Iran to understanding the history and development of mountaineering camps in Canada, and finally, the pressures on iconic glacier sites in Iceland. These chapters introduce the reader to, and provide a background and contextual framework for, understanding mountain tourism within natural surroundings.

References

7 summits (2009) The Highest Mountains on the Seven Continents. Available at: http://7summits.com (accessed 24 February 2015).

Antonucci, D.C. (2014) Tahoe Facts. Available at: http://www.tahoefacts.com/#/lake-tahoe/ (accessed 28 August 2015).

Antz, C. (2009) Spirituelles wandern. In: Dreyer, A., Menzel, A. and Endress, M. (eds) *Wandertourismus: Kundengruppen, Destinationsmarketing, Gesundheitsaspekte*. Oldenbourg, Munich, Germany, pp. 283–293.

Beedie, P. and Hudson, S. (2003) Emergence of mountain-based adventure tourism. *Annals of Tourism Research* 30(3), 625–643.

Beniston, M. (ed.) (2002) *Mountain Environments in Changing Climates*. Routledge, London.

Christie, I., Fernandes, E., Messerli, H. and Twining-Ward, L. (eds) (2014) *Tourism in Africa: Harnessing Tourism for Growth and Improved Livelihoods*. World Bank Publications, Washington, DC.

Eagles, P.F., McCool, S.F. and Haynes, C.D. (2002) *Sustainable Tourism in Protected Areas: Guidelines for Planning and Management*. Best Practice Protected Area Guidelines Series No. 8. Cambridge, UK, the United Nations Environment Programme and the World Tourism Organization.

Elert, G. (n.d.) Height of the tallest mountain on earth. *The Physics Factbook*. Available at: http://hypertextbook. com/facts/2001/BeataUnke.shtml (accessed 15 February 2015).

Holden, A. (2008) The environment-tourism nexus: influence of market ethics. *Annals of Tourism Research* 36(3), 373–389.

Johnston, J. (2014) The Importance of Quality Guides. Available at: http://www.alpineascents.com/ kilimanjaro-article.asp (accessed 15 February 2015).

Kyle, G.T., Mowen, A. and Tarrant, M. (2004) Linking place preferences with place meaning: an examination of the relationship between place motivation and place attachment. *Journal of Environmental Psychology* 24, 439–454.

Lake Tahoe (2014) Lake Tahoe Skiing and Snowboarding Directory. Available at: http://www.tahoeguide. com/skiing (accessed 15 February 2015).

Larmer, B. (2009) The real price of gold. *National Geographic* January, 34–61.

Mountain (2015) Encyclopedia of Everything Mountains. Available at: http://www.mountainprofessor.com (accessed 15 February 2015).

Mt Logan Climb (2014) Mt. Logan Climb via the King Trench Route with International Mountain Guides. Available at: http://www.mountainguides.com/logan.shtml (accessed 15 February 2015).

Oxford English Dictionary (2015) Mountain, n. and adj. *OED Online*. Oxford University Press, Oxford, UK. Available at: http://www.oed.com/view/Entry/122893?rskey=L3o88Q&result=1&isAdvanced=false' \l 'eid (accessed 15 February 2015).

Pearce, P.L. (2005) *Tourist Behaviour: Themes and Conceptual Schemes*. Channel View Publications, Clevedon, UK.

Pidwirny, M. (2006) Mountain building. In: *Fundamentals of Physical Geography*, 2nd edn. Available at: http://www.physicalgeography.net/fundamentals/10k.html (accessed 24 February 2015).

Pidwirny, M. (2014) Mountain. *The Encyclopedia of Earth*. Available at: http://www.eoearth.org/view/article/51cbee797896bb431f69819e%20 (accessed 24 February 2015).

Smith, J. (2014) Mountain Ecosystem. *Encyclopedia Britannica*. Available at: http://www.britannica.com/science/mountain-ecosystem (accessed 24 February 2015).

Snowdon, P., Slee, B. and Farr, H. (2000) The economic impacts of different types of tourism in upland and mountain areas of Europe. In: Godde, P., Price, M.F. and Zimmermann, F.M. (eds) *Tourism and Development in Mountain Regions*. CAB International, Wallingford, UK, pp. 137–154.

Strayed, C. (2013) *Wild: From Lost to Found on the Pacific Crest Trail*. Vintage, New York.

Sung, H.H., Morrison, A.M. and O'Leary, J.T. (1996) Definition of adventure travel: conceptual framework for empirical application from the providers' perspective. *Asia Pacific Journal of Tourism Research* 1(2), 47–67.

Swarbrooke, J., Beard, C., Leckie, S. and Pomfret, G. (2003) *Adventure Tourism: The New Frontier*. Butterworth-Heninemann, Burlington, Massachusetts.

UNEP (2007) *Tourism and Mountains: A Practical Guide to Managing the Environmental and Social Impacts of Mountain Tours*. United Nations Environment Programme, Nairobi.

West, J.B. (2002) Highest permanent human habitation. *High Altitude Medicine & Biology* 3(4), 401–407.

World Bank (2013) Tourism in Africa: Hiking Mount Kilimanjaro in Tanzania. Available at: www.worldbank.org/en/news/feature/2013/10/03/mount-kilimanjaro-tourism-africa-tanzania (accessed 15 February 2015).

Yosemite Park (2014) Park Statistic. Available at: https://irma.nps.gov/Stats/SSRSReports/National%20Reports/Annual%20Park%20Ranking%20Report%20%281979%20-%20Last%20Calendar%20Year%29 (accessed 7 January 2016).

17 Tourism, Environmental Pragmatism and Changing Attitudes Towards Mountains

C. Michael Hall*

University of Canterbury, Christchurch, New Zealand

Introduction

One of the most significant lessons of the history of tourism is that resources are socially and culturally constructed and therefore change over time (Cooper and Hall, 2008). Mountains provide an excellent example of this. For most of the history of Western civilization the dominant attitude towards mountains has been that they are wild places to be avoided. Mountains, and volcanoes in particular, were regarded as 'warts', 'boils', 'pox' and other 'unsightly excrescences' before the modern period of mountain appreciation (Porteous, 1986). It is only since the late 18th and early 19th centuries that there has been a shift in attitudes and mountains have come to be regarded in a positive aesthetic light (Nicholson, 1959). Such cultural change is vital for tourism, as, arguably, without them there would be little mountain tourism as we now recognize it, at least from Western tourists, ecotourism likely would not exist, and national parks may not have come into existence (McQuillan, 1995; Frost and Hall, 2009).

This chapter, therefore, provides a brief account of the emergence of positive attitudes towards mountains and how this has contributed to the development of tourism as a pragmatic conservation mechanism in mountain regions.

Examples are primarily drawn from the USA and Australia. The changing attitudes towards mountains are also grounded in broader debates over how and why nature should be conserved and they have continuing relevance to mountain tourism right up to the present day.

Mountains and the Judeo-Christian Tradition

Mountains have a peculiar place in the Islamic and Judeo-Christian traditions. For the most part, mountains, along with other wild country, have not been desirable places to visit. The historically predominant landscape ideal of ordered and managed nature is regarded as reflecting the Genesis account of creation that gives man dominion over nature (White, 1967). To go to the mountain, desert or wild country was to leave civil society. Rather than being an attraction in their own right, they were a place to be tested, as with the examples of the Israelites' 40 years of wandering in the Sinai or Christ's 40 days and nights in the wilderness. Psalm 140, which has often been quoted by thinkers sympathetic to the design argument and the physico-theological proof for the existence of God (Glacken, 1967) is unusual in that

---

* Corresponding author: michael.hall@canterbury.ac.nz

it contains a sympathetic attitude toward nature, noting that everything in nature has its place in a divine order: 'the high mountains are for the wild goats; the rocks are a refuge for the badgers … O Lord, how manifold are thy works! In wisdom hast thou made them all' (verses 18, 24).

From this perspective, God is separate from nature but he may be understood in part from it and provided a basis for the emergence of minority yet significant positive traditions towards nature in Christianity, such as the teaching of St Francis of Assisi, or the influential St Augustine who wrote: 'Some people in order to discover God, read books. But there is a great book: the very appearance of created things' (quoted in Glacken, 1967, 204). These perspectives were significant, as they helped lay the foundations for both natural science and more positive attitudes towards nature.

The dominant Judeo-Christian view of mountains and wild country can be contrasted with that of Eastern religions. The polarity that existed between city and wilderness in the Judeo-Christian experience did not exist so strongly outside European Christianity. The aesthetic appreciation of wilderness began to change far earlier in the Orient than in the West. By the fourth century AD, for instance, large numbers of people in China had begun to find an aesthetic appeal in mountains, whereas they were still seen as objects of fear in Europe (Nicholson, 1959). Eastern faiths such as Shinto and Taoism fostered appreciation of wild land rather than hatred (Nash, 1967). Shinto deified nature in favour of pastoral scenes. As Tuan (1974, 148) observed: 'In the traditions of Taoist China and pre-Dorian Greece, nature imparted virtue or power. In the Christian tradition sanctifying power is invested in man, God's vice regent, rather than nature.'

Attitudes Towards Nature

Dominant Judeo-Christian narratives about nature provided the language of encounter for European colonial societies in the new world. In the Colonial era, Cotton Mather disdained New England's dark, wolf-filled forests as a demon-ridden 'howling wilderness' that should be cleared into a 'fruitful field' (Leopold, 1989).

For both the Puritans and other settlers in North America and the early colonists in Australia, the 'howling wilderness' provided an environment in which their faith was to be tested, but also a landscape to be transformed and tamed (Nash, 1967; Hall, 1992; Manganiello, 2009).

In Australia wilderness, and mountains in particular, served as a symbol of the physical and mental barriers that the early European settlers faced. It not only prevented convicts from achieving freedom, but it also created the environment in which ordinary men and women were conditioned to suffer and despair. The biblical meaning of wilderness as a place of suffering and possible redemption was reinforced in Australian 19th-century novels, such as *For the Term of His Natural Life*. In Clarke's (1874) book the main character, Rufus Dawes, is struggling against the barrier of wilderness in his search for freedom.

> Footsore and weary, he lay on a thicket of thorny melaleuca, and felt at last that he was beyond pursuit. Dense scrub and savage jungle impeded his path; barren and stony mountain ranges arose before him. He was lost in gullies, entangled in thickets, bewildered in morasses.

The towering cliffs and gorges of the Blue Mountains were perceived by William Wentworth in his poem Australasia (1823; 1873) as part of 'the vast Austral wilderness':

> How mute, how desolate thy stunted woods, How dread thy chasms, where many an evil broods.

Wentworth could well have been writing about a formidable gorge of the Grose River in New South Wales, which led the explorer George Caley to name it the Devil's Wilderness because of its dreary appearance, abruptness, intricacy and dangerous nature (Else-Mitchell, 1939). A similar reaction to wilderness is found in the report of the government Surveyor, James Calder, on his examination of the country between Lake Saint Clair and Macquarie Harbour in south-west Tasmania. Commenting on 'the character of the western country', Calder noted:

> It is frequently open in the valleys, and on some of the secondary hills. On the mountainsides large forests are invariable. A wilder prospect

than that seen from hence can scarcely be imagined; for in almost all directions, the landscape ends in groups of broken mountains.

(Calder, 1849, 418)

However, attitudes towards mountains in the settler societies of the New World came to be dramatically transformed over the course of the century. Miller (1967), for example, argued that by the 1840s the USA had 'nationalized' nature, whereby nature's monuments such as the Niagara Falls and the Rockies were acclaimed as manifestations of America's independence from Europe. America's cultural independence from the Old World produced a desire to laud the moral purity of the wild forests and mountains of the New World, untainted as they were by the domination of things European (Nash, 1967). Yet, this cultural movement, somewhat ironically, sprang from the Romantic movement then sweeping Europe (Honour, 1975; Honour, 1981).

The notions of the sublime, and the development of a Romantic appreciation of nature, found its origins in the work of Immanuel Kant and another German philosopher, Alexander Baumgarten, who introduced the term 'aesthetics' in the 18th century (Perry et al., 2008). Baumgarten considered aesthetics a way of 'knowing', and related the sublime to the physical sensations and the emotions of fear and awe felt when confronted by landscape forms that exhibited the immense physical power of nature – such as volcanoes, rugged mountains, canyons and ancient forests. For Baumgarten, beauty was to be found away from the straight and rigid lines of formal aesthetics and in the smooth and sinuous lines of nature. From such perspectives grew the notions of picturesque landscape that came to be popularized in the poetry of the Romantic poets, such as Coleridge and Wordsworth, as well as the work of artists such as Turner and Caspar David Friedrich.

The Romantic movement provided the intellectual base for the writings of Thoreau, Emerson and, later, John Muir in the USA. The American transcendental movement, as it has come to be called, provided a significant counter to the majority of North Americans, who saw the land as something to be conquered and made productive, rather than conserved. Yet by the mid-19th century the sense of loss

and despoliation of nature in the form of industrialization and urbanization that contributed to the rise of the Romantic movement in Europe was also beginning to be felt in the USA and in other Anglo-colonial societies (Dunlap, 1999). Indeed, the notion of loss was intrinsic to Muir's writing and activism.

To Muir, unlike Emerson and Thoreau, the recording of what he observed was not enough; he felt compelled to try and help save wild country before it was damaged by agricultural clearing, commercial forestry, grazing, or unrestrained tourism. Muir's works represent some of the best natural history writing of their time and proved extremely influential in creating present-day perceptions of national parks and wilderness areas as 'storehouses of nature's treasure' (Hall, 2010). Muir's Romantic ecology was best expressed when he wrote:

> When we try to pick anything out by itself, we find it hitched to anything else in the universe ... The whole wilderness in unity and interrelation is alive and familiar ... the very stones seem talkative, sympathetic, brotherly ... No particle is ever wasted or worn out but eternally flowing from use to use.
>
> (Badè, 1924, 123–124)

John Muir, an avid climber, left a lasting impression on the manner in which mountains and wilderness are interpreted and observed. Muir helped chart the future direction of conservation and environmental thought throughout the world, and has therefore helped substantially shape present-day understanding of the nature of national parks (Nash, 1967). Yet as Mark and Hall (2009, 101) comment:

> The literature on tourism and national parks is surprisingly brief when it comes to discussing the role of activists and the use of tourism as a justification for the creation of national parks, although its role is generally recognized, particularly in its modern day incarnation of 'ecotourism'.

Narratives of Pragmatic Conservation, Tourism and John of the Mountains

The conventional narrative of American and, indeed to a substantial extent, environmentalism elsewhere in the world, is that of the contest between philosophies of wise use (economic conservation) and preservation (Romantic conservation). The first reservations for the preservation of mountain scenery tended to be established in areas that were judged to be waste lands that had no economic value in terms of agriculture, grazing, lumbering or mining but which did attract the tourist dollar via virtue of their aesthetic appeal. Historically, this has usually been illustrated by the contested approaches of Gifford Pinchot and John Muir in the late 19th and early 20th centuries (Nash, 1967; Smith, 1998). However, Minteer and Pyne (2013, 6) argue that in the American context at least, there is a failure to recognize the pragmatism that 'that has always been a part of the U.S. environmental tradition'. Such an observation is significant, as tourism has, arguably, long filled a pragmatic link between the two philosophies.

John Muir's attitude toward tourism is revealing because, 'as with many conservationists Muir regarded tourism as a less evil form of economic development than grazing or commercial clearcutting of forests' (Mark and Hall, 2009, 90). In the 1870s, his writing suggests 'that a growing tourist business might drive the more exploitative users' (Cohen, 1984, 206) out of the Sierra and Yosemite in particular. According to Cohen (1984, 206) Muir attempted to write 'moderate articles which would bring urban tourists' into contact with wild nature, and especially the mountains. There were the 'thousands of tired, nerve-shaken, over-civilized people' that Muir (1898, 15) wrote of, who were discovering the therapeutic value of nature as their real 'home', that 'mountain parks and reservation [were] useful not only as fountains of timber and irrigating rivers but as fountains of life'. Indeed, Cohen goes on to argue, 'in a sense, all of Muir's writings were for the tourist, since they involved the question of how to see. Most tourists did not want to hear philosophy, but wanted to know exactly where to stop and look' (1984, 207).

Significantly for mountain tourism, Muir's writings also helped extend the range of places that the tourist may visit by stressing the importance of encountering wild nature as opposed to the more pastoral nature of a Thoreau or Emerson. For example, in his *First Summer in the Sierra*, first published in 1911 but based on writings from 1869, Muir commented on a group of tourists in the Yosemite:

> Somehow most of these travellers seem to care but little for the glorious objects about them, though enough to spend time and money and endure long rides to see the famous valley. And when they are fairly within the mighty walls of the temple and hear the psalms of the falls, they will forget themselves and become devout. Blessed, indeed, should be every pilgrim in these holy mountains!
> (Muir, 1911, 104)

A theme he frequently returned to when discussing the encounter of visitors to the 'novel grandeur' of Yosemite:

> Most of those I saw yesterday were looking down as if wholly unconscious of anything going on about them, while the sublime rocks were trembling with the tones of the mighty chanting congregation of waters gathered from all the mountains round about, making music that might draw angels out of heaven.
> (Muir, 1911, 190)

As Hall (2010) suggested, Muir was transforming a more Gothic perception of wild nature to one that was not only Romantic and transcendental but which was also experiential. For example, Muir (1874, 267) sought to encourage the reader to get beyond the 'improved' and accessible aspects of the Yosemite Valley floor: 'Lovers of clean mountain wildness must therefore go up higher, into more inaccessible retreats among the summits of the range'. Unless they did so the tourist would be unable to have the same benefits as Muir in encountering the sublime.

> I leaped lightly from rock to rock, glorying in the freshness and sufficiency of nature, and in the ineffable tenderness with which she nurtures her mountain darlings in the very fountain of storms. The world seemed wholly new; young beauty appeared at every step. There was no end of feathery rock-ferns and gardenets of fairest flowers. I exulted in the wild cascades and shimmering crystalline lakelets. Never fell light in brighter spangles; never fell water in brighter foam. I floated through the rocky paradise enchanted, and was out in the lower sunshine ere I was aware.
> (Muir, 1874, 272)

Muir stressed the aesthetic and experiential virtues of the mountains and wild country of the

USA rather than the tamed lands of the Old World. In this, he was reinforcing the idea that the sublime American environment could provide national monuments for the New World that rivalled the cultural monuments of Europe. He suggested that: 'Americans are little aware as yet of the grandeur of their own land, as is too often manifested by going on foreign excursions, while the wonders of our unrivaled plains and mountains are left unseen' (Muir, 1888). As Mark (2009, 83) observed: 'Through a kind of perceptual lens attuned to seeing scenery as art in nature, pursuit of the sublime eventually helped link nascent regional identity with these seemingly wild places. Their sheer scale made them symbols of a "new" nation.'

Muir's activism is significant in the history of mountain tourism because it directly advocated tourism as an economic justification for the establishment of parks and the preservation of natural areas. While business interests, and railroads in particular, had supported the creation of some of the early national parks, including Yellowstone in the USA and Banff in Canada, Muir was integral to an emerging preservation movement that promoted tourism as an alternative form of economic development as well as the aesthetic, religious and sublime virtues of wilderness (Hall, 2010). Nevertheless, while tourism was seen as appropriate, other economic uses of mountain areas were not. For example, in the controversy surrounding the proposed damming of Hetch Hetchy valley in the Sierra Nevada in 1912, Muir was staunchly opposed to the 'purveyors of the dollar' that desired a dam: 'Those temple destroyers, devotees of raging commercialism, seem to have a perfect contempt for Nature, and, instead of lifting their eyes to almighty God of the Mountains, lift them up to the Almighty Dollar' (Muir, 1912).

From present-day perspectives, the extent to which tourism is beneficial in some mountain areas may be debatable. However, it needs to be remembered that numbers of visitors, as well as the total population, were much smaller than at present. The Sierra Club, formed of 'mountain-lovers' in 1901, served as the foundation for Muir's and others' activism as well as a means 'whereby the experiences and practical results of travel might be brought together and preserved for the use of others to follow' (LeConte, 1979, 42). Tourism was integral to the Sierra club's mission. Article III from the club's original articles of incorporation states:

> That the purposes for which this Corporation is formed are as follows, to-wit: To explore, enjoy and render accessible the mountain regions of the Pacific Coast; to publish authentic information concerning them; to enlist the support and co-operation of the people and government in preserving the forests and other natural features of the Sierra Nevada Mountains.
>
> (LeConte, 1979, 44)

As Hall (2010) suggested, inclusion of the phrase 'render accessible' in the Sierra Club's articles set a trajectory that has deeply affected the management and understanding of national parks throughout the world. Among all of the debates affecting national parks, 'the most enduring, and most intense, is where to draw the line between preservation and use' (Runte, 1990, 1). Cohen (1984) argues that:

> Buried in the phrase were the relationships among roads, developed accommodations in parks and reserves, and 'styles' of recreation. After all, ease of access, the comfort of accommodations, and the kind of recreational trails and facilities would determine the kind of ecological consciousness produced by the parks and reserves. From the beginning, the Sierra Club involved itself in decisions about access and development, advocating roads and trails in Yosemite and elsewhere, later encouraging private means of access by railroad and lobbying for improved and more extensive public roads.
>
> (Cohen, 1984, 306)

The environmental pragmatism of the Sierra Club at the beginning of the 20th century is now much more difficult to manage with respect to visitation and other economic and cultural demands. When visitors come into the mountains in some parks, they are now just as likely to find a traffic jam and a pollution haze as they are mountain glory. Rothman (1998, 151) even argues that the early national parks 'served as the transitional stage between the old and new forms of tourism' only to have their meanings transformed by the growth of the automobile (see also Shaffer, 2001). Indeed, with respect to the changing nature of access to and use of national parks, Leopold commented: 'if we think we are going to learn by cruising around the mountains in a Ford, we are largely deceiving ourselves' (Leopold, 1925, 19).

Conclusion: Valuing 'Mountain-top' Tourism

Virtually all national parks established in the USA until the 1930s were examples of rugged scenery. 'Mountain-top parks' comprised but 'a fringe around a mountain peak', a 'patch on one slope of a mountain extending to its crest', or 'but portions of a slope' (Wright et al., 1933, 37, 39). From Yellowstone through to parks that were established in the USA by Congress until 1919, including Mount Rainier (1899), Crater Lake (1902), Glacier (1910), Rocky Mountain (1910) and the Grand Canyon (1919), all were considered worthless for industrial or commercial uses. In one sense they were established not so much for what they were, but for what they were not (Hall, 1989). According to Runte (1973, 5):

> An abundance of public land that seemed worthless – not environmental concern or aesthetic appreciation – made possible the establishment of most national parks in the United States. Nothing else can explain how aesthetic conservationists, who in the past have represented only a small minority of Americans, were able to achieve some success in a nation dominated by a firm commitment to industrial achievement and the exploitation of resources. A surplus of marginal public land enabled the United States to 'afford' aesthetic conservation; national parks protected only such areas as were considered valueless for profitable lumbering, mining, grazing, or agriculture. Indeed, throughout the history of the national parks, the concept of 'useless' scenery has virtually determined which areas the nation would protect and how it would protect them.

Yet such mountain-top parks proved to have some economic value. The romantic appreciation of wild mountain landscape in the USA, Canada, New Zealand and Australia led to the development of a tourist industry associated with national parks and new forms of mountain tourism (Hall and Frost, 2009). The first reserve in Australia which may claim some association with the national park concept was

the reservation of an area in the Fish River (Jenolan) Caves district in the Blue Mountains in October 1866, intended to protect 'a source of delight and instruction to succeeding generations and excite the admiration of tourists from all parts of the world' (Powell, 1976, 114). These were the same mountains that only 30 years previously had evoked negative reactions from travellers. In 1870 the head of Jamieson Creek in the Blue Mountains was reserved, while the Bungonia Lookdown was reserved in 1872. Both areas were 'beauty spots', which provided views of spectacular gorges (Prineas and Gold, 1983). The Queensland *State Forests and National Parks Act* of 1906 was probably the first legislation in the world concerning the procedures to be followed in establishing national parks. The first national park created under the Act was an area of 131 ha at Witches Falls on Tambourine Mountain. However, the land was judged, according to Powell (1976, 114), as 'unfit for any other purpose', a clear restatement of the 'worthless lands' hypothesis attached to the creation of some of the early American national parks (Hall, 1989).

As Runte observed: 'tourism does not contradict the worthless lands hypothesis: it supports it. In the chess game of scenic preservation, ecology was the pawn – only economics could checkmate economics' (Runte, 1983, 140–141). The economic significance of tourism provided the mountain national parks with a pragmatic defence mechanism. Tourism gave areas of land that might otherwise be exploitatively used a material value. Aesthetics were important in the procurement of the tourist dollar and, perhaps just as significantly, have continued to evolve over time along a trajectory begun by the pragmatism of Muir and others like him to bridge the divide between economic and Romantic preservation (Jehlen, 1981). While such pragmatism is imperfect from a preservationist stance, it remains better than nothing; moreover, the dialectic between economic and Romantic preservation is ongoing. Given the prevalence of dualistic interpretations of conservation, a cautious, and defensible, reading might suggest that these oppositions have and will continue to be read/resolved in different fashions at different times, and as Muir has shown, even by the same individual.

References

Badè, W.F. (1924) *The Life and Letters of John Muir*, volume 2. Houghton, Boston, Massachusetts.

Calder, J.E., communicated by Lieut. R.N. Kay (1849) Some account of the country lying between Lake St. Clair and Macquarie Harbour. *The Tasmanian Journal of Natural Science Article XXXIII*, 3(4), 415–429.

Clarke, M. (1874; 1966) *For the Term of His Natural Life*. Oxford University Press, London.

Cohen, M.P. (1984) *The Pathless Way: John Muir and the American Wilderness*. University of Wisconsin Press, Madison, Wisconsin.

Cooper, C. and Hall, C.M. (2008) *Contemporary Tourism: An International Approach*. Butterworth-Heinemann, Oxford, UK.

Dunlap, T.R. (1999) *Nature and the English Diaspora: Environment and History in the United States, Canada, Australia, and New Zealand*. Cambridge University Press, Cambridge, UK.

Else-Mitchell, R. (1939) George Caley: his life and work. *Royal Australian Historical Society Journal and Proceedings* 25(6), 437–542.

Frost, W. and Hall, C.M. (eds) (2009) *Tourism and National Parks: International Perspectives on Development, Histories and Change*. Routledge, London.

Glacken, C. (1967) *Traces on the Rhodian Shore, Nature and Culture in Western Thought from Ancient Times to the End of the Eighteenth Century*. University of California Press, Berkeley, California.

Hall, C.M. (1989) The worthless lands hypothesis and Australia's national parks and reserves. In: Frawley, K. and Semple, N. (eds) *Australia's Ever Changing Forests*. Department of Geography Monograph Series, Australian Defence Force Academy, Canberra, Australia, pp. 441–456.

Hall, C.M. (1992) *Wasteland to World Heritage: Preserving Australia's Wilderness*. Melbourne University Press, Carlton, Melbourne, Australia.

Hall, C.M. (2010) John Muir. In: Butler, R. and Russell, R. (eds) *Giants of Tourism*. CAB International, Wallingford, UK, pp. 229–242.

Hall, C.M. and Frost, W. (2009) National parks and the 'Worthless Lands Hypothesis' revisited. In: Frost, W. and Hall, C. M. (eds) *Tourism and National Parks: International Perspectives on Development, Histories and Change*. Routledge, London, UK, pp. 45–62.

Honour, H. (1975) *The New Golden Land: European Images of America from the Discoverers to the Present Times*. Pantheon Books, New York.

Honour, H. (1981) *Romanticism*. Pelican, Harmondsworth, UK.

Jehlen, M. (1981) The landscape as totem. *Prospects* 6, 17–36.

LeConte, J.N. (1979) The Sierra Club (orig. 1917). In: Gilliam, A. (ed.) *Voices for the Earth. A Treasury of the Sierra Club Bulletin 1893–1977*. Sierra Club, San Francisco, California, pp. 41–45.

Leopold, A. (1925) Conserving the covered wagon. *Sunset* 53(3), 18–23.

Leopold, A. (1989) *A Sand Country Almanac: And Sketches Here and There*. Oxford University Press, Oxford, UK.

Manganiello, C.J. (2009) From a howling wilderness to howling safaris: science, policy and red wolves in the American south. *Journal of the History of Biology* 42(2), 325–359.

Mark, S.R. (2009) Framing the view: how American national parks came to be. In: Frost, W. and Hall, C.M. (eds) *Tourism and National Parks: International Perspectives on Development, Histories and Change*. Routledge, London, pp. 81–87.

Mark, S.R. and Hall, C.M. (2009) John Muir and William Gladstone Steel: activists and the establishment of Yosemite and Crater Lake National Parks. In: Frost, W. and Hall, C.M. (eds) *Tourism and National Parks: International Perspectives on Development, Histories and Change*. Routledge, London, pp. 88–101.

McQuillan, G. (1995) Mont Blanc, romantic tourism, and the legacy of travel writing. *Essays in Romanticism* 3(1), 35–54.

Miller, P. (1967) *Nature's Nation*. Harvard University Press, Cambridge, Massachusetts.

Minteer, B.A. and Pyne, S.J. (2013) Restoring the narrative of American environmentalism. *Restoration Ecology* 21(1), 6–11.

Muir, J. (1874). By-ways of Yosemite Travel. Bloody Canon. *The Overland Monthly* 13(September), 267–273.

Muir, J. (ed.) (1888) The passes of the High Sierra. In: Muir, J. (ed.) *Picturesque California and the Region West of the Rocky Mountains, from Alaska to Mexico*. The J. Dewing Company, San Francisco, California. Available at: http://www.sierraclub.org/john_muir_exhibit (accessed 1 February 2009).

Muir, J. (1898) The wild parks and forest reservations of the West. *Atlantic Monthly* 81(January), 15–16.

Muir, J. (1911) *My First Summer in the Sierra*. Houghton Mifflin, New York.

Muir, J. (1912; 1968) A voice for wilderness. In: Nash, R. (ed.) *The American Environment: Readings in the History of Conservation*. Addison-Wesley, Reading, Massachusetts, pp. 71–74.

Nash, R. (1967) *Wilderness and the American Mind*. Yale University Press, New Haven, Connecticut.

Nicholson, M.H. (1959) *Mountain Gloom and Morning Glory: The Development of the Aesthetics of the Infinite*. Cornell University Press, Ithaca, New York.

Perry, S., Reeves, R. and Sim, J. (2008) Landscape design and the language of nature. *Landscape Review* 12(2), 3–18.

Porteous, J.D. (1986) Bodyscape: the body-landscape metaphor. *The Canadian Geographer/Le Géographe canadien* 30(1), 2–12.

Powell, J.M. (1976) *Conservation and Resource Management in Australia 1788–1914, Guardians, Improvers and Profit: An Introductory Survey*. Oxford University Press, Melbourne, Australia.

Prineas, P. and Gold, H. (1983) *Wild Places: Wilderness in Eastern New South Wales*. Kalianna Press, Chatswood, New South Wales, Australia.

Rothman, H.K. (1998) *Devil's Bargains: Tourism in the Twentieth-Century American West*. University Press of Kansas, Lawrence, Kansas.

Runte, A. (1973) 'Worthless' lands – our national parks: the enigmatic past and uncertain future of America's scenic wonderlands. *American West* 10(May), 4–11.

Runte, A. (1983) Reply to Sellars. *Journal of Forest History* 27(3), 135–141.

Runte, A. (1990) *Yosemite: The Embattled Wilderness*. University of Nebraska Press, Lincoln, Nebraska.

Shaffer, M.S. (2001) *See America First: Tourism and National Identity, 1880–1940*. Smithsonian Institution Press, Washington, DC.

Smith, M.B. (1998) The value of a tree: public debates of John Muir and Gifford Pinchot. *Historian* 60(4), 757–778.

Tuan, Y.-F. (1974) *Topophilia: A Study of Environmental Perception, Attitudes, and Values*. Prentice-Hall, Englewood Cliffs, New Jersey.

Wentworth, W.C. (1823; 1873). *Australasia: A Poem*. Whittaker and Co., London.

White, L. Jr (1967) The historical roots of our ecologic crisis. *Science* 155(10), 1203–1207.

Wright, G.M., Dixon, J.S. and Thompson, B.H. (1933) *Fauna of the National Parks of the United States*. GPO & National Park Service, Washington, DC.

18 External and Internal Challenges of Glacier Tourism Development in Iceland

Johannes Welling* and Thorvarður Árnason
University of Iceland, Reykjavik, Iceland

Introduction

Glaciers in Iceland have been visited by foreign guests for centuries, but it is only in the last few decades that some of these have become highly popular tourist destinations on which a broad array of guided tour activities, ranging from soft to hard adventure, are now provided. Interest in these forms of tourist activities has grown rapidly in recent years, which has in turn led to the formation of many new tour companies specializing in this field, as well as increased overall product diversity. This chapter will examine the development of glacier tourism in Iceland and explore the challenges that this form of niche tourism is facing through gradual and sudden changes of the natural environment, as well as through the development of mountain tourism in Iceland more generally. The findings are based on data collected through a mix of quantitative and qualitative methods. Information concerning glacier tourism for this chapter was obtained by means of a literature study, analysis of tourist enterprises' websites, participant observations during two commercial glacier tours, and in-depth interviews with eight entrepreneurs specialized in glacier tour activities.

Historical Development of Glacier Tourism in Iceland

Due to its geographical isolation and fairly harsh climatic conditions, Iceland did not become a significant destination for foreign travellers until the end of the 18th century. Most foreign visitors in these early times were European scientists who came to Iceland to study its geological phenomena, later followed by upper-middle-class travellers and adventurers motivated to explore the wild and unfamiliar landscapes of volcanoes, lava field and glaciers, and experience untamed and sublime nature (Sæþórsdóttir *et al.*, 2011; Karlsdóttir, 2013). With the arrival of steamships in the late 1870s, Iceland became more accessible to foreign visitors, which led to a transition from the mostly scientist-explorer form of travel to a more touristic or pleasure-based form (Ísleifsson, 1996). It was not until after the Second World War, however, that the tourism industry in Iceland as such started to develop, taking advantage of the transportation infrastructure introduced and developed by the British and American occupation forces during the war.

The first international passenger flights from Iceland to Europe began in 1944, flying

---

* Corresponding author: hwelling@hi.is

Table 18.1. Types of glacier-based tourism activities provided by Icelandic tour companies (source: Icelandic Tourist Board, 2014b).

Types of tours provided	Number of companies	Types of tours provided	Number of companies
Super jeep/truck	16	Photography tours	4
Snowmobile	12	Ice cave tours	4
Glacier walks	9	Glacier hiking (> 1 day)	3
Glacier lake Zodiac/boats	5	Glacier training	1
Ice climbing	5	Other (e.g. scenic flights, dog sledding)	2

out of the US Air Force base in Keflavík, situated about 50 km from Reykjavík, the capital of Iceland. Soon afterwards a route network connecting mainland Europe and North America, using Iceland as a hub, was established, thus creating transport links that provided a major impetus to tourism development on the island (Johannesson *et al.*, 2010). In addition, after the end of the war, Icelanders obtained many of the large army trucks and jeeps with front-wheel drive that had been brought over by the occupation forces (Huijbens and Benediktsson, 2007). These vehicles opened up motorized access to the Central Highland (an uninhabited, largely pristine wilderness that covers about half of the island) and thus enabled travel to various icecaps and glaciers that had previously only been accessible on foot or by horseback. From then on, nature-based tourism in Iceland gradually expanded, mountaineer clubs and travel agencies started to organize tours across the Highlands for both domestic and foreign tourists, lodging cabins were built and travel routes laid out over the wilderness (Sæþórsdóttir *et al.*, 2011).

Because of the limited accessibility and dangerous terrain of glaciers, travelling on or across them was for a long time mainly limited to experienced alpinists and well-equipped scientific expeditions (Guðmundsson, 1995). It was not until the 1990s that local entrepreneurs started to develop commercial adventure and motorized tour activities on glaciers, which catered to less-experienced travellers. Tours taking place on glaciated terrain require specialized equipment (e.g. crampons or full-body harnesses) or modified vehicles (e.g. super-jeeps or snow-scooters), as well as experienced guides who can safely lead the tour groups through the glacial landscape (Buckley, 2007; Furunes

and Mykletun, 2012). Several types of activities also take place on the margin of the glaciers (e.g. hiking and boat trips). In the last decade or so, a broad assortment of guided tour activities that take place on or in the near vicinity of glaciers have been developed in Iceland (Table 18.1).

More recently, smaller or emerging Icelandic tour companies have attempted to explore new niche markets, such as ice cave tours, to differentiate themselves from the now fairly mainstream 'blue-ice' walking tours provided by the bigger companies. Another novel tourism initiative involves drilling a 300-m tunnel for sightseeing purposes in Langjökull, an icecap situated fairly close to the capital area and Keflavík International Airport (Icelandic Tourist Board, 2014a).

Development of Glacier Tourism in Iceland

Iceland has 269 glaciers, including 16 major icecaps, covering in total roughly 11% of Iceland's terrestrial surface (Sigurðsson and Williams, 2008). The large majority of glacier tourism activities, however, take place on just four of these glaciated areas, most of which are situated along the south coast of Iceland. Figure 18.1 shows a map of Iceland with the glaciated areas where most glacier tourism occurs (darkened areas on icecaps/glaciers). The Mýrdalsjökull and Vatnajökull icecaps, along with some of their outlet glaciers, are particularly important for glacier-based tourism services, both motorized and non-motorized, due to their easy and safe accessibility, as well as their proximity to Highway Number 1, the ring road that connects the capital to the

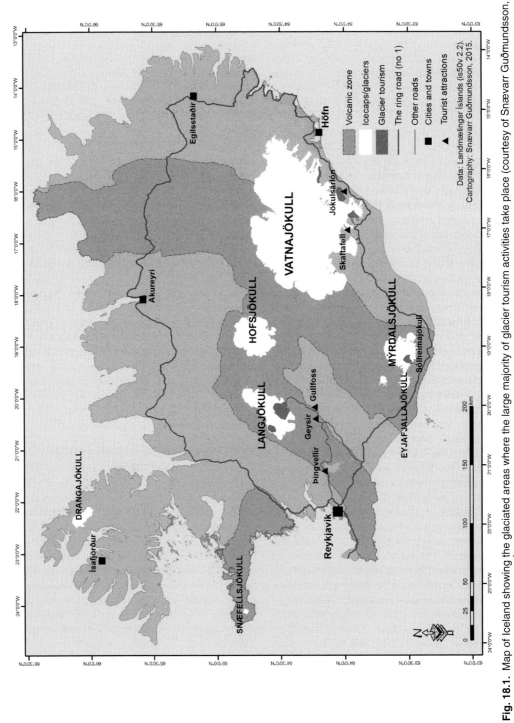

Fig. 18.1. Map of Iceland showing the glaciated areas where the large majority of glacier tourism activities take place (courtesy of Snævarr Guðmundsson, Johannes Welling and Thorvarður Árnason).

rest of the island. Langjökull icecap, on the western rim of the Central Highland, is also a popular site for motorized glacier tours, as is the outlet glacier Skálafellsjökull, on the south-east side of Vatnajökull. Many companies that offer jeep or snowmobile tours furthermore select their sites with regard to combining a glacier tour with visits to other popular nature destinations in the nearby vicinity, (e.g. colourful geothermal sites or spectacular waterfalls). Tours may also go to pro-glacial lakes such as Jökulsárlón on Breiðamerkursandur, which has in recent years become one of the best-known tourist attractions in Iceland. Amphibious boat tours have been available on the lake for roughly three decades and longer-lasting Zodiac tours were recently introduced. The latter type of tour is now also available on the nearby Fjallsárlón pro-glacial lake on the south-east margin of Vatnajökull.

Despite the increasing number and diversity of tour options, specialist outdoor activity companies who focus their product assortment entirely on glaciers or glacial landscapes still constitute a relatively small segment of the total tourism and leisure market in Iceland. As things currently stand, only about 40 companies (approximately 4% of all tour operators in Iceland) are specialized in providing glacier tours (Icelandic Tourist Board, 2014b). Glacier tourism in Iceland is furthermore characterized by the presence of a few relatively large companies with a diverse product range and a fairly large number of smaller and more specialized companies. The large companies have 30–50 full-time employees and a seasonal staff in the summer of more than 150 people. The majority of glacier tourism companies are middle-scale enterprises with between 10 and 30 employees, mostly based in the capital area and with operations on one or more glaciers. Businesses operating solely on Vatnajökull or its outlet glaciers are micro-companies, run by individuals or families, with only 1–5 employees. The number of the latter has increased considerably in the last few years, primarily due to the increase in winter tourism around Jökulsárlón and growing interest in ice cave tours.

Although the glacier tourism market in Iceland is relatively small, the demand for glacier tourism products grew rapidly in the last decade. In 2009 only around 2% of all recreation activities purchased by foreign tourists in Iceland were glacier or snowmobile trips, while by 2012 this had grown to 15% (Icelandic Tourist Board, 2014c). A number of different factors lie behind this strong increase. Glacial landscapes offer opportunities for nature-based recreation and tourism, in response to the ever-growing demand from foreign visitors for activity tours which explore Iceland's 'wild and untamed' nature (Sæþórsdóttir, 2010). Annual tourism surveys have repeatedly shown that the main motivation for travel to Iceland is to experience the island's nature. In the most recent survey, 80% of respondents cited this as the main reason for their trip (Icelandic Tourist Board, 2014c). Glaciers consist of physical features such as moraines, crevasses, moulins and especially the blue ice itself, which stimulate in their visitors feelings of wonder and amazement, as well as thrill, fear and the recognition of the glacier's dangerous power (Jóhannesdóttir, 2010). An encounter with a glacial landscape allows visitors to experience a unique and novel environment, which provides them with escape from their everyday life (Furunes and Mykletun, 2012). Glacier landscapes thus offer elements and attributes that meet the main travel goals of tourists in Iceland (i.e. to experience the pristine and sublime 'land of ice and fire', the last remaining wilderness of Europe). In addition to this, most tourists will not have experienced a glacier prior to their visit. For such tourists, glaciers have an iconic status which creates a 'must see or touch' feeling (Espiner and Becken, 2014). Glaciers furthermore open up opportunities for the provision of a wide range of soft and hard adventure tourism services (Pomfret, 2006; Buckley, 2007), which use the glacier as the setting or backdrop for their activities. Glaciers fulfil the desire of visitors to find something unique or different during their travels, as well as to take on adventurous challenges in a strange and potentially dangerous environment (Furunes and Mykletun, 2012).

Similar to the situation in Norway (Furunes and Mykletun, 2012), glacier tourism in Iceland is mainly the result of entrepreneurial activity by tour companies, which market and sell glacier-based activities as a tourist product. The increase of glacier tourism in Iceland is therefore also a result of the diversification of tour activities over the last 10 years. During this period, glacier tourism expanded from a fairly limited glacier mountaineering niche to a much more general nature-based or outdoor recreation sector, offering a broad activity assortment.

Glacier activities now include guided glacier walks, hikes and glacier traversing; ice-climbing; motorized tours with super-jeeps, trucks or snowmobiles on icecaps; boat and kayak tours on glacier lakes; photography tours in ice caves; training sessions for climbers; and scenic flights by plane or helicopter. The majority of these activities are available throughout the year, whereas some are only possible during the winter season, making glacier tourism an important stimulus for reducing the pronounced seasonality of tourism in Iceland. Furthermore, tour operators often provide tailor-made products for their customers, ranging from short and easy glacier walking trips for families to multi-day glacier tours intended for experienced mountaineers or scientific expeditions, which further diversifies their product range. Some of the larger glacier tour operators have extended their tour assortment enormously, providing more than 100 different kinds of organized trips on glaciers. The majority of glacier tour products consist of single or half-day tours which fit well into 1-day tour packages that are in high demand from tourists residing in the capital area and/or are easily combined with other tour activities taking place on that same day.

The large glacier tour companies have recently established strong networks with other tour operators, as well as transport and hotel chains, for cooperation and coordinated activities and have through this enhanced their marketing position vis-à-vis their competitors in other adventure tourism sectors. The majority of their employees consist of part-time contractors who are hired during the high season (June to August). Such contractors have a relatively easy entrance to the market due to the use of privately owned four-wheel-drive vehicles and often have basic mountain and glacier experiences and skills obtained through their membership of local search and rescue (SAR) teams which operate in every municipality in Iceland or through taking training courses for glacier guides, which are offered on a regular basis by the large glacier tour companies.

Challenges

The challenges facing glacier tourism in Iceland are of two basic kinds. First, external challenges constituting direct or indirect changes in the natural environment that affect glacier tourism but on which the tourism sector has no influence. Volcanic activity and climate change are examples of such challenges. Second, glacier tourism also faces internal challenges, which result from the changes in demand for and supply of glacier tourism activities themselves. The rapid growth of tourism in Iceland is an example of such a challenge.

Volcanic and geothermal activity

Iceland is one of the most active terrestrial volcanic regions, with a frequency of one eruption every 4 to 5 years (Gudmundsson et al., 2008). Approximately 60% of the Icelandic glaciers and icecaps are located on top of a volcanic zone (Fig. 18.1), the most extreme case being Vatnajökull, which covers nine major volcanic or geothermal areas. Since the time of settlement in Iceland (c.870 AD) at least 80 sub-glacial volcanic eruptions have taken place in Vatnajökull (Hannesdóttir, et al., 2010), the latest in Grímsvötn in 2011. The challenges facing glacier tourism mainly concern the indirect consequences of sub-glacial volcanic and geothermal processes. The three main impacts are glacier floods (jökulhlaups), tephra dispersion and diffusion of toxic gases through melt water.

Jökulhlaups

Jökulhlaups are outburst floods from glaciers caused either by sub-glacial volcanic eruptions or the draining of sub-glacial geothermal lakes, both types of floods occur quite frequently in Iceland. Jökulhlaups can change glacial landscapes dramatically: deposit fluvial and glacial sediments, flush away vegetation, endanger humans and livestock, and make large regions inaccessible by destroying bridges and roads (Björnsson and Pálsson, 2008). The most dramatic example of this in recent times is the

1996 Gjálp eruption underneath Vatnajökull, which destroyed two major bridges on the ring road. Most jökulhlaups caused by the draining of sub-glacial geothermal lakes are relatively minor and occur at fairly regular intervals but outburst floods caused by volcanic activity, in contrast, tend to drain without delay towards the glacier margin (Björnsson, 2002). A recent example of the latter is the volcanically generated jökulhlaup from Sólheimajökull, one of the most popular glacier tourism sites in Iceland, in the summer of 1999. This flood was unexpected and characterized by an unusually rapid rise of the melt water peak discharge draining into two former ice-dammed lake basins, which rapidly filled and drained catastrophically, filling the adjacent valley (Russell *et al.*, 2010).

Tephra dispersion

Another consequence of sub-glacial volcanic activity is the widespread dispersion of tephra (volcanic ash) during and following an eruption. Icelandic eruptions are often characterized by the production of large volumes of volcanic ash (Thordarson and Höskuldsson, 2008). The airborne dispersion of tephra can cover extensive parts of the glacier surface near the volcano. The tephra dispersion and disposition from sub-glacial eruptions in Eyafjallajökull in 2010 and Grimsvötn in 2011 affected the surface of almost all icecaps in Iceland. This can result not only in negative effects on the perceived glacial scenery but can also have major impacts on the accessibility of the area, whether by land or air.

Poisonous gas from floodwater

Sub-glacial geothermal activity can release poisonous gases into floodwater underneath an outlet glacier or icecap. A common volcanic gas that diffuses from melt water generated by the geothermal areas underneath Icelandic glaciers is hydrogen sulphide (H_2S) (Lawler *et al.*, 1996). Hydrogen sulphide has a malodorous smell and can irritate and eventually burn mucous membranes in both eyes and the respiratory system.

The glacier river that drains from Sólheimajökull often contains high concentrations of sulphur, which can reach poisonous levels by the glacier margin. In July 2014, high concentrations of H_2S in the floodwater emerging from the glacier required local authorities to advise travellers and tour companies to avoid going close to the glacier margin (Civil Protection in Iceland, 2014).

Responses to such events concerning tourists are mostly aimed at preventive measures and information dispersal. Local authorities, in cooperation with Search and Rescue (SAR) teams and regional tourism associations, have developed regional volcanic risk management strategies that consist of information meetings, onsite training sessions, distribution of information brochures to tourists, and the placing of hazard and emergency response information panels in mountain huts and in prominent positions along hiking trails (Bird and Gisladóttir, 2014). However, a recent study by Bird *et al.* (2010) showed that tourists in Iceland lacked knowledge of volcanic hazards, such as jökulhlaups, and that both tourists and tourism employees lacked knowledge of the early warning system and emergency response procedures.

Climate change

Icelandic icecaps and glaciers are all categorized as being temperate or warm-based (i.e. they have a high annual mass turnover where considerable melting is compensated for by high precipitation and, in turn, high rates of accumulation) (Aðalgeirsdóttir *et al.*, 2011). Such glaciers are highly dynamic and sensitive to climate variation, resulting in rapid responses (advance or retreat) to changes in temperature and precipitation (Björnsson and Pálsson, 2008; Guðmundsson *et al.*, 2011). The recorded changes in the volume and area of Icelandic glaciers are thus excellent indicators of global climate change. The first records of glacier volume in Iceland date back to the first centuries of settlement in Iceland (Aðalgeirsdóttir et al, 2011). After the onset of the Little Ice Age in the 13th century, glaciers started to advance and continued to do this until the late 19th century, when most of them had reached their maximum postglacial extent (Hannesdóttir et al., 2014). Around the beginning of the 20th century this trend was reversed, and since then all glaciers in Iceland have on the whole been receding. Glacier recession has been especially pronounced since the 1990s, with all monitored icecaps retreating and thinning at an unprecedented pace (Björnsson and Pálsson, 2008; Hannesdóttir et al., 2010). Langjökull, for example, diminished by about 7% in area from 1997 to 2006, and the outlet glaciers Virkisjökull–Falljökull, south of the Vatnajökull icecap, have shown an exceptionally fast retreat since 2007 (Guðmundsson et al., 2011; Bradwell et al., 2013). Dynamic glacier models coupled with future climate scenarios predict that the largest icecaps in Iceland – Vatnajökull, Langjökull and Hofsjökull – will lose 25–35% of their 1990 volume before 2040 and disappear almost totally within 150–200 years (Björnsson and Pálsson, 2008).

The recession of Icelandic glaciers, in particular, the upwards shift of the margins of outlet glaciers where most tourism activities take place, has already resulted in a number of negative impacts for glacier tourism, primarily concerning the maintenance of accessibility for tourism operations to popular glacier sites. As an example, the recession of the glacier terminus of Skálafellsjökull, south-east of the Vatnajökull icecap, to a higher elevation level made the glacier access point too steep for access by inexperienced tourists. A more wide-reaching concern of glacier tour companies is the extension of the distance between the parking place for their vehicles to the retreating glacier margin, which increases the time and walking distance that tour groups need to travel before they reach the glacier. In some cases, distances from the parking lot to the glacier have doubled in less than 20 years, resulting in the cessation of tours on such glaciers. Climate change in Iceland is also causing an earlier onset of the melting season, as well as enhanced late summer melting, resulting in an increase of glacier runoff and changes in the courses of glacial rivers, which can affect accessibility of different glacier sites (Björnsson et al., 2011).

Glacier recession also results in the emergence of pro-glacial lakes in front of most of the southern outlet glaciers of Vatnajökull, due to the uncovering of deep sub-glacial troughs carved out by the ice-age glaciers, which then fill up with melt-water runoff (Magnússon et al., 2012). This can restrict access for walking tours to the glacier margins but, in turn, provides opportunities for new types of activities, especially boat tours of various kinds. Future projections of glacier recession indicate that glacier lakes will become longer and wider and gradually replace the outlet glaciers totally (Magnússon et al., 2012). In the short run, this is likely to provide opportunities for more tourism activities on or around those lakes. However, the extension of glacier lakes may form serious barriers for tours on the glacier, as they can block access to the valley completely (Ritter et al., 2012). Glacier retreat also triggers the calving of ice-blocks from the termini of the glacier into lagoons, causing tidal waves, which can be hazardous to nearby visitors. Due to increased risk of calving at the margin of Sólheimajökull in August 2014, the nearby parking area was closed for weeks and the trail to the glacier had to be re-routed (Robert, 2014). This extended the walking time to the glacier by almost one hour, which in turn made the tour too difficult for less mobile visitor groups, such as families with young children and older people.

Increased tourism

The number of foreign visitors to Iceland tripled between 2002 and 2013 to reach 781,000 (Icelandic Tourist Board, 2014c). The long-term average increase in tourist arrivals was around 6–7% per year until 2011, when a new and much faster phase of increase started, with annual growth of 15–20% per year, which shows no signs of abating. This strong increase places growing pressure on fragile ecosystems and on local ways of life and traditions (OECD, 2014) and also has effects on glacier tourism. The number of glacier tours is thus rapidly growing while the number of glaciers accessible for such tours remains more or less the same. This results in increased tension between different tourist groups and between different tour companies. An example of this is ice-cave tours in south-east Iceland, which have recently become very popular, following an increase in winter tourism in Iceland. The number of easily accessible caves is very limited and tensions can thus arise between specialized tours for photographers, which involve small groups staying for fairly long durations, and larger groups of general tourists seeking the thrill of experiencing an ice cave.

Tensions have also risen between local tour operators who largely depend on such trips for their livelihood and the larger and more diversified adventure tour companies based in Reykjavík that offer day-tours to the ice caves from the capital area. The fact that these activities take place within the borders of Vatnajökull National Park suggests a possible solution in the form of specific management guidelines, which could limit the number of companies operating in such areas, but no such guidelines currently exist and, even if they were developed, they might prove difficult to enforce.

Conclusion

Glacier tourism in Iceland has grown from being a fairly small, niche-orientated sector to becoming one of the largest and most diverse adventure tourism sectors in the country in a relatively short period of time. These developments are largely due to the general increase in annual tourist arrivals to Iceland, but also to a considerable extent by the entrepreneurial activities of tour operators, who have both extended and diversified their operations. Glacier tourism faces several different types of external challenges, some catastrophic but short-lived (such as volcanic eruptions), some recurrent but localized (such as emission of poisonous gases) and some which are small-scale but cumulative and thus likely to have a significant long-term effect (such as global climate change).

The internal challenges facing this sector stem mainly from an unusually high rate of increase in tourist arrivals, which has been going on for a much longer period than any previous tourist boom and is putting large strains on the tourism infrastructure in Iceland. In some cases tensions have arisen between tourism companies due to competition for a limited resource (such as ice caves). Such tensions can be at least partly abated through increased cooperation or, in the case of protected areas, more stringent management guidelines.

The future development of glacier tourism in Iceland will mainly depend on the ability of tourism entrepreneurs to respond to the growing demand for distinctive glacier-based tour products that maintain the atmosphere of being in a sublime and untouched glacial landscape, while simultaneously coping with changes in the environment, both physical and perceived.

Acknowledgements

The authors wish to thank Snævarr Guðmundsson for his assistance in designing Fig. 18.1. Johannes Welling would also like to thank the Nature Conservation Fund of Pálmi Jónsson and the Icelandic Tourism Research Centre for their financial support of his research.

References

Aðalgeirsdóttir, G., Guðmundsson, S., Björnsson, H., Pálsson, F., Jóhannesson, T., *et al*. (2011) Modelling the 20th and 21st century evolution of Hoffellsjökull glacier, SE-Vatnajökull, Iceland. *The Cryosphere* 5, 961–975.

Bird, D.K. and Gisladóttir, G. (2014) Southern iceland: volcanoes, tourism and volcanic risk reduction. In: P. Erfurt-Cooper (ed.) *Volcanic Tourist Destinations*. Springer, Berlin-Heidelberg, Germany, pp. 35–46.

Bird, D.K., Gisladóttir, G. and Dominey-Howes, D. (2010) Volcanic risk and tourism in southern Iceland: implications for hazard, risk and emergency response education and training. *Journal of Volcanology and Geothermal Research* 189, 33–48.

Björnsson, H. (2002) Subglacial lakes and jökulhlaups in Iceland. *Global and Planetary Change* 35, 255–271.

Björnsson, H. and Pálsson, F. (2008) Icelandic glaciers. *Jökull* 58, 365–386.

Björnsson, H., Jóhannesson, T. and Snorrason, A. (2011) Recent climate change, projected impacts and adaptation capacity in Iceland. In: Linkov, I. and Bridges, T.S. (eds) *Climate: Global Change and Local Adaptation.* Springer, Dordrecht, Netherlands.

Bradwell, T., Sigurðsson, O. and Everest, J. (2013) Recent, very rapid retreat of a temperate glacier in SE Iceland. *Boreas* 42, 959–973.

Buckley, R. (2007) Adventure tourism products: price, duration, size, skill, remoteness. *Tourism Management* 28, 1428–1433.

Civil Protection Department in Iceland [Almannavarnir] (2014) Uncertainty phase – Update in English. Available at: http://www.almannavarnir.is/displayer.asp?cat_id=8&module_id=220&element_id=3137 (accessed 20 August 2014).

Espiner, S. and Becken, S. (2014) Tourist towns on the edge: conceptualising vulnerability and resilience in a protected area tourism system. *Journal of Sustainable Tourism* 22 (4), 646–665.

Furunes, T. and Mykletun, R.J. (2012) Frozen adventure at risk? A 7-year follow-up study of Norwegian Glacier tourism. *Scandinavian Journal of Hospitality and Tourism* 12(4), 324–348.

Guðmundsson, A.T. (1995) *Mountaineering in Iceland: Notes on Climbing, Hill-Walking and Glacier Tours.* Ari Trausti Gudmundsson, Reykjavik, Iceland.

Gudmundsson, M.T., Larsen, G., Höskuldsson, A. and Gylfason, A.G. (2008) Volcanic hazards in Iceland. *Jökull* 58, 251–268.

Guðmundsson, S., Björnsson, H., Magnússon, E., Berthier, E., Pálsson, F., *et al.* (2011) Response of Eyjafjallajökull, Torfajökull and Tindfjallajökull ice caps in Iceland to regional warming, deduced by remote sensing. *Polar Research* 30, 72–82.

Hannesdóttir, H., Zöhrer, A., Davids, H., Sigurgeirsdóttir, S.I., Skírnisdóttir, H. and Árnason, Þ. (2010) *Vatnajökull National Park: Geology and Geodynamics.* Northern Environmental Education Development. University of Iceland – Hornafjordur Regional Research Centre, Hornafjordur, Iceland.

Hannesdóttir, H., Pálsson, F., Algeirsdóttir, G. and Guðmundsson, S. (2014) Variations of Southeast Vatnajökull ice cap (Iceland) 1650–1900 and reconstruction of the glacier surface geometry at the little ice age maximum. *Geografiska Annaler: Series A, Physical Geography* 97(2), 237–264.

Huijbens E.H. and Benediktsson, K. (2007) Practising highland heterotopias: automobility in the interior of Iceland. *Mobilities* 2(1), 143–165.

Icelandic Tourist Board (2014a) Ice Tunnel to Open Next Year. Available at: http://www.ferdamalastofa.is/en/moya/news/ice-tunnel-to-open-next-year (accessed 20 August 2014).

Icelandic Tourist Board (2014b) *List of Icelandic Tour Operators and Travel Agencies.* Icelandic Tourist Board, Reykjavík, Iceland.

Icelandic Tourist Board (2014c) Tourism in Iceland in Figures, April 2014. Icelandic Tourist Board, Reykjavík. Available at: www.ferdamalastofa.is/static/files/ferdamalastofa/talnaefni/tourism-in-iceland-in-figures-april-2013.pdf (accessed 15 August 2014).

Ísleifsson, S.I. (1996) *Ísland framandi land.* Mál og menning, Reykjavík, Iceland.

Jóhannesdóttir, G.R. (2010) Landscape and aesthetic values: not only in the eye of the beholder. In: Benediktsson, K. and Lund, K.A. (eds) *Conversations with Landscape.* Ashgate Publishing, Farnham, UK, pp. 109–125.

Johannesson, G.T., Huijbens, E.H. and Sharpley, R. (2010) Icelandic tourism: past directions – future challenges. *Tourism Geographies* 12(2), 278–301.

Karlsdóttir, U.B. (2013) Nature worth seeing! The tourist gaze as a factor in shaping views on nature in Iceland. *Tourist Studies* 13(2), 139–155.

Lawler, D.M., Björnsson, H. and Dolan, M. (1996) Impact of subglacial geo-thermal activity on meltwater quality in the Jökulsa-a-Solheimasandi system, South Iceland. *Hydrological Processes* 10, 557–578.

Magnússon, E., Palsson, F., Björnsson, H. and Guðmundsson, S. (2012) Removing the ice cap of Öræfajökull central volcano, SE-Iceland: mapping and interpretation of bedrock topography, ice volumes, subglacial troughs and implications for hazards assessments. *Jökull* 62, 131–150.

OECD (2014) *OECD Environmental Performance Reviews: Iceland 2014.* OECD Publishing. Available at: http://dx.doi.org/10.1787/9789264214200-en (accessed 10 October 2014).

Pomfret, G. (2006) Mountaineering adventure tourists: a conceptual framework for research. *Tourism Management* 27, 113–123.

Ritter, F., Fiebig, M. and Muhar, A. (2012) Impacts of global warming on mountaineering: a classification of phenomena affecting the alpine trail network. *Mountain Research and Development* 32(1), 4–15.

Robert, Z. (2014) Level of uncertainty at Sólheimajökull. *Iceland Review On Line*, 05 August 2014. Available at: http://icelandreview.com/news/2014/08/05/level-uncertainty-solheimajokull (accessed 21 August 2014).

Russell, A.J., Tweed, F.S., Roberts, M.J., Harris, T.D., Gudmundsson, M.T., *et al.* (2010) An unusual jökulhlaup resulting from subglacial volcanism, Sólheimajökull, Iceland. *Quaternary Science Reviews* 29, 1363–1381.

Sæþórsdóttir, A.D. (2010) Tourism struggling as the wilderness is developed. *Scandinavian Journal of Hospitality and Tourism* 10(3), 334–357.

Sæþórsdóttir, A.D., Hall, C.M. and Saarinen, J. (2011) Making wilderness: tourism and the history of the wilderness idea in Iceland. *Polar Geography* 34(4), 249–273.

Sigurðsson O. and Williams, R. S. Jr (2008) *Geographical Names of Iceland's Glaciers: Historic and Modern*. Professional Paper 1746. US Geological Survey, Reston, Virginia.

Thordarson, T. and Höskuldsson, A. (2008) Postglacial volcanism in Iceland. *Jökull* 58, 197–228.

19 Hiking Tourism in Germany's Low and High Mountain Regions

Axel Dreyer* and Anne Menzel

Harz University of Applied Sciences, Wernigerode, Germany

Introduction

Over recent years, approximately 30% of the German population aged 14 and over chose regions in Germany as their preferred holiday destination (Schrader, 2013; Schmuecker and Koch, 2014; FUR, 2015). The most popular destinations for hiking holidays in Germany are mountains (BMWi, 2010). According to a study of PROJECT M *et al.* (2014), the low mountain ranges of the Black Forest (Schwarzwald), Bavarian Forest (Bayerischer Wald), the Harz Mountains, as well as the Allgäu (low mountain range and Alpine foothills – 'Alpen') are the preferred destination areas. Another hiking region, though less popular overall for Germans is the Alps, a high mountain range system that lies entirely in Europe and in the deepest south of Germany. Figure 19.1 shows the locations of the most important low mountain regions in Germany.

In Germany there are no world-famous hiking routes or trails like the Inca Trail in Peru, the West Coast Trail in British Columbia or the John Muir Trail in California, but there are numerous interesting and well-signposted routes in all federal German states, with the most interesting found in mountain regions. Some of these popular hiking trails in Germany are the 'Rennsteig' hiking trail in the Thuringian Forest ('Thüringer Wald'), the Rothaar Trail ('Rothaarsteig') in the Sauerland region, and the 'Westweg' Trail, which extends through the entire Black Forest, Germany's largest and highest low-mountain range, which has gained in national popularity.

Hiking – Recent Developments in the Context of Sports-related and Active Tourism

Only a couple of decades ago when holidays in the age of industrialization primarily focused on regeneration, rest and recreation came first in the list of travel priorities. The gradual structural shift towards a service-oriented society has led to a change in holiday interests not only in Germany, but also in many other countries of the Western world. Although rest and recreation are still important to people during their holidays, other interests have emerged that have either become as important or taken precedence over rest and recreation.

---

* Corresponding author: adreyer@hs-harz.de

Fig. 19.1. Most popular mountain regions for hiking holidays in Germany.

Since the end of the 1990s, the range of physical activities and sports carried out while on holiday has increased considerably, although the number of mere sport holiday bookings has not grown noticeably since then. Hiking has been a preferred leisure activity for Germans second only to swimming (IfD, 2005, 2008, 2011, 2014), and the low mountain regions are popular hiking areas due to their easy access. Although the number of other nature-based activity options that compete with hiking have increased, 40 million Germans enjoy hiking, and annual spending along chosen hiking trails has contributed up to €7.5 billion over approximately 370 million 1-day hiking tours. This market, therefore, offers a strong development potential especially in rural areas (DWV, 2013) and, as we show later, the low mountain

ranges are the most frequented type of landscape for hiking in Germany.

What distinguishes hiking from other activities on foot?

There are numerous facets of hiking, but no conclusive definition available for the term, which may vary according to context. Hiking is more than just walking, and differs from other kinds of running sports like jogging as the step sequence is defined as being without a flight phase (Dreyer et al., 2009). When does hiking start, and going for a walk end? Or, when does trekking start? To find and set up binding distinguishing limits has been challenging. Even the term 'trekking' is understood and interpreted differently between Germany, Nepal and New Zealand. In order to be able to differentiate as accurately as possible between hiking and other forms of walking, the essential characteristics of both sports have to be defined by fixing and formulating essential characteristics (Menzel *et al.*, 2013) like amount of time, landscape, planning, motives, trails, equipment and type of vacation.

The low mountain ranges – the most popular type of landscape for hiking in Germany

Hiking can be seen from various viewpoints:

- **Duration/length of time** (half-day, day, and several-day tours)
- **Motivational aspects or physical benefits** (i.e. sport-oriented hiking, pleasure-oriented hiking, health-oriented hiking, excursions and/or guided hiking tours)
- **Height parameters**

Important parameters for height are geographic (i.e. height profile, gradients or slopes) and climatic conditions (i.e. air pressure, temperature). These conditions affect and can impose strain on the cardiovascular and the musculoskeletal system (Scheumann, 2003).

Germany has three different types of landscape:

- The North German Plains or **lowlands**, which are flat.
- The middle and more southern part of Germany (which is the largest part) and to a large extent is a **low mountain** region with subdued mountains and a terraced landscape.
- The South German Alpine foothills and plateau, which gradually extends to the Alps, or the **high mountain** ranges.

Due to these geographic conditions, Germany can be divided into the following three hiking regions: lowland, low mountain and high mountain or alpine.

Hiking in the low mountain regions

The German low mountain regions are probably the most characteristic and typical landscape types in Germany. All mountain regions in Germany apart from the Alps and foothills of the Alps or alpine foreland are low mountain regions. The sparse population, a largely untouched nature, and the specific landscape features of this hilly region are particularly appealing and attract many holidaymakers and day-trippers. With hill heights ranging from 300 to 1500 m, and its many forests, valleys and rivers, the low mountain regions are not only important tourist regions but also the most popular landscapes for hiking. Approximately 40% of all active hikers in Germany prefer hiking in this landscape compared to other regions (BMWi, 2010).

Typical features of hiking in low mountain regions are the constantly changing landscapes and route profiles, as well as the beautiful scenic views (Menzel *et al.*, 2008; Trendscope, 2009; BMWi, 2010). Due to the moderate ascents and descents while hiking in the low mountain regions, the level of physical effort increases and muscular fatigue starts sooner than when hiking in the lowland (Scheumann, 2003).

Hiking in high mountain ranges (Alpine hiking)

Due to the fact that the percentage of high mountain ranges is rather small in Germany, the German high mountain alpine region is of little significance for hikers. Only 9% of the active hikers, hiking in Germany, mention it as their preferred hiking region (BMWi, 2010). Alpine hiking is the most demanding form of hiking requiring: hiking experience; knowledge of the route, track and weather conditions; the right equipment; good physical constitution, endurance and a sure foot (Scheumann, 2003).

Hiking – the Demand for Relevant Offers in Germany

Market research for the German market

Hiking has become increasingly popular in Germany throughout the last two decades.

During the so-called 'boom years' the percentage of hikers ('I go hiking regularly and/or every once in a while') among the total German population was over 60% (see Fig. 19.2). Since this time, a slight decrease has been noticeable (IfD, 1985–2014).

In contrast to relevant studies about leisure activities (i.e. AWA and VuMA), a hiking study developed by the German Hiking Association (PROJECT M *et al.*, 2014) concluded that there is an increasing demand for hiking in vacation and spare time. But a closer examination of this study shows that the demand only increased among the group of persons that had responded 'relatively seldom' hiking. This group increased from 18% in 2010 to 35% in 2013 and particularly applies to younger target groups. The percentage of regular hikers, who tend to be older ages, has declined. Among the group of occasional hikers, there have been no pronounced deviations in the years 2010 to 2014 (PROJECT M *et al.*, 2014). In this respect it is to be noted there was some inconsistency in methodology as in 2010, data was conducted by guideline-based telephone interviews, whereas in 2013, data was primarily collected via the Internet (BMWi, 2010; PROJECT M *et al.*, 2014). In general, however, it can be stated that hiking is a popular spare time activity for all age groups and has stabilized at a high level in Germany. Hiking is preferred over all other forms of spare time physical activities including cycling.

Reasons for being interested in hiking

One reason for the broad interest in hiking is the sales activities and marketing campaigns of the outdoor products and clothing industry that supports the increasing demand for close to nature offers. Since the end of the 1990s, German destinations increasingly have focused on improving the infrastructure of their hiking trails (cabin hiking/hut-to-hut hiking). New theme paths or themed hiking trails for excursions have been designed and new hiking target groups were explicitly addressed literally by creating 'hiking events' and offering appealing package tour holiday offers with organized pick-up and luggage transport (Menzel *et al.*, 2008). In 2002, enhanced quality awareness led to the first quality standards for hiking trails being implemented and since 2005, further criteria for hosts and lodging in Germany were added. For the first time in 2014 a complete hiking destination was rated as 'premium quality region/region of excellent quality' by the German Hiking Association.

The main reasons for hiking in Germany are: (i) to experience nature and the landscape; (ii) to relax; (iii) to regain and maintain health; and (iv) to feel and get to know something new (Dreyer *et al.*, 2009). The advantage of hiking compared to other types of sport and physical leisure activities is that as a so-called 'lifetime sport' it can be practised by people of nearly all age groups (Fig. 19.3).

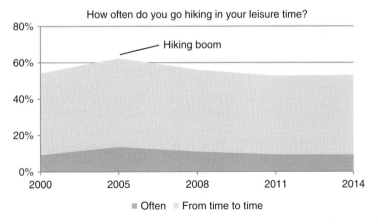

Fig. 19.2. Development of demand in the leisure time segment from 2000 to 2014 (from data in IfD, 2000, 2005, 2008, 2011, 2014).

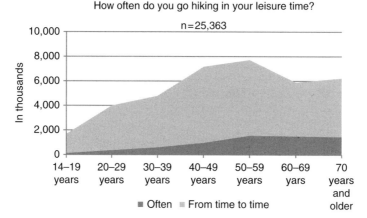

Fig. 19.3. Hiking popularity according to age group (from data in IfD, 2014).

Parallel to the positive development in the demand for hiking and as a result of a variety of factors such as technological innovations (Schneider and Dreyer, 2011), medical advances and demographic changes (Dreyer and Menzel, 2009), the hiking style and clientele has changed considerably throughout the last 20 years. Hikers are nowadays more often individualists with quite different motives and needs. For instance, hiking typologies are becoming more and more sophisticated and diverse (i.e. hut-to-hut hikes, hiking without backpacks, vineyard hiking).

Hiking Tourism in Germany – *Quo Vadis*?

Hiking tourism and general tourism trends

The development of hiking tourism should not be viewed detached from general tourism trends, which arise from, or are based on social megatrends (Gross and Klemmer, 2014). Framework conditions of this development include: climate change, technological progress and changes in population. Megatrend examples in Germany as a result of these conditions might include the rising demand for health care services (due to the growing number of older people in Germany) or the increasing tendency towards individualization. Further trends of relevance to tourism were shown by the UNWTO

(2001), who identified 11 tourism megatrends: globalization and localization – thinking globally and acting locally; polarization of tourism tastes – active/passive, big/small, consumptive/green, safety/risk; shrinking tourist world; electronic technology and fast track travel; consumers calling the shots; destinations seen as fashion accessories; theme-based marketing; increased destination focus on image – perceptions of potential visitors is critical; focus on Asian tourists; consumer-led campaigns – for sustainable development and fair trade tourism that better distributes benefits; and conscience vs consumption – growing conflict between socio-environmental consciousness and urge for travel consumption.

Tourism trends in Germany

Hiking might not only gain significance in the future as a result of changes in Germany's demographic characteristics but also because of the impact of general changes within society. The shift in the relationship of working to spare time started in the 1950s; by the 1990s the former work-oriented society changed to a leisure-oriented society in which values like pleasure, experience or event orientation, and environmental awareness emerged. Nowadays, the average work week is lengthening for some occupational groups, and as a result, leisure behaviour is also changing. According to Dreyer (2009, 2012), this includes German trends in tourism that will focus on the following priorities, each of which also can be associated with hiking activities: health, slower paced/deceleration, climate-friendly, more comfortable and individualized, cheaper and spontaneous, luxurious and exotic, experience-oriented, shorter and more frequent, safety and security. Further trends can be shown by Romeiss-Stracke (2005), who explains 'Sinngesellschaft' as a return to inner values; individualization, pleasure and lifestyle are becoming more and more important in Germany. Also the overall sense of well-being (naturally, emotionally and physically) is bound to change within a rapidly changing society (Romeiss-Stracke, 2005).

Trends in Hiking Tourism

Trends in hiking tourism not only depend on the classical megatrends in the tourism and travel sector, but also on the specific needs of the individual hiker. The hiking guest, like all consumers, is gradually becoming a multi-optional user who wants a larger variety of options and activities. The simplicity and naturalness of hiking is contrary to the increasing demands for quality and the desire for more comfort and convenience. Nevertheless, across all age groups, the principal motives are primarily to experience nature and to relax, as well as (often subliminal) seeking health benefits. The following pages attempt to give a picture of the six essential trends in hiking tourism: health; spirituality; quality; culture; experience; and technology.

Trend 1: Health

The general interest in health-related issues is becoming increasingly important in a societal context (Horx and Gatterer, 2013). In recent years, health has virtually become an independent consumer good as the demand for health products has increased considerably. This is a consequence of the demographic change and of industrialization. The LOHAS (lifestyle of health and sustainability) consumer segment is an emerging target market.

Health issues are not only gaining importance in the traditional or classic holiday sector, but also have an increasingly high priority for hikers. Besides being able to experience nature, the motives 'getting exercise' and 'do something for my health' have the highest priority for hikers (BMWi, 2010) and the significance of these motives increases with age.

The subject of health when hiking is not only of importance for older target groups, but also for younger persons in particular, who hike to reduce the increasing psychological and mental stress of their professional and family life. In their spare time, they seek rest and recuperation in natural surroundings (Leder, 2010). Dreyer and Duerkop (2011) discuss a special form of 'slow hiking'.

In future there will be, on the one hand, offers that explicitly promote the health-enhancing effects of hiking (for this reason training courses for specialized health hiking guides (so-called 'Gesundheitswanderführer') are meanwhile offered in Germany) and, on the other hand, more products will be available, which by choosing different combinations of components (i.e. hiking, wellness, tasty and healthy diet) will help to take proper account of the customer's specific needs and individual wishes to do something good for body and soul.

Trend 2: Spirituality

For more and more people a (hiking) holiday is also a search for meaning (Antz, 2009; Dreyer, 2012). This tendency to spirituality can also be explained by societal changes from a hedonistic society to a society on the lookout for meaning and purpose of life. In recent years an increase of spirituality in conjunction with hiking has become apparent, for instance by more visits to pilgrimage destinations. The pilgrims' office in Santiago de Compostela, Spain, for example, has noticed a steady growth in visitors for years. For the first time in 2006 more than 100,000 pilgrims were registered there, and in 2013 more than 200,000 registered. Nearly 15% of the foreign pilgrims at the Camino Francés are Germans (Pilgrims' Office in Santiago de Compostela, 2014).

Traditional pilgrimage in Europe as well as in the Christian culture area is not practised solely for religious reasons. The percentage of pilgrims who are not searching for God, but for a more general understanding of the meaning of life, is increasing steadily. The long stay in nature and the resulting stimulation of all senses gives people the feeling of returning (even if only for a short time) to their natural roots and helps them regain physical and mental energy (Horx and Gatterer, 2013; Opaschowski, 2013). This new and holistic view of 'pilgrimage' is therefore no longer compatible with the original meaning of the term; Antz (2009) provides the more comprehensive term 'spiritual hiking'.

Trend 3: Quality

It can also be observed that the demands of hikers have increased in recent years and will probably increase further. The demands on hiking trails in Germany are high. Ideally an optimal hiking trail system should have the following features:

- Narrow, naturally grown, and winding paths/trails.
- Cultural highlights along the hiking trail.
- Natural waters and attractions if possible.
- Clear and user-friendly marking or signposts.
- Good infrastructure, with parking facilities at the start of the hiking trail, refuges or shelters and resting places, and serviced huts for refreshments/food (Trendscope, 2009; BMWi, 2010; DWV, 2014).

The clear determination of quality standards for hiking trails is an orientation aid for travel decisions. The driving force for improving quality in the field of hiking tourism is the German Hiking Association (DWV) with its 600,000 members, which, among other things, takes care of more than 200,000 km of hiking trails (signposting, cleanliness, etc.) (DWV, 2014). Also of importance in this context is the German Alpine Club with over 1 million members (DAV, 2015) which, among other things, is responsible for operating numerous mountain huts and alpine lodges.

In recent years the German Hiking Association has launched numerous initiatives concerning quality (DWV, 2014).

- Certification of hiking trails (over 100 trails with the special quality distinction 'Qualitätswege Wanderbares Deutschland').

- Certification of accommodation and food (1450 certified hosts and lodgings 'Qualitätsgastgeber Wanderbares Deutschland').
- Training of hiking guides (5755 persons).
- Certification of health hiking guides (350 persons).

The certified hosts, referred to as 'Qualitätsgastgeber Wanderbares Deutschland' (DWV, 2014) offer high-quality services, such as: transport service to and from the hiking trail; information material about hiking options; hiking advice; facilities for drying clothes; and luggage transport to the next accommodation. In order to achieve an overall improvement in quality for the future, it will be necessary to consider and review the complete customer journey from arrival to departure and the activities during a stay. For this reason, the German Hiking Association has set itself another target and developed a further initiative to certify regions ('Qualitätsregion Wanderbares Deutschland'; DWV, 2014).

Trend 4: Culture

Hikers are also interested in cultural highlights during their hiking holiday. Apart from their hiking tours, they also like to make trips in particular to nearby towns and enjoy visiting museums, theatres and other places of interest (BMWi, 2010; Trendscope, 2013). While hiking, cultural-historical sites are often chosen as hiking destinations (PROJECT M et al., 2014); thus the attraction of a hiking region is not based solely on natural surroundings and the regional infrastructure, but also on the general character of towns, the ambience and the presentation of cultural highlights. Kimmel (2000) points out that it is not possible to clearly state which of the two holiday motives predominate – hiking or culture.

It should not be forgotten that culture also (or in particular) means tradition, lifestyle, regional identity and language or dialects (Croce and Perri, 2010). The design of the common social space where holidaymakers and locals meet or come together is a responsible task for regional development and destination management. It can be presumed that hiking holidaymakers will increasingly seek authenticity and thus want to enjoy regional specialities and typical regional dishes or traditional cuisine, as well as traditional celebrations. In the future, successful German hiking tourism destinations will be those that offer guests a customer-tailored tour with good hiking routes, cultural experiences, and regional food and beverages.

Trend 5: Experience

Consumer life in the 'Western' world is increasingly experience-oriented (Pine and Gilmore, 1999; Freyer, 2011); in response, tourism service providers are more often creating emotional experiences. Particular hiking routes may therefore largely be seen as products designed for tourism. As discussed earlier, paths staged with a thematic concept along a continuous thread provide visitors with experience (i.e. by means of storytelling, furnishings) (see Fig. 19.4). Examples of thematic trails or paths in Europe are: 'The Senses Trail' (Weg der Sinne) in Vico Morcote (Switzerland), the 'Experience Path' along the creek named Tuxbach, in Austria, and the 'Lovers' Bench Path' (Liebesbankweg) in the Harz mountains.

Many factors influence the hiking experience. For example, hiking through the landscape, with the varying weather and lighting conditions throughout the day, generates unique emotions. The paths and the natural surroundings (bushes, meadows, benches), the rest facilities or huts, the information provided on signs – all these influence the hiker's general perception of their experience. The more that the five human senses are appealed to, the more permanent and unique is the impression of a place.

When creating hiking trails, considering areas apart from the explorative experience (searching for information, exploring, playful experimentation, curiosity), the social experience (own hiking group, contact with other hikers while hiking) and biotic components (physical awareness, physical stimulation by means of a touch path) should be included in structure and organization. Landmarks and the choice of name are also of great importance.

Trend 6: Technology

It is now possible to request many features of holiday tours in areas along the tourist service chain through use of smart phones. Hikers can get detailed information (i.e. via Apps, web pages, assessment and comparison portals, social media), to book accommodation or travel arrangements, and to use GPS for orientation (for traffic and leisure activities like hiking). For the time being, smart phones will be the primary terminal in everyday life. With Google Glass and other innovations, the importance of augmented-reality applications, location-based services, mobile commerce, etc. will increase. Generally speaking, the question now arises: to what extent should technology be applied or used for activities in nature hiking?

It is already certain, though, that due to the increasing number of privately owned smart phones – in particular those with highly sensitive GPS transmitter functions – the possibilities for their use in the context of hiking or other holiday tours is increasing. In a survey that was carried out among hikers in the Harz region, over 25% of the interviewed hikers used a GPS-enabled system and device as a means of orientation while hiking. The respondents had all used GPS technology at least once before while hiking; comments indicated this had been a very positive experience, as the device provided a useful orientation aid (in less well-signed surroundings or areas without signposts), and thus gave a feeling of security (Gross and Dreyer, 2013).

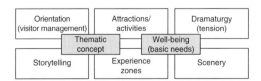

Fig. 19.4. Factors for staging an experience for tourists (source: Mikunda, 2005; based on Müller and Scheurer, 2007; according to Dreyer *et al.*, 2009).

Summary

Destinations will be successful if they manage to attract a certain select market of hikers by offering products in line with market requirements – i.e. by utilizing market segmentation. Six trends in the development of hiking tourism have been introduced, some of which can easily be combined, while others perhaps do not match at all (e.g. technology and spirituality, because hiking will always remain a product linked to nature, even if new technology is applied).

The ability of destinations to create a unique and distinctive name for themselves among the vast number of hiking possibilities in Germany and beyond is probably one of the most interesting tasks and challenges for the coming years in the field of destination management. Hiking destinations need to become more consumer-oriented and develop innovative product designs and marketing concepts.

References

Antz, C. (2009) Spirituelles Wandern. In: Dreyer, A., Menzel, A. and Endress, M. (eds) *Wandertourismus: Kundengruppen, Destinationsmarketing, Gesundheitsaspekte*. Oldenbourg, Munich, Germany, pp. 283–293.

BMWi – Bundesministerium für Wirtschaft und Technologie (2010) *Grundlagenuntersuchung Freizeit- und Urlaubsmarkt Wandern. Langfassung*. BMWi, Berlin, Germany.

Croce, E. and Perri, G. (2010) *Food and Wine Tourism. Integrating Food, Travel and Territory*. CAB International, Wallingford, UK.

DAV (Deutscher Alpenverein) (2015) Available at: http://www.alpenverein.de (accessed 7 September 2014).

Dreyer, A. (2009) Tourismus 2025. In: Bastian, H., Dreyer, A. and Gross, S. (ed.) *Tourismus 3.0 – Fakten und Perspektiven*. Schriftenreihe Dienstleistungsmanagement, Tourismus, Sport, Kultur, Band 9, Hamburg, Germany, pp. 15–22.

Dreyer, A. (2012) Entwicklungen in der Urlaubs und Freizeitgestaltung. In: Dreyer, A., Mühlnickel, R. and Miglbauer, E. (eds) *Radtourismus: Entwicklungen, Potentiale, Perspektiven*. Oldenbourg, Munich, Germany, pp. 9–12.

Dreyer, A. and Duerkop, D. (2011) Slow-Hiking – neue Langsamkeit im Wandertourismus? In: Antz, C., Eisenstein, B. and Eilzer, C. (eds) *Slow Tourism – Reisen zwischen Langsamkeit und Sinnlichkeit*. Martin Meidenbauer Verlag, Munich, Germany, pp. 105–122.

Dreyer, A. and Menzel, A. (2009) Wandern – die neue Lust. In: Bastian, H., Dreyer, A. and Gross, S. (eds) *Tourismus 3.0: Fakten und Perspektiven*. Schriftenreihe Dienstleistungsmanagement, Tourismus, Sport, Kultur, Band 9, Hamburg, Germany, pp. 263–290.

Dreyer, A., Menzel, A. and Endress, M. (2009) *Wandertourismus: Kundengruppen, Destinationsmarketing, Gesundheitsaspekte*. Oldenbourg, Munich, Germany.

DWV (Deutscher Wanderverband e.V.) (2013) Qualitätssprung für den Wandertourismus. Available at: http://www.wanderverband.de/conpresso/_data/PM_16_Qualitaetsregionen_.pdf (accessed 7 September 2014).

DWV (Deutscher Wanderverband e.V.) (2014) Qualitätsgastgeber. Available at: http://www.wanderbares-deutschland.de/gastgeber/qualitaetsgastgeber.html (accessed 7 September 2014).

Freyer, W. (2011) *Tourismus-Marketing: Marktorientiertes Management im Mikro- und Makrobereich der Tourismuswirtschaft*, 7th revised and amended edn. Oldenbourg, Munich, Germany.

FUR (Forschungsgemeinschaft Urlaub und Reisen e.V.) (2015) RA ReiseAnalyse 2015. Erste Ausgewählte Ergebnisse der 45. Reiseanalyse zur ITB 2015. Available at: http://www.fur.de/fileadmin/user_upload/RA_2015/RA2015_Erste_Ergebnisse_DE.pdf (accessed 28 July 2015).

Gross, S. and Dreyer, A. (eds) (2013) *GPS im Tourismus: Grundlagen – Einsatzbereiche – Produktentwicklung*. ITD, Elmshorn, Germany.

Gross, S. and Klemmer, L. (2014) *Introduction to Tourism Transport*. CAB International, Wallingford, UK and Boston, Massachusetts.

Gross, S., Gross, M.S. and Menzel, A. (2013) Bedeutung der GPS-Technologie beim Wandern. Ergebnisse einer Befragung im Harz. In: Gross, S. and Dreyer, A. (eds) *GPS im Tourismus, Grundlagen – Einsatzbereiche – Produktentwicklung*. ITD, Elmshorn, Germany, pp. 64–87.

Horx, M. and Gatterer, H. (eds) (2013) *Trend-Report 2014. Y-Events – Die positiven Überraschungen unserer Zukunft*. Zukunftsinstitut, Frankfurt, Germany.

IfD (Institut für Demoskopie Allensbach) (2014/2011/2008/2005/2000/1985) *AWA – Allensbacher Markt- und Werbeträgeranalyse 2014*. IfD, Allensbach, Germany.

Kimmel, D. (2000) Spaß-Philosophie statt Schulbank-Tourismus bei Wikinger-Reisen. *Touristik Aktuell* 36, 30–31.

Leder, S. (2010) Wandern aus sozial-psychologischer Perspektive. In: Dreyer, A., Menzel, A. and Endress, M. (eds) *Wandertourismus: Kundengruppen. Destinationsmarketing. Gesundheitsaspekte*. Oldenbourg, Munich, Germany, pp. 99–106.

Menzel, A., Endress, M. and Dreyer, A. (2008) *Wandertourismus in deutschen Mittelgebirgen: Produkte – Destinationsmarketing – Gesundheit*. Schriftenreihe Dienstleistungsmanagement. Tourismus, Sport, Kultur, Band 6. ITD, Hamburg, Germany.

Menzel, A., Dreyer, A. and Ratz, J. (2013) Trekking tourism as a special form of hiking tourism: classification and product design of tour operators in the German-speaking market. *Journal of Tourism* XIV(1), 23–46.

Mikunda, C. (2005) *Der verbotene Ort oder Die inszenierte Verführung*, 2nd updated and revised edn. REDLINE, Düsseldorf, Germany.

Müller, H. and Scheurer, R. (2007) *Tourismus-Destinationen als Erlebniswelt: Ein Leitfaden zur Angebots-Inszenierung*, 2nd edn. Universität Bern Center for Regional Economic Development (CRED), Bern, Switzerland.

Opaschowski, H.W. (2013) *Deutschland 2030. Wie wir in Zukunft leben*, new and updated edn. Gütersloher Verlagshaus, Gütersloh, Germany.

Pilgrims' Office Santiago de Compostela (2014) Statistics. Available at: http://peregrinossantiago.es/eng/pilgrims-office/statistics/ (accessed 7 September 2014).

Pine, B.J. and Gilmore, J.H. (1999) *The Experience Economy: Work Is Theatre & Every Business a Stage*. Harvard Business School Press, Boston, Massachusetts.

PROJECT M GmbH, Ostfalia Hochschule für angewandte Wissenschaften, Institut für Management und Tourismus and Deutscher Wanderverband (2014) *Wanderstudie. Der deutsche Wandermarkt* 2014. Berlin, Germany.

Romeiss-Stracke, F. (2005) *Was kommt nach der Spaßgesellschaft?* (3. Kulturpolitischer Bundeskongress 'publikum.macht.kultur', from 23 to 25 June 2005 in Berlin). Available at: http://www.kupoge.de/kongress/2005/dokumentation/romeiss-stracke.pdf (accessed 7 September 2014).

Scheumann, H. (2003) *Wandern Walken Joggen*. Meyer & Meyer Sport, Aachen, Germany.

Schmuecker, D. and Koch, A. (2014) *Reiseanalyse 2014. Kurzfassung der Ergebnisse. Struktur und Entwicklung der Nachfrage des deutschen Reisemarktes 2013*. FUR, Hamburg, Germany.

Schneider, S. and Dreyer, A. (2011) Innovationen im Wandertourismus – Erfahrungen bei der Realisierung einer iPhone-Applikation. In: Kagermeier, A. and Reeh, J. (eds) *Trends, Herausforderungen und Perspektiven für die Tourismus geographische Forschung*. MetaGIS, Trier, Germany, pp. 73–84.

Schrader, R. (2013) *Reiseanalyse 2013: Kurzfassung der Ergebnisse: Struktur und Entwicklung der Nachfrage des deutschen Urlaubsreisemarktes 2012*. FUR, Hamburg, Germany.

Trendscope (2009) *Wandern in Deutschland 2009*. Marktstudie. Trendscope, Cologne, Germany.

UNWTO (2001) *Tourism Vision 2020-Volume 7: Global Forecasts and Profiles of Market Segments*. World Tourism Organization, Madrid, Spain.

20 Sustainable Mountain Hiking Practices in Isfahan, Iran

Farhad Moghimehfar* and Elizabeth A. Halpenny
University of Alberta, Edmonton, Alberta, Canada

Introduction

This chapter presents two case studies that examined the constraints experienced by individuals attempting to engage in environmentally responsible hiking and camping practices in the mountains of Iran. With a population of over 75 million people, Iran (also known as Persia) is located in Western Asia. Two-thirds of Iran is covered with mountain ranges, namely the Zagros and Alborz.

Since the human settlement of Iran in the Lower Paleolithic era, people's lives have been intertwined with mountains. Modern mountaineering as a sport and recreation activity started in 1836 and soon became a popular leisure activity (Barjesteh and van Waalwijk, 2007). A considerable number of people participate in mountaineering activities at levels ranging from family day hikes to large-scale expeditions. These mountaineering activities are planned by individuals, not-for-profit organizations, travel agencies, and governmental bodies (e.g. Iran Mountaineering Federation). The most popular types of mountaineering activities are organized by not-for-profit organizations (also known as mountaineering clubs), which are the major focus of this chapter.

Using a qualitative approach, the first case study presented here explored pro-environmental behaviour constraints experienced during outdoor activities in mountain environments from the perspective of mountain guides. Twelve certified mountain guides were interviewed. A deductive approach, based on the hierarchical model of leisure constraints (Crawford *et al.*, 1991) was used to categorize these identified constraints. The second case study investigated the influence of constraints on hikers' intentions to engage in pro-environmental behaviours while hiking in the same mountains. Negotiation strategies that individuals used to overcome the barriers to behave in an environmentally responsible manner were also studied.

As with other recreational activities, individuals experience constraints to engaging in sustainable mountain hiking. To date, the authors could not find any study specifically concentrated on constraints to environmentally responsible mountain hiking. The present chapter pursues this topic to open an avenue for further social-psychological research on this topic.

---

* Corresponding author: farhad.moghimehfar@ualberta.ca

Pro-environmental behaviour constraints

Numerous studies have investigated the sustainability of human activities with the aim of predicting human behaviour, but not many of these have examined constraints. Tanner (1999) in a study of ecological behaviour constraints used the ipsative theory of behaviour. Tanner's study focused on three major types of constraints: objective, ipsative and subjective. Performing an action can be influenced by objective constraints. These constraints can be both facilitative and preventive, and include physical environments or structural factors (e.g. lack of time, income or knowledge) as well as social surroundings (e.g. social rules and norms) and mental or physical disabilities. Tanner defined ipsative constraints as 'factors that prevent the activation of the alternative' (p. 147). Tanner defined subjective constraints as barriers that affect the willingness to act and mainly influence preferences rather than participation itself (i.e. lack of motivation). Overall, Tanner concluded that the inclusion of inhibiting factors in pro-environmental behaviour studies contributed to human behaviour understanding.

Klöckner and Blöbaum (2010) mentioned that subjective and objective situational constraints to pro-environmental behaviour are responsible for 65% of variance in travel choice behaviour. Their results showed a strong association between constraints and ecological behaviour. Steg and Vlek (2009) characterized constraints as contextual factors that may facilitate or restrain human environmental behaviour. However, they mainly considered physical environment shortcomings such as physical infrastructure, technical facilities, and the availability of products as constraints to pro-environmental behaviour.

Miao and Wei (2013) indicated that 'constraints to motives are barriers between motives and pro-environmental behaviour' (p. 104). In their study they hypothesized that constraints to motives directly influences human pro-environmental behaviour. They compared this relationship in household versus hotel settings. However, their analysis did not show a statistically significant association between constraints to motives and pro-environmental behaviour.

Hines et al. (1986/87) suggested that situational factors directly influence responsible environmental behaviour. In this model situational factors represent economic constraints, social pressure, and different choices people have. However, Bamberg and Möser (2007) considered Hines et al.'s situational factors as perceived behavioural control over the action with direct association to intention rather than behaviour.

Although some studies on pro-environmental behaviour have considered constraints as important predictors of behaviours, a review of the literature reveals an absence of systematic classification of environmental behaviour constraints. In the next section we introduce an environmental behaviour constraints classification scheme with the aim of providing a better understanding of factors that restrain environmentally friendly actions during outdoor activities.

Classification of constraints to engagement in pro-environmental behaviour

Crawford et al. (1991) classified leisure constraints into three major categories: intrapersonal, interpersonal and structural constraints. Intrapersonal barriers refer to psychological aspects of individuals' characteristics that influence their preferences to perform the action rather than their participation. Anxiety, stress and religiosity are examples of intrapersonal constraints. Interpersonal constraints are the outcome of people's interactions with other individuals. What other people think about someone's participation in a particular behaviour constructs interpersonal constraints. Finally, structural constraints represent barriers that have their roots in an external physical environment that facilitates our participation in an action. Lack of infrastructure is an example of structural constraints. This classification of leisure constraints could also facilitate research on how pro-environmental constraints restrain people's participation in certain activities. However, later leisure scholars realized that constraints do not particularly foreclose the action. This is elaborated on next.

Constraints negotiation

Jackson *et al.* (1993) introduced constraints negotiation to the literature of leisure studies. Schneider and Wilhelm Stanis (2007) described constraints negotiation as 'the effort of individuals to use behavioural or cognitive strategies to facilitate leisure participation despite constraints' (p. 392). Jackson *et al.* (1993) believed that 'such negotiation may modify rather than foreclose participation'. This new concept in leisure participation is gaining increasing importance in a way that some researchers believe it is in the forefront of constraints research (Schneider and Wilhelm Stanis, 2007). These findings resulted in an extension to the hierarchical leisure constraints model with the inclusion of negotiation as a major predictor to the model (Jackson *et al.*, 1993). Based on the same assumption, Hubbard and Mannell (2001) tested different alternative models of constraints, negotiation, and motivation in the order of influencing participation in leisure activities. Their findings supported the proposition of the concept of negotiation in leisure constraints theories (Crawford *et al.*, 1991); for all three levels of constraints (i.e. intrapersonal, interpersonal and structural) individuals engage in constraints negotiation when engaging in leisure activities. This chapter adopted the concept of constraints negotiation from leisure studies to explore the effect of negotiation on individuals' participation in pro-environmental activities during outdoor recreation and, specifically, mountain hiking.

Place of study

Both the studies presented in this chapter were conducted in Isfahan, Iran. Isfahan is one of the biggest cities in Iran. With a population of more than 4 million, the city is surrounded by diverse geographical features, ranging from great salt deserts (Dasht-e-Kavir) to mountains with peaks above 14,000 feet (Zagros Mountain Range). Several mountaineering clubs are actively conducting hiking and mountaineering tours every weekend and holidays to these mountains. These clubs are mostly non-profit, non-governmental organizations that are managed by annually elected boards. Many of the tour guides in these clubs are certified by Iran Mountaineering and Sport Climbing Federation. Figure 20.1 displays the geographical location of Isfahan.

Study 1: Nature Tourism and Sustainable Behaviour Constraints: A Qualitative Study of Mountaineering Clubs

The first study was an exploratory study of constraints to pro-environmental behaviour during hiking. For this reason, a qualitative approach was used to identify these restraining factors from the view point of mountain guides. The aim of this investigation was to obtain an understanding of these constraints in this cultural setting.

Method and results

A phenomenological approach was used to investigate constraints that restrain hikers from engagement in pro-environmental behaviour. Twelve certified mountain guides from mountaineering clubs in Isfahan were selected and interviewed. The interviewed mountain guides were selected based on two major criteria: (i) they needed to have at least 2 years of active leadership experience; (ii) they had to be certified by the Mountaineering and Sport Climbing Federation of the country.

To collect information from these mountain guides, a series of video interviews was conducted. A semi-structured interview guide was used to lead the conversation. Questions such as: 'What are the main constraints for being an ecotourist?', 'How do you describe these constraints?' and 'Could you name some of the ecotourism constraints you had in your last tour?' were asked during the interviews.

Snowball sampling method was used to find information-rich key informants. Patton (2002) believes that the main reason of purposeful sampling in qualitative inquiries is in-depth understanding of the issue. For this reason, experienced tour guides were asked to provide us with the name of other tour guides who were very familiar with this topic. Twelve

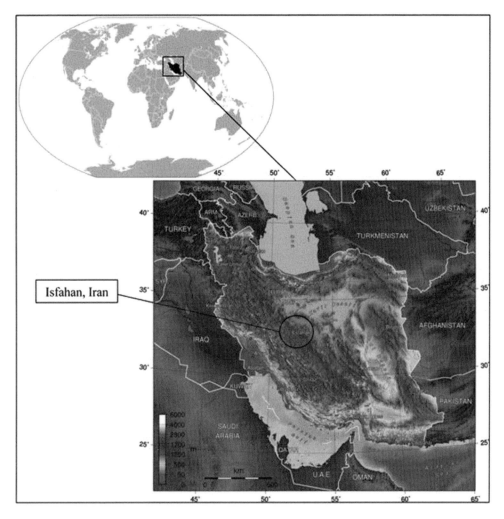

Fig. 20.1. Geographical location of Isfahan (source: Wikimedia, 2006).

certified mountain guides (among 19 identified) who agreed to participate in the research were interviewed. Interview times varied from 47 minutes to 81 minutes. Transcribed interviews were carefully reviewed, and themes and categories were identified. Finally, member checking (Mayan, 2009) confirmed the validity of the results. This entailed sending a list of themes and categories obtained from interviews to the interviewed mountain guides to confirm that an understanding of their perspectives was achieved.

Using a deductive approach for the analysis that was guided by leisure constraints theory, detected constraints in this study were categorized in three major groups of intrapersonal, interpersonal and structural constraints. The following intrapersonal constraints categories were identified: (i) purpose of the trip (e.g. day hike, alpine mountaineering, etc.); (ii) knowledge or awareness of the issue; (iii) emotions for nature; (iv) values; (v) environmental protection vs enjoyment; (vi) lack of efficacy; (vii) locus of control; (viii) gender difference; and (ix) frequency of participation in the activity. For instance, the majority of the interviewed mountain guides mentioned lack of knowledge about protecting environment as a major constraint for their tour participants. They believed that people do not participate in pro-environmental activities if they do not know it is harmful for nature or they are not aware of the consequences of their actions. 'How can we expect someone to protect nature when he doesn't know how to do that?! They burn their garbage in fire pit at the end of the day because they believe it doesn't harm the environment. However, some of them try not to burn plastic garbage', Mountain Guide 4 said.

Other significant intrapersonal issues mentioned in the interviews were the purpose of the trip and the difficulty of the trip. As an example, Mountain Guide 1 indicated that 'participants in difficult trips are more cautious about the environment. Although they usually prefer to visit remote areas, they have a better relationship with local people and also they are more concerned about flora and fauna.' They believed that serious mountaineers are more interested in pro-environmental activities and they try harder to stick to environmental protection rules.

Interviewed mountain guides also agreed on the contrast between enjoyment and environmental protection. They believed that too much emphasis on pro-environmental activities negatively influences people's behaviour through limiting their freedom, therefore their enjoyment during outdoor activities. Mountain Guide 4 reported:

> I mean … if we limit them too much – you know! Like … in certain activities [if we] always tell them what to do and what not to do, they don't continue with our club … we do it sometimes, but we don't want to lose our members.

They believed that they need to balance environmental concerns and enjoyment of outdoor activities. This research is congruent with Eiser and Ford's (1995, as cited in Miao and Wei, 2013), who found that people's behaviour during a trip is more liberated than their behaviour at home. Related to these types of intrapersonal constraints, some of the mountain guides indicated that they usually have a problem with new people on their tours who are not familiar with the rules. Mountain Guide 9 stated:

> It is more difficult to control people's behaviour when there are new people on the tour … We don't know them and they don't

know our rules. It takes time to teach them how to follow our rules and what [the] dos and don'ts are … Naive people are usually problematic.

The second category of constraints, interpersonal constraints, can be divided into external factors and subjective norms. External factors refer to constraints that relate to people other than tour participants. For example, Mountain Guide 2 mentioned that:

> Even when we don't have problem with people on our tour, local people can be the source of conflict. They are mostly friendly and helpful, but sometimes they don't like to have [that many] people in their lands and even when we want to be closer to their communities, they prefer to stay away from us.

External factors were considered as uncontrollable constraints from the viewpoint of our interviewees. In addition to the above, culture can be identified as another interpersonal factor. Mountain Guide 1 believed that:

> Sitting around a fire pit and singing traditional songs or playing musical instruments is intertwined with Iranian culture. Many people are interested in that, and it is difficult to convince them not to make fire when there is no fire ban or restriction, but when fire is a hazard in the area.

In another interview Mountain Guide 12 said: 'people usually follow others. If the majority of the participants are not familiar or loyal to ecotourism, or they don't behave pro-environmentally, other people usually follow them.' These are examples of subjective norms.

We categorized structural constraints, identified in the analysis of the interviews, into several themes: economy; super-structures and infra-structures; safety issues; management problems; type of tour; and lack of information resources. Almost all the participants agreed that lack of structures such as designated campsites and proper hiking trails was the most important structural constraint that prevented them from engagement in pro-environmental behaviour. Economic factors were identified as a barrier to pro-environmental behaviour. However, some of the mountain guides indicated that they force people to participate in environmentally friendly activities, such as carpooling. As an example, Mountain Guide 4 believed that:

Many people on the tours are students, or they are young. So they don't have enough money. So they may not own proper gear. But, on the other hand, we travel in bigger groups of people and use bus transportation, which is cheaper and definitely has less negative impact.

Interestingly, Mountain Guide 11 believed that:

Having rich people in the tour doesn't necessarily mean that it is easier to run a nature-friendly tour. Even sometimes it is more difficult because they don't want to follow rules. They [rich people] want to be comfortable. And sometimes they don't treat local people very well.

Lack of proper information about the issue was also considered as a constraint to pro-environmental behaviour. This issue was also considered as a management problem, as there is no authorized organization that provides reliable information. Findings from the first study were congruent with the categories of constraints introduced in leisure constraints theory. This exploratory study provides an insight into constraints to sustainable mountain hiking in Iran. This study was particularly designed to investigate mountain guides' point of view on this topic. The second study in this chapter, however, was designed to investigate these constraints from the viewpoint of mountain hikers and explored the influence of constraints on individuals' intention to participate in such activities.

Study 2: Constraints, Negotiation, and Peoples' Intention to Participate in Pro-environmental Behaviour

The second study in this chapter examined the relationship between pro-environmental behaviour constraints and people's intention to practise pro-environmental behaviour during outdoor activities. As we mentioned earlier, constraints do not necessarily foreclose participation in an activity, but people negotiate through their barriers. Based on this notion, negotiation through constraints to pro-environmental behaviour was also explored in this study. In this research we hypothesized that: (i) constraints have a direct negative impact on people's

intention to participate in pro-environmental behaviour during hiking; (ii) people's negotiation through constraints to pro-environmental behaviour during hiking directly and positively influences their intention to participate in pro-environmental behaviour; and (iii) negotiation through constraints to engage in pro-environmental behaviour mediates the influence of constraints on intention to behave pro-environmentally. Structural equation modelling (SEM) was used to test these hypotheses.

Method and results

A paper-based self-reported questionnaire was designed to collect data for this survey. A list of items was developed to investigate constraints to engaging in pro-environmental hiking in Iran. Nine items, informed by Study 1, were selected for the final version of the questionnaire: four items for intrapersonal, two items for interpersonal, and three items for structural constraints. Based on the same classification we used to measure constraints (intrapersonal, interpersonal and structural), six statements were developed to measure negotiation through constraint to pro-environmental hiking (two items for negotiation through each class of constraints). Participants' intention to participate in pro-environmental activities during mountain hiking was also measured with a single question. All the items were measured with a five-point Likert scale (1=Strongly Disagree to 5=Strongly Agree). As the questionnaire was developed in English and participants were Persian-(Farsi-)language speakers, back-translation (Brislin, 1970) was used to confirm clarity and accuracy of the final Persian survey instrument. Reliability of the questions was tested with the measurement of Cronbach's alpha coefficient for each construct (Table 20.1).

The target population of the second study was members of mountaineering clubs in Isfahan, Iran. Participants were approached by either their club managers or tour guides. Of the 265 respondents who were included in the final data set, 50.2% were male and the average age was 29. In terms of education, 51% had a Bachelor's degree, 23% had a college diploma, 18% had a high-school diploma or less, and 8% had a graduate degree. The average of reported years of membership in the outdoor clubs was 5.2 years (SD = 6.6). Table 20.1 describes respondents' level of agreement with the Likert-style questionnaire items designed to measure pro-environmental hiking intentions, constraints and constraints negotiation.

Figure 20.2 represents the associations between the study's main variables and Table 20.2 details the model's fit indices. IBM AMOS 21 was used to conduct the SEM, and SPSS 21.0 was used to calculate the descriptive statistics. Based on the results of SEM constraints had significant negative impact on pro-environmental intentions:

$$(\beta_{constraints \rightarrow intention} = -.416)$$

However, negotiation positively influences intention:

$$(\beta_{negotiation \rightarrow intention} = .359)$$

Finally as it was hypothesized negotiation mediates the influence of constraints on intention:

$$(\beta_{constraints \rightarrow negotiation} = -.268)$$

Discussion

The aim of this chapter was to present two studies on constraints that prevent mountain hikers from participating in pro-environmental activities during hiking trips. A qualitative approach was used in the first study to identify major constraints to pro-environmental behaviour from the viewpoint of mountain guides. Results showed that interpersonal (e.g. interaction with local people and cultural conflicts) and intrapersonal (e.g. lack of knowledge about protecting mountain environments, and place attachment)

Table 20.1. Constructs, negotiation, items, means, standard deviation and Cronbach's alpha coefficient.

Variables	M	SD	α
Pro-environment intention	**6.38**	**0.97**	
Constraints (Total)			.81
Intrapersonal	*3.13*	*1.66*	*.80*
I don't know how to protect nature	3.55	2.01	
I don't care about nature	2.94	2.24	
Physically I am not able to behave pro-environmentally	2.89	1.73	
I don't have the skills to protect nature	3.15	1.92	
Interpersonal	*2.87*	*1.68*	*.72*
Companions don't let me behave pro-environmentally	2.58	1.76	
People I know do not like to participate in pro-environmental activities	3.17	2.03	
Structural	*4.07*	*1.36*	*.48*
A lack of camping and trail facilities (e.g. signage) inhibits my ability to behave pro-environmentally	4.80	2.33	
Pro-environmental behaviour costs me a lot	2.49	1.74	
Eco-friendly outdoor gear is expensive	5.65	1.65	
Constraints negotiation (Total)			.66
Intrapersonal	*6.13*	*1.17*	*.83*
I try to learn how to protect nature	6.06	1.29	
I try to improve my environmental protection abilities	6.21	1.24	
Interpersonal	*5.79*	*1.27*	*.53*
I engage in pro-environmental actions even when my companions think this is unnecessary	5.75	1.55	
I try to travel with people who care about nature	5.83	1.53	
Structural	*4.74*	*1.52*	*.75*
I save money to buy environmentally friendly outdoor gear	4.44	1.72	
I spend more money to protect natural resources	5.05	1.68	

Note: Items were measured with a five-point Likert scale (1=Strongly Disagree to 5=Strongly Agree).

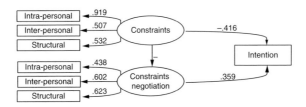

Fig. 20.2. A structural model of pro-environment behavioural intention constraints.

Table 20.2. Model fit indices.

Overall fit indices				
χ^2 / df	IFI	CFI	RMSEA	NFI
24.05 / 11	.981	.980	.057	.960

constraints are as important as structural constraints to pro-environmental mountain hiking, from the viewpoint of mountain guides. However, structural constraints (e.g. lack of proper hiking trails and campgrounds) were emphasized in the interviews. Both the deductive approach in the first exploratory study and the structural model in the second study confirmed that constraints to pro-environmental mountain hiking can be classified into three groups of interpersonal, intrapersonal and structural constraints. This classification provides a better understanding of constraints to engaging in pro-environmental behaviours during hiking in mountain areas. The literature indicated that pro-environmental behaviour constraints have been under-studied in previous research and need to be systematically examined (Steg and Vlek, 2009). Existing studies on constraints have mainly focused on structural constraints or contextual constraints. Therefore, a better understanding of interpersonal and intrapersonal constraints helps researchers and managers identify constraints that are not related to the physical environment. These constraints are linked to social-psychological characteristics of people. Investigating constraints to visitors' pro-environmental behaviour in mountain environments provides a context-specific knowledge that helps managers protecting remote mountain areas. Expanding on this issue was one of the major goals of the current chapter.

The structural model in the second study revealed that negotiation through constraints plays an important role in modifying the restraining effect of constraints on people's pro-environmental behaviour. This issue reveals the influence of social-psychological factors on people's intention to practise pro-environmental behaviour. Although constraints inhibit people from performing pro-environmental behaviour, negotiation modifies the effect of constraints. This means constraints do not prohibit the action, but they limit people's choice. This research was one of the first studies that considered the mediating effect of negotiation on the relationship between constraints to engaging in pro-environmental behaviour during mountain hiking and intention. Further investigations in this area are needed to reveal more details on the effect of negotiation on people's intention and decision-making process, as well as the factors that can facilitate individuals' pro-environmental behaviour in situations where constraints are not manageable or reducing constraints is not feasible.

Decreasing structural constraints through provision of proper facilities is an effective strategy to avoid negative impacts on tourism destinations. In mountain tourism, however, dealing with structural constraints is not the easiest visitor management tool. Mountain tourism often occurs in remote areas that are characterized by low levels of management resources; this is especially true in developing countries. In such contexts, providing adequate infrastructure and enforcement for the purpose of sustainable tourism activities is challenging. In these situations a focus on intrapersonal and interpersonal constraints can be a more effective approach to reducing negative impacts of mountain hiking on natural environments. This is possible through targeting factors that shape people's behaviour, such as individuals' attitudes toward protecting natural environment, subjective norms (influence of important others on someone's behaviour), and people's perception of their control over performing environmentally responsible behaviour or through internalization of motivational factors that can lead people to engage in environmentally friendly behaviours (Deci and Ryan, 1985). Literature on pro-environmental behaviour suggests that an increase in people's awareness can result in higher levels of environmental policy acceptance (Steg and Vlek, 2009). However, support of this is mixed (Jensen, 2002; Wurzinger and Johansson, 2006). Our findings suggested that facilitating people's negotiation through constraints may help reduce negative environmental impacts of mountain hikers.

This study is among the first to examine social-psychological aspects of mountain tourism in the Middle East (see also Moghimehfar et al., 2014). Although outdoor activities, and especially mountaineering, have been favourite activities of Iranians for centuries, recent rapid growth signals the importance of studying people's pro-environmental behaviour during outdoor activities, to prevent further negative impact on nature and culture of remote areas in this mountainous region.

References

Bamberg, S. and Möser, G. (2007) Twenty years after Hines, Hungerford, and Tomera: a new meta-analysis of psycho-social determinants of pro-environmental behaviour. *Journal of Environmental Psychology* 27, 14–25.

Barjesteh, F. and van Waalwijk, V.D. (2007) Introduction to Entertainment in Qajar Persia. *Iranian Studies* 40, 447–454.

Brislin, R.W. (1970) Back-translation for cross-cultural research. *Journal of Cross-cultural Psychology* 1, 185–216.

Crawford, D.W., Jackson, E.L. and Godbey, G. (1991) A hierarchical model of leisure constraints. *Leisure Sciences* 13, 309–320.

Deci, E.L. and Ryan, R.M. (1985) *Intrinsic Motivation and Self-Determination in Human Behavior*. Plenum, New York.

Hines, J.M., Hungerford, H.R. and Tomera, A.N. (1986/87) Analysis and synthesis of research on responsible environmental behaviour: a meta-analysis. *Journal of Environmental Education* 18, 1–8.

Hubbard, J. and Mannell, R.C. (2001) Testing competing models of the leisure constraint negotiation process in a corporate employee recreation setting. *Leisure Sciences* 23, 145–163.

Jackson, E., Crawford, D. and Godbey, G. (1993) Negotiation of leisure constraints. *Leisure Sciences* 15, 1–12.

Jensen, B.B. (2002) Knowledge, action and pro-environmental behaviour. *Environmental Education Research* 8, 325–334.

Klöckner, C.A. and Blöbaum, A. (2010) A comprehensive action determination model: toward a broader understanding of ecological behaviour using the example of travel mode choice. *Journal of Environmental Psychology* 30, 574–586.

Mayan, M.J. (2009) *Essentials of Qualitative Inquiry*. Left Coast Press, Walnut Creek, California.

Miao, L. and Wei, W. (2013) Consumers' pro-environmental behavior and the underlying motivations: a comparison between household and hotel settings. *International Journal of Hospitality Management* 32, 102–112.

Moghimehfar, F., Halpenny, E.A. and Ziaee, M. (2014) How big is the gap? Comparing the behaviours and knowledge of mountain hikers with ecotourism ideals: a case study of Iran. *Journal of Ecotourism* 13(1), 1–15.

Patton, M.Q. (2002) *Qualitative research and evaluation methods*, 3rd edn. Sage Publications, London, UK.

Schneider, I.E. and Wilhelm Stanis, S.A. (2007) Coping: an alternative conceptualization for constraint negotiation and accommodation. *Leisure Sciences* 29, 391–401.

Steg, L. and Vlek, C. (2009) Encouraging pro-environmental behaviour: an integrative review and research agenda. *Journal of Environmental Psychology* 29, 309–317.

Tanner, C. (1999) Constraints on environmental behaviour. *Journal of Environmental Psychology* 19, 145–157.

Wikimedia (2006) Topographical Map of Iran. Available at: http://upload.wikimedia.org/wikipedia/commons/9/99/Iran_topo_en.jpg (accessed 15 April 2015).

Wurzinger, S. and Johansson, M. (2006) Environmental concern and knowledge of ecotourism among three groups of Swedish tourists. *Journal of Travel Research* 45, 217–226.

21 Two Canadian Mountaineering Camps: Participant Motivations and Sense of Place in a Wilderness Setting

Robin Reid* and Terry Palechuk

Thompson Rivers University, Kamloops, British Columbia, Canada

Introduction

Since the early 1900s, the presence of the Alpine Club of Canada's (ACC) General Mountaineering Camp (GMC) on the Canadian landscape has been significant to the mountaineering, exploration and holiday activities in remote locations in the Rocky Mountain ranges of Western Canada. More recently the Boutique Mountaineering Camp (BMC) has also started offering unique opportunities for participants to engage in mountaineering and hiking activities in a Canadian wilderness setting. When one considers holiday experiences and the notion of 'place' in a wilderness setting, a question comes to mind: of all the available vacation options, why choose a mountaineering camp? What makes these particular wilderness place-experiences stand out from the multitude of other offerings on the 'brochure rack' of possible holidays?

These questions were explored with ACC's GMC and the BMC participants during the 5-week period the camps were in operation in the summer of 2013. Both camps are located in remote mountain locations in Western Canada and provide annual, unique opportunities for participants to engage in mountaineering and hiking activities.

Using a case study approach, participants (excluding guides and camp staff) were invited to complete a self-administered questionnaire. Information from this single-season study was used to provide a snapshot in time to investigate how sense of place prevails in a wilderness setting and to assess whether the motivations of the camp participants were related to concepts of place-identity and place-dependence. This chapter provides an overview of the research, and discusses the results as they pertain to place-identity, place-dependence and participant motivations to attend the GMC and BMC.

The GMC and the BMC

Traditionally, access to the backcountry and the basic comforts required by hunters, prospectors, surveyors and tourists was provided by outfitters. According to Rutledge (1989) 'a guide outfitter is an entrepreneur with sufficient leadership qualities, business acumen and organizing ability to capably assist a clientele to achieve a specific objective in British

---

* Corresponding author: rreid@tru.ca

Columbia's outdoors' (p. 1). The specialized service, provided by guides and outfitters, played an important role in facilitating visitors' access to the province's wilderness areas and building their connection to place (Beedie and Hudson, 2003). The outfitters' knowledge and experience in the mountains and coordination of all the necessary provisions was foundational to the success of the ACC's GMCs in the early 1900s. Their efforts, as reported from the 1907 camp, 'represented no small thought and toil' (Walker, 1908, 77). Food supplies, large canvas tents, lumber and other necessities were transported by horse train into remote areas that were not otherwise accessible for the average explorer, surveyor or tourist. Eventually, horses were replaced with helicopters as a means to transport participants and supplies into the GMC. Although modern technology made access into the camp easier, the modern GMC still provides a unique mountain experience reminiscent of its past, as shown in the photo of the 1935 camp in Fig. 21.1. The camps continue to be located in remote areas; large canvas-walled tents, supported by long wooden poles, bring a sense of nostalgia to the communal dining tent, tea tent, drying tent with a wood stove, and kitchen.

Segregated communal sleeping quarters for males, females and married couples have given way to smaller, modern, two-person tents for participants. Although the camp has seen considerable change, guest experience is still highly dependent on the knowledge, skills, background and support of the camp manager, cooks and guides.

The GMC, attended by ACC members since 1906, currently accommodates up to 30 guests per week (not including staff) in a 5-week rotation. The smaller BMC, established in 2012, accommodates 12 guests per week (not including staff) in a similar rotation. The GMC participants, staff and supplies are exchanged on Saturdays, while this same process for the BMC occurs on Sundays. It is worth noting that the owner-operator and camp manager of the BMC was also the camp manager of the GMC from 1985 until 2011, and had a long family history of outfitting for the GMC that dates back to the 1950s. This extends to a few of the guides, who continue to be a part of the camp experience at both the GMC and the BMC.

Fig. 21.1. Lake Magog (Assiniboine) ACC Camp 1935. (Photo by Lloyd McLeod. Permission granted by Carole McLeod.)

Participant Motivations and the Notion of Place-dependence and Place-identity

Based on participant numbers over the years, the specific camp locations selected by the management of the GMC and BMC appears to be relevant to participant motivations to attend the camps. There have been obvious logistical considerations in camp location decisions, such as helicopter costs, access to water, etc. This selective place-experience construct by the GMC and BMC, however, plays to the 'expectancy model of motivation to infer that people are attracted to natural environments in the pursuit of personal benefit' (Kyle *et al.*, 2004, 441).

From this expectancy theory perspective, the 'choice' of place to be used by the GMC and BMC may help in facilitating certain outcomes, which are seen as desirable by the participants. In a sense, these become the 'personal and behavioral mechanisms that bind individuals, in this instance, to geographic locales' (Kyle *et al.*, 2003, 253). Although this may simply be a connection to the mountains as a place, camp locations are selected by the camp organizers because of the geographical qualities and the climbing objectives available. In other words, specific attributes of the mountain wilderness – not just 'any place' – as suggested in Fig. 21.2.

The history of the camps has set the tone of what one might expect, which, in turn, from a participant perspective, suggests that participating in the camp will most likely yield the outcomes seen as desirable and carry a high valence (Daft, 2011). Examples of personal

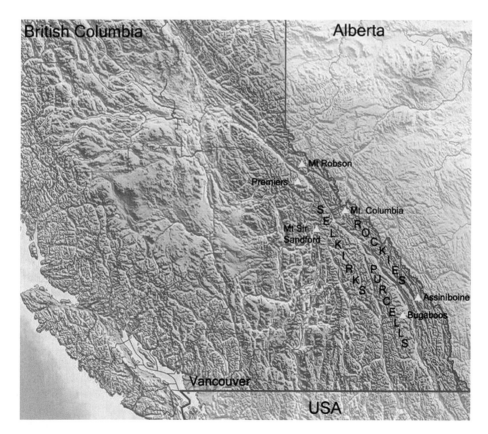

Fig. 21.2. Topographical map of British Columbia. (Note 1: white triangles indicate selected GMC locations. There are too many camp locations to include them all. Note 2: there are no BMC locations shown on this map.)

outcomes or objectives may include interest in summing a number of accessible peaks over 10,000 ft near the camps, or the amount of other climbing objectives available and achieved by either novice or more experienced climbers. That is, the participants would be highly motivated to participate, as they see the outcome of their effort as being of value and therefore worth the effort to invest in attaining those outcomes (Daft, 2011). White *et al.* (2008) suggest 'that an individual may see place as part of the self and simultaneously as a resource for satisfying goals or explicitly felt behaviors' (p. 649).

How people encounter places has been researched across various disciplines, with 'studies of place' theories focusing on differing approaches to how people encounter places. The suggestion is that one can approach the idea of place from a perspective of place-meaning (Manzo, 2005). Convery *et al.* (2012) identified two primary theoretical and methodological approaches to the subject of place in the literature.

> In the first instance, sense of place or genius loci is used to explore a range of factors, which together define the character, or local distinctiveness of a specific place. In the second, the term has been used to emphasize the ways in which people experience, use and understand place, leading to a range of conceptual subsets such as 'place identity', 'place attachment', 'place dependency' and 'insiderness/insidedness'.
>
> (p. 2)

With respect to experiences and place, there are a myriad of opportunities in which one can engage in activity – both built and natural. From a wilderness perspective, a sense of place-attachment is one of dependence or identity as suggested by several authors (Williams *et al.*, 1992; Bricker and Kerstetter, 2000; Blake, 2002; Kyle *et al.*, 2003; Presley, 2003; Kyle *et al.*, 2004; Convery *et al.*, 2012).

If one considers the notion of place-dependence and place-identity constructs, place may be interpreted with respect to what it offers, or what it represents. Williams and Vaske (2003) identify place-dependence as 'a functional attachment (that) is embodied in (an) area's physical characteristics' and place-identity as that of 'symbolic importance' (p. 831). With respect to the GMC and BMC, it may be a case of both. That is, with the GMC and its long

history of mountaineering, there may be an historical connection to its sense of exploration, in terms of what it offers and what it represents. In the sense of place-dependence, it might be suggested the GMC and BMC rely on certain attributes of the wilderness setting, thus fostering a place-attachment relationship for the camp, and further a place-identity relationship for the participants.

Sense of Place and the Wilderness Construct

With all the possible places where one may feel a sense of attachment, identity or dependence, why the wilderness? What is it about the wilderness environment that manifests it as something 'special' for some people to experience? Cronon (1996) explores the notion of wilderness as one that has been artificially constructed. That is, our early settlers set out to transform the rugged land they were faced with into one that was tamed. The frontier became civilization, while the mountains were seen as obstacles. 'There must have always been farmers who found they had to climb some wretched hill, taking time they could ill afford to rescue a recalcitrant sheep' (Bartlett, 2013, 145). At the same time there became a romantic attraction of both the natural, and perhaps primitive, world, as well as the struggle it represented. 'In just this way, wilderness came to embody the national frontier myth, standing for the wild freedom of America's past and seeming to represent a highly attractive natural alternative to the ugly artificiality of modern civilization' (Cronon, 1996, 15). In this sense, one might interpret an attachment to the wilderness place to that of a 'conditional form of permanence', as suggested by Cresswell (2004, 57). That is, it is an attachment to our past, albeit one that is 'a product of that civilization' (Cronon, 1996, 7). In the tourism literature, Jaworski and Lawson (2005) refer to a 'somewhat paradoxical reaction to globalization seen in the resurgence of local heritage sites and the exploitation of nostalgia as a dominant tourist theme' (p. 125). This supports Beedie and Hudson's (2003) premise that nostalgia and exploration may be a product of the 'modern social world' (p. 635) as a means of stability, or anchoring, with our past.

The GMC and BMC depend on certain attributes, which, as suggested by Kyle *et al.* (2003), 'implies knowledge of alternative leisure settings but also acknowledges an individual's decision to select a specific site from (the) alternatives' (p. 253). One cannot forget that the camp provides all of the amenities, guides, staff, food and lodging indicative of an all-inclusive holiday experience. As Beedie and Hudson (2003) suggest, this fits with the notion of contemporary lifestyles being complex, with longer working hours. The paradox, of course, is that the convenience of logistical formalities, being taken care of by a third party (the camp organizers), may play an important role in participant satisfaction within the wilderness setting. Thus logistical satisfaction may be included in the many factors in place-attachment.

From a commodification of 'place-experience' perspective, Kyle *et al.* (2004) suggest 'that the expectation of these outcomes draws people toward specific natural environments and, over time, attachments to the setting develop' (p. 440). In this sense, one might suggest a certain anticipation of the product offering that satisfies a need to be fulfilled.

Methodology

For the past two decades, the place-attachment construct has received the most attention from leisure researchers in an attempt to understand certain aspects of leisure behaviour. Drawing on the work of human geographers' conception of 'sense of place' and environmental psychologists' notion of 'place-attachment', leisure researchers have emphasized the importance of an effective and emotional bond between the person and a particular place. As a result, a variety of tools have been developed to determine what motivates one to participate in exercise and leisure. With respect to recreation, two of the earlier measures are the Paragraphs About Leisure (PAL) and the Recreation Experience Preference scale (REP). The main difference is that PAL explored the human needs satisfied by leisure, while the REP scale measured the degree of satisfaction after participating in a recreational activity (Driver *et al.*, 1991). An adaption of the Driver (1983) and Driver *et al.* (1991) REP

scale was used in this study to explore participant motivations for attending the GMC/BMC. Driver *et al.* (1991) describe the premise for the REP as being 'founded on the notion that leisure opportunities are important in helping people meet basic psychological needs, especially those that are not fulfilled in non-leisure times and space' (p. 264).

The REP scale, comprising 43 benefits within 19 domains, is most often applied to measuring recreation experience. Rodriguez *et al.* (2008), for example, used a sub-scale of the REP in their study of leisure and life satisfaction. The REP scale is one that is broad in scope when considering recreation in the natural environment, hence for the purpose of this study, a subset of the original 19 domains and 43 benefits outlined by Driver (1983) and Driver *et al.* (1991), five domains were utilized: (i) achievement; (ii) enjoy nature; (iii) escape; (iv) physical (fitness/health); and (v) social. Thirteen questions included an open-ended 'other' category, to explore why participants chose this particular type of mountaineering holiday. A five-point Likert scale enabled respondents to rate each statement from 1=Strongly Agree to 5=Strongly Disagree, to explore the significance of each of the five domains.

This project also drew from the work of Kyle *et al.* (2003; 2004) to explore the notion of being attracted to a place due to the construct of place-identity or place-dependence. In these studies, there was a departure from the REP scale, which explored what it was about the activity that satisfied one's participation. The work of Kyle *et al.* (2003) explored 'three dimensions of activity involvement (i.e., self-expression, centrality, and attraction)', as well as place-attachment and place-identity. For the purpose of this study, four place-attachment and four place-identity scale items were used and adapted for the GMC/BMC survey.

Sample Strategy and Data Collection

As both camps are located in remote wilderness, staff and participants are onsite for the duration of the programme, and it was impractical for the principal researchers to attend the camps to administer the questionnaires; therefore, the research process was facilitated by the camp managers at the mid-point of each camp. The camp managers explained the purpose of the project, as well as the process for administering the questionnaires, to ensure confidentiality. Participants were then left to complete the questionnaires (or not) by the Friday of that week (because Saturday is a very busy day, with the next group coming in) and deposit them in a large envelope that identified only the week of the camp, in a neutral location in the camp (i.e. the tea tent). The study period was for the entire mountaineering camp season (5 weeks) in the summer of 2013.

Results and Discussion

One might consider this a contained and captured convenience sample, which may help to explain the high aggregate response rate (72%), as outlined in Table 21.1. The response rate for the BMC participants was 98% and the GMC had a 60% response rate. There was a zero response rate in one week of the GMC because the questionnaire was not administered. From this perspective, because participants were not given the 'opportunity' to participate in the survey on week 2, one might suggest that the GMC response rate was in the order of 76.3% (an average of the 4 weeks in which questionnaires were administered). The open-ended question, exploring why participants chose this particular mountaineering holiday experience over other options, resulted in 117 responses out of a sample size of 131 and this was an 89.3% response rate.

Responses to the open-ended question were coded and grouped into themes of same or similar responses. The primary reason expressed by respondents for selecting this particular holiday experience over other alternatives was to 'get away from the city, love of the mountains, and nature' (25.6%) – escape and nature scales. One might infer that in this case, respondents made a place-connection based on what the camp represented (place-identity) – getting back to and experiencing nature. The next most suggested theme was sharing experiences and being with like-minded people

(12.8%) – the social scale. The third most-suggested theme was due to 'time and convenience' (11.1%). That is, respondents appreciated the time-saving element of logistics and infrastructure being taken care of by the camp organizers.

For some respondents (10.3%), it was the challenge of the mountaineering outings (achievement), while for others (8.5%) it was that they loved to climb (which could be categorized as 'achievement', 'social' or even 'enjoy nature') and this camp satisfied that need. There were three other categories, which, although listed separately, would fit under the 'past-positive' notion suggested by Shores and Scott (2007). These were: 'it was an annual event' (8.5%), 'past experiences' (3.4%) and 'familiarity with the camp' (9.4%) for a total of 21.3% of respondents. In this sense, one might suggest support for the notion of place-dependence vis-à-vis expectancy theory (motivations) of the camp itself. Although discussed as both place-identity and place-dependence as well as motivations, the notion of past-positive experiences appears to fit both constructs. In the end, it appears to support the complex relationship between place-dependence and place-identity as suggested by Williams et al. (1992).

The impressions found in this study suggest that participants feel a strong attachment to place vis-à-vis identity, dependence and motivation. That is, there is a connection to what the place represents (wilderness and camp history) as well as what it offers (an opportunity to satisfy one's connectivity to place through activities or shared experiences). It might further be suggested that in this case, there is support for the notion put forth by Williams et al. (1992) that 'place attachment is strongly related to mode of experience' (p. 37). Thus, the more one's motivations are satisfied, the more the place is valued, resulting in increased place attachment (Williams et al., 1992; Bricker and Kerstetter, 2000; White et al., 2008).

The link that can be suggested is that both the GMC and the BMC facilitate experiences that are seen as desirable. As described earlier, the GMC and BMC are not located in random places in the mountains; specific places are chosen that will best deliver and satisfy guest motivations. Participants expressed a strong desire to return after having experienced the

Table 21.1. GMC/BMC response rate.

Week	GMC			BMC			Total		
	Participants	Completed	Response rate (%)	Participants	Completed	Response rate (%)	Total participants	Total completed	Total response rate (%)
1	16	13	81.3	12	12	100	28	25	89
2	25	0	0.0	12	12	100	37	12	32
3	19	14	73.7	8	8	100	27	22	81
4	30	27	90.0	11	11	100	41	38	93
5	30	18	60.0	12	11	92	42	29	69
Total	120	72	60.0	55	54	98	175	126	72

camp. Of the 98% who indicated they would return, 67% were first-time participants at the camp. This may offer support for the notion of a past-positive experience shaping visitor expectations of the future, lending support for expectancy theory. The suggestion is that because one was satisfied, one will therefore invest in the effort to return, because of the value of the outcomes that can be achieved, which are seen as desirable (Daft, 2011).

So Where Does All This Take Us?

Institutions like the GMC and BMC have now placed themselves in the position of 'having to deliver'. After all, expectations have been created and participants have come to attach themselves to these camps as a means of satisfying experience outcomes (Beedie and Hudson, 2003; Kyle *et al.*, 2004). As suggested by Cronon (1996), our notion of wilderness is that of an artificial construct used to satisfy our nostalgic way of connecting with our past (the frontier) – a sense of permanence, as suggested by Cresswell (2004). In this way, new camp locations are selected each year as a means to satisfy the notion of exploration, or, dare we say 'wilderness'. Many participants finish their week actively anticipating where the camp will be located in the following year.

Respondents strongly identified with place (attachment and identity), motivations and amenities. In this sense there may be support for the wilderness as an artificial construct – respondents like what it offers and represents, but also like the notion of just showing up and participating, versus detailed front-end planning and organization. It might be suggested that in this particular wilderness construct, the respondents appreciate the camp as a mechanism to satisfy their motivations (and resultant place-attachment) as well as the amenities that facilitate their comfort and experience. As suggested earlier, as well as by one respondent, this is a very specific type of wilderness all-inclusive holiday. The thought, however, of GMC and BMC participants recognizing the camp as all-inclusive is likely to tarnish the romantic expectation of the wilderness attachment vis-à-vis frontier and exploration. Yet, as suggested by Beedie and Hudson (2003),

'these holidaymakers are tourists in so much as they buy an experience that is usually packaged for maximum efficiency' (p. 626). With respect to participant satisfaction with the GMC and BMC, it may be a complex synthesis of attachment to both the wilderness as a place as well as the 'built' camp through which satisfied outcomes are facilitated.

For the GMC and BMC as 'organizations', the wilderness that was once the 'unknown' has now become an object to be commoditized. Locations (specific locations) need to be found that will satisfy the past-positive expectancies of previous participants, as well as set it apart from other commercial holiday offerings. Place-attachment in this case takes on a different meaning from that of the participant. Place, for the GMC and BMC, becomes a logistical challenge to capitalize on what it offers, as well as towards a business construct of sustainability. As Hultman and Gössling (2006) suggest, 'nature and the environment are being staged and re-invented as commodities' (p. 80). For the GMC and BMC to be sustainable, this experience-commodity facilitative construct becomes their reality. Thus the perspective of place and place-attachment, as suggested by Cresswell (2004) and Braun (2001), depends upon the lens one looks through – that of the organizer versus that of the participant.

Summary

As has been discussed, this study has explored a strong identification with both place-identity and place-dependence by participants in the GMC and BMC mountaineering camps – what the camps represent and what they offer. Further, it has been suggested that motivations and, more likely, satisfaction of motivations, is the driver towards the notion of place-attachment. This may be explained by a past-positive experience of motivation satisfaction of desired recreation experiences resulting in future expectancies. To facilitate this, the authors suggest that camp organizers select 'specific' places that capitalize on what the specific location offers in terms of motivation-satisfaction. They also suggest that the GMC and BMC have taken the form of a wilderness all-inclusive experience albeit with a more demanding level of activities. It is a complex mosaic of relationships that influence and satisfy place-attachment. The end result is that the experience being facilitated by the GMC and BMC is strongly recognized by participants both in terms of place-attachment (identity and dependence) as well as satisfying their motivations for participating.

References

Bartlett, P. (2013) Is mountaineering a sport? *Royal Institute of Philosophy Supplement* 73, 145–157.

Beedie, P. and Hudson, S. (2003) Emergence of mountain-based adventure tourism. *Annals of Tourism Research* 30(3), 625–643.

Blake, K. (2002) Colorado fourteeners and the nature of place identity. *American Geographical Society* 92(1), 155–179.

Braun, B. (2001) Place becoming otherwise. *BC Studies Autumn* 131, 15–34.

Bricker, K. and Kerstetter, D. (2000) Level of specialization and place attachment: an exploratory study of whitewater recreationalists. *Leisure Sciences* 22, 233–257.

Convery, I., Corsane, G. and Davis, P. (eds) (2012) *Making Sense of Place: Multidisciplinary Perspectives*, 1st edn. Boydell Press, Rochester, New York.

Cresswell, T. (2004) *Place: A Short Introduction*. Blackwell, Malden, Massachusetts, pp. 53–79.

Cronon, W. (1996) The trouble with wilderness: or, getting back to the wrong nature. *Environmental History* 1(1), 7–28.

Daft, R. (2011) *The Leadership Experience*, 5th edn. South Western Educational Publishing, Mason, Ohio.

Driver, B.L. (1983) Recreation experience preference domains, scales and core statements. Unpublished manuscript.

Driver, B.L., Tinsley, H. and Manfredo, M. (1991) The paragraphs about leisure and recreation experience preference scales: results from two inventories designed to assess the breadth of the perceived psychological benefits of leisure. In: Driver, B.L., Brown, P. and Peterson, G. (eds) *Benefits of Leisure*, 1st edn. Venture Publishing, Inc., State College, Pennsylvania, pp. 263–286.

Hultman, J. and Gössling, S. (2006) *Ecotourism in Scandinavia: Lessons in Theory and Practice*. CAB International, Wallingford, UK and Cambridge, Massachusetts.

Jaworski, A. and Lawson, S. (2005) Discourse of polish agritourism: global, local and pragmatic. In: Jaworski, A. and Pritchard, A. (eds) *Discourse, Communication and Tourism*. Channel View Publications, Clevedon, UK.

Kyle, G., Graefe, A., Manning, R. and Bacon, J. (2003) An examination of the relationship between leisure activity involvement and place attachment among hikers along the Appalachian trail. *Journal of Leisure Research* 35(3), 249–273.

Kyle, G.T., Mowen, A. and Tarrant, M. (2004) Linking place preferences with place meaning: an examination of the relationship between place motivation and place attachment. *Journal of Environmental Psychology* 24, 439–454.

Manzo, L.C. (2005). For better or worse: exploring multiple dimensions of place meaning. *Journal of Environmental Psychology* 25(1), 67–86.

Presley, J. (2003) In praise of special places. *Parks & Recreation* 38(7), 22.

Rodriguez, A., Latkova, P. and Sun, Y. (2008) The relationship between leisure and life satisfaction: an application of activity and need theory. *Social Indicators Research* 86(1), 163–175.

Rutledge, L.G. (1989) *That Some May Follow: The History of Guide Outfitting in British Columbia*. Friesen Printers, Cloverdale, British Columbia, Canada.

Shores, K. and Scott, D. (2007) The relationship of individual time perspective and recreation experience preferences. *Journal of Leisure Research* 39(1), 28.

Walker, F.C. (1908) Paradise Valley Camp. *Canadian Alpine Journal* 1(2), 77.

White, D., Virden, R. and Riper, C. (2008) Effects of place identity, place dependence, and experience-use history on perceptions of recreation impacts in a natural setting. *Environmental Management* 42, 647–657.

Williams, D. and Vaske, J. (2003) The measurement of place attachment: validity and generalizability of a psychometric approach. *Forest Sciences* 49(6), 830–840.

Williams, D.R., Patterson, M.E., Roggenbuck, J.W. and Watson, A.E. (1992) Beyond the commodity metaphor: examining emotional and symbolic attachment to place. *Leisure Sciences* 14(1), 29.

22 Impacts and Solutions in Mountain Tourism: Overview, Contextual Development and Areas of Focus

John S. Hull* and Harold Richins

Thompson Rivers University, Kamloops, British Columbia, Canada

Introduction

Chapter 22 provides an introduction to Part V, which explores the diversity of impacts, approaches and solutions in mountain tourism, through utilization of a number of case studies and relevant writings. By gaining a greater understanding of the complex effects and approaches used to achieve viable outcomes and successful results, this may also provide substantially greater possibility in minimizing adverse consequences in mountain tourism.

Introduction to Literature on Impacts and Solutions in Mountain Tourism

Regional development and mountain tourism

Policy makers argue that tourism is an important tool for regional development that has the potential to improve quality of life in mountain destinations by providing employment opportunities for local residents, important tax revenues for governments, and economic diversification for local economies (Godde *et al.*, 2000; Andereck *et al.*, 2005; Hall and Boyd, 2005;

Lane, 2009; Kruk, 2010). Tourism is a forceful agent of change, creating impacts that are the product of development over time. Factors that influence impacts include: understanding where tourism is taking place; for how long and at what scale; who are the visitors; what activities are they engaging in; what infrastructure exists to support the tourism industry (Mathieson and Wall, 1982; Mason, 2008). Davison (1996) also identifies the importance of time and location in relation to assessing impacts as a result of tourism production and consumption taking place in the same location. As a result, impacts are spatially concentrated in the tourism destination, dependent upon climate and visitor holiday periods. With the rapid growth of tourism since 1950, most attention initially focused on the positive economic impacts of tourism with little attention being paid to the social and environmental consequences of development (Mathieson and Wall, 1982; Andereck *et al.*, 2005). As the tourism industry has continued to expand, however, there have been numerous studies examining not only the benefits but also the costs of tourism development at destinations (McCool and Martin, 1994; Jurowski *et al.*, 1997; Andereck *et al.*, 2005).

---

* Corresponding author: jhull@tru.ca

The mixed blessing of mountain tourism

Nepal and Chipeniuk (2005) point out that in socio-economic and environmental terms, tourism in mountain regions is a mixed blessing: it can be a source of problems, but also offers many opportunities for residents. There are three main consequences for mountain communities fostering tourism, which can be categorized into economic, socio-cultural and environmental elements (Godde *et al.*, 2000; Nepal, 2002; Andereck *et al.*, 2005; Mason, 2008).

Economically, mountain tourism generates important positive impacts by raising tax revenues for the public sector, promoting local investment and regional development, increasing jobs and providing income that improves the quality of life for local residents. Negative consequences include an increased cost of living,

expanding tax burdens, inflation, lack of linkages with local or regional production systems, low retention of benefits, high degree of seasonality and expanding government debt.

Socio-culturally, benefits from mountain tourism include increased intercultural communication and understanding, revitalization of local arts and crafts, increased pride in community, encouragement of cultural activities and improved cultural heritage. Negative consequences include overcrowding, loss of local identity and cultural traditions, increased crime rates, prostitution, drug-taking, social conflicts between hosts and guests and the commoditization of culture.

Environmentally, benefits from tourism in mountain regions have been identified as increased parks and recreation opportunities (see Figs 22.1 and 22.2), improved infrastructure and facilities, and heightened community appearance; while negative impacts include noise

Fig. 22.1. Historic Old Faithful Inn at Yellowstone National Park, Wyoming, USA (photograph courtesy of Harold Richins). Note: The Inn, a US national historic landmark built with local materials, was completed in 1904 and is considered the largest log structure in the world.

Fig. 22.2. Upper hot springs at Banff National Park built in 1932 (photograph courtesy of Harold Richins). Note: Original facilities operated nearby, commencing in 1886 and 1904.

pollution, garbage pollution, exploitation of resources, fire hazards, introduction of non-native species, air pollution from cars and airplanes, water pollution, wildlife disruption, loss of habitat, deforestation, trampling of soil and vegetation, and vandalism (Godde *et al.*, 2000; Nepal, 2002; Andereck *et al.*, 2005; Mason, 2008).

negative impacts while advancing sustainable development strategies. McKercher (1993) has identified eight fundamental truths, most of which have relevance to mountain tourism, that explain the complexity of the tourism industry and why various impacts are generated regardless of the tourism activity (Table 22.1).

Support for mountain tourism

Even though impact studies in the late 20th century suggest that negative impacts outweigh the positive, researchers (Jafari, 1990; Wall, 1997; Mason, 2008) point out that the majority of residents at tourism destinations still want tourist visitation. According to Hudson and Townsend (1992, 50), the benefits of tourism 'owes much to a policy climate that has been uncritical over a range of issues.' Wall (1997) argues that there is a need for destinations to make choices and trade-offs that minimize

Mitigating impacts

Buckley (2012) in his work on issues in sustainable tourism research and practice identifies the need to understand impacts, generate responses through policy and management recommendations, and develop indicators to evaluate and monitor results. He points out that regulatory instruments provide the foundation of sustainability in tourism as in other industry sectors. The adoption of standard planning, regulatory and technological approaches (see Fig. 22.3) is key to reducing pollution and

Table 22.1. The Fundamental Truths of Tourism.

Tourism consumes resources and creates waste.
Tourism has the ability to over-consume resources.
Tourism competes with other resource users and needs to do this to survive.
Tourism is private-sector dominated.
Tourism is multi-faceted and is therefore almost impossible to control.
Tourists are consumers, not anthropologists.
Tourism is entertainment.
Unlike other industrial activities, tourism imports clients rather than exporting a product.

Fig. 22.3. Integrated planning and the resulting mountain tourism resort of Sun Peaks, BC, Canada (photograph courtesy of Harold Richins).

associated impacts from tourism development at destinations (Buckley, 2009).

Williams and Ponsford (2009) also point out that minimizing impacts in mountain destinations does not only depend on the efforts of local residents and policy makers. Solutions must also consider that tourists become aware of the impact of their tourism pursuits and adjust their activities accordingly; businesses must recognize the effects of their production processes and modify them accordingly; and regulatory agencies must monitor the effect of their tourism policies on destination environments and revise them as necessary.

Summary of Chapters in Part V: Impacts and Solutions in Mountain Tourism

The chapters in this section provide an understanding of impacts, approaches and solutions to tourism in mountain environments. This introduction and the subsequent chapters in Part V provide a diversity of examples, showing both direct and indirect influences on mountain tourism.

Chapters in this section represent a wide range of subject areas including: community-based tourism within a Philippines World Heritage site; addressing seasonality of mountain tourism in Garmish-Partenkirchen; ethics, social responsibility, values and equity in the context of natural and historic mountain environments; building network connections in mountain tourism border regions in Spain and France; community developmental change in a Nepalese mountain adventure destination; and exploring distinctive methods of leisure and tourism connection among 11 small communities in a mountainous, rural regional area of New Zealand. Summaries of this section's chapters follow.

Chapter 23. Regional Collaboration in Community-based Mountain Tourism in World Heritage Sites: The Ifugao Rice Terraces of the Cordillera Central Mountains in the Philippines

Authors: Jovel Ananayo and Harold Richins

Mountain tourism does not just refer to high-level alpine environments, but embraces lower-level rural environments and geographically diverse areas with varying weather patterns, temperatures and climatic conditions. This chapter focuses on island-based tropical mountains in the northern region of the Philippines Archipelago. The authors provide insight into community-based tourism and governance in a World Heritage site in the Philippines.

Utilizing tourism as a catalyst, the regional community developed a community-based and integrated organization, called Save the Ifugao

Terraces Movement. This group attempted to integrate the local approach to governance with external knowledge from international agency groups regarding the development and success factors in the provision of local tourism experiences. This case explores the use of a community-based ecotourism programme, targeted at international tourists, that prioritized the conservation of the world-famous Ifugao Rice Terraces, encouraged sustainable practices and strengthened local and regional culture.

The challenges that exist in the preservation of both natural and cultural heritage are discussed, with a special examination of traditional farmers' children in the region who seek alternative income and lifestyle choices. Results have been encouraging thus far, as there is increasing awareness of local stakeholder needs, instigating more effective governance strategies, and opening up possibilities for viable employment streams to community members, including those who focus primarily on the preservation of the unique rural environment and ethnic culture of the region.

Chapter 24. Mountain Tourism Supply-chain Networks in Cross-border Settings: The Case of Intercerdanya, Spain

Authors: Dani Blasco, Jaume Guia and Lluís Prats

International borders are often delineated by significant mountain ranges. Steep valleys and high mountain passes often form natural barriers where communities have been historically built on the edge of borders based on needs for protection, or in some cases, for trade. Chapter 24's authors study border tourism within the context of the French and Spanish Pyrenees Mountains. The chapter brings to light the authors' points of view, provides suggestions and discusses challenges related to building connections in mountain tourism border regions. This includes aspects of sustainability, planning, community and regional tourism development, and the management of growth in mountain regions, including a criticism of the potential commodification of mountains due to tourism development.

This chapter provides an understanding of distinctive and diverse issues in mountain tourism development, as well as discussing both community and corporate modes of destination organizations. The primary focus of this chapter is to explore effective and efficient tourism and trade, limitations to the trade, and suggestions for proactive supply-chain trade network management approaches across traditional border areas of mountainous Spain and France.

Chapter 25. A Moral Turn for Mountain Tourism?

Authors: Lisa Cooke, Bryan Grimwood and Kellee Caton

The interdisciplinary nature of tourism provides the opportunity to study mountain tourism from many perspectives. Most tourism researchers have focused on the management or business perspective, or have been oriented toward enterprise, and/or community/ regional economic development. However, the nature of tourism as an area of study encourages a range of diverse perspectives, cultivating a critical eye or generating unique perspectives for consideration.

The authors explore an emerging area in tourism studies – moral philosophy. Creating understanding and meaning in outdoor experiences is explored through literature with a comprehensive emphasis on sustainability, including aspects of ethics, social responsibility, values and equity, in the context of natural and historic environments, the study of wilderness, indigenous studies, exploration and survival. This chapter, utilizing a case study of Sun Peaks Ski Resort, discusses challenges facing many mountain resorts throughout the world. It provides a refreshingly new, yet potentially confrontational analysis in attempting to understand tourism development in sensitive regions (where traditional use and/or habitation has existed) through a different perspective, rather than the dominant Western paradigm. By viewing mountain regions from a different viewpoint and casting a moral eye on the topic, perhaps, as the authors of this chapter suggest, readers may begin to understand destinations in natural environments as being layered with 'a complex cultural, historical, and political production'. More inclusionary values may allow decision makers and future stakeholders to have empathy and understanding of the multitude of views and moral platforms.

Chapter 26. Mountain Tourism in Germany: Challenges and Opportunities in Addressing Seasonality at Garmisch-Partenkirchen

Authors: Joel T. Schmidt, Christian H. Werner and Harold Richins

Many alpine towns have been dependent on winter tourism for hundreds of years. A range of factors have significantly influenced the evolution of mountain destinations, including: changing economic conditions; broader interests and expectations from visitors with a desire for more diverse experiences; changing long-term weather patterns; and greater demand for health and wellness activities and other special interests.

Garmisch-Partenkirchen is one of the most prominent mountain resort communities in Germany; the community chose, during the post-war period, to invest in tourism and recreation with a focus on adventure, mountains, tourism and trade instead of other industries. Challenges in Garmisch-Partenkirchen are representative of those faced by many alpine towns. The city is striving to maintain its position as a mountain tourism leader by transitioning from a winter to an all-season tourism resort destination, through the inclusion of special offerings in the areas of health, sport and culture. Chapter 26's authors present current tourism data about the region, reflect on the challenges, and examine the solutions for a long-term viable future implemented at this mountain destination. The authors believe the continued adjustment of goals and initiatives to meet regional, national and international trends in mountain tourism is commendable.

Chapter 27. Tourism and Change in Nepal's Mt Everest Region

Author: Sanjay Nepal

This chapter was written prior to two devastating earthquakes that hit Nepal – the first on 25 April 2015 (7.8 magnitude) and the second on 12 May 2015 (7.3 magnitude). The first caused numerous landslides and a serious avalanche that wiped out part of Everest base camp, killing at least 19 climbers, making it the 'deadliest day on the mountain', according to reports. As this book goes to the publisher, more than 8000 people have been reported dead and twice as many injured in these catastrophic events. The points raised here by Sanjay Nepal highlight the tremendous challenges faced when looking at tourism in this particular mountain region.

For over 150 years, people seeking adventure in mountain regions, looked to Europe (The Alps) and North America (The Rockies) as important destinations. However, until the early 1950s, some of the world's greatest mountain ranges were off-limits to the outside world. Once opened, and over the ensuing 50 or 60 years, the mountains of the Himalayas were explored and summits reached on numerous occasions through major expeditions that took a significant amount of time and resources to organize. Since the 1990s, and particularly in the last decade, a major change in visitor activity occurred in the Nepalese Himalayas, with a significant new form of mountain adventure tourism.

Chapter 27 explores the exponential growth and development of high-altitude climbing and trekking in the Mt Everest region of Nepal. Factors include: the growth in visitors to the Everest region over a 15-year period, from 1998 to 2012; the expansion of tourism and community infrastructure in the region; the growth and diversity in tourism employment in the region; the significant social changes affecting the villages and communities; impacts on the local people, such as changes in values, traditions and community identity; and the substantial pressures on the region's environment due to the extensive needs of climbing teams and adventure climbing tours.

The chapter concludes with a look at the future potential challenges in the region and the influence these will have on the communities.

It also explores the conceptual nature of mountain adventure in the context of the pressures of overuse in popular destinations. The question of what 'adventure' really means in this context is briefly explored.

Chapter 28. Rural Tourism and Small Business Networks in Mountain Areas: Integrating Information Communication Technologies (ICT) and Community in Western Southland, New Zealand

Authors: Carolyn Deuchar and Simon Milne

Chapter 28 examines the rural mountain regions of New Zealand as tourism destinations and includes a case study of building community and tourism connectedness through the use of information and communication technologies (ICT). The authors explore distinctive connecting methods of 11 small, rural mountain communities in New Zealand's South Island.

Concepts raised in this chapter demonstrate approaches to building effective tourism networks with an applied case of small community-based tourism. The authors discuss the lack of effective practice examples showing how to develop social relationships or work on community connections; they emphasize grassroots community capacity building that incorporates the provision of shared resources and information.

The chapter authors investigate the application of community informatics and combine this with information technologies, systems and communication to show the effectiveness in information provision and community tourism enhancement. This is demonstrated through the discussion of a programme referred to as 'web-raising' in a mountain and rural tourism environment. This tourism network approach is particularly successful in building community sharing of tourism resources and outcomes in peripheral areas including mountain and rural settings.

The outcomes from the established tourism network programme described in this case study showed that not only were the local enterprises motivated to use the network for promotional purposes, they were even further motivated to support community development related to economic and social enhancement of the regional community. This was different from what has been found in other remote tourism destinations in New Zealand.

Concluding Remarks

This chapter introduced the reader to issues and considerations of impacts and solutions regarding mountain tourism and presented an overview of the six chapters within Part V. Though solutions may be found for dealing with specific mountain tourism challenges, understanding the diversity of issues and considerations that impact tourism destinations in mountain settings may provide a strong foundation for developing more integrated, sustainable and comprehensive approaches for tourism in mountain destinations.

References

Andereck, K.L., Valentine, K.M., Knopf, R.C. and Vogt, C.A. (2005) Residents' perceptions of community tourism impacts. *Annals of Tourism Research* 32(4), 1056–1076.

Buckley, R. (2009) Evaluating the net effects of ecotourism on the environment: a framework, first assessment and future research. *Journal of Sustainable Tourism* 17(6), 643–672.

Buckley, R. (2012) Sustainable tourism: research and reality. *Annals of Tourism Research* 39(2), 528–546.

Davison, R. (1996) *Tourism Destinations*. Hodder and Stoughton, London.

Godde, P., Price, M.F. and Zimmermann, F.M. (2000) Tourism and development in mountain regions: moving forward into the new millennium. In: Godde, P., Price, M. and Zimmermann, F. (eds) *Tourism and Development in Mountain Regions*. CAB International, Wallingford, UK, pp. 1–25.

Hall, C.M. and Boyd, S.W. (2005) *Nature-based Tourism in Peripheral Areas: Development or Disaster?* Channel View Publications, Clevedon, UK.

Hudson, R. and Townsend, A. (1992) Tourism employment and policy choices in local government. In: Johnsen, P. and Thomas, B. (eds) *Perspectives on Tourism Policy*. Mansell, London.

Jafari, J. (1990) Research and scholarship: the basis of tourism education. *Journal of Tourism Studies* 1(1), 33–41.

Jurowski, C., Uysal, M. and Williams, R.D. (1997) A theoretical analysis of host community resident reactions to tourism. *Journal of Travel Research* 36(2), 3–11.

Kruk, E. (2010) *Marketing the Uniqueness of the Himalayas: an Analytical Framework*. ICIMOD, Kathmandu, Nepal.

Lane, B. (2009) Thirty years of sustainable tourism. In: Gossling, S., Hall, C.M. and Weaver, D. (eds) *Sustainable Tourism Futures: Perspectives on Systems, Restructuring and Innovations*. Routledge, New York, pp. 19–32.

Mason, P. (2008) *Tourism Impacts, Planning and Management*. Butterworth-Heinemann, Oxford, UK.

Mathieson, A. and Wall, G. (1982) *Tourism: Economic, Physical and Social Impacts*. Longman, London.

McCool, S. and Martin, S. (1994) Community attachment and attitudes towards sustainable development. *Journal of Travel Research* 32(3), 29–34.

McKercher, B. (1993) Some fundamental truths about tourism: understanding tourism's social and environmental impacts. *Journal of Sustainable Tourism* 1(1), 6–16.

Nepal, S. (2002) Mountain ecotourism and sustainable development. *Mountain Research and Development* 22(2), 104–109.

Nepal, S. and Chipeniuk, R. (2005) Mountain tourism: towards a conceptual framework. *Tourism Geographies* 7(3), 313–333.

Wall, G. (1997) Sustainable tourism – unsustainable development. In: Wahab, S. and Pigram, J.J. (eds) *Tourism, Development and Growth: the Challenge of Sustainability*. Routledge, London, pp. 33–49.

Williams, P. and Ponsford, I.F. (2009) Confronting tourism's environmental paradox: transitioning for sustainable tourism. *Futures* 41(6), 396–404.

23 Regional Collaboration in Community-based Mountain Tourism in World Heritage Sites: The Ifugao Rice Terraces of the Cordillera Central Mountains in the Philippines

Jovel Ananayo[1]* and Harold Richins[2]
[1]*Ifugao State University, Cordillera Administrative Region, Philippines;*
[2]*Thompson Rivers University, Kamloops, British Columbia, Canada*

Introduction

This chapter examines the role of tourism development on the conservation of world heritage sites, focusing on the Ifugao Rice Terraces of the Philippine Cordilleras. These terraces, bounded by rugged peaks, are located within the Cordillera Central Mountains on the northern part of the island of Luzon, in the northernmost region of the Philippines archipelago (see Fig. 23.1). The interrelationship between tourism development and world heritage site conservation are explored by analysing the tourism programme of the Save the Ifugao Terraces Movement (SITMo), which was intended to help conserve the Ifugao world heritage sites.

This case study includes a description of a locally developed method in addressing long-term conservation and community development issues within a world heritage cultural site. The case acknowledges, in the context of its broader plan, the background and approach in developing locally based tourism within the region (Drost, 1995; Borges *et al.*, 2011; Ananayo, 2014). This includes the SITMo Eco-Cultural Tourism Program. An important aspect of this programme has involved substantial collaboration, communication and engagement of key groups in the development, operation and management of the tours and their resulting outcomes. There were a few weaknesses in the development process and implementation; however, outcomes were generally constructive. These outcomes are described in this case study, including economic outcomes and contributions, environmental outcomes and contributions, and contribution to cultural conservation.

This case first examines SITMo's tourism activities, in order to provide an understanding of the development approach. After reviewing the tourism activities and providing a brief description of the SITMo model, SITMo's approach to community-based tourism and how it is translated into actual operations is examined, by looking into the stakeholder cooperative that was implemented to advance the tourism programme. The findings indicate that the current, as well as the envisioned, stakeholder cooperative is largely similar to stakeholder cooperation advocated for sustainable tourism

---

* Corresponding author: jovelfrancis_ananayo@yahoo.com

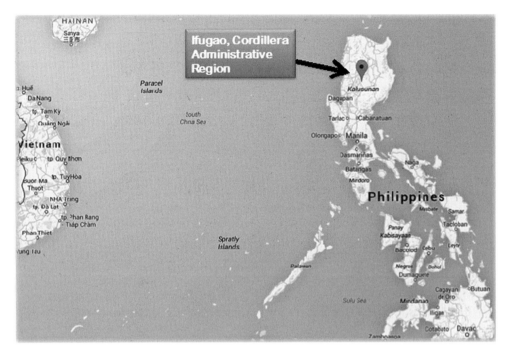

Fig. 23.1. Map of Philippines and Ifugao Rice Terrace Region.

(Swarbrooke, 2004) and other stakeholder approaches (UNESCO and Nordic World Heritage Foundation, 2001; Aas *et al.*, 2005; Sheehan and Ritchie, 2005; Beritelli, 2011; Borges *et al.*, 2011).

A significant move to advance the conservation of World Heritage Sites and historic towns and places was the Seoul Declaration in 2005 (ICOMOS, 2005). The Declaration outlined the importance of historic towns and areas, issues besetting them, and strategies or approaches for their conservation. However, the stipulations have generally included broad principles and guidelines. In most cases, these broad principles and guidelines are only useful if serious attempts are made towards translating them into operational plans regarding specific sites with due consideration to the distinct and diverse contexts of heritage-related destinations.

Previous papers describe and compare local models of ecotourism development to more established models for community-based ecotourism (Lyttleton and Allcock, 2002; Ananayo and Richins, 2010). The case analysis presented here focuses on providing an

illustration of the set-up of community-based stakeholder cooperation in the implementation of SITMo's ecotourism programme within the mountainous regions of Ifugao. The stakeholder cooperation involved in the organization's programme is evaluated based on the stakeholder cooperation model for sustainable tourism as prescribed by the World Tourism Organization, which was enhanced by Swarbrooke (2004). The general outcomes or contributions of SITMO's programme towards achieving conservation of the Rice Terraces are then presented.

The community-based ecotourism programme described in this chapter forms part of the Save the Ifugao Terraces Movement (SITMo), a local non-governmental organization designed to contribute to the conservation of the Ifugao Rice Terraces and culture (SITMo, 2015a). The Ifugao Rice Terraces of the Philippine Cordilleras were inscribed in the World Heritage List in 1995 (UNESCO World Heritage Centre, 2014b), but from 2001 have been included in the List of World Heritage Sites in Danger due to complex challenges threatening their long-term sustainability (UNESCO World

Heritage Centre, 2014c). By exploring various aspects of the Ifugao case, it may provide useful insights on the ways that tourism can effectively support World Heritage Site conservation.

The Ifugao Rice Terraces – A Brief Background

A description of the Ifugao Terraces and its people provides a context for the cultural heritage interests that are increasing due to tourism. Traditionally, the lives of the Ifugao people revolved around the rice terraces. The terraces were also a symbol of socio-economic status in the community and were previously considered the most valuable property a person or family owned mainly because of their economic and socio-cultural value to local families. Community livelihood heavily relied on the cultivation of the rice fields. Moreover, the Ifugaos considered the terraces as priceless treasures, as they had been maintained and handed down to them from their forefathers across many generations (Keesing, 1962; Conklin, 1980; UNESCO World Heritage Centre, 2014a).

Across the annual rice terrace cycle are cultural rituals and festivities that are interwoven with the different stages of rice production. Nonetheless, these practices are now slowly diminishing due to various interlocking factors. Two of the major factors contributing to this slow loss are the introduction of Christianity and the educational curriculum, which is increasingly patterned after the Western education system. Previous unrestrained tourism development has also been indicated as one of the major culprits for this diminishing emphasis on the cultural traditions in rice terrace regions. These factors, in addition to others, are undermining the continuation of Ifugao cultural values and practices, and therefore threatening the sustainability of the rice terraces.

Although the rice terraces are threatened with numerous challenges, their great beauty as well as their socio-economic, cultural and environmental significance is not completely diminished at this point. The Ifugao Rice Terraces were inscribed into the United Nations Educational, Scientific and Cultural Organization (UNESCO) World Heritage List in 1995, which

recognized the outstanding universal cultural value of the rice terraces. Though this was a significant step forward in the conservation of the rice terraces, UNESCO's periodic monitoring of Ifugao revealed that the rice terraces were showing signs of deterioration. A mission to the terraces from UNESCO reported that close to 30% of the terraces were showing some signs of being neglected or not being cultivated (UNESCO, 2001). The findings indicated that even with immediate measures being undertaken, there would be approximately a 10-year period of restoration and conservation needed.

From 2001, the Ifugao Rice Terraces were on the List of Word Heritage Sites in Danger (UNESCO World Heritage Centre, 2014b). This was due to key aspects, including: abandonment of the terraces because of the neglected irrigation system and people leaving the area; unregulated development threatening the property; tourism needs not being addressed; and lack of an effective management system (UNESCO, 2001). The world heritage site has been taken off the endangered list more recently, due to more than 10 years of concerted effort (Provincial Government of Ifugao, 2004; Better Conservation, 2014; UNESCO World Heritage Centre, 2014d). Responsible eco/cultural tourism, which includes a sustainable development programme, has improved, though a recent status report noted some concern and support for achieving further enhancement of sustainable tourism practices (UNESCO, 2001).

Proposed Strategies to Conserve the Rice Terraces

Anudon (2002), in his extensive study, recommended a Community-based Resource Management (CBRM) strategy to sustain the rice terraces. This strategy proposed that conservation and livelihood development be linked together to counter the ongoing trend in deterioration of the terraces. Conservation for the terraces incorporated schemes that deal with the deteriorating rice terraces, forests and swidden farms. These include restoration of damaged terrace walls, repairs of irrigation systems, introduction of Sloping Agricultural Land Technology (SALT), and reforestation in order to maintain biodiversity.

Conservation in rice terraces also includes making government social services accessible to farmers and building the natural resource capability within the sensitive site (Gonzales, 2000; Ciencia, 2007; Ananayo and Richins, 2010; Ananayo, 2014). This is intended to motivate them to settle in the area, and continue to cultivate their farms. On the other hand, livelihood development mainly refers to the enhancement of existing income-generating activities as well as the introduction of new revenue-oriented activities that are expected to add to the income of the farmers. These include rice–fish culture or the integration of freshwater fish production with rice cultivation, rice–vegetable farming such as the pingkol, and farm mechanization such as the introduction of the use of microtillers designed for upland farms.

Although the Local Government Units (LGUs) of the relevant regional areas are recommended as the key players in the implementation of the CBRM strategy, it has been stressed that farmers need to be mobilized, empowered and take an active role in the planning and implementation of the terraces programmes. An alternative strategy has been to set up a foundation or nongovernmental organization to help the LGUs. The foundation can tap potential funding agencies that do not typically work directly with government agencies, either locally or more regionally. In reviewing the CBRM model, however, the potential of tourism to help in the terraces' conservation and proposed livelihood activities is not explicitly addressed, nor acknowledged. Part of this case is to point out how tourism can significantly contribute to terrace conservation, which is consistent with other cases, regarding world heritage preservation, enhancement and success (Akagawa and Sirisrisak, 2008; Arezki et al., 2009; Frey and Steiner, 2011; Jimura, 2011).

The Save the Ifugao Terraces Movement (SITMo)

With strong support from the Philippine Rural Reconstruction Movement (PRRM), the largest and oldest non-governmental organization in the Philippines, the Save the Ifugao Terraces Movement (SITMo) was formally launched in 2000 (Ananayo, 2014; SITMo, 2015a). The overall purpose for setting up the organization was 'to advance the campaign for the protection and rehabilitation of the Ifugao Rice Terraces' (from unpublished SITMo Program Documents). The organization was established and registered at the Philippine Securities and Exchange Commission (SEC) as a non-profit organization. The following are the organization's vision, mission and goals:

- **Vision:** 'Ifugao is economically developed and sustained as a World Heritage Site and a world-class ecotourism destination with people who are healthy and well-nourished, self-sufficient, educated, globally competitive and God-loving, living in harmony with nature and proud of their cultural identity.'
- **Mission:** 'Build SITMo as a strong movement and the lead institution in the conservation of the Ifugao Rice Terraces and cultural heritage.'
- **Goals:** 'Mainstream indigenous knowledge, skills and practices; Improve and sustain quality of life of the people; Rehabilitate and protect critical watersheds, ecosystems, and biodiversity; Support and advocate efforts for good governance; Continuous efforts on resource mobilization and movement building.'

To achieve the above organizational goals, SITMo formulated an integrated approach. The approach put together at least seven interrelated programmes to tackle terrace conservation. These include: (i) sustainable agriculture; (ii) natural resource management and livelihood; (iii) renewable energy development; (iv) indigenous knowledge transmission; (v) community-based land use planning; (vi) ecotourism; and (vii) local governance. The organization has indicated that these initiatives will enhance and save the Ifugao Rice Terraces from gradual demise as they are aimed at addressing the factors that endanger its world heritage. While SITMo has a wide array of programmes, this case will focus on the ecotourism programme of the organization and how it is linked to the conservation of the Rice Terraces.

SITMo's Eco-cultural Tourism Program

Background and approaches to the Eco-cultural Tourism Program

Acknowledging the threats to the long-term sustainability of the rice terraces and recognizing that tourism is among the leading threats, SITMo designed its innovative eco-tourism programme as part of its strategy to conserve the terraces. In consideration of preserving and enhancing the rice terraces and the communities that live among them, SITMo designed and implemented a community-based tourism approach. The programme is referred to as the SITMo Eco-cultural Tourism Program. The new eco-cultural programme of SITMo provides for initiatives to address issues of cultural enhancement, economic stability, community engagement and authenticity of the visitor experience. Moreover, the programme is aimed at helping address the deterioration of the terraces' watersheds and the declining interest of younger generation Ifugaos in their culture and the rice terraces (SITMo, 2015b).

The experience for visitors includes observation of various stages of agricultural activities and the interwoven cultural rituals and festivals across the annual rice production cycle. By highlighting the various seasonal phases of rice production in the terraces and engaging community members in the eco-cultural tourism packages, a prioritized, core product has been developed for the rice terrace experience. Tourists have direct and more realistic interaction with the host terrace communities through brief encounters, and participation in the various terrace activities, festivals and other cultural and adventure activities makes sure they are brought together and immersed in the experience.

The host community and its farmers are consulted in order to provide the least invasive experience to their activities, while allowing for the highest possible immersion into their local culture. Activities for visitors are well designed, communicated, and agreed to in order to create the best possible experience, while minimizing any possibility of hostility, invasiveness or negative impact. Tour-guiding and other services are provided primarily by members of the local Ifugao Rice Terrace host communities to ensure that maximum economic benefit goes to the local stakeholders, and meals and snacks of local delicacies are provided by the local community using locally grown vegetables and livestock. Every attempt is made to diversify activities and to cater to a wide variety of interests. Sites chosen as host communities include heritage areas and upland communities that do not regularly receive tourists, but have heritage resources that may be developed for tourism purposes. To maximize the visitor experience and immersion in the local culture and natural areas, adventure tourism (caving, spelunking, and river rafting) is also incorporated with other activities.

Cooperation and stakeholder relationships in the SITMo Eco-cultural Tourism Program

In analysing the tourism and heritage conservation programme of SITMo, significant information was gathered and interviews conducted in the region. The analysis of SITMo's reports and information gathered through interviews reveals the organization's emphasis on a cooperative community approach to tourism and heritage conservation. Interviews included SITMo's Eco-cultural Tourism Program Coordinator, Chief Operations Officer, Finance Officer, ecotourism volunteers and guides, and the supervising Tourism Operations Officer at the Ifugao Provincial Tourism Office. The method used in the development and implementation of the programme was not based on established models, but rather on local and regional practical knowledge on how to help arrest the prevailing issues besetting the rice terraces.

The informal nature of the Eco-cultural Tourism Program's development resulted in significant challenges in understanding the approaches that led to successful outcomes. The following discussion provides a review of the interactions and cooperation approaches involved with the development and implementation of the SITMo's eco-cultural tourism offerings.

Understanding various key players or stakeholders (those who impact, are involved in, or are potentially impacted by the operation) is vital when embarking upon sustainable tourism programmes or tourism and heritage conservation initiatives (UNESCO and NWHF, 2001; Swarbrooke, 2004; Tucker and Emge, 2010; Beritelli, 2011; Borges *et al.*, 2011). In the case of SITMo's Eco-cultural Tourism Program, those involved included the village communities, municipal local government units, travel agencies and the Department of Tourism. Figure 23.2 illustrates the present stakeholder cooperation set-up in the implementation of SITMo's ecotourism programme.

The stakeholder cooperation set-up in the implementation of the tourism programme shows that SITMo is at the heart of the involved groups of stakeholders. The organization is, therefore, the focal point in coordinating, harmonizing and directing tourism initiatives for the conservation of the rice terraces. It likewise takes charge of eliciting support from other stakeholders, and connects together the heritage communities and other tourism stakeholders.

Additionally, SITMo acts as a local tour operator. It organizes, packages, sells and

facilitates tours across the heritage areas. The tours are promoted with the help of staff personal contacts, Manila-based travel agencies and via the internet. Since SITMo is a non-profit organization, its main objective is to distribute the economic benefits from tourism to the host communities. The breakdown of the economic contributions of the tours is presented in the following section. The municipal local government units and the Department of Tourism provide marketing, funding and technical support, while the host communities provide the services for tourists. The municipal and village governments also enact local legislations in support of the programme (Impact, 2008; A New Plan, 2013).

At the community level, local organizations such as farmers' groups and youth associations are active partners in the management of the tour packages. As hosts, the communities provide meals and snacks for visitors, giving them the opportunity to promote local delicacies, an important part of their intangible cultural heritage. Local farmers

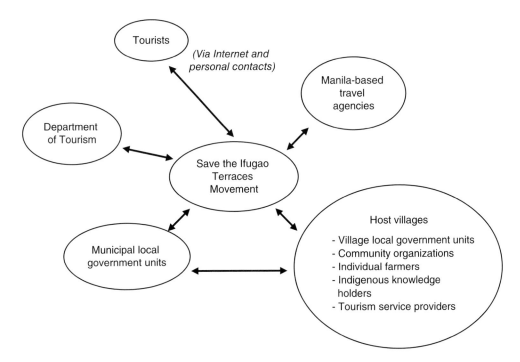

Fig. 23.2. Current stakeholder cooperation set-up (source: derived from SITMo reports and interviews).

provide the vegetables and livestock for the meals, thereby generating additional income. Other local stakeholders participate by producing souvenir items for sale. At this stage, however, it is still premature to determine the economic impact of the tourism programme on the farmers, since the programme is still in its infancy.

Although SITMo is taking the lead role in promoting tourism for the conservation of the rice terraces, it plans to transfer the task to the terrace communities in the future. For this reason, the organization's capacity-building activities are geared towards increasing tourism skills and management capabilities in the communities so that they can effectively

and efficiently handle their own tourism operations in the future. When the communities are considered capable enough to handle their tourism operations, SITMo may then shift its role to providing technical and marketing support to them. Moreover, SITMo may, in the future, also consider transferring its operations to other communities using the lessons learned from the existing pilot sites. Figure 23.3 illustrates that the host villages are expected to eventually take on a strong organizational role. Though this is yet to happen, host villages in the heritage areas are expected to eventually take charge in marketing their own tours and in coordinating their tourism initiatives with other stakeholders.

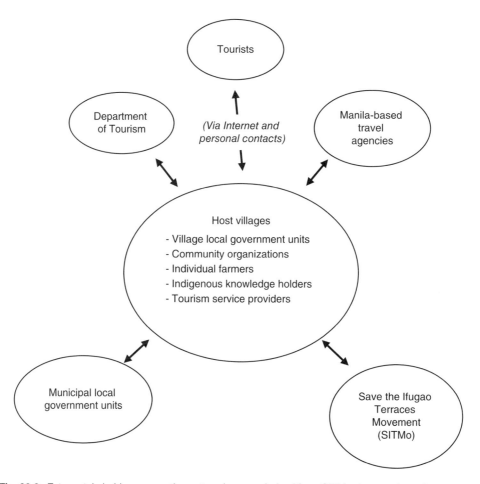

Fig. 23.3. Future stakeholder cooperation set-up (source: derived from SITMo documents and interviews).

Weaknesses of SITMo stakeholder cooperation in the Eco-cultural Tourism Program

While SITMo involved various stakeholders in the implementation of its programme, some key stakeholders were left out. These include the Ifugao Provincial Tourism Office (PTO), and the private sector; specifically, the local tourism businesses concentrated in Banaue municipality (Banaue Tourism, 2015). SITMo's weak relationship with the aforementioned key stakeholders might hinder the future success of its tourism programme, due to tensions between the organization and the operators of the existing businesses and the PTO.

Figure 23.4 illustrates SITMo's present stakeholder relationships in the context of the broader picture of stakeholder cooperation in the Province of Ifugao. The straight lines indicate strong relationships and open communication, while the broken arrows indicate otherwise. It can be observed that SITMo has strong relationships with local communities, travel

intermediaries and municipal governments, while its relationships with other stakeholders are relatively weak.

At present, the PTO and the local tourism businesses are the main players in the local tourism industry, and their initiatives are not directly designed to help conserve the terraces. Hence, while SITMo pursues its programme with the aim of contributing to the conservation of the rice terraces, the PTO and the local private sector might negate the organization's initiatives. In addition, the PTO and the local businesses might look at SITMo as a competitor instead of as a partner. For these reasons, SITMo might want to look for areas of convergence and trade-offs with the aforementioned stakeholders. If SITMo wants to mainstream its programme to the government, it might be advantageous to involve the PTO and tap its human and financial resources. In addition, the PTO is the Provincial Government's tourism arm, and has the capacity to influence municipal and village governments for tourism development.

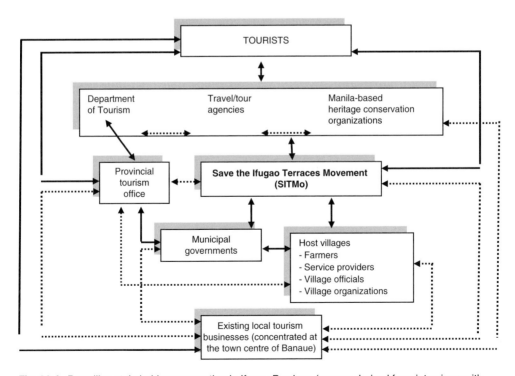

Fig. 23.4. Prevailing stakeholder cooperation in Ifugao Province (source: derived from interviews with key informants).

As per the Stakeholder Cooperation Model prescribed by the World Tourism Organization (Swarbrooke, 2004; Silk Road, 2012), the stakeholder cooperation envisioned by SITMo seems to be on the right track. The attainment of sustainable tourism requires the involvement of all stakeholders that perform different but complementary roles. Drawing from this model suggests that SITMo can only achieve its goal successfully by involving the local private sector, the PTO and other stakeholders to be successful with the Ifugao Terraces Movement. Figure 23.5 illustrates the adapted model for stakeholder cooperation for sustainable tourism (UNESCO and Nordic World Heritage Foundation, 2001; Swarbrooke, 2004; Aas *et al.*, 2005; Sheehan and Ritchie, 2005; Beritelli, 2011; Borges *et al.*, 2011). This adapted model does not suggest international organization involvement as is prevalent in other tourism stakeholder cooperation models.

Outcomes from the Ifugao Terraces Eco-cultural Tour Program

Economic outcomes and contributions

From the commencement of SITMo's Eco-cultural Tourism Program in 2006, the organization was able to facilitate 23 packaged tours. The tours involved at least 530 participants: 70% domestic and 30% foreign tourists. The domestic tourists

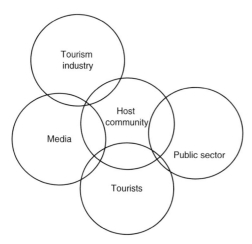

Fig. 23.5. Adapted stakeholder cooperation model for sustainable tourism.

included university students, families, media people, researchers, conservationists and other individual vacationers. In like manner, the foreign tourists were mainly families, researchers, backpackers and conservation-oriented individuals. By 2012, SITMo facilitated eco-cultural tours, including 1822 visitors to Ifugao, of which 11% were local and 89% were foreign (Ananayo, 2014). At present the organization does not have a systematic data gathering and recording system on tourists' profiles. The organization is considering, however, developing future data-gathering mechanisms crucial in understanding its tours, product development and marketing approaches.

SITMo's Ecotourism Program has been introduced slowly and steadily, acknowledging that tours may eventually move to a growth period, characterized by more tourists and increased sales. By this point, it will be important to have fully integrated techniques and sustainable tourism methods that incorporate community, cultural, economic, and world heritage needs and considerations into the management approach (Di Giovine, 2008; Hockings *et al.*, 2008; Okazaki, 2008; Landorf, 2009; Reid *et al.*, 2009; Borges *et al.*, 2011).

Although SITMo tour numbers are relatively low, those tourists are considered 'quality tourists'. For the purposes of this case study, quality tourists are hereby defined as those who are culturally and environmentally sensitive and are willing to spend their money in a way that benefits them and the terrace communities. They may not necessarily be high spenders, but they are conscious that their expenditures benefit the local hosts. Also, quality tourists behave in a manner that creates the least negative socio-cultural impact to the local communities. From a sustainable tourism standpoint, high tourist arrival rates may not necessarily be beneficial, as they may have greater negative impacts upon the community than benefits, whereas a focus on quality tourists whose behaviours and expenditures have positive impacts to the local destination has been indicated to have strong merit for the SITMo eco-cultural tours.

For the first year of operation, SITMo's Ecotourism Project was able to infuse a significant amount of money into the local economy, the Province of Ifugao (i.e. PhP or Philippine Peso1.6 million, which is the equivalent of

US$35,847). On average, each tour partici-
pant spent at least PhP3044 or US$68 per
tour package. Since the tours were usually
on a 3-day package, the average daily tourist expenditure for each packaged tour was
PhP1015 or US$23. A small part of the tour-
ism revenues are remitted to community organizations as their community trust fund. Figure
23.6 shows the breakdown of tourist expenditures for 2007 and Fig. 23.7 illustrates the
breakdown of tourist expenditures and benefits to the communities (SITMo, 2006–2007).

From 2010 to 2012, the organization's Eco-
cultural Tourism Programme had stabilized and
generated about PhP1.6–1.7 million to the province's economy. Figure 23.8 illustrates the breakdown of economic contributions of the eco-cultural
tours in 2012, including benefits to the communities. Although this provides an idea on where
the tourist money was spent, it does not realis-
tically provide information on the full economic
impact of the programme. Measuring economic
impacts requires the identification of target
beneficiaries and determining their income level
prior to the implementation of the programme.
Such information, when gained in the future,
will serve as a benchmark in measuring the impact of the programme on beneficiary income.

Environmental outcomes and contributions

To help address the depleting forests or terrace
watersheds, part of the SITMo Tourism Program included conducting awareness-building
activities in the communities and the inclusion
of tree-planting in the tours (see Figure 23.9).
SITMo, in partnership with the Ujah Youth
Organization in Banaue, jointly established a
community nursery for indigenous tree species. Part of the tour package is for tourists to
purchase seedlings from the nursery and plant
them in the forests. The planted trees are number-coded to correspond with the recorded
names of those tourists who planted them.
Hence, the tourists can identify which trees
they planted when they go back to the place in
the future. Over the years, a number of hec-
tares of the watershed have been planted with
trees. Figure 23.10 shows coded trees planted
by a tourist in a community nursery.

Another outcome of the programme was
the increase in awareness and revitalization
of organic farming. Although organic farming is still prevalent in the rice terraces, some
farmers had started to use chemical fertil-
izers and pesticides, which are harmful to the

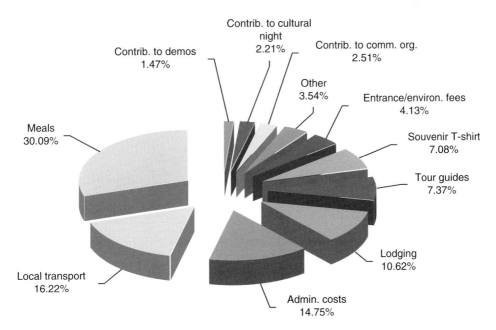

Fig. 23.6. Breakdown of tourist expenditures in 2007 (source: derived from SITMo tour packages).

environment. In the terrace areas where chemicals are used, endemic edible fish and shellfish or crustaceans diminished. The rice cycle tours, to some degree, increased awareness and helped develop an understanding of the importance of using traditional organic farming practices.

Cultural conservation poses a great challenge as the efforts might fall into the trap of fossilizing culture. Initiatives to preserve cultures can be disadvantageous as they might hamper the evolution or emergence of new or more dynamic cultures. On the other hand, the lack of conscious effort to conserve traditional cultures may lead to cultural homogenization and loss of cultural identity and diversity (Swarbrooke, 2004; Reid et al., 2009; Timothy and Nyaupane, 2009; Alberts and Hazen, 2010; Chen and Chen, 2010; Chirikure et al., 2010; Taylor et al., 2014). There are distinct advantages to maintaining important traditional cultures, while embracing modern and emerging ones.

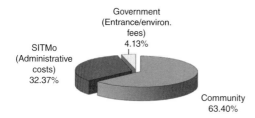

Fig. 23.7. Breakdown of economic benefits 2007 (source: derived from SITMo tour packages).

In the case of SITMo's tourism programme, the objective was not to convince the terrace communities to go back to their traditional lifestyles, freeze them at a certain point in time, or return the people to their ancestors' traditional lifestyles, but to help address the diminishing Ifugao indigenous knowledge systems contributing to the deterioration of the rice terraces. The rice cycle tours helped to maintain several aspects of indigenous knowledge, while diminishing ones were revitalized (SITMo, 2015b).

There is both potential opportunity and concern with other regional and international tour companies providing visitor access to the Ifugao Terraces, including additional seasonal rural and cultural experiences (Gray, 2008; Ananayo, 2014). Although these tours often utilize local and regional tour leaders and guides, this increased interest in customer experiences in the region will create a need for more strategic and operational sustainable tourism practices (Banaue Tours, 2014; GAdventures, 2014; It's More Fun, 2014; Ivanhenares, 2014; Mayoyao, 2014; Synotrip, 2014; Visitmy, 2014).

In the case of SITMo's tourism programme, it was recognized that one of the major factors for the deterioration of the rice terraces was the gradual loss of indigenous knowledge systems. As a result of the organization's initiatives, aspects of indigenous knowledge are being revived and their importance is being recognized. These include

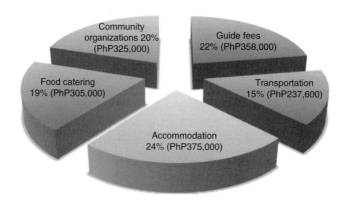

Fig. 23.8. Economic contributions of Ifugao Terrace Movement Eco-cultural Tours (2012 in PhP).

Fig. 23.9. Community-established nursery for indigenous tree species (photograph courtesy of Jovel Ananayo).

Fig. 23.10. Number-coded tree planted by tourist contributing to cultural conservation (photograph courtesy of Jovel Ananayo).

the revitalization or strengthening of the following knowledge systems:

- terracing;
- indigenous trades and crafts;
- performing arts;
- organic farming; and
- religious rites and rituals.

Conclusion

This chapter has examined the role of tourism development on the conservation of World Heritage Sites, focusing on the case of the Ifugao Rice Terraces of the Philippine Cordilleras, located in the Cordillera Central Mountains on the island of Northern Luzon. In addition, the interrelationship between tourism development and World Heritage Site Conservation were explored by analysing the tourism programme of the Save the

Ifugao Terraces Movement (SITMo), which was intended to help conserve the Ifugao World Heritage Sites.

This case study included a description of a locally developed method in addressing long-term conservation and community development issues within a World Heritage Cultural Site, including a review of the SITMo Eco-cultural Tourism Program. As an important part of this programme, various aspects of collaboration, communication and engagement with key groups in the development, operation and management of the tours, and their resulting outcomes were explored.

The findings of the SITMo Eco-cultural Tourism Program indicated that the current, as well as the envisioned, stakeholder cooperation set-up has been largely similar to the stakeholder cooperation model for sustainable tourism. When comparing SITMo to previous studies, however, based on the Sustainable Tourism Stakeholder Cooperation Model, the SITMo model may need to involve more stakeholders and improve on the interrelationships between stakeholders in order to successfully achieve the programme objectives.

Finally, this case illustrated how the programme contributed to World Heritage Site Conservation by presenting the particular outcomes of the SITMo tourism programme. Though some weaknesses have been shown in the process of development and implementation, outcomes of the SITMo tourism approach are generally constructive. These include economic outcomes and contributions, environmental outcomes and contributions, and contribution to cultural conservation.

The findings revealed that the particular outcomes of the programme made significant contributions to the conservation of the World Heritage Sites. This was shown in the revitalization of diminishing Ifugao cultural practices, provision and spreading of the tourism economic benefits to different heritage communities and stakeholders, especially the farmers, who barely benefitted from the industry throughout the history of tourism in the province. Some outcomes of the programme likewise showed a modest, but significant, contribution to the restoration of the environment, particularly the terrace watersheds.

References

A New Plan (2013) A New Plan to Revive Famous Ifugao Terraces. Available at: newsinfo.inquirer.net/416677/a-new-plan-to-revive-famous-ifugao-terraces#ixzz3W0NUelYu (accessed 17 November 2014).

Aas, C., Ladkin, A. and Fletcher, J. (2005) Stakeholder collaboration and heritage management. *Annals of Tourism Research* 32(1), 28–48.

Akagawa, N. and Sirisrisak, T. (2008) Cultural landscapes in Asia and the Pacific: implications of the World Heritage Convention. *International Journal of Heritage Studies* 14(2), 176–191.

Alberts, H.C. and Hazen, H.D. (2010) Maintaining authenticity and integrity at cultural world heritage sites. *Geographical Review* 100(1), 56–73.

Ananayo, J.F. (2014) Heritage and tourism in a 'living cultural landscape': role perspectives of multiple stakeholder groups in the conservation of the Ifugao rice terraces of the Philippine Cordilleras World Heritage site. PhD thesis, University of Otago, Dunedin, New Zealand.

Ananayo, J. and Richins, H. (2010) *Village Culture and Community Based World Heritage Management: A Case Study of the Ifugao Rice Terraces of the Philippine Cordilleras*. Asia Pacific Tourism Research Conference Publication, Macao, China.

Anudon, L. (2002) Strategy for the Ifugao Provincial Government to restore and preserve the rice terraces. MA thesis, Asian Institute of Management, Manila, Philippines.

Arezki, R., Cherif, R. and Piotrowski, J. (2009) *Tourism Specialization and Economic Development: Evidence from the UNESCO World Heritage List* (No. 9-176). International Monetary Fund, Washington, DC.

Banaue Tourism (2015) *VisitMyPhilippines.com The Ultimate Travel Guide for Tourists*. Department of Tourism, Philippines.

Banaue Tours (2014) Destinations. Available at: http://www.banaue-tours.com/about_us/destinations/ (accessed 15 February 2015).

Beritelli, P. (2011) Cooperation among prominent actors in a tourist destination. *Annals of Tourism Research* 38(2), 607–629.

Better Conservation (2014) Better Conservation in Pakistan and the Philippines Allow Committee to Remove Two Sites from World Heritage List in Danger – 2012. Available at: http://whc.unesco.org/en/news/891 (accessed 15 November 2014).

Borges, M.A., Carbone, G., Bushell, R. and Jaeger, T. (2011) *Sustainable Tourism and Natural World Heritage: Priorities for Action*. IUCN, Gland, Switzerland.

Chen, C.F. and Chen, P.C. (2010) Resident attitudes toward heritage tourism development. *Tourism Geographies* 12(4), 525–545.

Chirikure, S., Manyanga, M., Ndoro, W. and Pwiti, G. (2010) Unfulfilled promises? Heritage management and community participation at some of Africa's cultural heritage sites. *International Journal of Heritage Studies*, 16(1–2), 30–44.

Ciencia, S.L. (2007) MDG Midterm Report: The Case of Ifugao, in an Alternative MDG Midterm report. Social Watch Philippines 2007 Report. *Social Watch Philippines*. Available at: http://www.socialwatch.org/sites/default/files/pdf/en/12_missingtargets.pdf (accessed 24 July 2015).

Conklin, H.C. (1980) *Ethnographic Atlas of Ifugao*. Elliots Books, New Haven, Connecticut.

Di Giovine, M.A. (2008) *The Heritage-Scape: UNESCO, World Heritage, and Tourism*. Lexington Books, New York.

Drost, A. (1995) Developing sustainable tourism for world heritage sites. *Annals of Tourism Research* 23(2), 479–492.

Frey, B.S. and Steiner, L. (2011) World heritage list: does it make sense? *International Journal of Cultural Policy* 17(5), 555–573.

GAdventures (2014) Northern Philippines Adventure. Available at: www.gadventures.com/trips/northern-philippines-adventure/AQPN/2015/ (accessed 22 February 2015).

Gonzales, R. (2000) Bridging participation and GIS technology for Natural Resource Management: GIS with the Ifugao people of the Philippines. PhD Dissertation, International Institute for Aerospace Survey and Earth Sciences, Enshede, the Netherlands.

Gray, D. (2008) Personal Requiem: Asia's Lost Gems. Available at: http://www.nbcnews.com/id/23781125/ (accessed 28 August 2015).

Hockings, M., James, R., Stolton, S., Dudley, N., Mathur, V., *et al.* (2008) *Enhancing our Heritage Toolkit: Assessing Management Effectiveness of Natural World Heritage Sites*. World Heritage Papers No. 23, UNESCO World Heritage Centre, Paris.

ICOMOS (2005) The Seoul Declaration on Tourism in Asia's Historic Towns and Areas. Available at: http://www.international.icomos.org/centre_documentation/tourism-seoul2005.pdf (accessed 29 November 2014).

Impact (2008) *IMPACT Publication: Sustainable Tourism and the Preservation of the World Heritage Site of the Ifugao Rice Terraces Philippines*. UNESCO, Bangkok.

It's More Fun (2014) Cordillera Autonomous Region Top Things To Do. Available at: http://itsmorefuninthe-philippines.com/?page_id=4557 (accessed 25 November 2014).

Ivanhenares (2014) Ifugao: Plant Rice at the Mayoyao Rice Terraces! Pfukhay ad Majawjaw 2012! Ivan About Town Travel Blog, Philippines. Available at: http://ivanhenares.com/2012/01/ifugao-pfukhay-ad-majawjaw-2012-rice.html (accessed 25 November 2014).

Jimura, T. (2011) The impact of world heritage site designation on local communities – a case study of Ogimachi, Shirakawa-mura, Japan. *Tourism Management* 32(2), 288–296.

Keesing, F.M. (1962) *The Ethnohistory of Northern Luzon*. Stanford University Press, Redwood City, California.

Landorf, C. (2009) Managing for sustainable tourism: a review of six cultural World Heritage Sites. *Journal of Sustainable Tourism* 17(1), 53–70.

Lyttleton, C. and Allcock, A. (2002) *Tourism as a Tool for Development*. UNESCO–Lao National Tourism Authority (NTAL)/Nam Ha Ecotourism Project, 71. Macquarie University, Sydney.

Mayoyao (2014) WOW Ifugao - An Ecotourism Initiative at Mayoyao Ifugao. Available at: http://mayoyaoifugao.weebly.com/index.html (accessed 25 November 2014).

Okazaki, E. (2008) A community-based tourism model: its conception and use. *Journal of Sustainable Tourism* 16(5), 511–529.

Provincial Government of Ifugao (2004) *The Ten-Year Rice Terraces Conservation Master Plan.* Provincial Government of Ifugao, Lagawe, Philippines.

Reid, D.G., George, E.W., Mair, H. and George, E.W. (2009) *Rural Tourism Development*. Channel View Publications, Clevedon, UK.

Sheehan, L.R. and Ritchie, J.B. (2005) Destination stakeholders exploring identity and salience. *Annals of Tourism Research* 32(3), 711–734.

Silk Road (2012) *Silk Road Action Plan 2012/2013: Enhancing Collaboration for Sustainable Tourism Development*. World Tourism Organization, Madrid.

SITMo (2006–2007) Annual Financial Report. Save the Ifugao Terraces Movement, Ifugao, Philippines.

SITMo (2015a) History and Background. Available at: http://sitmo.org.ph/public/about-us (accessed 24 July 2015).

SITMo (2015b) The Ecotour Project. Save the Ifugao Terraces Movement. Available at: http://sitmo.org.ph/public/on-going-project-2 (accessed 24 July 2015).

Swarbrooke, J. (2004) *Sustainable Tourism Management*. CAB International, Wallingford, UK.

Synotrip (2014) Ifugao Rice Terraces. Available at: http://www.synotrip.com/philippines/amazingphilippines/ifugao-rice-terraces (accessed 24 November 2014).

Taylor, E., Daye, M., Kneafsey, M. and Barrett, H. (2014) Exploring cultural connectedness in the sustain-ability of rural community tourism development in Jamaica. *PASOS. Revista de Turismo y Patrimonio Cultural* 12(3), 525–538.

Timothy, D.J. and Nyaupane, G.P. (eds) (2009) *Cultural Heritage and Tourism in the Developing World: A Regional Perspective*. Routledge, London.

Tucker, H. and Emge, A. (2010) Managing a world heritage site: the case of Cappadocia. *Anatolia* 21(1), 41–54.

UNESCO (2001) State of Conservation (SOC): Rice Terraces of the Philippine Cordilleras (Philippines) 2001. Available at: whc.unesco.org/en/soc/2561 (accessed 17 November 2014).

UNESCO and Nordic World Heritage Foundation (2001) Cultural Heritage Management and Tourism: Models for Co-operation among Stakeholders. Available at: http://unescobkk.org/fileadmin/user_upload/culture/AAHM/Resources/CHMangmtTourism.pdf (accessed 17 November 2014).

UNESCO World Heritage Centre (2014a) Rice Terraces of the Philippine Cordilleras. Available at: http://whc.unesco.org/en/list/722 (accessed 17 November 2014).

UNESCO World Heritage Centre (2014b) World Heritage List. Available at: http://whc.unesco.org/pg.
    cfm?cid=31 (accessed 15 November 2014).
UNESCO World Heritage Centre (2014c) World Heritage in Danger. Available at: http://whc.unesco.org/
    en/158 (accessed 17 November 2014).
UNESCO World Heritage Centre (2014d) Analysis and Conclusion by World Heritage Centre and the
    Advisory Bodies in 2012. Available at: http://whc.unesco.org/en/soc/149 (accessed 17 November 2014).
Visitmy (2014) Available at: visitmyphilippines.com/index.php?title=TourPackages&Page=1&pid=110
    (accessed 17 November 2014).

24 Mountain Tourism Supply-chain Networks in Cross-border Settings: The Case of Intercerdanya, Spain

Dani Blasco,* Jaume Guia and Lluís Prats
University of Girona, Girona, Spain

Introduction

Mountain tourism refers to tourism activities that take place in mountain settings. Previous research has paid attention to many facets of mountain tourism, e.g. mountain tourism planning and development, environmental, sociocultural and economic impacts of mountain tourism and mountain tourists' motivations (Godde *et al.*, 2000).

Mountains are always natural divides between their neighbouring regions, and in many cases they become administrative international borders between sovereign states. It is well known that the presence of borders affects the development, management and consumption of tourism activities in border tourism destinations (Timothy, 2001; Nordin and Svensson, 2005; Dredge, 2006; Wachowiak, 2006; Beritelli *et al.*, 2007). Nevertheless, literature on mountain tourism has paid very little attention to the role and impact of international borders on tourism in mountain settings (Timothy, 1999; Saxena and Ilbery, 2008; Blasco *et al.*, 2014a).

A supply chain is a network of interrelated and interdependent enterprises that are engaged in different functions, ranging from the supply of raw materials through the production and delivery of end products to target customers (Zhang *et al.*, 2009). Tapper and Font (2004) define a tourism supply chain (TSC) as a chain that comprises the suppliers of all the goods and services that go into the delivery of tourism products to consumers. In the case of a winter sport tour operator, the supply chain comprises: (i) ski-product suppliers such as ski resorts, ski schools, ski rental companies, etc.; (ii) bed and food suppliers such as hotels, apartments, other accommodation services, restaurants and other food service suppliers; (iii) après-ski activities such as entertainment, shops, etc.; and (iv) other destination-level support activities such as banks, medical services, etc. (Flagestad and Hope, 2001).

The literature on tourism supply chains or its equivalents, such as tourism value chains or tourism industry chains, has grown in the last decade (Kaukal *et al.*, 2000; Tapper and Font, 2004; Alford, 2005; Yilmaz and Bititci, 2006; Zhang *et al.*, 2009; Song, 2011). Nonetheless, the analysis of tourism supply chains in cross-border settings has received little attention. To cover this gap, this chapter explores to what extent the creation of a mountain tourism supply chain is affected by the presence of borders; or, in other words, how a mountain tourism supply chain is created in a cross-border region. The case of the winter sports tour operator Intercerdanya and

---

* Corresponding author: dani.blasco@udg.edu

its supply chain in the cross-border Cerdanya Valley–Catalan Pyrenees region is thus analysed.

The results show that to create a supply chain in a cross-border region, a cross-border tourism business opportunity has to exist. Also required are entrepreneurial resources with the competencies to handle the inherent institutional differences on both sides of the border. This case proves that supply-chain structures can help to effectively set up and implement a profitable business quickly, but are not able to guarantee a competitive product by themselves (e.g. complimentary services such as après-ski activities).

Mountain Tourism and Borders

Mountain tourism is a topic that has received some attention in academic literature. The most comprehensive accounts are found in the books *Tourism and Development in Mountain Regions* (Godde *et al.*, 2000) and *Facilitating Sustainable Mountain Tourism* (Kruk *et al.*, 2007), and in the article *Mountain Tourism: Toward a Conceptual Framework* (Nepal and Chipeniuk, 2005).

Godde *et al.* (2000) discuss the motivations of mountain tourists, the multi-faceted character of mountain tourism, the negative impacts on mountain development, and the effects and potential of tourism in mountain regions. Kruk *et al.* (2007) focus on the principles of sustainable mountain tourism, its management and implementation, with an emphasis on issues such as participatory planning, gender and social inclusion, and tourism enterprise development. Nepal and Chipeniuk (2005) have developed a conceptual framework for a holistic understanding of mountain tourism on the basis of mountain-specific resource characteristics, types of mountain amenity users and mountain recreational zoning. Other relevant research on mountain tourism has focused on managing growth (Gill and Williams, 1994) and in the commodification of mountains due to tourism development (Beedie and Hudson, 2003).

In all, the main focus is set on the environmental, socio-cultural and economic impacts of tourism development in mountain destinations and on mechanisms to improve their competitiveness and sustainability. Less attention has been paid to issues like mountain tourism motivations, e.g. escaping from urban overcrowding, enjoying pristine landscapes, doing recreational mountain sports and getting to know mountain cultures; or to enterprise development and market linkages.

The role of borders on the development, management and consumption of tourism activities in border regions has been widely researched (Timothy, 2001; Sofield, 2006; Wachowiak, 2006; Saxena and Ilbery, 2008; Blasco *et al.*, 2014b). In general, the analysis of tourism and borders has centred on the types, scales, scope and functions of different borders on tourism; the social, economic and environmental benefits of developing cross-border destinations; the hindrances to developing cross-border destinations; and the politics of cross-border cooperation. In all this literature, only three cases analyse mountain regions: Timothy's (1999) research on cross-border partnerships in tourism resource management in the international parks along the USA–Canada border; Saxena and Ilbery's (2008) research on the England–Wales border; and Blasco *et al.*'s (2014a) analysis on the Pyrenees mountain range that divides Spain and France.

However, their focus is not on mountain tourism, but on national park tourism in the first case, on rural tourism in the second and on tourism zoning in the third. Moreover, if we look closely at the particular nature of these three cases, Timothy's (1999) analysis of cross-border tourism in national parks involves collaboration among a few public administrations on issues such as management frameworks, infrastructure development, human resources, conservation, promotion and international local level border concessions and treaty waivers; while Saxena and Ilbery's (2008) case involves many small private operators and a few resource controllers, emphasizing the difficulty of participation and inclusion to create an equitable, sustainable and integrated cross-border network; and Blasco *et al.*'s (2014a) main focus is on the attractiveness and advantage of cross-border destination over conventional destinations.

In order to complement these findings, this research has explored a case of mountain tourism cross-border development based on winter sport activities. Some literature has focused on the particular topic of winter sport tourism (Klippendorf, 1987; Gill and Hartmann, 1991; Todd and Williams, 1996; Hudson, 2004) dealing with issues such as the diversification of activities, destination development, consumer behaviour and sustainability, and also on winter sport destinations' organizational structures and their performance (Flagestad and Hope, 2001). In fact these authors identify two modes of winter sport destination organizational structures: the community mode and the corporate mode.

The community mode has been described by several authors (Heath and Wall, 1992). It reflects an organizational structure without much substance and with strong elements of politically driven management. It consists of specialized individual independent business units, which operate in a decentralized way, and where no unit has any dominant administrative power or dominant ownership within the destination. The management lies with the political and administrative institutions of the community, often the local government or a destination management organization with local government participation or influence.

The corporate mode of destination organization is dominated by a ski business corporation that manages a selection of business units of service providers incorporated by ownership and/or contracts. The major business units offer ski products, lift operations, ski schools, ski rentals, food and beverages, retail franchise, etc. A certain amount of the destination bed base is also operated by the ski corporation. These corporations have a dominant influence on how the destination is operated as a strategic business unit as well as strong political power in the community-related development of the destination.

No mention of winter sports destinations in cross-border regions is found in the literature, however. Therefore, this case study explores how a mountain tourism supply chain is created and evolves within a cross-border region, in the mountain winter sports tourism business. As outdoor winter sports activities only take place in mountain regions, the results of the case will be specific to cross-border mountain destinations where outdoor winter sports can be practised. Also, in opposition to Timothy's (2001) and Saxena and Ilbery's (2008) cases

above, only a supply-chain network involving larger private operators, rather than public administration or inclusive destination networks, is involved in this case.

Methods

The case of the tour operator Intercerdanya and its supply chain was selected for empirical analysis. This company is located and operates in the Cerdanya Valley–Catalan Pyrenees cross-border region between France and Spain. As stated earlier, there is little knowledge regarding the role of borders in mountain tourism in cross-border regions. Therefore, an exploratory approach is adopted, with the purpose of gaining insight into the topic (McNabb, 2010). Inductive analytical methods were thus chosen to interpret the collected data (Glaser and Strauss, 1967).

Data gathering was done through in-depth interviews with relevant stakeholders. Additional secondary data were collected from relevant websites. Interviews were semi-structured, with questions concerning the cross-border reality of the region as a tourism destination and, in the case of Intercerdanya, about the history of the company and the role that the border has played in the development of its supply chain. For instance: how the supply-chain partners were selected; how supply-chain relationships are managed; what role the border played and plays in the development and management of the supply chain; what are the differences, if any, between managing the supply chain with ski resorts, accommodation and food service suppliers, après-ski activities and destination-level support services; what benefits Intercerdanya has obtained as a result of its supply management activities; and what are the limitations, if any.

Interviews lasted between 1.5 and 2 hours, with the CEO of the tour operator Intercerdanya being selected as the first and main informant. Knowledge of additional relevant stakeholders was gathered by means of snowball sampling (Jennings, 2001) until a satisfactory saturation point was reached, which complies with the requirements of purposive sampling (Strauss and Corbin, 1990; Czernek, 2013).

Inductive thematic analysis, an analytical method through which the researcher constructs meaning from the data in relation to the research question, was chosen as the method of analysis (Janesick, 2000; Guest *et al.*, 2012). It consists of working through the texts to identify topics that are progressively integrated into higher-order themes, via processes of de-contextualization and re-contextualization. Validity and reliability was ensured through the crosschecking of results by the three researchers and their verification with the interviewees.

The Company Intercerdanya and the Cerdanya Valley–Catalan Pyrenees Cross-border Region

The Cerdanya Valley–Catalan Pyrenees tourism destination, straddling the border between Spain and France, is split into two parts, one in Spain and the other in France. The destination is 150 km from Barcelona, 170 km from Toulouse and 100 km from Perpignan, its main urban tourist markets. The two main towns in the Spanish Cerdanya are Puigcerdà (9957 inhabitants) and the Spanish enclave of Llívia (1689 inhabitants), while on the French side the largest town is Font-Romeu (1841 inhabitants). The Cerdanya Valley is one of the widest

mountain valleys in Europe, with an average width of 10 km, and has a dozen ski resorts in a 30-km radius catchment area from Puigcerdà.

The Treaty of the Pyrenees, signed by the French and the Spanish crowns in 1659, delineated the border between France and Spain along the watershed of the Pyrenees mountains, except for the Cerdanya Valley, which, after a long and curious process of negotiations (Sahlins, 1991), was split into two separate countries (see Fig. 24.1). It is noteworthy that one of the municipalities of the Spanish Cerdanya, Llívia, became an enclave within the French Cerdanya as a consequence of these negotiations. After more than three centuries, the commonality of the traditional culture has been eroded and the institutional divide has grown wider.

The Cerdanya Valley–Catalan Pyrenees region is a traditional mountain tourism destination. From the 1950s onwards, this picturesque mountain area became a popular ski and summer holiday destination, and thus ski resorts, hotels, campsites, second homes and other tourist facilities were built, alongside the progressive improvements in communications. Later, villages, towns and heritage sites were progressively developed as tourism attractions based

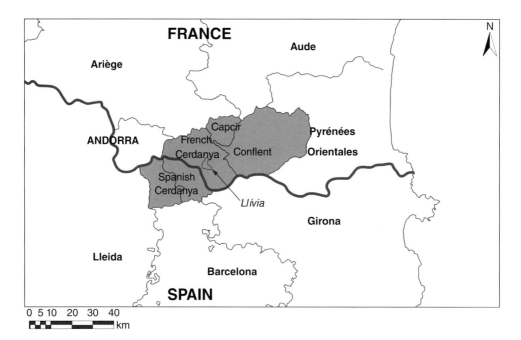

Fig. 24.1. The Cerdanya Valley–Catalan Pyrenees region and Llívia (from Sahlins, 1991).

on high-quality rural, rambling, wellness and heritage-based experiences.

Attempts to build a cross-border governance structure for the destination as a whole have been unsuccessful until very recently, when one such attempt has begun to crystallize in the form of a cross-border tourism cluster in the region (Blasco *et al.*, 2014b). There was only one exception in 1983, when an individual company, the winter sports tour operator Intercerdanya, started its operations in both sides of the border and was the first manifestation of cross-border activity in the region. Over the years the company has built a cross-border supply-chain network, involving ski resorts and services, hotels and other accommodation businesses, and restaurants. Their main markets are France, Spain, Portugal and the Canary Islands, and their main market segment is school groups on a half-term winter sports break. Intercerdanya is located in Llívia, the Spanish enclave in the area, and sells a diverse array of winter sports packages that include up to ten different ski resorts in the cross-border region (see Table 24.1 below), and the corresponding accommodation, food and transport services.

Results and Discussion

As a result of the inductive thematic analysis, we found four main themes, which were brought forward from the data, and which explain the creation and development of the company and its cross-border supply chain: (i) the existence of a business opportunity; (ii) entrepreneurial competences; (iii) dealing with institutional dissimilarities; and (iv) the limitation of supply-chain structures in terms of après-ski activity

problems. These findings are presented below and reported through paraphrasing the relevant narrations of the interviewees (Corden and Sainsbury, 2006).

The existence of a business opportunity

At the time the company started, more than 30 years ago, the ski resorts in the area were very different from what they are now. They had very few services, artificial snow production was not available, and connectivity by road was much slower. The vast majority of skiers came from domestic markets close by, mainly from Barcelona and Catalonia on the Spanish side of the region and from Toulouse and the Languedoc on the French side. It was mostly a weekend activity, therefore on weekdays in the winter season there were very few skiers in the resorts.

At that time Spain and Spanish society were going through enormous political change, which fostered the democratization of education and a desire for openness and new experiences. Schools adopted new curricula, which included educational outings. In this context, school pupils became a new segment of the ski market (Gómez and Sanz, 2003). In addition, this segment of the market was not going to consume the weekend product but was going to ski on weekdays, which was precisely when occupation was the lowest.

A potential problem was the fact that not all ski resorts could guarantee snow at any time in the winter season in the region, and there were no artificial snow production mechanisms. There was, however, one ski resort that had snow during the whole season, but this

Table 24.1. The ski resorts in the Cerdanya Valley–Catalan Pyrenees region.

Ski resort	Country	Highest peak	Slopes	Km skiing
Font Romeu	France	2213 m	43	43
Masella	Spain	2535 m	65	74
Les Angles	France	2400 m	45	55
La Molina	Spain	2535 m	54	61
Espace Cambre d'Aze	France	2750 m	21	35
Porté Puymorens	France	2471 m	33	50
Formigueres	France	2350 m	16	22
Puyvalador	France	2382 m	19	32

resort was on the French side of the cross-border region. Also, depending on the wind and other changing weather conditions, some ski resorts were better than others. Therefore, creating a supply chain that encompassed all the ski resorts would allow Intercerdanya to direct its customers to the best resort each day, thus always securing an attractive ski product for the customers. This implied looking at the cross-border region as a single ski destination and, as a result, designing a cross-border supply chain.

The founders of Intercerdanya saw this business opportunity and started operations with a small upstream network of suppliers that included a few local hotels in Llívia, the Spanish enclave town where the company is located, and the closest ski resorts in the French side of the border. As has already been said, over the years the network has grown to encompass all the resorts in the region and hotels outside Llívia, although always Spanish hotels. Regarding customers, the company's main focus is on the segment of school groups where the ski skills of individuals range from beginners to advanced. Therefore, Intercerdanya relied on building downstream distribution networks, where schools played the role of informal 'distributors' to the final customer, i.e. the school pupil. They started with a small network of schools from the nearby Catalonian provinces and over the years expanded the network of schools to faraway regions in Spain, the Canary Islands and Portugal, and more recently, also to nearby French provinces.

Entrepreneurial competencies

The company started up and continued to grow as a result of the entrepreneurial activity of the founders. They were three young skiers from Llívia, who had been ski enthusiasts and instructors and had entrepreneurial drive and a vision of the business opportunity described above.

In addition to having a vision of the business opportunity and the drive to start up the business, creating the company involved a large amount of networking and relationship building. Regarding the upstream network of suppliers, the entrepreneurs had the advantage

that in a region with a small population there is a high density of personal relationships and nearly all relationships have a social component (Hite, 2003). This fact can make starting business relationships easier and this advantage was used at the beginning to work with local hotels in the same town, Llívia. However, the fact that the ski resorts were across the border on the French side meant that they had to negotiate and create business relationships with people from outside their natural community.

In any case, due to the nature of the business and the particularities of the product, the existence of a personal component in the business relationships with suppliers was not essential. Hoteliers had already invested in their hotels and the ski resorts had already invested in their ski slopes, chairlifts and other facilities. They already had large numbers of skiers at weekends, but very low numbers during the weekdays of the winter season. Therefore, these suppliers did not have to make any specific investments and, at the same time, had the chance to increase their income by receiving these new customers during the weekdays of the season. It was a good enough business deal that could be implemented without the need of large doses of trust and relationships with a personal component. Therefore, the border was never a hindrance for this type of business. As the manager of Intercerdanya stated: 'When we first visited the French ski resorts, they realized they had an opportunity to make good business with Spanish schools during weekdays. Therefore, although at the beginning they preferred French skiers, our proposal was very interesting and they accepted.'

Over the years, the company increased the number of skiers steadily and always made payments to its suppliers on time. This enhanced its reputation among the ski resorts and hotels in the region, therefore expanding the network has been relatively easy. In this regard, the Intercerdanya manager explained that 'Our suppliers knew they were going to get all bills paid on time, and moreover we never tried to negotiate the prices they gave us'.

As for the downstream distribution network of schools, the company relied on personal visits to their premises. In autumn they travelled to their target markets, visited the school board directors and offered their product. The visits were repeated over the years with the intention of creating stronger relationships with the schools and in order to ensure continued business with them. Face-to-face visits contributed to making these relationships stronger, but learning about the pupils' changing needs and committing to continuous improvements to satisfy these needs were essential in maintaining their reputation and the relationship.

Finally, in terms of finances, the founders have always relied on private capital and bank loans. They have never applied to the public administration for grants, i.e. they have always contributed to the business using their own resources.

Dealing with institutional dissimilarities

All cross-border regions or destinations are characterized by a duality of institutional regimes. Blasco *et al.* (2014b) identify three types of institutional dissimilarities: cultural, functional and organizational. Regarding cultural dissimilarities, long periods of socio-cultural separation foster the emergence of mistrust, rivalry, suspicion and other negative feelings between the two communities. In our case, there is still a general perception among the people interviewed that the French behave with a sense of historical superiority. However, in the past few decades the cross-border French region has experienced some revival of their identity as French Catalans. This has reversed the process of separation and has contributed to an increase in cultural proximity and social trust across the border. In fact, this contributes positively when it comes to managing the cross-border supply network and expanding the French market of the company.

Functional dissimilarities are mainly found in language differences, life routines, taxes, and in the functional role of the actual border. In our case we found that language was not a problem for the founders of the company. They were from Llívia, the Spanish enclave within France, which means that in addition to Catalan and Spanish, they also learned French at school and had plenty of opportunities to use it due to the fact that the town is completely surrounded by French-speaking villages. Therefore, the inherent multi-culturality of citizens in border areas, and particularly in enclaves, solves the potential hindrance of this functional dissimilarity. It is different in the case of skiers or customers, where most of the Spanish and Portuguese visitors do not speak French. However they are always escorted and have ski instructors who speak the languages of the cross-border area. Indeed, experiencing two different institutional settings at the same time gives added value to the experience for the majority of skiers.

Regarding life routines, the case shows that differences in eating habits and in characteristics of hotels played a relevant role for Intercerdanya. French people tend to have lunch at midday and dinner early in the evening, while Spanish and Portuguese visitors have lunch in the early afternoon and dinner in the late evening. The hotels on the Spanish side of the cross-border area are used to the dinner schedule of most of Intercerdanya clients who come from Spain and Portugal, but are also ready to adapt the schedule and the menu when they have French clients. This is less so in the case of French hotels, which prefer to stick to their traditional eating schedules and menus. We also found that the Spanish hotels have a style that suits the taste of young visitors more than the French hotels. As the manager of Intercerdanya acknowledged: 'We work mainly with Spanish hotels because the French hotels … are not making any effort to adapt to the routines of our customers.' Furthermore, for a number of decades VAT in French hotels has been higher than that in Spain, which was an additional reason for Intercerdanya to only work with Spanish accommodation suppliers. The ski resorts are a different story, as both French and Spanish resorts have restaurants that are ready to adapt their time schedule for lunch, and on occasions also the type of food, to satisfy the demands of the visitors.

The actual border was also a potential hindrance, when it meant having to show a passport or similar document at the crossing. The area has a low population and a relatively small number of border crossings, so it was never a relevant obstacle in terms of time lost in queues when skiers had to go from the hotel to the ski resort. In recent decades, the Schengen treaty agreed between most EU countries involved the elimination of border checkpoints, therefore any inconvenience has totally disappeared.

Finally, organizational dissimilarities that are relevant to our case are found in the organizational forms of the ski resorts. On the French side of the region they are owned by the municipalities, while on the Spanish side they are mostly owned by private companies, with the exception of one case, which is owned by the Catalan regional administration. However, we see that this diversity is not exclusive of the dual institutional regime, but also exists on the Spanish side of the border. Intercerdanya acknowledges that problems arise when the resort managers cannot make quick decisions when needed, e.g. due to changing weather conditions changes have to be made fast and implemented effectively. The company confirms that both in privately owned resorts and also in those owned by the municipality, decisions are always made quickly as they are made 'locally', while in the case of state-owned resorts, decisions are centralized and fast responses are difficult to give. As a consequence of this, Intercerdanya stopped doing business with this ski resort and only resumed operations after they found a way to circumvent this obstacle. The owner of Intercerdanya explained: 'Sometimes we have to change plans rapidly due to change in weather conditions, and I can only rely on those who can take decisions up here in the mountains, and not in central headquarters located in distant places.' All these instances of institutional dissimilarities make it much more difficult to design and manage supply networks that involve suppliers from both sides of the border with their separated and different institutional regimes.

The limitations of supply-chain structures: the problem of après-ski

It is well known that among the components of the ski product or the ski package, there are après-ski activities (Flagestad and Hope, 2001). The vast majority of ski activities in this region take place on the weekends, which means that après-ski activities (e.g. shopping, restaurants, souvenir shops, etc.) are available only during weekends, but not during the week. This is a relevant problem for Intercerdanya, as they cannot 'force' these individual businesses to open. In other words, they cannot make these businesses join the supply network. If they opened, it is likely that they would do some business from the weekday school visitors, but Intercerdanya cannot guarantee how much business they will do. Additionally, most of the après-ski activities are targeted at weekend visitors, which are mostly families and small groups, but not designed for larger groups of young visitors. Therefore, in most cases the après-ski activities are confined to activities in the accommodation where they are staying. There are some exceptions, though, such as the natural spa in the nearby French village of Llo, and the city of Puigcerdà on the Spanish side of the border, where the shops are open most weekdays.

These facts prove that individual companies' supply networks are very effective when it comes to creating tourism products, but have limitations when the attractiveness of the products has to rely on complementary assets, which the supply network cannot mobilize, e.g. après-ski activities, shopping and other destination-level complementary services. The manager of the Intercerdanya operator explained that: 'It has not been possible to change the mind[s] of many service business owners, and...shops and other complementary services remain closed during the weekdays, and even in the winter peak season.' Therefore, only a full-blown collaboration at the destination level can guarantee full satisfaction to ski visitors. This would imply adopting the structure of a tourism cluster and having the mechanisms to supply all the multiple diverse 'parts' of the tourism product to be consumed by the different types of visitors, i.e. ski activities, accommodation and food services, après-ski and other destination-level services.

This problem could be mitigated by the recent creation of a new cross-border destination-level governance structure in which both private tourism businesses and public tourism bodies from the two sides of the border collaborate (Blasco *et al.*, 2014b). This destination-level governance structure has just been created and only time will tell whether it will be able to design and implement new strategies that can help to solve the problems stated above, i.e. the shortage of après-ski activities on weekdays, which a single company's supply-chain structure is unable to deal with.

In this regard, there is both hope and despair. The hope comes from this new initiative and the despair from the fact that many après-ski activity businesses in the region, i.e. shop owners, restaurateurs, etc., are family businesses and the owners have no interest in expanding. For them, dealing with new segments of the market that require changes in the running of the business (e.g. opening during the week) is a problem, and they prefer to preserve their lifestyle than expand their business. There is also the danger that those businesses willing to operate on weekdays might find that there is not enough business for it to be profitable. If this was the case, it would prove that the number of weekday visitors would be too low.

This situation contrasts with that of neighbouring Andorra. This small country, where the main economic activity is winter sport tourism, has made important investments in facilities to host après-ski activities, such as a large indoor spa, or entertainment resorts for young visitors. It also has the advantage of being (in effect) an immense open shopping mall, due to its history as a tax haven. The fact that it is a sovereign country that relies on tourism means that the Andorran government plans and invests in facilities and complementary activities, so that a visit is enhanced as much as possible. As we have seen, our case is just the opposite. The fact that the area is split between two countries makes the design and implementation of a common strategy for tourism development very difficult, and their peripheral position in both Spain and France is an additional challenge when it comes to attracting the required funds to invest in après-ski facilities. In any case, as a tax haven, Andorra has always been a mighty competitor for the neighbouring Cerdanya Valley–Catalan Pyrenees region. It is because of this 'unfair' competition that Intercerdanya does not do business with Andorran operators and ski resorts and is committed to keep on working with its supply-network operators and other tourism business in the cross-border Cerdanya Valley–Catalan Pyrenees

region in order to be competitive and increase the number of visitors to this destination year after year.

Conclusion

Winter sport is the main tourist activity in some mountain regions. In these destinations, these activities can be organized in different ways. Flagestad and Hope (2001) identified two main modes of winter sport destination organization, the community mode and the corporate mode, and have suggested that the latter is the more effective. No mention, however, is made of the fact that some winter sport mountain destinations are divided by an international border. Therefore, there is no knowledge of how cross-border activities are organized, or whether they are organized at all.

The case analysed here shows that each side of the border was organized without any type of cross-border integration, following the community mode, but also with very little internal integration. In this particular context, cross-border integration started by means of a single company, Intercerdanya, which in a very short time built an extensive supply-chain network involving operators from both sides of the border. The supply-chain structure can be depicted as a hybrid between the two modes of organization. The managerial approach is similar to that of the corporate mode, but the relationships within the supply chain are similar to those in the community model. It seems, though, that in cross-border settings, supply-chain structures might be an effective middle way to initiate cross-border integration in a winter sport region.

However, this research revealed that a middle-way mode, the supply chain, has limitations when it comes to guaranteeing the complementary services needed to have a competitive product. In this case, this was manifested by the limited capacity of the company to extend the supply chain to operators of après-ski activities. Therefore, to avoid this hindrance, the supply-chain mode should be complemented by some integrated community mode of organization in the destination, by means of which après-ski businesses and other supply-chain operators would agree to collaborate to secure satisfactory experiences during the whole winter season. Finally, for a supply chain to emerge, a cross-border tourism business opportunity needs to exist, together with entrepreneurial resources with competencies to handle the inherent institutional differences on both sides of the border.

These findings shed some light on the way winter sport cross-border mountain destinations can be organized in order to increase their competitiveness and achieve their potential as tourism destinations. A company's supply-chain organization type, where individual tour operators are the main coordinators of the supply chains, has been proposed as a new mode that lies between the two known modes

envisaged by Flagestad and Hope (2001), i.e. the corporate hierarchical mode, where the ski resorts are the coordinators of the supply chain activities, and the community horizontal mode, where the coordination capacity is found within a network that encompasses the whole array of supply-chain operators. This is, thus, one of the main contributions of the paper, together with the specificities involved in the creation of a tourism supply chain in a cross-border region and how it can be handled by the company that leads the supply network. This knowledge can also be useful for practitioners who operate in cross-border areas, in that it identifies the main issues involved in the creation and operation of tourism supply chains and their limitations.

References

Alford, P. (2005) A framework for mapping and evaluating business process costs in the tourism industry supply chain. *Information and Communication Technologies in Tourism* 2005, 125–136.

Beedie, P. and Hudson, S. (2003) The emergence of mountain based adventure tourism. *Annals of Tourism Research* 30(3), 625–643.

Beritelli, P., Bieger, T. and Laesser, C. (2007) Destination governance: using corporate governance theories as a foundation for effective destination management. *Journal of Travel Research* 46(1), 96–107.

Blasco, D., Guia, J. and Prats, L. (2014a) Tourism destination zoning in mountain regions: a consumer-based approach. *Tourism Geographies: An International Journal of Tourism Space, Place and Environment* 16(3), 512–528.

Blasco, D., Guia, J. and Prats, L. (2014b) Emergence of governance in cross-border destinations. *Annals of Tourism Research* 49, 159–173.

Corden, A. and Sainsbury, R. (2006) *Using Verbatim Quotations in Reporting Qualitative Social Research: Researchers' Views*. Social Policy Research Unit, University of York, York, UK.

Czernek, K. (2013) Determinants of cooperation in a tourist region. *Annals of Tourism Research* 40, 83–104.

Dredge, D. (2006) Policy networks and the local organisation of tourism. *Tourism Management* 27, 269–280.

Flagestad, A. and Hope, C.A. (2001) Strategic success in winter sports destinations: a sustainable value creation perspective. *Tourism Management* 22(5), 445–461.

Gill, A. and Hartmann, R. (1991) Mountain resort development. In: Gill, A. and Hartmann, R. (eds) *Proceedings of the Vail Conference April 18th–21st, 1991*. The Center for Tourism Policy and Research, Simon Fraser University, Burnaby, British Columbia, Canada.

Gill, A. and Williams, P. (1994) Managing growth in mountain tourism communities. *Tourism Management* 15(3), 212–220.

Glaser, B.G. and Strauss, A.L. (1967) *The Discovery of Grounded Theory: Strategies for Qualitative Research*. Aldine Publishing, Chicago, Illinois.

Godde, P.M., Price, M.F. and Zimmermann, F.M. (2000) *Tourism and Development in Mountain Regions*. CAB International, Wallingford, UK.

Gómez, M. and Sanz, E. (2003) La enseñanza del esquí alpino en las clases de educación física de la educación secundaria obligatoria. *Retos. Nuevas tendencias en Educación Física, Deporte y Recreación* 4, 11–24.

Guest, G., MacQueen, K.M. and Namey, E.E. (2012) *Applied Thematic Analysis*. Sage, Thousand Oaks, California.

Heath, E. and Wall, G. (1992) *Marketing Tourism Destinations: A Strategic Planning Approach*. Wiley & Sons, New York.

Hite, J.M. (2003) Patterns of multidimensionality among embedded network ties: a typology of relational embeddedness in emerging entrepreneurial firms. *Strategic Organization* 1(1), 9–49.

Hudson, S. (2004) Winter sport tourism in North America. In: Ritchie, B.W. and Adair, D. (eds) *Sport Tourism: Interrelationships, Impacts and Issues*. Channel View Publications, Clevedon, UK, pp. 77–100.

Janesick, V.J. (2000) The choreography of qualitative research design. In: Denzin, N.K. and Lincoln, Y.S. (eds) *Handbook of Qualitative Research*. Sage, London, pp. 379–399.

Jennings, G. (2001) *Tourism Research*. Wiley, Sydney, New South Wales, Australia.

Kaukal, M., Höpken, W. and Werthner, H. (2000) An approach to enable interoperability in electronic tourism markets. In: *Proceedings of the 8th European Conference on Information Systems*. Vienna University of Technology, Vienna, Austria, pp. 1104–1112.

Klippendorf, J. (1987) *The Holiday Makers: Understanding the Impact of Leisure and Travel*. Heinemann, London.

Kruk, E., Hummel, J. and Banskota, K. (2007) *Facilitating Sustainable Mountain Tourism: Volume 2: Toolkit*. International Centre for Integrated Mountain Development, Kathmandu, Nepal.

McNabb, D.E. (2010) *Case Research in Public Management*. M. E. Sharpe, New York.

Nepal, S.K. and Chipeniuk, R. (2005) Mountain tourism: toward a conceptual framework. *Tourism Geographies: An International Journal of Tourism Space, Place and Environment* 7(3), 313–333.

Nordin, S. and Svensson, B. (2005) The significance of governance in innovative tourism destinations. In: Keller, P. and Bieger, T. (eds) *Innovation in Tourism: Creating Customer Value*. AIEST, St Gallen, Switzerland, pp. 159–170.

Sahlins, P. (1991) *The Making of France and Spain in the Pyrenees*. University of California Press, Los Angeles, California.

Saxena, G. and Ilbery, B. (2008) Integrated rural tourism: a border case study. *Annals of Tourism Research* 35, 233–254.

Sofield, T. (2006) Border tourism and border communities: an overview. *Tourism Geographies: An International Journal of Tourism Space, Place and Environment* 8(2), 102–121.

Song, H. (2011) *Tourism Supply Chain Management*. Routledge, New York.

Strauss, A. and Corbin, J. (1990) *Basics of Qualitative Research: Grounded Theory Procedures and Techniques*. Sage, Newbury Park, California.

Tapper, R. and Font, X. (2004) *Tourism Supply Chains. Report of a Desk Research Project for the Travel Foundation*. Leeds Metropolitan University, Leeds, UK.

Timothy, D.J. (1999) Cross-border partnership in tourism resource management: international parks along the US-Canada border. *Journal of Sustainable Tourism* 7(3–4), 182–205.

Timothy, D.J. (2001) *Tourism and Political Boundaries*. Routledge, New York.

Todd, S.E. and Williams, P.W. (1996) From white to green: a proposed environmental management system framework for ski areas. *Journal of Sustainable Tourism* 4(3), 147–173.

Wachowiak, H. (2006) *Tourism and Borders: Contemporary Issues, Policies and International Research*. Ashgate Publishing, Burlington, Vermont.

Yilmaz, Y. and Bititci, U. (2006) Performance measurement in the value chain: manufacturing v. tourism. *International Journal of Productivity and Performance Management* 55(5), 371–389.

Zhang, X., Song, H. and Huang, G.Q. (2009) Tourism supply chain management: a new research agenda. *Tourism Management* 30(3), 345–358.

25 A Moral Turn for Mountain Tourism?

Lisa Cooke,[1]* Bryan Grimwood[2] and Kellee Caton[1]
[1]*Thompson Rivers University, Kamloops, British Columbia, Canada;*
[2]*University of Waterloo, Waterloo, Canada*

Introduction

The inseparability of the practice of tourism and the environments in which it takes place has long been noted in tourism studies (Fridgen, 1984). Similarly, tourism has long been understood as a practice with moral implications, although this has not always been articulated overtly. Jafari's (2001) 'advocacy' and 'cautionary' platforms, for instance, represent one well-known analytical tool to capture two long strands of scholarship highlighting tourism's powerful role in bringing about, respectively, desirable and undesirable changes for individuals, groups, cultures, landscapes and ecosystems. Increasingly, however, talk of morality within the tourism context has become more overt (Lea, 1993; Hultsman, 1995; Holden, 2003; Smith and Duffy, 2003; Macbeth, 2005; Fennell, 2006; Gras-Dijkstra, 2009; Jamal and Menzel, 2009; Smith, 2009; Feighery, 2011; MacCannell, 2011; Caton, 2012; Su et al., 2013; Mostafanezhad and Hannum, 2014; Grimwood, 2015). But tourism's 'moral turn' (Caton, 2012) is still in its early years, having yet to be enriched to any great degree by specific disciplinary knowledge bases that bear on tourism practice, perhaps principal among them, geography. In other

words, although tourism is fundamentally an environmental phenomenon and fundamentally a value-laden and power-inflected phenomenon, discussions of morality in tourism, as of yet, rarely unfold in the specific contexts of the particular types of environments where tourism takes place.

'Moral geography' can be defined as the epistemic domain in which moral and geographical arguments intersect. Evident in this body of scholarship are commitments to understanding how moral beliefs are distributed across space, and how morality is performed in particular contexts (Smith, 2000). Work in moral geography also examines the ways in which 'assumptions about the relationships between people and their environments may reflect and produce moral judgments, and how the conduct of particular groups or individuals in particular spaces may be judged appropriate or inappropriate' (Matless, 2009, 478). Typically, work in this domain fuses empirical observations with contextual interpretations (Proctor, 1999), in order to draw attention to both the embodied or lived experience of ethics and the relations of power that produce and reproduce a sense of moral order through environmental and spatial practices. Such a place-based approach to moral inquiry is helpful in fleshing

* Corresponding author: lcooke@tru.ca

out the typically much more abstract notions found in moral philosophy, bringing them to life in concrete times and places.

In this chapter, we seek to highlight mountain environments, which play host to tourism activities, as morally resonant spaces – spaces in which different meanings and values are asserted, contested, negotiated and resisted. Our discussion herein is in no way meant to be an exhaustive outline of the central moral issues that arise from tourism in mountain environments; indeed, as highlighted in this volume, mountain areas across the globe defy homogenization, and in any given environment, new issues are always emerging as the cultural, legal, political, economic and even geological terrain shifts. Instead, we aim to offer readers a bit of the intellectual flavour of moral geography by spotlighting a handful of common concerns that surround mountain tourism in North America, the continent where the three of us live and work.

We begin by exploring issues of representation in mountain tourism marketing, drawing on the example of ski tourism in the western USA to illustrate the way promotional discourse works to constitute mountains as geographies of exclusion and white privilege. Next, we consider tourism development as a colonial practice, exploring an example in which indigenous land claims are being overwritten by the counter land claims of a new corporate citizenry of 'lifestyle settlers' in British Columbia's first mountain resort municipality. Finally, we depart from the slopes for the waterways of Canada's mountain environments, to explore canoe travel as an embodied performance. Historically, this performance has been tied to the production of a hegemonic narrative of Canadian nationalism bound up with the valorization of nature as vanishing wilderness in need of preservation through white masculine settler systems of expertise, but imagined differently, through the joint moral agency of members from different groups for which riverscapes are deeply meaningful, canoeing can alternatively be a practice through which relational understandings of spaces and human experiences within them can be forged. These three explorations of moral geography aim to illuminate mountain areas as complex and layered spaces of meaning, and it is our hope

that they will raise awareness and curiosity about mountain tourism environments beyond their common imaginary as playgrounds for innocent pleasure.

Mountains as Moral Terrains

If we are to take a moral turn in tourism studies and practice, as Caton (2012) suggests, then we need to look at the ground under our feet. As noted, at the intersection of tourism as a set of discourses and practices, and moral philosophy as an epistemic domain, are real people in real places doing real things. Mountain places offer particularly textured sites for this inquiry because of the ways that they come into view as natural. Geographer Bruce Braun (2002) suggests that nature is artifactual, meaning that what we see and experience as nature is a complex cultural, historical and political production. To be sure, there is a materiality to the physical world. But how it comes into view is cultural and discursive (Hall, 1997). Places are not inert containers where culture occurs. They are culturally produced processes, whereby entire cultural systems come together to happen as places (Cooke, 2013). Complex relationships between space, power and knowledge are mirrored by places (Appadurai, 1988; Rodman, 1992; Gupta and Ferguson, 1997; Braun, 2001, 2002). What we see, why it matters, how it is valued, and how that value structures experience to reflect bodies of cultural knowledge that work to 'em-place' people (Escobar, 2001). These same processes also work to 'dis-place' others (Munn, 2003). What counts as nature is no exception. As a result, anything that comes into view as natural needs to be critically unpacked for the cultural, historical and power relations that operate to bring it into view as such.

Turning this approach back to the moral dimensions of mountain places, specifically in North America, where we locate the examples presented here, we must consider the ways that settler colonial interests and values structure dominant geographies of leisure and tourism, producing particular imaginaries (Salazar, 2012) of place. In this conversation, land and place are not just political matters tied to issues of land claims, fights for the acknowledgement of Aboriginal Title and the right of self-determination, or fights for the legal rights of particular kinds of bodies to occupy particular kinds of spaces. They are equally moral matters, demanding careful consideration of the way spaces are ideologically produced, more quietly, in a taken-for-granted sort of way, as nature-play places and touristic sites of leisure. Power relations, as they operate on and through settler colonial spaces, are not clearly visible. This is especially true of those 'naturalized' out of sight by settler colonial constructions of nature. As Braun (1997, 4–5) suggests, 'Instead, [such power relations] take the form of "buried epistemologies" or "bad epistemic habits" that have been naturalized as "common sense" in everyday relations and in social, economic, and political institutions.' If moral geography is an epistemic realm, and we are to take a critical turn toward this kind of thinking, then we must unearth these buried epistemologies that are deeply embedded in the strata of mountain places.

In the subsections that follow, we consider three examples of ideological production in mountain environments, as described in the introduction above. These vignettes represent three different moments in the tourism process: (i) the articulation of the dominant mountain imaginary prior to the tourist visit, through site marketing; (ii) the embedding of that imaginary, through the material production of the site itself on the ground; and (iii) the embodied enactment of tourism practice in mountain environments, through which tourist performances can reproduce – but also resist – this dominant imaginary.

Picturing the Ski Resort

Places are with us before we get there. From the comfort of our armchair, they come to us via *National Geographic* magazine or the Travel Channel, from lessons learned as schoolchildren, and through postcards, souvenirs, stories and endless photo reels shared by friends returning from afar. In turn, we consume guidebooks, brochures and websites as we prepare for our own journeys. There is no unmediated tourism encounter (Skinner and Theodossopoulos, 2011; Salazar, 2012).

The representations of tourism places that populate our hypermediated world are also rarely ideologically neutral. Most often, they are the products of sophisticated marketing systems designed to sell fantasy (Morgan, 2004). In the case of ski resorts in North America, the operative fantasy is that of an elite white leisure lifestyle, a discursive formation with component parts that can be spotted in such far-flung arenas as the sidewalk cafes of Monaco (d'Hauteserre, 2015), the Abercrombie and Fitch shop in the average US fashion mall (McBride, 2005), and the Skymall catalogues of humorous toys for the wealthy and eccentric that pass the hours for bored passengers criss-crossing the globe 30,000 feet up. To be sure, tourism in general has been represented as being largely the province of a white, Western lifestyle, as demonstrated through analyses of travel brochures such as those of Buzinde, Santos and Smith (2006) and Burton and Klemm (2011), both of which note the absence of people of colour depicted as tourists, contrasted with their presence as entertainers performing for white visitors. Ski resorts, however, are particularly problematic in this regard.

Historian Annie Coleman (1996) unpacks the 'unbearable whiteness of skiing', exploring how this leisure activity came to be appropriated as an expression of white ethnicity through resorts' advertising campaigns. As she argues, North American skiing had long seen European influence, due to the presence of Scandinavian immigrants in the 19th century, who brought snow sport knowledge and equipment-building expertise with them from the home country. In the 20th century, however, skiing took on a new meaning in the US context, as wealthy tourists experienced Europe's burgeoning recreational ski industry and carried this interest back home, helping to establish downhill skiing as a status sport and creating demand for highly sought-after European instructors. Despite the decline of immigration from Europe after the First World War, however, and also despite the location of most major North American ski spaces in the Mountain West, in areas characterized by rich ethnic diversity, the young ski industry did not fail to retain its 'enthusiasm for white ethnicities' (Coleman, 1996, 588). With the rise of consumerism in post-war

USA, the ski industry joined forces with the tourism industry to package ski vacations as a recreational product for middle- and upper-class families, embracing an advertising strategy that represented skiing as a healthy, athletic, fashionable and sexy leisure activity, generally through the trope of the handsome and fit blond skier, clothed in the classic Norwegian sweater, perhaps posed with a St Bernard dog or some other marker of northern European ethnicity. Coleman also identifies frequent overt parallels drawn with Europe (the Colorado Rockies advertised as 'the other Alps', for instance), as well as German words appearing in stylized fonts in resort advertising. And of course, there is the ubiquitous architecture of the 'Alpine village', with its quaint peaked roofs and colour-contrast half-timbering, its obligatory airy but cosy day lodge, and its European restaurant fare. Coleman relays the story of the Vail Village Inn, which in the 1960s hired construction crew cook Ed Kilby, famous for his chicken-fried steak, and rechristened him 'Pierre Kilbeaux', a newly arrived 'famous French chef', who would grace the restaurant menu with his *filet de boeuf au poulet frit*.

With European symbolism deployed to sign in for all things sophisticated, resort and gear advertising increasingly tended toward emphasizing the trappings of an elite ski lifestyle more than actual participation in the sport, with advertisements focusing on the après-ski experience (note the lack of translation from the French) and the fashion one could sport while standing in the lift line. Skiing itself became optional, less central to the experience than socializing and showing off one's 'achievements of consumption' (Coleman, 1996, 600). In this elite white Europhilic world, images of people of colour remained absent from ski resort promotional materials long after the USA had begun to make significant inroads into racial desegregation, long after referent European countries like France and Germany had themselves become widely multi-cultural, and despite the role of non-white ethnicities, particularly indigenous and Latino/a, in shaping the spaces in which much US ski culture is enacted. They are still absent today.

Although there does not appear to yet be a published comprehensive analysis of mountain resort advertisements with regard to depictions of race, a simple glance through the websites of major ski destinations, such as those throughout the US Southwest owned by the Vail resort group, renders immediately obvious the near absence of images of non-whites. A colleague of the present authors, who is currently undertaking a large-scale analysis of this issue, has noted to us that her preliminary outcomes reveal that the pattern noted from casual internet searching is not a fluke, but rather is indeed typical of ski advertising more broadly (A. Terwiel, British Columbia, 2014, personal communication). In a similar vein, Harrison (2013) notes that a search of the US magazine *Skiing* from 1993 to 2010 revealed no articles related to African American skiing, despite featuring pieces on disabled skiing and gay skiing. Such 'significant silences' (Echtner and Prasad, 2003) regarding racial diversity in skiing's promotional discourse continue to issue forth, heedless of the actual participation of people of colour in the sport. Perhaps contrary to the expectations of resort managers, Black people do ski recreationally – see Harrison's (2013) discussion of the more than 80 Black ski clubs existing in the USA. So too, for example, do indigenous people – consider the Ski Apache resort in New Mexico, owned and operated by the Mescalero Apache Tribe since the 1960s (and featuring notably different promotional imagery on its website than the likes of the resort group mentioned above). Skiing, as white as it still is, is not as white as it looks in tourism marketing discourse.

The representation of ski slopes as populated almost exclusively by whiteness helps to constitute them – even before the act of travel – as exclusionary geographies (Harrison, 2013), sending the message to people of colour that they are not particularly welcome in mountain recreational spaces and reassuring the dominant socio-economic order that prevailing moral and aesthetic norms associated with white ethnicity will not be challenged in this culturally valued leisure space, where racial homogeneity signs in for old-school Euro-chic, which signs in for modern elitism. But Canada and the USA, where nature-based recreation and tourism is big business, are multi-cultural, multi-racial societies – and nations which increasingly play host to diverse tourists from around the globe. How will the North American ski industry react, in the face of changing national demographics and to the temptation of West Egg wealth from a growing global middle class energized to experience the world through tourism? Will skiing's blueblood semiotic stick? Or will there someday be room for everybody on the mountain?

Skwelkwek'welt/Sun Peaks: Two Places, One Sign

About 45 minutes' drive from Kamloops, British Columbia, sits a site occupied by two distinctly different places: Skwelkwek'welt/Sun Peaks. As you drive out of the Thompson River Valley and ascend the hill towards 'the mountain' (which is actually three mountains), there are cabin-lined lakes, expansive farms and hamlet communities. On arrival at the site, the road is flanked with condominium complexes, hotels, large chalet-style houses and signs pointing out the various amenities: golf course, Nordic ski trails, chair lift parking and the village site. Welcoming you is a large sign: 'Welcome to Sun Peaks Resort'. A walk around the resort site uncovers large hotels, several restaurants and shops, a day lodge, a health centre, a skating rink and the bases of chair lifts. There are no indicators that any other places occupy this space. One space of visibility is opened here. At first glance, this is a ski and golf resort community – only.

But this place is not singular, nor uncontested. There is another place here, an othered place, called Skwelkwek'welt. Part of traditional Secwépemc territories, Skwelkwek'welt is an important high alpine hunting and gathering ground used for generations as part of seasonal subsistence rounds and ceremonial rites of passage. The significance of Skwelkwek'welt to the Secwépemc peoples cannot be overstated. This place emerges in the inextricability of economic, spiritual and cultural being (Billy, 2006). Before Sun Peaks emerged on this mountain, this was an intact high alpine environment in the heart of Secwépemc territory (Drapeau, 2010) – a territory to which Aboriginal Title was never extinguished by the treaty process and land that was never ceded to the Crown (Harris, 2002).

And yet there is only one sign: Welcome to Sun Peaks. One place is dominant here, the other buried. As Cole Harris (2002, xxiv) so

aptly reminds us: 'Whatever else it may also be, colonialism – particularly in its settler form – is about the displacement of people from their land and its repossession by others.' Sun Peaks is an example of what this displacement and repossession look like on the ground – not just as a spatial practice but also as a cultural and discursive one. Sun Peaks is a culturally produced place that happens, that takes place (Braun, 2001), in the image of settler colonial and capitalist desires.

Naturalizing this cultural production as the singular, natural, only version of this place requires sustained political and imaginative effort. In 2010, Sun Peaks incorporated as Canada's first 'mountain resort municipality' – a political gesture that could be read as a kind of antithetical land claim to local indigenous calls for an acknowledgement of Aboriginal Title of these same lands. In 2011 Sun Peaks Corporation commissioned the writing of a history of the resort that opens with Chapter 1, titled 'The Mountain Emerges', and tracks the evolution of the ski resort community from a local ski hill to a multinational-owned resort community (Scherf, 2011). This book works to narrate 'the mountain' (as Sun Peaks) into being as the only place there, by rooting its history in place, em-placing a community on this mountain. The book closes with an eloquent passage about the inclusiveness of this community: 'Sun Peaks is a true mountain community that takes care of its members … [and when you visit] … you can be sure that we will be here to welcome you. *The mountain, as always, will be waiting for you*' (emphasis added, Scherf, 2011, 96).

There are two notable moments in this closing passage that alert us to the need to shift our gaze towards the moral dimensions of this mountain geography. The first is on the matter of time. 'The mountain, as always, will be waiting for you.' This suggests that this place, this mountain, has always been singularly a ski resort community. The other is the reflection on the inclusive spirit of Sun Peaks. What matters about this assertion is that Sun Peaks is making a claim of inclusiveness only as Sun Peaks. Sun Peaks is the naturalized starting point, the terrain, upon which community formation is built. The ground under the feet of this community escapes questioning. This gesture of inclusiveness is fundamentally an exclusion, as it erases Secwépemc narratives of place and being – Skwelkwek'welt – from this mountain. All are welcome, as long as they do not challenge this site as exclusively a ski resort community. The result is that Secwĕpemc epistemologies are buried, paved over (figuratively and literally), and ski runs, a golf course and hotels are built on top of them.

If we don't look down and examine the terrains upon which we walk (and ski) we are participating in this work of exclusion. Harris (2002, xvii) writes that the establishment of the reserve system in British Columbia was a process by which 'One human geography was being superseded by another, both on the ground and in the imagination'. This is not just true of spatialized settler colonial structures like the reserve system. Settler colonialism operates as a cultural project (Veracini, 2011), and as discussed, places are culturally produced artifacts. So while there are two distinctly different places occupying this site, one is dominant – not because it is more important, but because historical and contemporary colonial power relations calibrate the relationship between the two. The work of maintaining these power relations is not up to elites and politicians alone. Rather, it is in the operation of settler colonial common-sense notions about the world, social relations and places that this work of domination gets done (Barker, 2009). Thus, how we imagine and engage with mountain places is as much a moral issue as it is a political one.

The Natures of Canoeing

When looking for leisure in mountain environments, we are often drawn to the freshwater lakes and rivers that provide opportunities for entangling our bodies in the rhythms of the landscape. In North America and, according to some pundits, Canada most specifically, canoeing is cherished as the ideal mode of water-based recreational travel for connecting with nature while minimizing ecological footprints. Helping to levitate this popular status of canoeing was former Canadian Prime Minister and the late Pierre Elliot Trudeau.

What sets a canoeing expedition apart is that it purifies you more rapidly and inescapably than any other. Travel 1000 miles by train and you are a brute; pedal 500 miles on a bicycle and you remain basically a bourgeois; paddle 100 miles in a canoe and you are already a child of nature.

(Trudeau, 1970)

Among his several other distinctions and political accomplishments, Trudeau's inscription of wilderness rivers and canoe expeditions into the Canadian imagination arguably shaped public support for the creation of mountain region protected areas (e.g. the Nahanni National Park Reserve in 1972) and the Canadian Heritage River System in 1984, which now includes several designated mountain waterways. Premised on conserving specific values associated with mountain and other environments, these initiatives have abetted a process of normalization 'whereby the *biophysical nature* traveled by canoe is held as an *intrinsic property* of the canoe trip activity' (Grimwood, 2011, 51).

That canoeing carries with it a presumed relationship to those places deemed 'natural' comes with undeniable benefits. On several occasions, authors have echoed Trudeau's sentiments above with observations that canoeing fosters one's sense of ecological rootedness and social belonging (Patterson *et al.*, 1998; Raffan, 1999; Hvenegaard and Asfeldt, 2007) and prompts a citizenry of wilderness ambassadors (Hodgins, 1988; Raffan, 2004). What the consideration of moral geographies alerts us to, however, are the multiple, dynamic and contested values packed within, and flowing from, the canvas of canoes. In other words, despite appearances, travelling mountain lakes and rivers by canoe is far from benign. For example, critical social researchers have illuminated how the 'nature of canoeing' reproduces a particular, hegemonic Canadian nationalistic identity based on whiteness, masculinity, class and colonialism (Baker, 2002; Newbery, 2003; Baldwin, 2009; Erickson, 2013).

Following Braun (2002), the canoe helps code wilderness as a fetishized and anachronistic space; that is, an uncivilized but endangered space located outside of history, mourned for and deemed in need of protection by the leisure class (see also Erickson, 2013). Similar to the silences discussed in our Skwelkwek'welt case above, the livelihoods, occupancy and experiences of indigenous and non-indigenous inhabitants in these places are systematically denied (Grimwood *et al.*, 2015). Even when canoeists explicitly recognize indigenous peoples as long-time stewards of so-called nature places – as several did in 2004 by identifying with First Nations on the moral grounds of Boreal Forest protection (Raffan, 2004) – histories and relations of privilege are not necessarily abandoned. Baldwin (2009) is quite clear on this, arguing that by mobilizing their subjectivity to identify with indigenous claims to land and protection, settler canoeists implicitly reinforce their hegemonic position of privilege and the assumption that certain groups occupy an authentic margin.

But as we have illustrated throughout this chapter, moral geography offers more than the opportunity to critique morally laden practices and performances in and of tourism. It also engenders possibilities for envisioning ethics in a new light, one that is situated in the events of place and values the relationships, encounters and vitality among social, material and perceptual domains (Popke, 2009). Grimwood (2015) has marshalled this promise into empirical research designed in part to reconfigure the ways nature and canoeing spaces are communicated, made sense of and performed.

Drawing on mobile ethnography of experiential journeys taken with canoe tourists and Inuit inhabitants of an Arctic riverscape, and a backdrop of geographical and anthropological literatures, Grimwood illuminated three relational, value-based metaphors that eschew conventional and divisive notions of nature. These metaphors (emplacement, wayfaring and gathering) convey fluid, ambiguous and place-based processes of connection, participation and becoming to craft cooperative and provisional linguistic spaces within the moral terrains of canoeing, and nature-based tourism more generally. Grimwood's argument is that more responsible and socially just forms of tourism may only proceed when our vocabulary becomes open and responsive to the plurality of voices and experiences layering a landscape. Here, we are reminded that:

> Ethics are not just socially imposed norms, they are also ways of composing who we are … [Ethics] provides a basis for questioning the way things are, informs how we might relate to others, and is a mode of being in which we exercise our individual responsibilities in

concert, though not necessarily agreement, with others.

> (Smith, 2009, 270–271)

Accordingly, taking the moral turn in the terrains of mountain tourism is not simply a matter of following prescribed standards or codes constraining self-interest. It is much more about perceiving and enacting ourselves and others as responsible agents who always seek possibilities for our individual, social and ecological betterment (Smith, 2009).

Conclusion

As we hope we have illustrated here, North American mountain environments are complex moral terrains, layered with diverse meanings, shot through by historical and contemporary relations of power. Moral geography helps us attend to these layers – to recognize that the leisure landscapes we typically take for granted are not innocent of power. From the construction through marketing materials of mountain spaces, who belongs there, and who doesn't, to the physical production of sites that emplace tourists and tourism brokers and displace those with alternate claims to the same lands, to the embodied journeys practised there, tourism takes place and makes place. Although the dominant mountain imaginary in North America has been that of a natural playground for the leisure class, where white ethnicity can display its superiority in terms of its wholesome athleticism, tasteful consumerism and high-minded ecological sensitivity, this place myth is not inevitable. Different and more inclusive futures are possible. By calling attention to place meanings that privilege dominant interests and highlighting alternative meanings of taken-for-granted leisure spaces – in short, by acknowledging and engaging with the multiplicity of place – we can perhaps begin to move from common sense to common ground.

Acknowledgement

The authors would like to thank Jessica Braidwood, research assistant for the first author, for her incredible support and insightful contributions to this project.

References

Appadurai, A. (1988) Putting hierarchy in its place. *Cultural Anthropology* 3, 36–49.

Baker, J. (2002) Production and consumption of wilderness in Algonquin Park. *Space and Culture* 5, 198–210.

Baldwin, A. (2009) Ethnoscaping Canada's boreal forest: liberal whiteness and its disaffiliation from colonial space. *The Canadian Geographer* 53, 427–443.

Barker, A. (2009) The contemporary reality of Canadian imperialism: settler colonialism and the hybrid colonial state. *The American Indian Quarterly* 33, 325–351.

Billy, J. (2006) Cultural survival and environmental degradation in the mountains of the Secwepemc. In: Moss, L.A. (ed.) *The Amenity Migrants: Seeking and Sustaining Mountains and Their Cultures*. CABI International, Wallingford, UK, pp. 148–162.

Braun, B. (1997) Buried epistemologies: the politics of nature in (post)colonial British Columbia. *Annals of the Association of American Geographers* 87, 3–31.

Braun, B. (2001) Place becoming otherwise. *BC Studies* 131, 15–24.

Braun, B. (2002) *The Intemperate Rainforest: Nature, Culture, and Power on Canada's West Coast*. Minnesota University Press, Minneapolis, Minnesota.

Burton, D. and Klemm, M. (2011) Whiteness, ethnic minorities and advertising in travel brochures. *The Service Industries Journal* 31, 679–693.

Buzinde, C., Santos, C. and Smith, S. (2006) Ethnic representations: destination imagery. *Annals of Tourism Research* 33, 707–728.

Caton, K. (2012) Taking the moral turn in tourism studies. *Annals of Tourism Research* 39, 1906–1928.

Coleman, A. (1996) The unbearable whiteness of skiing. *Pacific Historical Review* 65, 583–614.

Cooke, L. (2013) North takes place in Canada's Yukon Territory. In: Jørgensen, D. and Sörlin, S. (eds) *Northscapes: History, Technology, and the Making of Northern Environments*. University of British Columbia Press, Vancouver, British Columbia, Canada, pp. 223–246.

d'Hauteserre, A. (2015) Affect theory and the attractivity of destinations. *Annals of Tourism Research* 55, 77–89.

Drapeau, T. (2010) Spatialising new constitutionalism: the Secwepemc people versus Sun Peaks Resort Corporation in British Columbia, Canada. *Politics* 30, 1–10.

Echtner, C. and Prasad, P. (2003) The context of Third World tourism marketing. *Annals of Tourism Research* 30, 660–682.

Erickson, B. (2013) *Canoe Nation: Nature, Race, and the Making of a Canadian Icon*. University of British Columbia Press, Vancouver, British Columbia, Canada.

Escobar, A. (2001) Culture sits in places: Reflections on globalism and subaltern strategies of localization. *Political Geography* 20, 139–174.

Feighery, W. (2011) Consulting ethics. *Annals of Tourism Research* 38, 1031–1050.

Fennell, D. (2006) *Tourism Ethics*. Channel View Publications, Clevedon, UK.

Fridgen, J. (1984) Environmental psychology and tourism. *Annals of Tourism Research* 11, 19–39.

Gras-Dijkstra, S. (2009) *Values in Tourism: An Itinerary to Tourism Ethics*. Edu'Actief, Meppel, Netherlands.

Grimwood, B.S.R. (2011) Thinking outside the gunnels: considering natures and the moral terrains of recreational canoe travel. *Leisure/Loisir* 35, 49–69.

Grimwood, B.S.R. (2015) Advancing tourism's moral morphology: relational metaphors for just and sustainable Arctic tourism. *Tourist Studies* 15(1), 3–26.

Grimwood, B.S.R., Yudina, O., Muldoon, M. and Qiu, J. (2015) Responsibility in tourism: a discursive analysis. *Annals of Tourism Research* 50, 22–38.

Gupta, A. and Ferguson, J. (1997) Culture, power, place: ethnography at the end of an era. In: Gupta, A. and Ferguson, J. (eds) *Culture, Power, Place: Explorations in Critical Anthropology*. Duke University Press, Durham, North Carolina, pp. 1–29.

Hall, S. (1997) The work of representation. In: Hall, S. (ed.) *Representation: Cultural Representations and Signifying Practices*. Sage, London, pp. 13–74.

Harris, C. (2002) *Making Native Space*. University of British Columbia Press, Vancouver, British Columbia, Canada.

Harrison, A. (2013) Black skiing, everyday racism, and the racial spatiality of whiteness. *Journal of Sport and Social Issues* 37, 315–339.

Hodgins, B. (1988) Canoe irony: symbol and harbinger. In: Raffan, J. and Horwood, B. (eds) *Canexus: The Canoe in Canadian Culture*. Betelguese Books, Toronto, Ontario, Canada, pp. 45–57.

Holden, A. (2003) In need of new environmental ethics for tourism? *Annals of Tourism Research* 30, 94–108.

Hultsman, J. (1995) Just tourism: an ethical framework. *Annals of Tourism Research* 22, 553–567.

Hvenegaard, G. and Asfeldt, M. (2007) Embracing *friluftsliv's* joys: teaching the Canadian North through the Canadian wilderness travel experience. In: Henderson, B. and Vikander, N. (eds) *Nature First: Outdoor Life the Friluftsliv Way*. Natural Heritage Books, Toronto, Ontario, Canada, pp. 168–178.

Jafari, J. (2001) The scientification of tourism. In: Smith, V. and Brent, M. (eds) *Hosts and Guests Revisited: Tourism Issues of the 21st Century*. Cognizant Communication Corporation, Elmsford, New York, pp. 28–41.

Jamal, T. and C. Menzel. (2009) Good actions in tourism. In: Tribe, J. (ed.) *Philosophical Issues in Tourism*. Channel View Publications, Bristol, UK, pp. 227–243.

Lea, J. (1993) Tourism development ethics in the Third World. *Annals of Tourism Research* 20, 701–715.

Macbeth, J. (2005) Towards an ethics platform for tourism. *Annals of Tourism Research* 32, 962–984.

MacCannell, D. (2011) *The Ethics of Sightseeing*. University of California Press, Berkeley, California.

Matless, D. (2009) Moral geographies. In: Gregory, D., Johnston, R., Pratt, G., Watts, M. and Whatmore, S. (eds) *The Dictionary of Human Geography*. Wiley-Blackwell, Chichester, UK, p. 479.

McBride, D. (2005) *Why I Hate Abercrombie and Fitch: Essays on Race and Sexuality*. New York University Press, New York.

Morgan, N. (2004) Problematizing place promotion. In: Lew, A., Hall, C.M. and Williams, A. (eds) *A Companion to Tourism*. Blackwell, Malden, Massachusetts, pp. 173–183.

Mostafanezhad, M. and Hannum, K. (eds) (2014) *Moral Encounters in Tourism*. Ashgate, Farnham, UK.

Munn, N. (2003) Excluded spaces: the figure in the Australian Aboriginal landscape. In: Low, S. and Lawrence-Zúñiga, D. (eds) *The Anthropology of Space and Place: Locating Culture*. Blackwell, Oxford, pp. 92–109.

Newbery, L. (2003) Will any/body carry that canoe? A geography of the body, ability, and gender. *Canadian Journal of Environmental Education* 8, 204–216.

Patterson, M.E., Watson, A.E., Williams, D.R. and Roggenbuck, J.R. (1998) An hermeneutic approach to studying the nature of wilderness experiences. *Journal of Leisure Research* 30, 423–452.

Popke, J. (2009) Geography and ethics: Non-representational encounters, collective responsibility and economic difference. *Progress in Human Geography* 33, 81–90.

Proctor, J. (1999) A moral earth: facts and values in global environmental change. In: Proctor, J. and Smith, D. (eds) *Geography and Ethics: Journeys in a Moral Terrain*. Routledge, London, pp. 149–162.

Raffan, J. (1999) *Bark, Skin and Cedar: Exploring the Canoe in Canadian Experience*. HarperCollins, Toronto, Ontario, Canada.

Raffan, J. (ed.) (2004) *Rendezvous with the Wild: The Boreal Forest*. Bost Mills, Erin, Ontario, Canada.

Rodman, M. (1992) Empowering place: multilocality and multivocality. *American Anthropologist* 94, 56–69.

Salazar, N. (2012) Tourism imaginaries: a conceptual approach. *Annals of Tourism Research* 39, 863–882.

Scherf, K. (2011) *Sun Peaks Resort: An Evolution of Dreams*. Sun Peaks Resort Corporation, Kamloops, British Columbia, Canada.

Skinner, J. and Theodossopoulos, D. (eds) (2011) *Great Expectations: Imagination and Anticipation in Tourism*. Berghahn, Oxford, UK.

Smith, D. (2000) *Moral Geographies: Ethics in a World of Difference*. Edinburgh University Press, Edinburgh, UK.

Smith, M. (2009) Development and its discontents: ego-tripping without ethics or idea(l)s? In: Tribe, J. (ed.) *Philosophical Issues in Tourism*. Channel View Publications, Bristol, UK, pp. 261–277.

Smith, M. and Duffy, R. (2003) *The Ethics of Tourism Development*. Routledge, London.

Su, X., Wang, H. and Wen, T. (2013) Profit, responsibility, and the moral economy of tourism. *Annals of Tourism Research* 43, 231–250.

Trudeau, P.E. (1970) Exhaustion and fulfillment: the ascetic in a canoe. *Wilderness Canada*. University of British Columbia Press, Vancouver, British Columbia, Canada. Available at: http://www.canoe.ca/che-mun/102trudeau.html (accessed 1 November 2014).

Veracini, L. (2011) Introducing. *Settler Colonial Studies* 1, 1–12.

26 Mountain Tourism in Germany: Challenges and Opportunities in Addressing Seasonality at Garmisch-Partenkirchen

Joel T. Schmidt,[1]* Christian H. Werner[1] and Harold Richins[2]
[1]*University of Applied Management, Erding, Germany;*
[2]*Thompson Rivers University, Kamloops, British Columbia, Canada*

Introduction

Mountain tourism has traditionally had a preponderance of visitors during the winter high season, associated particularly with snow sports and related activities (Hudson, 2004; Mill, 2007; Pegg *et al.*, 2012). Over the last few decades, a number of changes and enhancements to the experiences people may have in mountain destinations has provided for an increased diversity of options (Godde *et al.*, 2000; Needham and Rollins, 2005; Flognfeldt and Tjørve, 2013; De Grave, 2014; Whistler, 2015).

Some mountain destinations have had challenges, however, in reinvigorating their infrastructure and amenity provision to accommodate an increased interest in other seasonal activities, as they have been more oriented toward snow sports experiences (Mill, 2007; Unbehaun *et al.*, 2008). These challenges may relate to: the built infrastructure and entrenched development policies, traditional purchase behaviour patterns of long-term visitors, awareness of destination offerings in non-prime times, imbedded community interests and practices which may hamper change, divergent and changing regional and customer demographics, and regional or local community issues regarding appropriate employment skills and management experience (Needham *et al.*, 2004; Moss, 2006; Mill, 2007; Glover and Prideaux, 2009; Nepal and Jamal, 2011; Pegg *et al.*, 2012; Morrison, 2013; De Grave, 2014; Falk, 2014).

Our case study, Garmisch-Partenkirchen, located in Southern Germany (see Figs 26.1 and 26.2), encompasses many of the current and future issues facing alpine towns as mountain tourist destinations as they transition from winter to all-season experiences. This chapter examines special aspects of the community and its current tourism data, reflecting on the challenges facing the regional area as it shifts from a winter-only to a year-round tourism focus, and the solutions implemented for a long-term, viable future.

'Discover your true nature – 365 days a year' (GaPa, 2014b) is one of the current slogans for the alpine town of Garmisch-Partenkirchen. Located at the foot of Mount Zugspitze (2962 m), it is the most famous town in the Bavarian Alps, and Germany's first choice for

---

* Corresponding author: joel.schmidt@fham.de

Fig. 26.1. Historical mountain town of Partenkirchen, Garmisch-Partenkirchen, Germany (photograph courtesy of Harold Richins).

winter sports. The town is re-inventing itself, as the motto stated above clearly communicates, as a mountain tourism destination that is defined by year-round tourism offerings instead of solely winter activities.

This shift is not limited to Garmisch-Partenkirchen; it is a global trend (Hudson, 2004; Needham *et al.*, 2004; Pegg *et al.*, 2012; De Grave, 2014), reflecting the increased interest in adventure tourism and numerous additional resort destination amenities in the last decade (Swarbrooke *et al.*, 2003; Beedie, 2008; Lepp and Gibson, 2008; Roberts, 2011; ATTA, 2013; Morrison, 2013). But this process is not without its challenges and difficulties. For Garmisch-Partenkirchen, the shift to year-round mountain tourism (GaPa, 2014c) is firmly imbedded in the town's future vision and political agenda. Yet this shift implies redevelopment and new expansion of infrastructure, which is not always easy, given Germany's stringent rules and regulations for building projects and environmental policies controlling the impact of sports expansion and development.

Garmisch-Partenkirchen: A Portrait

The official region of Garmisch-Partenkirchen extends across an area of almost 50,000 acres (GaPa, 2014a) offering tourists a rich palette of mountain experiences. With a current population of 28,040 in 2014, the city's growth has remained relatively stable over the last 10 years and is expected to continue with minimal variation into the next two decades, according to a study on the regional district forecasting population growth to the year 2032 (BLSD, 2014). However, while the population total may remain relatively stable, the demographic profile of residents will change, according to the study, which predicts a 28–33% increase in the number of people aged 60 years and over. This echoes the trend in Germany and elsewhere for an ageing population (Dwyer *et al.*, 2009; FSO, 2009; Glover and Prideaux, 2009; Scott and Becken, 2010; Sedgley *et al.*, 2011) and remains a critical issue for tourism development in Garmisch-Partenkirchen.

One interesting factor relating to the inhabitants of Garmisch-Partenkirchen is the

Fig. 26.2. Location of Garmisch-Partenkirchen, Bavaria, Germany (from Google Maps).

number of registered secondary residences. In 2014, the total number of secondary residences was 1329 (4.7% of the population). As a popular tourism destination, the number of secondary residents can have an effect on economic sustainability, as has been experienced in Scandinavian mountain regions (Williams and Kaltenborn, 1999; Müller, 2005; Flognfeldt and Tjørve, 2013) and North America (Moss, 2006; McIntyre et al., 2006; Chipeniuk and Rapport, 2008), where tourists are selecting secondary residences over hotels. However, this does not yet appear to have impacted on the Garmisch-Partenkirchen tourism industry as critically as in Scandinavia.

The Garmisch-Partenkirchen economy is solid and stable, with little variation in growth and definitely not in recession. A report from the Garmisch-Partenkirchen Chamber of Commerce and Trade (IHK), analysing data over a 5-year period starting in 2007 or 2008, shows that unemployment remains consistently below the German average (yet higher than the rate

listed for Bavaria); purchasing power remains above the German national average, but lower than Bavaria; and the region's contribution to the GDP has not changed significantly over the five years (IHK, 2014). One slightly downward trend the IHK indicated relates to available industrial real estate (short-, mid- and long-term). Land use is critical in this region and opportunities to expand into the beautiful natural landscape are decreasing, resulting in high real-estate prices (IHK, 2014).

The economy is clearly tourism-based, with over 50% of industry coming from the hotel, restaurant and service sectors. According to a market study conducted in 2013 (Neumann and Harrer, 2013), tourism in Garmisch-Partenkirchen generated total revenue of €287.8 million. This apparent stability is more indicative of a need for change, according to a study by Lohmann et al. (2014). These experts interpret the situation combining a relatively low GDP per capita, higher unemployment rates than other areas in Bavaria, above-average purchasing power and real-estate rates, as favouring older, affluent people rather than young families and companies new to the area, which are needed to boost the economy and generate new growth. A more detailed examination of tourism data and the city's long-term strategic plan is provided in later sections of this chapter, especially regarding the goal to be a year-round mountain tourism destination.

Description of the Mountain Areas of Garmisch-Partenkirchen

The local mountains surrounding the city include many summits that can be accessed without lifts or other transportation assistance, offering sport and adventure tourism experiences (Zugspitzland, 2014):

- Zugspitze (2962 m)
- Schneefernerkopf (2874 m)
- Wetterwandeck (2698 m)
- Alpspitze (2628 m)
- Osterfelderkopf (2050 m)
- Kreuzjoch (1719 m)
- Wank (1780 m)
- Kreuzeck (1651 m)
- Hausberg (1310 m)
- Waldeck (1236 m)
- Rießerkopf (1130 m)
- Katzenstein (880 m)

In general, there are three main mountain ski-resort areas offering assisted mountain access via trains, gondolas, lifts, cable-cars, rope-tows and tracks (GaPa, 2014a), namely:

- Zugspitze area: Germany's only glacier ski-resort with 22 km of runs, open from November to May
- Garmisch-Classic: offering 40 km of runs, open from December to April
- Mount Wank: concentrates on non-skiing winter activities

The Bavarian Zugspitze Railway is open year-round with its impressive 19-km route running from the main train station in Garmisch-Partenkirchen (707 m) to the peak of the Zugspitze. In addition, the Eibsee (Lake Eib) cable-car running from the Eibsee station to the Zugspitze peak is open in summer and winter. The other routes are in operation during the winter ski season.

Garmisch-Partenkirchen, with its impressive ski areas, is part of a larger network of German ski resorts in southern Bavaria (see Fig. 26.3), and visitors are able to access over 169 km of ski runs in a radius of 30 km. With these Zugspitze runs, Garmisch-Partenkirchen remains a leader in snow-guarantee for long season (given its high elevation), and other resorts in the region are not able to compete.

Brief History of Garmisch-Partenkirchen

Garmisch-Partenkirchen has a tradition as a world-class mountain resort spanning many decades, especially since hosting the IV Olympic Winter Games in 1936. The city, which is so strongly associated with winter sport, is deeply entrenched as a mountain tourism destination.

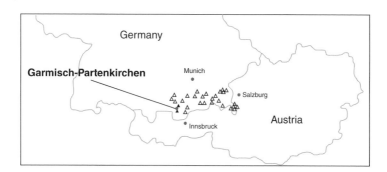

Fig. 26.3. Ski resorts in the Bavarian Alps (based on Skiresorts, 2014).

In Roman times, a way-station called Partanum (MGP, 2003) was established on what today is the section of the town called Partenkirchen. Roman soldiers and tradespeople travelled through this area as they made their way along the Via Claudia Augusta. This was a road leading from the Po River in Italy, north over the Alps, and into Germany via Augsburg to the Danube River at the site of the current town of Donauwörth, a distance of approximately 563 km (VCI, n.d.).

Records of the community of Garmisch suggest that, for approximately 800 years, both towns were governed through Werdenfels Castle (Zeune and Spichtinger, 2000; Werdenfels, 2014), situated on an escarpment north of Garmisch. It is only since 1 January 1935 (MGP, 2003) that the two towns have merged into one city (or 'markt' in German). Historic documents have referred to the two locations as far back as 802 AD, *Germareskauue*, and 1130 AD, *Barthinkirchen* (GPI, n.d.). The idea to amalgamate was also not so novel, since the region (including Mittenwald) was governed under the jurisdiction of the Grafschaft Werdenfels

(established by the Bishop of Freising in 1294 AD and dissolved in 1802 AD by the Bavarian monarchy; MGP, 2003). A boom in ocean shipping due to the discovery of America is thought to have led to a decline in overland trade and, coupled with periodic epidemics, crop failures, and other social and religious community disintegration, led a long-term economic decline over a few hundred years.

Fortunes finally began to change when visitor numbers increased as a result of improved train routes, tourism and mega-event sporting activities in the mid-1930s (Citizendium, 2014). Garmisch and Partenkirchen up to this time were essentially separate communities until planning began for the IV Olympic Winter Games (held in 1936; see Fig. 26.4; Winter Olympics, 2014).

Adventure, mountains, tourism and trade were the foundations of Garmisch-Partenkirchen. The city has remained true to its roots, with investment in tourism and recreation instead of other industries in the post-war period of reorganization and development. Today, the city strives to maintain its position as a leader in mountain tourism in Germany, with an

Fig. 26.4. Garmisch-Partenkirchen and the 1936 Olympic Stadium (photograph courtesy of Harold Richins).

all-season concept including special offerings in the areas of health, sport and culture. To achieve this, Garmisch-Partenkirchen continues to adjust its goals and initiatives proactively in accordance with regional, national and international trends in mountain tourism.

Transition to All-season Destination

Comparison of tourism data

In order to gain a clearer picture of the transition occurring in Garmisch-Partenkirchen, it is important to examine tourism data, especially relating to overnight guests staying in paid accommodation. Figure 26.5 displays the amount of overnight guests from 1954 to 2013 based on data from Nagel and Ries (2014).

The data listed are yearly figures with no differentiation between summer and winter visitors; the figure clearly indicates an increasing trend over 50 years. Also visible, is a sudden peak in a 10-year cycle starting in 1980 (see Fig. 26.5). This increase is due to the world-famous Passion Play, an outdoor musical theatre production drawing thousands of summer visitors in nearby Oberammergau. The production, which has run every 10 years since the 1600s, has been growing in popularity over the last 40 years. Although Fig. 26.5 helps to present the increasing attractiveness

of the city for guests over the years, it does not indicate specific seasonal information.

Figure 26.6 extends the examination of overnight guests in Garmisch-Partenkirchen to include a separate analysis of summer and winter seasons. With this differentiation of data, the importance of summer visitors becomes very clear. Compared to numerous winter sports resorts in various destinations within the Alps and internationally, Garmisch-Partenkirchen has long had the benefit of more balanced tourism interest. In some years, in fact, the amount of summer visitors is twice as high as the amount of winter visitors (Nagel and Ries, 2014). For the city and region to focus mainly on winter tourism offerings would be to neglect more than half of the tourism yearly market.

According to Buhalis (2000), it is important for destination management organizations to analyze the destination with regard to six important factors: attractions, accessibility, amenities, available packages, activities and ancillary services. Of these six factors, the tourism department already has rich information regarding attractions, amenities and activities, and with the implementation of internal vacation planning services via the Garmisch-Partenkirchen website (GaPa Tourismus), it will be possible to control available packages pre-arranged for special target groups. More data needs to be gathered regarding accessibility and ancillary services (or it already exists, but is not openly available for application in this current study).

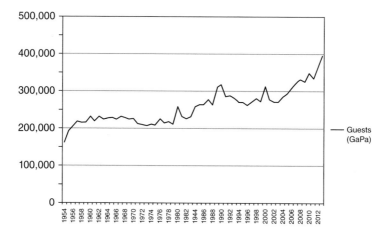

Fig. 26.5. Annual total of overnight guests (1954–2013) (based on data from Nagel and Ries, 2014).

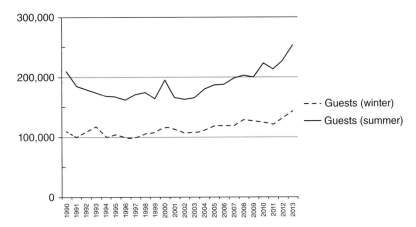

Fig. 26.6. Overnight guests comparison of summer/winter (1990–2013) (based on data from Nagel and Ries, 2014).

In an online visitor self-report survey in 2013, GaPa Tourismus identified popular recreation activities (2014c). Interestingly, the least popular activities identified in the study were biking, concert/music events, and sports events. The ten most popular activities reported in the survey were the following.

- Walking
- Hiking
- Restaurant and dining
- Café and ice-cream stands
- Day trips
- Shopping
- Swimming (indoor)
- Skiing
- Regional markets
- Museums and exhibitions

In this same study, visitors also reported the sightseeing attractions included in their itineraries. The five most popular attractions were:

- Historical Ludwig Street
- Olympic Stadium (including ski jump)
- Partnach Gorge
- Zugspitze (including the AlpspiX viewing platform at the top of the Zugspitzbahn)
- Michael-Ende-Spa-Park

The least of the popular attractions listed include the Königshaus am Schachen (a royal mansion), the Werdenfels Museum and the castle ruins of Werdenfels. The participation in recreation activities and types of attractions most visited matches the current profile and demographic trend for the area: low impact, high enjoyment and experience, high relaxation and rejuvenation – typical for guests in the age range of 41–60 (GaPa, 2014c). However, the range of activities possible in the area, and the focus on an all-season mountain tourism destination can also match the profile of an 'adventure traveler' (ATTA, 2013) referring to a traveller who chooses a certain type of tourism activity, rather than the degree of difficulty or risk in the chosen activity. There are ample soft-adventure activities that are immediately accessible in Garmisch-Partenkirchen, which could potentially increase the participation of guests in the 30–40 age range and represent a new target group for marketing. The tourism department of Garmisch-Partenkirchen is dealing closely with these types of challenging decisions relating to the future of the city.

Long-term strategic goals

The two strategic goals outlined in the 6-year business plan (Plan-GaPa Tourism 2012–2017) are expected to help Garmisch-Partenkirchen achieve long-term and enduring mountain tourism, independent from solely winter tourism. They are: (i) to become a leading destination in the Alps; and (ii) to become a year-round mountain destination (GaPa, 2014c). The city is committed to achieving these main goals, and has outlined additional goals and measures to move forward, including the following.

- Development of additional summer tourism offerings (especially in the areas of hiking, biking, health and wellness, and family).
- Strong positioning in terms of wide range of sporting activities, including soft winter sports (e.g. snow-shoeing, Nordic walking, etc.).
- Maintenance and expansion of existing mountain trails infrastructure.
- Acquisition of large-scale winter sport events.
- Acquisition of conferences, exhibitions and seminars.

For Garmisch-Partenkirchen these goals are realistic. Not only is the city a leading alpine ski-resort, it also has a long history (70 years) with special status as a premium spa city (specializing in natural healing therapies and wellness offerings). The combination of easy access to a beautiful, natural landscape, wide range of sports, and premium health and wellness facilities make the city a good partner for large-scale events, conferences and exhibitions during the winter or summer seasons. With these goals in place, the city can move forward with its strategic development plans to become a leading mountain tourism destination, aligned with a portfolio of measures that match theory and good practice of competitive alpine destinations; namely, the effective integration of offerings targeting business and leisure travellers (Buhalis, 2000; Morrison, 2013).

Garmisch-Partenkirchen Tourismus plays an integral role as a destination management organization, as it strives to manage the overall experience of travellers on an ongoing seasonal basis (Howie, 2003; Laws *et al.*, 2011). Visitors encounter Garmisch-Partenkirchen on many levels, so the tourism association interacts with as many different tourism principals as they are able (Buhalis, 2000; Wang and Pizam, 2011; Morrison, 2013), from taxi-drivers to lift personnel. Consequently, the development of guiding principles that can align behaviour and communication with guests is essential for effective experience management. Table 26.1 presents an overview of the expanded vision and mission for the city as a tourism destination.

Table 26.1. Guiding principles (GaPa, 2014c – translation by the authors).

Vision	Garmisch-Partenkirchen gives you 'butterflies in your tummy'
Mission	Personal 'storming-the-peak' experiences of the highest quality
Identity	Gateway to an alpine paradise of unlimited possibilities
Values	Inspiring people through character and sustainable quality
Skills	Living fully, 365 days a year
Behaviour/ communication	You've heard about me already, now let's get to know each other
Environment	Always in motion

The guiding principles are emotional, personal and dynamic, supporting the interactive experience creation with visitors. They also reflect the goal to bring guests back to Garmisch-Partenkirchen on return visits and different times of the year, thereby transforming day guests into overnight guests and multi-seasonal guests as well.

In order to gain a more comprehensive understanding of the breadth and depth of tourism initiatives currently undertaken by the City of Garmisch-Partenkirchen, the information presented in Tables 26.2 and 26.3 describes selected actions outlined in the 6-year plan (GaPa, 2014c), which has been extended and adapted for an additional period (the original time-frame spanned from 2007 to 2012, and has now been extended to include 2012–2017 as well). These actions are categorized as actions that have not yet been implemented, referred to as goals (G), actions that are currently in process (P), or actions that have already been completed (C). The actions listed in this study do not represent the comprehensive scope of actions and initiatives taken by GaPa Tourismus. Rather, these selected actions represent examples of the vision and commitment of their efforts to realize their exciting programme of change for an enduring future as a mountain tourism destination with a year-round palette of activities for a wide range of guests and visitors.

Garmisch-Partenkirchen Tourismus is indeed taking their role as a destination management organization seriously, with exciting success as these actions indicate. Their vision extends beyond winter and summer sport activities

Table 26.2. Selected actions for summer and winter seasons with identifier of goal (G), in process (P) or completed (C) (adapted from GaPa, 2014c).

Summer Season

Expansion of the Nordic Centre (Kaltenbrunn)	G
Improve bike trail connections with multi-region network	G
Implementation of all-season concept for the Gudiberg Lift	G
Paved inline skating route to Griesen/Ehrwald	G
Improvement of children's programmes (e.g. petting zoo, indoor playground, adventure play-grounds in valley and mountain)	G
Comprehensive development concept (Mount Wank)	G
Alpine pasture and cottage guide: 'At home in the mountains' (new publication)	P
New running trails: 4 Trails Run	P
Redevelopment of the high mountain trail Graseck–Gudiberg	P
Open-air cinema/nature cinema at Mount Wank	C
Suspension bridge at Faulken Canyon	C
Free courses at Michael-Ende Spa Park (e.g. Qi-Gong)	C
'Meditation' hiking trail	C
Improved signage at Mount Wank	C

Winter Season

Expansion concept for winter hiking trails (e.g. Hausberg–Kreuzeck)	G
Sledding route guarantee (Hausberg/Eckbauer)	G
Ice skating area with Christmas Market in the Partenkirchen sector	G
Improvement of transportation of guests (hotel shuttle service)	G
Differentiation of ski areas (according to usage: companies and associations, public, ski tours, etc.)	G
Snow-guarantee investment at Garmisch-Classic: 98 propeller artificial snow canon and 47 lances	C
Artificial snow coverage on all five descents to the ski villages/resorts	C
Continual support of soft winter sports through press coverage (incl. newsletter, website and print)	C
Development of expanded winter sport activities: Night touring at Garmisch-Classic, training course for ski-tours at Mount Wank	C

as they strive to create pathways for guests to truly experience Garmisch-Partenkirchen in ways that will bring them back for more. The efforts taken to create a GaPa Tourismus brand and image as a top mountain destination are systematic, planned and are beginning to have positive outcomes. Table 26.3 presents actions that have been identified as amenable, realizable and profitable (Buhalis, 2000; Murphy, 2009; Morrison, 2013; GaPa, 2014c; Lohmann *et al.*, 2014). With these actions, GaPa Tourismus targets a very relevant segment of the German tourism market: the business traveller. Conscious application of the MICE (meetings-incentives-conferences-exhibitions) approach to business travel is used to extend the range of experience beyond winter and summer mountain sports.

Health and wellness offerings are part of the GaPa Tourismus concept for strategic development, and as a recognized Spa-city there is already a long tradition in this sector (70 years as a recognized city). This is not without its challenges since the prerequisites and conditions need to be continually improved, evaluated and documented in order to maintain the privilege of using the prefix 'Spa', and maintaining a 'premium' location prefix intensifies the documentation processes. Integration of health and wellness into mountain tourism activities (see Table 26.3) helps bridge the gap between sport and sustainable interaction with nature and landscape. According to Unbehaun *et al.* (2008) such integration is a viable alternative to purely winter sport activities, and with the expanded focus on new target markets (such as Russia and China) these new offerings can be very effective.

Development of cultural management (see Table 26.3) extends the opportunities for natural experience at Garmisch-Partenkirchen into the area of visual and performing arts. Since 2008, the city has offered a cultural festival organized by a local event company in late August and into September. In the summer of 2014 (CULTUS, 2014), the festival included

Table 26.3. Selected actions for conventions, heath and culture with identifier of goal (G), in process (P) or completed (C) (adapted from GaPa, 2014c).

Conventions and Exhibitions	
Improvement of reservation management (CRM)	G
Unified rebate packages for special partners	G
Improved cooperation and collaboration with catering for events	G
Energy reduction concept (lighting, heating, power)	P
Creation of new apprenticeship programme: Expert in Event Engineering	P
ISO certification 9001: 2008 (as convention provider)	C
Convention reporting in selected key publications (e.g. *Convention International*, etc.)	C
Renovation of banquet room 'Werdenfels' at city hall, and redesign of Spa Park outdoor concert pavilion	C
Health & Spa Location Recognition	
Special target group offers for qualified health programmes and providers	G
Continuation and expansion of 'Mountain Sport Afternoons' (ski schools, mountain guides, rafting, paragliding, climbing, etc.)	G
Expansion and development of single-day and multi-day programming in health sector	G
Health events for employees and partners of GaPa Tourismus	G
Communication of 'Spa City' prefix on city signage and media coverage	P
Concept development for primary prevention region for corporate health sponsorship	P
Expanded offerings for overnight health programmes (thematic, 2–13 nights)	C
Advanced training certificate for 'Climate-Therapist'	C
Culture Management	
Establishment of a Youth Film Festival	G
Sponsoring of local and traditional customs (e.g. carnival festival)	G
Expansion of the culture pages (online: www.gapa.de)	G
Conceptualisation for the 'Michael and Edgar Ende Centre', and collaboration with local museums	G
Project Spa-House Garmisch, and Open Spa-Park	P
Creation of a new steering committee (consulting and coordination levels)	C
Development of an online event calendar	C

53 events (shows, productions, concerts, exhibitions, etc.). It is a priority of the city to engage in these ongoing events (such as the popular BMW Motorcycle Days, which have been operating for 20 years), as they establish a firm link within a specific target group and existing network of new and returning visitors. Additionally, affiliations with other alpine associations, such as 'Best of the Alps' (see Box 26.1 on p. 267), also play a key role in reaching new guests through existing networks. In this case, membership is also a benchmarking tool as it places Garmisch-Partenkirchen together with the 12 top mountain tourism destinations in the Alps (Ultimate Ski, 2015; Ski Europe, 2015).

Challenges and Future Implications

Many challenges face the city and region of Garmisch-Partenkirchen as they consciously make the shift from winter ski-resort to all-season mountain tourism destination. Many of these challenges have been addressed in the sections above. However, two of the recurring themes in the city's strategic planning, as well as in the literature on mountain tourism, are: (i) dealing effectively with climate change for a sustainable and low-impact on environment future; and (ii) finding viable solutions for developmental restrictions that impede the strategic plan initiatives. These are both long-term challenges that have considerable influence on the realization of the shift to year-round mountain tourism offerings.

Climate change

Climate change is clearly having an impact on the future of mountain resorts (Scott, 2003). In 2007, the Organisation for Economic Co-operation and Development (OECD) commissioned a study on the impact of climate change on the European Alps tourism industry, especially the big ski-resort communities. The general findings from the OECD indicate that the warming trend will continue in the future, bringing 'reduction in snow cover at lower altitudes, receding glaciers and melting permafrost at higher altitudes, and changes in temperature and precipitation extremes' (Agrawala, 2007). An additional study conducted in North America indicated similar findings. With the ski and snowboard industry supporting over 210,000 jobs and bringing in over US$1.2 billion to the US economy, there is a significant predicted decrease in winter revenue over the next 50 years due to climate change and the subsequent warming trend (Burakowski and Magnusson, 2012). German Alp regions will be greatly affected by the warming trend, and the estimate is that even a minimal 1°C increase in warmth will decrease the available snow-reliable areas by 65%, and an increase of 4°C will leave only the Zugspitze area as a skiable destination due to its higher elevation.

While this future warming trend is irrefutable, Mayer and Steiger (2013) recognize that it is unclear as to exactly how much time remains for the ski industry in the Alps, more specifically, the lower elevation region of the Bavarian Alps, including Garmisch-Partenkirchen. Mayer and Steiger examine two indicators for cost-effectiveness of alpine ski-destinations: the 100-day rule (cost-effectiveness requires 100 days of continuous operation) and the Christmas rule (cost-effectiveness requires uninterrupted operation during the 2-week Christmas vacation period). For both scenarios, if less than 50% of the runs are open, the sport is no longer economically viable. The Garmisch-Classic ski area currently boasts 70% snow-secure runs; however, with temperature increases of 1–3°C, it falls below the 50% level. A compensation measure such as creating artificial snow is only a short-term solution, which has high economic and environment costs (Mayer and Steiger, 2013).

Garmisch-Partenkirchen is committing resources toward expansion and maintenance of the artificial snow makers, and coverage on Garmisch-Classic is at 48.4%, including all five descents to the village/ski-resort, while the Zugspitze area is not using artificial snow at all, since it has a higher elevation (Mayer and Steiger, 2013). However, the shift towards tourism activities independent of winter skiing

has occurred, which will include a mix of offerings until it is no longer possible to proceed, due to economic or environmental barriers. By that time, the expectation is that alternative activities will be mature and already part of the mountain infrastructure.

Seasonal priority, a shift in perspective

Making seasonality a priority, and particularly moving towards all-season offerings, has been advocated as an important means of viability in the longer term for mountain resorts (Dickson and Huyton, 2008). It is precisely the shift in perspectives that can be so difficult for some resorts to make. Traditional winter-sport perspective takes a 'doom' approach, while for the all-season perspective could be seen as a 'boom' opportunity. Falk (2014) establishes the positive relationship between increase in sunshine and increased overnight guests in Austria, stating that the incremental increase in sunshine over the past 50 years has resulted in a 5.5% increase in domestic overnight stays and 10% in foreign overnight stays. Upon closer examination, Falk determines that domestic visitors react to short-term changes in sunshine and weather, while foreign visitors base their decisions on the reports from previous year. De Grave (2014) interprets the shift to year-round mountain tourism as also having positive benefits, especially relating to social and environmental factors, visitor and resident awareness, and value assessment of the natural landscape (interaction with forest areas and their preservation and use).

Based on the tourism data from 2013 (Nagel and Ries, 2014), a major challenge for Garmisch-Partenkirchen is dealing effectively with the change of seasons. Having made the shift in strategic priority to an all-season destination does not solve the problem of low visitor numbers in April; however, it does work to balance the visitor numbers throughout the year and lower the potential risk of relying only on one season – winter.

Regardless of what new activities and tourism offerings are made to compensate for the change of season periods, Needham et al. (2004) in their study within the Canadian mountain resort community of Whistler, British Columbia, express the need to consult with

Fig. 26.7. Example of summer activity near Garmisch: walking the Höllentalklamm (photograph courtesy of Harold Richins).

stakeholders before making significant changes, since each stakeholder group has different attitudes toward mountain development and usage. While this study is not from a region close to Garmisch-Partenkirchen, the findings are still worth noting for mountain destinations in transition phases. Whistler is much younger than Garmisch-Partenkirchen; however, it too suffers from the present and future challenges of being reliant upon tourism and recreation, seasonality, climate change, diverse priorities, and the challenges for enduring and sustainable development, particularly in the tourism resort sector (Needham *et al.*, 2004; De Grave, 2014; Whistler, 2015).

Developmental restrictions

Innovative infrastructure investment is a key factor for ensuring a competitive position in the mountain tourism industry, especially regarding Austria as a neighbouring rival. Mayer and Steiger (2013) in their analysis of the Bavarian Alps, report that ongoing investment in the

maintenance and extension of the mountain railway is necessary for economic stability of mountain tourism, acting as a compensatory factor to the impact of climate change on the area. The study maintains that investments need to support communities and resort areas to make the shift away from winter-dependent tourism services, meaning that there are more investment areas to consider other than artificial-snow facilities.

Garmisch-Partenkirchen is moving in a constructive direction regarding projects and investments for infrastructure improvement. Although they are active in maintaining and expanding the artificial-snow facilities, other areas are also receiving the necessary support for expansion (Mount Wank lift area, as well as ongoing investment in updating lift systems to include express and multi-person transportation services). An advantage for Garmisch-Partenkirchen is its reputation in hosting international large-scale events, such as the Winter Olympics and World Cup skiing. These events have ensured that the resort areas are modern and up to date with high capacity for mountain access. Yet, the challenge remains to shift the mindset of resort stakeholders and investors away from the winter-only perspective, as lift system infrastructure investment also benefits mountain sports other than skiing. In general, sustainable mountain tourism requires that lift systems and mountain access transportation be viewed as a multiplier, promoting tourism interactions with the landscape that exceed winter sport activities (Godde *et al.*, 2000; Thomas and Fredline, 2004; Nepal and Jamal, 2011; Fablet, 2013; Mayer and Steiger, 2013).

Conclusion

Garmisch-Partenkirchen as a mountain tourism destination has the characteristics that make it possible for an effective and long-term shift to an all-season destination, given its: (i) size (large, but not oversized); (ii) location (lower Alps region, but because it is in the Zugspitze area, it is positioned to maximize the benefits of both upper and lower elevation areas and it is also closer to Northern European populations); and (iii) profile (sport, health and convention focus is already in place).

The biggest challenge is creating a greater shift from the mindset of winter to year-round mountain tourism. Stakeholder management and working effectively with city political, economic and social leadership as a destination management organization will be critical for creating an enduring future as a leading mountain tourism destination that is able to escape the short-sightedness of status quo decision making (Buhalis, 2000; Mayer and Steiger, 2013), which pushes for ongoing subventions for maintenance of snow-guarantee until climate change makes it impossible to sustain. This one-sided approach to mountain tourism can have drastic effects for long-term mountain usage, as the efforts needed for maintaining snow-guarantee in the winter season may damage the environmental ecosystem in ways that are irreparable in the future, not to mention the massive economic drain such measures would entail.

Garmisch-Partenkirchen, along with 11 other mountain resorts in the European Alps has joined a network of top mountain tourism destinations, Best of the Alps (BOTA), to create a greater shift from the mindset of winter to year-round mountain tourism (BOTA, 2014). (See Box 26.1.)

Up until now Garmisch-Partenkirchen has been taking effective action in the constructive areas and has manoeuvred successfully through the complexities surrounding mountain tourism destinations. It is hoped that this impressive and historic mountain city will continue to thrive and successfully implement its vision for all-season

tourism in the future, discovering and continuing to commit to outdoor mountain recreation and tourism 365 days a year.

Box 26.1. 'Best of the Alps' (BOTA)

A network of top mountain tourism destinations, including Garmisch-Partenkirchen and 11 other mountain resorts in the European Alps (BOTA, 2014). It highlights winter and summer offerings and operates as an additional online branding strategy for increased dissemination of the partner locations. Special events include an annual car rally (classic cars) and golf tournament (moving from location to location).

According to Gloersen *et al.* (2013) BOTA is purely a marketing initiative for the benefit of the partner locations, but with little impact on an overall alpine tourism strategy. However, membership is advantageous, especially for Garmisch-Partenkirchen as one of two Bavarian Alps cities included in the network. Compared to some of the other members, Garmisch-Partenkirchen is still a comparatively small alpine city hosting fewer than 1 million winter visitors in a season. BOTA has partnerships with BMW and Rossignol, giving added leverage and media coverage for special regional initiatives, events and conferences. With a direct link to the GaPa Tourismus web pages (including online vacation planning portal) the BOTA website offers another entrance point for international visitors.

References

Agrawala, S. (2007) *Klimawandel in den Alpen – Anpassung des Wintertourismus und des Naturgefahrenmanagements*. OECD Publications, Paris. Available at: http://www.oecd.org/env/cc/38002265.pdf (accessed 30 September 2014).

ATTA (2013) *Adventure Tourism Market Study 2013*. Executive Summary. Adventure Travel Trade Association and the George Washington University, Washington, DC.

Beedie, P. (2008) Adventure tourism as a 'new frontier' in leisure. *World Leisure Journal* 50(3), 173–183.

BLSD (2014) *Regionalisierte Bevölkerungsvorausberechnung für Bayern bis 2032: Demographisches Profil für den Landkreis Garmisch-Partenkirchen*. Heft 546. Bayerisches Landesamt für Statistik und Datenverarbeitung, Munich, Germany.

BOTA (2014) Best of the Alps. Available at: www.bestofthealps.com (accessed 15 December 2014).

Buhalis, D. (2000) Marketing the competitive destination of the future. *Tourism Management* 21(1), 97–116.

Burakowski, E. and Magnusson, M. (2012) *Climate Impacts on the Winter Tourism Economy in the United States*. Natural Resources Defense Council, New York.

Chipeniuk, R. and Rapport, E. (2008) What is amenity migration and how can small mountain communities measure it? In: Moss, L.A.G., Glorioso, R.S. and Krause, A. (eds) *Understanding and Managing Amenity-led Migration in Mountain Regions*. Banff, Alberta, pp. 212–218.

Citizendium (2014) Garmisch-Partenkirchen. Available at: http://en.citizendium.org/wiki/Garmisch-Partenkirchen (accessed 5 December 2014).

CULTUS (2014) KULTurSOMMER Garmisch-Partenkirchen (21.8.–24.9.2014) Programmflyer. Cultus Production GmbH, Füssen, Deutschland. Available at: http://www.kultursommer-gapa.de/index.php (accessed 1 September 2014).

De Grave, A. (2014) Seasonal business diversification of ski resorts and the effects on forest management: Effects on trees and people due to a shift from winter only to year-round business of ski resorts in British Columbia. MSc thesis, University of British Columbia, Canada.

Dickson, T. and Huyton, J. (2008) Customer service, employee welfare and snow sports tourism in Australia. *International Journal of Contemporary Hospitality Management* 20, 199–214.

Dwyer, L., Edwards, D., Mistilis, N., Roman, C. and Scott, N. (2009) Destination and enterprise management for a tourism future. *Tourism Management* 30(1), 63–74.

Fablet, G. (2013) Real estate development in ski resorts of the Tarentaise Valley. Between cyclical variations and structural requirements. *Journal of Alpine Research/Revue de géographie alpine* (101–103).

Falk, M. (2014) Impact of weather conditions on tourism demand in the peak summer season over the last 50 years. *Tourism Management Perspectives* 9, 24–35.

Flognfeldt, T. and Tjørve, E. (2013) The shift from hotels and lodges to second-home villages in mountain-resort accommodation. *Scandinavian Journal of Hospitality and Tourism* 13(4), 332–352.

FSO (2009) Germany's Population by 2060: Results of the 12th Coordinated Population Projection. Federal Statistics Office. Statisitisches Bundesamt, Wiesbaden, Deutschland. Available at: https://www.destatis.de/EN/Publications/Specialized/Population/GermanyPopulation2060.pdf?__blob=publicationFile (accessed 30 November 2014).

GaPa (2014a) Garmisch-Partenkirchen: Facts and Numbers 2014. Garmisch-Partenkirchen Tourismus. Available at: http://www.gapa.de/download/2014_factsheet_engl.pdf (accessed 10 September 2014).

GaPa (2014b) The Perfect Alpine Holiday. Garmisch-Partenkirchen Tourismus. Available at: http://www.gapa.de/download/2014_the_perfect_alpine_holiday.pdf (accessed 30 August 2014).

GaPa (2014c) *6 Year Plan-GaPa Tourism: Updated as Tourism Business Plan 2012–2017 (1st update, April 2014)*. Garmisch-Partenkirchen Tourismus.

Gloersen, E., Bausch, T., Hurel, H., Pfefferkorn, W., del Fiore, F., *et al.* (2013) Strategy-development for the Alpine Space: Final Report. European Territorial Cooperation, Alpine Space Programme. Available at: http://www.alpine-space.org/2007-2013/fileadmin/media/Downloads_in_about_the_programme/SDP_Final_Report.pdf (accessed 11 January 2016).

Glover, P. and Prideaux, B. (2009) Implications of population ageing for the development of tourism products and destinations. *Journal of Vacation Marketing* 15(1), 25–37.

Godde, P.M., Price, M.F. and Zimmermann, F.M. (eds) (2000) *Tourism and Development in Mountain Regions*. CAB International, Wallingford, UK.

GPI Garmisch-Partenkirchen Info (n.d.) Geschichte. Available at: http://www.garmisch-partenkirchen-info.de/geschichte.php (accessed 30 August 2014).

Howie, F. (2003) *Managing the Tourist Destination*. Continuum, London.

Hudson, S. (2004) *Winter Sport Tourism in North America. Sport Tourism: Interrelationships, Impacts and Issues*. Channel View Publications, Clevedon, UK, pp. 77–100.

IHK (2014) *Strukturdaten des IHK-Gremiums Garmisch-Partenkirchen*. Industrie- und Handelskammer für München und Oberbayern, Munich, Germany.

Laws, E., Richins, H., Agrusa, J. and Scott, N. (2011) *Tourist Destination Governance: Practice, Theory and Issues*. CAB International, Wallingford, UK.

Lepp, A. and Gibson, H. (2008) Sensation seeking and tourism: Tourist role, perception of risk and destination choice. *Tourism Management* 29(4), 740–750.

Lohmann, M., Pechlaner, H., Smeral, E. and Wöber, K. (2014) *Österreich Tourismus vor Weichenstellung: Stagnation oder Wachstum? Bericht des Expertenbeirats 'Tourismusstrategie'*. Bundesministerium für Wissenschaft, Forschung und Wirtschaft, Vienna, Austria. Available at: https://www.bmwfw.gv.at/Tourismus/Documents/Bericht%20des%20Expertenbeirats_Endfassung-25.4.2014.pdf (accessed 5 September 2014).

Mayer, M. and Steiger, R. (2013) Skitourismus in den Bayerischen Alpen: Entwicklung und Zukunftsperspektiven. In: Job, H. and Mayer, M. (eds) *Tourismus und Regionalentwicklung in Bayern*. Akademie für Raumforschung und Landesplanung-ARL, Hannover, Germany, pp. 164–212.

McIntyre, N., Williams, D. and McHugh, K. (eds) (2006) *Multiple Dwelling and Tourism: Negotiating Place, Home and Identity*. CAB International, Wallingford, UK.

MGP Markt Garmisch-Partenkirchen (2003) Virtuellen Rathaus: Geschichte. Available at: http://buergerservice.gapa.de/de/cfb6d9ba-35bc-5ede-f43a-f6278651966b.html (accessed 30 August 2014).

Mill, R.C. (2007) *Resorts: Management and Operation*. John Wiley and Sons, New York.

Morrison, A.M. (2013) *Marketing and Managing Tourism Destinations*. Routledge, London.

Moss, L.A. (ed.) (2006) *The Amenity Migrants: Seeking and Sustaining Mountains and Their Cultures*. CAB International, Wallingford, UK.

Müller, D.K. (2005) Second home tourism in the Swedish mountain range. In: Hall, C.M. and Boyd, S.W. (eds) *Nature-Based Tourism in Peripheral Areas: Development or Disaster?* Channel View Publications, Clevedon, UK, pp. 133–148.

Murphy, P. (2009) *The Business of Resort Management*. Routledge, New York.

Nagel, P. and Ries, P. (2014) *Tourismusbericht für das Jahr 2013: Gästeankünfte und Übernachtungen Inlands- und Auslandszahlen*. Garmisch-Partenkirchen Tourismus, Garmisch-Partenkirchen, Germany.

Needham, M.D. and Rollins, R.B. (2005) Interest group standards for recreation and tourism impacts at ski areas in the summer. *Tourism Management* 26, 1–13.

Needham, M.D., Wood, C.J.B. and Rollins, R.B. (2004) Understanding summer visitors and their experiences at the Whistler Mountain Ski Area, Canada. *Mountain Research and Development* 24(3), 234–242.

Nepal, S.K. and Jamal, T.B. (2011) Resort-induced changes in small mountain communities in British Columbia, Canada. *Mountain Research and Development* 31(2), 89–101.

Neumann, A. and Harrer, B. (2013) *Wirtschaftsfaktor Tourismus in Garmisch-Partenkirchen 2012*. DWIF-Consulting GmbH, Munich, Germany.

Pegg, S., Patterson, I. and Gariddo, P.V. (2012) The impact of seasonality on tourism and hospitality operations in the Alpine region of New South Wales, Australia. *International Journal of Hospitality Management* 31(3), 659–666.

Roberts, C. (2011) Sport and Adventure Tourism. In: Robinson, P., Heitmann, S. and Dieke, P.U. (eds) *Research Themes for Tourism*. CAB International, Wallingford, UK, p. 146.

Scott, D. (2003) Climate change and tourism in the mountain regions of North America. In: *1st International Conference on Climate Change and Tourism*, Dierba, Tunisia, pp. 9–11.

Scott, D. and Becken, S. (2010) Adapting to climate change and climate policy: progress, problems and potentials. *Journal of Sustainable Tourism* 18(3), 283–295.

Sedgley, D., Pritchard, A. and Morgan, N. (2011) Tourism and ageing: a transformative research agenda. *Annals of Tourism Research*, 38(2), 422–436.

Ski Europe (2015) Best Alps Ski Resorts. Available at: http://www.ski-europe.com/best/wherebest.html (accessed 12 January 2015).

Skiresorts (2014) Ski Resorts: Bavarian Alps. Tourispo GmbH and Co. KG. Available at: https://www.snow-online.com/ski-resorts/bavarian-alps (accessed 11 January 2016).

Swarbrooke, J., Beard, C., Leckie, S. and Pomfret, G. (2003) *Adventure Tourism: The New Frontier*. Butterworth Heinemann, Oxford, UK.

Thomas, R.R.P. and Fredline, E. (2004) Mountain resorts in summer: defining the image. In: Hall, C.M. and Boyd, S.W. (eds) *Nature-Based Tourism in Peripheral Areas: Development or Disaster?* Channel View Publications, Clevedon, UK, pp. 75–90.

Ultimate Ski (2015) Ski the Best of the Alps. Available at: http://www.ultimate-ski.com/features/ski-destinations/best-of-the-alps.aspx (accessed 12 January 2015).

Unbehaun, W., Pröbstl, U. and Haider, W. (2008) Trends in winter sport tourism: challenges for the future. *Tourism Review* 63(1), 36–47.

VCI Via Claudia Info (n.d.) Via Claudia Augusta: European Axis of Culture. A Bit of History. Available at: http://www.viaclaudia.org/en/a-bit-of-history.html (accessed 30 August 2014).

Wang, Y. and Pizam, A. (eds) (2011) *Destination Marketing and Management: Theories and Applications*. CAB International, Wallingford, UK.

Werdenfels (2014) Werdenfels Castle. Available at: www.digplanet.com/wiki/Werdenfels_Castle (accessed 10 December 2014).

Whistler (2015) History. Available at: http://www.whistlerblackcomb.com/about-us/history.aspx (accessed 12 January 2015).

Williams, D.R. and Kaltenborn, B.P. (1999) Leisure places and modernity: The use and meaning of recreational cottages in Norway and the USA. In: Crouch, D. (ed.) *Leisure/Tourism Geographies. Practices and Geographical Knowledge*. Routledge, London, pp. 214–230.

Winter Olympics (2014) Garmisch-Partenkirchen 1936. Available at: www.olympic.org/garmisch-partenkirchen-1936-winter-olympics (accessed 12 December 2014).

Zeune, J. and Spichtinger, H. (2000) *Werdenfels Castle - Little Guide*. Garmisch-Partenkirchen, Germany.

Zugspitzland (2014) Karten. Tourismus-Service Zugspitzland. Available at: http://www.zugspitzland.de/karte.html (accessed 30 August 2014).

27 Tourism and Change in Nepal's Mt Everest Region

Sanjay K. Nepal*
University of Waterloo, Waterloo, Ontario, Canada

Introduction

Mountain regions around the world are one of the major hotspots for adventure tourism development. This is especially true in the Nepalese Himalaya; since the opening up of the country for the first time to the outside world in 1951 (the country had been closed to foreigners), international tourism has effectively positioned the Nepalese Himalaya as a premier mountain adventure destination (Nepal, 2003). Nepal has seen an unprecedented growth in mountaineering and trekking tourism over the last 10 years (Nepal, 2010).

A few classic Himalayan destinations, including the Annapurna and Everest regions in Nepal, continue to attract large numbers of adventure-seeking tourists. Even during the politically volatile period, international tourism in these two regions continued to thrive. As a result, remote mountain villages, such as Namche Bazaar in the Everest region, have transformed into cosmopolitan villages that cater primarily to international tourists (Nepal *et al.*, 2002). This chapter provides a brief account, and the implications of more recent developments in mountain tourism in the Everest region.

This author first travelled to the Everest region in 1996, for preliminary fieldwork related to his PhD thesis, which was quickly followed by two seasons of main fieldwork in 1997 documenting tourism development and associated environmental changes, and returning to the region in 2012, then again in 2014. During the intervening period, 1997 to 2012, dramatic developments had taken place, resulting in much more commercialized and organized tourism services and facility development. This chapter summarizes some of those changes to the built environment, and social cultural changes associated with tourism.

The Mt Everest Region

The Mt Everest region, known locally as Upper Khumbu, is part of the Sagarmatha National Park (SNP) located in north-eastern Nepal in the Solu-Khumbu District (see Fig. 27.1). The Park was designated a World Heritage Site in 1979. The world's highest mountain, Mt Everest (8850 m), also known to the Sherpa as *Chomolangma* and to the Nepalese as *Sagarmatha*, is no doubt the most well-known and ultimate destination for mountaineering and trekking.

The Mt Everest region witnessed exponential growth in tourism since the early 1960s,

---

* Corresponding author: snepal@uwaterloo.ca

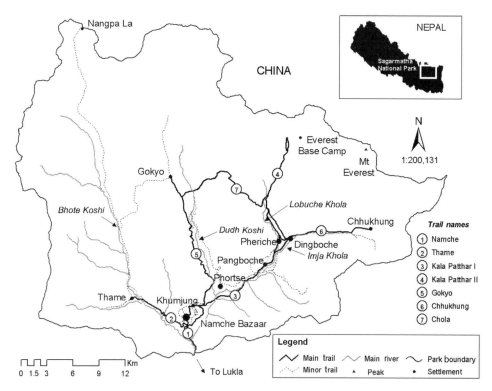

Fig. 27.1. Map of Mt Everest region showing main trekking trails and settlements (map courtesy of Sanjay Nepal, 2003, p. 36).

from around 20 visitors in 1964, the year when the Nepal government first allowed foreign visitors to make multi-day hiking tours in the region, to 18,200 during the 1997–1998 seasons. The escalating civil unrest throughout the country caused a major decline in tourism during 2001–2002 (Nepal, 2010). After 2003, however, the number of visitors to SNP rebounded in full force and has kept growing at a steady pace. In 2013, around 37,000 foreign trekkers visited the region. Most of the trekkers head to Tengboche monastery (3857 m) and further up to the Everest Base Camp (EBC, 5364 m), staying in lodges and teahouses operated by local Sherpa residents along the routes. Climbing expedition teams follow a similar route before arriving at EBC to prepare for the ascent to the summit of Mt Everest.

High-altitude climbing and trekking has been a significant component of the adventure tourism industry in the Mt Everest region, resulting in significant socio-economic and environmental implications. In general, tourists have greatly outnumbered the local Sherpa population since the late 1970s. More than four decades of intensive tourism development have had various positive influences, such as development of modern infrastructure, increases in household incomes and improved living conditions, international exposure and recognition of local culture, as well as cross-cultural exchanges (Stevens, 1993). However, negative influences, such as growing waste disposal problems, pressure on forests and biological systems, and deterioration of traditional values have also been witnessed in recent decades (Nepal *et al.*, 2002; Byers, 2005).

Tourism and Transformation in the Everest Region

2015 marks the 62nd anniversary of the successful British expedition to Mt Everest. Since 1966, when the first organized commercial trek to the Everest region commenced, tourism has remained the bread and butter of the Sherpa. The transformation of Khumbu to Everest did not occur overnight, but Hillary's and Norgay's scaling of the summit of Mt Everest in 1953 slowly but decidedly paved the way for its turn as one of the most famous adventure destinations in the world. Going by recent reports, some 37,000 foreign trekkers hike the trail to Everest Base Camp (EBC) every year, and more than 4000 mountaineers have successfully climbed Mt Everest since 1953 (Prasain, 2013). There are innumerable accounts of deaths and despair in Everest's harsh mountain environment (Ortner, 1999).

The Sherpa, a highland ethnic group, have become synonymous with mountain labourers, who with their charm, physical endurance and unflinching loyalty to their foreign guests, have epitomized the meaning of hospitality. Today, some 3000 Sherpa, during the two tourist seasons in spring and autumn, provide their services to trekkers and mountaineers from around the world. The Sherpa are aided by thousands of non-Sherpa porters and trekking staff. It should be pointed out that porters on the Everest trek today are almost all non-Sherpa, unlike before the early 1980s when most porters were Sherpa. This is testament to their successful transformation from porter to guide to entrepreneur to cultural icon.

As of May 2012, there were more than 300 lodges run by Sherpa in the Everest region. Ncell, a Nepalese telecommunications company, successfully built a satellite station at the EBC, making possible instant global transmission of mountaineering news, and allowing trekkers and mountaineers to 'stay connected' to the outside world. Restaurants along the trail serve lunch and snacks that are anything but local or traditional. Until the early 1990s, after dark, the streets of Namche Bazaar, the tourist hub of Everest, used to be dimly lit with the glow of kerosene lamps, solar lights and petromaxes emanating from the windows of tourist lodges. Today, Namche Bazaar and villages beyond it bask in a comfortable glow of electricity, the symbol of humankind's technological prowess. There are countless pubs and cafes – of the Internet variety too – and the main streets of Namche and Lukla are lined with offerings as diverse as one could find in a cosmopolitan city, including a local outlet of Sherpa Adventure

Gear, a high-end clothing company, owned by a Sherpa originally from Khumbu but now an American citizen based in Seattle.

Economic Changes

Growth in tourist numbers

The Mt Everest region has experienced more dramatic growth in tourist numbers since 2007. In 1997, fewer than 18,000 tourists had visited the area, but the number continued to rise until 2000 when it reached 25,251 (see Table 27.1). Due to government and political instability, the number of tourists declined by 15% in 2001 and a further 36% in 2002, before slowly rising in most of the following years. After peace was restored in 2006, tourist numbers increased significantly again and have been on a steady rise ever since. Between 2006 and 2012, tourist numbers increased by almost 82%. This has given a significant boost to guiding services; for example, it is estimated that there are more than 1800 trekking guides active in the region (Retzmann, 2013). That is a significant number compared to 1997 when there were fewer than 450 guides.

It is evident from Table 27.1 that trekking and mountaineering are seasonal activities. During the off-seasons, June to September, and December to January, many local residents turn their attention away from tourism to local affairs.

Growth in mountain lodges

Mountain lodges represent one of the most important tourist infrastructures in the region. A survey conducted in 1997 showed a total of 225 lodges, of which 25% were concentrated in the two major settlements of Namche Bazaar and Lukla (Nepal, 2003). By 2014, the total number of lodges had grown to 314. The number of tourist lodges in Namche Bazaar had increased from 32 in 1997 to 54 in 2014, an increase of 46%. In Lukla, the number of lodges had increased from 23 in 1997 to 44 in 2014, an increase of 91%. One consequence of this increase in lodges is the development of

Table 27.1. Growth in number of tourists to the Everest region between 1998 and 2012 (source: Sagarmatha National Park, Visitor Entrance Post, 2014, data collected May 2014).

Month	1998	1999	2000	2001	2002	2003	2004	2005	2006	2007	2008	2009	2010	2011	2012
January	553	594	474	579	235	427	592	426	486	566	643	576	721	619	694
February	708	781	876	682	496	518	751	524	455	592	852	658	923	923	1,041
March	1,863	2,255	2,883	2,540	1,995	1,802	2,696	2,343	1,977	3,029	3,688	3,041	3,676	3,318	3,931
April	2,784	3,440	4,238	3,834	2,313	2,759	3,914	2,458	3,433	4,246	4,661	4,513	5,112	6,651	6,657
May	1,108	1,408	1,259	1,313	692	1,624	1,301	937	886	1,679	1,986	1,629	2,134	2,395	2,611
June	142	115	61	145	90	221	127	201	110	284	297	298	431	434	473
July	94	153	39	114	78	77	160	204	184	209	294	229	349	241	263
August	195	315	145	203	126	252	183	260	352	434	450	509	421	403	439
September	1,103	1,521	1,196	1,160	877	1,253	976	1,036	1,190	1,458	2,135	2,135	2,301	2,374	2,588
October	5,987	7,263	7,537	6,440	3,530	5,470	6,390	6,242	6,595	7,750	9,260	8,831	9,407	10,392	10,367
November	3,964	4,533	4,862	3,479	2,488	3,714	3,208	3,448	3,329	4,188	4,830	4,769	5,056	4,968	5,415
December	1,513	2,183	1,681	1,081	866	1,183	1,098	984	1,039	1,379	1,503	1,596	1,593	1,853	2,020
Total	20,014	24,561	25,251	21,570	13,786	19,800	21,396	19,063	20,036	25,814	30,599	28,784	32,124	34,571	36,518

well-defined built-up areas. For example, Nepal *et al.* (2002) illustrates how the village of Namche Bazaar grew from its pre-tourism days, in 1955, to 1997. Research conducted subsequent to 1997 shows further expansion of Namche Bazaar (see Figs 27.2, 27.3, 27.4). In the past, most households simply converted their existing homes to tourist lodges, but since 1997 almost all lodges are new constructions. The vast majority of lodges are large in size, stone built, aesthetically pleasing in appearance, Sherpa-owned, and are quite different from the traditionally smaller Sherpa houses. The building costs of these lodges are prohibitively high, but thanks to the income from tourism, many Sherpa entrepreneurs seem to be able to afford them. An interesting development is the emergence of lodge chains owned by companies like Yeti Mountain Home, Asia Trekking, and Intrek, most of which are locally owned, but have foreign partners too.

Figures 27.2, 27.3 and 27.4 indicate a much more compact centre, and new dwellings extending towards the south-eastern part, or the lower-right section of the sketches. Apart

from the lodges, other types of tourism services have also come into existence. Today there are numerous souvenir shops (see Fig. 27.5), several adventure sports equipment stores, coffee shops and even Irish pubs (Nepal, 2015).

Tourism employment

Perhaps one of the most significant effects of mountain tourism in Everest is the number of tourism-related employment opportunities. Local residents can work as trekking and mountaineering guides, lodge entrepreneurs, shop owners, porters and kitchen staff. In addition to these direct employment opportunities, there is also other indirect employment; for example, carrying goods for merchants who sell their goods and wares to Sherpa entrepreneurs, working as household help and in various other capacities. It could be argued that income from tourism has enabled the locals to live and work in the region, in stark contrast to the rest of rural Nepal, where there has been an exodus of young people in search of better

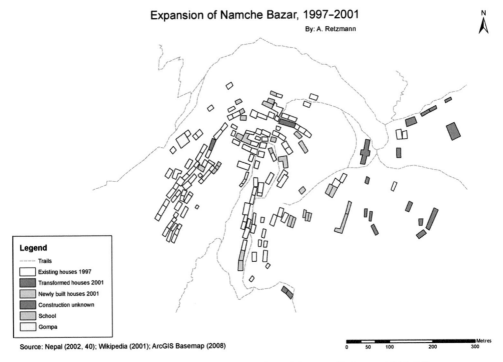

Fig. 27.2. Sketch of Namche Bazaar between 1997 and 2001 (source: Retzman, 2013, 24).

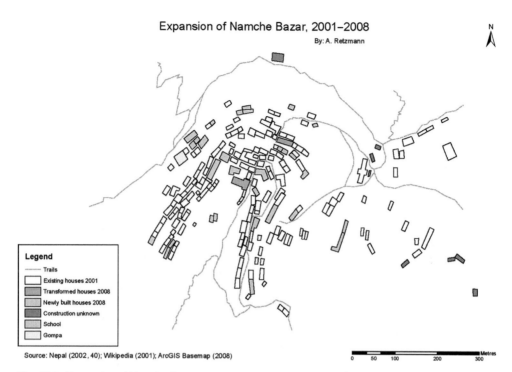

Fig. 27.3. Expansion of Namche Bazaar between 2001 and 2008 (source: Retzman, 2013, 25).

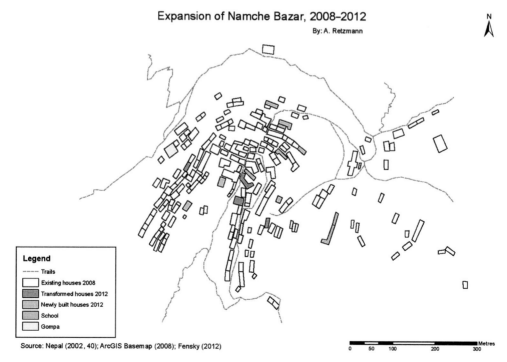

Fig. 27.4. Expansion of Namche Bazaar between 2008 and 2012 (source: Retzman, 2013, 27).

Fig. 27.5. Downtown Namche Bazaar, with its colourful shops, Irish pub and lodges (photograph courtesy of Sanjay Nepal, 2012).

prospects either in major cities in Nepal (mostly Kathmandu) or overseas (Middle East, Malaysia, South Korea, etc.). Earlier, it was noted that Everest tourism had a regional employment effect as it attracted people from many adjoining districts who came to the region looking for work (Nepal *et al.*, 2002).

The wealth accumulated by the Sherpa inhabitants has allowed them to look for more lucrative investment opportunities in tourism; for example, in luxury accommodation, airlines, trekking and mountaineering guide and outfitting businesses, while Sherpas from poorer households work as high-altitude porters. Today, it is difficult to find a local Sherpa resident working as a trekking porter; these jobs are now held by other highland ethnic groups such as Rai, Magar and Tamang. It is not uncommon to find many Rai men and women working as domestic helpers in Sherpa households.

Tourism has thus reversed the fortunes of highland ethnic groups: prior to the 1970s more prosperous households in the north-eastern highlands of Nepal belonged to the Rai and Magar ethnicities who occupied more favourable agricultural niches; today, it is the Sherpa who are much more prosperous than other ethnic highlanders. In 1997, a total of 777 people were employed in the lodging sector; today the number has risen to 1526 (Gehrig *et al.*, unpublished draft). While only 37 non-family female lodge employees were counted in 1997, today that number has risen to 367. Similarly, the number of non-family male employees increased from 173 in 1997 to 473 in 2011.

Social Changes

Perhaps the most noticeable social change in the Everest region is the increasing mobility of the resident Sherpa population. Many Sherpa entrepreneurs have multiple dwellings in the Everest region and in Kathmandu. Many also have friends and family overseas; for example, in the USA. It is common to find well-travelled local residents. Because of the increasing mobility of the Sherpa, particularly from villages like Namche Bazaar and Lukla, local food habits and tourist services are changing rapidly. The presence of fake Starbucks coffee shops in Lukla and additional hamburger joints offers the casual trekkers the familiarity of home, whether that is desirable or not. Similarly, Irish pubs and upmarket coffee houses are the latest trends made possible only because of international tourism. The global hybrid culture as represented by tourists has influenced how local residents think about the outside world and their place within it. For example, Pasang from Phakding states:

> At first I did not understand why all these tourists wanted to walk on foot for many days. I understood it much better when I visited my son and his family in New York. My son lives a very hectic life – the people in the subway, the hustle and bustle of life, the stress, the desire to succeed … when I saw this on the faces of people riding the subway I realized that the tourists who came to Khumbu were looking for something simpler, a slow pace in life. Here (in Phakding) life is less stressful … I stay here during tourist seasons and help in village affairs when I can. I live in Kathmandu when the tourist season is over.
>
> (Quoted in Nepal, 2015, p. 255)

While it may be tempting to conclude that international tourism has negatively impacted the social fabric and cultural values of host communities in the Everest region, recent research has indicated that the drivers of social and cultural changes are not just related to tourism but must be considered broadly in the context of globalization, of which tourism is a part (Nepal, 2015). Omnipresent electronic media and ease of access to information in remote locations have increased local residents' familiarity with the Western world, and have prepared them to respond to tourism accordingly. Sharp distinctions between traditional and modern, and local and cosmopolitan, are gradually disappearing. A local Sherpa may be tending to his yak herds in the morning, entertaining and interacting with tourists at his lodge during the day, communicating with his overseas friends and relatives in between household chores, and at night watching news on television of world events at distant locations.

The lived experiences of a Sherpa are thus rich and complex; as such, it is difficult to provide a deterministic account of the effects of tourism on Sherpa society. The Sherpa view themselves, just like anyone else, as steadily progressing and modernizing, while retaining essential elements of their community identity and cultural values. In a more recent study, this author has concluded that the Sherpa are very successful in negotiating between tradition and modernity, and that successful negotiation is largely due to a higher level of cultural competence gained through involvement in tourism (Nepal, 2015).

Environmental Changes

The rise in tourist numbers, construction of tourism-related facilities, and a higher level of commercialization of tourism services has resulted in several negative environmental changes. One of the most challenging is the accumulation of tourist-generated waste. The following statistics on waste collection demonstrate the severity of the problem. A report published by the Sagarmatha Pollution Control Committee (SPCC), a local NGO based in Namche Bazaar, indicates that between 2008 and 2011, SPCC disposed of 483 t of burnable and 75 t of non-burnable waste from the region (SPCC, 2011). During the same 3-year period, 53.7 t of burnable waste, 32 t of human waste and 9 t of kitchen waste were handed over by various mountaineering expedition teams to SPCC for proper disposal. In addition, 5561 empty EPI gas containers, 4297 empty oxygen cylinders, more than 15,000 batteries, 3.7 t of cans, and 1.8 t of empty glass bottles were sent to Kathmandu for recycling. The environmental stewardship shown by the SPCC is commendable, but it does not have the capacity to address what seems like an insurmountable problem. There are two small incinerators in Namche and Lukla, but their capacity to handle the locally generated waste is far too limited.

A more recent development in environmental clean-up and waste control has been the establishment of a waste management group in several villages. There are nine such groups in the villages, including Gokyo, Lobuche, Gorakshep, Somare, Dole, Thame, Thamo, Namche and Monjo. The groups are fully responsible for keeping their villages clean while SPPC concentrates its efforts on mountaineering-related waste removal. Another interesting development is the 2011 declaration of the Everest region as a plastic-free zone. This was achieved with grassroots activism shown by the *Sherwi Yondhen Tshokpa*, a local network of Sherpa students. Local awareness of environmental issues is rising in the region.

A positive development in many lodges is the decreasing reliance on firewood as the principal source of fuel energy. Nepal (2003) had estimated that tourism was responsible for 21% of fuelwood consumption in the region in 1997. There are no new estimates of fuelwood consumption. A recent study has suggested that kerosene is the dominant source of energy today (Gehrig *et al.*, unpublished draft). This is mainly due to the limited availability of fuelwood in the region rather than the desire to adopt kerosene, which is quite expensive, as it has to be carried all the way from Lukla after it is transported from Kathmandu by air. In villages between Lukla and Namche, fuelwood is still the dominant source of energy.

The main trekking trails within the Everest region today are maintained well, which was not the case in 1997, when this author completed an extensive trail damage assessment (Nepal, 2003). It was estimated that 10% of the almost 80 km of trail system in the region had been severely degraded in 1997. Today, the main trails from Lukla to Namche, and from Namche to Tengboche, have been widened, repaired and maintained well. Trails beyond Tengboche, especially those above 4000 m, are more degraded, due not only to increased human traffic, but also to the increasing practice of using horses to transport supplies to villages at upper elevation. The use of horses as packstock is also new, rarely observed before 1997.

Tourism and the Dynamics of Change

Globally, the Mt Everest region has evolved as a premier tourism destination, attracting both high-end as well as budget-conscious travellers. Following the footsteps of early explorers and travellers, the primary goal of many trekkers is to reach the Everest Base Camp and experience first-hand the grandeur and majesty of high mountains. Responding to global demand for adventure tourism, local Sherpas have built an impressive tourism infrastructure, supported by wide-ranging services and facilities. One of the major influences of this build-up of tourism infrastructure is the gradual urbanization of remote villages. If not for tourism, these villages would most likely have remained rural.

Physical transformation of the villages has lead to social transformation (e.g. it is rare to find a household in some of the major establishments that is not dependent on tourism). In other words, today an average Sherpa household spends more time engaging and interacting with tourists than in traditional village or community affairs; this is true at least during the two tourist seasons, spring and autumn. This engagement with tourism has afforded opportunities and mobilities which transcend geographical scales – globally, regionally and locally. Change is inevitable in any society, but the process of change has been greatly accelerated due to tourism. The primary influence of globalization and tourism is the emergence of a unique Sherpa identity as highly skilled mountain guides with global recognition. Whether this over-dependence on tourism is sustainable and healthy for households who rely on tourism for their material well-being is open to question.

Several related issues remain unexplored in the Everest region. For example, how trends in global warming and receding Himalayan glaciers will impact on future tourism remains to be seen. The economic and social adjustments necessary to cope with a warmer climate requires a critical assessment of other alternative opportunities besides tourism. Currently, such opportunities do not seem to exist. Sustainable mountain development requires a rethinking of opportunities beyond tourism. Similarly, the effects of modernization on tourists' expectations from Everest experience is uncertain.

The vast majority of international tourists expect an authentic mountain adventure experience in the region and many imagine it to be rugged, primitive and somewhat unspoiled by outside influence. Are these expectations real? What are the local Sherpa doing to ensure that these expectations are managed? Indeed, the Everest experience today is vastly different from the early days of tourism in the region, when ruggedness and primitivism were promoted as its main charms. While a trek to Everest Base Camp is still physically dangerous, psychologically challenging and emotionally draining, the Everest experience is a much more diluted affair than it used to be, thanks to the modern comforts and conveniences put together by the Sherpa, who seem to know more about the foreigners than the foreigners know about the Sherpa.

Overall, from the perspective of local Sherpa, tourism in the Mt Everest region has been a great economic success. The social and environmental challenges of tourism will not go away, but the Sherpa community is committed to addressing those problems, and in finding solutions that are culturally sensitive and locally appropriate. The five decades of tourism development have been a positive learning experience for the Sherpa community, and in finding their place in a modern and globalized world. The Sherpa have shown remarkable ability to adapt to changing local and global realities and will continue to do so in the decades to come.

References

Byers, A. (2005) Contemporary human impacts on alpine ecosystems in the Sagarmatha (Mt. Everest) National Park, Khumbu, Nepal. *Annals of the Association of American Geographers* 95(1), 112–140.

Gehrig, R., Nepal, S.K., Garrard, R., Sherpa, S.F. and Kohler, T. (unpublished draft) Community based tourism and lodge development in sagarmatha National Park, Nepal, 11 pp.

Nepal, S.K. (2003) *Tourism and the Environment – Perspectives from the Nepalese Himalaya*. Studien Verlag and Himal Books, Innsbruck and Kathmandu.

Nepal, S.K. (2010) Tourism and political change in Nepal. In: Butler, R. and Suntikul, W. (eds) *Tourism and Political Change*. Goodfellow Publishers, Oxford, UK, pp. 147–159.

Nepal, S.K. (2015) Irish pubs and dream cafes: tourism, tradition, and modernity in Nepal's Khumbu (Everest) region. *Tourism Recreation Research* 40(2), 248–261.

Nepal, S.K., Kohler, T. and Banzhaf, B.R. (2002) *Great Himalaya – Tourism and the Dynamics of Change in Nepal*. Swiss Foundation for Alpine Research, Berne, Switzerland.

Ortner, S. (1999) *Life and Death on Mt. Everest – Sherpas and Himalayan Mountaineering*. Oxford University Press, New Delhi, India.

Prasain, P. (2013) Making Records, Breaking Records. Available at: http://kathmandupost.ekantipur.com/printedition/news/2013-05-31/making-records-breaking-records.html (accessed 11 January 2016).

Retzmann, A. (2013) Together for tourism. Analysis of the trekking tourism development in Nepal. Bachelorarbeit im Studiengang Lehramt an Gymnasien, Eingereicht im Fach Geographie, University of Hamburg, Hamburg, Germany, 37 pp.

Sagarmatha Pollution Control Committee (SPCC) (2011) *Annual Progress Report*. SPCC, Namche Bazzar, Nepal.

Stevens, S.F. (1993) Tourism, change, and continuity in the Mount Everest Region, Nepal. *The Geographical Review* 83(4), 410–427.

28 Rural Tourism and Small Business Networks in Mountain Areas: Integrating Information Communication Technologies (ICT) and Community in Western Southland, New Zealand

Carolyn Deuchar* and Simon Milne
AUT University, Auckland, New Zealand

Introduction

Tourism offerings in mountain destinations are often diverse, fragmented and uncoordinated in terms of management, due to the wide variety of stakeholders involved (Strobl and Peters, 2013). This is compounded for small tourism enterprise (STE) owners/operators in rural areas where geographical isolation, distance from markets, and often limited transport and infrastructure impact on their ability to be competitive at a national and global level.

Western Southland is a rural destination located at the very south of New Zealand's South Island (see Fig. 28.1). Tucked between the towering peaks of Fiordland to the west, the Takitimu mountain range to the north, and the wild Southern Ocean, Western Southland boasts spectacular unspoilt scenery and coastline, lush rolling farmland, and is an area that is rich in Maori culture and early settler history. It is a lesser-known rural destination that, in terms of touristic activity, is considered 'well off the beaten track'.

Rural tourism in mountainous regions is often based in areas with very low population density, and this is particularly true in New Zealand (Albrecht, 2009; Bensemann and Hall, 2010). Main towns and settlements of Western Southland are: Riverton, Orepuki, Colac Bay, Tuatapere, Otautau, Ohai, Monowai/Lake Hauroko, Lorneville/Wallacetown, Nightcaps, Thornbury and Drummond with a combined population of approximately 3300 (Statistics New Zealand, 2013), spread over one of New Zealand's most sparsely populated land areas. Despite local attempts to engage with the visitor economy, these small communities do not feature to any significant extent in the plans of local government or the regional tourism organization (RTO) in terms of tourism development, management or marketing.

In this chapter we explore the drivers for local residents, community groups and tourism business operators/owners to engage with a community informatics project, designed to enhance collaboration between stakeholders and raise the profile of the small rural communities of Western Southland as a mountain tourism destination. We argue that information and communication technologies (ICT) offer

* Corresponding author: carolyn.deuchar@aut.ac.nz

© CAB International 2016. *Mountain Tourism: Experiences, Communities, Environments and Sustainable Futures* (eds H. Richins and J.S. Hull)

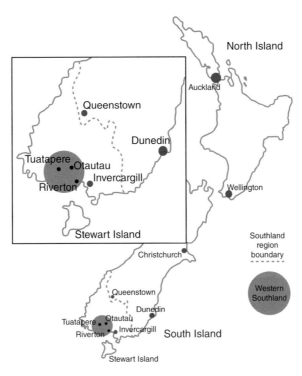

Fig. 28.1. Western Southland, New Zealand (from Clark, 2007).

significant opportunities to galvanize rural communities in mountain areas and so enhance community and STE cohesion and connectedness for destination development. Theoretically, this chapter draws on the bodies of knowledge associated with the use of ICT in tourism STE network development and adds to the literature via the use of a community informatics approach.

Tourism Networks, ICT and Community

Trends in tourism planning and management reflect the development of 'dense' networks of tourism enterprises as a contributing factor that propels the growth of tourism worldwide (Tzortzaki et al., 2006; Romeiro and Costa, 2010; Farsani et al., 2013). The opportunity to improve competitiveness, profitability and economic efficiencies are cited as key motivating factors for individual engagement in the majority of the literature concerning tourism SME

alliances, business partnerships and networks. Tourism planners commonly promote tourism enterprise collaboration as a way to develop high-end tourism products and experiences that appeal to high-spending, low-impact travellers (e.g. adventure or ecotourism products; Johnston, 2004). While the assumptions behind this approach to tourism planning may be sound, in practice regional coordination of tourism activities and network development among small tourism firms is largely at a nascent stage (Nordin, 2003; Braun, 2005).

Networking and inter-organizational learning are pivotal linkages for sustainable tourism development (STD), though relatively few studies discuss small business networks in the tourism sector (Pavlovich, 2001; Nordin, 2003; Braun, 2005), and even fewer are specifically related to tourism in peripheral areas (Hall, 2005; Aylward and Kelliher, 2009; Albrecht, 2010). This makes it difficult to judge the efficacy of regional initiatives to enhance the tourism experience through tourism STE collaboration and networks. Much of the extant literature associated with tourism networks and small firm collaboration in rural destinations also fails to embrace the important element of community.

STE often relies on personal connections embedded in geographic communities to share knowledge and experiences (Aylward and Kelliher, 2009; Beritelli, 2011). The concept of small firm embededdness is common in tourism network literature (Uzzi, 1996; Uzzi, 1997; Pavlovich and Kearins, 2004) where it is asserted that social factors affect business success. STE develops social relations and systems of connections in order to access knowledge, information and resources.

Murphy (1985) suggests community as a focal point for decision making, and presents an ecological model of tourism planning for local involvement in destination development. By adopting this approach, host communities guide processes for tourism development such as market segmentation and destination promotion, according to the types of tourism they wish to attract. Jamal and Getz (1995) similarly offer a set of theoretical constructs to strengthen the links between community and tourism planning with a focus on local collaboration and decision making. Milne *et al.* (2008, 662) highlight 'the role of locality and embedded cultural dimensions that need to be factored into government and/or community initiatives' to create sustainable collaborative outcomes and improved economic opportunity through rural tourism. The authors contend that a key factor in fostering 'dynamic and flexible STE, and communities that can effectively interact with the tourism sector', is collaboration and networking between enterprises and also between tourism businesses and the broader community.

The art of welcoming visitors as part of the 'community show' is reflected in Murphy's approach (1985, 169) to integrate the wishes, aspirations and traditions of local people into future tourism development. Several authors suggest that it is desirable to find ways and means to ensure that all sectors of community participate in tourism development (Butler and Hall, 1998; Murphy and Murphy, 2004; Hall, 2005; Ateljevic, 2009; Hamilton and Alexander, 2013). While this emphasis on community involvement appears sound in terms of STD,

there are often few opportunities for community to participate in tourism processes.

Globally, lesser-known rural destinations tend not to feature highly in central or local government tourism planning (Rosenfeld, 2002). In New Zealand, interest groups such as promotions associations and tourism groups often provide a grassroots collective effort to promote their 'place' as a great place to work, visit and live. However, other than the passion and energy of volunteers who may have a deep sense of community attachment, these groups and associations often have limited support and resources to develop and market their destination (Albrecht, 2009).

The 'adhesive' that bonds these associations is usually a deep sense of trust, reciprocity, loyalty and shared values and connections (social capital) which are usually familial and/or very locally based, perhaps limited to the geographical confines of a particular town or even neighbourhood (Albrecht, 2009). Social networks and the strong ties found in and between STE and community are useful in grassroots rural tourism development, but there is a risk of the associated social capital found in these networks not being optimized fully should they remain closed to 'others' (Braun, 2004; Novelli *et al.*, 2006). Closed social networks often lack the weak (external) ties that 'link networks within one community to the diverse resources that may be available in others' (Woolcock, 2001, 13).

In order to increase these ties, there is a need to find ways to tap into the social and economic aspirations of local communities and link STE and community interactions at a variety of scales – national, regional and local. It is vital to take into account the specificity (or uniqueness) of place, or the social, cultural, institutional, political and environmental dimensions of different places that add a level of complexity and richness to the context in which STE is embedded (George, 2010; Deuchar, 2012).

Lifestyle choices, aspirations and noneconomic motivations are important stimuli to rural tourism business formation (Hall, 2005; Ateljevic, 2009). These choices primarily relate to quality of life attributes such as the desire to live at a slower pace and focus on personal relationships and personal development, as well as an opportunity to showcase the local environment to those who visit (Goulding, et al., 2005).

Similarly, tourism in mountain and rural areas offers the visitor an opportunity to escape from busy urban lifestyles, slow down and enjoy a different pace of life. Nature-based activities and the experience of 'rurality' are increasingly attractive to travellers (George, 2010; Sharpley and Jepson, 2011) and the spiritual and emotional dimensions of the rural tourism experience offer the visitor an opportunity to establish a strong place attachment to those localities that resonate with their own past lived experiences, childhood memories, and culture and heritage (Sharpley and Jepson, 2011).

It could be said that this creates a 'match made in heaven' between the new 'moral' tourist (Butcher, 2003) who seeks a personally enriching encounter with the destination, and the lifestyle entrepreneur who has values-laden motivations for being in business that are not solely related to the accumulation of personal wealth (Shaw and Williams, 1994; Bensemann, 2009).

ICT can facilitate network development (Poon, 1993; Braun, 2004; Johnston, 2004; Braun, 2005). Tourism and technology go hand in hand as ICT enhances both the dissemination of information and the channels of communication between tourism consumers and suppliers. ICT, networks and relationships are critical factors that affect the visitor experience at the destination and have a 'significant influence on the regional distribution of economic advantage' (Braun, 2005, 3). The capacity of ICT to affect relationships, establish and build networks and communities (both virtual and real), and drive visionary business strategy development is the focus of considerable debate and discussion (Surman and Wershler-Henry 2001; Milne et al., 2004; Ali and Frew, 2010; Fotis, et al., 2011). ICT is the backbone of the tourism industry and a vital enabler of competitive improvements (Buhalis and Laws, 2001; Buhalis and O'Connor, 2006). These technologies offer STE the opportunity to get closer to the customer over a wider geographical area, improve operational effectiveness, provide the prospective tourist with quality of service and access to information, and assist with channels of communication and coordination (Braun, 2004; Ndou and Petti, 2007).

Community Informatics (CI) brings together the concepts of information technologies and information systems with the concept of community development (Wellman, 2001; 2002). CI offers a valuable avenue for community members to participate in tourism planning and development as it opens up technology-enabled channels of communication, enables digital storytelling, and facilitates information sharing (Gretzel et al., 2009). CI is the study of 'how ICT can help achieve a community's social, economic or cultural goals' (Gurstein, 2003, 3). CI is a relatively new area of research and practice that is concerned with the 'use of ICT for the personal, economic, cultural and social development of human communities' (Gretzel et al., 2009, 2). It is an approach that involves both grassroots movements and action research, and 'links economic and social development at the community level with emerging opportunities in such areas as electronic commerce, community and civic networks, electronic democracy, self-help, advocacy, and cultural enhancement' (Gurstein, 2007, 14). CI privileges people, information and communication ahead of the technology because it 'emphasises a grassroots perspective whereby community members are centrally involved in the application of ICT for community development' (Loader and Keeble, 2004, 4; Williamson, 2008; Gurstein, 2010).

Web-raising in Western Southland

The Western Southland web-raising programme is a rural tourism, small business and community development initiative that incorporates CI concepts. Milne et al. (2004, p. 185), draw on core themes of CI research and contend that they 'match closely with the linkage creation, stakeholder communication, and small business/community marketing that underpin the ability to enhance tourism's role in the development process'. Presenting a CI approach known as 'web-raising' (Milne and Mason, 2001), Mason and Milne (2002) contend that the process of bringing people together to 'talk tourism' and establish how they would like to be portrayed to the outside world has the potential to strengthen these relationships. Web-raising is thus defined as:

> The digital equivalent to a barn-raising – a community that works together to create a

collective asset. While it may take several forms, web-raising generally brings residents and local businesses together to share experience and skills and empower one another in the creation of web documents. While an effective and unique web-site is developed, the building process itself allows different groups to learn more about each other, in the same way that barn-raising helped to forge important notions of communal trust and reciprocity in the American West during the last century.

(Milne *et al.*, 2004, 186)

The first phase of this initiative was to develop the community-built website www.westernsouthland. co.nz. One of several aims of the site is to enhance the visitor experience and help visitors with planning a trip around the region. To do this, the site supports the visitor to gather more information both before they arrive and while they are there. This gives visitors more reason to stay longer and spend more money, thus raising the profile of the region as a visitor destination and building yield. It is also a community site for use by community members and diaspora. Phase 1 was the initial development of the website built using open source content management software that today houses 163 separate listings created and uploaded by STE owners/operators, other business owners/ operators, community organizations and individuals. The second phase was the Western Southland: Podzone Country project which equipped the community with the skills and equipment to create podcasts.

Tourism experiences in the region are highly diverse, with products ranging from trekking the Hump Ridge Track, time spent in a mountain holiday park, helicopter tours of mountain terrain, farm stays to boating and other outdoor adventures. The community-built website www.westernsouthland.co.nz creates a unique sense of place and communicates the passion of the locals for 'our place'. STE owners/ operators can create a page to advertise their business, free of charge. They can upload text and photos, and 'affiliate' with other businesses that they are happy to recommend or support. They can also link to a business or personal website, or other sites that they may have an association with.

The podcast project introduced, promoted and fostered skills in digital voice-recording,

editing and publishing. It also acted as an incentive for broadband uptake. The web-raised site www.westernsouthland.co.nz houses a series of 24 podcasts that were scripted, recorded, edited and uploaded by STE and locals who learnt the skills to do this through workshops, demonstrations and one-on-one training sessions. Podcast content ranges from local stories and history, through to family recipes, tips for visitors and commentary on native bird watching.

To present the main motivations for engaging with the web-raising programme, we draw on the findings of 25 semi-structured interviews with local STE owners/operators (many of whom would be classified as 'life stylers' – see Clark, 2007), key individuals and community leaders, members of community and residents, and representatives of local government and public agencies; as well as a project-evaluation focus group – all placed within a case study and informed by the literature.

Data collection follows a 4-year period of engagement with key individuals, research participants and others associated with the project. This enabled a comprehensive understanding of the tourism 'milieu' that surrounds STE owners/operators of this small mountainous sub-region. Open-ended interviewing techniques were used to explore and understand the attitudes, opinions, feelings and behaviour of individuals or groups of individuals towards 'working together' to promote the place where they lived. Interview questions were used to understand: the factors that motivated them to become involved, what value they found in doing so, and how they would describe the outcomes of the web-raising initiative. Each participant was interviewed in his or her own home or place of business, or at a location that suited them in one of the small towns of Western Southland. Each interview lasted between 1 and 3 hours.

Motivations for engaging with the web-raising programme

When asked what motivated them to engage with the web-raising and podcast project, informants expressed two common motivating factors. The first was to promote Western Southland as a great place to live, work and visit – and to provide better information for visitors. This was mostly driven by a desire to retain and regenerate population, and to craft a legacy for future generations (jobs for youth, retention of local knowledge, etc.). STE and community groups alike appreciated the ability to have a web presence that was free and part of a portal for the region. Informants also appreciated that the content was written totally by locals.

The second motivating factor was to capture the rich heritage information of the region. Informants were particularly interested in capturing the stories and history of the towns and settlements in Western Southland. This they did by working together to generate digital content for their website (podcasts, text, images). The schools and the school children were also active in offering support, strengthening the links between generations and between schools, community and business.

Research participants felt that there was a sense of urgency to do this as long-term residents (first and second generation of early pioneers) were getting older and passing away. There is a growing recognition that as long-term residents 'pass on', many of the local stories – especially those about early settler history – are dying out and need to be preserved. A local historian from Riverton comments:

> I think that history is our way forward in this region. Riverton is the oldest town – definitely in the South Island, perhaps the oldest town in all of NZ. So that history has to be recorded and put out there. It doesn't exist ... it's crazy not to have it, people are getting older ... they're dying.

Informants also considered the web-raising programme enabled them to engage with the visitor industry and be self-sufficient in doing so. An accommodation provider from Tuatapere comments:

> The podcast project is bringing the 'local feeling' out with the words and stories that belong to the area. Not just the picture or the text, but the spoken word. Western Southland has been neglected because of the high profile of Te Anau and Milford sound. We have to promote ourselves because there are people up there who consider we're not worth it ... so we have to use what we've got ... our stories, our history, our way of doing things. I met people who I knew are in the same game [in this instance, backpacker accommodation] over in [another town] and this allowed us to get together and think about the place we live and not just what business we were in ... Podcasting is another spanner in the toolkit to help us do this.

Due to the influx of new settlers, there was a desire to represent the community to newcomers, and to stay in touch with the diaspora. The web-raising programme provided a reason for various tourism stakeholders to get together, share ideas and work together on the logistical aspects of the projects. Therefore, these exchanges offered an opportunity to strengthen relationships among and between long-term residents of Western Southland as well as newcomers to the area, many of whom are tourism operators. The chair of a local promotions group was emphatic about the need to find a common interest to bring people together: 'We need to get people together, to find a way that they can work on something – where they have a common interest.'

Several informants commented that the web-raising programme brought much-needed energy, passion and direction to the promotions groups. These groups are made up of busy local farmers, STE owners/operators, residents, and interest groups who work both in tourism and elsewhere or who are heavily committed to a variety of community organizations. Informants also commented that through the workshops (where they were taught to create their own page for the site), they met people they didn't know before or caught up with acquaintances. For STE owners/operators, the workshops allowed them an opportunity to get together and discuss operational aspects of owning a tourism business or formally acknowledge their appreciation of another business by affiliating with them on their web page.

The 55 participants in the podcast workshops ranged from those who own and/or operate tourism businesses (18) or other businesses (8), and teachers and support staff from local schools (10), through to school children, members of community organizations and residents (19). Only four STE owners/operators created and uploaded podcasts to advertise their business. There was no parameter on the type of podcasts that could be developed. In fact, STE and other business owners were actively encouraged to advertise their own organizations in whatever way they wished. While uptake was high to create a listing on the website, few STE used the podcast training to create podcast advertisements to load on their web page. They were more interested in digitizing historical and heritage information for future generations or drawing attention to local landmarks, and this was their motivation to learn the ICT skills.

When community leaders put out a call in their communities to attend workshops or create a listing or podcast for the site, many people responded willingly. They gathered at schools, libraries, church halls, pubs and cafes and worked on podcast projects or shared tips on how to upload pictures to a page. Working together was simply considered the 'community spirited' thing to do and this was primarily because of what emerged as the main goal of the project in the eyes of research participants: to build a community resource of heritage information that was also useful to promote Western Southland as a destination. STE and residents were aware of the challenges they faced due to geographic isolation and there was an air of 'we're all in this together'. The workshops were also seen as a social activity. An interview participant (the leader of a community-based environmental group) comments:

> I think it becomes a living thing, a living active thing where locals have become involved in their own website. Being able to get together, have a meal or a drink and make podcast brings out the living 'funness' of it … recording podcasts at the Santa Parade, for example. Make sure you keep it fun and light. People have enough to do.

Informants were happy to be involved in project activities that related to logistics (booking venues, printing flyers, etc.). This reflected a desire to be able to participate in something that was good for their community but that was also short-term with a clear set of tasks and expectations attached to it. As long as the task was simple, clearly defined and achievable, then it was done. Logistics were in the comfort zone of many.

The community-built website www.westernsouthland.co.nz continues to offer a useful online resource for visitors and residents. The most recent request (August 2014) to be added to the site came from the new owner of a cafe in the very small settlement of Orepuki (population 92), and a new heritage trail was uploaded to the site in 2013. Attending workshops to learn how to create a page or a podcast for the site, or the opportunity to add a local business as an affiliate, meant that the website became not only an online presence for STE but also a useful point of collaboration; an opportunity to begin working together on a common interest, and a point of entry to the local tourism network.

Conclusions

STE owners/operators who engaged with the web-raising programme in Western Southland were not primarily motivated to do so because of the opportunity to promote their own businesses. Rather, they were driven by the desire to support community aspirations, i.e. economic and social development, at a very local level. The enterprise level benefits of forming networks and collaboration that are outlined in the literature (e.g. reduced costs and operational efficiencies, creating new services or experiences, knowledge transfer, marketing and distribution, and better access to resources) remain important, but they pale in comparison to the benefits that intensified STE relationships and linkages with community can offer both the firm and the destination.

This research highlights the need to change the way collaboration in rural/mountain areas is viewed by tourism planners and academic researchers. Collaboration works best when an enabling environment is created to encourage activities that are organic and originate from the grassroots level. Applied in this context, 'web-raising' offers an opportunity for residents and business owners/operators to work together as locals and engage in tourism processes. Using ICT to tap into the community interest and retain important cultural and heritage information through podcasting, offered a social activity that brought residents and businesses together in workshops and community meetings to learn about tourism and the internet, thus creating valuable human and social capital.

In simple terms, STE and community networks in rural/mountain destinations are best thought of in terms of systems of connection – or even local social movements as agents of social and economic change through community-led tourism development (Deuchar, 2012; McGehee *et al.*, 2014). This study shows that ICT can be used to foster collaboration among the 'lifestyle STE' and community found in mountain regions by simply tapping into what they – as locals – love about 'our place'.

References

Albrecht, J.N. (2009) The implementation of tourism strategies: a critical analysis of two New Zealand case studies. Unpublished PhD thesis. University of Otago, Dunedin, New Zealand.

Albrecht, J.N. (2010) Challenges in tourism strategy implementation in peripheral destinations – the case of Stewart Island, New Zealand. *Tourism and Hospitality Planning and Development* 7(2), 91–110.

Ali, A. and Frew, J.A. (2010) ICT and its role in sustainable tourism development. In: Gretzel, U., Law, R. and Fuchs, M. (eds) *Information and Communication Technologies in Tourism 2010. Proceedings of the International Conference in Lugano, Switzerland, 10–12 February 2010.* Springer, New York, pp. 479–491.

Ateljevic, J. (2009) Tourism entrepreneurship and regional development: example from New Zealand. *International Journal of Entrepreneurial Behaviour and Research* 15(3), 282–308.

Aylward, E. and Kelliher, F. (2009) Rural tourism development: proposing an integrated model of rural stakeholder network relationships. Paper presented at the *IAM Conference*, 2–4 September 2009, Galway Mayo Institute of Technology. Available at: http://repository.wit.ie/1393/ (accessed on 3 March 2013).

Bensemann, J. (2009) Copreneurship in rural tourism: exploring women's experiences. Unpublished doctoral dissertation. University of Canterbury, Christchurch, New Zealand.

Bensemann, J. and Hall, C.M. (2010) Copreneurship in rural tourism: exploring women's experiences. *International Journal of Gender and Entrepreneurship* 2(3), 228–244.

Beritelli, P. (2011) Cooperation among prominent actors in a tourist destination. *Annals of Tourism Research* 38(April), 607–629.

Braun, P. (2004) Regional tourism networks: the nexus between ICT diffusion and change in Australia. *Information Technology and Tourism* 6(4), 231–243.

Braun, P. (2005) Creating value to tourism products through tourism networks and clusters: uncovering destination value chains. Paper presented at the *OECD Conference on Global Tourism Growth: A Challenge for SMEs*, 6–7 September 2005, Korea.

Buhalis, D. and Laws, E. (2001) *Tourism Distribution Channels.* Continuum, London.

Buhalis, D. and O'Connor, P. (2006) Information communication technology – revolutionizing tourism. In: Buhalis, D. and Costa, C. (eds) *Tourism Management Dynamics: Trends, Management, Tools.* Elsevier Ltd, Oxford, UK, pp. 196–209.

Butcher, J. (2003) *The Moralisation of Tourism: Sun, Sand and Saving the World?* Routledge, London.

Butler, R. and Hall, C.M. (1998) Conclusion. In: Butler, R., Hall, C.M. and Jenkins, J. (eds) *Tourism and Recreation in Rural Areas.* John Wiley, Chichester, UK, pp. 249–258.

Clark, V. (2007) National strategies local realities: Small tourism businesses in Western Southland. Master's thesis. AUT University, Auckland.

Deuchar, C. (2012) Small tourism enterprise network formation in rural destinations: integrating ICT and community in Western Southland New Zealand. Unpublished doctoral dissertation. Auckland University of Technology, Auckland, New Zealand.

Farsani, N., Coelho, C. and Costa, C. (2013) Rural geotourism: a new tourism product. *Acta Geoturistica* (4)2, 1–10.

Fotis, J., Buhalis, D. and Rossides, N. (2011) Social media impact on holiday travel planning: the case of the Russian and the FSU markets. *International Journal of Online Marketing* 1(4), 1–19.

George, E.W. (2010) Intangible cultural heritage, ownership, copyrights, and tourism. *International Journal of Culture, Tourism and Hospitality Research* 4(4), 376–388.

Goulding, P., Baum, T.G. and Morrison, A. (2005) Seasonal trading and lifestyle motivation: experiences of small tourism businesses in Scotland. *Journal of Quality Assurance in Hospitality and Tourism* 5(2–4), 209–238.

Gretzel, U., Go, H., Lee, K. and Jamal, T. (2009) Role of community informatics in heritage tourism development. In: Höpken, W., Gretzel, U. and Law, R. (eds) *Information and Communication Technologies in Tourism (ENTER 2009)*. Springer, Amsterdam, Netherlands, pp. 1–11.

Gurstein, M. (2003) Effective use: a community informatics strategy beyond the Digital Divide. *First Monday* (8)12. Available at: http://firstmonday.org/htbin/cgiwrap/bin/ojs/index.php/fm/article/view/1107/1027 (accessed 16 August 2011).

Gurstein, M. (2007) *What is Community Informatics (and Why Does it Matter)?* Polimetrica, Rome, Italy.

Gurstein, M. (2010) Community Informatics and Community Development: CI Gave a Party and CD Didn't Come, CD Gives a Party and They Didn't Invite CI – What is Going on? Available at: http://gurstein.wordpress.com/2010/02/28/community-informatics-and-community-development-ci-gave-a-party-and-cd-didn%E2%80%99t-come-cd-gives-a-party-and-they-didn%E2%80%99t-invite-ci%E2%80%94what-is-going-on (accessed 18 June 2010).

Hall, C.M. (2005) Rural wine and food tourism cluster network development. In: Hall, D., Kirkpatrick, I. and Mitchell, M. (eds) *Rural Tourism and Sustainable Business*. Channel View, Clevedon, UK, pp. 149–164.

Hamilton, K. and Alexander, M. (2013) Organic community tourism: a cocreated approach. *Annals of Tourism Research* 42(July), 169–190.

Jamal, T. and Getz, D. (1995) Collaboration theory and community tourism planning. *Annals of Tourism Research* 22(1), 186–204.

Johnston, R. (2004) Clusters: a review of their basis and development in Australia. *Innovation, Management Policy* 6(3), 380–391.

Loader, B. and Keeble, L. (2004) *Challenging the Digital Divide: A Literature Review of Community Informatics Initiatives*. Joseph Rowntree Foundation, York, UK.

Mason, D. and Milne, S. (2002) E-Commerce and community tourism. In: Palvia, P., Palvia, S. and Roche, E. (eds) *Global Information Technology and Electronic Commerce: Issues for the New Millennium*. Ivy League Publishing, Atlanta, Georgia, pp. 294–310.

McGehee, N., Kline, C. and Knollenberg, K (2014) Social movements and tourism-related local action. *Annals of Tourism Research* 48(September), 140–155.

Milne, S. and Mason, D. (2001) Tourism, web-raising and community development. In: Sheldon, P., Wober, K. and Fesenmaier, D. (eds) *Information and Communication Technologies in Tourism (ENTER 2001)*. Springer, New York, pp. 283–293.

Milne, S., Mason, D. and Hasse, J. (2004) Tourism, information technology and development: revolution or reinforcement? In: Hall, M., Lew, A. and Williams, A. (eds) *A Companion to Tourism Geography*. Blackwell, London, pp. 184–195.

Milne, S., Clark, V., Speidel, U., Nodder, C. and Dobbin, N. (2008) Information technology and tourism enterprise collaboration: cases from rural New Zealand. In: Salmon, J. and Wilson, L. (eds) *Handbook of Research on Electronic Collaboration and Organizational Synergy*. IGI Publishing, Hershey, Pennsylvania, pp. 651–663.

Murphy, P.E. (1985) *Tourism: A Community Approach*. Methuen, New York.

Murphy, P.E. and Murphy, A.E. (2004) *Strategic Management for Tourism Communities: Bridging the Gaps*. Channel View Publications, Clevedon, UK.

Ndou, V. and Petti, C. (2007) DMS business models design and destination configurations: choices and implementation issues. *Information Technology and Tourism* 9(1), 3–14.

Nordin, S. (2003) Tourism Clustering and Innovation: Paths to Economic Growth and Development. European Tourism Research Institute (ETOUR) (2003)14. Available at: http://www.rmportal.net/library/content/nric/2507.pdf (accessed 16 August 2014).

Novelli, M., Schmitz, B. and Spencer, T. (2006) Networks, clusters and innovation in tourism: a UK experience. *Tourism Management* 27(6), 1141–1152.

Pavlovich, K. (2001) The twin landscapes of Waitomo: Tourism network and sustainability through the Landcare Group. *Journal of Sustainable Tourism* 9, 491–504.

Pavlovich, K. and Kearins, K. (2004) Structural embeddedness and community-building through collaborative network relationships. *M@n@gement* 7(3), 195–214.

Poon, A. (1993) *Tourism, Technology and Competitive Strategies*. CAB International, Wallingford, UK.

Romeiro P. and Costa C. (2010) The potential of management networks in the innovation and competitiveness of rural tourism: a case study on the Valle del Jerte (Spain). *Current Issues in Tourism* 13(1), 75–91.

Rosenfeld, S. (2002) Creating smart systems: A guide to cluster strategies in less favoured regions. European Union-Regional Innovation Strategies. Available at: http://ec.europa.eu/regional_policy/archive/innovation/pdf/guide_rosenfeld_final.pdf (accessed 18 January 2010).

Sharpley, R. and Jepson, D. (2011) Rural tourism: a spiritual experience? *Annals of Tourism Research* 38(1), 52–71.

Shaw, G. and Williams, A. (1994) *Critical Issues in Tourism: A Geographical Perspective*. Blackwell, Oxford, UK.

Statistics New Zealand (2013) 2013 Census QuickStats About a Place. Available at: http://www.stats.govt. nz/Census/2013-census/profile-and-summary-reports/quickstats-about-a-place.aspx?request_value= 15132&tabname=Populationanddwellings (accessed 3 January 2015).

Strobl, E. and Peters, M. (2013) Entrepreneurial reputation in destination networks. *Annals of Tourism Research.* 40(January), 59–82.

Surman, M. and Wershler-Henry, D. (2001) *Commonspace: Beyond Virtual Community*. Financial Times/ Pearson, London.

Tzortzaki, A., Voulgaris, F. and Agiomirgianakis, G. (2006) Experience-based tourism: the new competitive strategy for the long term survival for the tourism industry. Available at: https://www.researchgate.net/ publication/253881373_Experience-based_Tourism_The_New_Competitive_Strategy_for_the_Long_ Term_Survival_of_the_Tourist_Industry (accessed 11 December 2015).

Uzzi, B. (1996) The sources and consequences of embeddedness for the economic performance of organizations: the network effect. *American Sociological Review* 61(4), 674–98.

Uzzi, B. (1997) Social structure and competition in interfirm networks: the paradox of embeddedness. *Administrative Science Quarterly* 42(1), 35–67.

Wellman, B. (2001) The persistence and transformation of community: from neighbourhood groups to social networks. Report to the Law Commission of Canada. Available at: http://groups.chass.utoronto.ca/netlab/ wp-content/uploads/2012/05/The-Persistence-and-Transformation-of-Community-From-Neighbourhood-Groups-to-Social-Networks1.pdf (accessed 10 December 2015).

Wellman, B. (2002) Little boxes, glocalization, and networked individualism. In: Tanabe, M., Van den Besselar, P. and Ishida, T. (eds) *Digital Cities II. Computational and Sociological Approaches* (Second Kyoto Workshop on Digital Cities, Kyoto, Japan, October 18–20, 2001). Springer, London, pp. 10–25.

Williamson, A. (2008). A model for emergent citizen-focussed local electronic democracy. Unpublished PhD thesis. Monash University, Victoria, Australia.

Woolcock, M. (2001) The place of social capital in understanding social and economic outcomes. *Isuma Canadian Journal of Policy Research* 2(1), 11–17.

29 Development, Planning And Governance In Mountain Tourism: Overview, Contextual Development and Areas of Focus

John S. Hull* and Harold Richins
Thompson Rivers University, Kamloops, British Columbia, Canada

Introduction

This chapter provides an introduction to Part VI with a focus on development, planning and governance in mountain tourism through an exploration of associated literature and a summary of this section's chapters. Through this introductory summary it is understood that even though mountain tourism is an attractive and alternative livelihood, there are challenges to sustainable development. Development, planning and governance of mountain tourism are increasingly varied and complex across the globe, relying on collective efforts of public, private and non-government stakeholders.

Introduction to Literature on Development, Planning and Governance in Mountain Tourism

Mountain tourism as an attractive and alternative livelihood

Development of tourism in mountain regions has been recognized as one of the most promising alternative livelihood strategies for rural and remote areas (Kruk, 2010). Mountain regions are attractive to tourists for their pristine natural features, high natural/cultural diversity, wilderness characteristics and spectacular scenery (see Figs 29.1–29.3). These and other relevant factors have contributed to making mountain regions the second most popular tourism destinations globally (Mieczkowski, 1995; Nepal, 2002, 106). The overall value of the international mountain tourism market is estimated at US$140–188 billion per year, employing between 25 and 47 million people worldwide (Kruk, 2010).

The market for mountain tourism is nowhere near saturation point. The growth of tourism is regarded as an ongoing and given norm (Lane, 2009, 42). As the demand for trekking, hiking, camping, mountaineering, rock climbing, mountain biking, wildlife viewing, skiing and other forms of non-consumptive mountain activities increases, there is a need for mountain tourism to provide an avenue for transforming development constraints of the region into economic opportunities and assets through sustainable development (Nepal, 2003; Kruk *et al.*, 2007; Kruk, 2010).

---

* Corresponding author: jhull@tru.ca

Fig. 29.1. Mountain community of Steeg im Lechtal, Tirol, Austria; part of the Protected Area Tiroler Lech Nature Park (photograph courtesy of Harold Richins).

Challenges to sustainable mountain tourism

There are key challenges to sustainable development in mountain regions that include: (i) managing the exponential growth of visitation; (ii) adapting to the impacts of climate change; and (iii) addressing the health, safety and security of travellers (Kruk *et al.*, 2007). For developed regions (Nepal, 2002; Nepal and Jamal, 2011; Pavelka and Draper, 2015) additional concerns include: monitoring the growth associated with amenity migration from resorts, second-home and non-permanent populations; mitigating environmental changes occurring in and around communities from development pressure; and minimizing economic leakage due to shortages of local skills and labour. In developing countries, mountain development is faced with: high local population growth rates and rampant poverty; inaccessibility; underdevelopment and a subsistence way of life; high levels of stress on fragile natural resources; and highly skewed distribution of wealth and property (Nepal, 2002; Hall, 2007; Zhao and Ritchie, 2007).

As a result of these challenges, mountain tourism has been identified globally as an important component of sustainable mountain development and conservation (UNDESA, 1992). Since the 1992 UN Conference on Environment and Development, the need to address mountain concerns and the contribution that tourism can make to mountain communities has been recognized (Kruk *et al.*, 2007). Development strategies have focused on principles of sustainability – environmentally, to make optimal use of environmental resources by maintaining ecological processes and conserving natural resources and biodiversity; socioculturally, on respecting the authenticity of host communities, their tangible (built) and intangible (stories, traditions, values) heritage; and economically, on ensuring viable, long-term economic benefits that are fairly distributed, contributing to poverty alleviation (Edgell, *et al.*, 2008; Kruk, 2010).

Fig. 29.2. Mountain community tourism in Laos through Green Discovery Adventure and Eco Tours (photograph courtesy of Harold Richins).

Relationship between tourism and mountain development

The relationship between tourism and mountain development has featured prominently in a number of international global development strategies. As part of Agenda 21, mountain development has focused on encouragement and reinforcement of holistic management strategies, identification of multi-stakeholder roles, and multi-level approaches as cornerstones of successful tourism. Over the last decade, the Pro-Poor Tourism Partnership and the Millennium Development Goals have also emphasized the eradication of poverty and equitable development as a key global concern, which has featured in the mountain tourism agenda as part of pro-poor tourism strategies (Hall, 2007; Zhao and Ritchie, 2007; Kruk, 2010). Sustainable mountain tourism can be a promising vehicle for economic development and poverty reduction, unlocking opportunities for local economic diversification in poor and marginalized rural areas that lack significant development opportunities (Ashley and Haysom, 2004; UNWTO, 2004; Nepal, 2005; SNV, 2009; Kruk, 2010). At present, researchers argue that there is not a coherent approach to examining mountain-related tourism development issues (Nepal and Chipeniuk, 2005).

There is a need for integrated planning strategies and good governance to anticipate and regulate change in the tourism system to increase benefits if tourism is to deliver its promise of mountain development, economic prosperity, community development and conservation (Murphy, 1985; Kruk, 2010; Hull, 2012). In tourism, governance lies between government

Fig. 29.3. Top of Whistler Ski Resort, British Columbia, Canada (photograph courtesy of Harold Richins).

and management (Pechlaner *et al.*, 2012). Hultman and Hall (2012) distinguish between four types of governance structures in the literature that can be useful in considering strategies for planning and development in mountain regions: hierarchies, markets, networks and communities. These categories are based on the relationship between state/public authority on one hand, and stakeholder autonomy on the other. Hierarchical structures show the highest degree of state or public intervention; market governance the least. Network and community governance structures signal different modes of public–private partnerships and community demonstrates the highest degree of participation in destination development (Hall, 2011; Hultman and Hall, 2012).

Governance structures in mountain tourism

Governance structures in mountain regions vary across the globe, from continent to country to community. There are emerging cases of destination organisations and their stakeholders adopting comprehensive and consensus-based strategies designed to achieve greater levels of sustainability built on the collective efforts of public, private and non-government stakeholders (SNV, 2004; Nepal and Chipeniuk, 2005; Beritelli *et al.*, 2007; Kruk *et al.*, 2007; Murphy, 2008; Williams and Ponsford, 2009; Laws *et al.*, 2011). For mountain regions, the development process increasingly involves formal connections, collaboration, knowledge and trust, making that support the formation and evolution of networks (Richins, 1999; Murphy and Murphy, 2004; Beritelli *et al.*, 2007). Researchers argue that destination economies emerge as a result of network formations and stakeholder negotiation processes initiated by economic restructuring and policy implementation (Milne and Ateljevic, 2001; Hultman and Hall, 2012). Future sustainable development must therefore emphasize cooperation and collaboration as part of a bottom-up process, from the local to the regional and national levels that supports an integrated vision and strategies that are relevant in a mountain context (Kruk, 2010). Researchers argue (Gibson *et al.*, 2005; Del Matto and Scott, 2009), that sustainable tourism futures for mountain regions must consider: socio-ecological system integrity; livelihood sufficiency and opportunity; intragenerational equity; intergenerational equity; resource maintenance and efficiency; socio-ecological civility and democratic governance; precaution and adaptation; and immediate and long-term integration.

Summary of Chapters in Part VI: Development, Planning and Governance in Mountain Tourism

This introduction and the chapters following in Part VI provide a diversity of examples related to the direct and indirect influences on achieving effective development, planning and governance of tourism in mountain communities. This summary of Chapters 30 to 35 reveals the diversity of scholarship in this topical area, including cross-border governance in mountain areas, migration strategies to mountain regions, international snow sports destination planning, development and governance in family-focused destinations, national park administration, and spa and wellness strategic directions within mountain tourism settings.

Chapter 30. Protected Areas in the Alps: Governance and Contributions to Regional Development

Authors: Michael Volgger, Lena-Marie Lun and Harald Pechlaner

Given the difficulty of access, mountain areas have been less susceptible to development. Numerous large expanses of mountainous regions have remained relatively protected through various regional and national means. These mountain assets, which have often served as the basis for the initiation of regulations for protected areas in mountain regions, contribute to the enhancement of regional community development. Effective outcomes are dependent, to a large degree, upon effective governance practices. This chapter looks at effective governance practices as they relate to protected area management.

Volgger, Lun and Pechlaner explore this topic through the study of protected area management in alpine regions within Austria and Northern Italy.

The authors build concepts of protected areas and how tourism plays an important part in enhancing mountain regions. In addition, protected areas are reviewed based on their contribution to regional development in mountain areas. Protected mountain area governance within the regions of Bolzano-South Tyrol (Italy) and the Federal Province of Tyrol (Austria) is included and diverse approaches to governance in natural parks in these important mountain tourism regions of the Alps is compared. The exploratory findings from the research suggest that the success of mountain tourism management in protected areas is somewhat dependent on the particular approach taken toward protected area governance.

Chapter 31. Setting the Table for Mountain Tourism: The Case of a South African National Park

Authors: Linda-Louise Geldenhuys, Peet van der Merwe and Melville Saayman

Mountains, as attractions near urban areas, are also important areas for tourism research. The authors provide a developmental and historical understanding of Table Mountain, an important South African icon. They acknowledge mountain tourism destinations as important, and explore the unique attributes of the Table Mountain National Park, which is part of the Cape Floristic Region, a UNESCO World Heritage site, and one of the New7Wonders of Nature.

This case builds the historical progression of this mountain icon, from when it first developed as a tourist destination in the early 1900s to the present day. Table Mountain Aerial Cableway was one of the earliest cableways to be utilized for tourism, having been built just a little over a decade after the first tourist tramway at Bolzano, which was at that time located in Tyrolian Austria in 1913.

The chapter authors further elaborate on the mountains as prominent assets for tourism visitation and provide a profile of visitors to Table Mountain National Park, locally, regionally and internationally. They discuss the diversity of park visitor travel motivations and the historic and current importance of the attraction in distinguishing the Cape region of South Africa.

Chapter 32. Governance of French Ski Resorts: Will the Historic Economic Development Model Work for the Future?

Authors: Emmanuelle George-Marcelpoil and Hugues François

Sustainability has increasingly become a mainstream topic of concern regarding future longevity and viability of mountain tourism. Like other regional areas where mountains play an important part in tourism, planners in the mountainous areas of France have prioritized building and maintaining mountain tourism experiences for participants, which, in turn, sustains the enterprises and organizations that provide employment and other social and economic benefits to regional areas.

The chapter authors explore the concerns in mountainous France, other European communities, and in other mountainous locales address a number of crucial issues including: (i) future challenges of climate change and warming trends in some areas; (ii) societal issues based on changing population demographics; (iii) information communications and technology shifts; (iv) innovations and challenges to the effectiveness of traditional methods of promotion and marketing; and (v) viable habitability of communities affected by property values in mountain tourism destinations. These concerns, if not addressed, may have far-reaching impacts on the future success of both larger as well as smaller communities dependent on economic and social outcomes driven by mountain tourism.

Relatively recently, there have been growing concerns about the current model of economic and social development that has dominated the past seven or eight decades, upon which the winter mountain tourism sector has been based. The authors of this chapter discuss this and other issues, and acknowledge the disjointed nature of mountain tourism destinations in France. They point out the importance

of an approach that brings discussion and increased cooperation between operators and municipalities through a 'SCOT', which, in English, refers to a regional planning cohesive scheme.

Chapter 33. The Development and Design of Ski Resorts: From Theory to Practice

Authors: Simon Hudson and Louise Hudson

Resort development in mountain regions has seen an unprecedented maturity since 1936, when Sun Valley, Idaho, became what is considered by most to be the first purpose-built ski resort in the USA. The ski industry has matured from small, family-owned and local clubs determining ways to move people up to the top of a small hill, to investments in the development of all-season multi-billion-dollar summer and winter resort towns. All-season resorts are complex systems, involving small and large businesses, full-size community amenities, transportation systems, a variety of permanent and short-stay accommodations, sophisticated and integrated architecture, and engineering designed village spaces and infrastructure. This involves extensive mountain planning and development processes.

This chapter provides an historic context regarding resort development and explores the design and planning process for ski resorts in mountain destinations throughout the world. Important phases in designing these resorts are discussed, including approval processes, site feasibility, design guidelines, and styles of resort and village development. Utilizing the case study of one of the world's most prominent mountain resort designers, authors Simon Hudson and Louise Hudson provide an overview of the development and design process regarding mountain resorts, based on a case study of Ecosign. Located in Whistler, British Columbia, Ecosign is responsible for the development of more than 400 summer and winter mountain resort projects worldwide. A particular focus on the company's founder and visionary leader, Paul Mathews, is included, highlighting his significant contributions to the mountain resort industry.

Chapter 34. Non-government Organizations' Mountain Management: A Sustainable Support Model for Southern Oregon's Mountain Destinations

Authors: Byron Marlowe and Alison Burke

Sensitive mountain regions present unique concerns for stewardship, conservation and protection. These areas are often located in relatively remote regions with low population densities, and this creates challenges in building the necessary grassroots support to build effective practices in establishing successful management approaches. In this chapter, Byron Marlowe and Alison Burke describe a range of non-government organizations (NGOs) and their work in supporting and championing important natural attractions in mountain destinations in Southern Oregon. Three examples, Crater Lake National Park, Mt Ashland and Oregon Caves National Monument, are discussed. Each of these attractions is unique in its geological makeup, primary recreational interest and use, and management structure. This chapter describes the diversity and distinctiveness of NGOs working collaboratively, and primarily on a volunteer basis, to support these three different mountain tourist attractions.

These organizations are involved in a number of activities, including hospitality management, promotion of the experience, education and interpretation, building commitment and success in land stewardship, and acquiring funds for achieving the goals and objectives related to the natural mountain attraction.

Chapter 35. Development and Governance of a Family Destination in the Alps: The Case of Serfaus-Fiss-Ladis

Authors: Anita Zehrer, Frieda Raich, Hubert Siller and Franz Tschiderer

Chapter 35 examines collaboration and stakeholder governance by means of an exploratory study of a significant mountain tourism community within the Tyrolean Alps of Austria. The authors describe this large alpine destination and its significant stakeholders, and elaborate on the common and integrated nature of relationships, which create success for a mountain destination experience. The authors discuss key components and roles of the destination's experience providers: destination management organizations that provide common promotion, communication and facilitation of destination product and service provision; uphill lift enterprises that provide access to alpine sports; accommodation and gastronomy providers that deliver hospitality services; ski schools that provide learning and enhancement of on-snow experiences; and small municipalities that provide community administrative and political leadership and infrastructure.

Best-practice provision in the mountain tourism destination experience is viewed through the lens of the Serfaus-Fiss-Ladis case study, which offers insights into integrated governance success factors, including: cooperation and collaboration of stakeholders and service providers through the strategic integration of a shared vision; success factors in destination governance and management with priorities placed on leadership networks, market positioning, service innovation and entrepreneurial spirit, as well as having a strong emphasis on the customer experience; and examining future challenges that need to be addressed to ensure continued enhancement and viability.

Concluding Remarks Regarding this Chapter

Chapter 29 has provided an introduction to Part VI and has attempted to shed some light on the complexities of mountain tourism, relating more specifically to development, planning and governance within these complex and diverse regional geographical areas. Initiatives, actions and activities of significance to mountain tourism destinations may be distinctive and contentious in nature and may involve complicated and arduous processes in achieving successful outcomes and minimizing adverse effects of mountain tourism change and sustainable development. The broad coverage geographically, as well as the diverse nature of each subject area of relevance to mountain tourism planning and development, may advance the knowledge in this distinctive, but growing, area of impact and influence in mountain regions, as well as indicate and help facilitate areas of interest and emphasis, signalling the need for further effort and scholarship activity within this field of study.

References

Ashley, C. and Haysom, G. (2004) From philanthropy to a different way of doing business: strategies and challenges in integrating pro-poor approaches into tourism business. Paper presented at *ATLAS Africa Conference*, 2004. Pretoria, South Africa.

Beritelli, P., Bieger, T. and Laesser, C. (2007) Destination governance: using corporate governance theories as a foundation for effective destination management. *Journal of Travel Research* 46(1), 96–107.

Del Matto, T. and Scott, D. (2009) Sustainable ski resort principles: an uphill battle. In: Gossling, S., Hall, C.M. and Weaver, D. (eds) *Sustainable Tourism Futures: Perspectives on Systems, Restructuring and Innovations*. Routledge, New York, pp. 131–51.

Edgell, D., DelMastro Allen, M., Smith, G. and Swanson, J.R. (2008) *Tourism Policy and Planning: Yesterday, Today and Tomorrow*. Butterworth-Heinemann, Oxford, UK.

Gibson, L., Lynch, P.A. and Morrison, A. (2005) The local destination tourism network: development issues. *Tourism Planning and Development* 2(2), 87–99.

Hall, C.M. (2007) Pro-poor tourism: do tourism exchanges benefit primarily countries of the South? *Current Issues in Tourism* 10(2–3), 111–118.

Hall, C.M. (2011) A policy for governance and its implications for tourism policy analysis. *Journal of Sustainable Tourism* 19(4–5), 437–457.

Hull, J.S. (2012) Planning for tourism. In Robinson, P. (ed.) *Tourism: The Key Concepts*. Routledge, Abingdon, UK, pp. 156–158.

Hultman, J. and Hall, C.M. (2012) Tourism place-making: governance of locality in Sweden. *Annals of Tourism Research* 39(2), 547–570.

Kruk, E. (2010) *Marketing the Uniqueness of the Himalayas: An Analytical Framework*. ICIMOD, Kathmandu, Nepal.

Kruk, E., Hummel, J. and Banskota, K. (2007) *Facilitating Sustainable Mountain Tourism. Volume 1: Resource Book*. International Centre for Integrated Mountain Development (ICIMOD), Kathmandu, Nepal.

Lane, B. (2009) Thirty years of sustainable tourism. In: Gossling, S., Hall, C.M. and Weaver, D. (eds) *Sustainable Tourism Futures: Perspectives on Systems, Restructuring and Innovations*. Routledge, New York, pp. 19–32.

Laws, E., Richins, H., Agrusa, J. and Scott, N. (2011) *Tourist Destination Governance: Practice, Theory and Issues*. CAB International, Wallingford, UK.

Mieczkowski, Z. (1995) *Environmental Issues of Tourism and Recreation*. University Press of America, Lanham, Maryland.

Milne, S. and Ateljevic, I. (2001) Tourism, economic development and the global–local nexus: theory embracing complexity. *Tourism Geographies: An International Journal of Space, Place and Environment* 3(4), 369–393.

Murphy, P. (1985) *Tourism: A Community Approach*. Routledge, London.

Murphy, P. (2008) *The Business of Resort Management*. Butterworth-Heinemann, Oxford, UK.

Murphy, P. and Murphy, A.E. (2004) *Strategic Management for Tourism Communities: Bridging the Gaps*. Channel View Publications, Clevedon, UK.

Nepal, S. (2002) Mountain ecotourism and sustainable development. *Mountain Research and Development* 22(2), 104–109.

Nepal, S. (2003) Tourism and the environment. In: Nepal, S. (ed.) *Perspectives from the Nepal Himalaya*. Lalitpur, Innsbruck, Austria.

Nepal, S. (2005) Tourism and remote mountain settlements: spatial and temporal development of tourist infrastructure in the Mt Everest Region, Nepal. *Tourism Geographies: An International Journal of Tourism Space, Place and Environment* 7(2), 205–227.

Nepal, S. and Chipeniuk, R. (2005) Mountain tourism: towards a conceptual framework. *Tourism Geographies* 7(3), 313–333.

Nepal, S. and Jamal, T.B. (2011) Resort-induced changes in small mountain communities in British Columbia, Canada. *Mountain Research and Development* 31(2), 89–101.

Pavelka, J. and Draper, D. (2015) Leisure negotiation within amenity migration. *Annals of Tourism Research* 50, 126–142.

Pechlaner, H., Volgger, M. and Herntrel, M. (2012) Destination management organizations as interface between destination governance and corporate governance. *Anatolia: An International Journal of Tourism and Hospitality Research* 23(2), 151–168.

Richins, H. (1999) Community influencing characteristics in tourism development. *Fourth Conference of the Australian and New Zealand Association for Leisure Studies Proceedings of the National Tourism and Hospitality Conference*. Hamilton, New Zealand, pp. 205–211.

SNV (2004) *SNV Annual Report 2003*. Nepal Foundation, Kathmandu, Nepal.

SNV (2009) *SNV Annual Report 2009*. SNV, The Hague, Netherlands.

UNDESA (1992) *United Nations Conference on Environment and Development (UNCED). 1992 Summit.* UN Department of Economic and Social Affairs, New York.

UNWTO (2004) *Tourism and Poverty Alleviation: Recommendations for Action.* UNWTO, Madrid, Spain.

Williams, P. and Ponsford, I.F. (2009) Confronting tourism's environmental paradox: transitioning for sustainable tourism. *Futures* 41(6), 396–404.

Zhao, W. and Ritchie, B. (2007) Tourism and poverty alleviation: an integrative research framework. *Current Issues in Tourism* 10(2–3), 119–143.

30 Protected Areas in the Alps: Governance and Contributions to Regional Development

Michael Volgger,[1]* **Lena-Marie Lun**[1] **and Harald Pechlaner**[2]

[1]*European Academy Bozen/Bolzano (EURAC research), Bozen/Bolzano, Italy;*
[2]*Catholic University of Eichstaett-Ingolstadt, Ingolstadt, Germany*

Introduction

Mountain tourism is intrinsically linked to unique and diverse biophysical and cultural characteristics of mountain areas. Historically, limited opportunities for communication and interaction in mountain areas created exceptional variations in biotic life patterns, which also tend to be particularly sensitive and fragile (Godde et al., 2000; Nepal and Chipeniuk, 2005). Protected areas are considered to be suitable instruments to economically valorize and, at the same time, protect mountain areas; estimates suggest that mountain areas comprise more than 25% of all protected areas worldwide (Thorsell, 1997).

Originally, National Parks, Nature Parks and smaller protected areas were set up with the purpose of protecting valuable natural landscapes, or the habitats of endangered species against human-based threats. However, it has long become apparent that generating economic and socio-cultural benefits for the rural communities situated within and around protected areas are fundamental to increased acceptance and long-term protection (Eagles et al., 2002). The following quote, taken from one of the interviews that underlie this chapter,

indicates the paradigm shift that many protected areas are undergoing.

> [Protected area management] needs to take on regional development issues. There are a lot of possibilities in this context: sustainable forms of tourism, mobility, alternative energy sources or the marketing of regional products. The Nature Park status brings about direct and indirect advantages for regional development.
> (Interview with a mayor of a Nature Park municipality, 2014; own translation)

Tourism and particularly ecotourism, one of the growing and maturing types of alternative tourism (Page and Dowling, 2002; Weaver and Lawton, 2007), plays an important role in this context, since it provides local communities with financial returns and at the same time helps satisfy visitors' increasing wish to pursue recreational and sportive activities in an intact natural and authentic cultural environment. Thus, tourism can economically valorize and increase recognition and appreciation of protected areas, particularly in mountain regions (Eagles et al., 2002).

However, the societal and economic contribution of protected areas goes beyond tourism, in supporting wider regional development (Weixlbaumer et al., 2015). Promoting traditional

---

* Corresponding author: michael.volgger@eurac.edu

local agriculture and handicraft as well as using protected area labels for marketing a destination are becoming important issues in this context. Collaboration and mutual commitment to conservation efforts may reduce conflicts, especially at a local level when protected area management recognizes inhabitants' need for income generation and social cohesion (Leibenath, 2001).

Furthermore, the impact of a protected area is related to its organizational structure and mechanism of governance. Feyerabend-Borrini *et al.* (2006) argue that 'good governance' of protected areas greatly depends on the relationship between local government and civil society, the quality of governance and the engagement of local actors, as well as on respect for local peoples' rights and the intrinsic value of nature. Increasingly, it is recognized that the participation of local community actors can improve governance and management processes within protected areas, since they facilitate integration of local skills and knowledge and thus enhance the capacities of government institutions (Lockwood *et al.*, 2006).

This chapter and the underlying empirical study that compares four Alpine Nature Parks, investigates different approaches to develop and govern protected areas and links these governance approaches to protected areas' contributions to mountain tourism and regional development. The chapter is organized as follows.

The literature review introduces the concept of protected areas, establishes a link to tourism with particular regard to mountain tourism, and finally broadens the perspective to embed the discussion into a regional development approach in mountain regions. The literature review is followed by a description of methods and results of the aforementioned empirical study of four Alpine Nature Parks in two countries (Austria and Italy). Results are presented separately for the two Austrian (Tyrolean) and the two Italian (South Tyrolean) Nature Parks and they are discussed considering the main perspectives of the chapter (i.e. governance as well as contributions to tourism and implications for regional development). In a comparative view, the conclusion ties results together and refers these back to the main purpose of the chapter.

Protected Areas: Definition and Concept

The original idea behind protected areas is strongly linked to motivations to conserve biodiversity and landscapes. The IUCN (International Union for Conservation of Nature), one of the world's largest organizations for preserving nature, defined a protected area as '[a] clearly defined geographical space, recognised, dedicated and managed, through legal or other effective means, to achieve the long-term conservation of nature with associated ecosystem services and cultural values' (Dudley, 2008, 8). Although protected areas remain a fundamental tool to maintain the integrity of natural ecosystems, they have increasingly become an instrument for multiple uses, ideally integrating biodiversity protection, sustainable forestry with other aspects such as outdoor recreation and tourism (Job and Paesler, 2013; Pegas and Castley, 2014). In recent years, the paradigm shift towards this socio-economic component of protected areas has accelerated beyond conservation by integrating the concept of regional development into aspects of protected area governance (Mose and Weixlbaumer, 2007).

Tourism in Protected Areas

Recognized as a means for improving the welfare of rural communities, from an economic perspective, protected areas are clearly related to sustainable and nature-based tourism. Boo (1990) argues that tourism has increased considerably to protected areas, which provide ideal recreational opportunities due to their pristine natural environment. Tourism has thus become a powerful means of creating economic benefits for rural communities that lie near protected areas (Hvenegaard, 1994; Dharmaratne *et al.*, 2000; Stevens, 2002). Moreover, by creating tangible profits for the people living in protected areas, ecotourism can be fundamental in generating local acceptance of areas with protection status (Whelan, 1991). Policy discussions also take the importance of tourism for protected areas into consideration, regarding tourism as a significant instrument for improving the socio-economic conditions of host communities (Neto, 2003; Whitelaw et al., 2014).

The authors recognize that, in the context of protected area management, it can be challenging to strive simultaneously to develop tourism, conserve nature and improve the livelihoods of local people (Cochrane, 1996; Strickland-Munro and Moore, 2013). Spatial overlapping of touristic activities and conservation objectives may lead to conflicts between tourism stakeholders and park management representatives (Coghlan, 2012).

Increasingly, research – often case-study-based – also directly or indirectly focuses on the particular importance of sustainable tourism in protected areas in mountain regions (Nepal, 2000; Harmon et al., 2004; Hamilton, 2006). The success of touristic activities in protected mountain areas depends on various factors such as: target market orientation, marketing strategies, cooperation initiatives and a distinctive experience orientation (Hammer and Siegrist, 2008). Overall, approaches to tourism development and governance in protected mountain areas have broadened; suggestions to further develop tourism policies aim to foster mutual understanding between mountain inhabitants, guests and protected areas' management (Hamilton and McMillan, 2004). This seems especially important when recognizing the diverse but also sensitive ecological and socio-economic environment of mountain areas often facing distinct challenges such as depopulation and economic decline.

Protected Areas for Regional Development

Next to tourism, additional regional opportunities in protected areas are increasingly discussed in the literature. Protected areas are regarded as instruments for regional development in peripheral regions of Europe that face economic and socio-cultural challenges (Mose, 2007; Weixlbaumer et al., 2015). The potential socio-economic benefits of protected areas for rural communities, such as employment opportunities or infrastructure development, are extensively discussed in literature (Hamilton and McMillan, 2004; Bushell and Eagles, 2007).

Integrating sustainable development and conservation goals has led to a more innovative and dynamic type of protected area governance that strengthens regional economic cycles and moves human actions and nature to the centre of interest (Hammer, 2007). Protected areas can contribute to regional development in various ways (i.e. through involving various sectors such as handicraft, agriculture, trade, tourism, etc.); generating synergies through networks; and being an impulse for innovative projects (e.g. dealing with sustainable mobility or renewable energies) (Stevens, 2002; Mose, 2007). In particular, using the protected area's label as a tool for marketing a destination is important when discussing regional development dimensions since these are commonly connected to a positive image and guarantee certain quality standards (Voth, 2007). Protected areas that are strongly committed to the goal of promoting regional development seem to succeed in meeting expectations of the local population (Hammer, 2007).

In this context, the governance aspect is considered an important influence and success factor (Feyerabend-Borrini et al., 2006; Whitelaw et al., 2014). Compared to the national or international level, interest in using protected areas for regional development is particularly high at the local level. Thus, Hammer (2007) suggests it is fundamental to create appropriate regional administrative structures and to also consider mixed forms of state regulation and local or regional self-regulation. To better understand the role of such organizational structures and functional processes in the context of establishing and developing protected areas, the empirical part of this chapter discusses the governance of four Alpine protected areas and their contributions to mountain tourism and regional development in detail.

Methodology

The study had an exploratory character and followed a qualitative approach. The research team conducted ten semi-structured interviews with stakeholders of four regionally anchored Nature Parks (Kaunergrat, Ötztal, Texelgruppe/ Gruppo di Tessa, and Rieserferner-Ahrn/

Vedrette di Ries-Aurina) in mountain areas on the northern and southern side of the main ridge of the Alps (see Fig. 30.1). Two of these protected areas are located in Austria (Bundesland Tirol/Federal Province Tyrol) and two in Italy (Autonome Provinz Bozen-Südtirol/Autonomous Province of Bolzano-South Tyrol). This cross-boundary selection aimed to integrate protected areas that exhibit different organizational types and governance structures.

The interviewees were representatives of the park management, local administrative structures, tourism stakeholders in the Nature Park municipalities and other sectors such as agriculture. The semi-structured interviews, conducted between February and March 2014, lasted between 30 and 60 minutes each and concentrated on two main topics related to the mountain parks: (i) governance structures; and (ii) impacts on tourism and regional development. Regarding the governance structures, the open-ended questions related to the following points.

- Vision, strategy and their implementation.
- Success factors and potential challenges.
- Main tasks of the protected area management and ultimately its organizational structure.

Concerning the impact on mountain tourism and regional development, the interviews mainly focused on the effects of the protected areas on the respective economic conditions. Most of the questions regarded tourism and, in particular, the destination perspective. However, questions also referred to synergies between protected areas and other sectors and industries, such as agriculture and handicrafts.

The interviews were analysed using the GABEK technique (Zelger, 1994), a methodology that has proven particularly appropriate when dealing with unstructured and complex data, such as local stakeholders' opinions and perceptions. GABEK is a computer-supported analysis method for qualitative research that succeeds in combining the advantages of an open approach to data collection with those of a systematic analysis process (Pechlaner and Volgger, 2012). Overall, the advantages of the GABEK technique compared to other qualitative analysis tools include the intersubjective traceable validity, closeness to the original data

material, and the various options for visually representing complex and collective structures of meaning and understanding (Buber and Kraler, 2000; Zelger *et al.*, 2008).

The first step of a GABEK analysis aims at breaking down the transcribed interviews into coherent statements. Subsequently, each such statement is coded by three to nine keywords. These chosen keywords should be close to the actual words of respondents and should aim at representing the underlying statements (Buber and Kraler, 2000). With the help of the software WinRelan, the coded data can be visualized in the form of semantic networks; for instance, in the form of association graphs or causal net graphs (Zelger *et al.*, 2008). Whereas association graphs depict keywords that are related to each other by interviewees (i.e. appear in the same statements), causal net graphs also allow the identification and visualization of perceived direct as well as inverse cause and effect relationships (Buber and Kraler, 2000). To represent the findings in this chapter, we applied causal net graphs, where lines ending in arrowheads indicate direct (positive) and those ending in circles inverse (negative) correlations.

Results and Discussion

Results for the research around the four Alpine Nature Parks are discussed below.

Protected mountain areas in the Autonomous Province of Bolzano-South Tyrol (Italy)

Keywords that the interviewees related to the protected areas (Nature Parks) in their region regarding governance mechanisms and implications for tourism and regional development are depicted in Fig. 30.2.

Governance

Results of the interviews indicate that governance of protected areas (in particular Nature Parks) in the Autonomous Province of Bolzano-South Tyrol is rather centralized, as the provincial government takes on a major leadership role and is the primary decision-making authority. The designation of protected areas as well as

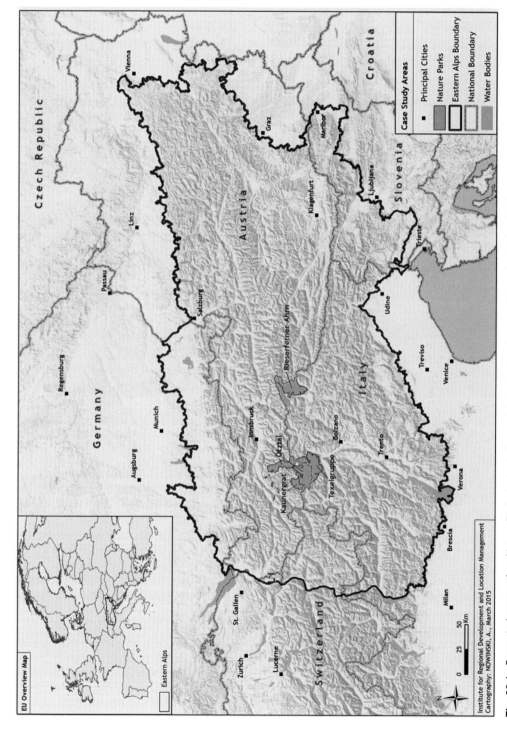

Fig. 30.1. Case study areas: four Nature Parks in the Italian and Austrian Alps (source: illustration Michael Volgger, Lena-Marie Lun and Harald Pechlaner; cartography A. Nowinski).

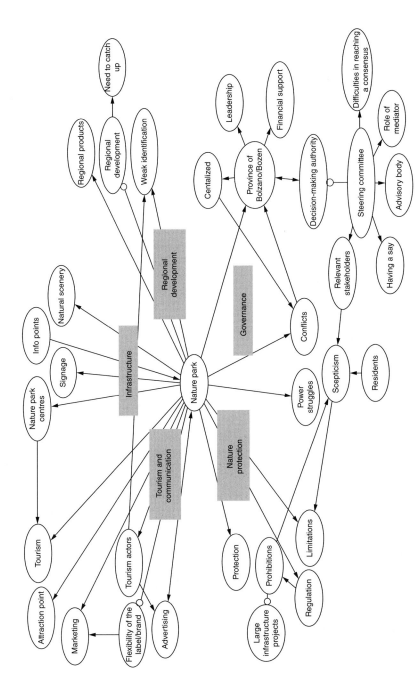

Fig. 30.2. Autonomous Province of Bolzano-South Tyrol – governance and implications of Nature Parks. Note: Lines ending in arrows indicate direct (positive) and those ending in circles inverse (negative) relationships.

their management and financing are subject to a centralized governance mechanism. Respondents suggested that this type of governance may give rise to conflicts of interests, since the local communities, located within park confines, have relatively limited possibilities to formally influence planning and management processes. Steering committees do exist that integrate most relevant local stakeholders. However, according to the interviewees, such committees mainly have an advisory role to the provincial government.

Moreover, interviewees explained that the original purpose of the protected areas in the Autonomous Province of Bolzano-South Tyrol (mainly established in the 1970s and 1980s) was to prevent large-scale infrastructural projects in the fields of tourism development and hydropower use. Although the development and utilization aspects became relatively more important over the course of time, the conservation and protection purpose appears to remain the central pillar of protected area governance in South Tyrol.

Contributions to tourism and implications for regional development

According to interviewees, protected mountain areas are relevant attraction points in mountain tourism in South Tyrol. This holds particularly when additional features such as Nature Park Centres and information points, or dedicated paths enhance the experience of natural attractions. Additionally, signposting is considered to be an important element. This includes the main messages delivered by the signposts. Whereas signposts focusing on the prohibition aspects of protected areas may increase the credibility of these parks from the guests' perspective, they can contribute to reducing acceptance of such protected mountain areas among local businesses and residents. Therefore, the emphasis that the protected area puts on communicating the protection or (sensitive) use aspects is relevant.

Furthermore, respondents underscored the role of branding in achieving synergies between protected areas and tourism. The relevance of adopting an umbrella brand for protected mountain areas is also emphasized from the perspective of regional development. Interviewees mention that such brands may help to support the utilization aspect in the governance of protected areas and thus increase their acceptance among residents and businesses (in particular among farmers and the craft sector). They may also push regional products and foster the adoption of regional value chains. However, interviewees recognize further development potentials in the relatively strict South Tyrolean protected mountain area governance.

Protected mountain areas in the Federal Province of Tyrol (Austria)

Some cause–effect relationships concerning protected mountain areas (in particular Nature Parks) in the Federal Province of Tyrol as perceived by the interviewees are illustrated in Fig. 30.3.

Governance

Compared to the South Tyrolean governance of protected mountain areas, the interviewees underscored the rather decentralized approach in the Province of Tyrol. The Tyrolean Nature Parks are governed at a local or regional level and take on the legal form of associations. While they require legal confirmation by the Tyrolean government, municipalities and other local and regional stakeholders are essential in decision making and financing within these structures. Additionally, Tyrolean Nature Parks are not one protected areas category in the narrow sense, but rather they unite various underlying – and often fragmented – protected areas under the common label of a Nature Park (Region). The protection depends on the underlying categories, whereas the umbrella branding as a Nature Park seems to facilitate the internal and external marketing according to the interviewees.

This set-up may have the advantage of both increasing the local acceptance of the protected mountain areas and furthering the use aspect in terms of tourism in regional development. Some interviewees, however, raise the concern that Tyrolean Nature Parks are slightly less dedicated to the issue of protection.

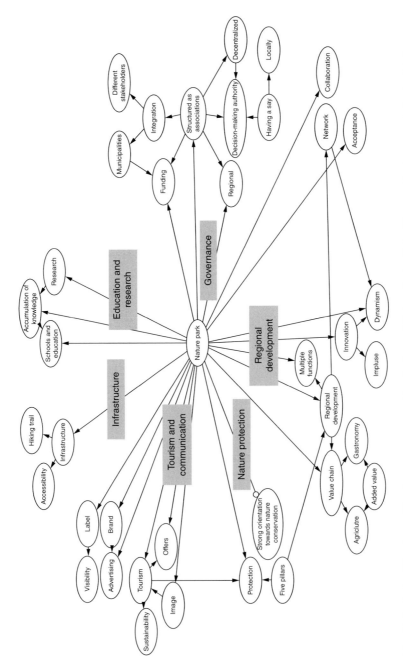

Fig. 30.3. Federal Province of Tyrol – governance and implications of Nature Parks. Note: Lines ending in arrows indicate direct (positive) and those ending in circles inverse (negative) relationships.

Contributions to tourism and implications for regional development

In Tyrol, the comparatively liberal use of 'Nature Park' as a label, building upon more technical protection categories, seems to increase the perceived value of these areas among tourism stakeholders and other local actors. Regional products, firms, accommodation businesses and offers can be 'branded' with the 'Nature Park' logo (if congruent with the values and territories of the park), which fosters integration of the economic interests present in the protected areas. The intensive use of Nature Parks as a brand or label has particularly led to synergies between agriculture and tourism for the profit of both.

Additionally, the strategies of the Tyrolean Nature Parks are explicitly and equally dedicated to five objectives, namely 'nature and landscape', 'tourism and recreation', 'education', 'research' and 'regional development'. In these five areas, the Tyrolean Nature Parks are oriented towards proactively giving new impulses and promoting innovation, according to the interviewees.

Conclusion

The mountain alpine protected areas in this study are fragile and relatively densely populated.

Hence, Alpine mountain areas overwhelmingly take the form of cultivated nature and nature shaped by humans. Therefore, when addressing the issue of protected mountain areas in the Alps, it is essential to consider the interests of natural conservation together with that of human use. It is especially critical to consider the interests of three target groups, namely residents, guests and businesses, in such densely populated areas.

Within the context of the Alpine area, different approaches to the governance of protected mountain areas co-exist. This chapter compares two approaches to governance in Nature Parks in the neighbouring Alpine regions of Tyrol (Austria) and South Tyrol (Italy). The study suggests that these governance approaches differ mainly in terms of the degree of centralized vs. decentralized governance on the one hand, and the emphasis on protection vs greater consideration of economic utilization of the Nature Park on the other hand (see Fig. 30.4). One might call the Tyrolean approach to protected mountain area governance somewhat more liberal and the South Tyrolean approach relatively more protectionist.

The relative impact of the two protected mountain area governance approaches on tourism and regional development are perceived to

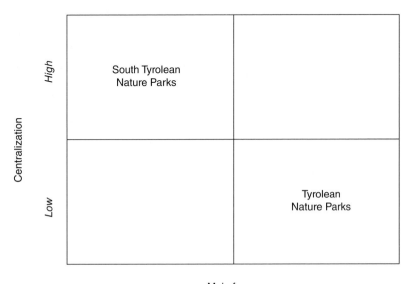

Fig. 30.4. Schematic categorization of the analysed governance approaches to the protected mountain areas in the Alps.

be slightly different. The more liberal governance seems to achieve higher acceptance among local and regional stakeholders and has advantages from a communication point of view. In contrast, the more protectionist approach might have advantages in long-term credibility. This might be particularly true since previous studies indicate that the protection status has an impact on tourism decision making (Reinius and Fredman, 2007). However, also in the relatively more protectionist approach, it seems favourable to enhance the experience level within the park by installing information points, dedicated paths and guided tours. Overall, these findings indicate that, first, various approaches to establishing, developing and governing protected areas exist and co-exist. This holds even within regionally limited areas, such as the Italian and Austrian parts of the main ridge of the Alps. Major differences concern, for example, the degree of centralization and the relative importance of protectionist compared to utilization perspectives. Second, findings indicate that protected areas' contributions to mountain tourism and regional development at least partially depend on the chosen approach to protected area governance.

References

Boo, E. (1990) *Ecotourism: The Potentials and Pitfalls – Country Case Studies*. World Wildlife Fund (WWF), Washington, DC.

Buber, R. and Kraler, C. (2000) How GABEK and WinRelan support qualitative research. In: Buber, R. and Zelger, J. (eds) *GABEK II. Zur Qualitativen Forschung. On Qualitative Research*. Studien-Verlag, Innsbruck, Austria; Vienna, Austria; and Munich, Germany, pp. 111–137.

Bushell, R. and Eagles, P.F.J. (eds) (2007) *Tourism and Protected Areas. Benefits Beyond Boundaries*. CAB International, Wallingford, UK.

Cochrane, J. (1996) The sustainability of ecotourism in Indonesia: fact and fiction. In: Parnwell, M.J.G. and Bryant, R.L. (eds) *Environmental Change in South-East Asia: People, Politics and Sustainable Development*. Routledge, London, pp. 237–259.

Coghlan, A. (2012) Linking natural resource management to tourist satisfaction: a study of Australia's Great Barrier Reef. *Journal of Sustainable Tourism* 20(1), 41–58.

Dharmaratne, G.S., Sang, F.Y. and Walling, L.J. (2000) Tourism potentials for financing protected areas. *Annals of Tourism Research* 27(3), 590–610.

Dudley, N. (ed.) (2008) *Guidelines for Applying Protected Area Management Categories*. IUCN, Gland, Switzerland.

Eagles, P.F.J., McCool, S.F. and Haynes, C.D. (2002) *Sustainable Tourism in Protected Areas: Guidelines for Planning and Management*. Prepared for the United Nations Environment Programme, World Tourism Organization and IUCN – The World Conservation Union. World Commission on Protected Areas (WCPA), IUCN Publication Services, Gland, Switzerland.

Feyerabend-Borrini, G., Johnston, J. and Pansky, D. (2006) Goverance of protected areas. In: Lockwood, M., Worboys, G. and Kothari, A. (eds) *Managing Protected Areas. A Global Guide*. Earthscan, London, pp. 116–145.

Godde, P.M, Price, M.F. and Zimmermann, F.M. (2000) Tourism and development in mountain regions: moving forward into the new millennium. In: Godde, P.M, Price, M.F. and Zimmermann, F.M. (eds) *Tourism and Development in Mountain Regions*. CAB International, Wallingford, UK, pp. 1–25.

Hamilton, L.S. (2006) Protected areas in mountains. *Pirineos* 161, 151–158.

Hamilton, L.S. and McMillan, L. (2004) *Guidelines for Planning and Managing. Mountain Protected Areas*. IUCN, Gland, Switzerland.

Hammer, T. (2007) Protected areas and regional development: conflicts and opportunities. In: Mose, I. (ed.) *Protected Areas and Regional Development in Europe: Towards a New Model for the 21st Century*. Ashgate, Aldershot, UK, pp. 21–36.

Hammer, T. and Siegrist, D. (2008) Protected areas in the Alps: the success factors of nature-based tourism and the challenge for regional policy. *GAIA* 17(1), 152–160.

Harmon, D., Worboys, G. and Verdone, D. (2004) *Managing Mountain Protected Areas: Challenges and Responses for the 21st Century*. Andromeda Editrice, Colledara, Teramo, Italy.

Hvenegaard, G.T. (1994) Ecotourism: a status report and conceptual framework. *Journal of Tourism Studies* 5(2), 24–35.

Job, H. and Paesler, F. (2013) Links between nature-based tourism, protected areas, poverty alleviation and crises – the example of Wasini Island (Kenya). *Journal of Outdoor Recreation and Tourism* 1–2, 8–28.

Leibenath, M. (2001) Entwicklung von Nationalparkregionen durch Regionalmarketing: Untersucht am Beispiel der Müritzregion. *Europäische Hochschulschriften*, Reihe 5, Volks- und Betriebswirtschaft, Bd. 2732. Peter Lang International Academic Publishers, Frankfurt am Main, Germany.

Lockwood, M., Worboys, G. and Kothari, A. (eds) (2006) *Managing Protected Areas: A Global Guide*. Earthscan, London.

Mose, I. (ed.) (2007) *Protected Areas and Regional Development in Europe. Towards a New Model for the 21st Century*. Ashgate, Aldershot, UK.

Mose, I. and Weixlbaumer, N. (2007) A new paradigm for protected areas in Europe. In: Mose, I. (ed.) *Protected Areas and Regional Development in Europe: Towards a New Model for the 21st Century*. Ashgate, Aldershot, UK, pp. 3–20.

Nepal, S.K. (2000) Tourism in protected areas: the Nepalese Himalaya. *Annals of Tourism Research* 27(3), 661–681.

Nepal, S.K. and Chipeniuk, R. (2005) Mountain tourism: toward a conceptual framework. *Tourism Geographies* 7(3), 313–333.

Neto, F. (2003) A new approach to sustainable tourism development: moving beyond environmental protection. *Natural Resources Forum* 27(3), 212–222.

Page, S.J. and Dowling, R.K. (2002) *Ecotourism*. Prentice-Hall, Harlow, UK.

Pechlaner, H. and Volgger, M. (2012) How to promote cooperation in the hospitality industry: generating practitioner-relevant knowledge using the GABEK qualitative research strategy. *International Journal of Contemporary Hospitality Management* 24(6), 925–945.

Pegas, F.D.V. and Castley, J.G. (2014) Ecotourism as a conservation tool and its adoption by private protected areas in Brazil. *Journal of Sustainable Tourism* 22(4), 604–625.

Reinius, S.W. and Fredman, P. (2007) Protected areas as attractions. *Annals of Tourism Research* 34(4), 839–854.

Stevens, T. (2002) *Sustainable Tourism in National Parks and Protected Areas: An Overview*. Scottish Natural Heritage, Edinburgh, UK.

Strickland-Munro, J. and Moore, S. (2013) Indigenous involvement and benefits from tourism in protected areas: a study of Purnululu National Park and Warmun Community, Australia. *Journal of Sustainable Tourism* 21(1), 26–41.

Thorsell, J. (1997) Protection of nature in mountain regions. In: Messerli, B. and Ives, J.D. (eds) *Mountains of the World: A Global Priority*. Parthenon Publishing Group, New York, pp. 237–248.

Voth, A. (2007) National parks and rural development in Spain. In: Mose, I. (ed.) *Protected Areas and Regional Development in Europe: Towards a New Model for the 21st Century*. Ashgate, Aldershot, UK, pp. 141–160.

Weaver, D.B. and Lawton, L.J. (2007) Twenty years on: the state of contemporary ecotourism research. *Tourism Management* 28(5), 1168–1179.

Weixlbaumer, N., Siegrist, D., Mose, I. and Hammer, T. (2015) Participation and regional governance: a crucial research perspective on protected areas policies in Austria and Switzerland. In: Gambino, R. and Peano, A. (eds) *Nature Policies and Landscape Policies: Towards an Alliance*. Springer International Publishing, Cham, Switzerland and Heidelberg, Germany, pp. 207–215.

Whelan, T. (1991) Ecotourism and its role in sustainable development. In: Whelan, T. (ed.) *Nature Tourism: Managing for the Environment*. Island Press, Washington, DC.

Whitelaw, P.A., King, B.E. and Tolkach, D. (2014) Protected areas, conservation and tourism – financing the sustainable dream. *Journal of Sustainable Tourism* 22(4), 584–603.

Zelger, J. (1994) Qualitative Auswertung sprachlicher Äußerungen. Wissensvernetzung, Wissensverarbeitung und Wissensumsetzung durch GABEK. In: Wille, R. and Zwickwolff, M. (eds) *Begriffliche Wissensverarbeitung: Grundfragen und Aufgaben*. B.I.-Wissenschaftsverlag, Mannheim, Germany, pp. 239–266.

Zelger, J., Fink, S. and Strickner, J. (2008) Darstellung von Erfahrungswissen durch GABEK. In: Zelger, J., Raich, M. and Schober, P. (eds) *GABEK III: Organisationen und ihre Wissensnetze. Organisations and their Knowledge Nets*. Studien-Verlag, Innsbruck, Austria, pp. 143–159.

31 Setting the Table for Mountain Tourism: The Case of a South African National Park

Linda-Louise Geldenhuys,* Peet van der Merwe and Melville Saayman
North-West University, Potchefstroom, Republic of South Africa

Introduction

For hundreds of years, mountains have seemed majestic to humans. They convey a sense of the extraordinary, of dramatic and exotic landscapes (Silva *et al.*, 2013, 17). Due to the attractive and symbolic image of mountains, tourism demand for such areas has grown and expanded to about 20% of global tourist flows (Silva *et al.*, 2013, 17). With their spectacular scenery, beauty and unique values (diversity, marginality and aesthetics), mountains make up one of the most popular destinations for tourists (Nepal and Chipeniuk, 2005, 313). As one of the tourism industry's fastest-growing markets, and one of the most upcoming areas, mountain tourism is second in global popularity and the chosen destination of 500 million tourists annually (Thomas *et al.*, 2006; Singh, 2007). In South Africa, the three largest mountain destinations are the Drakensberg Mountains, the Soutpansberg and the Swartberg, but the most renowned mountain/icon and, arguably, best-loved is Table Mountain, which forms part of the Table Mountain National Park (TMNP).

Three aspects make TMNP a unique national park. First, it is an urban national park, because it is situated in a densely populated urban setting (Bryant, 2006, 26). According to Chiesura (2004, 29) and Salazar and Menendez (2007, 296), an urban park can also be known as a municipal or public park, public open space or municipal gardens; it is a park in a city or other incorporated place that offers recreation and green space to residents of, and visitors to, the municipality. Urban parks are also viewed as spaces where a spectrum of recreational and leisure activities can be pursued such as walking, picnicking and relaxing, and they are seen as places that provide people with unique experiences as a result of the natural and cultural features present and the social communities that gravitate to them (Gobster, 2001, 35; Thompson, 2002, 59). Secondly, this park is also named a UNESCO World Heritage Site (Rössler, 2006; UNESCO, 2015), which is a place such as a forest, *mountain*, lake, island, desert, monument, building, complex, or city that is listed by the United Nations Educational, Scientific and Cultural Organization (UNESCO) as of special cultural or physical significance. As of 2015, 1031 sites are listed: 802 cultural, 197 natural and 32 mixed properties, in 163 countries (Rössler, 2006, 334). Thirdly, it is one of the Seven Wonders of Nature, which comprise the Amazon (South America), Ho Long Bay (Vietnam), Iguazu Falls (Argentina/Brazil), Jeju Island (South Korea),

---

* Corresponding author: linda-louiseG@prestigeacademy.co.za

Komodo (Indonesia), PP Underground River (Philippines) and Table Mountain (South Africa).

The aim of this chapter is to examine TMNP as a mountain tourism destination. Aspects of discussion in this regard will include a discussion on Table Mountain as a national park, the history and relevance of TMNP, benefits of mountain tourism, differences between urban and natural destinations, the socio-demographic profile of visitors to the park, the economic impact of TMNP, as well as the travel motivations of those visiting TMNP. The chapter will be concluded with the main findings and contributions of TMNP as a tourism destination in South Africa.

Table Mountain National Park (TMNP)

TMNP was established in 1998 and covers more than 25,000 ha, including a 1000-km coastline (Saayman et al., 2013, 440). The park stretches from Signal Hill in the northern parts of Cape Town to Cape Point in the south, along the seas and coastline of Cape Peninsula, as shown in Fig. 31.1 (South African History Online, 2014). The park covers 265 km^2 and is surrounded by the city of Cape Town (Forsyth and Van Wilgen, 2008, 3). Every year Table Mountain attracts approximately 2 million domestic and international visitors (South African History Online, 2014). Table Mountain is one of two renowned landmarks found inside the borders of TMNP, the other being the Cape of Good Hope. Bordering the park is a variety of communities ranging from wealthy to extremely poor (Saayman et al., 2013, 40). Known for its rich biodiversity, TMNP is home to more than 2200 different plant species, more than the total number found throughout the British Isles (Forsyth and Van Wilgen, 2008, 3; Cape Town, 2014). Of the plant species found at TMNP, 90 are endemic to the area (Forsyth and Van Wilgen, 2008, 3). Most of the plant species found on the mountain are part of the floral kingdom of Fynbos, the Cape Floral Kingdom (Capensis), which is the smallest of the world's six plant kingdoms (Daitz and Myrdal, 2012, 325).

TMNP is a hiker's paradise, with the highest peak reaching 1085 m (3560 feet), offering plenty of hiking trails to tourists and nature lovers starting from Camps Bay, and including Kirstenbosch National Botanical Garden and the city centre (South African History Online, 2014). The mountain may seem rather tame on a clear and sunny day, but the weather can change rapidly to being cloudy and misty (South African History Online, 2014). A number of ill-prepared hikers and tourists have lost their lives on the slopes of Table Mountain in an attempt to get to the summit on a day unsuitable for hiking up this natural wonder (South African History Online, 2014). Quite apart from hiking, viewing or photographing the scenery, activities that can be undertaken in the park also include scuba diving, mountain biking, hang gliding, paragliding, fishing, dog walking, surfing, wind surfing, rock climbing and horse riding. A multitude of barbeque and picnic areas are provided for approximately 2 million annual visitors to the mountain (Scholtz et al., 2011, 1; South African History Online, 2014).

History of TMNP

Antonio Saldanha, the Portuguese seafarer, anchored his fleet in Table Bay in May 1503. He first named the bay Aguada de Saldanha, or 'the watering place of Saldanha'. He also climbed Table Mountain, which he called Taboa do Capo, or Table of the Cape. On a clear day, the mountain is visible for many kilometres out to sea and across the city of Cape Town (South African History Online, 2014). The cloud cover visible on overcast days is popularly known as the tablecloth, or perruque (the wig) as the French call it, and is said to be the result of a tobacco-smoking contest between the Devil and Jan van Hunks, a retired privateer who inhabited the slopes of one of the smaller mountains flanking Table Mountain, known as Devil's Peak (South African History Online, 2014). The majestic Table Mountain, together with the two smaller mountains on either side, Devil's Peak and Lion's Head, forms part of the mountain range creating the backdrop of the Cape Peninsula, as shown in Fig. 31.2 (South African Tourism, 2014a).

In 1913, the Cape Town City Council commissioned an engineer, Mr H.M. Peter, to investigate the possibilities regarding transport to the top of Table Mountain. A suggestion

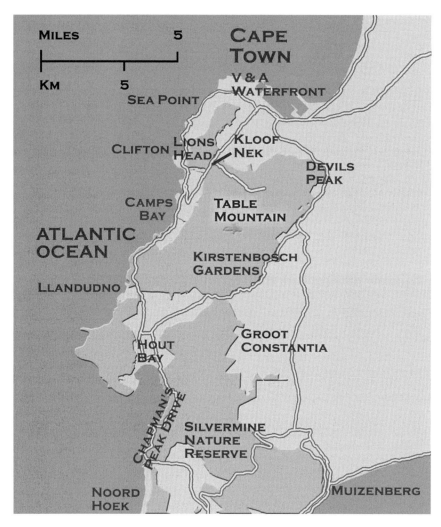

Fig. 31.1. Map of Table Mountain National Park (source: Findtripinfo.com, 2014).

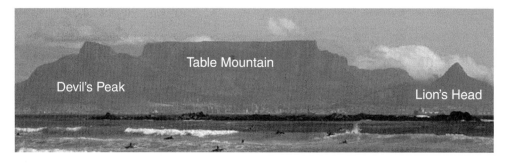

Fig. 31.2. Photo of Devil's Peak, Table Mountain and Lion's Head (source: Santillanis, 2009).

was made that the railway running between Oranjezicht and Platteklip be used. In 1913, the costs for this project were estimated at £100,000 (Cape Town, 2014), but plans were put on hold due to the First World War. The building of a cableway was proposed again in 1926 by a Norwegian engineer, Trygve Stromsoe. After Stromsoe approached Sir Alfred Hennessy with a functioning model of his idea, Hennessy and his fellow investors formed the Table Mountain Aerial Cableway Company (TMACC) to finance the construction of this transportation mode (Table Mountain Aerial Cableway, 2014). Construction for the cableway was commissioned to German contractor Adolf Bleichert, and the cableway was officially launched in October 1929, costing £60,000 (Table Mountain Aerial Cableway, 2014). The aerial cableway was the first man-made tourist attraction for Cape Town. An upgraded cableway was officially reopened in October 1997 (South African Tourism, 2014b). To date, more than 22 million people have made use of the cableway to visit the top of Table Mountain and to enjoy the scenery (South African History Online, 2014). The view from the top offers tourists a magnificent vista stretching over the city centre and surrounding suburbs to the Atlantic Ocean, and beyond to Robben Island (Cape Town, 2014).

June 2004 saw the declaration of the Cape Floristic Region (CFR) as a Natural World Heritage Site due to its universal significance to humanity (SANParks, 2015). The CFR is made up of eight separate areas, which are representative samples of the entire region. One of these regions is TMNP (SANParks, 2015). The reasons for the inclusion of TMNP lie in the fact that, as mentioned earlier, TMNP is home to close to 3000 plant species and one of only six plant kingdoms on earth to be found on one continent (Forsyth and Van Wilgen, 2008, 3; SANParks, 2015).

In 2012 Table Mountain was named as one of the New7Wonders of Nature (Times Live, 2012). According to the Times Live, an increased number of visitors flocked to the park in November of 2012, which supported the statement made by Cape Town Mayor Patricia de Lil that the inclusion of Table Mountain as one of the seven wonders will lead to an increase in direct and indirect economic and socio-economic benefits to the city of Cape Town, as well as for South Africa as a whole (Times Live, 2012).

Benefits of Mountain Tourism

Robertson and Hull (2001) point out that mountains are not only physical and natural; they are viewed as cultural spaces, socially, cognitively and emotionally constructed, and imagined sites that are both individually created and shared with others (Silva et al., 2013, 18). Several commentators argue that, based on impacts and relevance in a community setting, mountains can represent the following (Skeldon, 1985; McCool, 2002; Beedie and Hudson, 2003; Kastenholz and Rodrigues, 2007; Silva et al., 2013, 18):

- Typically, places of refuge and escape from the pressures of the urbanized world.
- Places of evasion from the hot, humid and, at times, uncomfortable climates of coastal and tropical regions.
- Places that offer excitement, stimulation and potential adventure.
- Places frequently sought by the global hiking and trekking market.

Mountains must be understood as destinations that appeal for a variety of reasons, each conveying a variety of meanings and effectively attracting different tourism markets (Silva et al., 2013, 18). While Table Mountain is an excellent example of an urban mountain destination, it must not be forgotten that Table Mountain is not only a national park, but also a protected area (Saayman et al., 2013, 441). Therefore the following benefits are also of relevance to Table Mountain and to the larger region (Saayman et al., 2013, 442):

- Positive economic benefits are derived from Table Mountain as a national park due to increased tourist numbers to the area.
- Communities view national parks as a positive aspect due to its aesthetic value as well as to its ability to draw tourists to the area.
- National parks contribute to the quality of life of the community.
- National parks increase the employment rate of underprivileged communities in which the national park functions.

A study conducted by Saayman *et al.* (2013) aimed to identify the socio-economic benefits derived from the largest urban national park in South Africa, TMNP. Saayman *et al.* (2013, 450) established that the perceptions of residents and community members in the park surroundings were seen as an overall positive in terms of economic and social impacts delivered by the park. This implies that businesses as well as sectors of the industry, such as the accommodation and catering sectors, greatly benefit from the additional economic benefit brought by TMNP (Saayman *et al.*, 2013, 446). It further implies that the quality of life of residents in Cape Town is positively impacted, thus improved, by TMNP (Saayman *et al.*, 2013, 449). This enhances the belief that the aesthetic value of a park such as TMNP has an overall positive impact on the quality of life of communities in the surrounding areas (Saayman *et al.*, 2013, 454). Hence, it was concluded that managers of the TMNP should communicate with community members on a regular basis concerning the policies, strategies and future plans of the park to better ensure the sustainable tourism development of TMNP (Saayman *et al.*, 2013, 454) and to gain the support of the surrounding communities for the policies and plans.

Mountain destinations such as TMNP normally have a positive impact on the surrounding communities, and provide positive contributions to the economy (i.e. increased tourism numbers, increased rate of employment), social improvements (e.g. improved quality of life, aesthetic value added) as well as offering a place for recreation, escape and relaxation with activities such as hiking, mountain biking and scuba diving (Scholtz *et al.*, 2011; Saayman *et al.*, 2013).

Differences in Destinations: Urban Versus Natural

There are a number of ways in which destinations differ from each other, and urban destinations, such as the city of Cape Town, differ considerably from places such as TMNP, a natural destination. Lubbe (2012, 144) identified the following aspects to show how one destination may differ from another:

- Size: each destination is different from another, based on the geographical area covered by the destination. A destination can, for example, be a region, a province, or a country.
- Physical attractions: one destination may be rich in cultural and heritage attractions, while another destination may have a magnificent coastline.
- Infrastructure: public transport, roads, airports, accessibility and general facilities will differ from those at other destinations, based on the level of development of the destination.
- Benefits offered to visitors: some destinations will seek to meet the needs of mass tourism, while other destinations will, for example, appeal to business travellers.
- Dependency on tourism: the level of development of a country, together with the country's economic base, will to some extent determine the dependence of the destination on tourism for growth and survival.

From the foregoing, it is clear that the market for one destination, the benefits it offers to visitors, as well as the reasons why visitors would choose to visit a specific destination, will differ. With this in mind, Van der Merwe *et al.* (2011, 465) state that the motives of visitors are destination-specific, thereby implying that each destination will have its own set of motivators that would draw or appeal to tourists, and suggesting that the motives for visitors to mountain destinations will differ from the motives of visitors to urban destinations (Van der Merwe *et al.*, 2011, 465). It therefore becomes imperative to explore the motives of the visitors to TMNP, and this will be discussed later in the chapter.

Socio-demographic Profile of Visitors to TMNP

TMNP, a renowned tourism destination enjoyed by both domestic and international visitors, may be regarded as having a positive influence on the life and economy of surrounding communities, and, therefore, it is important to determine the profile of visitors to this park (South African History Online, 2014). This information is useful for developing new products

Table 31.1. Summary of the profile of domestic and foreign visitors to TMNP (source: Scholtz *et al.*, 2011, 4).

Demographic Detail	Profile
Home language	English (50%), followed by Italian, Dutch and German (41%)
Gender	Male (52%); female, (48%)
Age	Average age of 37 years
Marital status	Married (44%); not married (36%); living together (14%)
Country of residence	Foreign visitors (69%); RSA (31%). Foreign visitors include Italy (11%) and USA (12%)
Province of residence	Western Cape (51%); Gauteng (24%); KwaZulu-Natal (12%)
Qualification	Diploma/degree (35%); postgraduate (29%); professional (23%)
Aware of the National Park	Yes (92%); no (8%)
Mode of transport	Sedan (51%); RV (28%); micro bus (15%)
Decision to visit the Park	Spontaneous (42%); more than a month ago (35%); a month ago (17%)
Initiator of the visit	Self (42%); friends (25%); family (14%)

or offerings, which can enhance the image of TMNP, as well as for the improvement of marketing the park.

TMNP receives both domestic and foreign visitors throughout the year. Research conducted by Scholtz *et al.* (2011, 4) indicated the profile of visitors as being mostly male, English-speaking, married and between 35 and 45 years of age, with an average age of 37 years. Respondents from foreign countries make up the majority of visitors to TMNP, and originate primarily from Italy and the USA. It is worth noting that TMNP is the only park in South Africa that receives more foreign visitors than domestic visitors per annum (Scholtz *et al.*, 2011, 4). The majority of domestic respondents originated from the Western Cape, followed by Gauteng Province within the South African borders (Scholtz *et al.*, 2011, 4).

Most visitors (both domestic and foreign) had a diploma or degree, and they were aware of Table Mountain as a national park. Visitors were first exposed to national parks in general (not TMNP specifically) at the age of 15 years, their chosen mode of transport to and from the TMNP was by sedan vehicle (either owned or rented), and the decision to visit TMNP was a spontaneous decision initiated by the respondents themselves. Table 31.1 offers a summary of the profile of visitors to TMNP.

Economic impact

Saayman *et al.*, (2013, 454) reports that residents' perceptions were that TMNP has a positive economic and social effect on the community of Cape Town. It must be noted, however, that the economic impacts made by the park are, perhaps, greater than the social impacts, given that the approximate amount generated by the park for the region of Cape Town is ZAR278million (Saayman *et al.*, 2013, 454). Foreign visitors to TMNP spent a significantly greater amount than visitors from the rest of South Africa (with exception of visitors from the Western Cape).

The average size of the groups of people travelling to TMNP was determined to be one to two people, and the annual income of visitors was estimated to be ZAR552,001 or more. At the time when this chapter was written, the rand–euro exchange rate was measured at ZAR12.91 per euro and the rand–dollar exchange rate was measured at ZAR12.18 per US dollar. Most respondents indicated that they visit TMNP once or twice during the course of a year, yet the majority of visitors had never spent a night at the park. The main reasons for visitors not making use of the park's overnight accommodation facilities were:

- Visitors were not aware of the overnight facilities in the park.
- TMNP is an urban park and visitors already had other accommodation in Cape Town.
- Visitors did not have enough time to spend a night in the park.
- Visitors lived in or around Cape Town.

A Wild Card is a loyalty card scheme implemented by South African National Parks

(SANParks) for regular visitors to parks across South Africa where holders of this card can enjoy benefits such as free entry into all SAN-Parks. For visitors to TMNP, having a Wild Card was not of importance and the majority of visitors tended not to have one.

Visitor spending included fees for entrance and conservation (ZAR141.45), restaurants (ZAR129.26), accommodation (ZAR364.72), food (ZAR57.00), beverages (ZAR26.85), transport to and from the park (ZAR134.39), souvenirs and jewellery (ZAR17.85), and spending on clothes and footwear (ZAR22.74). The average amount spent by visitors per trip to TMNP was calculated at ZAR894.26.

In terms of job creation, TMNP employs 871 individuals whose income is solely dependent on the park and its activities (Saayman *et al.*, 2013, 454). Due to the size of the park, and because it is an urban park, the number of employees needed for performing daily work is low compared to other national parks in South Africa. For instance, the Kruger National Park employs 10,150 people (Saayman *et al.*, 2013, 454). If TMNP wishes to increase the number of employees in the future, more facilities and activities would have to be initiated, which will create a demand for more workers to be employed at the park, so as to ensure that the service delivery at the park does not falter (Saayman *et al.*, 2013, 454).

Travel Motivations of Visitors to TMNP

Travel motivations significantly aid in the determination of marketing strategies for destinations and are, therefore, of paramount importance if TMNP visitor numbers (as well as awareness of the destination) are to be increased (Slabbert, 2002). The research conducted found that the main motivations of visitors to TMNP as a recreation destination were in line with the motivations of visitors to TMNP as identified by Scholtz *et al.* (2011, 18), and can be summarized as follows:

- Visitors have the desire to explore a new destination.
- They visit the park for the scenic beauty and view.

- They visit TMNP for photographic purposes.
- Visitors want to learn more about specific marine life found within the park, such as penguins.
- They visit because Table Mountain is a world-renowned attraction, World Heritage site and one of the New7Wonders of Nature.
- Visitors have a need to relax.
- Visitors want to spend time with family for recreation, or to spend time with someone special.

Other motivations of visitors to TMNP included factors such as:

- TMNP offers a value for money experience.
- The park enables a break from a daily routine.
- Visitors are able to learn more about nature and conservation practices.
- Visitors want to take part in activities such as hiking, dog walking, fishing, surfing and wind surfing, rock climbing and mountain biking.

Conclusion

The purpose of this chapter was to examine TMNP as a mountain tourism destination. The history of Table Mountain and the establishment of TMNP was reviewed. This was followed by a discussion on mountains as tourism destinations and how they impact on surrounding communities, and ended with an exploration of the profile and travel motivations of visitors to TMNP.

From the very first construction projects on Table Mountain, involving the establishment of transportation methods up the mountain, to the latest improvements to the Table Mountain Aerial Cableway, this mountain destination has gone from being one of mere aesthetic benefit to one of the New7Wonders of Nature, in a World Heritage site designated region, and a national park. Further conclusions that can be drawn from the analysis include the fact that, overall, TMNP has a positive impact on the community and economy of Cape

Town, South Africa, and results in a variety of benefits to both community members and the country as a whole. Such benefits include growth of the economy, increased employment rate, value added to the quality of life of community members, positive social impacts such as beautiful scenery, and an easily accessible recreation area close to residents of Cape Town.

In conclusion, TMNP is a destination that differs significantly from destinations in the surrounding area, based on size, relevance and benefits. By publishing research concerning both knowledge and understanding of the profiles of the visitors to TMNP and their motivations to visit, the literature concerning the mountain tourism industry is increased, thereby aiding in the development and expansion of this industry across the world (Slabbert, 2002).

As a further explanation of the importance of establishing the profile and motives of the market for mountain tourism, Slabbert (2002) suggests that the determination of the travel motivations of a specific market is a critical step in the segmentation of the market, without which effective marketing of the destination, in this case TMNP, would be impossible.

It is clear that mountain tourism, even though not a new concept in South Africa, provides areas for potential future research and development to better understand the full impact of this sector of the tourism industry. Such fruitful areas for research could include further market research at mountain tourism destinations, as well as correlation studies in order to compare mountain tourism across South Africa, as well as with international mountain tourism destinations.

References

Beedie, P. and Hudson, S. (2003) Emergence of mountain based adventure tourism. *Annals of Tourism Research* 30(3), 625–643.

Bryant, M.M. (2006) Urban landscape conservation and the role of ecological greenways at local and metropolitan scales. *Landscape and Urban Planning* 76, 23–44.

Cape Town (2014) Table Mountain Aerial Cableway. Available at: http://www.capetown.travel/attractions/entry/table_mountain_cableway (accessed 23 May 2014).

Chiesura, A. (2004) The role of urban parks for the sustainable city. *Landscape and Urban Planning* 68, 129–138.

Daitz, D. and Myrdal, B. (2012) Table Mountain National Park. In: Suich, H., Child, B. and Spenceley, A. (eds) *Evolution and Innovation in Wildlife Conservation: Parks and Game Ranches to Transfrontier Conservation Areas*. Earthscan, London.

Findtripinfo.com (2014) The Summit of Cape Town's Table Mountain. Available at: http://www.findtripinfo.com/south-africa/cape-town/table-mountain-cape-town.html (accessed 3 October 2014).

Forsyth, G.G. and Van Wilgen, B.W. (2008) The recent fire history of the Table Mountain National Park and implications for fire management. *Koedoe* 50(1), 3–9.

Gobster, P.H. (2001) Visions of nature: conflict and compatibility in urban park restoration. *Landscape and Urban Planning* 56, 35–51.

Kastenholz, E. and Rodrigues, A. (2007) Discussing the potential benefits of hiking tourism in Portugal: an exploratory study of the market profile and its expenditure levels. *ANATOLIA – An International Journal of Tourism and Hospitality Research* 8(1), 5–22.

Lubbe, B.A. (2012) *Tourism Management in Southern Africa*. Pearson Education South Africa, Cape Town, Republic of South Africa.

McCool, S. (2002) Mountains and tourism: meeting the challenges of sustainability in a messy world. In: McKay, J. *et al.* (eds) *Celebrating Mountains: Proceedings of an International Year of Mountain Conference*. Australian Alps Liaison Committee & Canprint Communications. Jindabyne, Australia 99, 311–318.

Nepal, S. and Chipeniuk, R. (2005) Mountain tourism: toward a conceptual framework. *Tourism Geographies* 7(1), 313–333.

Robertson, D. and Hull, R. (2001) Which nature? A case study of Whitetop Mountain. *Landscape Journal* 20, 176–185.

Rössler, M. (2006) World heritage cultural landscapes: a UNESCO flagship programme 1992–2006. *Landscape Research* 31(4), 333–353.

Saayman, M., Saayman, A. and Rossouw, R. (2013) The socio-economic impact of Table Mountain National Park. *Journal of Economic and Financial Sciences* 6(2), 439–458.

Salazar, S. and Menendez, L.C. (2007) Estimating the non-market benefits of an urban park: does proximity matter? *Land Use Policy* 24, 296–305.

SANParks (2015) Table Mountain National Park: World Heritage Site Status. Available at: http://www.sanparks.org/parks/table_mountain/conservation/heritage.php (accessed 11 March 2015).

Santillanis, A. (2009) Early Views of Table Mountain. Primitive culture. Available at: http://primitiveculture.blogspot.com/2009/11/early-views-of-table-mountain.html (accessed 18 March 2015).

Scholtz, M., Van der Merwe, P. and Saayman, M. (2011) *Table Mountain National Park: A Marketing Analysis*. TREES (Tourism Research in Economic Environs and Society), Potchefstroom, South Africa.

Silva, A., Kastenholz, E. and Abrantes, J.L. (2013) Place-attachment, destination image and impacts of tourism in mountain destinations. *ANATOLIA – An International Journal of Tourism and Hospitality Research* 24(1), 17–29.

Singh, T. (2007) Mountain resort planning and development in an era of globalisation. *Annals of Tourism Research* 34(1), 1090–1091.

Skeldon, R. (1985) Population pressure, mobility and socio-economic change in mountainous environments: regions of refuge in comparative perspective. *Mountain Research and Development* 5(1), 233–250.

Slabbert, E. (2002) Key success factors in market segmentation. Unpublished MA dissertation. North-west University, Potchefstroom, Republic of South Africa.

South African History Online (2014) Table Mountain. Available at: http://www.sahistory.org.za/places/table-mountain (accessed 23 May 2014).

South African Tourism (2014a) From Cape Point to Table Mountain: Table Mountain National Park. Available at: http://www.southafrica.net/za/en/articles/entry/article-southafrica.net-table-mountain-national-park (accessed 10 March 2015).

South African Tourism (2014b) Table Mountain, Cape Town. Available at: http://www.southafrica.net/za/en/articles/entry/article-southafrica.net-table-mountain (accessed 23 May 2014).

Table Mountain Aerial Cableway (2014) About the Cableway. Available at: http://www.tablemountain.net/about/the_table_mountain_aerial_cableway/ (accessed 23 May 2014).

Thomas, C., Gill, A. and Hartmann, R. (2006) *Mountain Resort Planning and Development in an Era of Globalisation*. Cognizant Communications Corporation, New York.

Thompson, C.W. (2002) Urban open spaces in the 21st century. *Landscape and Urban Planning* 60, 59–72.

Times Live (2012) Table Mountain Becomes One of the World's New7Wonders of Nature. Available at: http://www.timeslive.co.za/travel/2012/12/03/table-mountain-becomes-one-of-the-world-s-new-seven-wonders-of-nature (accessed 11 March 2015).

UNESCO (2015) World Heritage List. Available at: http://whc.unesco.org/en/list/ (accessed 27 November 2015).

Van der Merwe, P., Slabbert, E. and Saayman, M. (2011) Travel motivations of tourists to selected marine destinations. *International Journal of Tourism Research* 13(1), 457–467.

32 Governance of French Ski Resorts: Will the Historic Economic Development Model Work for the Future?

Emmanuelle George-Marcelpoil* and Hugues François
Irstea Research Unit DTM, Grenoble, France

Introduction

Mountain tourism, particularly winter sports has over the past century provided a number of economic opportunities for mountain regions. Many high mountain communities and villages are significantly dependent on winter snow sports as an economic driver of these locales. By way of example, in Savoie region of France, winter sports generates over 33% of the territory's gross domestic product; almost 50% if indirect economic impacts are included (SMBT, 2014). This has often been referred to as a bounty of 'white gold' during the *Trente Glorieuses*, that is, the three post-war decades, but which is currently under threat in the global context.

The focus of this chapter is on the future of resorts in France and in other tourist contexts, using parameters such as climate (increase in the vulnerability of resorts to climate changes (Abegg *et al.*, 2007)); factors concerning society (ageing of the target skier population, erosion of the clientele); and technology (the role of social networks in the reputation of tourist destinations). In addition, ski resorts, emblematic of mass tourism, especially in France, are directly concerned with the evolution of a development model towards greater sustainability (Marcelpoil *et al.*, 2010).

This evolution toward more sustainability can be illustrated by several initiatives conducted at different levels (Luthe, 2013). In the USA (George, 2003), in a response broadly to the increasing interest in sustainable mountain resort practices, and in particular in responding to the pressures of violent actions regarding the 'eco-terrorist' movement Earth Liberation Front against a Vail Mountain Resort extension project in Colorado, the National Ski Areas Association invested in the creation of the Sustainable Slope Charter in 2000 (Sottovia, 2013). Sustainable development emerged in Europe with the Convention on the Protection of the Alps (Abegg, 2011). In France, a charter for the development of mountain resorts by the National Association of the Mayors of Mountain Resorts was created in 2007 (ANMSM, 2007). In addition, ski lifts in France, with the development of ISO 14001 procedures, the international standard covering the certification of ski lifts, attempt to guarantee in particular the establishment of environmental management systems.

With changing demand patterns, long-term climatic challenges and far more diverse travel interests of regional and international tourists, these and other factors call into question the economic model on which ski resorts are based and,

---

* Corresponding author: emmanuelle.george-marcelpoil@irstea.fr more specifically, the fundamental relationship between tourist accommodation and ski lift infrastructures. This chapter will begin by reminding readers that the creation and expansion of resorts in the various mountain regions of France during the period between the Second World War and the 1980s was based on a cyclic relationship between accommodation and ski lifts. Describing in detail the current trends regarding ski lifts and accommodation respectively, the second part of the chapter will emphasize that the economic model still operates based on the same accommodation–ski lift relationship, but with some real differences as compared to the initial period. In practice, the pursuit of urbanization for tourism purposes calls into question the viability of various economic scenarios available to the local stakeholders. Can those connected with the ski resort industry influence the land dynamics in their regional areas? Do they have the financial and land capacities, and how do they manage with the economic operators? These are issues this chapter will examine in the final section.

The Historical Background of the French Economic Model

France, like its European neighbours, underwent a development in winter tourism at the end of the 19th century and in the early 20th century. Much has been written about the role of the elite in the spread of this new type of tourism, supplementing the summer recreational activities already well established in the mountains (Larique, 2006). As such, resorts came into being early in the 20th century, which have become emblematic of the French tourism industry, such as the mega-mountain resorts of Val d'Isère, Megève or Chamonix. With these first tourist resorts, specifically recognized for skiing, the most important factors are the progressiveness and variety of the actions and initiatives leading to their creation. Many different stakeholders were involved including public figures with the unprecedented role of elected representatives, in particular the mayors who believed in the tourism adventure, and also economic stakeholders, both local and external, who contributed ideas and property as well as their financing networks. Resorts grew up, often based on existing villages, sometimes at very

high altitude (as in the case of Val d'Isère, 1850 m above sea level, on the road between France and Italy) without any real master plan with regard to urbanization or architecture.

The Rising of a Snow Plan: the Local Roots of a National Doctrine

In this context, once the law governing annual paid leave was voted on in 1936, the state endeavoured to set up a real tourism structure able to offer recreational activities. A survey was therefore launched in the French mountains to identify the best sites to host resorts and thus facilitate France's rise to prominence as a European winter holiday destination. This aim was continued under the Vichy government with 'Mission 42', the conclusions of which remained at the recommendation stage during the Second World War but which became relevant once more in the climate of post-war reconstruction, through the Savoie department in the Alps. This department, like many others, was seeking a path to economic reconstruction and initially looked into hydroelectric power. However, this option was quickly discarded as the state had decided to nationalize electricity production. Savoie then turned to winter sports tourism and adopted the conclusions of 'Mission 42' applicable to its scope of operation for itself (François and George-Marcelpoil, 2012).

After setbacks in several municipalities (François and George-Marcelpoil, 2012), Saint-Bon-en-Tarentaise was selected to create a resort, Courchevel, from scratch. The stakes were high: a resort was to be built from nothing, *ex-nihilo*, and provide local economic development. Courchevel was thus launched in 1946 and took several years to build under the leadership of two famous sons of the mountain regions, the architect Laurent Chappis and the civil servant Maurice Michaud. What is striking about the Courchevel project is the desire to plan the site rationally, facilitated from a real estate point of view by the Alpine pastures located above the level of 1850 m in altitude made available by the municipality. At Courchevel, it was the creation of tourist infrastructures, in this case the drag lifts, which would initially be seen as the source of profit, justifying the total development. However, this first calculation was quickly put aside given the practicalities and the burden of the investments for the ski lifts. It was the development of cheap agricultural land that was to allow the construction and subsequent sale of tourism real estate. The money quickly generated could then be invested in the development of facilities, especially the installation of ski lifts, and the enlargement and improvement of the ski area. As the latter grew, it was logical to construct new tourist accommodation.

The tourism real estate–ski lift cycle thus took shape starting with Courchevel, with the aim of attracting private investors for the accommodation. Hopes were quickly fulfilled and then exceeded with a poorly controlled expansion in urbanization at Courchevel 1850 m and below (in the sites at lower altitude), thus exceeding the 23,000 beds initially planned (Perret, 1992; Marcelpoil *et al.*, 2012).

Rules and Legal Means to Build Ski Resorts

The lessons learned at Courchevel were incorporated into the *Plan Neige* (Snow Plan) in the 1960s. This allowed the French state, which was very much in favour of a strong sector-specific planning rationale at this point in time during the booming *Trente Glorieuses*, to encourage the emergence of a real tourist industry with resorts of international renown. To this end, it applied the Courchevel model on a large scale, based on planning (particularly real estate) and rationalization, but orchestrated not by a public figure like the Savoie department, but by a private one-man-band, which it considered to be the only suitable solution in order to achieve such ambitions. This marked the advent of so-called integrated resorts, *ex-nihilo*, such as Les Arcs and La Plagne, managed by sole promoters and their financing systems, in addition to the support of the State through the 1958 order authorizing expropriation for public purposes (see French Ordinance n°58-5597 23 November 1958, relating to the revision of expropriation rules for public interest).

The number of resorts grew and the tourism real estate–ski lift equation was in full swing. On the one hand, the quick return on investment offered by the tourism real estate allowed the long-term amortization of the ski lifts. On the other hand, the profitability of this economic model favoured accommodation based on low ratios of 9–12 m² per bed, which, in addition to satisfying customers attracted by the urban model, allowed maximum potential to be obtained from the real estate and resulted in the creation of a large supply of accommodation. Thus the resort of La Plagne today has 65,000 beds for tourists (François *et al.*, 2012; see also interactive version, available at http://www.observatoire-stations.fr).

This model continued to develop into the 1980s, when demand first started to slacken off. The first winters with no snow in the 1989/1990/1991 seasons underlined how dependent resorts were on snow resources and marked the end of the growth in the number of resorts in France, which then stood at approximately 350 sites. The era of managing the existing resorts had arrived, which meant securing the long-term future of the sector.

Resorts Today: Ski Lift Operation, a Key Issue for Tourism Real Estate

Since the early 1990s, the winter sports sector has been faced with various issues, which have very real impacts on its viability. The first issue concerns the falling numbers of customers over a number of years. Even if the representatives make every effort to confirm France's leading position in terms of winter sports, with a total of 58 million skier-days in 2013 for all the French sites, the reality of the situation is less black-and-white. The number of French people going on skiing holidays is stagnant at approximately 8.2%, and only 7.5% actually ski. More worrisome is the recent report for the 2013/2014 winter season (DSF, 2014) that highlights a 4% fall in national attendance compared to the previous season with sometimes severe drops – 30% for the Vosges area and 15% for the Jura.

Same Tourism, New Expectations

Beyond the falling numbers of holidaymakers, the change with regard to the clientele is above all qualitative. Expectations have diversified, with tourists who ski less during the day, who want safe skiing and who want a resort experience that is far removed from a standard product (Holbrook and Hirschmann, 1982; Batat and Frochot, 2013). In this context, the tourism sector has not been spared by the explosion of digital technology in society, with the arrival of new information and communication technologies (ICTs), which have fundamentally shaken up methods of communication, promotion and loyalty in resorts (Buhalis and O'Connor, 2006). What is at stake is the differentiation of the tourism offer, in line with knowledge of the clientele, customer profiles and reactivity, etc. Thus, as the manager of Val Thorens Tours, Eric Bonnel, points out, the creation of a shared brand, Live United, makes it possible to

> maintain a presence among customers all year round, position the resort in its global environment, its region, create new activities [in order to] create a lasting link, and offer our customers great experiences so that they will be our ambassadors, our communicators [using] social networks.

This communication strategy paid off. Val Thorens won the World Ski Awards in 2013, ahead of 188 resorts from 20 nations.

The positioning of French resorts, particularly in the category of the largest resorts, is based on a quantitative evaluation of performance. Indeed, there are countless marketing pitches boasting the number of kilometres of ski runs in resorts and the power of the ski lifts, in order to appear and remain among the elite of international resorts. Thus, the construction of the largest cable car in the world in 2003, carrying 200 people per gondola and connecting La Plagne with Les Arcs in Savoie, was part of this strategy. The challenge is to attract an international clientele. However, a German study published in autumn 2013 (Schrahe, 2013) denounced the methods of calculating the length of ski runs, which lead resorts to overestimate the lengths by 34% on average, sometimes even twice that figure, highlighting the difference between the number of kilometres stated and the reality, and, ultimately, the race in quantitative criteria. For example the 3 Vallées ski area (which includes Courchevel), whose slogan is 'the largest ski area in the world', in reality has 493 km of ski runs instead of the 600 km stated, an exaggeration of 22%. The revelations of this study have led many sites to stop giving the length of their ski runs on their websites.

From Performance to Investment: Resorts Inequalities

This reading of resort performance highlights the critical importance of the ski lifts (Sottovia, 2013). This is backed up by recent scientific works concerning resort performance (Botti et al., 2012; Goncalves, 2013) that all strongly favour criteria linked to the physical material of the facilities (the slopes) and the infrastructures (ski lifts, snow machines, etc.). In practice, the global performance of a resort is assessed based on the key figure of turnover generated by ski lifts together with additional indicators, such as the number of skier-days, trips on the ski lifts, slopes, number and kind of ski lifts, and the volume of investments; in other words, only measurable criteria. In France, this qualitative pre-eminence has led to the production of a synthetic indicator, the power moment, defined as the product of the flow (people/hour) by the height travelled (in metres). This indicator gives a uniform vision of the equipment, and makes it possible to assess the global volume of a resort's ski lifts. Based on this, DSF defines four categories of resort: 'Small' with a power moment (PM) less than 2500, 'Medium' between 2500 and 5000, 'Large' between 5000 and 15,000 and 'Very Large' when the PM is higher than 15,000. The issue concerns the size of the ski area, its commercial character with new, fast infrastructures, allowing customers to be transported quickly to the top of the ski area without breakdowns and in suitably comfortable conditions.[1] This 'headlong dash' to equip the ski area and to achieve customer satisfaction, in the context of a mature market, is illustrated by Fig. 32.1, which highlights the high rate of expansion of the power moment according to the types of category of resort over the last 25 years.

The investments made by the very large and internationally renowned resorts have become a standard, influencing the other categories of resort, and justifying considerable investments in

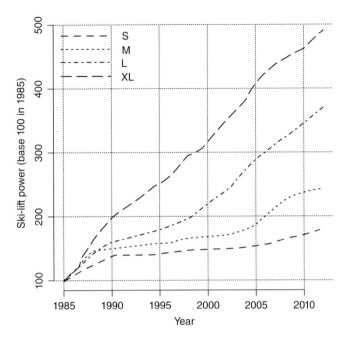

Fig. 32.1. Expansion of the 'Power Moment' in ski lifts.

all the French resorts in order to compete with foreign destinations.

In view of the maturity of the market, this type of movement to equip resorts obviously questions the capacity of the ski lift operators, which comes under the specific French institutional context with regard to the management of ski areas. Indeed, since the mountain law of 1985, ski lifts have been a public service, entrusted to the municipalities, which cannot deny their management responsibilities. Local authorities may choose to manage the lifts themselves through an agency, or to delegate management by delegating public services to private operators or semi-public companies. In practice, most international resorts are managed by private operators (see Fig. 32.2) among which the Compagnie des Alpes (CDA) occupies centrestage, managing the largest French resorts, resorts which in theory are less concerned by climate change (see Fig. 32.3). The CDA, whose turnover reached €678 million in 2013, has real means to invest in ski areas and slope maintenance, tasks which traditionally fell to the ski lift operators, to which have now been added newer operations (CDA, 2013). In different previous research projects (François et al.,

2014; Spandre et al., forthcoming), we could observe a major trend to manage slope profiling and snow production, and more recently, the rising of a detailed knowledge of the clientele, becoming a market specifier.

What Room for Manoeuvre is Available to the Resorts: Alliances Between Stakeholders?

Above and beyond the financial surface necessary to fulfil this equipment policy, the operators must also possess a suitable product in the accommodation sector. We are a long way from the period of the integrated resorts, where the resort manager held both the ski area and the tourist accommodation. This area of activity is now under the control of accommodation operators such as the Pierre et Vacances (PV) group, MGM, a group from the Haute-Savoie area, and construction of high-end chalets and residences. Since the decentralization laws of 1982–1993, the local authorities have increased means at their disposal, particularly in the context of real-estate management with

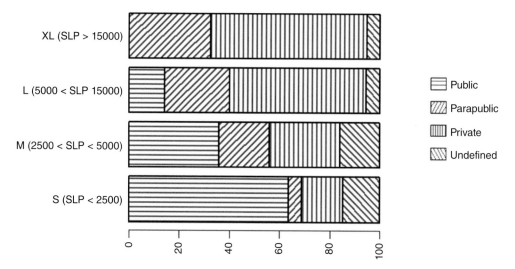

Fig. 32.2. Resort management by public, parapublic, private and undefined.

the PLU (Local Town Planning), which contributes to the allocation of land and its use. In practice, Local Town Planning was introduced by the SRU Solidarity and Urban Renovation law of 2000, replacing the POS (Land Use Plan). The PLU is a town-planning document that, for a group of municipalities or an individual municipality, establishes a global town planning and development project and sets out the general rules for land use for the area in question in line with this project. The local authority is therefore under pressure from two sources: on the one hand, from the ski lift operators, who justify the creation of new beds by the argument of their increased costs; and on the other hand, from property developers who, in response to the demand of the clientele, boast new forms of tourist accommodation.

Real Estate in Resorts: The Limits of the Growth

This saw the appearance of alliances between stakeholders at several levels. The relationship first of all concerns the ski lift operators in connection with the property developer-builders and tourism real-estate managers (George-Marcelpoil and François, 2013). As confirmed by interviews with some resorts stakeholders, the CDA and Pierre et Vacances (PV) have

become noticeably closer, verging on a real collusion of interests (George-Marcelpoil et al., 2012).

> Very strong synergies can be seen between the Compagnie des Alpes and Pierre & Vacances, for example. These synergies go well beyond ... deals, which may exist for certain operations.

The interest for PV is to create joint products with the CDA, thus improving its profitability:

> And ... it is in its (PV) interest to say to itself: 'If we make an alliance with the Compagnie des Alpes, we show joint products with joint tools and joint visibility, we are at ... to simplify, 70% of the occupancy rate for the season. We might be able to get to 75 or 80%.' And it's pure margin.

The stakeholder system then widens to alliances between ski lifts and local authorities. The key challenge for operators is to convince the local authorities, initially the mayors, to open new building rights for new accommodation. To do so, the main arguments put forward are a continual loss of so-called professional commercial beds and the failure of beds for tourists to match the needs of the clientele. The aim is, on the one hand, to establish the reduced profitability of the accommodation for the winter season and, on the other, the need to respond to customers by particularly promoting hotels and tourist residences.[2] The latter form of accommodation[3] does indeed correspond best to customer expectations

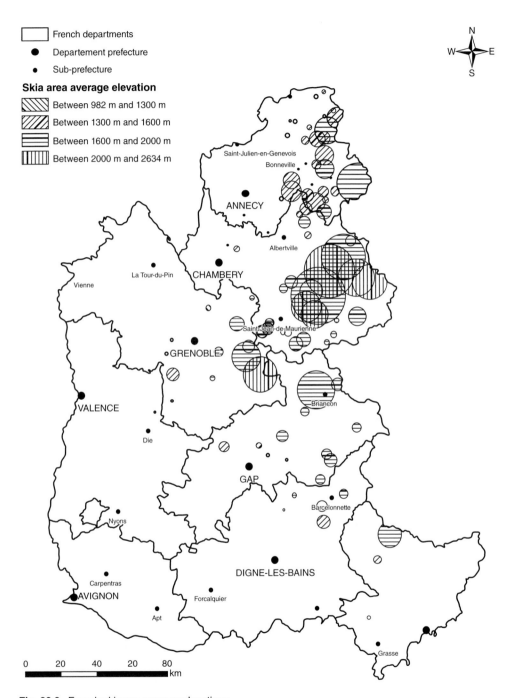

Fig. 32.3. French ski area average elevations.

with new, high-quality accommodation and associated services. In practice, since 2000, almost 420,000 m² of habitable surface area on average is built each year in the Alpine resorts (Fablet and George-Marcelpoil, 2013). Most of the recent development operations in resorts concern the creation of beds for tourists in tourist residences.

The stakes are high: the attractiveness of the resorts needs to be supported by investment in new ski lifts, the operation of which is secured by the development of the real estate and its performances in terms of occupancy. Although the economic and commercial context of winter sports has profoundly changed, we find ourselves faced with the same foundations for the economic model of the resorts. But for how long?

In addition to the consumption of natural resources involved in this type of process, the actual viability of the economic model is on hold. The land available in the mountains, in addition to the related natural hazards and the associated extra cost of construction, is not unlimited and some sites, such as Val d'Isère, no longer have any areas to build on. On a more fundamental level, it is the economic viability of pursuing the real-estate trend, which is in question. A recent diagnosis in *Eco des Pays de Savoie*[4] reports difficulties in the new-build market in resorts over the past few seasons. In Savoie, Haute-Savoie and Isère, 6800 beds for tourists were authorized in 2013, of which sale is only guaranteed for 4.4%, a percentage that reflects real tensions.

Which Ways to Improve the Management of Existing Resources?

Such difficulties should encourage resorts to seek solutions and room for manoeuvre. Among the available possibilities, the rehabilitation of the existing tourism real estate – particularly that created in the 1970s – is becoming a key issue (Miquel *et al.*, 2010). Many initiatives have been launched in particular by French lawmakers through the SRU (Urban Solidarity and Renewal) law of 2000 and operations to renovate tourism real estate (ORIL). The lack of success can be put down to the cumbersome administration linked to these approaches, but also to the easier option of creating new beds. However, as renovation is urgent to avoid what some are already referring to as tourist wastelands (Vlès, 2006, Hatt, 2011), the CDA has turned to its parent company, the Caisse des Dépôts et Consignations (CDC), and banks to found real-estate companies in several resorts. These real-estate companies make it possible

to buy beds for renovation, renovate them and sell the rehabilitated beds, the sale of which then allows the rehabilitation process to be continued. These companies have the combined financial capacity of the CDA and the CDC to enter the tourism real-estate market and thus have a lever effect on the thorny question of the rehabilitation of tourist accommodation. In this context, local authorities can try to review the new bed/rehabilitated bed ratio to encourage at least a balance or even a preference for rehabilitation in the future.

There is a second institutional factor. Indeed, French lawmakers are seeking to encourage municipalities to come together in administrative groupings to combat the fragmentation of municipalities often criticized in France. They have also tackled the question of regional planning with the necessity of setting up a SCOT (regional planning cohesion scheme). This urban planning document, resulting from the SRU law, establishes a coherent, joint regional project for several municipalities or groups of municipalities. However, the reality is that few SCOTs are approved in mountain regions and particularly in areas linked to ski resorts,[5] whereas this urban planning tool is currently the only route for new urban planning. It is proving even more difficult for resorts to fit their future into a much vaster spatial region and to have their strategy dictated by a higher level, in this case the inter-municipality group.

In any case, at a more local level, a differentiation in the strategies of resorts is making an appearance, as shown in Fig. 32.4, representing several real-estate trends in resorts situated in the Tarentaise Valley. Although the upward trend is generalized, that of Courchevel born in the 1940s is more marked than that of Valmorel, a resort that was created towards the end of the 1970s. The real-estate choices are more measured for the latter, but the local authority does not hesitate to use spatial resources to build new accommodations. The creation of a Club Med at Valmorel in 2011 thus corresponds to the creation of new beds, managed by a large group, which, together with beds in flats rented out by professionals, supplements the accommodation offer of hotels and holiday homes.

A final element in terms of sustainability results from the concept of habitability. Indeed,

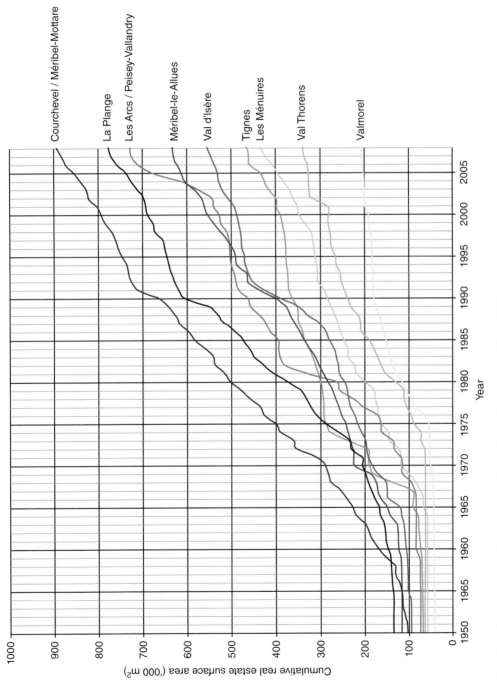

Fig. 32.4. Real-estate trends in resorts in Terentaise Valley (source: Fablet, 2013).

the rise in the price of real estate is often very significant in resorts,[6] with both spatial and socio-economic consequences. In practice, this rise limits the possibility for certain categories of the population to get a foot on the property ladder, particularly local or seasonal workers. These populations are therefore obliged to reside outside the resorts, often in the valleys, thus leading to significant numbers of commuters and the resulting effects on facilities and services (François and Marcelpoil, 2008).

Conclusion

In the future, research work should focus on qualifying the development trends of the resorts. Areas of development for resorts are already apparent under the joint effect of factors specific to the destination and also to the overall context. As such, some resorts are pursuing their model based on tourists staying in the resort for their entire holiday, whereas others have moved on towards recognizing and taking into account excursion tourism. Some sites remain structured by the winter tourism economy, whereas others are hesitating or actively seeking to interlink the development of tourism and residential development. Finally, some sites are adopting an integration model, bringing them closer to an American concept of the resort. All these trends and paths must be specified both in their fields and the way they are changing. Thus, the future of the winter sports sector is clearly bound by the assessment of both local

and global evolution factors. Two dimensions would seem to be important in this context.

The first concerns the way in which the system of stakeholders in the economic model of a resort does or does not share the same vision of the destination and of its future to contribute to a renewal of the resort's economic model. Amid the changes of town councils during the latest local elections, the local authorities can be seen to be adopting different positions with regard to development and the intensity of the levels of development hoped for. It will be a matter of how the perception of these issues by the new stakeholders can contribute to changing the direction that development is taking.

The second dimension concerns climate change and the way in which resorts will adapt to this. Adaptation strategies will have a technological aspect, reflecting the progress made in the production of artificial snow to compensate for the lack of natural snow. Adapting will also involve to an even greater extent organizational and economic responses, depending on the degree of vulnerability of the resorts and their evaluations.

Such changes will inevitably have an impact on the landscape of French resorts, leading to a form of selection among them. This includes quantitative selection, with no doubt a reduction in the number of resorts in the long term, and qualitative selection with a renewal of the economic models, or even new models, and development for these winter destinations.

Notes

[1]Moreover, the ski lift profession pushed hard but unsuccessfully for this comfort criterion to be included in the calculation of the ski-lift power.

[2]The recent study carried out in 2014 for the Syndicat National des Résidences de Tourisme (SNRT) highlights the fact that in June 2014 the number of beds in the network stood at 775,000, i.e. 25% of the tourist accommodation buildings. This figure rises to as much as 55% in the Savoie and Haute-Savoie areas, which are deeply involved with the resorts.

[3]A tourist residence is a 'classified commercial accommodation establishment' that is operated permanently or during the holiday season. It comprises a uniform group of rooms or furnished flats organized in collective units or houses, offered for rental by the day, by the week or by the month to a tourist clientele, which does not live there permanently. It is provided with a minimum of equipment and shared services (source: http://www.insee.fr, accessed 14 August 2014).

[4]*Eco des Pays de Savoie*, no. 32–33, 8 August 2014.

[5]See the relevant map available at: http://www.rhone-alpes.developpement-durable.gouv.fr/les-scot-en-rhone-alpes-a366.html (accessed 14 august 2014).

[6]For example, the average price of property may reach €15,000/m² for accommodation near the slopes at Courchevel, and €7000/m² overall in most of the 'international' resorts (source: http://www.challenges.fr, accessed 14 August 2014).

References

Abegg, B. (2011) Tourism in Climate Change, Compact n1, Background Report. Cipra International. Available at: http://www.cipra.org/fr/pdfs/110223f_compactTourismus.pdf/at_download/file (accessed 14 August 2014).

Abegg, B., Agrawala, S., Crick, F. and De Montfalcon, A. (2007) Climate change impacts and adaptation in winter tourism. In: Agrawala, S. (ed.) *Climate Change in the European Alps: Adapting Winter Tourism and Natural Hazards Management*. OECD, Paris, France, pp. 25–60.

ANMSM (2007) National charter in favour of sustainable development in mountain resorts. Document produced in partnership with ADEME and MountainRiders. Available at: http://admin.anmsm.fr/Upload/Mediatheque/mini-site-developpement-durable/presentation/Charte-DD-GB.pdf (accessed 14 August 2014).

Batat, W. and Frochot, I. (2013) *Towards an Experimental Approach in Tourism Studies*. Handbook of Tourism Marketing, Scott Maccabe editions, Routledge, London.

Botti, L., Goncalves, O. and Peypoch, N. (2012) Benchmarking Pyrenean ski resorts. *Journal of Alpine Research/Revue de géographie alpine* 100(4). Available at: http://rga.revues.org/1855 (accessed 14 August 2014).

Buhalis, D. and O'Connor, P. (2006) Information and communications technology – revolutionising tourism. In: Buhalis, D. and Costa, C. (eds) *Tourism Management Dynamics – Trends, Management and Tools*. Elsevier, Burlington, Vermont.

CDA (2013) Document de référence & rapport financier annuel 2013. Available at: https://www.compagniedesalpes.com/amf_fr/2014/document-reference-CDA-2013.pdf (accessed 14 August 2014).

DSF (2014) Saison d'hiver 2013/2014. Un bilan globalement moyen. *La montagne en mouvement*, no. 36, pp. 3–4. Available at: http://www.domaines-skiables.fr/downloads/Mag36-DSF-Juillet2014-BD.pdf (accessed 14 August 2014).

Fablet, G. (2013) Real estate development in the ski resorts of the Tarentaise Valley. *Journal of Alpine Research/Revue de géographie alpine* 101(3). Available at: http://rga.revues.org/2196 (accessed 14 August 2014). DOI: 10.4000/rga.2196.

Fablet, G. and George-Marcelpoil E. (2013) Formes et impacts des dynamiques foncières et immobilières en stations de montagne: l'exemple du massif alpin. In: Joye, J.F. (ed.) *L'urbanisation de la montagne. Observations depuis le versant juridique*. University of Savoy, Chambéry, France, pp. 43–59.

François, H. and George-Marcelpoil, E. (2012) Vallée de la Tarentaise: de l'invention du Plan neige à la constitution d'un milieu innovateur dans le domaine du tourisme d'hiver. *Histoire des Alpes* 17, 227–242.

François, H. and Marcelpoil, E. (2008) Mutations touristiques, mutations foncières: vers un renouvellement des formes d'ancrage territorial des stations, chapitre 13, 177–195. In: Clarimont, S. and Vlès, V. (ed.) *Tourisme durable en montagne: entre discours et pratiques*. Editions Afnor, La Plaine-Saint-Denis, France.

François, H., George-Marcelpoil, E., Fablet, G., Bray, F., Achin, C., *et al.* (2012) Atlas des stations du massif des Alpes. Available at: http://cemadoc.irstea.fr/cemoa/PUB00036588 (accessed 14 August 2014).

François, H., Morin, S., Lafaysse, M. and George-Marcelpoil, E. (2014) Crossing numerical simulations of snow conditions with a spatially-resolved socio-economic database of ski resorts: a proof of concept in the French Alps. *Cold Region Science and Technology* 108, 98–112.

George, A. (2003) Managing ski resorts: perceptions from the field regarding the sustainable slopes charter. *Managing Leisure* 8, 41–46.

George-Marcelpoil, E. and François, H. (2013) From creating to managing resorts. Emerging stakeholder group rationales in the Tarentaise Valley. *Journal of Alpine Research/Revue de géographie alpine* 100(3). Available at: http://rga.revues.org/1925 (accessed 14 August 2014).

Goncalves, O. (2013) Efficiency and productivity of French ski resorts. *Tourism Management* 36, 650–657.

Hatt, E. (2011) Requalifier les stations touristiques contemporaines: une approche des espaces publics. Application à Gourette et Seignosse-Océan. Unpublished MSc thesis. University of Pau and Pays de l'Adour, Pau, France.

Holbrook, M.B. and Hirschmann, E.C. (1982) The experiential aspects of consumption: consumer fantasies, feeling and fun. *Journal of Consumer Research* 9, 132–140.

Larique, B. (2006) Les sports d'hiver en France: un développement conflictuel. Histoire d'une innovation touristique (1890–1940). *Flux* 1(63–64), 7–19.

Luthe, T. (2013) Comparaison et analyse des labels de durabilité pour la montagne, en Europe et dans le monde. Les stations de montagne en transition: Labels touristiques et durabilité. Conference presentation. Mountain Riders, 28 November 2013, Chambéry, France. Available at: http://www.mountain-riders. org/FLOCONVERT/TABLERONDE/LABEL%20DE%20DURABILITE-Tobias%20Luthe.pdf (accessed 6 August 2015).

Marcelpoil, E., Bensahel-Perrin, L. and François, H. (2010) *Les stations de sports d'hiver face au développement durable. Etat des lieux et perspectives*, L'Harmattan, Paris, France.

Marcelpoil, E., François, H. and Billet, S. (2012) L'ancrage du financement des stations de la vallée de la Tarentaise: une lecture territoriale. Rapport de Synthèse – Phase 2. FACIM, Chambéry, France.

Miquel, F., Mougey, J. and Ribières, G. (2010) *La réhabilitation de l'immobilier de loisirs en France*. Ministry of Ecology, Sustainable Development and Energy, Paris, France.

Perret, J. (1992) *Le développement touristique local. Les stations de sports d'hiver*. Editions Cemagref, Paris, France.

Schrahe, C. (2013) *The List of the World's 50 Largest Ski Areas*. Ski Weltweit, Montenius Consult International, Cologne, Germany.

SMBT (2014) Savoie Mont Blanc Tourisme website. Available at: http://pro.savoie-mont-blanc.com/Observatoire/ Nos-publications/Chiffres-cles (accessed 14 August 2014).

Sottovia, C. (2013) Durabilité et développement touristique des stations de ski: des modalités pratiques aux recommandations. L'exemple de la charte nationale en faveur du développement durable dans les stations de montagne. Unpublished Master's thesis, Sciences Po (Paris School of International Affairs), Paris, France.

Spandre, P., François, H., Morin, S. and George-Marcelpoil, E. (forthcoming) Dynamique de la neige de culture dans les Alpes Françaises: une stratégie d'adaptation au changement climatique? *Journal of Alpine Research/Revue de géographie alpine*.

Vlès, V. (2006) *Politiques publiques d'aménagement touristique: objectifs, méthodes, effets*. Editions Afnor, La Plaine-Saint-Denis, France.

33 The Development and Design of Ski Resorts: From Theory to Practice

Simon Hudson[1]* and Louise Hudson[2]
[1]*University of South Carolina, Columbia, South Carolina, USA;*
[2]*Freelance Travel and Ski Writer, Columbia, South Carolina, USA*

Introduction

The origins of skiing are open to debate. Petroglyphs depicting archaic skiing scenes have been discovered in the Altay Mountains of China as well as in Russia, with both countries staking their own claim to the first skiers. What is widely accepted, however, is that whoever first strapped on a pair of skis probably did so to hunt animals (Jenkins, 2013). Documentation of skiing's earliest emergence as a leisure pastime associated with tourism dates back to mid-19th-century Norway. Recreational skiing emerged in Australia and North America a few decades later, and soon after, socially focused skiing clubs began to develop in Australia and across Europe and North America, facilitating the creation of more and better ski facilities (Batchelor *et al.*, 1937).

The 1960s saw the start of the great ski boom. Europe witnessed the creation of a new generation of fully integrated ski stations, while in North America, larger resorts in New England, Colorado, California, the Canadian Rockies and the Eastern townships of Quebec emerged to meet the growing demand for winter vacations. While the 1970s were a period of massive market and product expansion, the 1980s presented a decade characterized by industry

consolidation and product management (Williams, 1993). By the mid-1980s ski facility supply had in many regions outstripped demand, and poorly managed ski destinations were experiencing financial difficulties (Kottke, 1990). The industry received some impetus from the snowboarding boom and 'shaped' skis in the 1990s, but the 2000s saw little increase in ski visits as major mature markets (like the USA, Canada and other Alpine countries) stagnated or declined, as was also the case with Japan, while other markets were emerging, such as China and Korea. The 2000s were also characterized by diversification in the industry. Winter resorts realized that they had to offer more activities than just skiing and boarding, both on- and off-snow. The more progressive resorts began to expand the range of activities they offered, such as ice skating, snow scooting, sledging and dog sledging, ice driving, paragliding, snowmobiling and tubing (the increasingly popular activity of sliding down the slope on the inner-tube of a truck tyre).

Today, the industry continues to be characterized by diversification and consolidation. Technological advances and rising infrastructure costs are the primary reason for increasing concentration in the industry, and further consolidation is possible as smaller regional resorts

---

* Corresponding author: shudson@hrsm.sc.edu

are acquired by larger resort operators with more sophisticated management capability. The ski industry is also highly vulnerable to climate change, which can have a devastating economic impact on ski resorts, requiring them to diversify their products and services and focus on alleviating the negative consequences of seasonality. If we factor in demographic shifts which are also dramatically affecting the ski industry landscape, then we have an environment of increasing uncertainty – where ski resort planning and development takes on a greater significance.

This chapter takes a look at the design and planning process for ski resorts, finishing with a case study about arguably the world's most successful ski resort designer, Paul Mathews, and his company, Ecosign, based in Whistler, British Columbia. The chapter begins, though, by examining the key stages in the design of ski resorts: gaining development approval; analysing site feasibility; deciding on design guidelines; and choosing development styles.

Development Approval

After the initial concept has been created, general design guidelines are established and the ski and base area capacities are determined. The ski runs will dictate the layout and size of the ski lift network, which will, in turn, influence the layout of the base area. Usually an environmental statement is then drafted, a profitability or pro-forma analysis made, and final design approval sought. This approval can sometimes take many years. The final approval for the Jumbo Glacier Resort in British Columbia, Canada, for example, took an unprecedented 21 years to go through the approval process, including four major public reviews of the proposal.

Many ski areas in North America are partially or completely located on public lands; over 90% of ski areas in the US Rocky Mountains and Pacific West, for example, operate under US Forest Service permits. In addition to a use fee, ski areas are asked to prepare Master Development Plans (MDPs) that identify the existing and desired conditions for the ski area and the proposed improvements on the National Forest System lands within the permit

boundary. These plans help the ski areas articulate their long-range vision for the use of public lands, and they help the Forest Service anticipate future use. A similar system is in place within the National Parks of Canada. Ski resorts will often employ specialist consultants to create such master plans, companies like International Alpine Design (IAD), Brent Harley & Associates (BHA), and Ecosign (profiled in this chapter).

An example of a ski resort MDP is the one produced by BHA for Big White in British Columbia, Canada (see Fig. 33.1). The MDP describes the proposed transformation of the ski resort into a major all-season world-class destination. The ski area was analysed in terms of slope, elevation, aspect and fall-line in order to gain an understanding of the alpine skiing development potential and its capability to physically and environmentally support additional four-season recreation activities. The plan suggested that at build-out, the facilities could accommodate a comfortable carrying capacity of 24,240 skiers and snowboarders per day. One of Big White's distinguishing features is the 'ski in–ski out' resort residential offering. Direct linkages to and from the base areas and the resort residential development areas are established by return ski trails, the pedestrian trail network and gondola lift.

Development approval varies depending on the country. In Germany, for example, the political acceptability of the project is a major factor in determining whether or not it will be approved. Politics was clearly the driver at Sochi, home of the 2014 Winter Olympics. The Russian President, Vladimir Putin, pushed development of the mountain area near Sochi with two agendas: to prepare for the Olympics and to foster in Russia the kind of world-class ski area available in other parts of Europe (Bachman, 2014). A long-term plan to expand ski facilities kicked off in 2007 when Sochi won the bid for the Games. Organizers built a train that takes visitors from the Sochi Airport to Rosa Khutor, the largest of the region's ski areas, and then accelerated lift construction. In total, 21.6 km (13 miles) of cable-car routes were built for the Games. One gondola took people to a peak near the start of the Olympic cross-country skiing and biathlon events.

Fig. 33.1. Master Development Plan for Big White in British Columbia (courtesy of Brent Harley & Associates).

It is the world's longest and fastest detachable-car ropeway, travelling at up to 8.5 m per second.

Site Feasibility

Naturally a key component of the planning process is site feasibility. As has often been said, the three most important factors necessary to ensure a successful business are 'location, location, location'. This old adage definitely applies to alpine ski resorts, as location, elevation and relief influence the reliability of snow cover and, added to this, the skiable area and configuration of a resort's slopes and physical environment, which are particularly crucial in its success. In addition to its ability to make snow, a ski resort's success entails the melding of key additional geographical factors such as continentality, climate and microclimate, elevation of the base and summit, elevation of the seasonal snowline, slope aspect and, as mentioned above, reliable natural snow cover. These and other geographical factors significantly influence how a resort's location influences the degree of its vulnerability to the long-term effects of climate change.

The location for Jumbo Glacier Resort in British Columbia was chosen for its optimal snow conditions and high elevations. The resort will provide lift-serviced access to four nearby glaciers at an elevation of up to 3419 m (11,217 feet). In winter, the ski area will offer 5627 feet of vertical, and in summer, up to 2300 feet of natural snow vertical will be available on the glaciers. The resort is planned in three phases and will ultimately include 5500 bed-units (plus 750 beds for staff accommodations) in a 110-ha resort base area. At build-out, the resort will see up to 2000 to 3000 visitors per day in high season.

Accessibility is also a critical component of site feasibility. For most winter sports enthusiasts, travel time and cost are critical variables when deciding to head to the mountains. In the USA, for example, 67% of resorts' areas are within 74 miles or easy commuting distance to major metropolitan areas. A high proportion of weekend resort areas require 2 or more hours of driving time, while vacation destinations are typically in more remote locations where snow conditions are more consistent. Because of the need for snow, appropriate terrain and climate, resort areas tend to be clustered, offering skiers several choices when they reach the mountains. This is the case in Canada, where substantial ski area facilities are clustered around the eastern, most densely populated provinces, Ontario and Quebec, which are close to the American border. However, the most popular resorts, are in western Canada, as about half of all international visitors head for British Columbia or Alberta.

In Europe, vacation skiers from the northern countries such as Germany, the Benelux countries, the UK and Scandinavia, represent half the skier market for the European Alpine countries. Austria is in the top position for the European winter vacation market, with nearly half of European winter sports enthusiasts traveling to Austria (largely from Germany and the UK). About 14% travel to France (largely from the UK) and about 11% visit Switzerland and Italy. Accessibility to the latter two countries has improved with a new Eurostar Swiss service, complementing its existing French one, and the opening of a new international airport at Turin in Italy. However, the British skiers are increasingly favouring France as a destination, using low-cost airlines and high-speed rail and road links via the Channel Tunnel. Andorra, located between France and Spain, has benefitted from easy access from Barcelona, and has over 2.3 million skier visits per year. Large numbers of Russians travel to Andorra each winter, attracted as much by the low prices in the retail shops as by the skiing.

Outside Europe and North America, access is similarly an important consideration in ski area development. In China, for example, where skiing is growing faster than anywhere else in the world, numerous studies have been made to determine the best locations within easy reach of the major populated cities. To date, the best option for the Chinese capital, Beijing, is Saibei, a rather basic resort created within 170 miles (272 km) of the capital. Alongside Jilin province, Heilongjiang, in the north-eastern corner of China, appears to be the country's major boom area for resort development, especially around the city of Harbin, which has seen heavy investment in a modern airport and road network. The Provincial Government has announced plans to open up 250 new ski centres in that province alone in the next decade. It would join Austria's Tyrol and Canada's Quebec as one of the few 'regions' in

the world to boast an exceptionally high concentration of ski centres.

Some resorts have been quite innovative in recent years in order to improve their accessibility for skiers and boarders. In 2013, Aspen Skiing Company successfully lobbied for taxpayer-funded incentives to be offered to Delta to lure the airline back to Aspen airport. The incentive reportedly cost a total of US$350,000 and resulted in Delta launching a daily route to and from Atlanta and Saturday-only flights from Minneapolis. The same year, Jay Peak in Northern Vermont applied to join a pilot programme that would allow for the supplemental funding of border-cross services. Jay Peak attracts more than half of its customers from Canada, so was keen to cut down on border-crossing times and make the trip more appealing to customers.

Design Guidelines

Certain design guideline principles provide an umbrella for the specifics of site planning and these include avoiding land conflicts, designing access roads based on expected peak traffic, and considering the varied abilities of skiers and snowboarders (Mill, 2012). Ski slopes that offer a range of slopes result in attracting a variety of skiers. Sibley (1982) suggested some time ago that novice slopes should be under 20 degrees, intermediate slopes 20–45 degrees, and advanced slopes 45 degrees or steeper. Experienced skiers and boarders will also look at the variety of runs available and the total vertical drop. Considerable care must be taken in locating both the base and uphill facilities, in order to avoid avalanche paths.

The significance of flat, stable land close by to provide adequate building sites has been seen as an advantage to resort development success. Ski areas are increasingly using land development as a way of maximizing profits. Vail Resorts' recent acquisition of Park City Mountain Resort, for example, was heavily influenced by the real-estate opportunities. Vail plans to link Park City to neighbouring Canyons Resort, where there are already over 90 acres of undeveloped land. At Park City there are another 15 acres of developable land within and around existing parking lots. Another example of property development driving the growth of ski areas comes from the Niseko United ski area of Japan, where in the last decade more than 7000 new beds have been developed and an estimated US$800 million has been invested.

Resorts have considered the needs of snowboarders by including terrain parks, and also the needs of non-skiers by considering other activities such as skateboard parks and zip-lines. In fact, winter zip-lining is spreading around North American ski resorts, adding yet another activity-based après-ski alternative. The Canopy Tour at Crested Butte Mountain Resort, for example, has five lines ranging from 120 to 400 feet long, connected by three wooden suspension bridges and massive platforms designed for winter use with tough grips and snow grates. 'It's about a two-hour tour, with two guides, that make it fun and interactive', says Director of Innovations, Erica Mueller. 'It is something different for people to do on a day off from skiing or after skiing and really attracts all age groups' (E. Mueller, Crested Butte, personal communication, September 2014).

Resorts identify capacity of the area when planning, and the usual process is to use the amount of skiable area for each skier classification, which in turn is used to determine the necessary ski lift and base area facilities. The capacity of the ski lifts to bring skiers up the mountain must be balanced against the capacity of the ski trails to take them down. The goal is to spread the skiers and snowboarders over the mountain while ensuring that the time spent queuing is not too uncomfortable. Experts believe that the ideal lift system covers 1000 to 2000 vertical feet over a slope length of 4000 to 5000 feet. From an economic point of view, the earning potential of the lift increases as the length increases while cost per foot decreases. However, some resorts prefer to put a cap on the number of skiers on the hill. Deer Valley in Utah, for example, has a cap of 7500 skiers, even though the ski hill has the capacity to hold many more. The thinking behind this cap is that the visitor experience will be much more pleasant if there are limited lift lines and fewer skiers on the slopes. Of course, there is always a price to pay for such extra comforts – the daily lift ticket price at Deer Valley in the 2014–15 season was US$114.

Linking smaller resorts together has been seen to be beneficial in addressing capacity problems and builds more attractiveness for skiers and snowboarders. For example, in Switzerland, Grimentz and Zinal and also Arosa and Lenzerheide have recently linked up; and in Austria, Lech and Warth have joined together with new lifts. Earl Knudsen, partner at Alpine Partners, believes that these kinds of collaborations make smaller resorts more attractive to customers: 'The link between Grimentz and Zinal will provide skiers with some of the best off-piste in Switzerland, while the Lech and Warth connection will offer 50 per cent more terrain', he says (Chomé, 2013). On a larger scale in the USA, some stakeholders in the Utah ski industry are pushing to interconnect up to seven resorts in the future – including Snowbird, Alta, Solitude, Brighton, Canyons, Deer Valley and Park City – believing that such interconnection could be vital to Utah's ability to compete both nationally and internationally.

Finally, ski resorts have increasingly been sensitive to environmental limitations, such as the presence of wildlife habitats that are home to endangered species, the existence of special cultural or archaeological sites deemed worthy of preservation, and a scarcity of natural resources such as water for snow-making. As Smith (2013) has commented, one of the biggest changes in the past 20 years has been the need for ski resorts to embrace environmentally friendly practices, from recycling waste and implementing public transportation systems to adopting energy-saving strategies and constructing LEED-certified buildings. Sixty per cent of the world's 250 leading ski resorts are now using at least some renewable energy and one-third are using 100% renewable energy (Thorne, 2014).

Development Styles

Smith (2013) has explored the evolution of ski resorts in America from a design and architectural perspective. She traces this evolution of resorts from modest beginnings as rustic cabins and unpretentious lodges in the 1930s; to second homes for the newly upwardly mobile middle class pursuing the good life in the post-war period when skiing exploded in popularity; and finally to supersized postmodern vacation homes and corporate-owned, carefully planned mountain villages offering a total vacation experience in the 1980s. Vancouver-based Intrawest would be a good example of a company involved in this latter phase of development. Operating seven North American ski resorts, Intrawest invests heavily in real-estate developments and tourism infrastructure, adding retail, lodging and restaurants to attract people to the resort and keep them there.

Intrawest has developed a business model consisting of four distinct 'waves'. Wave 1 is the starting point when the company first becomes involved in a resort; Wave 2 is characterized by increasing development and longer-staying guests; in Wave 3, the village is well established and there is a dramatic increase in the number of destination visitors; and finally, in Wave 4, the resort is transformed and destination guests are visiting year-round, maximizing the use of shops, hotels, convention facilities and restaurants.

An edited book by Clark *et al.* (2006) contains several chapters that examine planning issues and problems of resort development in North America. Dorward (2006) discusses the appeal of the village concept for the design of mountain resorts, but argues in favour of regional planning strategies that are more typical of urban regions and that support the growth of healthy resort communities. Hartmann (2006)

takes a critical look at the sprawling resort landscapes of the Colorado High Country and the loss of community in the original resort areas. He discusses an expanding new entity – the 'down valley' in current mountain resort areas. Finally, Johnson *et al.* (2006) look at the important subject of regional transportation and focus on a rapidly changing rural area near Jackson Hole/Yellowstone Park that has seen a considerable influx of amenity migration. The authors conclude that future research should include better cost accounting of rural residential development that results from changes to the local transportation infrastructure, as well as ecological and qualitative amenity accounting for rural residents.

Case Study: Paul Mathews – The World's Most Extensive Ski Resort Designer

Since 1975 Paul Mathews (see Fig. 33.2) has been designing ski resorts all over the world, numbering in the 400s by 2015. In the course of his work he has met many world leaders including the Prime Minister of the Russian Federation, President of Montenegro and the King of Spain, Juan Carlos, who offered to trade jobs with him for a winter season. 'I declined, saying that being a King was really too

Fig. 33.2. Paul Mathews in Niseko, Japan (photograph courtesy of Ecosign).

hard work; shaking hands and smiling at people you did not know and did not particularly care for', says Mathews. 'To which he laughed and said my job was definitely better than his' (P. Mathews, personal communication, February 2015).

Having grown up skiing in Colorado, early in his career Paul Mathews designed a brand new resort on Vancouver Island, Mount Washington Ski Resort, which opened in 1978. With his academic background in forest ecology and landscape architecture, he was able to satisfy environmental prerequisites at Mount Washington, preserving soil, water and forests while creating a viable resort. 'It was critically acclaimed and it quickly became the second most visited ski resort in British Columbia', says Mathews. 'Word of mouth led to jobs down in Washington, Idaho, Montana and Oregon.'

In 1975, Mathews became Chairman of the initial Resort Municipality of Whistler Planning Commission with some oversight of the design of the new Whistler Village. He also commenced planning for Whistler Mountain ski area (see Fig. 33.3), with responsibility for

the extensive system of lifts and slopes. From his Whistler-based company, Ecosign, Mathews has gone on to design over 400 resorts in 38 countries, always with an eye to creating an Alpine flavour, looking at the resort holistically and centralizing services. This is not an easy task, but Ecosign has researched how far the average skier will willingly walk around a resort and how much uphill walking they will tolerate. Moreover, Mathews does not allow stairs in an Ecosign resort, favouring ramps instead. Slope capacity is also taken into account, as well as the difficulty level of runs and the carrying capacity of lifts. Ecosign is now able to use a software program to detect the best snow on the mountain and the warmest spots to construct restaurant patios.

With annual revenues around CAN$3 million, Ecosign remains a relatively small company with 20 employees. Their modus operandi is to identify terrain for the ski area and base village, bearing in mind climate – especially snowfall, sun and wind. Next they map out the best slopes and send in foresters and surveyors to fine-tune the layout to match the natural

Fig. 33.3. Whistler Municipality in British Columbia Canada (source: Google Maps).

topography. Lifts, ski runs and base areas are then pencilled in. 'A greenfield project could take four years', says Mathews. 'An addition or renovation to an existing project could perhaps take just one year.' The team travels extensively, dealing with different cultures, languages and international media, and attends trade shows in the USA, Canada, Europe and China on an annual basis.

The name Ecosign is actually a contraction of 'ecological design', a new concept back in the 1970s. Mathews says:

> Needless to say, I was very optimistic when I started Ecosign and frankly, would have been happy just working in British Columbia and Alberta in western Canada and indeed I did start with Whistler Mountain and Hemlock Valley in British Columbia.

Forty years later, the forward-thinking company has become a worldwide reputable brand for international mountain resort design.

Mathews' innovative ideas were honed by negative experiences in his youth skiing at badly executed ski areas in Washington State: 'That led to interest later in life to undertake university studies in forest ecology and landscape architecture at the University of Washington in Seattle as the educational foundation needed to design good mountain resorts.'

Ecosign was responsible for identifying possible sites in readiness for the 1988 Calgary Winter Olympics. This job was a big break for the company, launching it into Olympic limelight, and also giving employment to the staff for several years during an economic downturn. Mathews explains:

> We ended up identifying 17 different potential areas, narrowed that down to approximately three and finally, the Government of Alberta chose development of Nakiska at Mount Allan to host the Olympic Alpine Skiing events, the legacy training site and a commercially viable recreational ski area ... Nakiska at Mount Allan filled all of those goals and was built for CAN$23 million and continues to host about 200,000 skier visits annually.

This work led the Austrian lift company Doppelmayr to recommend to Nippon Cable, Japan that they hire 'Olympic Planners', which resulted in Ecosign's first job in Mount Zao, Japan in 1984. 'We have since made plans for 34 areas in

Japan, including 13 new greenfield projects', Mathews adds.

Next followed work preparing master plans for Swiss resorts in Laax, Arosa and Savognin, which, in turn, led to assignments in Austria, Spain and France. 'The company's reputation and breadth of projects just grew organically, averaging about ten new projects per year plus of course taking care of a lot of existing customers', says Mathews.

A career coup was getting the contract in 2010 to redesign the ski lift system at Courchevel, one of France's ritziest resorts. The same year Mathews redesigned Canyons Resort in Park City, Utah. He was also responsible for choosing the location and designing the resort of Rosa Khutor, as well as mapping out the competitive courses for the 2014 Sochi Winter Olympics. This job proved to be one of the most difficult of his career. It began as a project for the Russian Federation, looking at tourism potential in the North Caucasus. Mathews explains:

> Once we identified Rosa Khutor and the Gazprom Laura projects, we designed them for commercial ventures and then later we were asked if these resorts could host Olympic Winter Games ... We put the snow cluster venue Master Plan together for the Russian Olympic Committee and I personally presented the venues to the International Olympic Committee in February 2007.

When Sochi won the right to host the 2014 Olympic Winter Games in July 2007, Ecosign was immediately hired to redesign the Rosa Khutor Ski Area. Mathews recounts:

> Once Russia had the Olympics, all hell broke loose in the Sochi region, with everyone claiming they owned the lands where the competition venues were planned ... Finally, a freeze was put into place by Mr Vladimir Putin, saying that the Federal Government owned all of the land. Even Interros, our customer, lost our rights to the lease that we had signed to develop Rosa Khutor.

With the project on hold for almost 16 months, precious time was wasted, which could have been better used on design and construction. Mathews says:

> We worked continuously through 2011, but when the big construction was underway we did not know how to play the Russian game of 'kickbacks', and so we were replaced by other

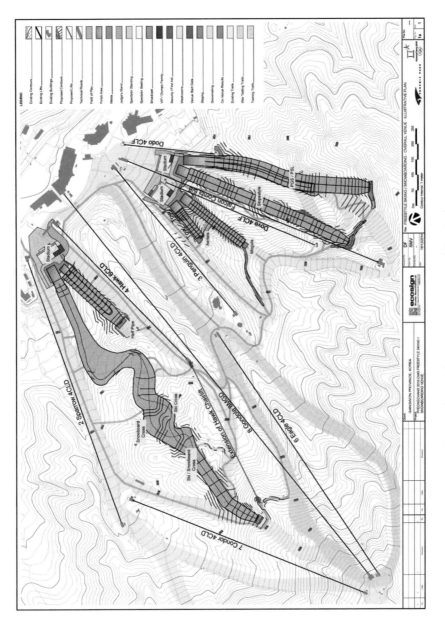

Fig. 33.4. Plans for Phoenix Park, Pyeong Chang, South Korea (courtesy of Ecosign).

Russian companies … Ultimately, these companies made a real mess of the Rosa Khutor mountain site with unprofessional practices.

He does grant that in the end Sochi hosted a 'pretty decent' Olympic Winter Games, adding that Rosa Khutor was enjoying good business and visits during its first year of commercial operation: 'Time will tell how the project lasts into the future', he says.

After this high-profile endeavour, Ecosign was chosen to plan Pyeong Chang, Korea for the Freestyle Skiing and Snowboarding venues for the 2018 Winter Olympics (see Fig. 33.4). The company also won an international competition to design the Snow Cluster competition venues for the Beijing bid to host the Olympic Winter Games in 2022.

During Mathews' long career he has noticed three important technological improvements that have assisted ski area planning. He explains:

Detachable grip chairlifts, snowmaking systems and winch cats for grooming ski slopes have very substantially changed how we design ski resorts … In fact, I was considered the first 'early adopter' in seeing the tremendous potential benefits of detachable grip chairlifts and gondolas. Given rope speeds two to three times faster than conventional fixed grip lifts allows us to go two or three times longer distances for equivalent travel times, and due to the carrier spacing allows us to go much higher verticals up to 800 or even 1000 metres with existing wire rope construction methods. Winch cats allow grooming of steep slopes and snowmaking has improved tenfold from when I started in the business, in efficiency and quality and quantity of snow.

And the future for Ecosign when Mathews retires? There's a transition plan in place whereby several senior VPs will team up with Mathews' son and daughter to continue the lasting legacy.

References

Bachman, R. (2014) The dangling future of Sochi's ski gondolas. *Wall Street Journal* 24(February), B10.

Batchelor, D.E., Brewster, F., Carscallen, A.N., Douglas, H.P., Hall, F.A., *et al*. (1937) Skiing in Canada. *Canadian Geographical Journal* 14(2), 57.

Chomé, L. (2013) Ski holiday trends. *TourismLink*. Retrieved from: http://www.tourismlink.eu/2013/12/ski-holiday-trends-20132014 (accessed 3 December 2014).

Clark, T., Gill, A. and Hartmann, R. (eds) (2006) *Mountain Resort Planning and Development in an Era of Globalization*. Cognizant Communications Corporation, New York.

Dorward, S. (2006) The evolution of village form and its relevance as a model for resort design and development. In: Clark, T., Gill, A. and Hartmann, R. (eds) *Mountain Resort Planning and Development in an Era of Globalization*. Cognizant Communication Corporation, New York, pp. 253–277.

Hartmann, R. (2006) Downstream and down-valley: essential components and directions of growth and change in the sprawling resort landscapes of the Rocky Mountain West. In: Clark, T., Gill, A. and Hartmann, R. (eds) *Mountain Resort Planning and Development in an Era of Globalization*. Cognizant Communication Corporation, New York, pp. 278–293.

Jenkins, M. (2013) On the trail with the first skiers. *National Geographic* December, 85–101.

Johnson, J., Maxwell, B., Brelsford, M. and Dougher, F. (2006) Transportation and rural sprawl in amenity communities. In: Clark, T., Gill, A. and Hartmann, R. (eds) *Mountain Resort Planning and Development in an Era of Globalization*. Cognizant Communication Corporation, New York, pp. 294–320.

Kottke, M. (1990) Growth trends: going both ways at once. *Ski Area Management* 29(1), 63–64, 96–97.

Mill, R.C. (2012) *Resorts: Management and Operation*, 3rd edn. Wiley, Hoboken, New Jersey.

Sibley, R.G. (1982) *Ski Resort Planning and Development*. Foundation for the Technical Advancement of Local Government Engineering in Victoria, Melbourne, Australia.

Smith, M.S. (2013) *American Ski Resort. Architecture, Style, Experience*. Oklahoma University Press, Norman, Oklahoma.

Thorne, P. (2014) What are Ski Resorts Doing to Combat Climate Change? Available at: http://www.snowcarbon.co.uk/ski-resorts/what-are-ski-resorts-doing-combat-climate-change (accessed 12 November 2014).

Williams, P.W. (1993) The evolution of the skiing industry. In: Khan, M.A., Olsen, M.D. and van Var, T. (eds) *VNR's Encyclopaedia of Hospitality and Tourism*. Nostrand Reinhold, New York, pp. 926–933.

34 Non-government Organizations' Mountain Management: A Sustainable Support Model for Southern Oregon's Mountain Destinations

Byron Marlowe[1]* and Alison Burke[2]

[1]*Washington State University, Pullman, Washington, USA;* [2]*Southern Oregon University, Ashland, Oregon, USA*

Introduction

Mountains are increasingly dependent upon the support of non-governmental organizations (NGOs). These usually involve grassroots efforts, mobilized by ordinary citizens. NGOs and communities are representative of a broad spectrum within a targeted region and are indicative of the heterogeneity of their various community groups (Maxwell, 2005). Their non-profit status allows them the freedom to tackle different objectives specific to the region, such as climate considerations, sustainability and community support. In southern Oregon, NGO employees and volunteer workers are increasingly valuable in the sustainable future of the region's mountain recreation and tourism.

Non-governmental organizations in the Southern Oregon region within the USA are responsible for several management strategies including land stewardship, fundraising, hotel operations, food service, travel marketing and education. Each NGO is comprised of local individuals and private citizen donations, there is a unique devotion and commitment to long-term goals, protecting the ecology of the region,

and facilitating a healthy growth model. Unfortunately, these also provide unique challenges and concerns, especially in the rural parts of the region, where climate change affects tourism opportunities and financial resources are scarce. This chapter highlights NGO management and governance of a mountain, national park and national monument in southern Oregon and the engagement, efforts and collaborations of respective NGO partners.

Literature review

The mountains of the world occupy around 24% of the Earth's total surface and are attractive as tourism destinations for adventure, excitement and an opportunity to experience 'serious leisure' (Hamilton-Smith, 1993; Beedie and Hudson, 2003; Ujvári, 2009). One of the most important challenges facing the 21st century is creating a sustainable future for mountain populations through the use of sustainable management of mountain resources (Ujvári, 2009). This is often accomplished with the investments from the community and grassroots organizations;

---

* Corresponding author: marloweb@sou.edu

however, obstacles such as climate change and rural economies temper the development potential of mountain tourism in some regions.

Climate change is a salient concern to mountain tourism. With the change in weather patterns and snowfall, many ski resorts turn to non-snow sport opportunities to utilize the area for land-based services. But as Ujvári (2009) notes, the absence of snow leads to greater exposure of wildlife and fragile vegetation, which are disturbed with the increase of trekking, biking and other activities. This can have severe and lasting effects on mountain ecosystems. And the changes in precipitation levels may cause ski resorts to close permanently, which impacts services and employment in the area. Climate change presents very real and lasting challenges when attempting to develop a sustainable tourism base.

The World Tourism Organization has identified core metrics of sustainable tourism. 'These indicators can be applied to all destinations and include: site protection, stress, use intensity, social impact, development control, waste management, planning process, critical ecosystems, consumer satisfaction, local satisfaction and tourism contribution to local economy' (Ujvári, 2009, 161). Similarly, Lee and King (2006) suggest seven categories of tourism relating to resources and sustainability: (i) natural resources; (ii) cultural assets; (iii) special attractions; (iv) accommodations; (v) cuisine; (vi) transportation; and (vii) safety and security. This is what Wilson et al. (2001) called a 'complete tourism package'. A complete tourism package consists of events highlighting the local attributes, along with lodging, food services and other attractions. Marketing is also a major component of successful tourism, in order to draw visitors to the region (Sainaghi, 2006). Yet many rural communities that rely on non-profit, volunteer and other non-governmental agencies for the management of their mountain resorts sometimes lack the resources to attain the total tourism package.

Kline et al. (2011) note the importance of fostering and supporting tourism entrepreneurship in rural communities. Rural communities have unique attributes that can be nurtured and expanded. Community buy-in and support for the tourism industry can be an important part of the climate for tourism. If a community culture does not encourage residents to consider tourism as an alternative form of economic development, it creates a situation where outside entrepreneurs may eventually dominate a community's tourism industry (Blank, 1989; Gunn and Var, 2002). Community investment is a crucial aspect of sustainable mountain tourism.

Ecology, economy and socioeconomic attributes make up the triangle of suitability. These are achieved, in part, through community buy-in and community-based mountain tourism, but must be carefully balanced and integrated in order to keep tourism sustainable (Godde, 1998). Non-governmental organizations in Southern Oregon are emerging as exclusive partners in the sustainable future of mountain management within the region. Their greater involvement in the management of governance and the use of mountain resources for water extraction, education and recreational activities, such as tourism, are essential to the region's sustainable future. Moss and Godde (2000) suggest that the information gap that hinders potential for empowerment by many mountain communities needs special attention, and 'champions', striving to both balance the scales and pass on their skills to local people as swiftly as possible, should play a key role. This suggests that information should be effectively communicated through NGO partnerships within mountain communities to lead to cohesive management strategies being implemented and executed. Through a case study of protected mountain areas of regional and national significance, the following highlights meaningful NGO management and governance approaches of mountain, national park and national monuments in Southern Oregon and the active engagement, relationships and involvements of their associated NGO partners. Three mountain areas are covered including Mount Ashland, Crater Lake National Park, and Oregon Caves National Monument (Fig. 34.1).

Mountain: Mount Ashland NGO Management

Mount Ashland is a scenic mountain location boasting spectacular views of Mt Shasta to the

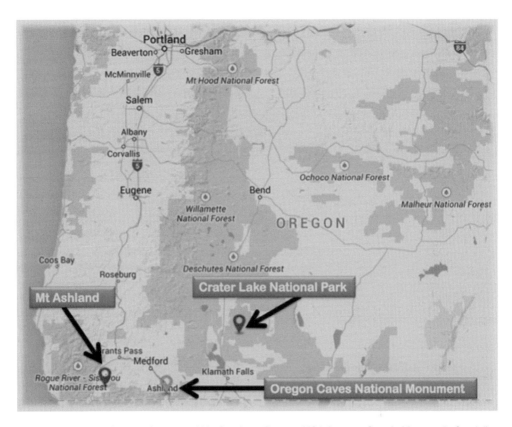

Fig. 34.1. Location of mountain areas within Southern Oregon, USA (source: Google Maps and eSpatial).

south and the Rogue Valley and Mt McLaughlin to the north. Every year, thousands of hikers seek out the Pacific Crest Trail, which traverses this mountaintop. Outdoor enthusiasts seek out the tranquil quiet, the sweeping meadows of wildflowers, the steep and rugged mountain biking and running trails, and the windswept bowls and fresh powder for skiing. However, despite the beauty and multiple offerings for nature aficionados, Mt Ashland as a recreation resort has been plagued with financial hardships. It has been bought and sold numerous times throughout the years and has brought together the local population in fundraising activities. Yet financial solvency is reliant on and hampered by two major issues: snow and the Ashland watershed.

Mount Ashland, the highest peak in the Siskiyou Mountains, is located 8.6 miles south of the city of Ashland, Oregon and 5 miles north of the California border, and soars at an elevation of over 7000 feet (actual elevation:

7532 feet). Mt Ashland is part of the Rogue River-Siskiyou National Forest. In the 1940s and 1950s, Mt Ashland became a destination for backcountry skiing. The plentiful snowfall and picturesque scenery inspired the Mount Ashland Corporation to build a ski resort in the early 1960s. Between 1961 and 1963, the Mount Ashland Corporation raised money to build roads, clear trees for ski slopes, erect chairlifts and towropes, and construct a ski lodge. A local businessman, Glenn Jackson, donated more than US$60,000 to help build the ski lodge.

Unfortunately the plentiful snowfall did not last and in 1970, after 3 years of winter drought conditions, the Mount Ashland Corporation folded. Jackson County financed the purchase of the ski area and Southern Oregon College Foundation took over management. This ownership lasted only 2 years before Dick Hicks purchased the ski area and incorporated it as Ski Ashland, Inc.

Harbor Properties, a Seattle-based company, purchased the property from Hicks in 1983. Sadly, drought struck again in the late 1980s, and although the ski area had expanded in the past decade with additional chairlifts and lighting, the number of skiers declined and revenue diminished. In 1991, it was again for sale (Korbulic, 1991). Thousands of people from southern Oregon and Northern California came together in a grass-roots effort to raise money to save the ski area. They raised over US$2 million to help save Mt Ashland from bankruptcy. The city hired Mount Ashland Association (MAA), a not-for-profit corporation, to maintain and operate the ski area. MAA is a prime example of a community-based organization (Mount Ashland, 2010). At this time, the City of Ashland entered a lease agreement with MAA, which will expire and be terminated or renewed on 30 June 2017.

Mount Ashland Association

There are several benefits to the ski area being owned by a non-profit organization. First, MAA is able to accept donations. In 2014, the ski area raised over US$300,000 in donations (J. Schectman, Oregon, 2014, personal communication). Second, as a non-profit, MAA receives preferential rates and treatment. For example, they are able to secure reduced or no-cost media advertising and donated airtime. And third, when the organization does make a profit, they do not have to pay taxes on it, which helps them financially in the lean years. There are only 20 ski resorts in America that are owned by non-profits.

To be tax-exempt, however, under section 501 c (3) of the USA Internal Revenue Code, the following conditions are imposed (Internal Revenue Service, 2015a).

- An organization must be organized and operated exclusively for exempt purposes.
- None of its earnings may inure to any private shareholder or individual.
- The organization may not attempt to influence legislation as a substantial part of its activities and it may not participate in

any campaign activity for or against political candidates.

- It is commonly referred to as a charitable organization.
- Other than testing for public safety organizations, the organization is eligible to receive tax-deductible contributions.
- The organization must not be organized or operated for the benefit of private interests.
- The organization's net earnings may not inure to the benefit of any private shareholder or individual.
- The organization is finally restricted in how much political and legislative (lobbying) activities they may conduct.

The future of Mount Ashland might rest with the ability to market itself as a destination area independent of snow; the ability to create non-snow revenue from events such as weddings, music festivals and other outdoor events. There is also a need for collaboration and local support; it recently partnered up with the local university to provide resources and services, for example. And, of course, there is the need for fundraising and grants. 'Mt Ashland has demonstrated great success with soliciting donations, crowdsourcing, hosting specific events such as auctions to garner funds. Fundraising works best with a tangible goal. It is much harder to raise funds to keep a ski resort open when one, two, or maybe even three years sees the area with no snow and no winter sports' (J. Schectman, Oregon, 2014, personal communication).

Ashland Watershed

The ski area has struggled with drought conditions off and on over the years, sometimes remaining closed for an entire season, at other times only opening a handful of weekends when the conditions permit. Other ski areas have the luxury of making snow to help augment the winter conditions. This is not an option for Mount Ashland because of the watershed.

The city of Ashland's sole water supply is provided by the Ashland Creek watershed, which covers approximately 15,000 acres. In 1893, President Cleveland honoured the Ashland

Board of Trade's (now the Chamber of Commerce) request to preserve the Ashland Watershed for the purpose of securing the city's water supply. In 1929 a Memorandum of Understanding (MOU) gave the city oversight in the watershed management. The forest service agreed to work with the City of Ashland on any forest management projects that would affect the quality of the water supply. A new memorandum was signed in 1975 wherein the city agreed to hire consultants to monitor the conditions of the watershed and the forest service continued to agree to implement any necessary measures to maintain the quality of the watershed. As a result, there are relatively few roads and few acres where commercial logging has taken place (Ashland Forest Resiliency Stewardship Project, 2010).

Yet the watershed management is affected whenever new construction is undertaken on Mt Ashland. For example, after the ski area installed a chairlift, there were reports of sediment running down into the creek. Artificial snow would therefore severely disrupt the watershed and is not negotiable for the ski area (Ashland Forest Resiliency Stewardship Project, 2010).

Youth Summer Service Program (YSSP)

In 1994, Mount Ashland launched the Youth Summer Service Environmental Camp. This 4-day educational programme is offered in July and August to incoming eighth and ninth graders in the Rogue Valley. Conceived and implemented entirely by volunteers, the programme engages in projects such as re-vegetation on the slopes, erosion control, litter removal and preservation. The participants learn about the environment, make a positive impact, and assist Mt Ashland and maintain the health of Ashland's watershed. In return, the youth receive 20 hours of community service and a discounted season ski pass. More importantly, the participants develop a sense of environmental awareness and stewardship. In 2002, the YSSP received the Silver Eagle Award for Excellence in Environmental Education. Presented by Mountain Sports Media, the youth programme was recognized for making the connection between recreation and responsibilities. In 2013,

Mt Ashland was awarded with the National Ski Area Association's Best Employee Programme Award.

Ashland Woodlands and Trails Association (AWTA)

The Ashland Woodlands and Trails Association (AWTA) is a private, non-profit organization responsible for preserving and maintaining Ashland's trails and woodlands for the community. Comprising volunteers, the AWTA receives donations and grants to fund trail construction and maintenance. Local fundraising events for AWTA include the Mt Ashland Hill Climb Run (13+ miles long, 1 mile up), Mt Ashland Hill Climb Bike Race (24-mile road bike race, 18-mile mountain bike race), the Siskiyou Outback Trail Run along the Pacific Crest Trail (15 km, 50 km and 50 miles) and other smaller races within the community. Fundraising has also included proceeds from film festivals and individual contributions. The organization has no membership fees and relies on volunteer participation from the community.

Mountain National Park: Crater Lake National Park NGO Management

Crater Lake National Park situated in southern Oregon on the crest of the Cascade mountain range in south-central Oregon is well known for being home to the deepest lake in the USA, Crater Lake (Fig. 34.2). Crater Lake National Park comprises 183,224 acres; ranging elevations throughout the park provide diverse habitats for an array of wildlife and make for an outstanding outdoor laboratory as well as an emerging sustainable tourism destination. In 2013 Crater Lake National Parks received over 500,000 visitors. Surrounded by cliffs almost 2000 feet high and boasting a picturesque island from a violent volcanic past, Crater Lake is also home to hikes in old-growth forest and cross-country ski trips in the winter months. Many of the roads and facilities close during the winter, but the park is open and accessible all year long. Most visitors come to Crater Lake National Park during the months

Fig. 34.2. Crater Lake National Park (photograph courtesy of Harold Richins).

of July through to mid-September, when the weather is generally mild with little precipitation. Due to the elevation of the park (6500 feet at Park Headquarters and 7100 feet at Rim Village), weather conditions change quickly and in the winter are very severe. Hiking, backpacking, camping, picnicking and sightseeing are popular pursuits within the park year-round, but one must be prepared. Boating and scenic driving around Rim Drive can be enjoyed by visitors during the summer months. In winter snowshoeing and cross-country skiing provide solitude and a little-known view of the park.

Crater Lake National Park Trust

The Crater Lake National Park Trust is an independent 501 c (3) with a board of directors who are responsible for the strategic leadership and the oversight of the tactical management of the Trust, which envisions and plays an active role in the park's role in the southern Oregon community. As such, Crater Lake National Park is recognized internationally as a treasure trove of activities, because of the work of the community and the financial support of the Trust. Made up of a board, the Trust is known for its deep support of education at Crater Lake National Park. Formed in 2002, The Crater Lake National Park Trust works to help protect, promote and enhance Crater Lake National Park, its unique water purity and its value for human inspiration and knowledge (C. Hill, Oregon, 2014, personal communication). The Crater Lake National Park Trust became independent from the Oregon Community foundation in late 2006 with the support of board members and the southern Oregon communities with an emphasis to support the mission of the park to educate local Oregonians.

The Crater Lake National Park Trust conducts fundraising to increase sales of the Oregon Crater Lake License Plate, a special fundraising initiative that was started in cooperation with Travel Southern Oregon. The Crater Lake National Park Trust contracts with Travel Southern Oregon (aka the Southern Oregon Visitors Association, or SOVA) for constituent and donor management, fundraising, grant writing, marketing, administrative coordination, PR and more. SOVA was formed in 1984 and supports the marketing efforts of Crater Lake. SOVA is designated as a tax exempt 'business league' under IRS 501 c (6), which means that none of the net profits from fundraising can benefit any shareholder or individual (Internal Revenue Service, 2015b). The profits are completely devoted to improving the businesses it supports. The board of directors of SOVA works to increase and lengthen visitor stays at Crater Lake park by marketing the region as a destination and by encouraging cooperative efforts with the National Park Service in outreach marketing, research and education of the park (C. Hill, Oregon, 2014, personal communication).

Friends of Crater Lake

Formed in 1993, the Friends of Crater Lake ask for and make donations to the many aspects of interpretation and education conducted at Crater Lake National Park for the parks visitors and attending students. The Friends of Crater Lake is a 501 c (3). The classification of this non-profit status for the Friends allows for the organization to be exempt from federal income tax. The Friends of Crater Lake has a board of directors that works with the National Park Service to maintain a stewardship of the natural and cultural resources of Crater Lake National Park. Supporting appropriate visitor opportunities to observe, experience and understand the character of the area; working with park staff in completing special projects; and taking the lead in fundraising are also activities undertaken by the Friends. Many Friends are alumni of the park, the concessionaire or a contractor. The Friends work closely with park staff to identify and prioritize unfunded needs and then meet those challenges through the use of volunteers (C. Hill, Oregon, 2014, personal communication).

Crater Lake Natural History Association

Formed in 1942 to benefit Crater Lake National Park and the Oregon Caves National Monument

under a memorandum of understanding with the National Park Service, the Crater Lake Natural History Association is a 501 c (3) with a board of directors responsible for the strategic leadership and the oversight of the tactical management of the association. The Crater Lake Natural History Association is responsible for the operation of bookstores at Crater Lake National Park and Oregon Caves National Monument. Profits from the bookstores are distributed back to The Crater Lake National Park and The Oregon Caves National Monument for National Park Service approved projects that increase the knowledge of the natural history of Crater Lake and The Oregon Caves or aids in their interpretation for the benefit of visitors. Employees and volunteers of these NGO partners with Crater Lake National Park and their responsibilities are highlighted in Fig. 34.3.

National Monument: The Oregon Caves National Monument NGO Management

Located in the Siskiyou Mountains of southwestern Oregon, this includes the main part of the 488-acre park located 20 miles east of Cave Junction, Oregon. The elevation of the monument is just above 4000 feet. Above ground, the monument encompasses an old-growth forest, including a Douglas fir tree with the widest-known girth in Oregon. In 2013, Oregon Caves National Monument received 72,770 visitors. Tours through the Oregon Caves are seasonal, and offered from late March through to the end of November. The Monument is located in the wooded slopes of the Siskiyou Mountains, part of the coastal mountain range of Oregon and California. When you visit, expect comfortable summer temperatures, snowy winters, and rain during spring and autumn. The surrounding bioregion offers unique geology and botany, wild and scenic rivers, wilderness areas, and historic features for visitors to southern Oregon to discover while visiting the monument (C. Hill, Oregon, 2014, personal communication).

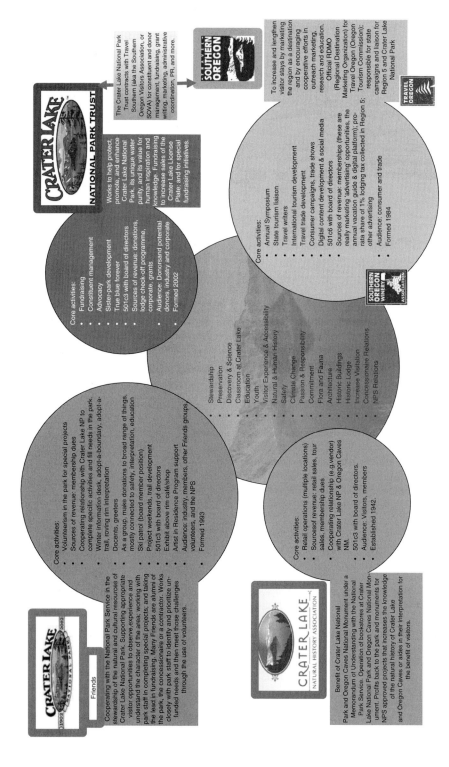

Fig. 34.3. NGO support at Crater Lake National Park.

The Friends of the Oregon Caves

Formed in 2008, The Friends of the Oregon Caves and Chateau is a non-profit organization cooperating with the National Park Service (NPS), a bureau of the United States Department of Interior, in the preservation, stewardship and improvement of cultural and natural resources of the Oregon Caves National Monument, a 501 c (3) with a board of directors. The Friends of the Oregon Caves Board of Directors is responsible for the strategic leadership and the oversight of the tactical management of the Friends organization. An example of the board of directors' responsibilities is the ongoing fundraising efforts for The Chateau at The Oregon Caves National Monument. The Oregon Caves and the Chateau are unique assets of national significance that contribute to the identity and economic well-being of the local community. The Oregon Caves Chateau, a national landmark and the primary historic structure in the Oregon Caves National Monument, is one of the three publicly owned, historic lodges of Oregon that provide overnight accommodations. The furnishings and setting create a feeling of nostalgia that is unforgettable. The Friends are responsible for raising the necessary funds to restore the interior and the furnishings of the Chateau and to show local, statewide and national support for a priority in the National Park Service budget for the full structural restoration of the Chateau.

The Illinois Valley Community Development Organization

Supporting the Oregon Caves National Monument is the Illinois Valley Community Development Organization (IVCDO). The IVCDO, is a 501 c (3) non-profit, working to improve economic and social conditions in Oregon's rural southwest through programs designed to enhance the standard of living, create jobs and encourage sustainable community development. The classification of this non-profit status for the IVCDO allows for the organization to be exempt from US federal income tax. The IVCDO has a board of directors who are responsible for the strategic leadership and the oversight of the tactical management of the organization. Starting in 2001, the IVDCO has managed both the Illinois Valley Visitors Center and The Château at the Oregon Caves as part of their relationship with the National Park Service (see Fig. 34.4). As a component of fundraising to support the IVCDO, the Friends of the Oregon Caves 501 c (3) was formed. The IVCDO communicates frequently with The Friends of the Oregon Caves organization. By partnering with the Friends of the Oregon Caves organization, the National Monument receives increased exposure through both organizations. Recently, The Chateau at Oregon Caves was a beneficiary of this partnership between the IVCDO and The Friends by becoming a member of The Historic Hotels of America. Through the increased fundraising of The Friends, the marketing of IVCDO and the leadership of each board of directors, the investment into this hotel designation commenced. The contract with the National Parks Service benefits the communities around the monument by offering a high-quality marketing outlet for local artists, musicians and artisan food and wine producers. It is also providing local employment with an annual payroll of US$450,000 in the Illinois Valley, which is located in south-western Oregon and the mountains of Josephine County, a rural disadvantaged area of Oregon. In 2002, the organization entered into an agreement to manage The Chateau at the Oregon Caves National Monument under the name Oregon Caves Outfitters. The management of two forest service campgrounds followed in 2004. Figure 34.4 highlights the employee and volunteer responsibilities of NGO partners with The Oregon Caves National Monument.

Conclusion

The future of southern Oregon mountain destinations would benefit further through increased partnerships with NGO governance, to secure the required skills and for their sustainable future. Currently, partnerships are fostered through education programmes, fundraising activities geared toward outdoor enthusiasts, donations from bookstores (in the case of Crater Lake), private donations and volunteer hours. The buy-in from the community engenders a

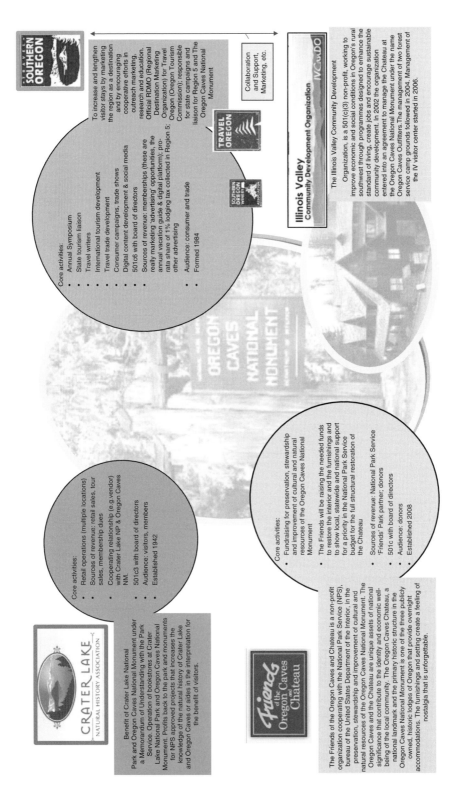

Fig. 34.4. NGO support at Oregon Caves National Monument.

sense of collective efficacy and ownership of the land. This in turn fosters agency and personal investment in the future of the region (Blank, 1989; Gunn and Var, 2002).

As discussed, climate change has significantly impacted on the development of Mount Ashland and the surrounding area, in its objective to be a viable destination ski resort. Ujvári (2009) notes that mountain landscapes are particularly fragile and susceptible to change and degradation. Similarly, Tigu *et al.* (2013) found that other ski resorts have needed to rely on non-snow sports, such as cycling and hiking, in order to continue and sustain viable mountain tourism.

The difficulties for achieving collaboration and participation success lie in generating and maintaining revenue and continuing a strong cohesive volunteer foundation. Zahra and McGehee (2013) highlight volunteer tourism in the Philippines: volunteers act as a bridge between the host community and the NGOs they represent, helping to get community feedback on which educational programmes are seen as most valuable in the community.

Opportunities for collaboration between NGO organizations that are involved in mountain management strategies have been under-researched. Specifically, within southern Oregon, the education outreach efforts of The Natural History Association and The Friends of Crater Lake in connection to the classroom at Crater Lake National Park has been shown to duplicate and dilute each NGO's connection to the classroom. Clarity in their respective missions will support a more sustainable management structure into the future. Further investigation into the proposed Travel Center at Crater Lake National Park, supported by The Crater Lake Trust, would be supported by the Trust's communication with the Illinois Valley Community Development Organization. To date, there is no report of the Trust or the IVCDO conversing about the Illinois Valley Visitor Center. Despite the difficulties, southern Oregon's mountain, national park and national monument non-governmental organizations have solid management and working governance structures in place to support the region as a sustainable recreation and tourist destination.

References

Ashland Forest Resiliency Stewardship Project (2010) A Community Engagement Plan for the Ashland Forest Resilience Project. Available at: http://www.ashland.or.us/Files/AFR%20Community%20Engagement%20 Plan%2004.08.10.pdf (accessed 15 March 2015).

Beedie, P. and Hudson, S. (2003) Emergence of mountain based adventure tourism. *Annals of Tourism Research* 30(3), 625–643.

Blank, U. (1989) *The Community Tourism Industry Imperative: The Necessity, the Opportunities, its Potential.* Venture Publishing, State College, Pennsylvania.

Godde, P. (ed.) (1998) Community-based mountain tourism: practices for linking conservation with enterprise. Synthesis of an electronic *Conference of the Mountain Forum*, 13 April–18 May, 1998. Available at: http://www.mtnforum.org/sites/default/files/publication/files/community-basedmountaintourism.pdf (accessed 11 January 2016).

Gunn, C.A. and Var, T. (2002) *Tourism Planning: Basics, Concepts, Cases.* Routledge, New York.

Hamilton-Smith, E. (1993) In the Australian bush: some reflections on serious leisure. *World Recreation and Leisure* 35(1), 10–13.

Internal Revenue Service (2015a) Exemption Requirements 501(c)(3) Organizations. Available at: http://www.irs.gov/Charities-&-Non-Profits/Charitable-Organizations/Exemption-Requirements-Section-501% 28c%29%283%29-Organizations (accessed 20 April 2015).

Internal Revenue Service (2015b) Business Leagues. Available at: http://www.irs.gov/Charities-&-Non-Profits/Other-Non-Profits/Business-Leagues (accessed 8 August 2015).

Kline, C., Swanson, J. and Milburne, L.A. (2011) Rural tourism and arts entrepreneurship in the North Carolina Appalachian Mountains. *Journal of Tourism Challenges and Trends* 4(1), 77–102.

Korbulic, M. (1991) A downhill run for Ski Ashland? *Oregon Business Media* 14(11), 11.

Lee, C.F. and King, B. (2006) Assessing destination competitiveness – an application to the Hot Springs Tourism Sector. *Journal of Tourism and Hospitality Planning and Development* 3(3), 179–197.

Maxwell, J. (2005) *Qualitative Research Design: An Interactive Approach.* Sage, Thousand Oaks, California.

Moss, L.A.G. and Godde, P.M. (2000) Strategy for future mountain tourism. In: Godde, P.M., Price, M.F. and Zimmermann, F.M. (eds) *Tourism and Development in Mountain Regions*. CAB International, Wallingford, UK, pp. 323–338.

Mount Ashland (2010) Youth Summer Service Environmental Camps. Available at: http://mtashland.dev.projecta. com/Page.asp?NavID=44 (accessed 11 January 2016).

Sainaghi, R. (2006) From contents to processes: versus a dynamic destination management Model (DDMM). *Tourism Management* 27(5), 1053–1063.

Tigu, G., Calaretu, B.V. and Bulin, D. (2013) Tourism destination management - new approaches in Romania. *International Journal of Academic Research in Business and Social Sciences* 3(7), 720–728.

Ujvári, K. (2009) Mountain tourism: climate change and sustainability. *Journal of Tourism and Trends* 1(1), 153–163.

Wilson, S., Fesenmaier, D, Fesenmaier, J. and Van Es, J.C. (2001) Factors for success in rural tourism development. *Journal of Travel Research* 40, 132–138.

Zahra, A. and McGehee, N.G. (2013) Volunteer tourism: a host community capital perspective. *Annals of Tourism Research* 42, 22–45.

35 Development and Governance of a Family Destination in the Alps: The Case of Serfaus-Fiss-Ladis

Anita Zehrer,* Frieda Raich, Hubert Siller and Franz Tschiderer
Management Center Innsbruck (MCI), Innsbruck, Austria

Introduction

The attractiveness and viability of a mountain tourism destination relates to various factors as constitutive elements of competitiveness, such as resources, destination management, demand and situational conditions (Crouch and Ritchie 1999; Bornhorst, *et al.*, 2010; Crouch, 2011). This can create significant challenges for communities dominated by visitation and with tourism enterprises operating as a key driver for economic success.

Tourism businesses in European countries may be characterized by small and medium-sized structures, i.e. individual and independent business units operate in a decentralized way, with no unit having any dominant administrative power or dominant ownership within the community-structured destination (Scott, *et al.*, 2009; Fueglistaller *et al.*, 2010; Beritelli and Laesser, 2011). The lack of coordination and cohesion within tourism destinations is a well-known problem to destination managers (Inskeep, 1991; Jamal and Getz, 1995). Hence, taking advantage of entrepreneurial opportunities within a mountain destination by bundling resources through collaboration plays a crucial role within tourism policy in community-type tourism areas, particularly for the strategic orientation and the development of the destination (Volgger and Pechlaner, 2014; Zehrer *et al.*, 2014). This research acknowledges the importance of considering stakeholders in the broadest sense suggested by Freeman (1984), applied to a mountain destination setting.

This chapter presents a single exploratory case study of the community-type destination Serfaus-Fiss-Ladis, located in the Tirolean Alps of Austria. The research is based on the examination of relevant literature and primary data gathered in Serfaus-Fiss-Ladis from destination stakeholders (i.e. private entrepreneurs in the areas of accommodation, restaurant, destination management organization (DMO), transportation/cable car and the municipality). The chapter will describe findings on:

- The role of the DMO in a community-type destination, its status, tasks and strategies.
- The cable-car industry and its challenges in the destination development.
- The public administration (community) as one of the key stakeholders.
- The status of the accommodation sector and its challenges towards innovative business models.
- The role of the ski schools within the development and governance of the destination.

---

* Corresponding author: anita.zehrer@mci.edu

- The collaboration of stakeholders and their role within the planning and development of the destination.
- Future challenges that have to be considered to maintain competitiveness.
- The success factors summarizing future strategies for sustainable development.

The Destination of Serfaus-Fiss-Ladis

Serfaus-Fiss-Ladis (SFL) is a tourism destination and ski area in the Tirol, Austria (see Fig. 35.1). The ski area is located between 1200 m and 2820 m above sea level, and has 39 ski lifts and 28 carpet lifts ('magic carpets'), opening up a total of 212 km of ski runs. The core target group is the family, consisting of parents and children of all age groups. Besides the nuclear family, SFL also targets extended families and connoisseurs, which could be couples without children, who appreciate the high quality of the infrastructure and premium service features.

The core brand promise is to be 'the most stunning mountain experience park with service

excellence for families and connoisseurs'. Furthermore, the key component of the brand is to be:

> The most renowned family destination in Europe, offering unique skiing comfort world-wide, free of stress, with utmost pleasure, premium level quality, in balance with nature, ideal for kids, a mountain experience park in summer and winter on the Tirolean sun terrace.
>
> (DMO, 2012, 20)

The attractiveness of the tourist product is formed by means of a broad offer of services, children's entertainment programmes, quality infrastructure and high-level service quality. Customer satisfaction and loyalty have been recognized as the immediate and ultimate aims of the destination, respectively (Ariffin, 2013).

The most essential service providers of the destination are the DMO (destination management organization), the cable-car companies, the community (public administration), the accommodation providers with gastronomy, and the ski schools. These stakeholders will be described in the next sections.

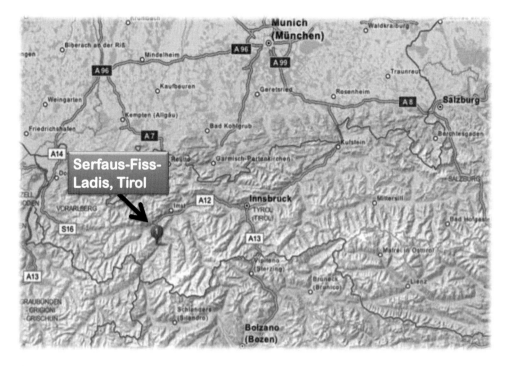

Fig. 35.1. Map of Serfaus-Fiss-Ladis, Tirol (source: Google Maps).

The DMO of Serfaus-Fiss-Ladis

The DMO of Serfaus-Fiss-Ladis has elaborated the following vision:

We want to become the most renowned DMO in the Alps. Based on our high quality claim we will provide the best service features compared to other destinations. By continuing improvements we want to become the competence center and the driving force for the region. We continue to be an attractive place to work with motivated employees and guarantee further development and training of employees.

(DMO, 2012, 16)

Indeed, the destination management organization plays a very crucial leadership and networking role within the broader locale and also for other Alpine destinations (Volgger and Pechlaner, 2014). The DMO's main tasks lie in the field of product development as well as internal and external communication. In practice, the DMO incurs the following tasks and functions.

- Consulting and coordination tasks for guests, members and partners.
- Marketing tasks, including brand communication; in fact, the marketing and promotion of the destination is now a ubiquitous activity, aided by the rise in new technological innovations such as social media (Pike and Page, 2014).
- Destination internal communication: within the destination 95% of the communication is undertaken via the DMO. Hence, the DMO plays a central role as a communication interface to its members, primarily to its accommodation providers.
- Product development and idea generation for destination innovations: the central tasks of product development comprise the maintenance and development of the infrastructure (e.g. enlargement of the ski area, themed hiking paths, etc.) and project management (as well as co-financing of projects). Again, the DMO operates as an interface among all service providers involved. Customer orientation herein is the highest imperative.

Members of the DMO meet twice a year in different destinations (e.g. Italy, Norway, Canada) to generate ideas, exchange experiences and communicate with like-minded colleagues. The aim is to identify and recognize trends of the industry in time to react with new and innovative products and services. The DMO in SFL represents the overarching organization of the destination and unites political and private interests. As the main coordination body, the DMO shows a high networking ability (Volgger and Pechlaner, 2014). The DMO's strength in organizational and financial matters, as well as its tradition, enables it to fulfil tasks at a high level and thus reach legitimacy, high recognition and trust among all interest groups and stakeholders of the destination.

The extended model of the determinants of DMO success, according to Volgger and Pechlaner (2014), involves the networking capability (i.e. the ability to interact and collaborate effectively with stakeholders in the destination, including developing and sustaining inter-organizational relationships); the professional performance of operational and strategic activities (marketing, service provision, product development, management etc.); the ability to provide sufficient human resources and funding; and transparent evidence of performance. These factors are true for the DMO of Serfaus-Fiss-Ladis.

Cable-car Companies of Serfaus-Fiss-Ladis

The Austrian Alps are one of the most popular ski destinations in Europe. Austria's ski resorts differ widely in their characteristics, such as the quality of skiing (e.g., length of ski runs and availability of modern transport facilities), average snowfall, average slope altitude, mountain scenery, distance of the resort from the nearest population centre, and number and quality of accommodations, amenities, and promotional activities.

(Falk, 2008, 1172)

Hence, scholars like Chew (1987), Pearce (1987), Gunn (1988), Martin and Witt (1988), Inskeep (1991), Dickman (1994), Prideaux (2000), and Khadarooa and Seetanahb (2008), among others, have argued that the infrastructure base of a country is the determinant of the attractiveness of a tourism destination. In particular, transport infrastructure, which provides the vital base for transportation services, is presumed to be an important determinant in this respect.

The ski resort of Serfaus-Fiss-Ladis is operated by two economically independent companies: one is the Seilbahn Komperdell GmbH (Serfaus); the other is the Fisser Bergbahnen GmbH (Fiss-Ladis). Their goal is clearly defined and agreed: to offer a unique experience on the mountain for families and connoisseurs of life enjoying nature and high-quality food. Over the years, the cable-car companies have continually promoted and pushed the quality of the infrastructure on the mountain. Today, the SFL cable-car companies rank among the top cable-car companies in the Alpine region when it comes to total revenue (i.e. in 1999/2000 the two companies reached net sales of €22.18 million). Since the turn of the millennium, the companies increased their revenue 280% and generated net sales of €61.9 million in 2013. More than 90% of the total revenue is earned during the winter season, and in the summer of 2013, the revenue amounted to €5.78 million. The share of gastronomy on the mountain amounts to 26% (€16.54 million). The cable-car companies of SFL yearly invest €18.4 million on average into the improvement of the ski resort. Since 1999, more than €276 million has been invested into the expansion and enhancement of the mountain infrastructure.

An average of 13,400 visitors per day, with a peak of 23,000, stay in Serfaus-Fiss-Ladis during the winter season. More than 1.7 million guests visited the resort during the 2012/13 winter season. In the summer season, 4200 guests on average per day use the mountain with a peak of 9000 per day in the high season (July and August). Between 2005 and 2013, the cable-car companies invested more than €9 million into relaunching the summer product and, in the summer of 2013, 564,000 visitors were recorded on the mountain, representing a 148% increase since the 2005 summer season.

Both existing cable-car companies can be regarded as core service providers within the destination Serfaus-Fiss-Ladis. The following are among the main responsibilities of cable-car companies in the destination:

- Biggest employer in the destination.
- *Zugpferd* (key service provider) of the destination: the continuing improvement and

enlargement of offerings on the mountain retains the demand in the villages, and thus reduces the entrepreneurial risk of the accommodation providers and restaurants.

- Innovative pioneer in the industry (development from transport company to holistic service provider).
- Stakeholder value: the profits of both cable-car companies are not distributed, but fully retained and reinvested. Thus, the cable-car companies of Serfaus-Fiss-Ladis are not driven by the shareholder-value principle, but rather by the stakeholder-value principle. This is reflected in the high investment volume of the last couple of years, which has largely impacted on the overall destination development.

This investment policy will be continued in the next couple of years to retain the competitiveness of the destination. Hence, the SFL cable-car companies plan to invest more than €20 million into the infrastructure in summer 2014 and have the following plans for the future:

- A new ski depot with 6000 storage facilities to improve the convenience of the skiers.
- A subterranean logistics system for deliveries with the aim to reduce the traffic congestion, particularly in the high season.
- Increase in capacity in the mountain restaurants in order to reduce capacity bottlenecks.

In this connection, it is useful to consider the theory of diffusion introduced by Rogers (1995), which classifies organizations and firms on the basis of timing of technology adoption: (i) innovators; (ii) early adopters; (iii) early majority; (iv) late majority; and (v) laggards. Considering the plans for the future mentioned above, the cable-car companies of SFL would be regarded as innovators; they have contributed tremendously to the overall success of the destination and play a crucial role for their competitiveness of the future.

The Communities of Serfaus, Fiss and Ladis

The public administration is one of the key stakeholders besides the DMO, the cable-car companies, the accommodation providers and the ski schools. The communities Serfaus, Fiss and Ladis take over various political functions and give the direction for future destination development. The communities are therefore the central node between the residents and the service providers and incorporate an important economic role. The communities are also responsible in land-use planning and have to support those projects, which use the limited space in an optimal and sustainable way. In doing so, the communities have an impact on company sizes and bed capacities. A challenge, therefore, is to enable residents to afford to live in the destination and thus avoid out-migration (Pedrazzini and Satiko, 2011), since the impacts of tourism upon locals and their communities is an issue (Yang et al., 2013). Thus, understanding and assessing tourism impacts in the community is important, in order to maintain sustainability and long-term success of the destination (Diedrich and García-Buades, 2009). Resident perceptions of tourism and its associated impacts have been used repeatedly to study the dynamics of the transformation of a destination from the perspective of local communities (Ap, 1992; Johnson et al., 1994; Besculides et al., 2002; Horn and Simmons, 2002; Harrill, 2004; Andereck et al., 2005; Andriotis, 2005).

The three communities of Serfaus, Fiss and Ladis fulfil the following tasks with regard to tourism.

- Provide various administrative duties (e.g. the registration system is done by the communities).
- Supply various infrastructure for tourists and locals alike (water supply, internet, gas supply, alternative energies, etc.).
- Support provision of social infrastructure, such as day-care institutions or kindergartens.
- Provide and maintain efficient access to and from the destination, and manage intense peak visitation periods.

The political and economic situation of the communities Serfaus, Fiss and Ladis is closely tied to the fact that a majority of the ownership of the two cable-car companies is in the hands of the communities. This enables a withholding of the distribution of earnings and a reinvesting of profits. The political as well as the economic function (public administration and ownership) of cable-car companies is a challenge, which might well lead to a conflict of interests since political players usually have an influence on the success of the cable-car companies.

Accommodation providers and gastronomy

Serfaus-Fiss-Ladis provides 13,774 beds (Serfaus: 6706 beds; Fiss: 5260 beds; Ladis: 1808 beds), of which 11,400 are commercial beds. Furthermore, the destination includes 50 restaurants, a discotheque, 20 bars and 15 Alpine pasture huts. The number of beds and overnight stays of the destination both show an increase that amounted to 1.5 million in the winter season 2012/13 and around 770,000 in the summer season. The majority of overnight stays are generated by 4- and 5-star hotels. The average length of stay amounts to 6.2 days in summer and 6.1 days in winter and is, therefore, considerably above the Tirolean average.

The value of the hotel and restaurant industry in the destination Serfaus-Fiss-Ladis is very high, with key providers being impulse-generators and initiators of the overall destination development and strategy (family hotels). These stakeholders are also important employers within the destination. The notion of families and connoisseurs provides space for effective positioning of the hotel and restaurant sector. While the ski schools and cable-car companies work across all three communities, the hotels and restaurants are managed by a variety of operators, and this is acknowledged as being a potential challenge.

Ski schools

In Serfaus-Fiss-Ladis there are two ski schools. They are among the best ski schools in the Tirol and have been awarded various prizes, such as 5 Snow Crystals in gold and silver, or the Quality Award of the Tirolean Ski Instructor Association (Snowsport Tirol). In peak season, each ski school employs around 300 ski instructors, who take care of about 2000 guests per day. The ski instructors come from various nations, such as Austria, Germany, the Netherlands, Australia or even Japan. The main challenges for the ski schools are managing peak times, the increasing demand to provide lessons in a variety of languages and providing accommodation for the ski instructors.

The Serfaus and Fiss-Ladis ski schools are the biggest in Austria, which has both pros and cons. An advantage certainly is the economic strength, the varied offerings, the low competition rate, the team spirit, and coherence when it comes to new investments, as well as the variety in language capabilities of the ski instructors. A disadvantage could be the lack in pressure for innovation, due to the monopoly-like situation, the low need for ski instructors in off-peak seasons, and the risk of losing contact with the guests and employees. Altogether, the ski schools are very significant to the destination, as they convey the 'snow experience'. The ski instructors add enthusiasm and emotionally connect the guest to the destination, and therefore play a considerable role as innovators even though they are only active in winter. Ski instructors convey direct and vital information received from the guests that might improve offered services and help the various service providers in the ski school and beyond.

Collaboration of Stakeholders

Cooperation plays a central role in the development of a tourism destination and a crucial part in the sustainable planning and development of a destination (Beritelli and Laesser, 2011). Thus, the essential service providers in the destination of Serfaus-Fiss-Ladis (cable-car companies, ski schools, communities, hotels and restaurants, and the DMO) need to collaborate, to provide an attractive tourism product and to remain competitive. This is the basis for the success of the destination. The mutual dependence, spatial closeness, common goals and strategies, an established culture of trust, as well as the various stakeholder roles within the destination, lead to an intense sense of connection for all service providers. Everyone is aware that the high quality of life is a result

of the high tourism intensity, which can only be maintained through cooperation, a common strategy and a joint vision (Zehrer *et al.*, 2014).

Cooperation is seen as a crucial success factor by tourism actors and is prevalent on various levels and among various projects. Cooperation is especially important for the sustainable product development of the destination. Thus, the destination of Serfaus-Fiss-Ladis strives to integrate all stakeholders into the future development of the destination by means of joint projects, such as the development of packages which are largely initiated by the DMO and the accommodation providers. The cable-car companies are generally willing to reduce the prices in the off-peak season, and thus support accommodation providers by generating demand in the communities. Well-elaborated examples of packages are the 'Snow Start' package, the connoisseurs' weeks in winter or the 'Super.Summer.Card' (Serfaus, 2014).

Cable-car companies and ski schools also cooperate, since the family ski area is very much dependent on both actors to fulfil the wishes and needs of the families. While the cable-car companies provide the hardware, the ski schools provide the software. Their collaboration contributes to the service quality and enables, for instance, a relief at peak lunch time. Furthermore, at peak times, half of the ski courses start at 9.30 am, the other half at 10.30 am. This guarantees no crowding in the kids' restaurants in peak times, as well as providing relief for the ski bus shuttles into the area. Also, the guests do not consume breakfast at the same time in their accommodation. These measures result in improved comfort and higher convenience along the whole destination service chain.

Collaboration, however, does not occur by accident. The DMO holds a very important interface role among the various service providers (cable-car companies, ski school, communities, hotels and restaurants). The DMO thus encompasses essential roles and functions among the participating destination actors.

- The professional positioning of the destination is the main task of the SFL Marketing GmbH, which is the associated company of the DMO, in which the cable-car companies hold 20%. Based on the common marketing of the DMO and the cable-car companies, the actors all benefit from synergies such as know-how and financial power.

- Staff of the ski school are also active in the DMO and the municipal council.
- The gastronomy on the mountain is operated by the cable-car companies.

Future Challenges

Serfaus-Fiss-Ladis is a successful destination, with clear positioning strategies and an increasingly competitive market. The important challenges that have been indicated include sustainability, competition, strategic focus and human resources. These strong challenges have to be considered for the future to achieve and maintain its sustainable destination development strategic outcomes. These are discussed further below.

Sustainable development

There is a tendency towards unsustainable mass tourism in the destination, as a result of continuous growth in overnight stays and visitor numbers. To prevent negative perception among guests, the future development of the destination needs to be publicly discussed. A big challenge in this context is visitor service, as guests are concentrated in select places within the destination during the peak winter season. The guests therefore might feel uncomfortable with crowding, which might result in a negative holiday experience.

According to visitor surveys, the guests in the destination are largely very satisfied with the size of the ski resort; however, they express some tendency towards dissatisfaction when it comes to longer waiting times for cable cars and ski lifts. The destination introduced various measures (e.g. starting times of ski schools) to relieve main hot spots and zones and counteract guests' perception of crowding. Future measures that address sustainable development at the resort include governance of lodging capacity and protection of natural resources of the destination.

Currently, the destination of Serfaus-Fiss-Ladis has rededicated land for building about 5000 additional beds, but continually increasing bed numbers might lead to over-capacity. Bed capacity thus has to be governed to overcome potential negative effects such as overcrowding, competition within the destination, or a negative price spiral.

The destination benefits a lot from its natural resources, combined with advanced infrastructure. Development and commercial activities within a mountain resort may result in an enormous intervention into nature (e.g. construction of new ski lifts and development of ski runs affect mountain flora and fauna). Future projects thus have to pay attention to resource protection that safeguards the natural resources and provides an attractive place for both locals and tourists, both currently and in the future.

Strong competition

Competitors of Serfaus-Fiss-Ladis include other destinations focusing on similar target groups of families and connoisseurs, and large destinations offering substitute products such as amusement parks, resorts and cruises. These artificially constructed attractions are less influenced by natural conditions, allowing the rival destinations to provide targeted services and products along a fully harmonized service chain.

The corporate identity of these competitors is much easier accomplished and implemented compared to community-based destinations, where a number of autonomous service providers and entrepreneurs are responsible for the tourism product along the value chain. Thus, it is necessary to deal with these competitors and to develop scenarios for potential strategies that could be applied in an increasingly difficult competitive environment. The overall economic situation might additionally lead to conflicts and competitiveness among actors, potentially leading to a price discussion and a generally negative effect for the destination.

In the future it will be essential to detect potential cost-savings for the destination, but these should not be achieved at the expense of the guests. The benefits and costs of investment projects must be objectively checked; the investments need to align with the objectives and strategy of the destination, its positioning and the guests' needs. The threat of a price drop in the accommodation sector of the destination results from the increase in bed capacity and a generally difficult competitive environment. Such a price strategy is difficult to reverse and demoralizes the quality strategy of the destination.

Opening up new target markets requires new competencies (e.g. language and intercultural competencies), which need to be acquired by the actors in the destination. In addition, the improvement of quality, the fulfilment of guests' needs and wishes, as well as the reaction towards external impacts, are essential for maintaining the success of the last few years. Serfaus-Fiss-Ladis is a 'best practice' destination, often observed by other stakeholders and competitors, putting the actors of the destination under pressure.

Strategic focus

The destination manages to hold an excellent and consistent position on the market. The challenge will be to continually retain all service providers and not to dilute the well-established position on the market. The tourist offering of Serfaus-Fiss-Ladis, originally concentrated in the villages, is continually shifted from the village to the mountain, due to the very active and dominant cable-car companies. This, however, might become a threat for other service providers of the destination, since the shifting demand might result in a loss in attractiveness of the village centres. The financially strong cable-car companies, also continually providing services such as accommodation and gastronomy, may potentially result in increased competition for revenue between these companies and the traditional providers of services for visitors within the villages.

In general, winter sport has lost much of its attraction and also in the most important German market (the core target market for Alpine regions), winter sports affinity has decreased; one-third of the German skiers are 60 years or older and 40% of the skiers have a household income of less than €2500 per month. This increases the strategic necessity to develop an all-year-round destination and provide alternative activities on the mountain.

According to Cooper (2006), tourism has been slow in adopting the knowledge management approach in its strategic areas of focus. However, the generation, use and sharing of knowledge is critical to the competitiveness of tourism destinations (Hjalager, 2002). Although the collaboration among actors and their interconnectedness is good, information and knowledge processing shows some potential, although vital guest feedback should be collected and processed in a more effective way.

Human resources

The final important challenge includes the human resources factor. Family businesses are the predominant form of enterprise in Serfaus-Fiss-Ladis. Planning for the integration of the younger generation into the family firm is an issue of strategic importance and constitutes a challenge, particularly for core service providers. Succession should thus be anticipated and planned in advance, since core entrepreneurs play an essential role in the future development of the destination.

Migration of the local population is a risk, as only limited income possibilities exist outside the tertiary sector. Furthermore, living expenses such as land prices have increased in the last few years, which results in a situation where locals may no longer be able to afford to live in Serfaus-Fiss-Ladis. The tourism intensity of Serfaus-Fiss-Ladis is very high, which leads to economic success. However, this success might also result in tourism fatigue (Swarbrooke, 1999). Maintaining local human resources and their positive attitude to tourism is essential to provide the level of hospitality that visitors seek.

The challenges described above demand continued cooperation among all actors to achieve the destination's strategic development, a task that must be fulfilled by the informal leadership network and the formal entities of the destination.

Success Factors and Conclusion

Serfaus-Fiss-Ladis can be regarded as a successful mountain tourism destination. However, the analysis shows that the destination will come across a series of challenges, which have to be faced by the stakeholders. To overcome these challenges, the following success factors might be helpful.

- Leadership network: leadership personalities (leaders) of core service providers such as cable-car companies, ski school, communities, hotels and restaurants, as well as the DMO, form an informal network, where the development of the destination, strategic issues, projects, etc. are informally discussed and decided.
- Clear positioning and focus: the destination Serfaus-Fiss-Ladis focuses on a particular market segment and thus aligns its products and marketing on this target group. This enables the destination to best fulfil the needs and wishes of the target group.
- Customer orientation: market research, problem solving and the focus on the customer are key success factors of the highly customer-oriented destination.
- Further development: the region strives for continuing improvement and development. Innovation and entrepreneurial spirit drive the destination into the future.

The combination of the above success factors represents a strategy to promote destination development and competitiveness. Thus, the collaboration among the various stakeholders and their willingness to mutually develop the destination further is of utmost importance.

References

Andereck, K., Valentine, K., Knopf, R. and Vogt, C. (2005) Residents' perceptions of community tourism impacts. *Annals of Tourism Research* 32, 1056–1076.

Andriotis, K. (2005) Community groups' perceptions of and preferences for tourism development: evidence from Crete. *Journal of Hospitality and Tourism Research* 29, 67–90.

Ap, J. (1992) Residents' perceptions of tourism impacts. *Annals of Tourism Research* 19, 665–690.

Ariffin, A.A.M. (2013) Generic dimensionality of hospitality in the hotel industry: a host–guest relationship perspective. *International Journal of Hospitality Management* 35, 171–179.

Beritelli, P. and Laesser, C. (2011) Power dimensions and influence reputation in tourist destinations: empirical evidence from a network of actors and stakeholders. *Tourism Management* 32(6), 1299–1309.

Besculides, A., Lee, M.E. and McCormick, P.J. (2002) Residents' perceptions of the cultural benefits of tourism. *Annals of Tourism Research* 92, 303–319.

Bornhorst, T., Ritchie, J.R.B. and Sheehan, L. (2010) Determinants of tourism success for DMOs and destinations: an empirical examination of stakeholders perspectives. *Tourism Management* 31(5), 572–589.

Chew, J. (1987) Transport and tourism in the year 2000. *Tourism Management* 8(2), 83–85.

Cooper, C. (2006) Knowledge management and tourism. *Annals of Tourism Research* 33(1), 47–64.

Crouch, G.I. (2011) Destination competitiveness: An analysis of determinant attributes. *Journal of Travel Research*, 50(1), 27–45.

Crouch, G.I. and Ritchie, J.R.B. (1999) Tourism, competitiveness, and societal prosperity. *Journal of Business Research* 44(3), 137–152.

Dickman, S. (1994) *Tourism: An Introductory Text*. Edward Arnold, Sydney, Austrailia.

Diedrich, A. and García-Buades, E. (2009) Local perceptions of tourism as indicators of destination decline. *Tourism Management* 30, 512–521.

DMO Serfaus-Fiss-Ladis (2012) *Annual Report*. DMO Serfaus-Fiss-Ladis, Austria.

Falk, M. (2008) A hedonic price model for ski lift tickets. *Tourism Management* 29, 1172–1184.

Freeman, R.E. (1984) *Strategic Management: A Stakeholder Approach*. Pitman, Boston, Massachusetts.

Fueglistaller, U., Volery, T. and Weber, W. (2010) *Strategic Entrepreneurship: The Promise for Future Entrepreneurship, Family Business and SME Research?* KMU Verlag HSG, St Gallen, Switzerland.

Gunn, C.A. (1988) *Tourism Planning*. Taylor and Francis, New York.

Harrill, R. (2004) Residents' attitudes toward tourism development: a literature review with implications for tourism planning. *Journal of Planning Literature* 18, 251–266.

Hjalager, A. (2002) Repairing innovation defectiveness in tourism. *Tourism Management* 23(5), 465–474.

Horn, C. and Simmons, D. (2002) Community adaptation to tourism: comparisons between Rotorua and Kaikoura, New Zealand. *Tourism Management* 23, 133–143.

Inskeep, E. (1991) *Tourism Planning: An Integrated and Sustainable Development Approach*. Van Nostrand Reinhold, New York.

Jamal, T.B. and Getz, D. (1995) Collaboration theory and community tourism planning. *Annals of Tourism Research* 22(1), 186–204.

Johnson, J., Snepenger, D. and Akis, S. (1994) Residents' perceptions of tourism development. *Annals of Tourism Research* 21, 629–642.

Khadarooa, J. and Seetanahb, B. (2008) The role of transport infrastructure in international tourism development: a gravity model approach. *Tourism Management* 29, 831–840.

Martin, C.A. and Witt, S.F. (1988) Substitute prices in models of tourism demand. *Annals of Tourism Research* 15, 255–268.

Pearce, D.C. (1987) *Tourism Today: A Geographical Analysis*. Longman Scientific and Technical, Harlow, UK.

Pedrazzini, L. and Satiko, R. (2011) *From Territorial Cohesion to the New Regionalized Europe*. Maggioli, Milan, Italy.

Pike, S. and Page, S.J. (2014) Destination Marketing Organizations and destination marketing: a narrative analysis of the literature. *Tourism Management* 41, 202–227.

Prideaux, B. (2000) The role of the transport system in destination development. *Tourism Management* 21, 53–63.

Rogers, E.M. (1995) *Diffusion of Innovation*. The Free Press, New York.

Scott, N., Baggio, R. and Cooper, C. (2009) *Network Analysis and Tourism – from Theory to Practice*. Channel View Publications, Clevedon, UK.

Serfaus (2014) Serfaus-Fiss-Ladis homepage. Available at: http://www.serfaus-fiss-ladis.at/en (accessed 1 August 2014).

Swarbrooke, J. (1999) *Sustainable Tourism Management*. CAB International, Wallingford, UK.

Volgger, M. and Pechlaner, H. (2014) Requirements for destination management organizations in destination governance: understanding DMO success. *Tourism Management* 41(1), 64–75.

Yang, J., Ryan, C. and Zhang, L. (2013) Social conflict in communities impacted by tourism. *Tourism Management* 35, 82–93.

Zehrer, A., Raich, F., Siller, H. and Tschiderer, F. (2014) Leadership networks in destinations. *Tourism Review* 69(1), 59–73.

36 Mountain Tourism: Implications and Sustainable Futures

John S. Hull* and Harold Richins

Thompson Rivers University, Kamloops, British Columbia, Canada

In Awe of Mountains

Mountains hold visitors or residents in awe as we venture into these scenic regions to explore and experience the front-country and picturesque resort mountain communities, or to journey into the remote backcountry with its inherent risks, challenges, and rewards. As said so beautifully by Lord Byron, 'There is pleasure in the pathless woods, there is rapture in the lonely shore, there is society where none intrudes, by the deep sea, and music in its roar; I love not Man the less, but Nature more' (Byron, 1905; Byron and McGann, 1986). The vistas, the deeply wooded wild forests, the rock, the clean air and the sound of rushing water – these are what we find when venturing into the mountains. Maybe at a deeper level, what we really seek in the mountains is a personal or perhaps a spiritual benefit from experiencing nature's sights, sounds and smells. These entice and invite us to reconnect with ourselves and with place. Romance and mystique are a common theme of visiting, exploring and/or being in mountain regions.

Numerous impacts and challenges face mountain communities. The recent earthquakes in Nepal raise the concern for natural hazards. Diminishing snow levels have raised awareness of climate change in the Alps. Poverty and marginalization emphasize the need for sustainable development in the Himalayas. Exponential growth in visitation raises concerns about the fragility of Machu Picchu's cultural assets. The organizations and enterprises providing tourism in these complex mountain environments make the creation and provision and study of mountain tourism experiences often challenging.

Broad Coverage on Mountain Tourism

This book, *Mountain Tourism: Experiences, Communities, Environments and Sustainable Futures*, has provided a wide coverage of five thematic sections with applicable case studies. Numerous approaches and processes have been explored and woven throughout the chapters of the book to describe and address key present and future management issues related to mountain tourism. Incorporating an overview of the historical context, relevant concepts, theories and areas of focus, the sections of this book on mountain tourism have endeavoured to provide a broad coverage and understanding of this important component of the tourism industry. *Mountain Tourism*

---

* Corresponding author: jhull@tru.ca

has offered significant insight into current and best practice, as well as the substantial nature of mountain tourism as a topic. The second section, following the introductory chapter, has presented a focus on experience creation in mountain tourism environments. Part III has provided an emphasis on people and communities in mountain tourism locations, while the fourth section centred on natural environments and their connection to mountain tourism. Finally, the last two sections focused on impacts and solutions in mountain tourism, followed by an examination of approaches for mountain tourism development, planning and governance.

Future Challenges for Sustainable Mountain Tourism

Through each section of the book, present and future challenges for mountain tourism have been mentioned, some of which are summarized here. These include: issues of increased visitation; the provision of engaging tourism and leisure experiences; long-term effects of climate change; issues of safety and security; impacts and management challenges in living and offering tourism within sensitive natural environments; the economic and socio-cultural challenges of transient people living and working within mountain communities; diversity of values and needs that may potentially result in user conflicts; natural hazards that may affect mountain regions such as earthquakes; and issues related to underdevelopment, where residents of mountain regions are attempting to secure future livelihoods that are equitable and sustainable.

A Sustainable Mountain Tourism Experience Model (SMTE)

In addressing these and other challenges, a model of relevance for sustainable mountain tourism experience has been generated, acknowledging current scholarship (Nepal and Chipeniuk, 2005; ICIMOD, 2007; Musa *et al.*, 2015), to provide a method of guidance or stewardship in advancing sustainability success within mountain regions. Figure 36.1 describes attributes of a Sustainable Mountain Tourism Experience Model (SMTE). The model is based on three major elements – Place, People and Practice – which are important for advancing sustainable mountain experiences. This is examined in further detail below.

The mountain tourism framework proposed by Nepal and Chipeniuk (2005) argues that there is a need to evaluate mountain resource characteristics, mountain amenity users and mountain recreational land use to examine recreation and tourism issues in mountain regions. The ICIMOD (2007) facilitation model from Nepal contends that, in order to build capacity in mountain regions, there is a need for considering project cycle facilitation at the strategy, institution and project levels and that at each of these levels there must be analysis and planning, action and monitoring, and assessing results and evaluation to support sustainable benefits. Finally, the framework by Musa *et al.* (2015), adapted from Weed and Bull (2004), focuses on the connection of activity, people and place within a dynamic sport and tourism context related to mountaineering.

The present book has introduced the advancement of an SMTE model that adopts a management focus. Similar to previous models, the elements of the SMTE model include reference to place with direct relevance to mountain experiences, and to people as integral to mountain tourism; however the model places more focus on practice as related to planning, management and governance of tourism in mountain environments similar to the facilitation model proposed by the ICIMOD (2007). There is a need for action and a participatory process to manage tourism development in mountain regions. The SMTE model is discussed in further detail below.

Place in mountain tourism

PLACE is one of the foundations for production and consumption of mountain experiences. Place is a 'space that is transformed into place as it acquires definition and meaning' (Tuan, 1977, 136; Cresswell, 2004). Agnew (1987) identifies three elements that every place should have: first

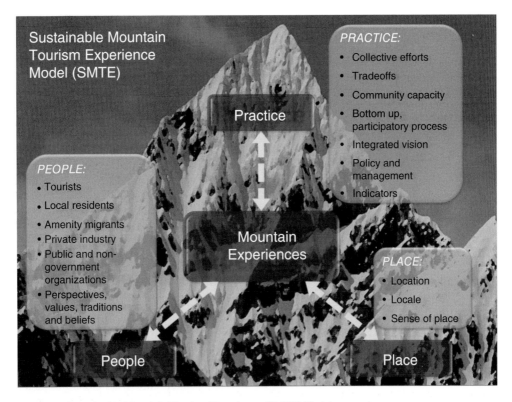

Fig. 36.1. Sustainable Mountain Tourism Experience (SMTE) Model.

is the identification of a 'location' (e.g. the Alps, or GPS coordinates). The second element is a 'locale', where one encounters, interacts, experiences, produces and consumes the meaning of place. Higham and Hinch (2009) argue that the consumption of meaning at a locale, such as in a mountain destination, is the result of the marketing, signage, facilities, infrastructure and assets that are encountered, as well as the services delivered. Whistler, Canada's Peak to Peak 360 Experience provides an example of this.

> The longest and highest lift in the world, the Guinness World Record-breaking PEAK 2 PEAK Gondola is just the beginning. As your connection between the tops of Whistler and Blackcomb Mountains, walk, sightsee, hike, dine, and play amongst giants – all summer long.
> (Whistlerblackcomb.com, 2015)

Third is 'sense of place', which is a participant's feelings and emotions from interacting with a place. As an example, this might be the sense of

accomplishment and reverence gained from hiking with a local guide along the Salkantay Trail to Machu Picchu in Peru. Tuan (1977) argues that these three elements of 'place' are not static, but are individualistic and actively constructed and renegotiated as an individual spends more time and adds more experiences while in a 'place' – the mountains. The result is an increasing attachment to place (Tuan, 2009) and the end result is a rich mountain tourism experience.

People in mountain tourism

PEOPLE are the second foundation of the model. The people that we meet and engage with in mountain destinations are an integral part of the mountain tourism experience. These people include long-time permanent residents, amenity migrants and tourists (Nepal and Chipeniuk, 2005). They are also the men, women and families working in the private sector as tour operators, accommodation providers, cooks, artisans and guides to deliver services for mountain visitors. Also included are the individuals working for public institutions and non-government organizations (NGOs), planning and managing the tourism industry. Overarching considerations related to people's perspectives, values, traditions and beliefs are also included, as these make a positive or negative impact on the mountain tourism experience (Nepal and Chipeniuk, 2005; ICIMOD, 2007).

Practice in mountain tourism

Third, PRACTICE is the planning, governance strategies and guidelines adopted by communities and local people to develop, manage and monitor tourism's impacts on mountain destinations. Wall (1997) argues that destinations wanting to advance sustainable development strategies need to make choices and trade-offs that minimize negative impacts and enhance positive impacts. Sustainability is built upon aspects of economic, environmental, social and cultural stewardship (Richins, 2008), achieved through the collective efforts of public, private and non-government individuals and the formal connections, collaboration, knowledge and trust-making that supports the formation and evolution of community capacity (Moscardo, 2009; Beritelli et al., 2007; Hultman and Hall, 2012). Sustainable research and practice includes a bottom-up, participatory multi-scale process, from the local to the regional and national levels, that understands impacts, supports an integrated vision through policy and management recommendations, and develops sustainable indicators to monitor and evaluate results that are relevant in a mountain context (UNEP/UNWTO, 2005; Kruk, 2010; Buckley, 2012).

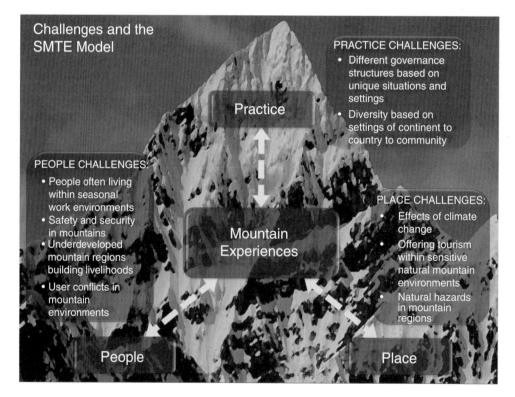

Fig. 36.2. Sustainable Mountain Tourism Experience Model used as a participatory tool for addressing major challenges in mountain tourism experiences.

Provision of mountain experiences

By acknowledging place, people and practice in mountain destinations, policy makers have an opportunity to promote sustainable tourism experiences. As an important component of the Sustainable Mountain Tourism Experience Model, the provision of tourism and leisure experiences is acknowledged as a central tenet of mountain tourism. The creation and development of experiences becomes successful through the integration of many of the following aspects: the engagement and participant involvement in the experience; the importance and mindfulness of place; the focus and emphasis in which the experience happens; the offering and provision of the experience; the style and messaging that may add value in the perception of the experience; the themes or authentic narrative of the experience; and the memories, actions and outcomes that emerge as a result of the experience

(Quan and Wang, 2004; Mossberg, 2007; Moscardo, 2009; Richins, 2013).

SMTE and Addressing Future Challenges

The Sustainable Mountain Tourism Experience Model acknowledges the numerous challenges in the production and consumption of mountain experiences. These challenges can be categorized into the elements of place, people and practice, as indicated in Fig. 36.2. The examples provided are not meant to be comprehensive, but rather to assist those aiming to utilize the model by providing a management framework or tool for identifying, prioritizing and understanding the challenges unique to a mountain destination as part of a participatory process.

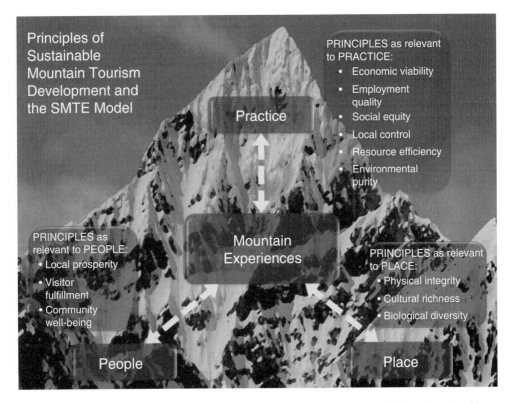

Fig. 36.3. Sustainable Mountain Tourism Experience Model used to prioritize principles of sustainable mountain tourism development.

SMTE and Sustainable Mountain Tourism Principles

Another major consideration for policy makers, planners, organizations and individuals engaged in mountain destinations in the context of the SMTE model is the importance of the principles of sustainable mountain tourism development proposed by UNEP and the UNWTO (2005). These principles have been grouped in Fig. 36.3 into the elements of place, people and practice. For mountain destinations across the globe, it is acknowledged that priorities will generally be different and that the diversity of stakeholders can work to build the capacity to recognize, prioritize and integrate these principles into a local or regional mountain context.

Whether mountain experiences are planned, designed, coordinated, spontaneous, organic and/or unstructured, it is necessary to incorporate the unique aspects of place, people and practice in the mountain context to overcome challenges and ensure greater potential for future success and sustainability. These three unique aspects of place, people and practice are integral and critical to building dynamic, innovative and forward momentum in the creation and provision of mountain tourism experiences, and in meeting the challenges of people and communities in mountain tourism environments. Place, people and practice are also critical considerations in understanding and acknowledging impacts and solutions with regard to mountain tourism, in working toward preserving and enhancing the natural environments where mountain tourism exits, and in developing, planning and achieving integrated governance approaches within highly diverse and dynamic local, regional and international mountain tourism settings.

References

Agnew, J.A. (1987) *Place and Politics: The Geographical Mediation of State and Society*. Allen and Unwin, London.

Beritelli, P., Bieger, T. and Laesser, C. (2007) Destination governance: using corporate governance theories as a foundation for effective destination management. *Journal of Travel Research* 46(1), 96–107.

Buckley, R. (2012) Sustainable tourism: research and reality. *Annals of Tourism Research* 39(2), 528–546.

Byron, G.G.B.B. (1905) *The Complete Poetical Works*. Houghton Mifflin, Boston, Massachusetts.

Byron, L.G. and McGann, J.J. (1986) *Childe Harold's Pilgrimage in Lord Byron: The Major Works*. Oxford University Press, Oxford, UK.

Cresswell, T. (2004) *Place: A Short Introduction*. Blackwell, Oxford, UK.

Higham, J. and Hinch, T. (2009) *Sport Tourism*. Butterworth-Heinemann, Oxford, UK.

Hultman, J. and Hall, C.M. (2012) Tourism place-making: governance of locality in Sweden. *Annals of Tourism Research* 39(2), 547–570.

ICIMOD (2007) *Facilitating Sustainable Mountain Tourism,* Volume 1. Resource Book. ICIMOD, Kathmandu, Nepal.

Kruk, E. (2010) *Marketing the Uniqueness of the Himalayas: An Analytical Framework*. ICIMOD, Kathmandu, Nepal.

Moscardo, G. (2009) Understanding tourist experience though mindfulness theory. In: Kozak, M. and Decrop, A. (eds) *Handbook of Tourist Behavior Theory and Practice*. Routledge, London.

Mossberg, L. (2007) A marketing approach to the tourist experience. *Scandinavian Journal of Hospitality & Tourism* 7(1), 59–74.

Musa, G., Higham, J. and Thompson-Carr, A. (eds) (2015) *Mountaineering Tourism*. Routledge, London.

Nepal, S. and Chipeniuk, R. (2005) Mountain tourism: towards a conceptual framework. *Tourism Geographies* 7(3), 313–333.

Quan, S. and Wang, N. (2004) Towards a structural model of the tourist experience: an illustration from food experiences in tourism. *Tourism Management* 25(3), 297. DOI: 10.1016/S0261-5177(03)00130-4.

Richins, H. (2008) Building sustainable tourism as an integral part of the resort community. *International Journal of Tourism Policy* 1(4), 315–334.

Richins, H. (2013) Experience studies in tourism: a movement, or just another way of offering specialized service or authentic tourism? Extended abstract for the *International Critical Tourism Studies Conference V. Tourism Critical Practice: Activating Dreams into Action*. Sarajevo, Bosnia and Herzegovina. Available at: http://cts.som.surrey.ac.uk/files/2013/10/Book-of-Abstracts.pdf (accessed 24 July 2015).

Tuan, Y.-F. (1977) *Space and Place: The Perspective of Experience*. University of Minnesota Press, Minneapolis, Minnesota.

Tuan, Y.-F. (2009) *Religion: From Place to Placelessness*. University of Chicago Press, Chicago, Illinois.

UNEP/UNWTO (2005) *Making Tourism More Sustainable. A Guide for Policymakers*. UNEP/UNWTO, Paris and Madrid.

Wall, G. (1997) Sustainable tourism – unsustainable development. In: Wahab, S. and Pigram, J.J. (eds) *Tourism, Development and Growth: The Challenge of Sustainability*. Routledge, London, pp. 33–49.

Weed, M. and Bull, C. (2004) *Sports Tourism: Participants, Policy and Providers*. Butterworth and Heinemann, Oxford, UK.

Whistlerblackcomb.com (2015) Peak 2 Peak 360 Experience. Available at: http://www.whistlerblackcomb.com (accessed 10 May 2015).

Index

_____